MW01165287

A Companion to John of Salisbury

Brill's Companions to the Christian Tradition

A SERIES OF HANDBOOKS AND REFERENCE WORKS ON THE
INTELLECTUAL AND RELIGIOUS LIFE OF EUROPE, 500–1800

Editor-in-Chief

Christopher M. Bellitto (*Kean University*)

VOLUME 57

The titles published in this series are listed at *brill.com/bcct*

A Companion to John of Salisbury

Edited by

Christophe Grellard
Frédérique Lachaud

BRILL

LEIDEN | BOSTON

Cover illustration: miniature at the beginning of Book 1 of the Policratique in the translation by Denis Foulechat. Courtesy Bibliothèque nationale de France, Manuscrit Français 24287, folio 12r.

Library of Congress Cataloging-in-Publication Data

A companion to John of Salisbury / edited by Christophe Grellard, Frederique Lachaud.
    pages cm. -- (Brill's companions to the Christian tradition, ISSN 1871-6377 ; VOLUME 57)
  Includes bibliographical references and index.
  ISBN 978-90-04-26510-3 (hardback : alk. paper) 1. John, of Salisbury, Bishop of Chartres, -1180. I. Grellard, Christophe, editor.
  B765.J44C66 2014
  189'.4--dc23

                                                            2014035753

This publication has been typeset in the multilingual "Brill" typeface. With over 5,100 characters covering Latin, IPA, Greek, and Cyrillic, this typeface is especially suitable for use in the humanities.
For more information, please see www.brill.com/brill-typeface.

ISSN 1871-6377
ISBN 978-90-04-26510-3 (hardback)
ISBN 978-90-04-28294-0 (e-book)

This book is printed on acid-free paper.

Printed by Printforce, the Netherlands

Contents

List of Contributors

Julie Barrau
is Lecturer in Medieval British History at the University of Cambridge. She specializes in political and intellectual history (12th and 13th centuries), and her recent publications include *Bible, lettres et politique – L'Écriture au service des hommes à l'époque de Thomas Becket* (2013).

David Bloch
is Professor of Classics at the University of Copenhagen. He specializes in ancient and medieval philosophy, focusing in particular on Aristotle and the Aristotelian tradition. His publications include *Aristotle on Memory and Recollection. Text, Translation, Interpretation, and Reception in Western Scholasticism* (2007) and *John of Salisbury on Aristotelian Science* (2012).

Karen Bollermann
is an Assistant Professor of English at Arizona State University. Her research engages Anglo-Saxon culture and Old English literature throughout the British Middle Ages and across its multi-lingual and -cultural history.

Cédric Giraud
is an Assistant Professor at the University of Lorraine and a junior member of the Institut universitaire de France. He specializes in the history of medieval schools and of Christian spirituality. His recent publications include *Notre-Dame de Paris 1163–2013. Actes du colloque de 2012* (2013) and *Per verba magistri. Anselme de Laon et son école au XIIe s.* (2010).

Christophe Grellard
is an Assistant Professor at the University of Paris I (Panthéon-Sorbonne) and a junior fellow of the Institut universitaire de France. He specializes in the history of medieval philosophy. His publications include *Jean de Salisbury et la Renaissance médiévale du scepticisme* (2013).

Laure Hermand-Schebat
is an Assistant Professor at the University of Lyon. She specializes in Latin literature of the Renaissance and her recent publications include *Pétrarque épistolier et Cicéron: étude d'une filiation* (2011).

Frédérique Lachaud

is Professor of Medieval History at the University of Lorraine. She specializes in the history of English political culture from the 12th to the 14th century. Her publications include *L'Éthique du pouvoir au Moyen Âge. L'office dans la culture politique (Angleterre, vers 1150–vers 1330)* (2010).

Constant Mews

is Director of the Centre for Studies in Religion and Theology at Monash University, Australia. He specializes in the religious and intellectual history of the 12th and 13th centuries. His books include *The Lost Love Letters of Heloise and Abelard*, 2nd edition (2008) and *Abelard and Heloise* (2005).

Clare Monagle

is a Senior Lecturer in the School of Philosophical, Historical and International Studies at Monash University. She specializes in the intellectual history of the 12th-century schools of Paris, with particular emphasis on the reception of Lombard's *Sentences*. She has recently published *Orthodoxy and Controversy in Twelfth-Century Religious Discourse: Peter Lombard's Sentences and the Making of Theology* (2013).

Cary J. Nederman

is Professor of Political Science at Texas A&M University. His research concentrates on the history of political thought. His latest book is *A Companion to Marsilius of Padua* (2012).

Ronald E. Pepin

is Professor Emeritus of Humanities at Capital Community College in Hartford, CT. He specializes in Anglo-Norman writers of the 12th century. His published translations include *The Vatican Mythographers* (2008); *Anselm & Becket: Two Canterbury Saints' Lives by John of Salisbury* (2009); *Amarcius: Satires* (2011).

Yves Sassier

is "agrégé" of the Faculties of Law (Roman law, legal history) and professor of medieval Western institutional history at the University of Paris-Sorbonne. He has published several books and contributions in the field of political and institutional history of medieval France and on the thought of clerics on power from the 7th to the 12th century.

Sigbjørn Sønnesyn

is post-doctoral Research Fellow at the Saxo Institute at the University of Copenhagen. His main research interest is the place of moral theology and ethics in 12th-century intellectual culture. His recent publications include *William of Malmesbury and the Ethics of History* (2012).

Short Titles

Works by John of Salisbury

Entheticus maior: *Entheticus maior et minor*, ed. and trans. Jan van Laarhoven, 3 vols. (Leiden, 1987), vol. 1, pp. 104–227.

Entheticus minor: *Entheticus maior et minor*, ed. and trans. Jan van Laarhoven, 3 vols. (Leiden, 1987), vol. 1, pp. 230–49.

Entheticus, ed. Pepin: Ronald E. Pepin, ed., "The *'Entheticus'* of John of Salisbury: A Critical Text," *Traditio* 31 (1975): 127–195.

The Early Letters: *The Letters of John of Salisbury*, vol. 1, *The Early Letters (1153–1161)*, ed. W.J. Millor and H.E. Butler, and C.N.L. Brooke (Oxford, 1986).

The Later Letters: *The Letters of John of Salisbury*, vol. 2, *The Later Letters (1163–1180)*, ed. W.J. Millor and C.N.L. Brooke (Oxford, 1979).

Historia pontificalis: *Ioannis Saresberiensis Historia pontificalis. John's of Salisbury's Memoirs of the Papal Court*, ed. and trans. Marjorie Chibnall (London, 1956[1]; Oxford, 1986[2]).

Metalogicon: *Metalogicon*, ed. J.B. Hall and Katharine S.B. Keats-Rohan, cccm 98 (Turnhout, 1991).

Metalogicon, trans. McGarry: *John of Salisbury, The Metalogicon: A Twelfth-Century Defense of the Verbal and Logical Arts of The Trivium*, trans. David McGarry (Berkeley, 1955, repr. Philadelphia, 2009).

Metalogicon, trans. J.B. Hall, Corpus Christianorum in Translation (Turnhout, 2013).

Policraticus I–IV, ed. Keats-Rohan: *Ioannis Saresberiensis Policraticus I–IV*, ed. Katharine S.B. Keats-Rohan, cccm 118 (Turnhout, 1993).

Policraticus, ed. Webb: *Ioannis Saresberiensis episcopi Carnotensis Policratici sive de nugis curialium et vestigiis philosophorum libri VIII*, ed. Clement C.J. Webb, 2 vols. (Oxford, 1909).

Policraticus trans. Nederman: *Policraticus: of the Frivolities of Courtiers and the Footprints of Philosophers*, trans. Cary J. Nederman (Cambridge, 1990).

Policraticus trans. Pike: *Frivolities of Courtiers and Footprints of Philosophers, Being a Translation of the First, Second and Third Books and Selections from the Seventh and Eighth Books of the* Policraticus *of John of Salisbury*, trans. Joseph B. Pike (Minneapolis, 1938).

Policraticus trans. Dickinson: *The Statesman's Book of John of Salisbury: Being the Fourth, Fifth and Sixth Books and Selections from the Seventh and Eight Books of the Policraticus*, trans. John Dickinson (New York, 1963).

Vita Anselmi: *Giovanni di Salisbury, Anselmo e Becket, due vite*, ed. Inos Biffi (Milan, 1990), pp. 22–120.

Vita Anselmi, trans. Pepin: *Anselm & Becket. Two Canterbury Saints' Lives, by John of Salisbury*, trans. Ronald E. Pepin (Toronto, 2009), pp. 17–71.

Vita Thomae: *Giovanni di Salisbury, Anselmo e Becket, due vite*, ed. Inos Biffi (Milan, 1990), pp. 151–212.

Vita Thomae, ed. Robertson: *Materials for the History of Thomas Becket, Archbishop of Canterbury*, ed. James C. Robertson and Joseph B. Sheppard, 7 vols. (London, 1875–85), vol. 2, pp. 299–352.

Vita Thomae, trans. Pepin: *Anselm & Becket. Two Canterbury Saints' Lives, by John of Salisbury*, trans. Ronald E. Pepin (Toronto, 2009), pp. 78–95.

Other References

Cartulaire de Notre-Dame de Chartres: *Cartulaire de Notre-Dame de Chartres*, ed. Eugène de Lépinois and Lucien Merlet, 3 vols. (Chartres, 1862–5).

The World of John of Salisbury: *The World of John of Salisbury*, ed. Michael Wilks (Oxford, 1984[1], 1994[2]).

MB: *Materials for the History of Thomas Becket, Archbishop of Canterbury*, ed. James Craigie Robertson and Joseph B. Sheppard, 7 vols. (London, 1875–85).

Introduction

Christophe Grellard and Frédérique Lachaud[1]

John of Salisbury is one of the main figures of the "12th-century Renaissance" and a major contributor to the political debates that took place between 1150 and 1180. His work stands at a crossroads between administrative and diplomatic activity on the one hand – as shown by his correspondence in the service of the archbishops of Canterbury and his *Historia pontificalis*; and philosophical and political thought on the other – as expressed in two exceptional works: the *Metalogicon* and the *Policraticus*. His place in contemporary debates and the sheer scale of his work have long made John of Salisbury a subject of interest. A conference held in 1980 to mark the eight-hundredth anniversary of his death offered an overview of advances in research and opened new avenues for study. Its contributions were later published in *The World of John of Salisbury*.[2] Since then, numerous studies and new editions of major texts have deepened our knowledge of John of Salisbury's work and of his place in his contemporary world,[3] and it is the aim of this collection to review recent progress and to highlight avenues for future enquiry. The following pages will first outline the origins and career of John of Salisbury, then discuss questions concerning his life and work that have led to specific debates.

The Life and Work of John of Salisbury

The biography of John of Salisbury has already been the subject of numerous studies. These either focus on one particular aspect of his life, or are cross-disciplinary and synoptic, presenting a general account of available data.[4] His

---

1   The authors wish to thank Alison Culliford for correcting the English version of the introduction.

2   Michael Wilks, ed., *The World of John of Salisbury* (Oxford, 1984[1], 1994[2]).

3   For a defence of a holistic approach to the work and career of John of Salisbury, see esp. Cary J. Nederman, "Friendship in Public Life during the Twelfth Century: Theory and Practice in the Writings of John of Salisbury," *Viator: Medieval and Renaissance Studies* 38 (2007), 385–397.

4   The life and work of John of Salisbury have been the subject of several general accounts. See esp. Hans Liebeschütz, *Mediaeval Humanism in the Life and Writings of John of Salisbury* (London, 1950[1], 1968[2]); Mario Dal Pra, *Giovanni di Salisbury* (Milano, 1951); Sister M. Anthony Brown, "John of Salisbury," *Franciscan Studies* 19 (1959), 241–297; Klaus Guth, *Johannes von*

high public profile and the partly autobiographical dimension of his writings account for the large number of sources one can draw on for the reconstruction of his life. These must, however, be used with some caution, as already in his time John raised controversy – particularly because of the positions he adopted on such issues as the relations between temporal power and the Church. Furthermore, if he does mention in his work a number of events that occurred in his life, this is not with any autobiographical purpose (such an ambition would largely have been alien to him): rather, his intention was to situate these personal events within an exemplary scheme, where the actions and gestures accomplished by others may be used as a model (or counter-model) of action. In medieval works that are traditionally seen as autobiographical (such as the *Liber de temptationibus* of Othlo of Saint-Emmeran, the *De uita sua* of Guibert of Nogent or the *Historia calamitatum* of Peter Abelard), individuality always appears within a certain typological framework, and is inserted into existing narrative schemes.[5] John of Salisbury is no exception to the rule. With these few cautionary statements in mind, one may proceed to outline the main aspects of his biography.

The first date in John's life that is known with any certainty is that of his arrival in Paris as a student, one year after the death of Henry I of England (*Metalogicon* 2.10) – in 1136. Given that "higher studies" at that time began at about the age of fifteen, this leads us to date John's birth at around 1120; unless one accepts that he would have started his cycle of studies in England, in which case a date of around 1115 would be more likely. John was born on the former site of the present-day Salisbury (Old Sarum), to a family that is generally thought to have been of modest origins. Two facts seem to confirm this point. John says that his nickname was "small," an adjective which could refer to a physical characteristic (he was small in size), but also to a social one (small in social status). And we know that John often found himself in a critical financial situation during his student years. In spite of this modest social standing, John and his family seem to have kept up a close relationship with the clergy of

Salisbury. Studien zur Kirchen-, Kultur- und Sozialgeschichte Westeuropas im 12. Jahrhundert (St. Ottilien, 1978); David Luscombe, "Salisbury, John of (late 1110s–1180)," *Oxford Dictionary of National Biography* (Oxford, 2004); Cary J. Nederman, *John of Salisbury* (Tempe, Arizona, 2005).

5   See, e.g. Sverre Bagge, "The Autobiography of Abelard and Medieval Individualism," *Journal of Medieval History* 19 (1993), 327–350; Chris D. Ferguson, "Autobiography as Therapy: Guibert de Nogent, Peter Abelard, and the Making of Medieval Autobiography," *Journal of Medieval and Renaissance Studies* 13 (1983), 187–212; Evelyn B. Vitz, "Type et individu dans l'autobiographie médiévale," *Poétique* 24 (1975), 426–445.

Salisbury Cathedral. Roger le Poer, bishop of Salisbury (1102–39) may have been John's patron,[6] and the deep, lifelong affection John felt for his city of birth has been highlighted on many occasions;[7] furthermore, there is proof that John was a canon at Salisbury in 1164,[8] and he backed Bishop Jocelin of Bohun (1142–84) against Becket. The studies of Frank Barlow have thrown some light on John's family.[9] His mother, Gille Peche, had children by at least two husbands, who were perhaps dignitaries or canons of Salisbury Cathedral. There is evidence that John had two half-brothers, Richard Peche and Robert; however it was his younger brother, Richard of Salisbury, who was closest to him, who took up his cause during the conflict between Henry II and Thomas Becket, and who followed him into exile; he also enjoyed the protection and friendship of Peter of Celle, who dedicated two prefaces of his *De claustrali disciplina* to Richard.

It was usual for the local clergy to teach the rudiments of Latin and grammar (in the medieval sense); nevertheless, John's first master seems to have been somewhat idiosyncratic (from the little we know about him in the available sources), given that John mentions him not for his gifts as a teacher but for his attempts at divination. Indeed, in his "most tender youth" (*in teneriori etate*), an expression that seems to refer to the first phase of his education when he was about seven years old, John was placed with a priest, together with another child, in order to learn the Psalms.[10] But this master, who was supposed to teach the basic principles of Latin and Scriptures, took advantage of the state of virginity of his two pupils and attempted to make use of them as

---

6   Yoko Hirata, *John of Salisbury and his Correspondents: A Study of the Epistolary Relationships between John of Salisbury and his Correspondents* (PhD Diss., University of Sheffield, 1991), vol. 1, p. 10 (after Edward J. Kealey, *Roger of Salisbury, Viceroy of England*, (London, 1972) p. 93).

7   Particularly by John McLoughlin, "Nations and Loyalties: The Outlook of a Twelfth-century Schoolman (John of Salisbury, c. 1120–1180)," in David Loades and Katherine Walsh, eds., *Faith and Identity. Christian Political Experience. Papers Read at the Anglo-Polish Colloquium of the British Sub-Commission of the Commission Internationale d'Histoire Ecclésiastique Comparée, 9–13 septembre 1986*, (Oxford, 1990), pp. 39–46. John describes the Church of Salisbury as *mater mea*; he also establishes a link between Salisbury and ancient Rome, claiming, for instance, that the name of the city derives from that of the emperor Severus.

8   *Fasti Ecclesiae Anglicanae 1066–1300*, vol. 4, *Salisbury* (London, 1991), p. 125.

9   Frank Barlow, "John of Salisbury and his Brothers," *Journal of Ecclesiastical History* 46 (1995) 95–109.

10   *Policraticus* 2.28, ed. Webb, vol. 1, p. 164.

mediums in divinatory practices, more precisely scrying.[11] It is quite typical of
John that he gave this personal anecdote the status of an *exemplum*, given that
he uses it to illustrate his theory of magic practice but also to stress its dangers.
In fact, in this passage of the *Policraticus*, John's purpose is not so much to provide a biographical element as to offer an *exemplum* whose value is reinforced
by the direct experience of the person who tells the story. Nevertheless, this is
precise enough to deduce that John received his first training in Salisbury, from
a priest, who, according to John's writings, later became a canon. Apart from
the reference to his "tender age," there is no conclusive element in this tale that
would make it possible to decide whether the priest was active in the service of
a parish or of a school linked to Salisbury Cathedral.

John probably continued his education in Salisbury; from the late 11th century, at the latest, the city could boast a teaching of grammar and perhaps the
arts, as well as singing. An *archischola* is mentioned in the statutes of Osmond,
bishop of Salisbury from 1078 to 1099, and a *magister scholae* in about 1139.[12]
There is nothing, however, to confirm that John would have started his cycle of
higher studies at Exeter, unless one takes into account the later links of his
family with this centre, as well as the intellectual significance of Exeter
Cathedral school; a grammar school existed in Exeter in the second half of the
12th century, as well as the teaching of theology. For the previous period, it has
been suggested that Robert Pullen may have taught there before leaving for
Paris in 1133.[13] We shall meet Robert later on in Paris.

The period when John was a student is probably the part of his life that has
been studied in the most depth, notably because it is documented in *Metalogicon*
2.10.[14] Here, again, John does not have a direct autobiographical purpose: what he
attempts to do by using the example of his own education is to show the damag-
ing consequences of an exclusive practice of dialectic. His overall aim is to

---

11   Jean-Patrice Boudet, *Entre Science et nigromance. Astrologie, divination et magie dans
      l'Occident médiéval (XIIᵉ–XVᵉ siècle)* (Paris, 2006), pp. 89–107. Jean-Patrice Boudet high-
      lights the fact that John of Salisbury is "le premier à utiliser le terme de *specularii* pour
      désigner les devins spécialisés dans la pratique de la catoptromancie (divination par les
      miroirs, les bassins et d'autres surfaces réfléchissantes) et de l'onychomancie (divination
      par les ongles utilisés comme des miroirs miniatures). Ce faisant, il latinise le vocabulaire
      relatif à des techniques divinatoires utilisées depuis l'Antiquité dans la magie grecque,
      mais aussi dans la magie juive." (ibid., pp. 104–105).
12   Nicholas Orme, *Education in the West of England 1066–1548. Cornwall, Devon, Dorset,
      Gloucestershire, Somerset, Wiltshire* (Exeter, 1976), pp. 65–66.
13   Ibid., pp. 46 et 52.
14   Katharine S.B. Keats-Rohan, "The Chronology of John of Salisbury's Studies in France:
      A Reading of 'Metalogicon', II.10," *Studi medievali* 28 (1987), 193–203.

promote a specific pedagogic model based on the practice of the whole spectrum of disciplines and on the link between dialectic and the other arts. Nevertheless, *Metalogicon* 2.10 yields much information on John's days as a student: he states that he studied for twelve years and describes his studies in some detail.

The first significant aspect of this narrative is John's relationship with Abelard. John's text seems to suggest that it was the very desire to be taught by Abelard that drew him to Paris. At the time Abelard's reputation as a logician was indisputable. But while Abelard also taught theology during those years, John does not mention it. This silence may be due to John's youth: he had not yet reached the age where he would have studied theology (in spite of the freedom students had to organise their own curriculum, it was unusual to start immediately with theology). John states that he received the rudiments of logic from Abelard – a statement that also argues against him having started his higher studies in England. For a whole year he attended Abelard's lessons (which may have been close to what Abelard writes in the *Glossule*), which he admits not to have understood fully, due to his own intellectual limitations. After the departure of Abelard in 1137, he joined the school of Alberic, who defended positions opposite to those of Abelard. But he also followed the teaching of Robert of Melun. Several reasons may account for this: firstly, it was Robert who took over from Abelard on the Montagne Sainte-Geneviève, secondly, he was English (John stresses this point), and finally he also shone for his intelligence. In any case, why one would choose a particular master over another remains rather obscure: John is usually content to stress the reputation of his various masters in the field of dialectic. He probably went to Paris specifically to study logic, and his choice of masters may have depended on their *fama*.

The departure of Alberic and of Robert after two years (around 1138–9) – one leaving for Bologna, the other deciding to stop teaching logic in order to dedicate himself fully to theology – led to John's growing awareness that dialectic by itself was a vain and sophistic pursuit. He then felt the need to start his cycle of studies afresh and "transferred" to the grammarian William of Conches, who taught him until 1141, either in Chartres or in Paris. During the same period, neglecting logic, he learned grammar under Richard l'Évêque, rhetoric under Thierry of Chartres and then Peter Helias, and the arts of quadrivium under Hardewin the German. But he also mentions friendly exchanges with another Englishman, Adam of Balsham or of the Petit-Pont (*de Paruo Ponte*), who was without doubt one of the best logicians of the time (and whom John criticized later in his *Entheticus*).[15]

---

15   See David Bloch, *John of Salisbury on Aristotelian Science* (Turnhout, 2012), esp. pp. 191–205; Jean Jolivet, Alain de Libera, dir., *Gilbert de Poitiers et ses contemporains* (Naples, 1987).

During that period John may have developed other friendships that were to last beyond his formative years. It was probably in Paris that he met Gerard Pucelle, Adam of Evesham and Bartholomew of Exeter, who all appear on several occasions in his correspondence. Also at this time John, who was in financial straits, taught pupils, not as a schoolmaster but rather as a private tutor to children of the nobility. The only pupil he mentions (rather in a negative way because of his leaning for formal logic) is William of Soissons, to whom he taught logic. Peter of Blois may have been another of his pupils, and it is often assumed that it was during his Parisian years that he met Peter of Celle, but in this particular case the proximity in age does not argue in favour of a master/pupil relationship.[16]

At the end of these three years spent learning afresh the fundamentals of the trivium, John went back to logic with Gilbert of Poitiers, and added theology to his curriculum. He does not seem to have been taught by him for more than a year, since Gilbert became bishop of Poitiers in 1142. John then turned to Robert Pullen in order to perfect his training in theology. After one year, however, Robert also left Paris, for Rome, and John replaced him with Simon of Poissy, who is not known otherwise, but with whom he completed his theological training between 1143 and 1147. Overall, John of Salisbury's studies lasted from 1136 to 1147, and the narrative he offers of what has been called – perhaps improperly – his "scholarly wanderings" (a narrative that is not unique, as suggested by that of William of Tyre, for instance) reflects the authority of masters within the educational system of the first half of the 12th century.

The years 1147–8 are not as well documented. One cannot rule out that John may first have been for some time in the service of Peter of Celle, who boasted, after the election of his former protégé to the bishopric of Chartres, that the new bishop had once been his clerk, *quondam clericus noster*.[17] Peter became abbot of Montier-la-Celle between 1140 and 1145 and John may have stayed with him; he may also have started writing the *Entheticus* during that period.

---

16   According to Léon Maître (*Les Écoles épiscopales et monastiques de l'Occident depuis Charlemagne jusqu'à Philippe Auguste (768–1180). Étude historique sur la filiation des écoles, la condition des maîtres et des élèves, et le programme des études avant la création des universités* (Paris, 1866), pp. 97–99, Peter of Celle and John shared the same masters: William of Conches, Richard l'Évêque and Peter Helias. Therefore he would be more a classmate than a student. This is also the hypothesis of Gérard de Martel in his introduction to Peter of Celle, *L'École du cloître*, ed. Gérard de Martel (Paris, 1977), p. 12. However, Peter speaks of John as being his *magister* and John of Peter as being his *alumnus* (see Christopher Brooke in his introduction to *The Early Letters*, p. xvii).

17   *The Letters of Peter of Celle*, ed. Julian Haseldine (Oxford, 2001), no. 183, p. 690: *Magister Iohannes de Anglia, quondam clericus noster, electus est Carnotensis.*

Entheticus is a criticism of formal logic, a eulogy of grammar and a defence of a type of Christian philosophy of Augustinian inspiration, as practised in the cloisters. Indeed, it was mostly during phases of more or less voluntary *otium* that he produced his work, and Peter was often an intellectual spur for him, for instance enticing him to write the *Historia pontificalis* during his exile in Reims in 1164.

It was also through the intermediary of Peter that John may first have been put in contact with Bernard of Clairvaux. Apart from his unquestionable intellectual influence (although less than Abelard's or Gilbert's), Bernard held a significant place in John's life and operated as a powerful lever to propel him into his ecclesiastical career. Probably in 1147, Bernard wrote to Theobald of Canterbury – an oral recommendation that is difficult to date may also have been instrumental – in order to recommend John to the archbishop.[18] Whether John used this letter immediately is more uncertain. In March 1148 he was at the Council of Reims, which he narrates in the *Historia pontificalis*: he may have gone there on account of Peter of Celle, but he simply indicates that he was a direct witness of the proceedings, without stating the reason for his presence in Reims. In the second half of the year 1148, however, one finds him in Canterbury in the service of the archbishop. He then entered a circle that probably was as important for his education as the years he had spent in the French schools, though it is less well documented. There he met a number of exceptional personalities, many of whom had also been taught in Paris, and some of whom were later called to high positions in the Church: besides, of course, Thomas Becket, these were men such as John of Canterbury, the future bishop of Poitiers and then archbishop of Lyon. What all these well-educated men had in common was probably the fact that their tastes or their intellectual capacities had not led them to teach logic and theology in the schools. Giving up speculation in the strict sense in favour of ecclesiastical and/or political action does not mean, however, that they had abandoned all intellectual ambition. This is clearly visible in John's correspondence: when writing to a former student or master he starts his letter with an allusion to philosophical theory or with an *exemplum* that introduces the subject. And in their daily exchanges these *literati*, some of whom were well versed in Latin antiquity, must have

---

18   *S. Bernardi Opera*, vol. 8, *Epistolae. I. Corpus epistolarum 181–310. II. Epistolae extra corpus 311–547*, ed. Jean Leclerc et Henri Rochais (Rome, 1977), Letter 361, pp. 307–308. See the commentary by Christopher N.L. Brooke, *The Early Letters*, p. xv. For the date of the first contact between John of Salisbury and Bernard of Clairvaux, see Maria Lodovica Arduini, "Contributo alla ricostruzione biografica di Giovanni di Salisbury," *Rivista di filosofia neoscolastica* 90 (1998), 198–214, esp. p. 207.

behaved in a similar way. *Policraticus* 8, which partly draws its inspiration from the *Saturnalia* of Macrobius in order to defend the concept of the philosophical symposium, perhaps transcribes in theory a practice that was common to the men of the archbishop's entourage. Beyond this circle of clerics, John perhaps knew the Bolognese master Vacarius, who resided in Canterbury and who may have been one of the masters who provided him with knowledge of Roman law.

In 1154, John appears as secretary and personal adviser to Theobald. Before that date, as Julie Barrau shows in the following pages ("John of Salisbury as ecclesiastical administrator"), his precise role in the archbishop's entourage remains vague, and he seems to have been employed mainly on missions to the papal Curia. As early as 1149 he was sent to Pope Eugenius III in Rome. In the prologue to *Metalogicon* 3, written in 1159, he states that he has travelled extensively in France and England, and that he has crossed the Alps ten times, even staying in Apulia for a lengthy period. This means that during these ten years of service he would have travelled to Italy on average once a year and stayed there for considerable lengths of time. These travels are significant both socially and intellectually. John was able to create or strengthen links with some influential men in the Church or in lay circles. It was, for instance, during one of his journeys to the Curia that he became close friends with Cardinal Nicholas Breakspear, a fellow Englishman who became pope in 1154 under the name of Adrian IV and with whom John stayed for a long period, as he narrates in the *Policraticus* and in his letters. This friendship, which John mentions on several occasions (e.g. Letter 50; *Metalogicon* 4.42), probably strengthened his position at the Curia, but it did not enable him – for lack of time, unless it was because Adrian IV did not wish to displease Henry II – to get promoted to the cardinalship, a position John seems to have coveted.

These travels were also intellectually significant. John may have acquired some of his legal knowledge in Italy, contrary to what is often assumed. His links with the kingdom of Sicily must also be emphasized: the periods John spent at the Curia between 1149 and 1154 coincided with the rapprochement between Eugenius III and Roger II, and, although the latter is described in the *Historia pontificalis* as acting "in the manner of other tyrants" because of his ambition to interfere with the affairs of the Sicilian Church,[19] John seems in the course of his missions (mainly in Apulia) to have created contacts with the Sicilian court and in particular with its chancellor, the Englishman Robert of

---

19   Helene Wieruszowski, "Roger II of Sicily, Rex-Tyrannus, in Twelfth-Century Political Thought," *Speculum* 38 (1963), 46–78, esp. p. 68.

Selby, to whom he refers in *Policraticus* and in his letters as well. The Sicilian court was an important intellectual centre and in particular a point of contact with Greek culture. A later letter by Henricus Aristippus to an Englishman called Robert bears witness to the high number of translations of scientific and philosophical works that were done there. These contacts may have enabled John to discover some new texts in Greek, a language he did not know since he had to employ a translator when he travelled to Apulia (a Greek dialect was spoken in some areas of Apulia).[20] It was also during his travels in Italy that he must have met Burgundio of Pisa; but it is more difficult to know whether it was through this intermediary that he came to know of the existence of the translations of James of Venice.[21]

During all these years spent close to – and perhaps in the intimate circle of – Pope Eugenius III and then Adrian IV, John of Salisbury probably confirmed his intellectual and social position. But it was also this very proximity that damaged his position in the eyes of King Henry II. During his stay at Benevento with Adrian IV in 1155–6, John may have been asked by the English king to obtain the authorization of the Pope for the subjection of Ireland, among other missions.[22] Henry II wished to give some legitimacy to his project of invasion: he may have hoped at best for a crusade, following the example of William the Conqueror during his invasion of England, or at least for the permission to govern Ireland. It is not the place here to examine the issue of the authenticity of *Laudabiliter*,[23] but one may follow John of Salisbury when he asserts that the negotiations were a success (*Metalogicon* 4.42), although one

---

20   See Jean-Marie Martin, *La Pouille du VIᵉ au XIIᵉ siècle* (Rome, 1993), pp. 509–518.

21   James of Venice was in Constantinople in 1136 with Burgundio of Pisa. It is around that date that he may have begun his work as translator. Before 1148 he produced legal advice for the archbishop of Ravenna for use in a case against the archbishop of Milan, which was eventually settled by the papacy. It is difficult to say how John of Salisbury may have had access to the translations of James of Venice (insofar as that he would have known them in their entirety). See Lorenzo Minio-Paluello, "Iacobus veneticus Grecus, Canonist and Translator of Aristotle," *Traditio* 8 (1952), 265–304; Sten Ebbesen, "Jacques de Venise," in M. Lejbowicz, dir., *L'Islam médiéval en terre chrétienne. Science et idéologie* (Lille, 2008), pp. 115–132; Giancarlo Garfagnini, "Giovanni di Salisbury, Ottone di Frisinga e Giacomo da Venezia," *Rivista critica di storia della filosofia* 27 (1972), 19–34, esp. p. 34.

22   On the Irish question, see esp. Giles Constable, "The Alleged Disgrace of John of Salisbury in 1159," *English Historical Review* 69 (1954), 67–76; Christopher N.L. Brooke, "Adrian IV and John of Salisbury," in Brenda Bolton and Anne J. Duggan, eds., *Adrian IV The English Pope (1154–1159). Studies and Texts* (Aldershot, 2003), pp. 1–13; Anne J. Duggan, "*Totius christianitatis caput*. The pope and the princes," ibid., pp. 105–155.

23   On this subject, see esp. Anne J. Duggan, "*Totius christianitatis caput*."

does not know whether John was a member of the royal embassy or whether he was there as a representative of the Archbishop of Canterbury.[24] At the end of *Metalogicon*, John relates that Adrian IV gave him a ring for the king of England as a token of the hereditary concession of Ireland.[25] But back in England John talked about his disgrace in letters to the Pope and to Peter of Celle, where he questioned the role of Arnulf, Bishop of Lisieux, an intimate of Henry II and a member of the embassy. From what John says, one of the accusations made against him was that he had lowered the royal dignity: this probably means that John was considered to have worked in favour of Theobald's interests at the expense of those of the English Crown. But in reality it was Adrian IV who was the great victor in these negotiations: John had obtained for the king the authorization to invade Ireland, but it seems that this was to be placed under the authority of the papacy. Furthermore, the reference in the discussions to the Donation of Constantine raised implicitly the status of England itself – another insular land – in relation to the papacy.[26] The favour shown to John by the Pope in Benevento probably fed suspicions concerning the former's attitude.[27]

At the time John may have considered exile, before rejecting a project that could be interpreted as a confession of guilt. Did he find himself in a situation of "internal exile"? His disgrace may have prevented him from fulfilling his office for the archbishop, insofar as his contacts with royal officers as well as his travels may have been curtailed. And it was during this period of compulsory *otium* that he may have started writing the *Policraticus*.[28] John attempted – probably in vain – to obtain the backing of Thomas Becket, who was then the king's chancellor, in order to put an end to this situation; in fact it was certainly the intervention of the Pope himself who won him back the king's favour. He started again on his missions to Rome, where he was present at the election of Alexander III, the former chancellor of Pope Adrian, in 1159. The new Pope

---

24   Constable, "The Alleged Disgrace of John of Salisbury in 1159," p. 68.

25   Brooke, "Adrian IV and John of Salisbury," *passim*.

26   Constable, "The Alleged Disgrace of John of Salisbury in 1159," p. 75; Nicholas Vincent, "Beyond Becket: King Henry II and the papacy (1154–1189)," in Peter D. Clarke and Anne J. Duggan, eds, *Pope Alexander III (1159–81). The Art of Survival* (Farnham, 2012), pp. 257–299.

27   This interpretation of the disgrace of John in 1156 is not unanimously accepted by historians: Anne Duggan, for instance, suggests that John's reformist and pro-papal positions were more likely to harm his reputation with the king (Duggan, "*Totius christianitatis caput*," p. 143).

28   Max Kerner, *Johannes von Salisbury und die Logische Struktur seines Policraticus* (Wiesbaden, 1977), pp. 114–116.

seems to have shown him some degree of affection and John immediately became a fervent defender of Alexander's cause in England, and a ferocious critic of Antipope Victor IV.

John of Salisbury's role in Canterbury became more significant during Theobald's illness (*Metalogicon* 4.42). Also, in 1159, in spite of his administrative tasks, John was able to complete his two main works, *Policraticus* and *Metalogicon*, which were both dedicated to Thomas Becket. Theobald died in April 1161, and in 1162 he was replaced by Becket. As suggested by Becket's caution during the Irish business, there is no proper evidence of a real friendship between the two men at this date. But the necessity of providing a degree of continuity with Theobald's pontificate, probably combined with the desire to benefit from John's numerous connections, in particular at the Curia, led the new archbishop to retain his services. John was a member of the embassy that was to receive the *pallium* at Montpellier from the hands of Pope Alexander III and, while not being the closest adviser to Becket, he seems to have retained his position as secretary.

By revealing himself as an ardent defender of ecclesiastical privileges, Thomas Becket disappointed the hopes Henry II had of a close collaboration with the new archbishop. In 1164 the conflict focused on the Constitutions of Clarendon, by which clerics were to be subjected to royal jurisdiction. Having first consented to the diktat of Henry II, Thomas then decided to reject the Constitutions and chose exile. As for John, he may have left England already in 1163: whether he was exiled by Henry II, who strove to deprive Thomas of his advisers (this is implicit in William FitzStephen's account), or sent on a mission by Becket, Letter 136 testifies to the contacts he made on the Continent (Philip of Alsace, then count of Amiens, and Louis VII) in order to back the cause of Canterbury.[29] It was also on this occasion that he went back to the Montagne Sainte-Geneviève in order to visit his former colleagues. Seeing their lack of progress in philosophy, this was a deeply disappointing experience for him: his attitude may reveal, however, his inability to understand the transformations that were affecting the schools at the time. As his mission became more difficult due to the lack of subsidies (Henry II had suppressed the income he could draw from his ecclesiastical benefices), John ended up taking refuge at the abbey of Saint-Remi at Reims with Peter of Celle, who had recently been elected abbot there.

During their exile Thomas Becket and John of Salisbury never seem to have stayed together, for Thomas was first at Pontigny and then at Sens, while John remained at Reims with Peter of Celle and under the protection of the King of

---

29   *The Later Letters*, pp. 2–10; Nederman, *John of Salisbury*, p. 29.

France and of the king's brother, Henri, Archbishop of Reims. During the first phase of his exile John was fairly ambivalent: with Thomas he called for moderation, while attempting to make a separate peace with Henry II. He even congratulated John of Canterbury, bishop of Poitiers, who was close to Becket, for having made his peace with the king.[30] On the other hand, in a letter written in 1167 to a cleric in the entourage of the bishop of Poitiers, he seems to warn against the temptation to abandon Becket's cause. Between those two dates it was probably his meeting with the king during Easter 1166 that made him join the archbishop's camp and place his sharp pen as well as his deep biblical culture at his service. And it was probably during this period of compulsory *otium* that John wrote one of his last important works (apart from the *Vita Thomae*), the *Historia pontificalis*, which he presents as a continuation of the chronicle of Sigebert of Gembloux, and which he never completed.

John's exile ended in November 1170 following the agreement between Henry II and Becket. John landed in England and travelled directly to Exeter to visit his dying mother, before going back to Canterbury in order to prepare for the return of the archbishop. There he had to deal with the obstruction and humiliations inflicted by royal officers, as he writes in a letter to Peter of Celle. The renewal of the conflict between the king and the archbishop eventually led to the murder of Becket in his cathedral on 29 December 1170. The testimony of William FitzStephen suggests that John was among those who fled during the attack; it is not impossible, however, as suggested here by Ronald Pepin ("John of Salisbury as a writer") that he took refuge somewhere in the church and witnessed the event. In any case he describes it at length in a letter, *Ex insperato* (Letter 305), a text he then used as a model for his *Vita Thomae*, the first hagiographic account of the martyr.[31] This narrative contributed to the inscription of the martyrdom in collective memory, and helped spread an interpretation of the murder to the advantage of Canterbury: a situation of political defeat was thus transformed into posthumous victory.

John spent the next few years in Exeter; while closely following what was going on in Canterbury, he helped Bishop Bartholomew on several occasions,

---

30 Recent studies by Hugh Thomas have stressed the violence and the systematic intimidation that marked the acute phase of the conflict between Henry II and Becket. This dimension should be kept in mind when attempting to make sense of the behaviour of the different parties: Hugh Thomas, "Shame, Masculinity, and the Death of Thomas Becket," *Speculum* 87 (2012), 1050–88.

31 E. Walberg, *La Tradition hagiographique de saint Thomas Becket avant la fin du XII* siècle* (Paris, 1929, repr. Geneva, 1975); Michael Staunton, *Thomas Becket and his Biographers* (Woodbridge, 2006).

and was also able to draw on his assistance.[32] As we have seen, it is difficult to argue in favour of John having been educated in Exeter prior to his departure for the Paris schools. Nevertheless, his links with the Church of Exeter played a significant role during his exile, and more largely during his whole career: this probably has to be put in the context of the close connections between the Churches of Salisbury and Exeter. Richard Peche and Robert FitzGille (later archdeacon of Totnes and eventually canon of Plympton in Devon), but also Richard of Salisbury, were all canons at Exeter, and their mother settled there.[33] John himself was a canon of Exeter perhaps from 1160, and in 1165 he may have considered settling in this city. In 1160–1, he seems to have played a significant role in the election to the bishopric of the archdeacon of Exeter, Bartholomew, who was a former member of Theobald's entourage in Canterbury. John became treasurer of the cathedral in 1173, an office he may have kept until 1176.[34] On several occasions in his correspondence he alludes to his friends and relatives in Exeter, and several letters written during the period of exile are addressed to the clergy of Exeter, with whom he enjoyed privileged connections. The Church of Exeter backed John and Richard, and John used his correspondence with Exeter to spread his views on the conflict between Henry II and Becket, although the clergy of Exeter refused to adopt an extreme position.[35]

John was probably in Canterbury for the ceremony of the reconciliation of the cathedral in December 1171. He also played a major role in obtaining the agreement of the Pope for the election of Richard of Dover to the archbishopric, and his help was certainly invaluable for the monks of Christ Church during this period of crisis.[36] John's intervention seems to have been decisive in the face of hostility, and must also have weighed considerably in favour of the canonisation of the martyr. Nevertheless, for a long time John's attitude towards Becket had probably been close to that of Peter of Celle, who was quite critical of the chancellor, to the point that he may have refused him his friendship.[37]

---

32   Yoko Hirata, "John of Salisbury and the clergy of Exeter," in *Collected Papers on John of Salisbury and his Correspondents* (Tokyo, 1996), pp. 157–181, esp. p. 172.

33   *Fasti Ecclesiae Anglicanae 1066–1300*, vol. 10, *Exeter* (London, 2005), pp. 25, 66, 69.

34   Barlow, "John of Salisbury and his Brothers," pp. 101 and 104; *Fasti Ecclesiae Anglicanae 1066–1300*, vol. 10, *Exeter*, p. 18.

35   Hirata, "John of Salisbury and the clergy of Exeter." Frank Barlow has identified the members of this group as Archdeacon Baldwin, Richard fitzReinfred, Roger of Sidbury and Roger of Limesy.

36   Barlow, "John of Salisbury and his Brothers," pp. 106–107.

37   Lynn K. Barber, "MS Bodl. Canon. Pat. Lat. 131 and a Lost Lactantius of John of Salisbury: Evidence in Search of a French Critic of Thomas Becket," *Albion* 22 (1990), 21–37, esp. p. 34,

Although he was the dedicatee of John's works, Becket may have felt rightly that he was the target of the criticism aimed at curial clerics in the *Policraticus*. For Karen Bollermann and Cary Nederman ("John of Salisbury and Thomas Becket") the ostentatious praise of Becket inserted into the dedications of *Policraticus* and *Metalogicon* may be interpreted as the means for John to express his disapproval of the chancellor; and in some respects wasn't the chancellor an ecclesiastical tyrant? The failed meeting with Henry II in 1166 modified John's behaviour. But it was Becket's murder that provoked a radical transformation in John's attitude towards the archbishop. He may have interpreted the manner of this death as a divine sign, and this may have led him to see the whole of Thomas's life in a new light. His conception of the martyr as the one who suffers for justice, probably forged while he was writing the *Vita Anselmi*, may also have led to a shift in his attitude.[38] A reliquary now at the Metropolitan Museum of Art has been linked with John, but this hypothesis has not been met with wide approval.[39] Nevertheless, a reliquary containing some relics of Becket was left by John to the Church of Chartres, and a window of the cathedral picturing the martyrdom attests to the growth of Becket's cult in Chartres. John's election as bishop of Chartres in 1176 was helped by the backing of William White Hands, archbishop of Sens, and proves the significance of the networks John had been able to create in Capetian circles; William may also have calculated that this promotion could counter the ambitions of Henry II. But it is also a testament to the central place immediately acquired by the cult of Thomas Becket, to whom John had the reputation of having been close. As Julie Barrau, Karen Bollermann and Cary Nederman suggest in the following pages, it was certainly to a large extent as a form of homage to Becket that the canons of Chartres elected John of Salisbury. In any case, Thomas played a decisive role in John's life, both in his political positioning and in his work.

John's decisions as bishop of Chartres were viewed controversially, as the correspondence of Peter of Celle and that of Peter of Blois testify. For a long time it was thought that very few traces remained of his activity as bishop,

---

which refers to Letter 24 (72 in the edition by Haseldine) of Peter of Celle and to the marginal notes of the manuscript of Lactantius. Conversely, recent studies on friendship in the 12th century may lead one to interpret the criticisms uttered by John as the signs of real friendship: Yoko Hirata, "John of Salisbury and Thomas Becket: the Making of a Martyr," in *Collected Papers*, pp. 121–133.

38   Both points have been put forward by Hirata, "John of Salisbury and Thomas Becket: the Making of a Martyr."

39   J. Breck, "A Reliquary of Saint Thomas Becket made for John of Salisbury," *The Metropolitan Museum of Art Bulletin* 13 (1918), 220–224; see *English Romanesque Art 1066–1200, Hayward Gallery, London 5 April–8 July 1984* (London, 1984), cat. no. 302.

apart from his participation in the Council of Lateran III. In fact, the contribution of Julie Barrau to this volume shows that many documents concerning this period of John's life still remain to be studied, which could provide important avenues for future research on John's last years. He died on 25 October 1180; he left some of his books (if not all of them) to his Church,[40] and was buried in Josaphat Abbey, close to Chartres, where the remains of his tomb are still to be seen.

Medievalists have long shown an interest in John of Salisbury's work, and his various writings are available in critical editions of varying quality, as well as in modern language translations. The contribution of Ronald Pepin in this volume offers the state of the art on the various works of John of Salisbury. Here some brief indications may be given on the dates of these writings – still a subject for disagreement among historians – and on their content:

> *Entheticus de dogmate philosophorum* or *Entheticus maior*.[41] This didactic poem written between 1147 and 1154 shares the same themes as *Policraticus*, but in different proportions: the criticism of a certain form of education, a eulogy of Christian philosophy coupled with a history of ancient philosophy, and a criticism of curial life and tyranny (that of Stephen, rather than that of Henry II). John may have started writing this text, which survives in four manuscripts, during his student years (or at the latest during his stay with Peter of Celle in 1147–8). Indeed, the criticism of logic, in particular that of Adam of Petit-Pont, and the praise of grammar – meaning the literary study of the classics – seem contemporary with his scholastic disillusionment, whether this took the form of a growing awareness of his weaknesses in the field of logic followed by his conversion to grammar under William of Conches around 1138–9, or, more radically, of his later renunciation of scholastic life in 1147. On the other hand, the second part of this work, which is dedicated to curial life and a criticism of tyranny, may have been written when he was active in the service of Theobald, and would bear witness to the hopes raised by the accession of Henry Plantagenet, after the disastrous reign of Stephen.

---

40   Most of these volumes were destroyed in the fire at the library of Chartres in 1944, but some had been dispersed beforehand (such as the Lactantius); others are undergoing restoration at the Institut de Recherche et d'Histoire des Textes.

41   *John of Salisbury's Entheticus de dogmate philosophorum, Critical Text with English Introduction and Notes*, ed. D.J. Sheerin (Chapel Hill, 1969); Ronald E. Pepin, "The *Entheticus* of John of Salisbury, a Critical Text," *Traditio* 31 (1975), 127–193; *Entheticus maior et minor*, ed. and trans. Jan van Laarhoven, 3 vols. (Leiden, 1987).

Policraticus siue de nugis curialium et uestigiis philosophorum:[42] John of Salisbury's masterwork is a composite text made up of three distinct parts that seem to be reflected in the wording of the title under which the work is known. The first part (Books 1 to 3) is a criticism of curial life (*de nugis curialium*), that is to say the behaviour and practices of *curiales* (their passion for entertainments such as hunting and music, mimes and *histriones*,[43] their belief in astrology, or their general hypocrisy). The second part (Books 4 to 6) is a treatise of good government, which corresponds to *Policraticus*, a term that may mean "the various forms of power" or "power over the city."[44] Within this section, Books 5 and 6, the *Institutio Traiani*, were attributed by John of Salisbury to Plutarch, and some passages circulated separately. Finally, the last part, which corresponds to *de uestigiis philosophorum*, describes what an authentic philosophical life should be, leading to happiness, in contrast to the life of the court. In spite of this relatively elaborate structure it is certain that *Policraticus* is the result of several successive layers of writing. It is highly probable that the parts of the text that pertain to the genre of consolation, and which are dedicated to the exemplarity of philosophers, the criticism of the curial cleric, and tyrannicide (Books 7 and 8), were written during John's disgrace in 1156. This may also be the case with the praise of philosophical symposia, an allusion to the intellectual community of Canterbury, which John had more leisure to spend time with during this period. The first and second parts may be dated to 1157–8: while not sparing the defects of court life, what John expresses here is a more detached view of political life. Finally, in 1159, he may have completed the work with a prologue and the end of Book 8. Of all the works of John of Salisbury, the *Policraticus* had the most significant posterity, as Frédérique Lachaud stresses in the following pages ("Filiation and Context: the Medieval Afterlife of the *Policraticus*"). The *Policraticus* was first read within a small circle of initiates; its knowledge was then spread in France and, in the later Middle Ages, in the

---

42   *Policraticus sive de nugis curialium et vestigiis philosophorum*, ed. Clement C.J. Webb, 2 vols. (Oxford, 1909); *Policraticus I–IV*, ed. Katharine S.B. Keats-Rohan (Turnhout, 1993). English translations: John Dickinson, *The Statesman's Book of John of Salisbury*, [*Policraticus* Books IV,V, VI, and excerpts from Books VII and VIII] (New York, 1963); Joseph Pike, *Frivolities of Courtiers and Footprints of Philosophers* [*Policraticus* books I, II, III and excerpts from VII and VIII] (New York, 1972); M. Markland, *Policraticus* [selections] (New York, 1979); Cary J. Nederman, *Policraticus* [selections] (Cambridge, 1990).

43   The term *histriones* (*Policraticus* 1.8) refers both to the "jongleurs" and mimes of John's day, and to ancient theatre. See Donnalee Dox, *The Idea of the Theater in Latin Christian Thought: Augustine to the Fourteenth Century* (Cambridge, 2004), pp. 87–92.

44   *Policraticus I–IV*, ed. Keats-Rohan, p. viii.

whole of the West. This does not mean that the identity of its author was always known. In any case, the way the text was read, whether in its entirety or not (it is often the *Institutio Traiani* that is quoted, and not the other books of the *Policraticus*), and reused, in environments very different from the one that prevailed during its conception, raises the question of the significance of its transmission. Over time some themes were dropped in favour of others, which were extracted from their context and adapted to entirely novel situations.

Metalogicon[45] was also completed in 1159 and is explicitly presented as an introduction to *Policraticus*: the choice of a liberal or humanistic education is the precondition for a philosophical life, as opposed to courtly life. At the end of 2.10, John states that he went back to Paris twelve years after the completion of his studies, in 1147. And at the beginning of the prologue to Book 3, he explains that for the past twenty years he has ceased to be interested in logic, both for financial reasons and on the advice of friends. From these converging allusions one may conclude that *Metalogicon* was probably written over a stretch of time at around 1158–9, on the basis of material that was already extant in the *Entheticus*. The contribution by Constant Mews and Cédric Giraud ("John of Salisbury and the Schools of the 12th Century") shows that against the figure of "Cornificius" John develops the ideal of an education that hones the critical judgement of each individual through the practice of liberal arts. This accounts for the large place given in this scheme to the teaching of grammar, whose role is to civilize individuals by enabling them to express themselves correctly on the basis of a specific literary culture. Grammar is seen, therefore, as the first step towards philosophy (in particular in its ethical dimension), but this must be completed by dialectic in the sense of the capacity for reasoning. Eventually the study of the arts of language must lead to theology, which completes this education by linking wisdom and grace. It remains difficult, however, to explain why John needed to criticize "Cornificius" at a stage in his life where he did not belong to scholastic circles anymore. The repeated allusions to his adversaries' attacks may pertain to literary fiction; but there is no doubt that what John criticizes here is the distortion of Epicurus's thought, in particular among curial clerics, and the incitement to seek an immediate return on investment in studies. This criticism – which is the precise opposite of his praise of the liberal arts – is the intellectual equivalent of the dichotomy between the vanities of the court and the exemplarity of philosophers. At a time when John saw arriving at court an increasing number of clerics fresh from their studies in law and logic, his purpose was to denounce the intellectual foundations of the

---

45   *Metalogicon*, J.B. Hall and Katherine S.B. Keats-Rohan, eds. (Turnhout, 1991); trans. D. McGarry, *The Metalogicon of John of Salisbury* (Berkeley, 1962).

spontaneous epicureanism of the *curiales*, and to remind those keen to take part in public life of the necessity of practising the liberal arts.

In 1164 John wrote the *Historia pontificalis*,[46] most probably at the request of Peter of Celle. In this work, which may have been planned to include a portrait of Pope Adrian IV,[47] but which stops in 1152, John's intention was to give a narrative of events at the Curia from 1148, mainly but not exclusively based on his own experience. As Clare Monagle shows in this volume ("John of Salisbury and the Writing of History"), the *Historia pontificalis*'s interest is multifold. It conveys a conception of history that is relatively original, marked by the author's attention to modest human actions and to the egotistical motives of its protagonists. The narrative highlights two major episodes: the trial of Gilbert de la Porrée at the Council of Reims in 1148, and the Second Crusade. In both cases John analyses conflicts and contradictions in some detail. According to Clare Monagle, John of Salisbury considered these to be the consequences of an incorrect use of language: instead of enabling communication between men, this can be a locus for misunderstanding, rivalry and conflict. Language has been given to Man by God, but it is also the sign of the Fall. In fact *Historia pontificalis* merges "modern" features (the historian ought only to rely on trustworthy sources) and "classical" ones (history has a place within a general scheme of edification and of the glorification of Creation).[48] The work was never completed, which may be due to Peter of Celle's disapproval of its tone.[49]

John is also the author of a *Vita Anselmi* written in 1162–3 at the request of Thomas Becket with a view to the canonization process of the former archbishop of Canterbury; it is based mainly on Eadmer's work.[50] The *Vita Thomae*, on the other hand, is a spontaneous development of the description of Becket's murder in *Ex insperato*. This hagiographical text aimed to ensure Becket's canonization but it also sets out some of John of Salisbury's philosophical and political ideas.[51] Finally, John twice reorganized his correspondence: once after Theobald's death and once again after his accession to the bishopric. This collection of letters, whose text was probably reworked, is an essential account

---

46   *Historia Pontificalis*, ed. and trans. Marjorie Chibnall (Oxford, 1986); see Christopher N.L. Brooke, "Aspects of John of Salisbury's *Historia Pontificalis*," in Lesley Smith and Benedicta Ward, eds., *Intellectual Life in the Middle Ages: Essays Presented to Margaret Gibson* (London, 1992), pp. 185–195.

47   This is the hypothesis of Brooke, "Adrian IV and John of Salisbury," p. 7.

48   See also the contributions published in Ernst Breisach, ed., *Classical Rhetoric and Medieval Historiography* (Kalamazoo, 1985).

49   Brooke, "Aspects of John of Salisbury's *Historia Pontificalis*," p. 195.

50   *Anselmo e Becket, due vite*, ed. Inos Biffi (Milan, 1990).

51   *MB*, vol. 2, pp. 299–322.

of the life of John of Salisbury, his understanding of the practice of philosophy and administration, and his talent as a polemicist in the service of the Church.[52]

Debates and Prospects

Some aspects of the life and work of John of Salisbury remain to be settled. A first series of questions turn on his educational years. The contribution of Constant Mews and Cédric Giraud to this volume analyses the link between John of Salisbury and 12th-century schools: starting with the reconstruction of his educational curriculum, from Salisbury to Paris, it then deals with the *quaestio uexata* of John's stay in Chartres in 1139–41. Did John follow William of Conches's teaching in Chartres or in Paris? The main tenet of the debate is not so much John's travels as the place of Chartres in the scholastic geography of Northern France and the intellectual orientations of the various schools in this period. Secondly, what incited John to give up the prospect of a career as a master, beyond his distaste for the direction logic was to take after the *logica uetus*? Did he leave Paris on account of his failure to establish himself there as a master? Yoko Hirata suggests that John felt envious of renowned masters such as Gerard Pucelle, who had been able to attract students to Paris as well as to Cologne. John's charisma and his work aroused admiration, but his reputation was in no way based on his teaching.

One would have to identify more clearly the loyalties and friendships he made during his educational years. Also in need of clarification is the nature of his relationships with Peter Abelard and Gilbert of Poitiers – although he professes to admire both. The influence of Abelard's thought on that of John of Salisbury is probably one of the questions that scholarship will throw new light on in the coming years.[53] This influence was certainly deeper than is usually

---

52 *The Letters of John of Salisbury*, ed. and trans. W.J. Millor and H.E. Butler, 2 vols. (Oxford, 1979 and 1986).

53 John also seems to have followed Abelard's example in his high estimation of the character of Trajan: Gordon Whatley, "The Uses of Hagiography: the Legend of Pope Gregory and the Emperor Trajan in the Middle Ages," *Viator: Medieval and Renaissance Studies* 15 (1984), 25–63, esp. p. 33. Another point of contact between the thoughts of Abelard and John has been brought to attention by John Marenbon in his introduction to the *Collationes*: this is the positive perception of Epicurus, who is distinguished from his Epicurean followers (Peter Abelard, *Collationes*, ed. and trans. J. Marenbon et G. Orlando (Oxford, 2001), p. xci, note 216). See also Luisa Valente, "Philosophers and other Kinds of Human Beings according to Peter Abelard and John of Salisbury," in Jakob L. Fink, Heine Hansen and Ana Maria Mora-Marquez, eds., *Logic and Language in the Middle Ages. A Volume in Honour of Sten Ebesen* (Leiden-Boston, 2013), pp. 105–124.

assumed, and raises all the more acutely the significance of the rejection of dialectic in the *Metalogicon* – which may or may not be a proper intellectual rejection of this discipline. This also raises the question of the way he viewed theology, in particular the scholastic theology that was developing at the time. The contribution of Christophe Grellard to this volume deals with this matter: this chapter analyses the nature of the theological education he received in Paris, and then examines the place of theology in the context of John's scepticism. In fact, the questions raised by scholastic theology (such as divine prescience, for which John provides a precise case study) pertain to the group of problems open to doubt, for which arguments pro and contra have to be examined. Above all, this inclusion of theological matters in the field of scepticism leads John to qualify the value of rational theological speculation in favour of a kind of fideism and even negative theology. Consequently, once the unknowable character of the divine is admitted, John can stress the essentially political dimension of theology understood as the transmission and administering of the divine law given by God to compensate for the cognitive deficiencies of man.

Regarding John's admiration for Gilbert de la Porrée, and the preference he expresses for him above Bernard of Clairvaux at the time of their confrontation at the Council of Reims in 1148, this has been the subject of recent analysis. According to Clare Monagle, John's position was unambiguously in favour of the schools: for him, the intimate knowledge Gilbert had of the liberal arts meant he could not err.[54] She has also compared the narrative of the Council in *Historia pontificalis* with that of Otto of Freising. In both cases, the story stresses the importance of humility and knowledge (that of Gilbert de la Porrée) in the face of immoderate action.[55] For John of Salisbury, Gilbert de la Porrée was also a mind capable of analysing the world and giving it some meaning.[56] The conflict, however, was not only the result of the confrontation between two systems of thought – the schools and the cloister – but also the consequence of political tensions between the papal Curia and the French and English Churches.

One finally has to mention the possibility of John's training in the field of law. He may have acquired notions of civil law when staying in Italy. The presence of Vacarius in Theobald's entourage probably also influenced his

---

54   Clare Monagle, "Contested Knowledge: John of Salisbury's *Metalogicon* and *Historia Pontificalis*," *Parergon* 21 (2004), 1–17.

55   Clare Monagle, "The Trial of Ideas: Two Tellings of the Trial of Gilbert of Poitiers," *Viator: Medieval and Renaissance Studies* 35 (2004), 113–129, esp. p. 125.

56   Monagle, "The Trial of Ideas," p. 126.

knowledge of Roman law. This shows in *Policraticus*, which may even have been read as an accessus to Roman law. The contribution of Yves Sassier to the volume aims at identifying the place of law in John of Salisbury's political thought: while clearly not a technician of civil law, John of Salisbury had a good knowledge of this discipline (in particular of the recent *Summa Trecensis*) and used the resources of law to feed his reflection on the hierarchy of norms. He relies on the Digest, but limits its impact in favour of a theological foundation to law. The will of the lawmakers is, as it were, captive, as the analysis of the principle *a legibus solutus* demonstrates.

John's approach to Canon law may probably be analysed anew in the light of recent studies on Gratian's *Decretum*. Indeed, the work of Anders Winroth suggests that this may have been compiled earlier than one assumed for a long time. Did John of Salisbury know the work?[57] The obituary of Robert FitzGille, John's half-brother, mentions the gift of a copy of the *Decretum* to the abbey of Plympton.[58] And in the correspondence between John and Baldwin of Totnes the two men appear under pseudonyms: Baldwin is Benedict, while John is Gratian.[59] Nevertheless, John's position towards the law of the Church was relatively ambiguous: while he defended it against royal interference, he seems to have been hostile to the introduction of new canons, preferring the text of the Gospel.[60] This point is discussed in this volume by Julie Barrau, who considers the insertion into a canonical collection at Worcester of the decretal *Cum Sacrosancta*, which was written in answer to some questions by John. Indeed, beyond his theoretical approach to law, John made a more practical use of it, as Yves Sassier shows. In particular he reuses some dispositions of Roman law in order to limit the action of the prince and his officers. This practical dimension crops up again in his letters and in some passages of the *Policraticus* where John expresses the point of view of a legal practitioner, although his implication in court proceedings remains difficult to gauge.

John's entry into the service of the archbishop of Canterbury also gives rise to a number of questions: what were the precise links between John and Bernard and more widely the Cistercian order? Interpreting John of Salisbury's

---

57   Anders Winroth, *The Making of Gratian's Decretum* (Cambridge, 2000).

58   Barlow, "John of Salisbury and his Brothers," p. 169: "...*legavit eidem ecclesiae decreta Gratiani.*" (Oxford, Bodleian Library, MS Bodley James 23).

59   Hirata, "John of Salisbury and the clergy of Exeter," p. 167.

60   See Jan van Laarhoven, "*Non iam decretam, sed Evangelium!* Jean de Salisbury au Latran III," in Mario Fois, Vincenzo Monachino, Felix Litva, eds., *Dalla Chiesa antica alla Chiesa moderna. Miscellanea per il cinquantesimo della Facoltà di Storia Ecclesiastica della Pontifica Università Gregoriana* (Rome, 1983), pp. 107–119.

attitude towards Bernard of Clairvaux in his *Historia pontificalis* as censorious
is somewhat problematic, given that it was Bernard who recommended him to
Canterbury[61]; furthermore, the impact of Bernard's work – in particular his *De
Consideratione* – on John of Salisbury cannot be denied. Perhaps the *Historia
pontificalis* should be seen as the outcome of an approach that is content to
display probable truths.[62] Indeed, in John's determination to concede beatific
vision to both Bernard and Gilbert one may discern an attempt to preserve
access to truth and to the love of God through two different paths, the cloisters'
and the schools'.[63] John of Salisbury's initial years in the service of Theobald
also raise the issue of the connection between John and the archbishop's
entourage – and also the nascent court of Henry II – as well as with the intellectual and social workings of the so-called "Canterbury circle." Henry II probably wished to preserve harmonious relations with the Church and in particular
with the papacy, and his relationship with Theobald was not confrontational.
However, as Karen Bollermann and Cary Nederman demonstrate, the behaviour of Thomas Becket as chancellor, and the fact that he continued to draw
income from his benefices while serving the temporal administration, certainly contributed to deteriorating the relations between Theobald's entourage
and the royal court.

John of Salisbury's work has long been studied almost exclusively for the
political theories it contains. But how did John perceive politics? Cary
Nederman ("John of Salisbury's Political Theory") shows here how John strove
to adapt elements from the classical tradition to the conditions of his time. In
particular, he took up the idea that rulers and their agents ought to use their
office for the public good. His considerations on virtues and vices in courts also
tally with his political thought. And in the *Policraticus* his defence of tyrannicide logically proceeds from his conception of the *res publica*. Another line of
enquiry may be provided by a comparison with Carolingian and Gregorian
antecedents, and by placing John's political ideas in the context of the growth
of royal administration in England. In particular, the place of John of Salisbury
in the tradition of reform ought to be reconsidered, beyond a simple opposition between temporal power and the authority of the Church.[64] Also, it is only

---

61   One should stress that John is even more censorious towards his former master Robert of
       Melun and also Peter Lombard, whom he accuses of acting out of envy and the desire to
       please Bernard (*Historia pontificalis*, p. 16).

62   See esp. Matthew Kempshall, *Rhetoric and the Writing of History, 400–1500* (Manchester,
       2011), pp. 408–427.

63   *Historia pontificalis*, pp. 16–17.

64   It is in particular this kind of re-evaluation that Nicholas Vincent invites to in a recent
       article on the policy of Henry II towards the papacy (Vincent, "Beyond Becket: King Henry
       II and the papacy (1154–1189)").

recently, in the light of work done on 12th-century historiography, that one has considered again the vision John had of the past – in particular the English and "British" past – and his conception of writing history.[65] And it is in the light of renewed inquiry on the way John perceived his own identity – native of Salisbury, a member of the Church of Canterbury, English by birth and by his loyalties, *Francus* (as he describes himself on occasion) and cosmopolitan –[66] that one may hope to understand the significance his circles of friendship held for him.[67]

Nevertheless, John of Salisbury's political ideas should not be artificially separated from the philosophical theories he developed on other subjects. Considering his work as a whole is an essential step for a precise understanding of it. For instance, while it is necessary to have a more accurate idea of the way he viewed political prophecies or the political use of some prophecies (such as those of Merlin),[68] this should also be understood in the wider context of Book 2 of *Policraticus*, which constructs a general framework for understanding the connections between the natural and the supernatural. In fact, Book 2 has not been much studied, although it includes numerous reflections on divination (notably by the intermediary of dreams), miracles, natural

---

65   See esp. McLoughlin, "Nations and Loyalties"; Yoko Hirata, "Colliding with Histories: John of Salisbury's Uses of the Past during the Becket Conflict," in *Collected Papers*, pp. 183–196; Ilya Afanasyev, "'*In gente Britanniarum, sicut quaedam nostratum testatur historia...*': National Identity and Perceptions of the Past in John of Salisbury's *Policraticus*," *Journal of Medieval History* 38 (2012), 278–294.

66   On the cosmopolitanism and the English identity of John of Salisbury, see esp. Christopher N.L. Brooke, "Cristianità e regni: Inghilterra," in Luigi Prosdocimi et al., eds., *La Cristianità dei secoli XI e XII in Occidente: coscienza e strutture di una società. Atti della ottava Settimana internazionale di studio, Mendola, 30 giugno-5 luglio 1980* (Milan, 1983), pp. 45–66, esp. pp. 63–64.

67   The place of John of Salisbury in different circles of friendship and the significance of friendship in his career and work have been the subject of numerous studies in the past two decades. See esp. John McLoughlin, "Amicitia in Practice: John of Salisbury (c. 1120–1180) and his Circle," in Daniel Williams, ed., *England in the Twelfth Century* (Wooldbridge, 1990), pp. 165–181; Laurence Moulinier-Brogi, "Jean de Salisbury: un réseau d'amitiés continentales," in Martin Aurell, dir., *Culture politique des Plantagenêt (1154–1224). Actes du colloque tenu à Poitiers du 2 au 5 mai 2002* (Poitiers, 2003), pp. 341–361; Nederman, "Friendship in Public Life during the Twelfth Century"; Julian Haseldine, "Understanding the Language of *Amicitia*: the Friendship Circle of Peter of Celle (c. 1115–1183)," *Journal of Medieval History* 20 (1994), 237–260.

68   This point has been treated by Hirata, "Colliding with Histories"; however, for Jean-Patrice Boudet, John completely rejects Sibylline prophetism (Boudet, *Entre Science et nigromance*, pp. 97–98).

philosophy or divine prescience, all themes that are essential if one is to understand how John's thought is rooted in medieval culture.[69]

John's work raises a number of important issues in the field of intellectual history. Indeed, it may be necessary to give him back his proper philosophical stature, a dimension specialists often hesitate to recognize in him. There can be no doubt that John missed the "scholastic turning point" that was on its way when he was a student. But it could be argued that his interest in Cicero and in humanism place him within another tradition that has been pushed aside by the triumph of university institutions: this tradition extends as far as Montaigne, via Petrarch and even Gerson, and this qualifies the impression that John of Salisbury may create of being relatively isolated within the history of ideas.[70] John also bears witness to the permanence of a sceptical tradition in the Middle Ages, as well as to a perception of philosophy as a way of life, as practice rather than theory. This re-evaluation of John of Salisbury's place in the history of medieval philosophy ought to go hand in hand with a better understanding of his view of Augustine's work. John proclaims his debt to Plato, Aristotle and Cicero but does not situate himself explicitly in relation to Augustine, unless it is to turn him into a follower of a form of scepticism. Nevertheless, John obviously knew Augustine's work extremely well, and used it in significant ways: on the theory of sin, on the question of knowledge (the knowledge of essence, the question of illumination, the relation to sensation), on the issue of virtue and grace and so on, John resorts to Augustinian arguments, sometimes implicitly, while distancing himself from them in many

---

69   For a general view of Book 2, see Barbara Hebling-Gloor, *Natur und Aberglaube im Policraticus des Johannes von Salisbury* (Zurich, 1956); on dreams, S. Bordier, "Aenigma Somniorum," *Bulletin de l'association Guillaume Budé* 50 (1991), 306–314; Dean Swinford, "Dream Interpretation and the Organic Metaphor of the State in John of Salisbury's *Policraticus*," *The Journal of Medieval Religious Cultures* 38 (2012), 32–59. On medicine, Cary J. Nederman and T. Shogimen, "The Best Medicine? Medical Education, Practice and Metaphor in John of Salisbury's *Policraticus* and *Metalogicon*," *Viator: Medieval and Renaissance Studies* 42 (2011), 55–74; on miracles, Christophe Grellard, *Jean de Salisbury et la renaissance médiévale du scepticisme* (Paris, 2013), pp. 97–105; on magic, Boudet, *Entre science et nigromance*; on divine prescience, *infra*, "John of Salisbury and Theology."

70   On John of Salisbury and Petrarch, see Laure Hermand-Schebat, *Pétrarque épistolier et Cicéron. Étude d'une filiation* (Paris, 2011), esp. pp. 236–256; on John of Salisbury and Gerson, Frédérique Lachaud, "'Plutarchus si dit et recorde...' L'influence du *Policraticus* de Jean de Salisbury sur Christine de Pizan et Jean Gerson," in Patrick Gilli and Jacques Paviot, dir., *Hommes, cultures et sociétés à la fin du Moyen Âge. Liber discipulorum en l'honneur de Philippe Contamine* (Paris, 2012), pp. 47–67. On John's scepticism, Grellard, *Jean de Salisbury et le renaissance médiévale du scepticisme*.

respects. This is the reason why it is necessary to identify more precisely the influence of Augustine's thought on that of John of Salisbury.[71]

John of Salisbury's contribution to medieval epistemology has frequently been highlighted.[72] In his chapter David Bloch reconsiders the internal tension that exists in John's epistemology: this rests both on a renewed reading of Aristotle (in particular his theory of demonstration as laid out in the *Posterior Analytics*) and on John's acceptance of a moderate form of scepticism inspired by Cicero. This contribution first turns on the influence of Aristotle upon the implementation of demonstrative procedures (inspired by the *Posterior Analytics*) and dialectical procedures (inspired by the *Topics* and *On Sophistical Refutations*), John clearly favouring the latter. This Aristotelian contribution is put into perspective by a genealogical approach to human knowledge – from sensation to intellection – which is based on Boethius and Augustine. The privilege granted to dialectic has to do precisely with the fact that it helps narrow the chasm between the instability of sensation and the stability of reason. It also allows for the reintroduction, within an epistemological reflection inspired by Aristotle and Boethius, of a strong "humanistic" turn that was perhaps inspired by the teaching at Chartres and Saint-Victor, and which rehabilitates reading and meditation alongside disputation.

In a similar way, issues concerning ethics have already been highlighted by several studies, on the supreme good, on virtue, on free will etc, although this rich seam of enquiry may still have much to yield.[73] In this volume Sigbjørn

---

71   Some avenues for research are suggested *infra* in the contribution by Christophe Grellard and in his *Jean de Salisbury et la renaissance médiévale du scepticisme*.

72   Hans Daniels, *Die Wissenschaftslehre des Johannes von Salisbury* (Freiburg-im-Breisgau, 1932); Brian P. Hendley, *Wisdom and Eloquence: A New Interpretation of the Metalogicon of John of Salisbury*, PhD Diss. (Yale, 1967); David Bloch, *John of Salisbury on Aristotelian Science* (Turnhout, 2012); Grellard, *Jean de Salisbury et la renaissance médiévale du scepticisme*.

73   See esp. Philippe Delhaye, "Le bien suprême d'après le *Policraticus* de Jean de Salisbury," *Recherches de théologie ancienne et médiévale* 25 (1953), 203–221 and "L'enseignement de la philosophie morale au XIIᵉ siècle," *Medieval Studies* 11 (1949), 81–94, repr. in his *Enseignement et morale au XIIᵉ siècle* (Paris-Fribourg, 1988), pp. 58–81; studies by Yves Sassier collected in his *Royauté et idéologie au Moyen Âge: Bas-Empire, monde franc, France (IVᵉ–XIIᵉ siècles)* (Paris, 2002); Klaus Guth, "Standethos als Ausdruck hochmittelalterlicher Lebensform. Zur Gestalt des ethischen Humanismus in der Briefwelt des Johannes von Salisbury," *Freiburger Zeitschrift für Philosophie und Theologie* 28 (1981), 111–132; Cary J. Nederman, "Aristotelian Ethics and John of Salisbury's Letters," *Viator: Medieval and Renaissance Studies* 18 (1987), 161–173; idem, "Knowledge, Virtue and the Path to Wisdom: The Unexamined Aristotelianism of John of Salisbury's *Metalogicon*," *Mediaeval Studies* 51 (1989), 268–286; idem, "Aristotelian Ethics Before the *Nicomachean Ethics*: Sources of

Sønnesyn seeks to clarify the status of ethics as the most important part of philosophy. Taking the opposite view from interpretations that stress the importance of freedom, he defends the idea that John of Salisbury's ethics is based on a concept of the good set in Aristotle's teleological perspective: his ethics may be called naturalistic. At the same time, the influence of Aristotle on John's thought is qualified by Augustine's significance for him: the eudaemonism that John applies is, as a last resort, completed by the love of God and the beatific vision. Augustine's influence acts on a second level: this is the place of grace in the ethical system constructed by John. As with Augustine, grace makes liberty effective and human action efficient; it implements what virtues and ethical dispositions cultivated by individuals set in motion. The ethics of John of Salisbury is not a body of doctrine but a practice, a form of life.

John of Salisbury's life and work are still in need of research. In spite of recent publications, the manuscript tradition of *Policraticus* in particular remains to a large extent to be studied.[74] John of Salisbury's writing methods also partially escape us. John's devotion to letters, his precocious and excellent mastery of Latin (especially Latin prosody), the fact he most often wrote for a small group of literature devotees account for some of his stylistic characteristics, as Ronald Pepin stresses here. His writings are also characterized by a taste for *exempla*, proverbs and aphorisms, all expressed in a humorous style. The influence of classical sources – often through the intermediary of *florilegia* – is also a notable feature of the way John of Salisbury writes: in recent decades this has been the subject of significant studies,[75] in particular in order to clarify

---

Aristotle's Concept of Virtue in the Twelfth Century," *Parergon*, n. s., 7 (1989), 55–75; idem, "Nature, Ethics and the Doctrine of *Habitus*: Aristotelian Moral Psychology in the Twelfth Century," *Traditio* 45 (l989/90), 87–110; idem, "Beyond Aristotelianism and Stoicism: John of Salisbury's Skepticism and Moral Reasonning in the Twelfth Century," in István P. Bejczy and Richard G. Newhauser, eds., *Virtue and Ethics in the Twelfth Century* (Leiden, 2005), pp. 175–195; Grellard, *Jean de Salisbury et la renaissance médiévale du scepticisme*, Chapter 4, pp. 153–213.

74   See esp. Rossana E. Guglielmetti, "Varianti d'autore nel Metalogicon e nel Policraticus di Giovanni di Salisbury," *Filologia Mediolatina* 11 (2004), 281–307; eadem, *La tradizione manoscritto del Policraticus di Giovanni di Salisbury, primo secolo di diffusione* (Florence, 2005).

75   Notably Anne J. Duggan, "Classical Quotations and Allusions in the Correspondence of Thomas Becket: an Investigation of their Sources," *Viator: Medieval and Renaissance Studies* 32 (2001), 1–22; Barker, "Ms Bodl. Canon. Pat. Lat. 131 and a Lost Lactantius of John of Salisbury"; Janet Martin, "Uses of Tradition: Gellius, Petronius and John of Salisbury," *Viator: Medieval and Renaissance Studies* 10 (1979), 57–76. It is a matter of regret that the doctoral dissertation of Janet Martin is still unpublished. See also Jean-Yves Tilliette, "Jean de

which were the potential sources of the *Institutio Traiani*. In the eyes of medievalists John of Salisbury has always been distinguished by his remarkable
knowledge of the Latin classics. Our improved understanding of *florilegia*
makes it possible to define more precisely the way John used classical sources:
these he seems to have privileged in works or letters that he knew would be
read by a literate public capable of understanding his literary allusions. Above
all, John of Salisbury gave himself over to a "deliberate confusion" of classical
and Christian matter and language, alongside other authors of the intellectual
avant-garde of the middle of the 12th century.[76] The contribution of Laure
Hermand-Schebat to the volume reviews the main classical texts to which
John had access and which really fed his thought. Her chapter examines the
main Greek and Latin authors John knew in the field of philosophy and literature. Any analysis of the place of ancient culture in John of Salisbury's work
must rest on two significant elements. Firstly the relation John had with the
classics was based on the idea of self-transformation. Reading the classics
enriches and modifies the personality of the reader who appropriates these
texts. Therefore concern for classics cannot be neutral; it must be part of the
dynamics of creation. Secondly, the relationship with classical authors remains
determined by the Patristic framework: the classics must be subject to the
authority of faith (on the model of the pagan captive in Dt 21: 10–13), so that
classical works ought to be read prudently and in an enlightened way, with
orthodoxy as a guide.

The borrowings made from classical authors often seem to divert John from
his main purpose, and his meaning may be obscured by his irony or his authorial strategy. Analysing the letters of John of Salisbury, Christopher Brooke has
suggested that he did not completely master the technique of opposing arguments.[77] Rather one may choose to follow Stephen Jaeger on this point: when
writing about the issue of tyrannicide in the *Policraticus*, he argues that John
deliberately placed in his text some statements that went counter to his main
argument. He even compares him to a chameleon, always concerned about the
impression he ought to make on his reader. As for the discursive strategy of
Policraticus, this would be explained by John's concern not to offend any

---

Salisbury et Cicéron," *Helmantica* 50 (1999), 697–710; Wim Verbaal, "Teste Quintiliano.
Jean de Salisbury et Quintilien: un exemple de la crise des autorités au XIIe siècle," in
Perrine Galand-Hallyn, Fernand Hallyn, Carlos Lévy, dir., *Quintilien ancien et moderne*,
(Turnhout, 2008); Christine Veyrard-Cosme, "Jean de Salisbury et le récit de Pétrone, du
remploi à l'exemplum," *Cahiers d'Études Anciennes* 39 (2003), 69–88.

76 Whatley, "The Uses of Hagiography," p. 34.
77 Brooke, "Aspects of John of Salisbury's *Historia Pontificalis*," p. 187.

particular individual, while mocking everybody.[78] Above and beyond the question of his style, or the use of pseudonyms taken from ancient texts – all devices that are meant to create a degree of complicity with a lettered audience – John developed a way of writing based on the accumulation of *exempla*, on implicit or explicit references, on associations of ideas that have often misled readers, in particular modern readers. The invasive use of metaphor in John's work is also in need of a proper analysis.[79] In any case, a better understanding of these modes of writing is an essential preliminary to any evaluation and analysis of his thought.

Without any doubt John of Salisbury was a key figure of the 12th century; the fact that he belonged to different worlds that were sometimes impenetrable to one another – the schools, the Curia, the princely courts, the cloister – turns him into an invaluable witness of his time. At the same time, these multiple affiliations render him difficult to situate, and his heterogeneous work, which mobilises different fields of medieval history, is in itself a challenge to medieval studies, which often suffer from the fact that disciplines are compartmentalized. The aim of this book is to offer some keys for an interdisciplinary approach to his work and to pay homage to the multiple talents of a man who was both bewildering and engaging.

---

78   C. Stephen Jaeger, "Irony and Role-playing in John of Salisbury and the Becket Circle," in *Culture politique des Plantagenêt (1154–1224)*, pp. 319–331.

79   On the use of metaphors in 12th-century Latin literature, see Giles Constable, "Medieval Latin metaphors," *Viator: Medieval and Renaissance Studies* 38 (2007), 1–20.

PART 1

Historical Context

∴

CHAPTER 1

John of Salisbury and the Schools of the 12th Century

Cédric Giraud and Constant Mews

Hunc unum fecit natura scientia proles,
Quadruplici studio, quatuor unus erat
Paulus, Aristotiles, Plato, Tullius unicus unus.[1]

[Nature, learning, lineage made this person one;
By fourfold study, he was four people in one:
Paul, Aristotle, Plato, Tully -- a unique individual.]

This epitaph touches on the complexity of the character of John of Salisbury. He seemed to be a Christian, an Aristotelian, a Platonist and a Ciceronian, rolled into one. Not only is the eclectic character of his thought difficult to classify, but his career also raises many questions relating to the intellectual life of the 12th century as a whole – in particular about his connection to the intellectual and literary traditions traditionally associated with the cathedral school at Chartres, where he became bishop in the last phase of his life (1176–80). Where does John fit within the educational spectrum of the 12th century? Because he chose the career of a diplomat and administrator rather than that of a teacher, he has often been interpreted as more an observer of the 12th-century schools than as an innovative thinker. Yet John's two verse summaries of philosophical wisdom, the *Entheticus de dogmate philosophorum* and *Entheticus in Policraticum*, as well as his two major prose syntheses, the *Metalogicon* and *Policraticus* (both presented to Thomas Becket in 1159), demonstrate a remarkable capacity both to absorb new ideas and texts coming into circulation in the 12th-century schools, and to critique the potential dangers created by inadequate teachers, less than fully aware of the significance of what they were committed to teach. Through regular correspondence with his friends in the schools, John was able to articulate a unified vision of educational ideals, much more difficult for practising teachers to maintain because of the intensely competitive environment in which they promoted their particular vision of the curriculum.

---

1 Epitaph of John of Salisbury, cited by Katherine S.B. Keats-Rohan, *Policraticus I–IV*, p. 3.

© KONINKLIJKE BRILL NV, LEIDEN, 2015 | DOI 10.1163/9789004282940_003

John's *Metalogicon* provides particularly important testimony not just about the 12th-century schools, but about his own vision of what an ideal education should provide. He was particularly troubled by studies pursued for the sake of self-interest and personal ambition at the expense of a love of learning for its own sake. Near the outset of that work he celebrated a group of teachers, whom he considered to embody this ideal: Gilbert, chancellor at Chartres and then bishop of Poitiers; Thierry, "a very assiduous investigator of the arts"; William of Conches, "the most accomplished grammarian since Bernard of Chartres," and the Peripatetic of Le Pallet, "who won such distinction in *logica* over all his contemporaries that it was thought that he alone really understood Aristotle."[2] John's eulogy provides us with a problem, however. Did these masters (all except Abelard traditionally associated with Chartres), constitute a coherent school of thought to which John of Salisbury was witness? This at least was the image promoted by the abbé Clerval and developed by Poole in his pioneering studies of John of Salisbury.[3] Is it legitimate, however, to speak of John of Salisbury as a product of the school of Chartres or is he much more a product of the various schools at Paris?

The Education of John, From Salisbury to Paris

As for many other scholars of the 12th century, the early education of John of Salisbury remains unclear.[4] The weakest of glimpses into his youth is offered by John himself in the *Policraticus*, when he explains that while still a boy (*puer*), he had been required to learn the Psalter from a priest, who practiced divination.[5] Furthermore, it is often assumed that he was educated at Salisbury itself in the *rudimenta litterarum*, but that he benefited from further education

---

2 *Metalogicon* 1.5, p. 20, ll. 1–16.

3 Alexandre Clerval, *Les Écoles de Chartres au Moyen Âge du Ve au XVIe siècle* (Chartres, 1895; repr. Chartres, 1994); Reginald L. Poole, *Illustrations of the History of Medieval Thought and Learning* (London, 1920², repr. New York, 1960), pp. 95–115; idem, *Studies in the Chronology and History* (Oxford, 1934), pp. 223–247.

4 There are few studies seeking to situate John in the educational context of his time. The best studies are still those of Klaus Guth, *Johannes von Salisbury (1115/20–1180). Studien zur Kirchen-, Kultur- und Sozialgeschichte Westeuropas im 12. Jahrhundert* (St. Ottilien, 1978), pp. 23–81 and of Pierre Riché, "Jean de Salisbury et le monde scolaire du XIIe siècle," in *The World of John of Salisbury*, pp. 39–61.

5 *Policraticus* 2.28, ed. Webb, vol. 1, p. 167, ll. 87–88: "Dum enim puer ut psalmos addiscerem sacerdoti traditus essem qui forte speculariam magicam exercebat...."

at the cathedral school of Exeter, because of the connections both he and his brother maintained with that town until the 1170s, on the assumption that it offered a more advanced education than Salisbury.[6] This quite plausible hypothesis does not exclude another possibility suggested by recent studies on the cultural role of Salisbury from the late eleventh to mid 12th century. Teresa Webber, drawing on close analysis of the manuscripts copied by or connected to the canons of Salisbury, has demonstrated that Salisbury was one of the most important cultural centres in England after the Conquest, at least attested by the production of manuscripts.[7] She has shown above all the interest of the canons in written culture, particularly in texts that were rare or never previously preserved in England. In this respect it is noteworthy that Salisbury scribes reserved a particular place for classical texts like the plays of Plautus, certain works of Cicero (*Disputationes Tusculunae, De officiis*), the *De beneficiis* of Seneca, as well as an anthology compiled from a Norman model, making known texts of Valerius Maximus and of Aulus Gellius.[8] The study of the textual traditions represented at Salisbury indicates that there were clear links between the canons and other continental centres, all the more remarkable given that this was not an establishment already integrated into other networks. Also noteworthy is the presence of school texts like extracts from the commentary of Remigius on Martianus Capella, an extract from the *Liber glosarum*, an important encyclopedia of an Isidorean type, compiled in the early Carolingian period, a fragment of the commentary on the *Timaeus* by Chalcidius, although without any indication that these were for school use. This demonstrates at least contact between Salisbury and continental centres favouring the trivium. Former pupils of Anselm of Laon, like Alexander (bishop of Lincoln, 1123–48) and Nigel (bishop of Ely, 1133–69) are linked to Salisbury, but the study of manuscripts and of textual transmission does not allow connections to be made between witnesses from Salisbury and the *studium* of Laon.[9] Educational activity was guaranteed by the presence of masters like Guy of Étampes, probably taught by Anselm of Laon and present at Salisbury around 1107, or a certain Ailwin, of whom nothing else is known.[10] Another

---

6   Cary J. Nederman, *John of Salisbury* (Tempe, Arizona, 2005), pp. 3–4.

7   Teresa Webber, *Scholars and Scribes at Salisbury Cathedral c. 1075-c. 1125* (Oxford, 1992), p. 1.

8   Ibid., pp. 63–65, even if this was not a compilation known by John of Salisbury.

9   Ibid., pp. 84–85; on Alexander and Nigel, see Cédric Giraud, *Per verba magistri. Anselme de Laon et son école au XII* siècle* (Turnhout, 2010), p. 121.

10   On Guy of Etampes, see Giraud, *Per verba magistri*, pp. 121–124; on Ailwinus, Webber, *Scholars and Scribes*, p. 83.

such master educated in France and potentially known to the young John of
Salisbury was Robert of Béthune, an Augustinian canon and from 1125 prior of
Lanthony, near Gloucester, subsequently bishop of Hereford (1130–48), who
had studied under Anselm of Laon and William of Champeaux in the second
decade of the 12th century.[11] The fact that in the year following the death of
Henry I (1 December 1135), John advanced directly to the study of dialectic
under Peter Abelard at the schools of the Montagne Sainte-Geneviève, suggests that he then thought he had already received sufficient background in
grammatica, and that he wished in Paris to study a discipline still new to him.
It nonetheless remains that John's education at Salisbury, perhaps longer than
has hitherto been assumed, enables us to explain certain remarkable features
of the intellectual identity of the future bishop of Chartres: the importance of
classical authors, the memory of Anselm and Ralph of Laon, links with French
scholars and great continental centres of learning. With the accession to the
English throne of Stephen of Blois, John may have felt this was a good time to
pursue his studies in the kingdom of France.

In this, John of Salisbury is a good representative of one of typical features
of "the renaissance of the 12th century": travel for the sake of study.[12] In fact,
love of learning, the danger of travel, meeting with another constitute the
obligatory stages of educational mobility as much for masters as for students.
While the Church was traditionally distrustful of wandering scholars, suspecting of making their travels an opportunity for dissipation, 12th-century scholars accorded such travel a new moral purpose: the most striking is that of
master Hugh of Saint-Victor (†1141), who himself left his native region, the
Empire, to come to the kingdom of France. In his famous pedagogical treatise,
the *Didascalicon* (likely composed before 1121), Hugh praises navigation.[13]

---

11   On Robert of Béthune as canon and prior of Lanthony, see Giraud, *Per verba magistri*,
      pp. 126–130.
12   On the region of France, see in particular Peter Classen, "La Curia Romana e le scuole
      di Francia nel secolo XII," in *Le istituzioni ecclesiastiche*, I: *Le istituzioni ecclesiastiche
      della societas christiana dei secoli XI–XII: Papato, cardinalato ed episcopato* (Milan, 1974),
      pp. 432–436; Joachim Ehlers, "Deutsche Scholaren in Frankreich während des 12.
      Jahrhunderts," in Johannes Fried, ed., *Schulen und Studium im sozialen Wandel des hohen
      und späten Mittelalters* (Sigmaringen, 1986), pp. 97–120 and Astrik L. Gabriel, "English
      Masters and Students in Paris during the Twelfth Century," in *Garlandia. Studies in the
      History of the Medieval University* (Notre Dame, 1969), pp. 1–37.
13   On the date and structure of this treatise, see most recently the article of Dominique
      Poirel, "*Tene fontem et totum habes*: l'unité du *Didascalicon* d'Hugues de Saint-Victor," in
      Cédric Giraud and Martin Morard, eds., *Universitas scholarium. Mélanges offerts en hom-
      mage à Jacques Verger par ses anciens étudiants* (Paris, 2011), pp. 293–328.

As the third of the mechanical arts, navigation consists above all in commerce, understood in the broad sense of communication between goods and people. In these new conditions, travel for the sake of study was distinguished by all the virtues, given that it was driven by a disinterested search for knowledge and as such could lead to exaltation of the Church. As Hugh of Saint-Victor recalls, travel and even exile are part of the conditions that endow study with calm, zeal and poverty.[14] These reasons, naturally formulaic and not a monopoly of the 12th century, were often complemented by more pragmatic considerations. It was a gathering of teachers which attracted large numbers of students. The reputation of a master, his *fama*, thus gave a direction to these migrations, creating an educational geography, but in a single direction, namely from England to France.[15] In this sense, the travel of John of Salisbury to the continent, in particular to the Parisian schools, was part of a larger, well known educational movement which brought dozens of English clerics to the Capetian capital. Thus, in a classic study, Astrik Gabriel identified no fewer than thirty students who went through Paris and became teachers of the first rank.[16] John personally knew many of these scholars, including Robert of Melun (†1167), an Englishman, who taught at Melun before becoming one of his teachers in Paris, and Richard of Saint-Victor (†1173), who came to Paris in the 1130s, to study under Hugh of Saint-Victor. They were his peers and sometimes also his friends.

John's choice of Paris and of Peter Abelard as his teacher reflects a new configuration of the educational landscape. Schools, attached to cathedrals and major collegiate churches and directed by a teacher (*scholasticus*), were experiencing a new importance by the first half of the 12th century in the French kingdom. The confluence of circumstances favourable to the development of urban schools was particularly evident in the north. At least as important as the desire for urban self-government was the re-assertion of royal power under Louis VI (1108–37) and Louis VII (1137–80) supporting and framing the politics of ecclesiastical reform as educational development. Whether they were situated in the royal domain or in neighbouring principalities like Blois, Normandy or Anjou, the schools of Reims, Chartres, Laon, Paris, Angers, Tours or Orléans, to cite only the most famous, benefited from political support that favoured

---

14   Hugh of Saint-Victor, *Didascalicon*, ed. C.H. Buttimer (Washington, 1949) 3.16–9, pp. 67–69.

15   On *fama*, see Giraud, *Per verba magistri*, pp. 104–105.

16   Gabriel, *Garlandia. Studies in the History of the Medieval University*, pp. 5–25.

their development.[17] These urban schools also benefited from being established in rich dioceses which possessed numerous chapters, the means of
maintaining masters and of welcoming students coming from all over the
Latin world. Meanwhile, in this pre-university period, the success of these
schools did not rest principally on a strong institutional organisation, but on
the capacity of a master to attract students. If the master should die, the school
would then fall back to a local level of being a centre for the education of diocesan clergy. In this sense, it is as appropriate to follow the success of a school
at the local level ("school at") as at its capacity to be a point of reference
("school of"). It is in this way that masters might end up creating schools of
thought identified by their name, particular in Paris (*Porretani, Adamiti,
Montani*).[18] This phenomenon occurred at the same time as great centres of
education were asserting themselves at the expense of schools of lesser importance, just as John of Salisbury was travelling to France. The development of
Paris, evident from the time of Peter Abelard, as capital for study of theology
and disciplines of the trivium makes it possible to speak of "reorganisation" of
the scholarly network in France.[19] John's arrival also occurred at the time of a
mutation in Parisian educational geography. Just as the schools were asserting
themselves in the time of William of Champeaux, namely in the first third of
the 12th century, around the cathedral cloister of Notre-Dame, the situation
was changing from the time of Bishop Stephen of Senlis (1123–41). In a move
(c. 1127) that suggests he wished to assert episcopal control over the schools, he
issued an edict forbidding teaching in a part of the cloister known as the
Tresantia (perhaps behind the sanctuary), and students from outside taking
lodging in the houses of the canons. He argued that this was to restore peace to
the cathedral cloister. As there was, nonetheless, no question of giving up a
school close to the cathedral, it was decided to give courses in a place adjacent
to the episcopal court, towards the Petit Pont. After the agreement of 1127,

---

17   Emile Lesne, *Histoire de la propriété ecclésiastique en France*, t. 5, *Les Écoles de la fin du VIIIe
      siècle à la fin du XIIe siècle* (Lille, 1940); Jacques Verger, "Une étape dans le renouveau sco-
      laire du XIIe siècle?," in Françoise Gasparri, ed., *Le XIIe siècle. Mutations et renouveau en
      France dans la première moitié du XIIe siècle* (Paris 1994), pp. 123–145, at pp. 126–128; Verger,
      La renaissance du XIIe siècle (Paris, 1996), pp. 101–102.

18   Yukio Iwakuma et Sten Ebbesen, "Logico-Theological Schools from the Second Half of the
      12th Century: A List of Sources," *Vivarium* 30 (1992), 173–210.

19   Verger, "Une étape dans le renouveau," p. 126; idem, "Des écoles du XIIe siècle aux pre-
      mières universités: réussites et échecs," in Ángel J. Martín Duque, dir., *Renovación intelec-
      tual del Occidente Europeo (siglo XII). Actas de la XXIV Semana de Estudios Medievales de
      Estella. 14 al 18 de julio de 1997* (Pamplona 1998), pp. 249–273, at p. 262.

schools continued to develop south of the Île de la Cité in a movement that progressively transformed the left bank into the region of the schools.[20]

John of Salisbury is a major witness in the *Metalogicon* to these changes, as much with regard to the quality of his observations as because of the way his account has shaped modern historiography of the schools. It must be observed, however, that this work, composed probably in two stages, between 1157 at the latest and 1159, is not the account of a life, namely a report of educational life in the second quarter of the 12th century, but more generally a reflection on the position of the arts of the trivium.[21] Among them, John devotes the second book of his *Metalogicon* to dialectic.[22] Careful to establish its correct usage, because of its increasingly popularity, John promotes a kind of ethics of dialectic, insisting above all on the fact that it can only help someone who has the substance to reason and thus sufficient knowledge to apply appropriately the rules of the discipline. In order to illustrate the principle that he has enuntiated, John then turns in the famous Chapter 10 of the second book, towards his own course of study, which is less a pretext for autobiographical narrative than a demonstration of the emptiness of studies devoted solely to dialectic. John's intent is thus a type of apology for searching out an education for the need to have several masters in different disciplines. His propensity for mentioning the names of so many teachers (no fewer than twelve are cited) is in fact a conscious literary strategy. His highly mobile educational career, an inverted apologia for the success of his own education, seeks to denounce those who remained immobile studying the same discipline at the same place. They stagnate and – even worse – go backwards. John wants to inform us not about the chronology of his studies or the working of the schools, but about what constitutes a good education: learning from different teachers, not limiting oneself to a single discipline, reconsidering what one thinks one knows. With that said,

---

20   Astrik L. Gabriel, "Les écoles de la cathédrale Notre-Dame et le commencement de l'université de Paris, " in *Huitième centenaire de Notre-Dame de Paris (Congrès des 30 mai-3 juin 1964). Recueil de travaux sur l'histoire de la cathédrale et de l'église de Paris* (Paris, 1967), pp. 141–166.

21   According to the new chronology offered quite convincingly by Nederman, *John of Salisbury*, pp. 24–27, against the traditional date of 1159, based on the dedication to Thomas Becket in the final chapter of the work; see in particular Hans Liebeschütz, *Medieval Humanism in the Life and Writings of John of Salisbury* (London, 1950), pp. 11–22; Daniel D. McGarry, *The Metalogicon of John of Salisbury. A Twelfth-Century Defense of the Verbal and Logical Arts of the Trivium* (Gloucester, 1971), p. xix, note 26.

22   *Metalogicon* 2.4, p. 60, ll. 2–3.

one can still try to seek out precisely what was the career of John from the testimony given in this chapter.[23]

Having arrived quite young (*adulescens*) in France in 1136, John took himself to the Montagne Sainte-Geneviève, with Peter Abelard, then a master renowned and admired by many.[24] After Abelard's unexpected departure, John turned for two complete years to two other masters in dialectic, Alberic and Robert of Melun. He judged the former to be "subtle and profuse," Robert of Melun to be "penetrating, brief and to the point."[25] John, however, does not forget that his purpose is not to make an educational prosopography, but to judge the education that he had received. While recognizing the merit of these two masters, he deplored their narrow specialisation in dialectic and a kind of infatuation that made them prefer their own discoveries to the teaching of the ancients.[26] According to a procedure dear to John, for whom the subsequent path of his life demonstrates human capacity, the educational trajectory of these two masters illustrates two possible paths for study: Alberic, leaving for Bologna, ended up by unlearning what he had taught; Robert on the other hand, once a theologian acquired the glory of higher wisdom and a famous name.[27] Well educated, John recognises the temptation of thinking that he had arrived at the end of his education and had become fully knowledgeable.[28] He follows his account of the brilliance and ambition of both Alberic and Robert with a passage in which he describes how he transferred for three years to a teacher, William of Conches, under whom he profited immeasurably: "I unduly exaggerated my own knowledge. I thought of myself as educated in that I was

---

23   There are numerous studies on this issue. The most important include: Liebeschütz, *Medieval Humanism*, "Appendix I: The Structure of *Metalogicon* II 10 and the Twelfth-Century Curriculum," pp. 111–113; John O. Ward, "The Date of the Commentary on Cicero's *De inventione* by Thierry of Chartres (ca. 1095–1160?) and the Cornifician Attack on the Liberal Arts," *Viator* 3 (1972), 219–273, at pp. 230–237; Guth, *Johannes von Salisbury*, pp. 34–39, Olga Weijers, "The Chronology of John of Salisbury's Studies in France (*Metalogicon* II.10)," in *The World of John of Salisbury*, pp. 109–116, Keats-Rohan, "John of Salisbury and Education in Twelfth-Century Paris from the Account of his *Metalogicon*," *History of Universities* 6 (1986–7), 1–45, eadem, "The Chronology of John of Salisbury's Studies in France: a Reading of *Metalogicon* II.10," *Studi medievali* 28 (1987), 193–203. In general we follow the latter's reconstruction, although with certain significant differences.
24   *Metalogicon* 2.10, pp. 70–71, ll. 2–9.
25   Ibid. 2.10, p. 71, ll. 9–24. It is probably to this period to which John refers at the beginning of book three of the *Metalogicon*, p. 101, ll. 2–5.
26   Ibid. 2.10, p. 71, ll. 25–30.
27   Ibid. 2.10, p. 71, ll. 30–35.
28   Ibid. 2.10, p. 71, ll. 35–40.

quick at those things that I had been taught. Then, coming back to myself and assessing my own capacities, I took myself, by permission of my teachers, to the grammarian of Conches. During this time I studied much, nor will I ever regret that time."[29] Frustratingly, John does not reveal where William of Conches was teaching, whether it was at Chartres, or Paris or some other location. John's silence on the matter has opened up a major debate about whether he studied at Chartres and the extent to which he was influenced by its intellectual traditions.

Did John of Salisbury Study at Chartres?

Without revisiting the detail of an extensive historiographical debate, complex even though there are relatively limited sources, it may be worthwhile to recall its key elements.[30] There certainly was, during the episcopates of Ivo of Chartres (1090–1115) and of Geoffrey II of Lèves (1115–48), a remarkable succession of chancellors, all celebrated by John of Salisbury as evoking a remarkable breadth of intellectual spirit, untouched by a contemporary tendency to self-interest and intellectual narrowness: Bernard, who taught at Chartres (1114–6), was its chancellor (1124–6), and composed a recently identified commentary on Plato's *Timaeus*; Gilbert, its chancellor between 1126 and 1142 before becoming bishop of Poitiers, and author of a series of commentaries on the *Opuscula sacra* of Boethius; Thierry of Chartres, its chancellor from 1142 until around 1150, famous for the range of his intellectual interests, which embraced dialectic, rhetoric, the quadrivium, and the Boethian *Opuscula sacra*.[31] From the time of Barthélemy Hauréau, these

---

29 Ibid. 2.10, p. 71, ll. 41–44: "Videbar mihi sciolus, eo quod in his quae audieram promptus eram. Deinde reuersus in me et metiens uires meas, bona praeceptorum meorum gratia consulto me ad grammaticum de Conchis transtuli, ipsumque triennio docentem audiui." On William of Conches and the uncertainties surrounding his career, see *Guillellmi de Conchis Dragmaticon philosophiae*, ed. Italo Ronca (Turnhout, 1997), pp. xvi–xix.
30 See the lively summary of the controversy given by Édouard Jeauneau, *L'Âge d'or des écoles de Chartres* (Chartres, 1995), pp. 15–24, trans. Claude Paul Desmarais as *Rethinking the School of Chartres* (Toronto, 2009), pp. 16–25.
31 Valuable biographical data on these masters is given in the introduction to the editions of their key works: *The Glosae super Platonem of Bernard of Chartres*, ed. Paul Edward Dutton (Toronto, 1991); *The Commentaries on Boethius by Gilbert of Poitiers*, ed. Nikolaus M. Häring (Toronto, 1966); *Commentaries on Boethius by Thierry of Chartres and His School*, ed. Nikolaus M. Häring (Toronto, 1971); *The Latin Rhetorical Commentaries by Thierry of Chartres*, ed. Karen M. Fredborg (Toronto, 1988).

figures have been often been characterised as shaped by a common Chartrian spirit, defined by neo-Platonism and intellectual curiosity, in particular for the subject matter of the quadrivium. John of Salisbury was widely interpreted as our most important witness to this tradition.[32] Yet in a paper, originally given in 1965, Richard Southern questioned the assumption that William of Conches, Thierry and Gilbert taught at Chartres, as well as the traditional claim that its cathedral nurtured an innovative and distinctly Platonist tradition as had often been claimed.[33] Southern questioned whether there was a school of Chartres of any significance after the death of Bernard of Chartres, both in the sense of there being a continuing institutional structure, with a fixed framework of masters, students and manuscripts ("school at") and in the sense of a unified intellectual tradition, even if represented in different places ("school of").[34] Southern's scepticism about whether William of Conches, Gilbert of Poitiers and Thierry actually taught at Chartres has been challenged by a number of scholars on very specific grounds, as also his broader claim that these masters "had the strength to make old thoughts live again, but they could not add to them."[35]

32   Jeauneau, *L'Âge d'or*, pp. 20–23.

33   The paper given in 1965 was published by Richard W. Southern, "Humanism and the School of Chartres," in *Medieval Humanism and Other Studies* (Oxford, 1970), pp. 61–85, arguments that he reaffirmed in *Platonism, Scholastic Method and the School of Chartres*, The Stenton Lecture 1978 (Reading, 1979) and in "The School of Paris and the School of Chartres," in Robert L. Benson and Giles Constable, eds., *Renaissance and Renewal in the Twelfth Century* (Cambridge, Mass., 1982, repr. Toronto, 1991), pp. 113–137, as well as in *Scholastic Humanism and the Unification of Europe*, vol. 1, *Foundations* (Oxford, 1995), pp. 58–101.

34   John J. Contreni, *The Cathedral School of Laon from 850 to 930. Its Manuscripts and Masters* (Munich, 1978), pp. 1 and 4.

35   Southern, "Humanism and the School of Chartres," p. 83; Peter Dronke, "New Approaches to the School of Chartres," *Anuario de Estudios medievales* 6 (1971), 117–140; Nikolaus Häring, "Chartres and Paris Revisited," in J. Reginald O'Donnell, ed., *Essays in Honour of Anton Charles Pegis* (Toronto, 1974), pp. 268–329; Roberto Giacone, "Masters, Books and Library at Chartres, according to the Cartularies of Notre-Dame and Saint-Père," *Vivarium* 12 (1974), 30–51; Jeauneau, *L'Âge d'or*, pp. 23–24 and idem, "Les maîtres chartrains," in Jean-Robert Armogathe, ed., *Monde médiéval et société chartraine. Actes du colloque international organisé par la ville et le diocèse de Chartres à l'occasion du 8ᵉ centenaire de la Cathédrale de Chartres, 8–10 septembre 1994* (Paris, 1997), pp. 97–111; Jacques Verger, "Le cadre institutionnel de l'école de Chartres jusqu'à Jean de Salisbury," in Monique Cazeaux, ed., *Aristote, l'école de Chartres et la cathédrale. Actes du Colloque européen des 5 et 6 juillet 1997* (Chartres, 1997), pp. 19–32.

There can be no doubt that Gilbert did teach at Chartres, as its chancellor, although to a much smaller group of students than at Paris, where he was certainly teaching by 1141 – four students, compared to three hundred, according to Eberhard of Ypres, who later recalled his having listened to Gilbert in both places.[36] That Thierry, celebrated in the *Metamorphosis Goliae* as the *doctor ille Carnotensis*, was under obedience to the bishop of Chartres in 1121 is confirmed by Abelard's comment that he had to be reprimanded by "his bishop," Geoffrey of Lèves, at the Council of Soissons.[37] While it is quite possible that Thierry, like Gilbert, also taught in Paris, he was officially based at Chartres, succeeding to Gilbert as its chancellor. Although much of its cathedral library was tragically destroyed in 1944, there can be no doubt that it possessed many rare scientific texts in Latin translation, often incorporated by Thierry of Chartres into his *Heptateuchon*, reflecting his particular interest in combining study of the trivium and quadrivium.[38] The various critical editions and studies produced by Édouard Jeauneau and other scholars confirm a common concern to harmonize the disciplines of the trivium and quadrivium, linking Platonist intellectual concerns with Christian wisdom, but in many different ways.[39] Southern's comment that there was nothing exceptional about Bernard of Chartres has been countered by Dutton's identification of Bernard as author of a relatively widely diffused commentary on Plato's *Timaeus* from the early 12th century.[40] Bernard certainly promoted awakening of interest in a text that had been known through the translation of Chalcidius, but previously attracted only limited attention. The fact that the early version of William's commentary on Priscian (but not his revision of the work from the late 1140s) frequently

---

36   Eberhard of Ypres, *Dialogus*, ed. Nikolaus M. Häring, "A Latin Dialogue on the Doctrine of Gilbert of Poitiers," *Mediaeval Studies* 15 (1953), 243–289, at p. 252.

37   Peter Abelard, *Historia calamitatum*, ed. Jacques Monfrin (Paris, 1967), p. 88. *Metamorphosis Goliae*, ll. 48–49, ed. R.B.C. Huygens, in *Serta Mediaevalia* (Turnhout, 2000), p. 813.

38   For an attempt to reconstitute the significance of the scientific manuscripts preserved at Chartres, many exceedingly rare, see Charles Burnett, "The Content and Affiliation of the Scientific Manuscripts Written at, or Brought to, Chartres in the Time of John of Salisbury," in *The World of John of Salisbury*, pp. 127–160.

39   See the studies of Édouard Jeauneau collected in *Lectio philosophorum*, those published in Haijo J. Westra, ed., *From Athens to Chartres: Neoplatonism and Medieval Thought. Studies in Honour of É. Jeauneau* (Leiden, 1992), as well as the editions of Chartrian texts indicated in Peter Dronke, ed., *A History of Twelfth-Century Western Philosophy* (Cambridge, 1988), pp. 459–486.

40   See note 31 above and Paul Dutton, "The Uncovering of the *Glosae super Platonem* of Bernard of Chartres," *Mediaeval Studies* 46 (1984), 192–221.

refers to Chartres supports the likelihood that William of Conches, from whom John of Salisbury received much instruction about Bernard of Chartres, did in fact teach there.[41] While John never reveals explicitly where William taught, he does say that he moved away from Sainte-Geneviève (as indicated by the verb *transferre*).[42] This has led many scholars to conclude that he probably did study under William of Conches at Chartres.[43] Keats-Rohan, by contrast, has argued that John's account refers to a continuous period of instruction in Paris.[44] Given John's discretion, it might seem that the most prudent solution would be simply to admit ignorance about the exact place where John studied, given that he does not mention it by name.[45] The question remains, however, whether it is legitimate to connect John of Salisbury to an intellectual tradition, stimulated by the Platonism of Bernard of Chartres, and distinct from the special focus on dialectic for which the Parisian schools were celebrated.

John insists that he learned a great deal over the three years he spent studying under William of Conches.[46] He presented Bernard as the selfless ideal of a teacher, very different from Alberic and Robert of Melun, who may have had fine minds, but lacked the foundations of a broad literary education. The precise chronology of John's studies under various masters mentioned in this

---

41   See the allusions to Chartres in the glosses of William of Conches on Priscian, studied by Édouard Jeauneau, "Deux rédactions des gloses de Guillaume de Conches sur Priscien," *Recherches de théologie ancienne et médiévale* 27 (1960), 212–247, repr. in *Lectio philosophorum*, pp. 335–370, at pp. 353–355, and new testimonies provided by Fredborg, *The Latin Rhetorical Commentaries by Thierry of Chartres*, pp. 7–8.

42   Ward, "Thierry of Chartres," p. 232; Guth, *Johannes von Salisbury*, pp. 40–41.

43   In this interpretation: Poole, *Illustrations*, pp. 180–181; Ward, "Thierry of Chartres," pp. 232–235; Weijers, "The Chronology," p. 115; Ronca in his introduction to *Dragmaticon*, p. xvii.

44   As John's account presents problems of interpretation underpinning the controversy, it seems excessive of Keats-Rohan to claim: "it can nevertheless be read as both in a perfectly logical and coherent fashion, describing, as I understand it, twelve years of study spent at the schools of Paris" ("The Chronology," p. 194, and "John of Salisbury," p. 12). John's account is not as clear-cut or as specific as this claim seems to suggest.

45   Thus Clerval, *Les Écoles*, pp. 180–181; Philippe Delhaye, "L'organisation scolaire au XIIe siècle," *Traditio* 5 (1947), 211–268, p. 262, note 4; Enrico Tacchella, "Giovanni di Salisbury e i Cornificiani," *Sandalion* 3 (1980), 273–313, p. 275, note 7. On Adam, see in particular *Adam Balsamiensis Parvipontani Ars Disserendi*, ed. Lorenzo Minio-Paluello (Rome, 1956) and the notice of Raymond Klibansky, "Adam," in *Oxford Dictionary of National Biography*, vol. 1 (Oxford, 2004), pp. 191–192. Nonetheless, there can be no question of the hypothesis once raised of a return to Oxford between 1141 and 1148, advanced by Christian Petersen, *Johannis Saresberiensis Entheticus de dogmate philosophorum* (Hamburg, 1843), pp. 68–83: "De philosophiae conditione et commercio inter Parisios et Oxoniam."

46   *Metalogicon* 1.24, p. 54.

passage, often perceived as an excursus, is not clear.[47] While on one occasion John mentions only William of Conches as his teacher during these three years, he elsewhere mentions that he had learned about Bernard's teaching from both William and Richard, known as "the bishop," and subsequently archdeacon at Coutances in Normandy. Richard, not a figure about whom much is known, impressed John by virtue of the range of his knowledge, which included certain "unheard of" things about the quadrivium (*inaudita quaedam ad quadruuium pertinentia*), that John had previously studied under a certain German teacher, called Hardewin, presumably a student or collaborator of Thierry of Chartres.[48] John says he also studied rhetoric, a discipline on which he had heard master Thierry lecture with certain other people, but without understanding much – but which he says he subsequently studied with greater profit under Peter Helias.[49] John's evident reserve towards Thierry, erudite, but apparently less accessible as a teacher than Bernard, might explain why he does not mention that they were brothers, a detail reported by both Abelard and Otto of Freising.[50] John's comment that he did study "unheard of things" relating to the quadrivium under Hardewin and Richard might indicate that he was studying at a place where there was interest in these disciplines. Nonetheless,

---

47 Ibid. 2.10, pp. 71–72, ll. 45–51; Weijers, "The Chronology," pp. 112–114.

48 On Richard, see Keats-Rohan, "John of Salisbury," pp. 14–15. Another German student of Thierry before 1137 was Adalbert of Mainz. Anselm of Havelberg, in his *Vita Adalberti*, ed. Philipp Jaffé, in *Monumenta Moguntina* (Berlin, 1866), pp. 589–592, ll. 684–784 asserts that Thierry, although a *Brito*, was brought up in France, and that Adalbert studied in its most famous schools, namely Reims and Paris, implying (although not explicitly asserting) that he studied under Thierry in Paris; Fredborg, *The Latin Rhetorical Commentaries by Thierry of Chartres*, p. 4. The fact that John says he absorbed the quadrivium from Richard, implies that Thierry (presumably Richard's teacher) might not have been as active as a teacher in Chartres.

49 *Metalogicon* 2.10, p. 72, ll. 52–54. On Thierry, see the studies already cited of Jeauneau as well as of: Ward, *passim* (in particular pp. 263–266 Appendix I, on relations with Bernard of Chartres); Fredborg, *The Latin Rhetorical Commentaries by Thierry of Chartres*, pp. 1–9; Max Lejbowicz, "Le premier témoin scolaire des Éléments arabo-latins d'Euclide: Thierry de Chartres et l'*Heptateuchon*," *Revue d'histoire des sciences* 56 (2003), 347–368, at pp. 348–354 on his life and work.

50 Abelard refers critically to the teaching of two brothers, "one of whom attributes such power to the words of consecration of the sacrament, that they were effective, even if pronounced by a woman," the other who was "so involved in philosophical texts that God could not exist before creation," in *Theologia Christiana* 4.80, ed. Eloi-Marie Buytaert (Turnhout, 1969), p. 302. See also Otto of Freising, *Gesta Friderici I*, ed. Georg Waitz and Bernhard von Simson (Hannover, 1912), p. 68: "duo fratres Bernhardus et Theodericus, viri doctissimi."

John did not develop expertise in the field. While aware of Thierry's interest in a wide range of disciplines, his aptitude was not for natural science. John was never a strict Platonist, like Bernard of Chartres. He was more interested in the ethical dimension that William of Conches drew out of the study of classical texts in general (following the technique of Bernard), whether relating to grammar, dialectic and rhetoric. In this respect, it may be deceptive to impose a Platonist label on the intellectual traditions of Chartres, when Plato was just one of many sources of inspiration.

The fact that John of Salisbury never mentions that Abelard ever returned to Paris after 1137, coupled with the brevity of his account in the *Historia pontificalis* of the accusations made against Abelard by Bernard of Clairvaux, so different from his detailed account of the trial of Gilbert of Poitiers at Reims in 1148, could be construed as suggesting that John was not in Paris during the years 1139–41. If John remained in Paris during these years, it seems strange that he should not mention Abelard's evident return to the city by 1139/40, when Bernard would preach against his influence. In the *Historia pontificalis* he mentions simply that Arnold of Brescia attached himself to Abelard in the period immediately after his expulsion from Italy at the Second Lateran Council in April 1139, but without any precise detail about these years.[51] The place where John most likely learned about Bernard of Chartres was at Chartres itself. Bernard of Chartres was a significant intellectual influence on William of Conches, Gilbert of Poitiers and Thierry. Given that Chartres was the residence of Theobald IV (c. 1090/95–1152), count of Chartres, Blois, Meaux and Châteaudun, and brother of both Stephen king of England (1135–54) and Henry of Blois, bishop of Winchester (1129–71), John could have perceived some political advantage to studying in Chartres, in the years following the accession of the young king of France, Louis VII. In 1138, following the temporary ousting of Ralph of Vermandois from the French court, Suger advised Louis VII to seek the support of Theobald of Blois, an alliance that lasted until 1141, when Count Theobald IV moved towards a war with Louis VII that lasted until 1144.[52] By the late 1150s, however, with the death of Stephen of Blois and

---

51   *Historia pontificalis* 31, p. 63.

52   On the temporary fall from grace of Ralph of Vermandois, Suger's approach to Theobald, and Theobald's subsequent conflict with Louis VII, following the collapse of the marriage of his sister to Ralph of Vermandois, see Suger's *De glorioso rege Ludovico, Ludovici filio*, ed. Françoise Gasparri (Paris, 2008), pp. 163–167 and Achille Luchaire, *Études sur les actes de Louis VII* (Paris, 1885), pp. 46 and 133. When John wrote the *Metalogicon*, the Angevin Henry II had supplanted the claim of Blois to possess the English crown, perhaps a reason for not identifying Chartres by name.

the accession of the Angevin Henry II, it could be that John felt it inappropriate to specify that he had studied at Chartres. Wherever John spent those years 1138–41 he was delighted to look back to a group of masters who celebrated Bernard of Chartres as their mentor, more broadly cultured than the dialecticians he had studied with in Paris, without specifying exactly where he was at this time.

John's Return to the Montagne Sainte-Geneviève

Towards the end of the period 1138–41, John indicates that economic necessity obliged him to give tuition to young nobles, which at least had the pedagogical advantage that he was obliged to recall what he had learned.[53] Young masters and freshly formed students often needed to resort to this practice to pay for their studies. There are many other examples of teachers offering private tuition, well known through the testimony of Guibert of Nogent and Peter Abelard. This remark of John recalls to us that besides masters of the first rank there was also a large cohort of masters and assistants who guaranteed the functioning of the schools and created what one could call a *Lumpen-intelligentsia*. The importance of such personnel and the diversity of tasks needing to be done (lectures, watching over students, assistance in divine office) effectively required the presence of many teachers subordinated to the *scholasticus* or head teacher of a school. The latter reserved to himself the most prestigious teaching and left to his assistants the task of instruction of the youngest. In this, John benefited from the help of Adam of Petit-Pont, master at Paris from 1132, canon of Notre-Dame from around 1146, who gave him the fruit of his teaching in a relationship that one could describe as more that of a supporting colleague than that of a teacher to a student.[54] Among the students taught by his care, John also mentions the name of William of Soissons, who gained a reputation through the audacity of his logical propositions.[55] This situation of assistant teacher nonetheless ended under the pressure of circumstances, the request of colleagues and the advice of his friends, who pressed him to take the *officium docentis*, likely meaning responsibility for a school that John would have established.[56]

---

53   *Metalogicon* 2.10, p. 72, ll. 54–58.
54   Ibid. p. 72, ll. 59–64.
55   Ibid., p. 72, ll. 64–75.
56   Ibid., p. 72, ll. 75–77.

To do this, John decided to complete his education by studying under Master Gilbert, also known as *Porreta*, without specifying exactly where this was other than that "he returned to find him again," following lectures *in logicis* as well as *in diuinis*.[57] John's term *repperi* implies that he had previously studied under Gilbert (who had been chancellor at Chartres since 1126), but now found him teaching in Paris. Gilbert's election to the bishopric of Poitiers in 1142 put an end to this phase of his study. John turned to Robert Pullen (subsequently made a cardinal in Rome in 1143) and then the little known Simon of Poissy to complete his studies in theology.[58] By this time, John specifies that almost twelve years had passed, implying that this was in 1147, when he was sometime between twenty-seven and thirty-two years of age. As if drawing a moral to his story, he reports that he then decided to return to the Montagne Sainte-Geneviève in order to see his companions still engaged in the study of dialectic.[59] Discovering what seemed to be their stagnation, even regression, in such marked contrast to John's own trajectory, enabled him to establish experimentally what seemed, to him to be a general truth: dialectic considered on its own was sterile, and must be fertilized by the contribution of other disciplines.[60]

John's account thus presents all the classical *topoi* that are found in other narrative sources about the schools of the 12th century. They are relevant not just to the facts reported, but to the intellectual climate that they reveal: attachment to an admired teacher (Peter Abelard), criticism laced with irony towards others (Alberic), and the importance of reputation being made and unmade by rumour. All these elements, including John's own crisis of conscience find echoes in the writing of his contemporaries.[61] This well-known chapter confirms our picture of the schools of the 12th century. Masters and students travelled a good deal, John had been educated by masters from England and

---

57   Ibid., p. 72, ll. 77–79: "Reuersus itaque in fine triennii repperi magistrum Gillebertum, ipsumque audiui in logicis et in diuinis, sed nimis cito subtractus est."

58   Ibid., p. 72, ll. 79–80.

59   Ibid., pp. 72–73, ll. 82–93. This seems to be a clear conclusion to the logical and chronological flow of the preceding account, making it uncertain that John remained in Paris throughout this time, as claimed by Keats-Rohan, who separates chronologically the end of the chapter from the flow of events to which it is a conclusion; "The Chronology," p. 203, "John of Salisbury," pp. 19–20.

60   *Metalogicon* 2.10, p. 73, ll. 93–96.

61   Cédric Giraud, *"Per verba magistri*. La langue des maîtres théologiens au premier XIIe siècle," in Peter von Moos, ed., *Zwischen Babel und Pfingsten//Entre Babel et Pentecôte, Sprachdifferenzen und Gesprächsverständigung in der Vormoderne (8.-16. Jahrhundert). Différences linguistiques et communication orale avant la modernité (VIIIe–XVIe siècle)* (Zurich, 2008), pp. 357–373.

Normandy, the kingdom of France and the Empire. John's studies do not correspond to a clearly defined curriculum, since the same masters teach both arts and theology and since students can repeat certain courses, while respecting a certain progression that leads from arts to sacred science. Finally, we should note that John shows himself to be very vague about the content of his studies of the quadrivium, presumably because this was not relevant to the genre of the *Metalogicon*. The same relative indifference to identifying space and time and to methods of teaching, characterised more by *lectio* than by *disputatio*, is explained by the author's purpose, more concerned with the intellectual personalities of the masters with whom he studied than with a precise reconstruction of his studies. Even if John had fully absorbed the practice of disputation, he was cautious about its misuse, and retained a preference for synthetic reflection on the wisdom of the classical authors, not just of philosophers like Plato and Aristotle, but also the great Latin authors, above all Cicero.

The Pedagogical Ideas of John of Salisbury

After situating the general education of John in the educational context of his time, it may be useful to turn towards what John tells us about his pedagogical ideas, particularly in the *Metalogicon*. Without studying his thought in detail, as it has been the subject of numerous studies, two main points nonetheless deserve attention.[62]

First, John writes in what he considers to be the context of a crisis. The *Metalogicon* opens with a lively preface, whose goal is to defend *logica* from the attacks to which it is victim. John's educational ideal is not just a collection of positive prescriptions, but a response to an enemy that, through charity, he does not wish to identify by name, but whom he ridicules with a conventional name

---

62   See in particular D. McGarry, "Educational Theory in the *Metalogicon* of John of Salisbury," *Speculum* 23 (1948), 659–675 and *Metalogicon*, pp. xxi–xxvii; Liebeschütz, *Medieval Humanism*, pp. 63–94; Brian P. Hendley, "John of Salisbury's Defense of the *Trivium*," in *Arts libéraux et philosophie au Moyen Âge. Congrès international de philosophie médiévale* (Montréal, 1969), pp. 753–762; G.C. Garfagnini, "'Ratio disserendi' e 'ratiocinandi via': il Metalogicon di Giovanni di Salisbury," *Studi medievali*, 12 (1971), 915–954; Guth, *Johannes von Salisbury*, pp. 47–56 and 61–81; Hanna-Barbara Gerl, "Zum mittelalterlichen Spannungsfeld von Logik, Dialektik und Rhetorik. Die Programmatik des *Metalogicon* von Johannes von Salisbury," *Studia Mediewistyczne* 22 (1983), 37–51; Riché, "Jean de Salisbury," pp. 54–59; Keats-Rohan, "John of Salisbury," pp. 2–7; Nederman, *John of Salisbury*, pp. 62–75.

borrowed, according to Donatus from a detractor of Virgil: Cornificius.[63] He is
clearly a literary fiction rather than a specific individual. Implicitly situating
itself in the tradition of Jerome's polemical writing, the *Metalogicon* thus seeks
to be a treatise *Against Cornificius*. John thus attaches this work to several currents that seek to reform the working of the schools, particularly in Paris,
through the 12th century. Cornificius is particularly dangerous because he is at
the head of a group against which Thierry, William of Conches and Peter
Abelard have struggled in vain, and which throws jibes against Anselm and
Ralph of Laon, Alberic of Reims and Simon of Paris, William of Champeaux,
Hugh of Saint-Victor and Robert Pullen. Above all, these Cornificians elevate
speed and *ingenium* as a privileged source of knowledge.[64] In contrast to the
educational cursus followed by John, they advocate an accelerated path of
study allowing two or three years for encompassing the whole of philosophy.
Worse, these self-professed "philosophers" advocate worldly success and take
riches alone to be the fruit of wisdom. This denunciation of study for the sake
of money making and its adherents recalls, as proved by John's career itself,
that frequenting the schools and acquiring educational skills facilitate social
mobility. During the course of the 12th century, possibilities multiplied for

---

63   *Metalogicon* 1.1–2, pp. 13–15. The important bibliography on this topic includes:
      Liebeschütz, *Medieval Humanism*, pp. 90–91 and "Appendix IV: The Personality of
      Cornificius," p. 118 where he prudently concludes that he is simply a personification;
      Franco Alessio, "Notizie e questioni sul movimento cornificiano," *Atti dell'Accademia delle
      scienze di Torino* 88 (1953–4), 125–135, Garfagnini, "'Ratio disserendi' e 'ratiocinandi via': il
      Metalogicon di Giovanni di Salisbury," pp. 927–951, Ward, "Thierry of Chartres," pp. 221–225,
      particularly p. 223, note 3; Guth, *Johannes von Salisbury*, pp. 56–61; Tacchella, "Giovanni di
      Salisbury," pp. 278–285 and 297–310; Rosemary B. Tobin, "The Cornifician Motif in John of
      Salisbury's *Metalogicon*," *History of Education* 13 (1984), 1–6; Riché, "Jean de Salisbury,"
      pp. 47–50; Pedro Belmar-Lopez, "La destruccion de la razon metodica en el siglo XII:
      Cornificius," *Estudios Filosoficos* 37 (1988), 275–296; Nederman, *John of Salisbury*, pp. 67–68
      (the proposed connection with Bernard of Clairvaux does not seem so plausible); David
      Bloch, "John of Salisbury, Adam of Balsham and The Cornifician Problem," *Cahiers de
      l'Institut du Moyen Âge grec et latin* 79 (2010), 7–24. The attacks raised against those who
      misuse the trivium by William of Conches, Hugh of Saint-Victor, Robert of Melun, Thierry
      of Chartres and the *Metamorphosis Goliae* (references listed by Ward, "Thierry of Chartres,"
      p. 222, note 2) do not seem to all have the same goal, and therefore are probably not all
      referring to the same target.
64   This enables, among other possibilities, the teaching of Cornificius and his followers to
      include a wry reference to the educational theories of Adam of Petit-Pont; see Bloch,
      "John of Salisbury," pp. 11–17.

pursuing a career in courts and bureaucracies, both lay and ecclesiastical.[65] Contemporaries often observed this, generally to deplore the practice. Criticism of money-making skills, like law and medicine, became a common topos of moralizing preachers, as it was for John of Salisbury.[66]

Besides being involved in this controversy, John also defines education from the positive perspective of education of the human being. To arrive at perfection, human nature needs to be developed and submitted to an exercise that improves both moral and intellectual capacities.[67] John's optimism and pedagogical humanism do not constitute pious faith in an infinite capacity for progress in human nature, because if any natural faculty is so low that it cannot be raised, none is so high that it cannot be lowered by neglect. The improvement of the human person is achieved through a process of animation, which allows nature to give birth to custom and exercise, the latter producing arts which develop talent. In this noetic process which enables a person to move from the state of nature to one of being cultivated, memory plays a key role since it collects and keeps the trace of perceptions. It also supplies its subject matter to the investigation of reason.[68] It is in this light that one must read the famous phrase of Bernard of Chartres cited by John of Salisbury: "we are like dwarves sitting on the shoulders of giants, with the result that we can see more and further than them, not because of sharper sight or great height, but because we are carried and raised above because of their stature as giants." Unlike Bernard of Chartres, for whom the comparison was important above all for keeping to intelligent imitation of ancient texts, John of Salisbury recognised in each period the capacity to improve the cultural legacy of preceding periods.[69] If one transposed to the level of humanity what John affirmed about the individual *in abstracto*, there was a kind of "collective memory," which transmitted to the

---

65   Peter Classen, "Die höhen Schulen und die Gesellschaft im 12. Jahrhundert," *Archiv für Kulturgeschichte* 48 (1966), 155–180.

66   Riché, "Jean de Salisbury," pp. 50–52; Stephen C. Ferruolo, *The Origins of the University. The School of Paris and their Critics 1100–1215* (Stanford, 1985), pp. 184–277.

67   *Metalogicon* 1.8, pp. 25–26.

68   Ibid. 1.11, p. 29. There is thus a close connection between pedagogy, noetics and philosophy as affirmed by McGarry: "John's philosophy of education is the foundation for his whole pedagogical theory, and the key to his philosophy of education is his general philosophy" ("Educational Theory," p. 664); see also Gerl, "Zum mittelalterlichen Spannungsfeld," pp. 41–42.

69   Jeauneau, "Nains et géants," in Maurice de Gandillac and Édouard Jeauneau, eds., *Entretiens sur la Renaissance du XIIᵉ siècle* (Paris, 1968), pp. 21–52, at pp. 31–33, with previous bibliography cited at p. 35, note 2.

ingenium of each generation the achievements of past centuries. In an implicit manner, this collective heritage that teachers receive as a deposit can only become valuable if it transforms an individual from his natural state to that of culture. An individual's appropriation of culture is achieved through four exercises that John defines with precision: reading, which enables texts to be known; teaching, which attaches itself as much to knowledge contained within texts as to those preserved in the memory; meditation, which rises to consideration of what is beyond comprehension; continuous action which transforms knowledge into action.[70]

The conception that John evokes of *logica* resembles the two aspects of pedagogy, namely blame and praise. Blame touches all those who seek out complexity to make themselves important, illustrated by an unflattering portrait of certain masters like Adam, who, according to John, uses his *Ars disserendi* to make obscurity seem like depth.[71] More broadly, John paints a portrait of the type of bad master of logic, defined by three faults: he does not adapt to his listeners; he does not offer reasoned progress, and he resorts to doctrinal concords that do violence to both Aristotle and Plato.[72] The education praised by John, particularly in logic, seeks to be based on the progress of a student, with the goal of pedagogy being to establish understanding of the context of what is taught, and not to make it obscure.[73] The patience of the teacher is evident towards the youngest, whose verbosity must be tolerated in order to make their spirits grow. This development for which the teacher has responsibility rests on a true regime of teaching, adapted to the character of the students, and based on effort.[74] In this sense, the account of the completion of education in logic in the last chapter of Book three connects to the account of human faculties in Book one: the process of developing the cultivation of the human spirit advances by implementation in practice, similar to the rules of any craft or to the art of war.[75] The extended praise that John makes in Book eight of the Topics, whose practical goal is to assemble the logical materials presented in the seven preceding books, insists on the importance of putting into practice what belongs to memory (*memoriter*) and sustained application (*iugi exercitio*).

---

70   *Metalogicon* 1.23, p. 51.
71   Ibid. 4.3, p. 142.
72   Ibid. 2.19, p. 85.
73   Ibid. 3.1. p. 103.
74   Ibid. 4.28, pp. 164–165.
75   Ibid. 3.10, p. 130.

John of Salisbury and Grammar: A Reading of *Metalogicon* 1.13–25

John presents grammar according to two different perspectives in Chapters 13 to 25 of Book one of the *Metalogicon*, the eight first chapters being of a technical character, the remaining ones being more moral. John's purpose is above all one of definition, as it is about transmitting the rules of the discipline that he wishes to defend. Drawing on Isidore of Seville, John defines grammar as the science of speaking and writing well and the foundation of all the liberal arts. Its status as foundational principle is inextricably bound up with chronology, since grammar receives and forms all people from the cradle, and organic in that it is itself the cradle of philosophy. From its first definition, grammar plays a civilizing role, since it teaches man to express himself.[76] Filling a maternal role, language must not be confused, however, with nature: keeping its status as a discipline while being the foundation of other disciplines, grammar imitates nature without being confused with it. This mimetic function is stretched quite widely by John, since while reserving the practical modalities of grammar to human institution, he maintains that grammar reproduces the working of nature in the very structure of the various duties of parts of speech (substantives, adjectives, verbs and adverbs).[77] This allows John to posit rules of grammatical construction and to define grammatical absurdity as distinct from logical absurdity.[78] A certain flexibility is at the same time dominant not just because nature allows metaphorical usages in human language, that transfer to speech the properties of things, but also because usage, with the variability that it takes for granted, constitutes the supreme tribunal of language.[79] The mimetic nature of grammar also explains the poetics that belongs to it, language having also the role of imitating moral nature. The poet, following a process of exteriorisation of emotions distinct to an individual, must first experience sentiments that he wishes another to experience, not only by attitude and gesture, but also by speech.[80]

After having defined the relationships of grammar with nature, John comes back to the definition of grammar as the art of expression and to grammatical norms. The study of orthography and of the rules of discourse allows a distinction to be made between *ars* (the norm to follow), *uitium* (the fault to reject) and *figura*, the license, above all, of the great authors, that keeps a balance

---

76   Ibid. 1.13, p. 32.
77   Ibid. 1.14, pp. 33–34.
78   Ibid. 1.15, pp. 35–36.
79   Ibid. 1.16, p. 41.
80   Ibid. 1.17, p. 42.

between the first two. Their study enables grammar to develop from technique to interpretation, since only understanding, respectively of *ars*, *uitium* and of *figura* allows comprehension of a text.[81] In studying tropes and other figures of style, the grammarian must be a semiotician to make sense of any text that employs *figurae*. In practice John advocates only a moderate usage of trope, insofar as the supreme rule of speech is to make oneself understood.[82] The mention of punctuation and of the articulation of discourse by *colon, coma* and *periodus* completes this examination of the content of grammar which concludes with a recommendation of Isidore as a path to access this discipline.[83]

With Chapter 21, John effects a shift in perspective, given that having indicated the entire range of grammar, John comes to its praise. His defence of grammar is part of a broader educational programme in which it is the foundation of philosophy, considering as much its intrinsic value as its propaedeutic role for the rest of the educational curriculum.[84] Drawing on the testimony of Quintilian, he critiques the followers of Cornificius, by insisting that one must pass through its study, without stopping there. Significantly, John – despite an allusion to Paul on charity as that which alone does good for man – does not develop a theory of redemption of the arts by theology, and uses ancient precedent to be the *auctoritas* that legitimates grammar.[85]

By connecting the study of grammar to description of the four tasks that lead to both philosophy and virtue, John presents this discipline as the foundation of a true art of living, which develops into ethics. Inasmuch as the first three tasks (reading, teaching, meditation) create the knowledge that allows for right conduct, grammar, the basis of reading and of communication, acts in cooperation with prevenient grace. In this way, John restores grammar to the Christian economy of learning and re-establishes for the society of his own day the Ciceronian ideal of the *homo bonus*.[86] After this peak, the return to pedagogy enables the implementation of this programme. The description of *praelectio* or explanation given by the teacher serves to illustrate a lesson in grammatical instruction that brings together all the other liberal arts: by explaining a text, or "penning it," to pick up a metaphor of John, the teacher must show all the pens at his disposal to describe the palette of disciplines, culminating in ethics.[87]

---

81   Ibid. 1.18, pp. 42–44.
82   Ibid. 1.19, pp. 45–46.
83   Ibid. 1.20, pp. 46–47.
84   Ibid. 1.21, p. 48.
85   Ibid. 1.22, p. 49.
86   Ibid. 1.23, pp. 50–51.
87   Ibid. 1.24, p. 52.

John deepens his explanation of this technique by taking the example of Bernard of Chartres and by giving a description of a class that he never followed. John reportedly insisted on the technique of summarizing by students the lessons of the previous day, describing as well an evening exercise of *declinatio*, relying on reasoned imitation of ancient models.[88] The figure of Bernard thus became a paradigm of grammatical teaching, as opposed to the pedagogical practices of his contemporaries.[89] This description, itself, participates in a characteristic educational tradition of elevating the figure of a previous generation as a model for the functioning of a discipline, just as Peter the Chanter, for example, does with Anselm and Ralph of Laon in the case of theology.[90] Significantly, the examination of grammar closes with a eulogy borrowed from Quintilian, and addressed by John to the grammarians of his day, showing through this the task of the *Metalogicon* to provide a connection to the ancient examples and to guarantee their relevance to the present.

John of Salisbury on Dialectic

If John of Salisbury was particularly keen to re-assert the importance of *grammatica* as the foundation of all literary study, it was part of his broader conviction, shaped by Cicero's *Topics*, that dialectic needed to be understood as part of *logica*, "the reasoning behind speaking or dissertation" (*ratio loquendi uel disserendi*).[91] Whereas Hugh of Saint-Victor had composed his *Didascalicon* without any detailed appreciation of Abelard's contribution to dialectic, but with a thinly veiled distaste for any teacher driven by love of novelty and intellectual vanity, John wanted to show why dialectic was integral to the pursuit of philosophy, even if it might be abused by poor practitioners. Hugh considered the arts of language (*logica*) only after he had described *theorica, practica* and

---

88   The density of the description makes its interpretation not easy, in particular as regards the relationship between the recitation of lessons, the evening *declinatio* and the *collationes* between students; see also Tacchella, "Giovanni di Salisbury," pp. 310–312.

89   On Bernard, see Keats-Rohan, "John of Salisbury," pp. 6–7.

90   This eulogy is not without a certain irony towards Bernard of Chartres and his students in their quest to reconcile Plato and Aristotle (*Metalogicon* 2.17). Other references in the index refer particularly to sayings, of which the last identifies Bernard and the most perfect of the Platonists (*Metalogicon* 4.35), see also *Policraticus* 7.9–13, ed. Webb, vol. 2, pp. 144–145. On Anselm and Ralph of Laon see Giraud, *Per verba magistri*, pp. 491–492.

91   *Metalogicon* 1.10, p. 28; 2.1, p. 56. See Garfagnini, "'Ratio disserendi' e 'ratiocinandi via': il Metalogicon di Giovanni du Salisbury."

mechanica, summarizing the arts of grammar, dialectic, and rhetoric at a relatively elementary level.[92] While clearly aware of the teaching of Bernard of
Chartres (whom he quoted without citing by name in the *Didascalicon*), Hugh
never absorbed William of Champeaux's interest in applying Aristotelian dialectic to the analysis of words, arriving in Paris a few years after William had
moved away from Saint-Victor in 1113. Although Hugh's *Didascalicon*, with its
focus on liberal arts as a foundation for the study of scripture, enjoyed wide
influence by the mid 12th-century, John believed that the liberal arts were
worth studying for their own sake. He felt it necessary to present what dialectic
had to offer for the study of philosophy, while signalling the dangers of insufficient foundation in reading the classical authors, the domain of
grammatica.

As has already been argued, John used the story of his own career within the
second book of the *Metalogicon*, about dialectic, to illustrate his argument that
dialectic without a foundation in grammar could lead to sterility. When he first
went to Paris, he reports that he was a devoted follower of Abelard, "from
whom I learned the elementary principles of this art." Yet he never became a
partisan follower of Abelard's dialectic, perhaps as a result of his tuition under
Alberic, a dialectician with a reputation for being very critical of the nominal-
ism associated with Abelard. Yet John also studied the discipline under Robert
of Melun, an Englishman who gained his nickname from teaching at the royal
palace at Melun (perhaps in the 1120s), but had moved to teaching at Sainte-
Geneviève by 1137, where he would remain until 1163, when he became bishop
of Hereford. While Robert was not strictly a nominalist, his subsequent respect
for Abelard's theological opinions suggests that he could have been seen as
Abelard's successor at Sainte-Geneviève.[93] John's comment that Alberic was
full of questions and Robert was penetrating in his replies, but both lacked a
deep foundation in letters, "preferring to delight in their own inventions" than
to stick to the paths of the ancients, hints at disappointment that they lacked
Abelard's breadth of learning. This disappointment may have contributed to
his decision to resume studies of *grammatica* under William of Conches and

---

92   On the varying ways in which Hugh located *logica* in relation to these other areas, see
      Poirel, "*Tene fontem et totum habes*: l'unité du *Didascalicon* d'Hugues de Saint-Victor."
93   William fitz Stephen mentions that Robert of Melun taught dialectic and theology for
      forty years, prior to becoming bishop of Hereford in 1163. His cognomen suggests that he
      initially established his reputation at the royal palace in Melun in the 1120s (possibly
      through the influence of Stephen of Garlande, Abelard's patron), before moving to
      Sainte-Geneviève by 1137, again perhaps through Stephen's influence: *Vita S. Thomae
      Cantuariensis*, in *MB*, vol. 3, p. 60; PL 190, col. 139CD.

move beyond a narrow focus on dialectic, such as he observes was increasingly the fashion in the Parisian schools.

Not the least interesting aspect of John's presentation of dialectic in the *Metalogicon* is his refusal to identify himself firmly with any particular school of dialectic. He prefers to focus attention on the broader concept of *logica* as encompassing all the arts of language, not just dialectic. While he clearly counted Abelard as a great scholar, well-known for his familiarity with Aristotle, he was cautious about accepting a number of specific teachings. He admired Abelard's gift for making difficult concepts accessible, which led, John suggests, to his putting forward a "somewhat childish" interpretation of genera and species.[94] John benefited from Abelard's instruction that one should always pay attention to the different possible meaning of words, and to the need to recognise that figurative speech should not be stretched to mean something beyond its original intention, without accepting the detail of his teaching.[95] John also recalled with respect a comment of Abelard about it being easier for someone to summarise the teaching of the ancients on dialectic than to acquire authority with such a synthesis, and the ancients ought to be respected because of their genius, as they made it possible for a newer generation to advance its ideas.[96]

John distrusted Abelard's view of universals as *sermones* (a view that he only fully articulated in the *Logica 'Nostrorum petitioni sociorum'*), recognizing that it still had followers, even among his friends, who declared that it was monstrous to predicate a thing (*res*) of a thing – even if Aristotle himself had authorized this practice.[97] In criticizing a purely nominalist approach to universals, John may well have been influenced by the teaching of Alberic, whose criticisms of Abelard's opinions are recorded in a tract on dialectic, probably compiled during the time John was his student. Significantly, this tract also refers to the teaching on dialectic of William of Champeaux, as if Alberic saw himself as extending the philosophically realist teaching of William, but with reference to a greater range of texts (notably the *Sophistici Analytici* of Aristotle), coming more into use in the 1130s, than when Abelard had first written on dialectic.[98]

---

94   *Metalogicon* 3.1, p. 102.
95   Ibid. 3.1, p. 105.
96   Ibid. 3.4, p. 116.
97   Ibid. 2.17, p. 81, ll. 18–26.
98   Lambert Marie De Rijk, "Some New Evidence on Twelfth-Century Logic: Alberic and the School of Mont Ste Geneviève (Montani)," *Vivarium* 4 (1966), 1–57; Abelard refers to the *Sophistici Elenchi* in his Ep. 13 (from the eary 1130s), ed. Edmé Renno Smits (Groningen, 1983), p. 273.

It may well be through Alberic's influence that John came to respect the teaching of William of Champeaux, distancing himself from a contemporary tendency (indirectly encouraged by Abelard) to dismiss his teaching as "condemned by his own writings."[99]

John never attaches himself to the views of any particular master. He was familiar with a range of arguments about universals that had been put forward over the last fifty years. In a celebrated chapter of the *Metalogicon* (2.17), he comments on various opinions on the subject, some in a way quite similar to those discussed by Abelard at the outset of his *Logica 'Ingredientibus'* – a text he may have known, even if he did not accept its arguments. He implicitly castigates dialecticians for being excessively preoccupied with the issue, not because universals were not important, but because they were too often bathing in unintelligibility for its own sake, when the question ought to be reserved for more advanced study. As if presenting a chronological overview, he begins with the view that universals were simply *uoces*, but declares that this position had almost completely disappeared with its author, namely Roscelin of Compiègne.[100] Then there was the view of Abelard that universals were *sermones*, a position that Abelard had advanced in a later revision of his glosses on Porphyry, the *Logica 'Nostrorum petitioni sociorum'*, and which John acknowledges still has some adherents.[101] Another view, difficult to identify precisely, was one reportedly justified by reference to Cicero and Boethius as well as Aristotle, that genera and species were simply understandings, existing *in intellectibus*.[102]

Among those who preferred to identify universals as things, he identifies several views, beginning with a position that he says was once held by Walter of Mortagne that considered universals to be states of existence of a specific individual. Walter, he reported, subsequently turned to accepting the view of Bernard of Chartres that universals were eternally true ideas, whose manifestations were infinitely varied.[103] John then reflects that Bernard, for all his brilliance as a follower of Plato, was engaged in a pointless task when trying

---

99   *Metalogicon* 1.5, p. 21, ll. 40–41.

100   Ibid. 2.17, p. 81, ll. 18–20.

101   Ibid. 2.17, p. 81, ll. 20–29; see *Peter Abaelards Philosophische Schriften. Die Logica 'Nostrorum petitioni sociorum'*, ed. Bernhard Geyer (Münster, 1973²), p. 522.

102   *Metalogicon* 2.17, p. 81, ll. 29–36; unlike John, Abelard reports this as a realist view, relying on the authority of Priscian's teaching that genera and species were forms of things created in the divine mind; *Logica 'Nostrorum petitioni sociorum'*, ed. Geyer, pp. 513–514.

103   *Metalogicon* 2.17, ll. 37–49.

to combine the ideas of Plato and Aristotle.[104] By contrast, John reports much more favourably the view of Gilbert of Poitiers, which he describes as consonant with Aristotle, redefining a Platonic concept, that identified universals with *formae natiuae*, which inhered in created things, rather than in the divine mind.[105] He is more critical of the view of Joscelin of Soissons that universals were collections of individuals rather than an individual thing in itself, and of another teacher who claimed that universals were the *maneries* of things – a neologism that he did not understand or care for.[106] John was not simply a reporter of opinions in the schools. He refused to align himself with any single perspective, whether on universals or on any other matter. He acknowledged that most teachers of logic tended to promote their own opinions against those of their teachers, in the end debating words rather than meanings.[107] Those who taught the doctrine of Plato while professing commitment to Aristotle, were naïve in trying to combine their views. In a chapter devoted to his own interpretation of universals, John explained that Aristotle did not believe in naïve existence of universals as such, but considered that they were abstract conceptions through which things could be understood. Genera and species may proceed from the mind of God, from whom all things came into being, but they did not exist except within specific things. It was still legitimate, however, to say that they existed, even if not in the way that specific things existed. John concluded the second book of the *Metalogicon* by presenting his own commitment to the views of Aristotle on universals, clearly differentiating himself from the Platonic views of Bernard of Chartres.[108] While John sided with the view that universals were more than just words, he did not think they were entities in themselves. Rather he accepts that universals provided a way of contemplating particular individuals, drawing on their common form – a position not dissimilar to that which he attributed to Gilbert of Poitiers. John identifies his approach as fully in accord with Aristotle rather than Plato, but as one that acknowledges that forms do have a reality, in that they are made by God, even if never as separate entities existing outside the individuals that they

---

104   Ibid. 2.17, ll. 81–84.

105   Ibid. 2.17, ll. 84–91.

106   Ibid. 2.17, ll. 92–107.

107   Ibid. 2.18, p. 84.

108   Brian Patrick Hendley, "John of Salisbury and the Problem of Universals," *Journal of the History of Philosophy* 8 (1970), 289–302.

inform.[109] While John had sympathy for those who followed Abelard's emphasis on predication as the task of language, his natural sympathy was more with Gilbert of Poitiers in acknowledging that universals were strictly speaking forms that existed only within individuals.

John's reserve with regard to Abelard's teaching on universals (at least by the time he wrote the *Metalogicon*) echoed a broader reserve about the way Abelard tended to identify *dialectica* with *logica*. John preferred the Ciceronian view of *logica* as embracing both dialectic and rhetoric, a view followed by Isidore, Hugh of Saint-Victor, and the author of the *Glosule* on Priscian's *Institutiones grammaticae*, an influential commentary from the late 11th century (preserved in an early manuscript of Chartres) that exercised a strong influence on the commentary of William of Conches on Priscian.[110] William of Champeaux drew on this broader, Ciceronian tradition in recognizing that grammar, dialectic, and rhetoric each considered language in a particular way, and each according a particular meaning to a word – a perspective that Abelard refused to accept. Abelard's focus, by contrast, was always on dialectic – a term that he used interchangeably with *logica*, understanding it as the science of evaluating an argument, extracting truth from falsehood.[111]

---

109   *Metalogicon* 2.20, p. 88 ll. 108: "Nihil autem uniuerale est nisi quod in singularibus inuenitur; seorsum tamen a multi quaesitum est. sed tandem nihil inuenerunt omnes in manibus suis, quoniam seorum a singularibus nihil est. nisi forte qualia sunt uera, at similia complexorum significata sermonum." On the difference between Gilbert and Abelard on universals see Jean Jolivet, "Trois versions médiévales sur l'universel et l'individu: Roscelin, Abélard, Gilbert de la Porrée," *Revue de métaphysique et de morale* 97 (1992), 111–155.

110   Isidore, *Etymologiae* 2.24.7, ed. Wallace M. Lindsay (Oxford, 1912): Didascalicon I, ed. C.H. Buttimer (Washington, 1939), p. 21: "*logica* sermocinalis genus est ad grammaticam, *dialecticam* atque rhetoricam, et continet sub se dissertiuam." On this theme in William of Champeaux, see Mews, "*Logica* in the Service of Philosophy: William of Champeaux and his Influence," in Rainer Berndt, ed., *Schrift, Schreiber, Schenker. Studien zur Abtei Sankt Viktor zu Paris und zu den Viktorinern* (Berlin, 2005), pp. 77–117. It is formulated in the prologue to the *Glosule* on Priscian, edited by Margaret T. Gibson, "The Early Scholastic 'Glosule' to Priscian, 'Institutiones Grammaticae': The Text and its Influence," *Studi medievali*, 3a ser. 20 (1979), 235–254. On its influence, see I. Rosier-Catach (ed.), *Arts du langage et théologie aux confins des XIᵉ et XIIᵉ siècles*, Studia Artistarum 26 (Turnhout, 2011).

111   *Logica 'Nostrorum petitioni sociorum'*, ed. Geyer, p. 506: "Logicam vero idem dicimus quod dialecticam et indifferenter utroque nomine in designatione utimur eiusdem scientiae." On Abelard's critique of William of Champeaux in this respect, see Mews, "Peter Abelard on Dialectic, Rhetoric, and the Principles of Argument," in Constant J. Mews, Cary J. Nederman and Rodney M. Thomson, eds., *Rhetoric and Renewal in the Latin West 1100–1540. Essays in Honour of John O. Ward* (Turnhout, 2003), pp. 37–53.

John preferred the more balanced approach of William, whom he described as "of happy memory" when recalling how he had described the study of the topics (*loci*), "even if imperfectly," as the science of finding a middle term and thus of extracting an argument.[112] John not only respected William's teaching on the foundations of argument, but was puzzled by Abelard's insistence that the consequence in a hypothetical proposition could only be valid if the consequence was included in its antecedent.[113] Abelard's teaching on this followed from his strict interpretation of a hypothetical consequence as no kind of thing, and therefore only having validity through its being implied in its antecedent.

At the opening of the third book of the *Metalogicon,* John confesses that it had been almost twenty years since he had abandoned the schools of the dialecticians – presumably around 1138 – and that professional obligations had since deprived him of the opportunity to look back on their writings. This did not prevent him, however, from presenting an overview in its third and fourth books of the various texts that made up the study of dialectic: Porphyry's *Isagoge,* Aristotle's *Categories* and *Periermeneias* and *Topics* (the latter more known through the summaries of Cicero and Boethius). In its fourth book, he explained the utility of Aristotelian texts with which Abelard had been largely unfamiliar, but were only just beginning to enter the curriculum of dialectic: the *Prior Analytics* about forms of arguments and the more complex *Posterior Analytics* and *Sophistical Refutations,* reflecting on the larger themes of sensation and imagination as the foundation for every branch of philosophy, on which prudence must be based. The cultivation of reason is the true concern of philosophy, transcending sense perception. John concludes by re-asserting the value of Aristotle's instruction in logic, against the criticisms made by Cornificius. Logic needs to be rightly employed to be used to the full. While John recognised the achievement of recent scholars in producing syntheses of dialectic, he offered his own reading of what Aristotle was trying to achieve in systematizing the rules of argument. Only when logic was linked with other studies was it useful. On its own, it simply became a pretext for verbosity. Drawing on Martianus Capella, he presents the cultivated mind as pursuing and loving true goodness, wisdom and reason, and (by grace) eventually obtaining the object of its affection.[114]

---

112   *Metalogicon* 3.9, p. 129.
113   Ibid. 3.6, p. 122.
114   Ibid. 4.29, p. 166.

John of Salisbury and Theology

John implies in the *Metalogicon* that he first embarked on the study of theology in 1141, when he "returned" to Paris after his three years study under William of Conches and Richard "the bishop." "Finding Gilbert again," he chose to follow the lectures of Gilbert *in logicis* as well as *in diuinis*. Presumably this was now in the much larger classes that Gilbert maintained in Paris, rather than the small elite group who had followed his teaching at Chartres. Nonetheless, John evidently applied himself to absorbing Gilbert's philosophical theology, through study of his commentaries on Boethius. Gilbert's approach to the doctrine of the Trinity, based around recognizing the distinction between that which a divine name referred to (i.e. Father, God), and the attribute (like fatherhood, divinity) by which it existed, appealed to John's fascination with a theological system that acknowledged the reality of forms, embodied within individuals. It relied on familiarity with the philosophical system on which it was based. Although John had only a limited time studying theology under Gilbert (appointed bishop of Poitiers by late 1142), he was sufficiently committed to Gilbert's theological teaching to compose an important defence of his arguments in the *Historia pontificalis*, when reporting the accusations made against him by Bernard of Clairvaux.[115] When he wrote that account, he was keenly aware that there were many people who were suspicious of Gilbert because they found his teaching hard to understand. John, for whom clarity of exposition was always a virtue, insisted that Gilbert's expertise lay in the depth of his familiarity with all the Fathers of the Church, as well as with the liberal arts, in which he was fully informed. He emphasised that Gilbert was assiduous in arguing against many heresies, and could cite the favourite passages of Hilary, Ambrose and Augustine that Gilbert admired.[116] John demonstrates sophisticated awareness of Gilbert's teaching that theology follows the norms of any other discipline, in its analysis of propositions of faith. Inevitably, human knowledge is subject to the limitations of language. True understanding lifted the mind away from words to contemplation of God. Gilbert emphasised that one had to follow the teaching of Hilary in looking beyond the specific words of any doctrinal formulation to consider the purpose of what was being said.[117]

---

115   *Historia pontificalis* 10–14, pp. 21–41.
116   Ibid. 13, pp. 28–32.
117   Ibid. 13, p. 41.

After Gilbert's departure, John attached himself to Robert Pullen, an Englishman who taught at Exeter in 1133 and then at Oxford before being invited to teach in Paris sometime between 1138 and 1142, prior to being made a cardinal in Rome in 1143. His large book of sentences shows that while a critic of certain theological views of Abelard, he made greater use of dialectic than Hugh of Saint-Victor.[118] Between 1143 and 1147 John attached himself to Simon of Poissy, who may well be the author of an innovative *Tractatus de sacramentis* (important for being one of the first to include marriage as one of seven sacraments), written c. 1145–60, quite independent of the teaching of Peter Lombard. The close relationship between this treatise and the *Sententie diuinitatis*, composed within the school of Gilbert of Poitiers c. 1141–8, suggests that Simon might himself have been influenced by Gilbert, although focusing more on pastoral than speculative questions.[119] Significantly, John never mentions Peter Lombard in the *Metalogicon*, even though he was already celebrated in the *Metamorphosis Goliae* (c. 1142) as a famous theologian. John's only comment about him is a remark in the *Historia pontificalis* that he could not say whether Peter Lombard and Robert of Melun were motivated by jealousy of Gilbert's reputation and a desire to propitiate Bernard of Clairvaux.[120] John disliked a contemporary tendency to sneer at teachers like William of Champeaux, Hugh of Saint-Victor and Robert Pullen, "whom all good men hold in happy memory."[121] While Robert Pullen and Simon were not speculative thinkers in the manner of Gilbert of Poitiers, John clearly acquired from them a training that would be of benefit for his subsequent career at Canterbury. In his *Entheticus de dogmate philosophorum*, an early work in which he first set out to synthesise the fruit of his learning from the schools, John comments on grace and wisdom, as well as on scripture, and concludes the work by reflecting on love and grace. Nonetheless, his approach emphasizes accord between the wisdom of the ancient philosophers and the call of grace.[122] The *Entheticus*

---

118 PL 186, cols. 639C–1010B; see F. Courtney, *Cardinal Robert Pullen: An English Theologian of the Twelfth Century* (Oxford, 1954), p. 278.

119 While Simon's possible teaching of John was not mentioned by Henri Weisweiler, *Maitre Simon et son groupe. De sacramentis* (Louvain, 1937), this Gilbertine link is suggested by Weisweiler's extended discussion of parallels with the *Sententie divinitatis* (pp. xlvi-lxii), as well as of its date (pp. ccxii-ccxiv) suggest this possibility.

120 *Historia pontificalis* 8, p. 16.

121 *Metalogicon* 1.5, pp. 21–22.

122 *Entheticus maior* Part I, Section E-G and Part IV, Section Y, vol. 1, pp. 120–127, ll. 223–324, pp. 222–225, ll. 1797–1834; see the notes in vol. 2, pp. 279–287, 417–421.

was an attempt to bring together the various perspectives, philosophical and theological, that he had imbibed in the course of his education.

Conclusion

John continued to maintain close friendships he had made with masters and fellow students in the schools of Paris through the rest of his life. It was precisely because he was so concerned by potential abuse of the educational ideals to which he had been committed that he applied himself to synthesizing the principles that he considered ought to prevail in the trivium, drawing from his own experience. He was unusual in the range of disciplines to which he applied himself, in particular to grammar and dialectic. His particular interest, however, was in drawing on classical letters to develop ethical principles that he considered too often lacking in contemporary educational practice. In idealizing Bernard of Chartres, William of Conches, Gilbert of Poitiers and Thierry of Chartres, he was drawing a sharp contrast with the narrow self-interest of many of the teachers of dialectic that he had encountered in Paris. Yet these teachers were not simply traditionalists. They had all been exposed to the teaching of Bernard of Chartres, but had each developed a particular intellectual tradition, none of them confined to remaining attached to Bernard's fidelity to Plato. Rather each developed a particular synthesis of classical and Christian wisdom, in such a way that it may not be possible to speak of a single "school of Chartres" as a unified intellectual tradition. John of Salisbury did not continue the scientific tradition associated with Thierry of Chartres or the Boethian approach to divinity developed by Gilbert of Poitiers, but rather developed an ethical approach, not just to grammar and dialectic in the *Metalogicon*, but to public life in the *Policraticus*. John's educational career was remarkable for the way it had been nourished by a range of ancient authors, embracing (in the words of his epitaph) Plato, Aristotle, Cicero, and Saint Paul. When John eventually became bishop of Chartres in the last years of his life, he could benefit from the holdings of a cathedral library that preserved memories of the complex variety of intellectual traditions by which he had been shaped.

CHAPTER 2

John of Salisbury and Thomas Becket

Karen Bollermann and Cary J. Nederman

Nearly 850 years after his death, Thomas Becket remains one of the most controversial and enigmatic figures in English history. As chancellor to King Henry II, as Archbishop of Canterbury, and ultimately as a martyr and saint, Becket has taken hold of the historical imagination, among scholars and students as well as in the popular consciousness through literature, theatre, and cinema. Much of the problem with making sense of Becket's career stems from his wild swings of allegiance and behavior. Although Becket had been an apparently dedicated servant of Archbishop Theobald of Canterbury, his transfer to the court of King Henry II occasioned a fundamental change of loyalty from ecclesiastical to secular causes, which in turn was contradicted by his conduct when appointed to the archbishopric following Theobald's death. A plethora of interpretations, none entirely satisfactory, has been advanced over the centuries to make sense of the twists and turns that characterized Becket's life and death.

One of the most important contemporary sources for understanding the trajectory of Becket's career is found in the writings of John of Salisbury, an active and prominent member of Archbishop Theobald's court from 1148 to 1161 and a partisan of Becket while he was exiled from England during his conflict with Henry II. John's close association with Becket is documented by the fact that his two major works, the *Policraticus* and the *Metalogicon*, were dedicated to the future martyr, as well as by the proximity in which they worked over a period of many years. John was identified by another of Becket's advisors, Herbert of Bosham, as among the so-called *eruditi* who served the Archbishop's cause.[1] John later took a leading role in the push to canonize Becket in the 1170s following the infamous assassination at Canterbury Cathedral, evidence for which is found in both his second letter collection and in his *Vita* of Becket. In sum, John's writings provide significant evidence for the course of Becket's life from about the time he became Chancellor in 1155 until (and beyond) his murder in 1170.

Oddly, there has been no sustained scholarly investigation focused on the intertwined careers of Thomas Becket and John of Salisbury. To be sure, John's works (especially his correspondence and his *Vita* of Becket) are commonly

---

1   Herbert of Bosham, *Eruditi sancti Thomae*, in MB, vol. 3, pp. 523–532.

employed by historians as a central primary source for the study of Becket. Yet little attention has been paid to the role Becket played in the development of John's literary endeavors. The present chapter aims to remedy this lacuna. Specifically, we concentrate on the question of how John's attitudes toward Becket as a person and as a political figure, reflected in the range of his writings, shaped the broader contours of his thought and activity. Our main hypothesis is that "the Becket problem," as we term it, was decisive at every stage in John's intellectual evolution, as well as formative in his own decisions about how to behave when confronted with serious political choices before, during, and after Becket's conflict with Henry II. By tracking the role played by the figure of Becket, we hope to illuminate a key feature of John's writings and career.

The general characterization of John's relationship with and opinion of Becket has varied widely. Those who have not made a careful study of the subject tend to assume that they were personal friends or intimates. Scholars who have investigated the nature of the private relationship between John and Becket in great depth have tended to propose more nuanced views. Summarizing the state of the literature about John's "personal attitude toward Becket," Anne Duggan accurately observes that some (such as Beryl Smalley) have "called it ambivalent; others have considered it circumspect; while a hostile critic might question its general integrity."[2] In contrast to the preceding scholarship, we hold that, from at least the mid-1150s, John articulated principled doubts about Becket's character, concerns that did not abate over the course of the latter's career. Even when John, during their mutual exile, chose to serve Becket's cause against Henry, he did so not out of personal loyalty to the Archbishop (from whose household he had voluntarily departed[3]), but rather out of devotion to the liberty of the Church and the supremacy of Canterbury. However, we also maintain that, once Becket lay slain on the floor of Canterbury Cathedral, John's view of his erstwhile colleague and superior changed dramatically. Whereas Becket's behavior in life was morally and politically problematic for John, he became in death a very useful saint for promoting the ecclesiastical agenda dear to John's heart.

The Early Years

When did John of Salisbury first become acquainted with Thomas Becket? Scholars have sometimes speculated that they may have known one another

---

2 Anne Duggan, "John of Salisbury and Thomas Becket," in *The World of John of Salisbury*, pp. 427–438, esp. p. 429.

3 See *The Later Letters*, pp. 23 (Letter 139) and 49 (Letter 150).

from the schools of Paris, where (as the autobiographical account in the *Metalogicon* details) John studied between 1136 and 1148.[4] Some of Becket's biographers claim that he journeyed to Paris to advance his education, apparently between 1138 and 1141.[5] But, as Frank Barlow notes, John himself never mentions Becket's presence there.[6] Rather, the earliest documented encounter between John and Becket, as we are told in the *Historia pontificalis*, was in 1148 at the Council of Reims, which the former attended in the company of his friend Peter of Celle and the latter in his capacity as a member of Archbishop Theobald's household.[7] Whether the two men had previous familiarity with one another thus remains an open question. Once John entered into the service of Theobald, which seems to have occurred at or immediately following the Council of Reims, he would, of course, have regularly interacted with Becket. But this is not to say that they were constantly together starting in 1148, since John seems to have spent the early portion of his Canterbury career travelling on diplomatic missions (in particular, to the papal court) on behalf of the Archbishop.[8] Based on the fact that John's first letter collection commences around 1154 with letters that he composed on behalf of Theobald, it seems likely that only in about that year did he begin residing mainly in Canterbury.

In December of 1154, Archbishop Theobald presided over the coronation of Henry Fitz Empress as the King of England, followed in February by Becket's appointment as the royal chancellor.[9] These events, in turn, seem to be intimately connected with John's composition of his earliest known literary work, the *Entheticus de dogmate philosophorum* (or *Entheticus maior*). A Latin poem running to 1852 lines, its purposes are both didactic and satirical. The *Entheticus maior* instructs the reader about the sources of philosophical wisdom and virtue, the relationship between human reason and divine truth, and the good order of the school and the court. It also contains a number of scathing caricatures of the personalities whom John encountered both in the Parisian classrooms and at European courts. It seems probable that John wrote the first major section of the *Entheticus maior* (comprising Parts I and II in modern editions) while a student at Paris in the 1140s.[10] The remainder of the poem (a prologue and Parts III and IV) seems to date to the middle of the 1150s, most

---

4   *Metalogicon* 2.10 (pp. 70–73).

5   Frank Barlow, *Thomas Becket* (London, 1986), pp. 20–21 surveys the evidence.

6   Ibid., p. 20.

7   *Historia pontificalis* 8 (p. 17).

8   Cary J. Nederman, *John of Salisbury* (Tempe, Arizona, 2005), pp. 14–16.

9   See Barlow, *Thomas Becket*, pp. 42–43 concerning Theobald's role in securing the chancellorship for Becket.

10   Nederman, *John of Salisbury*, pp. 10–11.

likely before the end of 1156. It is addressed explicitly to a member of the Canterbury circle (almost certainly Becket, although he is not mentioned by name) who has gone off to serve at the royal court.

The likelihood that John composed the later portion of the *Entheticus maior* with Becket in mind can be deduced from a number of the poem's features. John employs, for example, a unifying stylistic thread, stemming from a technique pioneered by Ovid called *prosopopoeia*, through which the author addresses his book as though it were a person. As Jan van Laarhoven remarks, *prosopopoeia* "provided a good way for an author to shield himself behind such a conversation with his brain-child, whilst the identity of the true addressee is kept uncertain, being mentioned at the most by allusions."[11] When John speaks to his book, giving it instructions and guidance, his words are meant for its addressee, presumably Becket. Thus, when the book is told "be mindful of yourself,"[12] its author employs a piece of advice that echoes what he had already remarked to Becket more directly.[13] More overtly still, John lectures his text: "Canterbury, parent of bishops and kings, has fostered you and prepares a hospice for you, indeed a home. She asks that you return and rest in that seat which is the head of the kingdom and the home of justice. You must obey a mother who admonishes rectitude in particular, and who seeks to extend your days."[14] When read in conjunction with a preceding statement that Becket was Theobald's heir apparent,[15] John's application of the *prosopopoeia* technique in this passage is especially transparent. It becomes impossible to distinguish between the identities of the poem and the chancellor.

A second connecting thread within the *Entheticus maior* is its recurrent use of the motif of the journey. This aspect is closely related to the *prosopopoeia* device, insofar as John couches much of his advice to his book in terms of guidance to a traveler. In particular, John recommends to his poem the safest modes of conduct while away from home and warns it about the dangers of both the trip and the destination. The travel theme is introduced almost immediately in the prologue: "The court rejoices in new friends, disdains old ones, only the cause of pleasure and profit pleases. Who are you who comes? What is the

---

11   *Entheticus maior*, vol. 1, p. 48.

12   Ibid., vol.1, p. 227, l.1851 (trans., p. 226): "...memor esto tui!"

13   Ibid., vol.1, p. 203, l.1513 (trans., p. 202).

14   Ibid., vol.1, p. 211, ll.1637–42 (trans., p. 210): "Pontificum regumque parens te Cantia fovit,/ hospitiumque tibi praeparat, immo domum./Haec petit, ut redeas et in illa sede quiescas,/quae caput est regni iustitiaeque domus./Parebis matri praesertim recta monenti,/ quaeque tuos tendit perpetuare dies."

15   Ibid., vol.1, p. 189, ll.1293–6.

reason for the journey? Where do you go? And for what reason? Perhaps it will be asked. Respond briefly, little book."[16] The response suggested by John forms the bridge from the prologue to the doctrines of truth and virtue that form the substance of Parts I and II. In Parts III and IV, written with the court and its new denizen especially in mind, the *viator* motif returns. John first explains to the poem what perils await it amongst courtiers, counseling it in particular not to speak indiscriminately or rashly: "Either be utterly silent or speak little at court, or find out in what faraway land you can hide; for if you do not spare your words, no one will spare you, and the impious crowd will overtake your days."[17] Dissemblance is promoted as the best course of action for the *Entheticus maior*, until it can have a private word with its "patron" (who is also engaging in pious dissimulation) and return home to Canterbury. But the journey back will itself be fraught with the temptations of the flesh, which take particular root in those who frequent inns and roadhouses.[18] Having summarized his advice for a safe trip, John sets his poem on its way: "But why do I delay any more? You are anxious to go. Watch out, what you may do; cautiously complete the journey once started."[19] From virtually beginning to end, the book is portrayed as preparing for its journey. It awaits only John's final instructions before its departure.

The convergence of the *prosopopoeia* technique with the *viator* motif helps to define the purpose of the *Entheticus maior*. If the book stands in for the chancellor as the recipient of John's advice and if that counsel is couched as guidance for the uninitiated traveler to court, then the impression is reinforced that John completed the poem soon after Thomas's departure for court. Indeed, we might speculate that the *Entheticus maior* was a sort of parting gift to Becket: John was warning Thomas about how to behave at court so as to advance Canterbury's interests, while reminding him that his "true home" was back in the archbishop's household. The poem was thus following in its patron's footsteps (one of John's favorite metaphors) along the route to court, while also mapping out the path for the return journey to Canterbury (possibly as Theobald's successor). The *Entheticus maior* reads as a travel guidebook to the alien world of secular

---

16   Ibid., vol.1, p. 105, ll.7–10 (trans., p. 104): "Aula novis gaudet, veteres fastidit amicos,/ sola voluptatis causa lucrique placent./ Quis venias? quae causa viae? quo tendis? et unde?/) forsitan inquiret. Pauca, libelle, refer."

17   Ibid., vol.1, p. 203, ll.1509–12 (trans., p. 202): "Aut taceas prorsus, aut pauca loquaris in aula,/ aut quaeras, in quo rure latere queas;/ nam si non parcis verbis, nemo tibi parcet,/ praevenietque dies impia turba tuos."

18   Ibid., vol.1, pp. 205, 207, ll.1533–60.

19   Ibid., vol.1, p. 227, ll.1849–50 (trans., p. 226): "Sed quid multa moror? properas exire. Videto,/ quid facias; coeptum perfice cautus iter."

political affairs and as a reminder to Becket that he was not ultimately a member of the temporal realm, but instead belonged in the spiritual sphere.

This impression is reinforced when one considers the thematic substance of the second section. At the beginning of Part III, John focuses his attention on the court, the denizens of which he pointedly rebukes for their moral impurity and intellectual vacuity. But the new courtier, affirmed in his faith, must ignore them, since he has a more pressing enterprise in which he must engage: the cancellation (a pun on *cancellarius*, chancellor) of the unjust decrees that had been imposed on the realm by the prior kings of England.[20] Yet John also acknowledges the moral complexity and ambiguity of courtly business and avers that the well-intentioned courtier must at times adopt the tricks of his surroundings in order to survive and to pursue his program of reform.

John may hardly be called optimistic about the possibility of Becket's success in this regard. "I fear that the chancellor is striving in vain that the proud court should change its customs," he says, inasmuch as corrupt "morals have been introduced into the court by that rope-dancer [Henry II] who defends by the law of his grandfather whatever he attempts."[21] John warns of the "little snares" that await a courtier "who speaks the truth." He advises instead to "take care that you do not perish by your garrulity," since those who state their minds honestly are targeted for exile by "the false philosopher," that is, the tyrant.[22] John is thus not above recommending a bit of pious deception in order to negotiate the duplicity of the court and to achieve one's goal: "That trick is good by which one profits in a useful manner, when through it rejoicing, life, and salvation are procured."[23] John's ultimate aim is to set out for Becket the philosophical and religious principles that ought to guide his conduct as a new courtier. The prologue advises its reader to locate and to converse with only that man who is a true "friend of God," identifiable by his devotion to truth and virtue.[24]

John returns to this theme in the final section of the *Entheticus maior*, a brief coda of fewer than one hundred lines that meditates on the lessons of the

---

20   Ibid., vol.1, p. 189, l.1297.
21   Ibid., vol.1, p. 201, ll.1485–6 and 1471–2 (trans., p. 200): "Sed vereor, frustra ne cancellarius instet,/ ut mutet mores aula superba suos," and "Hos aulae mores funambulus intulit ille,/ qui, quod praesumit, lege tuetur avi."
22   Ibid., vol.1, p. 203, ll.1503, 1496, and 1499–1500 (trans., p. 202): "Horum tendiculis dicenti vera parantur," "...cura, ne pereas garrulitate tua," and "...suntque tiranni/ falsus philosophus."
23   Ibid., vol.1, p. 199, ll.1441–2 (trans., p. 198): "Ille dolus bonus est, qui proficit utilitati,/ quo procurantur gaudia, vita, salus."
24   Ibid., vol.1, p. 105, l.12 (trans., p. 104): "...amica Deo."

work. He repeats his counsel that keeping oneself in the company of true philosophers – that is, men of good morals and deep faith – constitutes the key to resisting vice. In order to reach an accurate judgment about whom to befriend, in turn, one must seek the advice of the ancient writers and wise teachers. The lessons of these authorities form the necessary and indispensable guide to the virtues. Whether John's advice reflects early doubts about Becket's personal qualities or simply John's general fear of the corrupting effects of courtly life, he was proven largely prescient. As is well known, Becket threw himself wholly into the support and defense of Henry's political agenda, as well as into the libertine lifestyle of the court.[25]

Becket in John's Philosophical Works

Becket's unwavering devotion to Henry contributed to a serious breach between Canterbury and the royal household, occasioned by a series of disputes over the rights and privileges of each. For example, Theobald and Henry were at odds, beginning in Lent 1155, concerning the authenticity of some charters of Battle Abbey; over the archbishop's strenuous objections, the king twice confirmed their genuineness, despite the fact that they were clearly fraudulent.[26] Likewise, in early 1156, Henry imposed upon the Church (as well as laymen) a scutage to finance military action against his brother, Geoffrey, despite Theobald's loud complaints that this special tax infringed upon ecclesiastical liberty.[27] In both cases, Becket performed his duties as chancellor in a manner strictly consistent with the desires of the king, without giving any indication that he felt a pull to oppose his master in the name of loyalty to Canterbury.

Becket himself incurred the wrath of Theobald when, sometime around the middle of 1156, in his unrelinquished role as archdeacon of Canterbury, he sought to collect a tax on the churches under his jurisdiction as a "second aid," in addition to the archbishop's own exaction. John drafted a letter (sent in the name of Theobald) to Becket, ordering him to desist in this abuse and indeed threatening to anathematize anyone who would seek to profit from the impost.[28] The language of this letter is quite stinging: Eternal salvation is endangered for those who perpetuate the "evil custom" of collecting such an aid. By 1160, the year following the completion of the *Policraticus*, John's letters,

---

25   See Barlow, *Thomas Becket*, pp. 44–49.

26   Ibid., pp. 49–50.

27   Avrom Saltman, *Theobald, Archbishop of Canterbury* (London, 1956), pp. 43–44.

28   *The Early Letters*, pp. 35–36 (Letter 22).

both those written personally and those composed on Theobald's behalf, openly admonish Becket for his disobedience to the archbishop.[29] In sum, the documentary evidence from the late 1150s suggests considerable alienation (even rancor) between Canterbury and Becket.

It seems that John had strong reasons to view Becket as the professional servant of secular power about which he had expressed fear in the *Entheticus*. Nor, despite pleas for aid, did Becket intervene with Henry in 1156/7 when John fell afoul of the king's wrath, finding himself *persona non grata* at the royal court and also forbidden to travel overseas (for reasons that remain somewhat mysterious). John implored Becket directly for help, employing the trope of *amicitia*: "If the devotion of my insignificant self has any power with your excellency, if the memory of our old familiarity still counts for something, if the onslaught of Fortune does not undermine the faith of friendship, then do what you can to assuage the indignation which our most serene lord the king has conceived against me without cause."[30] There is no indication that Becket ever interceded with the king, nor even acknowledged his former colleague's predicament.

In light of these circumstances, it may seem strange that, when John turned, during the late 1150s, to compose the two writings that have sustained his reputation through the centuries – the *Policraticus* and the *Metalogicon* – he chose to dedicate them to Becket. Yet, scholars have come to realize that the dedication of advice works to powerful and well-placed people does not necessarily indicate endorsement of their behavior – indeed, quite often the opposite.[31] Such forms of ostensive praise are often meant instead to evince criticism (sometimes implicit, but sometimes overt) of the dedicatee's conduct. This appears a quite apt conclusion about John's decision to address both the *Policraticus* and the *Metalogicon* to Becket. The concluding chapters of these works refer explicitly to the chancellor's secular engagement at Henry's side in pursuing the siege of Toulouse during the second half of 1159, noting that Henry's "thunderbolts in the vicinity of the Garonne" are being hurled "(so we are told) with your advice and

29   Ibid., pp. 221–225 (Letter 128).

30   Ibid., p. 45 (Letter 28): "Si quid ergo potest apud excellentiam uestram paruitatis meae deuotio, si qua est antiquae familiaritatis memoria, si spectatae amicitiae fidem fortunae inpetus non subuertit, id agite quo serenissimi domini nostri regis gratis in me concepta indignatio mitigetur..." On the trope of friendship in John's letters generally, see Cary J. Nederman, "Textual Communities of Learning and Friendship Circles in the Twelfth Century: An Examination of John of Salisbury's Correspondence," in John N. Crossley and Constant J. Mews, eds., *Communities of Learning: Networks and the Shaping of Intellectual Identity in Europe, 1100–1450* (Turnhout, 2011), pp. 75–85.

31   See Judith Ferster, *Fictions of Advice* (Philadelphia, 1996); and Cary J. Nederman, "The Mirror Crack'd: The *Speculum Principum* as Political and Social Criticism in the Late Middle Ages," *The European Legacy: Toward New Paradigms* 3 (1998), 18–38.

guidance."[32] John's tone is one of evident lament and perhaps disapproval of Becket's worldly activities: John complains (perhaps somewhat hyperbolically) that the Toulouse expedition reflects "vanity" and disappoints his own hope "for peace" between "the English and the French," causing "kings whom we had seen the best of friends" to "become each other's implacable enemies."[33] John cautions Becket about his own role in stirring up this conflict: "In the midst of such turmoil, keep, I beseech you, your innocence; perceive, reiterate, and preach justice; do not deviate from the straight path, influenced by either love or hate, hope or fear; the just shall inherit the earth and, as is ordained by the authority of the Most High, the seed of the wicked shall perish."[34] Of course, by the time Becket would have read these words, the siege itself had been suspended, Henry having been outwitted by King Louis VII of France.

The impression of John's critical (or at least wary) stance toward Becket in the works dedicated to him seems to be reflected in the selection of the themes that he discusses, especially in the *Policraticus*. Most evidently, Becket would appear to be implicated in John's lengthy analysis (in Books 7 and 8) of the problems posed by the ecclesiastical or clerical tyrant, that is, a member of the clergy whose will is oriented toward private interests or purposes. The *Policraticus* is emphatic about the reality of ecclesiastical tyranny: "Priests should not be indignant with me, however, if I acknowledge that even among them one can find tyrants." Citing Ezek. 34:2–5, John asks: "Does this not seem to express the manifest tyranny of priests and to depict the lives of those who in all matters seek those things which are their own and who render the things which belong to Jesus Christ last of all?"[35] Throughout Books 7 and 8, John demonstrates a persistent awareness of the ubiquity of tyrannical behavior at all ecclesiastical grades during his day, and his condemnation of such conduct is framed in terms of the Epicurean proclivities of so many clerics.[36]

---

32 *Policraticus* 8.25, ed. Webb, vol. 2, p. 424, trans. Pike, p. 410: "...circa Garonnam et (ut dicitur) te auctore te duce fulminat..."

33 *Metalogicon* 4.42, p. 183, trans. McGarry, pp. 273–274: "...uanitati. Expectauimus enim pacem...Anglos et Gallos...reges quos amicissimos uidimus, se insatiabiliter persequuntur."

34 *Policraticus* 8.25, ed. Webb, vol.2, p. 424, trans. Pike, pp. 410–411: "In tantis rerum tumultibus quaeso custodi innocentiam et uide et dicta et praedica aequitatem; nec amore nec odio, timore uel spe declines a uia recta. Iusti enim hereditabunt terram et, ut auctoritate constat Altissimi, semen impiorum peribit."

35 Ibid. 8.17, ed. Webb, vol.2, p. 349, trans. Nederman, p. 194: "Michi uero indignari non debent sacerdotes, si et in eis fatear inueniri posse tirannos...Nonne tirannidem sacerdotii uidetur exprimere manifestam, et uitam illorum depingere qui in omnibus quae sua sunt quaerunt et quae Iesu Christi sunt post tergum faciunt?"

36 See Cary J. Nederman and Karen Bollermann, "'The Extravagance of the Senses': Epicureanism, Priestly Tyranny, and the Becket Problem in John of Salisbury's *Policraticus*," *Studies in Medieval and Renaissance History*, 3rd series 8 (2011), 1–25.

John's disdain for clerical tyranny can be easily connected, in turn, to the documented historical situation of the relationship between Canterbury and the royal household (especially Becket) in the later 1150s. For example, one sort of clerical tyrant about whom John inveighs is the priest who derives income from ecclesiastical office-holding, while also serving in a temporal administration:

> You must consider into which category would seem to be placed those for whom the license of divine right to shear and devour the flock does not suffice but who also appeal to the aid of secular laws and who, making themselves officials of princes, are not afraid to commit deeds which would readily embarrass any other tax collector. Meanwhile, they serve their own pleasures or avarice, and they pillage and oppress those who selected or admitted them into custody over themselves.[37]

This precisely describes the circumstances of Becket in a way that seems to us to be beyond coincidence. As mentioned above, it deeply troubled Archbishop Theobald that Becket continued to profit from his ecclesiastical office by collecting income while serving as England's chancellor. The implication is clear: Becket's conduct suggests that he had succumbed to the avarice associated with clerical tyranny and thus has imperiled his soul.

In a similar vein, John commences the closing portion of the last chapter of the *Policraticus* with a remark, directed specifically to Becket, that is easily interpreted as ironic, if not pointedly critical. Summarizing the practices that he attributes to Epicureans, John states,

> Behold that you [Becket] possess the truest and most faithful path and have achieved the state [happiness or the *summum bonum*] which is desired by Epicurus...This path alone can suffice for good and happy living, to such a great degree that the external world adds either little or nothing to perfection. And I do not prohibit you from wrapping yourself in a variety of glittering garments overlaid with gold, nor from feasting splendidly every day, nor again from occupying the foremost public offices, and – so that I may express much in a few words – from yielding to the times and even perverse morals (even though you are yourself

37   *Policraticus* 8.17, ed. Webb, vol.2, p. 357, trans. Nederman, p. 200: "Tu uide in quo gradu ponendi uideantur quibus non sufficit diuini iuris licentia tondere et deuorare pecus nisi secularium legum implorent auxilia et officiales principum facti ea committere non uerentur quae facile alius quilibet publicanus erubescat. Interim uoluptati seruient aut auaritiae, et qui eos elegerunt uel admiserunt in custodiam sui depopulantur et premunt..."

righteous in all moral matters), and from laughing with a world which is amused by its own enticements. For you are so great that you ought not and cannot be captured by these traps (although many have already been taken prisoner by them).[38]

Perhaps we should take these words at face value, namely, that Becket has demonstrated his ability to refuse the "frivolities" of courtly life and the underlying philosophy of Epicureanism that supports it. But John's apparent readiness to forgive Becket his comforts might also be read in the context of previous remarks in the *Policraticus*. For example, in Book 5, John highlights courtly hypocrisy in terms that directly echo the passage just quoted:

> Yet among all courtly fools, those who do harm most perniciously are those who are accustomed to glossing over their wretched frivolities under the pretext of honor and liberality, who move about in bright apparel, who feast splendidly, who often urge strangers to join them at the dinner table, who are courteous at home, benign when abroad, affable in speech, liberal in judgment, generous in the treatment of kin, and distinguished for the *imitation* of all the virtues. (...) He above all commits acts of license under the guise of virtue; and, for this reason, he pursues glory through means which are scarcely appropriate to the expectation of pardon. The greatest amount will be extorted with impunity by those who cannot, or indeed disdain to, be content with a little.[39]

---

38 Ibid. 8.25, ed. Webb, vol.2, pp. 423–424, trans. Nederman, pp. 229–230: "Ecce habes uiam uerissimam et fidelissimam, assequendum statum quem desiderat Epicurus...Haec ad bene beateque uiuendum potest sola sufficere; adeo quidem ut extraposita uniuersa aut nichil aut minimum perfectionis adiciant. Nec inhibeo quin uestibus niteas deauratis circumdatus uarietate, quin epuleris cotidie splendide, quin primos honores habeas; et, ut paucis multa complectar, quin tempori sed et peruersis moribus, rectus tamen ut es ipse, in omnibus morem geras et suis lenociniis irridentem irrideas mundum. Maior enim es quam ut debeas aut possis (licet iam sic ceperit multos) capi tendiculis eius."

39 Ibid. 5.10, ed. Webb, vol. 1, p. 325, trans. Nederman, p. 87: "Illi tamen perniciosius nocent inter omnes curiae nugatores, qui sub praetextu honestatis et liberalitatis miseriae suae solent ineptias colorare, qui nitidiores incedunt, qui splendidius epulantur, qui propriam ad mensam saepius extraneos compellunt accedere, humaniores domi, foris benigniores, affabiliores in sermone, liberiores in sententiis, in proximorum cultu munifici et omnium uirtutum *imitatione* praeclari...His utique uirtutis umbra licentiam facit; et unde uix oportuerat sperari ueniam, gloriam assequuntur. Possunt impune plurima extorquere qui paruo non possunt, immo dedignantur esse contenti" (emphasis added).

Placed in the context of excusing Becket's conduct, this general critique supports an ironic reading of the passage directed explicitly to the chancellor. Becket's well-known behavior appears to fit entirely within John's condemnation of foolish courtiers who seem to be one thing but are, in fact, quite the opposite.

It is noteworthy that John opens the final chapter of the *Policraticus*, in which Becket is explicitly invoked as the addressee of the work, with an insistence that one need not consciously subscribe to the Epicurean school in order to adopt Epicureanism. John observes that "although there are many Epicureans, that is, adherents to futile pleasures, few profess this name. For they are embarrassed to be called what they are and they endeavor to conceal their own private wickedness with another name, insofar as they desire to seem rather than to be good."[40] Given our previous survey of Canterbury's fraught relationship with the royal household by 1159, by which time Becket had come to be very closely associated with the causes championed by Henry II, there is every reason to suppose that these words were meant to apply to the English chancellor and to imply his complicity in a mode of clerical tyranny. We may be reasonably sanguine about the true thrust of John's comments regarding Becket's capacity to decline the blandishments of courtly comfort and pleasure on an Epicurean scale. The historical circumstances suggest that the tone of the critical ironist undercuts John's overt expressions of confidence in Becket's refusal to internalize the luxury of the court.

Becket as Archbishop

After Becket's selection as archbishop in 1162, John remained in the service of Canterbury, although his role seems to have been greatly diminished in contrast with his responsibilities under Theobald. He was one of the members of the embassy that received the archbishop's *pallium* from Pope Alexander III at Montpellier in July 1162. Upon his return to England, John compiled a brief *Life* of Saint Anselm, apparently at the instruction of Becket, who planned to pursue the canonization of his forerunner at the Council of Tours in May 1163.[41] It is unknown whether John played any further part in the process of preparing

---

40   Ibid. 8.25, ed. Webb, vol.2, p. 418, trans. Nederman, p. 225: "...cum Epicurei sint plurimi, id est uani sectatores uoluptatis, nomen hoc pauci profiteantur. Erubescunt enim dici quod sunt et propriam turpitudinem occultare nituntur nomine alieno, dum nom tam boni esse cupiunt quam uideri."

41   Nederman, *John of Salisbury*, p. 80.

for the Council, which, in any case, never took up the case for Anselm's sainthood. At the age of about 45, John had in effect graduated to *emeritus* status:
a symbol of continuity with the previous archbishop, and a figurehead to be
displayed to the world outside Canterbury. Given that John had cultivated personal relationships with leading ecclesiastical (and also secular) figures
throughout Europe, his "public relations" value in diplomatic matters was far
greater than any other contribution he might make to Becket's *curia*. It might
be speculated that Becket did not feel entirely comfortable keeping in his
immediate circle an individual who had been publicly critical, in letters and
writings, of his own errant ways while chancellor.

The events of Becket's conflict with Henry II, his exile, and his eventual martyrdom have been recounted and scrutinized so often in scholarly as well as
literary form that it seems hardly necessary to recount them.[42] John's activities
during the course of the unfolding crisis within the English Church were in
many ways marginal to and separate from Becket's cause, which again highlights the lack of intimacy that characterized their relationship. John left
England in late 1163 or early 1164 – a full year before the archbishop – for reasons that remain obscure. John's letter to Becket, reporting his journey to
France and his contacts with various communities and lords, contains ambi-
guities. On the one hand, John suggests that he is carrying out Thomas's
instructions by meeting with Count Philip of Amiens, from whom a promise of
support is extracted in the event that the archbishop is forced into exile.[43] John
also visited (apparently on his own initiative) King Louis, seeking royal support
and patronage for the cause of Canterbury. From the perspective of the letter,
then, John appears to be serving as Becket's advance herald, utilizing his extensive network of political connections to offer a pro-Canterbury account of the
deteriorating condition of Church-State relations in England. John reminds
Becket that his instructions involved making his way to Paris, renewing his ties
with the schools, and doing his best to avoid suspicion that he was working as
an agent of the archbishop (a plan that soon proved simply unaffordable).[44]
On the other hand, John's letter to Becket also contains the statement that
"I am under the king's disfavor (undeservedly, I swear on conscience) and if
I withstand his envoys, that disfavor will be greater."[45] Taken in conjunction
with a later recollection by William FitzStephen, another intimate of Becket's,

---

42   A useful survey may be found in Barlow, *Thomas Becket*, pp. 74–250.

43   *The Later Letters*, pp. 2–5 (Letter 136).

44   Ibid., pp. 10–13 (Letter 136).

45   Ibid., pp. 12–13 (Letter 136): "...regis indignationem gratis, conscientia teste, sustineo, et si
      me nuntiis eius opposuero, grauius sustinebo."

that John had been sent into exile by Henry II in order to prevent him from counseling the archbishop,[46] some scholars have concluded that the real reason for the departure was royal proscription.[47]

Whatever the case, John soon settled with his friend Peter of Celle, who had become abbot of Saint-Remi in Reims in 1162. It was here that John would remain in residence almost exclusively until his return, along with others of Becket's supporters, to England in 1170. When Becket and his entourage arrived in France in late 1164, they sought refuge first at the abbey of Pontigny, and later at Saint-Columba in Sens, both some distance from Reims. There is no evidence that John ever remained with Thomas for any extended period, which is perhaps fortunate, given that their communications were instead recorded in a body of correspondence that was eventually collected by John. Such geographic distance may also indicate John's sense of his relationship with the incumbent archbishop: John was a servant of Canterbury, not a personal aide to Becket.

John's letters from the initial period of his continental residence continue to express doubts about the qualities of Becket's personality. John displays an acute awareness of the archbishop's defects, which John ascribes to a tendency to exceed moderate bounds, a running theme in his thought as a whole. To Humphrey Bos, John bluntly states, "I have kept the faith owed to the Church and archbishop of Canterbury, and I have stood by him faithfully in England and on the continent when justice and moderation seemed to be his. If he ever seemed to detour from justice or exceed the mean, I stood up to him to his face."[48] Becket shows little sense of discretion with regard to judgments of circumstance, John observes, telling Bishop Bartholomew of Exeter, "He who inspects our hearts and judges our words and acts knows that I – more than any other mortal – have upbraided the lord archbishop on the grounds that he has from the beginning unadvisedly provoked the resentment of the king and court by his zeal, since many provisions should have been made for place and time and persons."[49] In other words, during the earliest stages of the dispute between king and archbishop, John held the latter as well as the former responsible.

---

46   *MB*, vol. 3, p. 46.

47   Duggan, "John of Salisbury and Thomas Becket," pp. 429–430.

48   *The Later Letters*, pp. 20–23 (Letter 139): "Ecclesiae et archiepiscopo Cantuariensi debitam seruaui fidem et ei, ubi iustitia et modestia uidebantur adesse, et in Anglia et in partibus cismarinis fideliter astiti. Sicubi uero aut exorbitare a iustitia aut modum excedere uidebatur, restiti ei in faciem."

49   Ibid., pp. 48–49 (Letter 150): "Nouit enim cordium inspector et uerborum iudex et operum quod saepius et asperius quam aliquis mortalium corripuerim dominum archiepiscopum de his, in quibus ab initio dominum regem et suos zelo quodam inconsultius uisus est ad amaritudinem prouocasse, cum pro loco et tempore et personis multa fuerint dispensanda."

Even after John had been forced to commit himself entirely to Becket's cause, he could not resist counseling a moderate course for the archbishop. In July 1166, John, fearing his master's propensity toward rash behavior, exhorted him to display virtuous moderation in his negotiations with his opponents. "It is especially expedient that your moderation be known to all," John recommends, "With moderation write and state the conditions [of a reconciliation], since it seems to be certain that the souls of the enemies of God's Church are so hardened that they will admit no condition at all."[50] Hinting at the Ciceronian view that what is expedient and what is honorable are ultimately inseparable, John suggests that Becket position himself as a conciliatory figure, not as an extremist. Whenever someone accuses Thomas of acting out of pride or hatred, rather than out of virtue and religious conviction, "this opinion should be answered by exhibiting moderation in deeds and words, in conduct and dress."[51] The archbishop is advised to imitate "the most modest David," in order that "you can moderately reply" to "those who reprove, indeed severely deride you."[52] John thus enunciates an unbreakable principle that should direct Becket: "In all things behave such that your moderation may be known by all. (...) Attend to the state of the times, the condition of the Roman Church, the needs of the English realm."[53] This advice the archbishop largely chose to ignore, even after his return to England in December 1170. A more moderate Becket may have made a far less dramatic martyr, but he would also very likely have done less damage to either the Church or the Crown in England.

The question of John's loyalty to Becket during the period of the exile is thus a vexed one. John McLoughlin has proposed the highly plausible hypothesis that John's correspondence displays a decisive change in thinking about the conflict around the middle of 1166.[54] Prior to that point, John seems to regard Henry and Becket to be engaged in a largely personal quarrel between two offices (king and archbishop) that need not – indeed, ought not – embroil the

---

50   Ibid., pp. 168–169 (Letter 176): "...modestia uestra, quod plurimum expedit, omnibus inno-tescat...eoque modestius scribendum et condiciones censeo exigendas, quo michi certior esse uideor animos aduersantium ecclesiae Dei sic induratos esse ut nullam omnino con-ditionem admittant..."

51   Ibid., pp. 170–171 (Letter 176): "...huic opinioni occurrendum est exhibitione moderationis, tam in factis et dictis quam in gestu et habitu..."

52   Ibid., pp. 172–173 (Letter 176): "...modestissimus Dauid...[u]os...istis increpatoribus, immo detractoribus uestris...poteritis modeste respondere."

53   Ibid., pp. 190–191 (Letter 179): "...et ita per omnia incedatis ut modestia uestra omnibus innotescat...Attendenda enim est instantia temporis, condicio ecclesiae Romanae, neces-sitas regni Angliae..."

54   John McLoughlin, "The Language of Persecution: John of Salisbury and the Early Phase of the Becket Dispute," in W.J. Sheils, ed., *Persecution and Toleration* (Oxford, 1984), pp. 73–87.

whole of the English Church. Henry's attacks on Thomas constituted, for John, a personal "tribulation" for the archbishop and a "test" of his resolve. Beginning in the summer of 1166, however, John's discourse shifts decisively toward what McLoughlin terms "the language of persecution," characterized by insistent references to the passion of Christ and the Roman repression of the early Church. John now views the conflict in terms of principle and recognizes that its resolution has implications for the whole of the English Church and, perhaps, for the organization of secular-temporal relations throughout Christendom. This is a position that Becket and his defenders had already started to enunciate in 1163, but that John was late in coming to embrace.

It is likely that a very specific event triggered John's change of attitude: his face-to-face meeting with Henry II at the end of April or beginning of May 1166. John had been seeking such a conference for some time, in the hope of making peace with the king and restoring himself to England. In a letter written during 1164 or 1165, he explains how he had attempted to chart an independent path in the conflict between Henry and Becket.[55] Likewise, John insists, "I have done nothing intentionally against the honor due to the king or his interests, as I am prepared to expound, if I am free to do so safely."[56] He expresses his readiness to take an oath to this effect and also to pay whatever penalty is required of him, if he is found guilty of having diminished the royal honor. John reports that discussions have commenced to restore him to royal favor,[57] but that Pope Alexander has cautioned him "to wait until the king's wrath has subsided a little."[58] John's ambivalence toward Becket is palpable: John will do nothing to diminish the position of the archbishop, but he renounces his status as a member of the Canterbury *curia*. "The lord of Canterbury himself knows that I have removed myself from his household (*consortio*), but I remove neither faith nor charity,"[59] John states in a letter to Humphrey Bos. John clearly believed that a separate peace with the king could be negotiated, on terms that would not dishonor the cause of Canterbury.

---

55   *The Later Letters*, pp. 22–23 (Letter 139).

56   Ibid., pp. 22–23 (Letter 139): "...contra honorem domino regi debitum aut utilitatem ex proposito nichil feci, sicut dictante iustitia docere paratus sum, si liberum et tutum fuerit."

57   Possibly a reference to the efforts of Peter of Celle to open channels of communication; see ibid., pp. 30–31 (Letter 144). John also pleaded with other influential friends to intercede with the king; see ibid., pp. 14–17 (Letter 137) and 48–49 (Letter 150).

58   Ibid., pp. 22–23 (Letter 139): "...expectarem ut ira eius aliquantulum deferueret."

59   Ibid., pp. 22–23 (Letter 139): "...bene nouit dominus Cantuariensis, a cuius me subtraxi consortio, sed nec fidem subtraho nec caritatem."

That belief shatters, however, after John meets with the king around Easter 1166. He reports that Henry demanded of him what he could not in good conscience offer, namely, that he swear an oath renouncing obedience to Becket.[60] Such a promise would have constituted a direct breach of John's own principles regarding the primacy of Canterbury in matters of faith, especially binding upon a cleric like himself. Henry, in short, wished to interfere with the good order and liberty of the English Church by demanding that its servants place loyalty to the crown above fidelity to their ecclesiastical superiors. That John's experience with the king clearly demonstrated to him what was at stake in the conflict with Becket seems evident from the immediately changed tone of his correspondence, as analyzed by McLoughlin. No longer did he contemplate compromise and negotiation with Henry: The king was now, in John's mind, the implacable oppressor of the Church, against whom opposition must be complete and unrelenting. In addition to immediately adopting the "language of persecution" identified by McLoughlin, John's letters now begin to describe Henry with reference to tyranny.[61]

The failure to reach accommodation in 1166 shaped John's ensuing efforts on behalf of Becket. Although too poor to travel extensively, John began to put his pen (and the literary reputation behind it) to use in advocating the cause of the archbishop and in defending his strategies, as well as in offering him advice (albeit perhaps not always wanted). John's collection contains perhaps two dozen letters on various matters written between early 1164 and Easter 1166, including three missives to Becket. During the next four-and-a-half years, until his departure for England in November 1170, John produced nearly 150 letters – seven addressed to Becket – nearly all of which are directly related to furthering the archbishop's position. This significant increase in output hints at John's recognition that the king's goals were incompatible with the liberties of the English Church. John begins to accumulate and to disseminate information helpful to negotiating the tortuous politics that swirled around the Becket conflict. Here, John's rhetorical skills and noted reputation as a correspondent served him admirably. Drawing on his network of acquaintances, he filtered news from Germany and Italy, as well as from France and England, about the machinations of the English crown and its allies, such as Emperor Frederick Barbarossa and the anti-popes whose claim he defended. John's letters testify to his role as a sort of "clearinghouse" for propaganda favoring Becket, as

---

60   Ibid., pp. 84–87 (Letter 164), 94–99 (Letter 167), and 198–199 (Letter 199).
61   Ibid., pp. 427–428 (Letter 234), 434–435 (Letter 235), 580–581 (Letter 275), and 614–617 (Letter 281).

well as for the flow of knowledge about the latest schemes both pro- and contra-Canterbury.

The eventual end of Becket's continental exile resulted from a prolonged set of negotiations in which John seems to have played a relatively minor role. John traveled in 1167 and again in 1169 to conduct meetings with papal legates charged with resolving the dispute.[62] In February 1170, he may also have journeyed to Pontoise to attend a conference between Becket and Henry II that was ultimately cancelled. John gives a narration of the events in a letter to Archdeacon Baldwin of Totnes, but does not specifically identify himself as present.[63] By 1169, it is clear that both Becket and Henry were under a great deal of pressure, from both ecclesiastical and temporal lords throughout Europe, to reach a settlement on what had become a somewhat embarrassing episode in the history of Church-State relations. Yet each, for his own reasons, refused to yield. Only on July 22, 1170, was an agreement reached, permitting the archbishop and those in exile with him to reclaim their offices and lands in England.

John was assigned to serve on a transition team to prepare Becket's return, and he crossed the English Channel in mid-November. Writing to Peter of Celle several weeks later, he reports that he found the situation at Canterbury in confusion. Rights and goods that were to have been restored to the jurisdiction of Canterbury remained in the hands of royal officials. Meanwhile, as appointed representative of the archbishop, John received neither cooperation nor respect from the king's men. Even the return of Becket himself in early December did nothing to improve circumstances. The king seems to have violated the terms of the agreement and returned to his old ways of bullying and interfering with the business of the archbishop. By contrast, John's life as an exile at Saint-Remi now appears to him "the likeness of paradise."[64]

Then, on December 29, the fateful and fabled murder of Becket in Canterbury Cathedral occurred. John was present in conference with the archbishop when the knights of Henry's court arrived to confront their nemesis. For all of the narration based on eyewitness accounts, the events of that day remain blurred.[65] In spite of the claim by one assassin that his sword had wounded the arm of John of Salisbury, this identification is mistaken; he had actually attacked another churchman, Edward Grim, who had remained by Becket's

---

62   Ibid., pp. 406–423 (Letters 230–231) and 660–663 (Letter 290).

63   Ibid., pp. 690–697 (Letter 298).

64   Ibid., pp. 714–725 (Letter 304); quote at pp. 724–725: "...instar paradisi."

65   See Edwin Abbott, *St. Thomas of Canterbury, His Death and Miracles*, 2 vols. (London, 1898), vol.1, pp. 27–212.

side. John instead fled the scene of the ambush, along with most of the other members of the archbishop's group, hiding elsewhere in the cathedral. One account of Becket's martyrdom, by Garnier of Pont-Sainte-Maxence, in fact reports that John objected to the archbishop concerning the handling of the would-be assassins: "'My lord, you have invariably gone against our advice, and done what you had determined on in your own heart'... 'We', said Master John, 'are not so well prepared that we wish to be handed over to death, for we lie in sin and weakness. I see no one but you choosing to die.'"[66] Whether or not these words are accurately placed in John's mouth, they certainly resonate with the misgivings that John had evinced about Becket recurrently over the years.

The Martyrdom and Its Aftermath

Whatever John's opinions about Becket during the lifetime of the future saint, he was perhaps the most active and vocal advocate for the archbishop's reputation during the early 1170s. John's Letter 305 – addressed to John of Canterbury, bishop of Poitiers – is generally accepted as having been written in early 1171, just weeks, possibly only days, after the murder.[67] On the basis of this dating, John's letter (which was widely distributed and recopied) would seem to give the first known account of Becket's martyrdom.[68] It is beyond dispute that John incorporated (with slight editing) much of this letter into the final portion of his *Vita et Passio* of Becket (to be discussed below); indeed, John's evident "self-plagiarism" is one reason why his *Life* has been subject to scholarly criticism.[69] While the dating of John's *Life* has been widely debated,[70] the same has not been the case for Letter 305.

---

66   Janet Shirley, *Garnier's Becket:Translated from the 12th-Century Vie Saint Thomas le Martyr de Cantorbire of Garnier of Pont-Sainte-Maxence* (London, 1975), p. 142.

67   This is the view propounded by Brooke in his introduction to *The Later Letters*, p. xliv. It has become largely canonical in the literature on Becket. See Barlow, *Thomas Becket*, p. 4, who dates Letter 305 to "immediately after the event"; Anne Duggan, *Thomas Becket* (London, 2004), p. 228, who says "probably after Easter 1171"; and Michael Staunton, *Thomas Becket and His Biographers* (Woodbridge, Suffolk, 2006), p. 20, who asserts "early in 1171."

68   See Duggan, "John of Salisbury and Thomas Becket," p. 427 and note 3.

69   Among those who have previously dismissed the intellectual merits and literary values of the *Vita* of Becket are Staunton, *Thomas Becket and His Biographers*, p. 20 and Nederman, *John of Salisbury*, pp. 80–81.

70   On the controversy concerning the dating of the *Life*, see Staunton, *Thomas Becket and His Biographers*, p. 26.

Although it lies beyond the scope of this chapter to offer a full investigation into the claim that Letter 305 was both an immediate and the first (though *not* eyewitness) account of the martyrdom, we will briefly summarize the grounds (drawn directly from the text itself) on which this view can no longer be sustained.[71] Significantly, John himself acknowledges that his letter is *not* the first account of Becket's murder, asserting, "I have no doubt that you [John of Canterbury] are well-informed about the passion of the glorious martyr Thomas, archbishop of Canterbury."[72] John then explains that his own narration will be brief precisely because he "know[s] that the event [and its details] is *already* widely and commonly known throughout almost the whole Latin world by the *reports of very many [others]*."[73] Later, John states that "great throngs of people gather" in Canterbury Cathedral to experience Becket's miraculous power; the church was not, however, opened to the public until after Easter, in mid-April 1171.[74] The sheer number and variety of miracles John mentions as having occurred there cannot have accumulated before the public had access to the martyr's remains (and associated holy spaces) within the cathedral.[75] Indeed, although miracles reputedly began to proliferate fairly soon after the reopening of the cathedral, the magnitude to which John attests cannot have been realized even in the first month or more of public visitation.[76] Finally, John's claim that Becket has worked "many mighty wonders...

---

71   The present authors plan further study of this subject and its many implications – including, importantly, the issue of potential sources for the account John provides – in light of our re-dating of Letter 305. We also argue for re-dating of John's Letters 306–310.

72   *The Later Letters*, pp. 724–727 (Letter 305): "...uobis de passione gloriosi martiris Thomae Cantuariensis archiepiscopi...constare non dubito." J.C. Robertson notes that two Becket emissaries (who had been sent to the pope prior to the martyrdom) received news of the archbishop's murder when they were at Sens with Archbishop William White Hands. On hearing the shocking news, White Hands penned a letter for them to carry on to the pope – Robertson claims that this is the first written account of the martyrdom. See James Craigie Robertson, *Becket, Archbishop of Canterbury: A Biography* (London, 1859), pp. 294–295.

73   *The Later Letters*, pp. 726–727 (Letter 305): "...ut opinor, iam fere per orbem latinum *ex relatione plurimorum* sit nota et uulgata materia" (emphasis added).

74   Ibid., pp. 736–737 (Letter 305): "...cateruatim confluentibus populis." See Rachel Koopmans, *Wonderful to Relate: Miracle Stories and Miracle Collecting in High Medieval England* (Philadelphia, 2011), pp. 144–145 on the reopening of the cathedral to the public.

75   Koopmans, *Wonderful to Relate*, pp. 142–144.

76   A useful guidepost to the occurrence and proliferation of Becket miracles at Canterbury can be found in Koopmans' account of these early days of public access, and especially in her account of when and why Benedict of Peterborough commenced his miracle collection there (ibid., pp. 145–153).

not only [in] his own church but [in] *both* of the English provinces" (that is, in Henry's French domains, as well as in the island kingdom proper) renders the dating of this letter not only *not* in early 1171, but possibly not even in mid-1171.[77] Its date of composition is delimited by the earliest time when Becket miracles occurring in Plantagenet France were being reported back to Canterbury in sufficient numbers to substantiate John's claim.[78]

John does, however, provide evidence of his motivation for writing the letter, one that accords well both with a date in later 1171 and with his established record as an epistolary propagandist *par excellence*. Scholars have drawn attention to the closing of Letter 305, wherein John raises the question of "whether it is safe, *without papal authority*, to address him [Becket]...among the catalogue of martyrs."[79] John expresses concern that "a devotion *not yet assured* may suggest some shadow of doubt, even after such signs and wonders."[80] John explains that he cannot himself obtain a papal answer to these questions because "permission to cross the sea is quite excluded without written leave from the king."[81] Therefore, for his part, John has resolved to "lend aid to God's will, and revere as a martyr...him whom God deigns to honor as a martyr...*not waiting* on the authority of any man."[82]

To what might these several references to a lack of papal confirmation of Becket's sanctity and to an inability to travel allude? And what might we then glean about both the likely dating and purpose of this letter? In light of the many miracles occurring at Canterbury, the Christ Church monks – who had not only evinced a certain degree of hostility toward their archbishop during his protracted conflict with the king and his long exile, but who had also initially

---

77   *The Later Letters*, pp. 726–727 (Letter 305): "...non modo ecclesiam propriam sed *utramque* prouinciam Anglorum miraculis multis et maximis..." (emphasis added).

78   See note 145 below.

79   *The Later Letters*, pp. 736–737 (Letter 305): "...an *citra Romani pontificis auctoritatem* tutum sit...eum in cathalogo martirum...inuocare..." (emphasis added). It should also be noted that, in this final paragraph of his letter, John switches from the personal "I/ you" to the formal "We/ You," likely signaling his request, on behalf of the entire Canterbury community, that the universal Church support them in recognizing Becket as a saint, despite the pope's refusal, thus far, to do so.

80   Ibid., pp. 736–737 (Letter 305): "...incredulitatis praetendat imaginem, post tot signorum exhibitionem, *nondum secura deuotio*" (emphasis added).

81   Ibid., pp. 736–737 (Letter 305): "...facultas transeundi adeo omnibus praeclusa est, ut nullus ad nauigium admittatur nisi litteras regis ante porrexerit."

82   Ibid., pp. 736–739 (Letter 305): "...assistamus Domini uoluntati, et quem ipse honorare dignatur ut martirem, ...ut martirem ueneremur...*non expectata* cuiuscumque hominis auctoritate..." (emphasis added)

resisted the spontaneous popular veneration of their murdered leader – eventually came to embrace and even encourage the growing cult of Becket there.[83] Sometime in the (possibly late) summer of 1171, a delegation of Canterbury monks was sent to Pope Alexander III to secure Becket's canonization; their petition was met with delay, if not outright rejection.[84] Then, in October 1171, Henry departed on a campaign to subdue Ireland; he was isolated there and could not be reached to grant any travel dispensations until he returned to Wales in April 1172, from whence he quickly traveled across England on his way to Normandy.[85]

News of the pope's delay in canonizing Becket[86] would surely have reached Canterbury sometime in the early fall; Henry's extended absence from the realm commenced shortly after that. Therefore, the most likely dating for John's Letter 305 is between October 1171 and April 1172. Indeed, John's opening remarks affirm that he had merely taken what was a "lucky break" to write: "Quite unexpectedly, quite in passing…I have just learned that the bearer [of this letter] was on his way across the sea to you. I am delighted at this heaven-sent opportunity to write, and have snatched it gratefully."[87] There is no suggestion of immediacy in relation to Becket's murder; rather the opposite, as John then makes reference both to "the long-drawn-out catastrophe" and the attendant "heap of difficulties."[88] This, too, accords well with the events that had befallen the Canterbury community, particularly in the months after the murder

---

83 On the monks' fraught relationship with Becket, see Barlow, *Thomas Becket*, p. 265 and Koopmans, *Wonderful to Relate*, p. 141.

84 Koopmans, *Wonderful to Relate*, pp. 145–146.

85 Robertson, *Becket*, pp. 301–302 and Barlow, *Thomas Becket*, p. 257.

86 Interestingly, Alexander III issued an 1170 bull which proclaimed that only the pope can confer canonization. This was meant to address the problem of local, popular veneration and to thereby systematize/legalize the process. Where Roberston, *Becket*, p. 293 note b thinks that "John of Salisbury would not seem to have been aware of this decree," we suspect that he did indeed know of it, but rejected the pope's "power grab" – for John, *only* God can decide such matters. Hence, his questions about venerating Becket without papal confirmation and his claim that sanctity "does not wait on the authority of any man" (*The Later Letters*, pp. 738–739); in this matter, even the pope himself is only a mortal human, as John intimates in Letter 308 (ibid., pp. 752–753).

87 Ibid., pp. 724–725 (Letter 305): "Ex insperato et in transitu michi, …nuper innotuit quod ad uos erat lator praesentium transiturus. Gauius ergo diuinitus ministratam occasionem scribendi, eam gratanter arripui…" The letter-bearer was either not a subject of Henry's or had already received prior authorization to travel as a messenger.

88 Ibid: "longae calamitatis" and "angustiarum cumulum."

and then in relation to their stymied efforts to obtain Becket's canonization. And, it is the latter that provides the motivation for John's having seized a fortuitous opportunity to send what amounts to a mini-dossier to his well-placed friend and ally, John of Canterbury, in the hope of stirring up continental support for Becket's (now-stalled) canonization. Indeed, as remarked above, this letter was widely circulated and recopied.[89] What John could not do himself, he could rally others to do for him.

Sometime after John penned Letter 305, he wrote a *Vita et Passio* of Becket, likely composed in late 1172-early 1173,[90] perhaps as yet another propaganda effort to "encourage" Pope Alexander III to confer sainthood on the archbishop, which eventually occurred on February 21, 1173.[91] As with Letter 305, numerous copies of John's *Life* of Becket circulated on the continent.[92] Despite its obvious contemporaneous importance,[93] scholars have almost uniformly taken a very dim view of it. On the one hand, it has been deemed a "hasty" composition not worthy of John's manifest literary talents; on the other hand, it has been labeled a "slight" work and mere "expansion" of Letter 305.[94] These negative judgments can only be sustained through a failure to examine closely the relationship between Letter 305 and the *Life* and a fundamental lack of appreciation for John's purposes and motivations for his *Life* of Becket.

---

89   Peter of Celle, who received a copy of this letter, shared John's opinion that one need not await formal canonization to commence veneration of so obviously holy a figure. See Peter of Celle, *Letters*, ed. Julian Haseldine (Oxford, 2001), pp. 662–663 (Letter 171).

90   John added, to his original Letter 305 list of miracles ascribed to Becket's powers, a new type of miracle – resurrection miracles. Benedict of Peterborough's Becket miracle collection (c. summer 1171-spring 1173) does not include any resurrection miracles until his Book 4 (the last of his original composition); William of Canterbury, who made use of Benedict's notes in crafting his own Becket miracle collection (c. mid-1172–1175), does not record any resurrection miracles until the beginning of his Book 2 (which commences with 13 such accounts in a row). Thus, John's addition of Becket resurrection miracles to his own list in the *Life* suggests a dating roughly between late 1172-early 1173. See Koopmans, *Wonderful to Relate*, pp. 145–154.

91   Staunton, *Thomas Becket and His Biographers*, pp. 3–4. It is unknown whether John's *Life* was, in fact, used in support of Becket's canonization. According to Alexander's biographer, the pope reportedly canonized Becket "at the request of *the clergy and people of France*" (Barlow, *Thomas Becket*, p. 269; emphasis added).

92   Duggan, "John of Salisbury and Thomas Becket," pp. 427–428 and note 4.

93   See, for example, Barlow, *Thomas Becket*, p. 5.

94   In addition to the references given in note 69 above, see *The Lives of Thomas Becket*, ed. Michael Staunton (Manchester, 2001), p. 7 and Beryl Smalley, *The Becket Conflict and the Schools* (Totowa, NJ, 1973), p. 107.

The fact that John had previously produced a *Life* of Anselm establishes that he was clearly conversant with the literary conventions governing the hagiographical arts. While admittedly John's *Life* of Becket falls short of the expected scope and length of a standard saint's life, it seems that much of the criticism leveled against this text stems from its seeming disregard of the conventions of the genre. Several reasons for John's choices in preparing the *Life* in a perhaps "unusual" way may be adduced. First, John himself tells us, in the *Life*'s prologue, that he intends to write a brief account: "[L]et this concise and quite brief discourse review the sum of his way of life."[95] John reiterates this point, while also clarifying his own purpose in writing: His text is "a short account that does not describe individual acts, but that assembles the sum of events and strives *to set forth the reason for his martyrdom*."[96] John refers those who desire a fuller account of "the whole sequence of his deeds" to "the vast volumes which have been written by him and about him…His letters…and the writings of others [are] full of credibility and worthy to repeat."[97] John evinces no suggestion of "haste" impelling him to write, as critics have claimed.[98] On the contrary, his studied use of much of his earlier letter, as well as echoes of his far earlier *Life* of Anselm (and of other of his works), suggest, on the face of it, the work of a careful (if singular) hagiographer.[99]

---

95   *Vita Thomae*, Prologue (ed. Biffi, p. 154, trans. Pepin, p. 74): "…summam conversationis eius succinctus et admodum brevis sermo percurrat." John's intented scope is confirmed in Alan of Tewksbury's own preface to John's *Life* of Becket, which acts as the introduction to the compilation (with which John assisted) of Becket letters and other materials.

96   Ibid. 4, ed. Biffi, p. 160, trans. Pepin, p. 76: "…praesertim compendiario non singula exprimenti, sed colligenti summam rerum et *causam martyrii eius exponere gestienti*" (emphasis added).

97   Ibid., Prologue, ed. Biffi, p. 154, trans. Pepin, p. 74: "…gestorum eius seriem…a magnis, quae ab illo et de illo scripta sunt, voluminibus…epistolae eius, et scripta aliorum, fide plena et digna relatu…" The "vast volumes" may refer, in part, to Benedict of Peterborough's substantial miracle collection, begun in mid-1171 and still underway, as well as, possibly, to the collection that William of Canterbury began to compile in mid-1172. More significantly, as discussed below, John is likely referring to his own substantial second letter collection and, possibly, also to the weighty compilation of Becket correspondence and documents he helped to compile.

98   Indeed, it is Letter 305 which John himself admits he is writing in haste; see *The Later Letters*, pp. 724–725.

99   A thorough comparison of the Letter 305 excerpt found in the *Life* reveals a consistent pattern of slight but deliberate editing. Additionally, most of the *Life* (70%) is completely new material; the Letter 305 material comprises only the very end of the *Life*. Finally, John's Becket *Life* prologue echoes his Anselm *Life* prologue in three respects: his use of the bright star/constellation metaphor for a saint, his stated intention to write a succinct narrative covering only some portion of the saint's life and deeds, and his referral to other, fuller accounts for those who wish to know more. See *Vita Anselmi*, Prologue (ed. Biffi, pp. 22–24) with *Vita Thomae* Prologue (ed. Biffi, pp. 152–154).

Yet, despite John's explicit avowal that he is writing a *Vita et Passio S. Thomae martyris*, from the standpoint of the conventions of the genre, John's text seems the proverbial "odd duck" indeed.[100] For example, of its 28 paragraphs, the first two alone address Becket's birth, childhood, and youth, and only in the most general of terms. Similarly absent from John's account are any early and continuing signs of Becket's living holiness (and of others' recognition of it) and of him having routinely faced obstacles to and suffered tribulations on account of leading a life of faith. By way of contrast, both of these themes are recurrent and important features in John's *Life* of Anselm. Rather, in some sense, John's *Life* of Becket reads more like an extended resume, a career profile. Far from dismissing his text as a peculiar and peculiarly failed hagiography, however, we would do well to bear in mind John's clear statement of purpose for it: He is laying out "the sum of events" that will "set forth the reason for [Becket's] martyrdom," pure and simple. John's narrative is not the tale of a man led deeper and deeper into the spiritual life, but of a man led inexorably to the martyr's demise. In foregrounding Becket's professional life, John charts his development from king's man to *defensor ecclesiae in extremis* against the very secular power he had once served.

A careful reading of John's account of Becket's career – from his early years in the courts, through his service in Archbishop Theobald's *curia* and his tenure as Henry's chancellor, to his own troubled reign as England's (mostly exiled) primate, culminating in his glorious martyrdom in the name of the Church and her liberty – reveals a number of tensions. On the one hand, as we have seen, John had expressed, over a considerable period and in a variety of writings, a range of concerns about Becket's character and behavior, including pointed criticisms of the archbishop's conduct during the course of his protracted conflict with Henry and associated exile. How was John to rewrite his own narrative of Becket so as to reveal a man drawn ever closer into the embrace of the Holy Church? On the other hand, Becket's cause – the liberty of the Church – was one to which John was deeply and permanently committed, and Becket had died in its service. How could John *not* celebrate the glory of the English Church's martyr? These, then, are the twin thematic foci of John's *Life* of Becket, the tensions between which lie just below the surface.[101]

---

100 Contra Duggan, *Thomas Becket*, p. 229, who calls it "the unabashed hagiography of a saint."

101 John's *Life* of Anselm likewise reveals John's deliberately focused attention on Church-Crown conflicts; Anselm, unlike Becket, was an obviously holy man, and so entirely unproblematic in this regard.

Evidence for John's somewhat tortured rehabilitation of Becket the man, in
the service of Becket the martyr, can be found in the many echoes to pertinent
parts of John's earlier works in which the archbishop had been implicated. For
example, John avers, against evidence to the contrary, that Becket was led to
seek a position in Theobald's household through "the inspiration and guidance
of grace rather than the counsel or intervention of friends."[102] Similarly, John
portrays Becket the chancellor as a man beset by constant "hardships...afflic-
tions...ambushes...[and] snares," even though "the world in all its flatteries
seemed to fawn on him and applaud him."[103] Thus, Becket, *"not* unmindful" of
his duty to the Church, "was forced to struggle daily...and by various stratagems
to elude various wicked deceptions."[104] John's personal letters and those he
penned in Theobald's name, as well references to Becket's chancellorship in his
major works, however, paint the picture of a man both utterly unmindful of his
duties to Canterbury and fully enjoying the luxury attendant on his exalted
position in Henry's court.

The *Life* provides hints of the luxurious lifestyle that Becket clearly did not
immediately renounce, despite John's protestations otherwise, upon taking up
the archbishop's mitre. John notes "the beauty of his vesture," his "table richly
and refreshingly made grand," and the fact that "his household was renowned
for opulent furnishings and various trappings of business."[105] Of particular
note is John's implicit praise of Becket's many qualities, couched in the context
of attacks on him occasioned by the beginning of his disagreements with the
king:

> [W]icked men...ascrib[ed] to superstition the fact that [Becket] was
> leading a stricter life. They falsely asserted that his zeal for justice was
> cruelty. They attributed to avarice the fact that he procured advantages
> for the Church. They said that his contempt for worldly favor was the
> pursuit of glory, and the magnificence of his court was made out to be

---

102   *Vita Thomae* 4, ed. Biffi, p. 160, trans. Pepin, p. 75: "...instinctu potius gratiae et ducatu
       quam consilio amicorum aut interventu..." But see Barlow, *Thomas Becket,* pp. 28–33.
103   Ibid. 7, ed. Biffi, p. 164, trans. Pepin, p. 77: "...laboribus...afflictionibus...insidiis...
       laqueis...Licet enim ei mundus in omnibus lenociniis suis adulari et applaudere
       videretur..."
104   Ibid., ed. Biffi, p. 164, trans. Pepin, p. 77: "...immemor erat...quotidie...contendere cogeba-
       tur et variis artibus varios eludere dolos."
105   Ibid. 11, ed. Biffi, pp. 170–172, trans. Pepin, pp. 79–80: "...honestate vestium...ditius et refec-
       tius nobilitari mensam...domus eius pro more gentis utensilibus pretiosis et gerendorum
       variis instrumentis nobilitaretur..."

pride. That he followed a divinely instructed will…was branded a mark of arrogance. That he often seemed to surpass the goals of his predecessors in defending justice was judged to be a sign of rashness.[106]

Interestingly, John himself had levied many of these criticisms against Becket's character, not only initially, but well into the later stages of the conflict.

With the narrative commencement of what John implicitly identifies as the irrevocable split between Church and Crown – the October 1163 council at Westminster – leading, as John knows, to Becket's eventual martyrdom, any implied criticisms of or contradictions regarding Becket fall away. John's account moves swiftly through the events of this council, as well as of the January 1164 Council of Clarendon, and the final, disastrous October 1164 Council of Northampton, from which Becket – to whom John for the first time refers as "Christ's confessor, the future martyr" – was "driven into exile."[107] Although the king's powerful advisers and even some members of the English Church (notably, Archbishop Roger of York) all receive a portion of the blame, John singles out Henry's "savage fury" as the principal cause of Becket's long and unjust persecution.[108]

In surprisingly short order, John dispenses with the six-plus years of Becket's exile in two paragraphs – quite likely, because he had already planned (perhaps even begun) to compile his second letter collection, which documents the events of the exile in great detail – moving quickly to the dramatic denouement. One paragraph serves as the transition from the end of John's original work in the *Life* to the beginning of his edited interpolation of the material drawn from Letter 305. This paragraph, which relates events immediately following Becket's return to England in December 1170, commences with a reference to Becket as "Saint Thomas," paving the way for the inevitable climax.[109]

---

106 Ibid. 13, ed. Biffi, p. 176, trans. Pepin, p. 82: "…impii…superstitioni ascribentes, quod vitam duceret arctiorem. Zelum iustitiae crudelitatem mentiebantur; quod ecclesiae procurabat utilitates, avaritiae attribuebant; contemptum mundani favoris venationem gloriae esse dicebant, curialis magnificentia fingebatur elatio; quod divinitus edoctam voluntatem sequebatur…nota supercilii inurebatur; quod antecessorum metas in tuendo iure saepe videbatur excedere, temeritatis arbitrabantur indicium."

107 Ibid. 16, ed. Biffi, pp. 182–183, trans. Pepin, p. 85: "…confessor Christi, futurus martyr" and 19, ed. Biffi, pp. 184–185, trans. Pepin, p. 86: "actus…in exsilium."

108 Ibid. 19, ed. Biffi, p. 186, trans. Pepin, p. 87: "…furor immanis." Interestingly, the language of persecution that characterizes the latter half of the *Life* accords well with the similar tone found in John's letters from 1166 onward, as discussed above.

109 Ibid. 21, ed. Biffi, p. 192, trans. Pepin, p. 89: "…sancto Thoma."

Among the very many interesting aspects of John's account of the martyrdom, two stand out as particularly noteworthy: John's discussion of the justification for viewing the victim *qua* martyr; and, his emphasis on the *imitatio Christi* features of the murder, to the extent that he portrays the sacrilegious nature of Becket's "crucifixion," in some ways, as surpassing even that of Christ's. While these twin prongs of John's argument are to some extent interrelated, John addresses each distinctly and at some length. John commences his discussion of the first prong with a rhetorical question: "*[I]f the cause makes the martyr*, which no right-thinking person doubts, what cause was more just, more holy than his?"[110] John then enumerates five clements in support of Becket's "cause":

1. He rejected riches, all glory, and the companionship of his friends and relatives "for love of Christ";
2. After realizing he'd erred in capitulating to Henry's demands at Clarendon, Becket thereafter insisted that he would preserve "the honor of God and the integrity of the Church";
3. During his exile, he (and his men) were exposed to poverty and many perils;
4. Because he possessed "so great a virtue of constancy," he was compelled to "prolong...his exile and bitter proscription...[as he] could not be broken by the force of cruel fortune nor weakened by blandishments"; and,
5. "He fought even unto death to defend [God's] law...and to cancel the abuses of ancient tyrants."[111]

Thus, Becket's unwavering dedication to preserving the liberty of the Church – into the seventh long year of a persecutorial exile fraught with a range of hardships, deprivations, and threats and through his final, fatal stand in defense of that paramount cause – unquestionably, John argues, confirms that the dead archbishop is indeed a martyr and not simply a murder victim.

On the other hand, John was well aware that, despite his rhetorical attempt to bootstrap "cause" into martyrdom on the slim authority of "right-thinking

---

110 Ibid. 22, ed. Biffi, p. 194, trans. Pepin, p. 90: "...*si causa martyrem facit*, quod nulli rectum sapienti venit in dubium, quid iustius, quid sanctius causa eius" (emphasis added).

111 Ibid. 22, ed. Biffi, p. 194, trans. Pepin, p. 90: "...pro Christi amore"; "...honorem Dei et honestatem ecclesiae"; "...tanta quidem virtute constantiae...exsilium et acerbam proscriptionem...protelavit...ut invictus eius animus nec fortunae saevientis impetu frangi posset, nec blanditiis emolliri"; and, "...pro lege Dei sui tuenda et evacuandis abusionibus veterum tyrranorum certavit usque ad mortem..."

person[s]," while "cause" *may* make the martyr, not all "right-thinking person[s]" agree as to which causes qualify as true "causes." Indeed, a decade earlier, John had encountered the difficulty of this distinction while penning his *Life* of Anselm,[112] wherein he relates a debate between Lanfranc (then Archbishop of Canterbury) and the visiting Anselm (his old colleague from Bec) regarding the legitimacy of the local (i.e., Anglo-Saxon) veneration of Saint Elphege as a martyr.[113] Lanfranc eventually accepted Anselm's argument that the reason for and manner in which Elphege was slain were themselves sufficient to justify his martyr status. On this reasoning, John might have felt secure in simply offering Becket's final moments and death as evidence of the rightness of his cause. That he did not, and instead offered up the whole of the exile as additional proof, bespeaks the underlying tension between a life clearly lived in holiness and devotion (i.e., Anselm's) and a life far more ambiguously lived and judged (i.e., Becket's).[114]

When John turns to the circumstances of the assassination itself – the second prong in his argument, in which he employs the *imitatio Christi* trope – he again reveals this anxiety over proof. John clearly feels the need to indulge in hyperbole so as to secure his assertion of Becket as a true martyr for the faith. John's single-mindedness of purpose in framing Becket's death, it should be noted, comes dangerously close to, if it is not in fact, sacrilege. In drawing out the ways in which Becket's death resonates with Christ's, at each point, John asserts that the archbishop was treated in a more odious, more impious manner than was Christ:

1. Although condemned unjustly, Christ had been formally charged, had had a legitimate trial, and had had the opportunity to mount a defense; Becket, on the other hand, had had no charges brought against him, had been brought before no valid tribunal, and had been given no opportunity to offer a formal defense.

2. After being convicted and sentenced to death, Christ had been taken outside the city gates for execution and had been executed on an ordinary day (i.e., the day before the Sabbath); Becket, however, was murdered not

---

112 John wrote his version at Becket's instruction, using Eadmer's much longer *Life* as his base text, with some additions from Eadmer's companion volume, *Historia Novorum*.

113 Elphege was the first martyred Archbishop of Canterbury, murdered by his Viking kidnappers for failing to reveal the hidden location of the cathedral's treasury. For the entire debate in John's *Life* of Anselm, see *Vita Anselmi* 6, ed. Biffi, pp. 58–60.

114 See Jennifer L. O'Reilly, "The Double Martyrdom of Thomas Becket: Hagiography or History," *Studies in Medieval and Renaissance History*, 2nd Ser. 7 (1985), 185–247.

only within the city, not only within his own church, but before the high altar *and* on the Feast of the Holy Innocents.

3. Once Christ had been hung on the cross, four soldiers divided his garments amongst themselves; after Becket lay dead in the church, his four assassins utterly pillaged the archiepiscopal palace and stables, taking care to remove and then send all documents to Henry (then in Normandy) to use against Becket's memory and the Church's liberty.

4. With Pilate's authorization, Christ's body was allowed to be removed from the cross, carefully prepared for burial, and then buried appropriately; in contrast, Becket's assassins and their cohorts threatened to cast his body into a swamp or to hang it from a gibbet, and, in any case, to ensure that it was not only *not* interred as befitted his office but not even in holy ground, such that it was necessary to prepare the archbishop's body in haste and to entomb it without ceremony in the cathedral's crypt.[115]

On John's comparative account, one might almost wonder if it isn't Christ who is a type of Becket, rather than the reverse. At any rate, John provides a full passion narrative that more than makes the case for Becket's death as a martyrdom.

A few further relevant points of interest remain. Inasmuch as, by the midpoint of his *Life* of Becket, John seems to have resolved his own inner conflicts over Becket the man versus Becket the *defensor ecclesiae* and martyr, he was aided in his rehabilitation of the former by the addition of two proleptic elements: Becket's famous and famously secret hair garments; and, a vision Becket reputedly had, on the eve of being driven out of Pontigny, predicting his future martyrdom. Near the end of the *Life*, John recounts the shocking discovery of Becket's hair garments (hitherto known to "very few"), revealed only when the martyr's body was being prepared for burial.[116] Yet, near the beginning of John's narrative, he avers that, following Becket's consecration as archbishop, he had *"immediately* put on the hair shirt."[117] In his narration of the events of the martyrdom itself, John again refers to Becket's "use of a rough hair shirt" as evidence

---

115 See *Vita Thomae* 23–26, ed. Biffi, pp. 196–202.

116 Ibid. 26, ed. Biffi, p. 202, trans. Pepin, p. 94: "...pauci familiares eius noverant."

117 Ibid. 11, ed. Biffi, p. 168, trans. Pepin, p. 79: "...*statim*...cilicium...induit" (emphasis added). John adds that Becket "put on the monk," a reference to the monk's habit Becket also supposedly wore hidden and likewise shockingly discovered during the burial preparations. John, however, makes no further reference to Becket's hidden monk's habit, although other contemporaneous accounts do.

that Becket "had *for a long time* shown himself to be a *living victim*, holy and pleasing to God."[118] Not only had Becket's clear, though hidden, long-standing holiness prepared him for the divinely ordained fate of the martyrdom,[119] but, much earlier, the archbishop's future had been revealed to him in a vision: "[B]efore the archbishop left [Pontigny], he was comforted by a divine revelation, a sign shown to him from heaven, that he would return with glory to his own church and from there depart to the Lord with the palm of martyrdom."[120] These several elements, related proleptically, aided John's efforts to smooth over his own well-documented difficulties with Becket the man and so to present a largely consistent narrative of his "saintly" subject.

John continued to work on Becket-related material even after the canonization was achieved, thus reinforcing his attachment to the martyr and his cause. First, probably in 1173–4, when John was largely resident in Exeter,[121] he compiled his second letter collection, which covered his involvement in the events of the Becket exile, as well as the assassination and its aftermath. This is very likely one of the "vast volumes" to which John alluded in the prologue to his Becket *Life*. As with his Letter 305 and *Life* of Becket, the dissemination of this edition was relatively broad, both in England and on the continent.[122] Second,

---

118   Ibid. 22, ed. Biffi, pp. 194–196, trans. Pepin, p. 91: "...asperiorus cilicii usu...*a multo tempore* exhibuerat *hostiam vivam*, sanctam, Deo placentam" (emphasis added). John's deployment of the "living sacrifice" trope, even as he is now relating the events surrounding the martyrdom, reflect his continuing anxiety over the "cause" argument he had offered; Becket's hair garments reveal him to have been, in fact, a white martyr as well as, now, a red martyr.

119   John states: "all the circumstances so came together in the archbishop's struggle that they forever illustrate the glory of his suffering" (ibid. 22, ed. Biffi, p. 194, trans. Pepin, p. 90: "... omnes circumstantiae concurrant in agone pontificis, ut patientis titulum perpetuo illustrarent...").

120   Ibid. 19, ed. Biffi, p. 188, trans. Pepin, p. 87: "...antequam inde progrederetur, divina revelatione confortatus est, coelitus sibi ostenso indicio, quod ad ecclesiam suam rediturus erat cum gloria, et inde per martyrii palmam migraturus ad Dominum." Henry ordered the Cistercians to oust Becket in mid-September 1166; Becket and his household left Pontigny in mid-November (Barlow, *Thomas Becket*, pp. 157–158). Presumably, Becket received the vision John reports during this interval.

121   See, however, Frank Barlow, "John of Salisbury and His Brothers," *Journal of Ecclesiastical History* 46 (1995), pp. 101, 104, and 106, suggesting that, during this period, John may well have been largely resident in Canterbury and not in Exeter.

122   See *The Later Letters*, p. lxiii; and Karen Bollermann and Cary J. Nederman, "John of Salisbury's Second Letter Collection in Later Medieval England: Unexamined Fragments from Huntington Library HM 128," *Viator: Medieval and Renaissance Studies* 40 (2009), 71–91.

in collaboration with Guy of Southwick and, later, Alan of Tewksbury (a monk, and then prior, of Christ Church, Canterbury), John worked, between 1174 and 1176, on editing Becket's letters and related documents.[123] John's *Life* of Becket serves as an introduction to this compilation, which was likewise widely disseminated. This project, too, added to John's status as perhaps the leading proponent of Becket's sanctity in the years following the martyrdom. Taken together, John's Becket-related literary endeavors in the early 1170s very likely played a signal role in the final stage – one that took John back to France – of his "relationship" with the martyred saint.

John and the Cult of Becket

On August 8, 1176, John of Salisbury was consecrated bishop of Chartres, a position he held until his death on October 25, 1180. The standard view of events is that word of John's selection as head of the Chartrian community (announced in letters from King Louis and from the cathedral chapter itself, both dated July 22, 1176) came as surprising news to him. John was, at the time, treasurer of Exeter, but the letters informing him of his episcopal elevation were sent to him at Canterbury, where he in fact received them. He then appears to have been placed under some duress to hie himself to France to take up the mantle post-haste, a feat which he accomplished with what can only be viewed as extraordinary speed, given the travel realities of the time.[124]

Why was John of Salisbury, a man who was a well-regarded clerk but relatively inexperienced in official Church leadership roles, handed the position of an important French bishopric? The evidence suggests that John's episcopal elevation stemmed from his long-standing relationship with William White Hands. White Hands came from one of the most powerful families in France, son of the count of Blois and closely related to the Capetian royal house. White Hands had been formally elected bishop of Chartres in January 1165 and was chosen to serve as archbishop of Sens in 1168; he was, at the time of John's consecration, in transition to the office of archbishop of Reims.[125] White Hands

---

123 Anne Duggan, *Thomas Becket: A Textual History of His Letters* (Oxford, 1980), pp. 94–98.
124 Ralph de Diceto, *Opera Historica*, 2 vols., ed. William Stubbs (London, 1876), vol. 1, pp. 410–413.
125 See Ludwig Falkenstein, "Wilhelm von Champagne, Elekt von Chartres (1164–1168), Erzbischof von Sens (1168/9–1176), Erzbischof von Reims (1176–1202), Legat des apostolischen Stuhles, im Spiegel päpstlicher Schreiben und Priviligen," *Zeitschrift der Savigny-Stiftung für Rechtsgeschicte. Kanonist. Abt.* 89 (2003), 107–284.

was only ever bishop-elect of Chartres and never formally consecrated, although he continued to administer the see until John took up the office of bishop. Hence, White Hands does not appear in the Chartres cartulary's litany of bishops (indeed, John is – mistakenly – identified there as bishop during White Hands' years, as well as his own).[126] White Hands also had been among the chief supporters of Becket (and later, of both the English king's punishment and the martyr's canonization) during his protracted conflict with Henry II.

For his part, John had long been an admirer of White Hands. Writing to the bishop of Poitiers, John of Canterbury, soon after White Hands' elevation to Sens, John described him (whom he calls "Carnotensis electi") as "a person in whom great hope is placed, of very noble reputation, and of high authority and great power in the French kingdom. ...For it is my sincere opinion that there is no one among the French clergy who surpasses him in good sense and eloquence."[127] Likewise, White Hands knew John, probably personally and certainly by strong reputation, perhaps from the time that the latter entered into French exile on account of his advocacy of Becket's cause. Indeed, John's second correspondence collection contains two letters, composed during the quest to confirm Becket's sainthood, addressed to White Hands.[128] Given the reach of his ecclesio-political sphere of influence, White Hands would have desired the episcopal seat of Chartres to be occupied by someone trustworthy as well as respected. John assuredly fit the bill.

This was certainly the judgment of John's long-time friend and associate, Peter of Celle. In a letter written to White Hands around the time of John's election and consecration, Peter cleverly posits a convergence between divine inspiration and a steady human hand, leading to the selection of the new bishop. Peter declares,

> In the admirable election of master John to the see of Chartres God has produced the morning star out of his treasuries (*thesauriis*) [an apparent reference to John's previous status as Exeter's treasurer]. Present there, assisting at this bringing forth of the predestination of God, was the most vigilant wisdom of my lord, and he provided the supporting hand of a

---

126   *Cartulaire de Notre-Dame de Chartres*, vol. 1, pp. 19–20.
127   *The Later Letters*, pp. 578–579 (Letter 274): "...uiri quidem magnae spei et famae clarissimae, et magnae auctoritatis et uirium multarum in regno Francorum. ...Non est enim in clero Francorum, ut ex animi sententia loquar, qui eum prudentia et eloquentia antecedat."
128   Ibid., pp. 742–753 (Letters 307 and 308).

midwife lest the preferred choice of the unchangeable God be aborted. To you, God, be praise, to you, thanks; to you, archbishop, a reward, to you, eternal repayment.[129]

Neither simony nor political maneuvering, Peter goes on to remark (perhaps somewhat disingenuously), induced the selection of John as bishop: "When and where was the like done in the kingdom of France, that, all semblance of simony being removed, no inducements of gifts being added to the scales, with no canvassings of clients making the ears itch, only the honor of God and the salvation of the people was sought in an episcopal election?"[130] Peter avers that, though John may be "a man of another people" (i.e., English), this only demonstrates that it was "solely by the love of God" that his election was secured.[131]

Can we glean from Peter's letter any indications of why White Hands might have promoted the cause of John's elevation? In our view, Peter's enumeration of John's characteristics and qualifications is revealing: "Truly this man John, *dipped in the precious blood of the blessed bishop and martyr Thomas*, fully learned in divine law, adorned with good conduct and kindly deeds, well described by the list of virtues addressed by the Apostle to Timothy, has been set up as a pillar in the Church of God to the honor of God and to your everlasting praise."[132] Beyond the somewhat hyperbolic enthusiasm expressed in Peter's encomium, the reference to Becket should hold our attention. In King Louis's July 22 letter to John, the monarch himself mentions the bishop-elect's relationship with "the blessed martyr Thomas" as a primary consideration in his selection for the post. (Interestingly, the longer letter from the Chartres chapter makes no allusion to Becket.) Moreover, Louis twice indicates the

---

129   Peter of Celle, *Letters*, pp. 416–417 (Letter 102): "In insigni electione Cartonensi de magis-
         tro Iohanne stellam matutinam produxit Deus de thesauris suis. Affuit, affuit huic predes-
         tinationis Dei partui uigilantissima sagacitas domini mei, et manum obstetricantem
         supposuit ne aborsum pateretur incommutabilis Dei preelectio. Deus, tibi laus, tibi grati-
         arum actio; archiepiscope, tibi merces, tibi eterna remuneratio."

130   Ibid., pp. 416–417 (Letter 102): "Quando et ubi simile factum est in regno Francie ut remo-
         tis omnibus simonie speciebus, nullis munerum suffragiis incumbentibus, nullis clien-
         tum uellicationibus pruritum aurium excitantibus, solus Dei honor et populi salus in
         episcopali electione quereretur?"

131   Ibid., pp. 418–419 (Letter 102): "...hominem de alia gente, amore Dei tantummodo..."

132   Ibid., pp. 418–419 (Letter 102): "Vere uir iste Iohannes *pretioso sanguine beati Thome ponti-
         ficis et martyris intinctus*, lege diuina ad plenum instructus, bonis moribus et piis actibus
         ornatus, apostolico ad Timotheum catalogo uirtutum bene depictus, ad Dei honorem et
         ad uestram perpetuam laudem columpna factus est in ecclesia Dei" (emphasis added).

involvement of "the archbishop of Sens" in the electoral process: first, that White Hands had counseled the chapter about his successor; and, second, that he had apprised the king of his personal approval of the choice of John.[133] Perhaps this should not surprise us, given White Hands' strong support of Becket and Louis's own efforts to reconcile the Archbishop of Canterbury with Henry II. But, beyond gazing back to the past, Louis's letter suggests to us something of the expectations that he and White Hands shared regarding John's potential *future* accomplishments as bishop – namely, to promote the cult of Becket in Capetian France as a political tool against the English monarchy. White Hands, in particular, had actively engaged in pursuing (by means of anathema and interdict) Henry's submission and capitulation to the Church in the wake of Becket's murder.[134] It seems entirely reasonable to view his championing of John's elevation to the Chartrian episcopacy as yet another stick with which to beat the king of England. Louis, of course, had his own reasons for wanting to see Henry reduced.

Long before John took up the mantle of leadership at Chartres, the cathedral was already well-known for its possession of the so-called *sancta camisia*, the chemise (or nightgown) of the Virgin Mary.[135] In addition, the cathedral possessed remains of a local saint, Leobinus, who had been bishop there in the mid-6th century, as well as various other relics.[136] But, the cathedral also claimed two significant items associated with the newly sainted Becket – namely, a vial of the martyr's blood and a small blade or knife once owned by him. Both of these relics can be safely associated with John of Salisbury's episcopacy, and both led to Chartres becoming an important secondary center (after Canterbury) for the veneration of Becket. While William White Hands, during his term as bishop-elect of Chartres, may have contributed to this development, significant documentary evidence implicates John directly in the promotion of Becket's reputation during his tenure as bishop. John took pains to draw attention to his connection with the martyred archbishop in his own correspondence after 1176, repeatedly referring to himself as "divina dignatione

---

133 Ralph de Diceto, *Opera historica*, vol. 1, p. 412.

134 Barlow, *Thomas Becket*, pp. 252–257.

135 See Dawn Marie Hayes, *Body and Sacred Place in Medieval Europe, 1100–1389* (New York, 2003), pp. 33–36. For a detailed description of the *camisia* itself, see *Cartulaire de Notre-Dame de Chartres*, vol.1, p. 59 note 1.

136 See Leobinus' obituary in *Cartulaire de Notre-Dame de Chartres*, vol. 3, pp. 5–6. For further details about Leobinus's life and career, see the references contained in *The Later Letters*, pp. 804–805 note 4. See also a brief catalogue of some of Chartres' relics in *Cartulaire de Notre-Dame de Chartres*, vol. 1, pp. 58–60 and notes.

et meritis sancti Thomae [or 'beati martiris'], Carnotensis ecclesiae minister humilis."[137] Throughout his episcopate, John reminded all those to whom he wrote both of Becket's memory and of his own close ties to the saint.

John's association with the vial of Becket's blood is attested (twice) in the Chartres cartulary. In his obituary, John's moral and spiritual qualities are praised effusively, and we are told that he left to Chartres various sacerdotal vestments and paraphernalia. Thereafter, the text continues:

> Also he [John] gave to the Church two precious vessels, in one of which he had placed (*posuit*) the blood of the glorious martyr Thomas, archbishop of Canterbury, as we saw, even now liquid, [and] in the other [of which he had placed] relics of the martyred saints Crispin and Crispinian. Also he gave us the glorious relics of the soldier-saint Gereon and of the group (*consortio*) of the Virgin of Cologne [namely, Saint Ursula and the 11,000 Virgins].[138]

The description of John's episcopacy, found in the cartulary's biographical litany, reiterates his donation of relics: "He gave to the Church two precious vessels: one containing the blood of saint Thomas, still liquid; the other, relics of the saints Crispin and Crispinian, [and] he also gave other relics of saint Gereon and of the sainted Virgins of Cologne."[139] Arguably, Chartres regarded these relics as the most significant and substantial of John's gifts to the Church, far more noteworthy than the donation of his sizeable library. Such a conclusion may not be surprising, given the reputational (not to mention financial) benefits that accrued to a cathedral from its possession of important relics: They were a magnet for pilgrims, as well as a source of diocesan pride. The addition of John's further cache of relics – and, in particular, the vial of Becket's "still liquid" blood – to the holdings of Chartres was surely an event of great moment.

It is hardly remarkable that John possessed an extremely valuable relic of Saint Thomas. When precisely John acquired his small container of this

---

137 PL 199, cols. 375D–387D; *The Later Letters*, p. 802 (Letter 325). Indeed, according to his obituary, John even imitated Becket by wearing a hair shirt of his own; see *Cartulaire de Notre-Dame de Chartres*, vol. 3, p. 202.

138 *Cartulaire de Notre-Dame de Chartres*, vol. 3, p. 202: "Duo vasa preciosa eidem ecclesie contulit, in altero quorum sanguinem gloriosi martiris Thome, Cantuariensis archiepiscopi, videntibus nobis, adhuc stillantem, in altero reliquias sanctorum martirum Crispini et Crispiniani posuit. Reliquias etiam gloriosas nobis contulit de Comitatu sancti Gereomi et de consortio Virginum Coloniensium."

139 Ibid. vol.1, p. 20: "Duo vasa preciosa, unum cum sanguine beati Thome adhuc stillante, aliud cum reliquiis sanctorum Crispini et Crispiniani, alias eciam reliquias sancti Gereonis et sanctarum Virginum Colonensium eidem ecclesie dedit."

precious fluid is difficult to determine: It could have been any time from immediately after the assassination up until his departure for Chartres in mid-1176. John acknowledged his ownership (and even use) of this Becket relic in a document now known as Letter 325, his last extant epistle, which was first published only in 1936.[140] This letter has been dated (on internal grounds) to the period between 1177 and 1179 and is addressed to the sitting Archbishop of Canterbury, Richard of Dover, and other members of the cathedral chapter and clergy. In it, John narrates his direct participation in a miracle that he ascribes to the intercessory power of Becket's relics. John tells the story of one Peter, a local stone-cutter who derided his fellow workers' "reverence" of Becket and "gratitude" for his reputed miracles. Soon after uttering this blasphemous denunciation, Peter was overcome with a serious illness, which John refers to as Becket's *first* miracle in this tale: "the wretched man whom saint Thomas' right hand had struck."[141] Eventually, Peter's mother and friends sought John's aid, whereupon, John reports,

> I hastened to the cathedral. The mute wretch was brought [to me]...and to the reliquary which contains the undergarment – that is, the chemise [i.e., the *sancta camisia*] – of the Blessed Virgin...I ordered the phial – in which I had placed (*reposueram*) the blood of saint Thomas which I had brought with me to Chartres – and water, in which to bathe the phial, to be brought [to me]. We prayed a little before the relics, and, when we had finished, I handed the phial to the wretched man to kiss. Instantly, in a loud voice which could be heard by all the bystanders, [he cried out,] "Saint Thomas, Saint Thomas, have mercy on me." He drank the water in which I had washed [both] the phial *and* the good martyr's knife; at once, his former health returned.[142]

---

140 The existence of this letter was apparently long known or at least rumored, but was only published for the first time by Raymonde Foreville, "Une lettre inédite de Jean de Salisbury, évêque de Chartres," *Revue d'histoire de l'Église de France* 22 (1936), 179–198. On the dating of and background to Letter 325, see *The Later Letters*, pp. 802–803 notes 1–2.

141 *The Later Letters*, pp. 804–805 (Letter 325): "...miserum quem dextra beati Thomae percusserat..."

142 Ibid., pp. 804–807 (Letter 325): "Profectus sum ad ecclesiam. Adductus est miser mutus... et ad capsam in qua est interula, id est camisia beatissimae Virginis...Praecepi igitur afferri philaterium in quo reposueram sanguinem beati Thomae, quem mecum Carnotum detuli, et aquam in qua philaterium lauaretur. Orauimus paulisper ante reliquias et, oratione completa, philaterium misero tradidi osculandum; qui statim uoce magna, ut a circumstantibus omnibus posset audiri, 'Sancte Thoma, sancte Thoma, miserere mei'. Hausit aquam in qua philaterium laueram *et* cultellum boni martiris, et illico pristinam recepit sanitatem..." (emphasis added).

According to John, Peter thereafter declared his intention to visit Canterbury in order to give thanks to the saint and to make amends for his "blasphemy." That Peter in fact did so is attested by the epistle, which John evidently composed as an official confirmation of the stone-cutter's story;[143] Peter is identified by John as "the bearer of this letter."[144]

Beyond the specifics of John's use of Becket's blood at Chartres lies a larger point: The story John narrates in Letter 325 cannot have taken place any later than 1179 and, hence, seems to be the earliest known *confirmed* account of a miracle attributed to Becket's intercessory powers occurring in France or, indeed, anywhere on the European continent outside of Plantagenet-dominated territories.[145] Why should Chartres have been the site of ostensibly the first Becket miracle beyond the realm controlled by Henry II? As we have already remarked, William White Hands had been among the leading advocates for the cause of Canterbury against King Henry during the 1160s (largely coinciding with the period 1164–8, during which White Hands was in residence at Chartres). Moreover, Becket himself had reportedly been well-received in Chartres during a brief visit in early 1169, following his retreat from a disastrous meeting at Montmirail with Kings Henry II and Louis VII of France.[146] Thus, the ground had already been prepared there for the veneration of Becket once he had been martyred. John's well-known association with the archbishop and his possession of the vial of blood not only reinforced but also invigorated the emergent cult of Becket at Chartres. Perhaps even more than Pontigny and Sens, where the archbishop had spent most of his time while in exile (and at

---

143   Koopmans, *Wonderful to Relate*, pp. 159–180 details the emerging "tradition" of requiring confirmation from "reliable" (i.e., clerical) sources of Becket miracles performed elsewhere and later reported to Canterbury.

144   *The Later Letters*, pp. 802–803 (Letter 325): "...lator praesentium."

145   Anne J. Duggan, *Thomas Becket: Friends, Networks, Texts and Cult* (Aldershot, 2007), IX. Two miracles associated with *aqua sanctificata* were reported on the Continent at around the time of John's letter, but one occurred in Normandy and the other in Aquitaine; see Raymonde Foreville, "La diffusion du culte de Thomas Becket dans la France de l'Ouest avant la fin du XIIᵉ siècle," in *Thomas Becket dans la tradition historique et hagiographique* (London, 1981), IX, p. 353. Of course, many miracles occurring after contact with Becket's relics were reported at Canterbury and other sites around England from 1171 onward; see Barlow, *Thomas Becket*, pp. 265–267 and Koopmans, *Wonderful to Relate*, pp. 139–200. John himself presents accounts of several such miracles in Letter 323 (*The Later Letters*, pp. 794–799).

146   As documented by Herbert of Bosham in his *Vita* of Becket, ch. 27, in *MB*, vol.3, pp. 436–437.

which no miracles had yet been reported[147]), Chartres was a natural location for the occurrence of an initial, distinctively French miracle attributed to Becket's intercession. That this miracle was first facilitated, and then reported, by John, who had already done so much to attach himself to Becket's saintly reputation, seems equally unremarkable. Clearly, the early hope that King Louis and William White Hands had implicitly placed in John for the establishment of Becket's cult at Chartres had begun to be fulfilled.

Following John's death on October 25, 1180, Chartres continued to be firmly associated with Becket's sanctity. The presence and importance of Becket's blood and knife, for example, are attested in an account of the *Miracles of Our Lady of Chartres* (c. 1206), originally written in Latin by an anonymous author and then rendered (with a few later additions), by Jean le Marchant, into French verse (c. 1252–62).[148] The bulk of the datable miracles described in the Latin original (and recounted in the French version) come from the period between 1197–1206.[149] Miracle 26 in this collection, dated internally to 1206, confirms the presence of *two* relics of "the martyr-saint Thomas, a little of whose blood and his own small knife (*cultellus ipsius*) were there."[150] Indeed, Becket's knife figures on its own in this final contemporary Latin miracle.

The text of Miracle 26, which opens with a brief reference to Becket's salvific powers, relates the cure of one William, a poor villein who violated the prohibition against working on a feast day. As a consequence, William found his hands stuck fast to a sickle and a sheaf.[151] He was eventually brought to

---

147   Barlow, *Thomas Becket*, p. 268.

148   See Jean le Marchant, *Miracles de Notre-Dame de Chartres*, ed. Pierre Kunstmann (Ottawa and Chartres, 1973), p. 7, for the possible attribution of the authorship of the Latin original to one Giles of Altisiodore; on Giles, see *Cartulaire de Notre-Dame de Chartres*, vol. 3, p. 69.

149   The Latin original, which Kuntsmann includes in the footnotes to his edition of the French text, is basically chronological, beginning c. 1197 (see the reference to "three years after the fire" which ravaged the Cathedral of Notre-Dame in 1194 in the first of the Latin miracles [*Miracles de Notre-Dame de Chartres*, pp. 77–78]) and completed in or after 1206 (the date appended to Miracle 26, which is also the only Becket miracle in both versions). Miracle 27 (the end of the Latin collection) is historiographic only and serves as a *coda* to the collection. The Latin text's author (as Kunstmann documents on pp. 7–8) reveals himself as either a direct eyewitness or as having heard a miracle account first-hand in nine of the twenty-six contemporary miracles.

150   Jean le Marchant, *Miracles*, p. 211: "...beatum Thomam martirem, de cujus sanguine portiuncula erat ibi et cultellus ipsius."

151   Ibid., pp. 206–209. The narrative similarity between William's story and that of Peter ought to be noted: Each had dared a saint (Germain in the former case, Becket in the latter) to punish him, leading to his respective ailment and to his eventual cure *only* via Becket's intervention.

Chartres' cathedral, where neither the famed *sancta camisia* nor the venerable relic of Saint Leobinus proved efficacious. At this point, "the guardian of the afore-mentioned relics grabbed the aforesaid knife (*cultellum*) and touched it to the right hand of the miserable man, where the sickle had adhered. On contact, the fingers of the hand that had been stuck to the sickle detached...In like manner, at the touch of this knife, his left hand was released from the sheaf."[152] Becket's knife alone effected William's cure.

More significant is that this miracle, which both occurred and was then documented some 25 years after John's death, indicates that his early efforts to promote the cult of Becket at Chartres proved resoundingly successful. This impression is reinforced by physical evidence, still visible today, in the cathedral itself. The Chartres Cathedral as John knew it was almost totally destroyed by a devastating fire in 1194, and the project of its rebuilding lasted for several decades. When it was finally restored, the cathedral incorporated, both within and without, a number of physical features that drew attention to the continuing importance and vitality of Becket's memory and veneration within the Chartrian community. Most notably, an entire stained glass window program is devoted to the saint's martyrdom.[153] Elsewhere in the cathedral is located a stained glass depiction of Becket flanked by two knights, topped by a rose.[154] Becket is also represented in a lower section of one of the cathedral's large rose windows, and an external statuary figure has been tentatively identified as Becket as well.[155] As Claudine Lautier has argued, the windows at Chartres in general reflected and promoted those saints whose relics were housed in the cathedral.[156] Moreover, the way in which Becket's life is represented in the Chartrian stained glass program suggests a highly selective, politicized

---

152   Ibid., pp. 211–212: "Apprehendit autem custos dictarum reliquiarum dictum cultellum et tetigit cum eo manum dextram persone miserabilis cui adheserat falcicula, ad cujus tactum soluti sunt digiti manus adherentis falcicule...Similiter, ad tactum ejusdem cultelli, soluta est manus sinistra a manipulo." (The "custos" mentioned may have been one Guibert; see his obituary in *Cartulaire de Notre-Dame de Chartres*, vol. 3, p. 201, where he is described as "custos fidelissimus hujus ecclesie.")

153   This can be viewed at Alison Stones, "Images of Medieval Art and Architecture, France: Chartres (Cathedral of Notre-Dame)" http://www.medart.pitt.edu/image/france/ chartres/chartres-cathedral/windows/choir-windows/018A-Becket/chartres-18ABecket -main.html.

154   Hayes, *Body and Sacred Place in Medieval Europe*, p. 87 and note 120.

155   Clark Maines, "A Figure of St. Thomas Becket at Chartres," *Zeitscrift für Kuntsgeschichte* 36 (1973), 163–173.

156   Claudine Lautier, "Les vitraux de la cathédrale de Chartres: reliques et images," *Bulletin Monumental* 161 (2003), 3–96.

understanding of events leading to his murder and canonization, one that places a premium on his quarrel with Henry II and its aftermath. The program also offers an implicit contrast between the French King Louis, portrayed as a mediator and friend of the Church, and the tempestuous and temperamental Henry.[157]

John of Salisbury's posthumous hand can be seen at work, at least indirectly, in inspiring the representations of Becket throughout the cathedral. Most obviously, John's donation of the vial of Becket's blood to Chartres, and his prior use of it (along with the martyr's knife) in facilitating the miracle of Peter the stonecutter, suggests a vital context for the impetus to create the later Becket images. Moreover, it has been suggested by Alyce Jordan that John's writings (housed at Chartres) helped to guide the choices made by the program's designers for its general themes, as well as for the specific events portrayed therein.[158] It seems clear that, despite John's relatively brief tenure as bishop of Chartres, he effected both an immediate and a lasting impact on the cult of Becket there, amply fulfilling the early promise placed in him by Louis VII and William White Hands when they selected him to become the first French bishop associated with the recent English martyr.

Conclusion

John of Salisbury spent over three decades writing, in a variety of ways and for a wide range of purposes, to and about Thomas Becket. In that time, Becket came to function, in large part, as an "organizing principle" for John's literary career, the figure around whom his central intellectual and political concern – protecting the liberty of the Church in the face of secular tyranny – coalesced. Interestingly, John's views of and attitudes toward Becket trace a developmental arc that neatly parallels Becket's own changing stance toward the Church – both move, respectively, from uncomfortable associate to zealously devoted advocate. It would likely never have occurred to John, when he directed thinly veiled criticisms to the chancellor in the 1150s, that Becket would (or even

---

157   See Marie-Pierre Gelin, "Heroes and Traitors: The Life of St. Thomas Becket in French Stained-Glass Windows," *Vidimus* 14 (January 2008) http://vidimus.org/issues/issue-14/feature/ (accessed 23 June 2011).

158   Alyce Jordan, "Thomas Becket in the Windows of Sens and Chartres: The Saint as Church Reformer and the Monarchic Conscience," lecture at Arizona State University, 2006 (cited by Natalie A. Hansen, *Making the Martyr: The Liturgical Persona of Saint Thomas Becket in Visual Imagery* [Urbana, IL, University of Illinois thesis, 2011], p. 36 note 20).

could) transform into the quintessential defender of the Church's liberty. And, it would have been equally difficult for John to imagine, prior to Becket's murder, that he himself would ever become one of the most active and effective promoters, first, of the archbishop's sanctification and, then, of the cult of Saint Thomas.

In the end, despite Becket's many character flaws, John valued, over and above all else, the cause for which the archbishop fought and died. Indeed, one wonders if John was not speaking primarily to himself when he asked (in his *Life* of Becket, as quoted above), "If the cause makes the martyr...what cause was more just, more holy than his?" For John, *no* cause was more just or holy than the liberty of the Church. As many of John's letters from the period of the exile reveal, the living Becket was far from an ideal *defensor ecclesiae*; in his martyrdom, however, he was perfected. It would not be an overstatement to say that John, in many ways, played a signal role, at a crucial historical moment, in securing Becket's enduring legacy, both in the Church and in the popular imagination. Nor would it be wrong to say that Becket inadvertently enabled John to leave his own lasting (if largely unrecognized) monument – physically, within and throughout Chartres Cathedral; and, intellectually, in the libraries of Europe. Truly, John of Salisbury's long and complex relationship with Thomas Becket was a match made ultimately and *only* in heaven.

CHAPTER 3

John of Salisbury as Ecclesiastical Administrator

Julie Barrau

John of Salisbury's career as an ecclesiastical administrator may seem the least remarkable and interesting aspect of his life; it is certainly not the reason for his enduring fame. He nonetheless spent most of his life, once he had finished his long course of studies in France, in some form of administrative service or office. John left his student years behind in 1147–8, according to a chronology now firmly established.[1] What happened next has been long debated. According to R.L. Poole, the new *magister* was first employed, until about 1154, at the papal court.[2] However, it was later demonstrated, particularly by Avrom Saltman, that Poole was probably wrong, given that John appeared, at a very modest rank, in the witness lists of two of the few charters surviving from the early part of Archbishop Theobald's time at Canterbury;[3] it is very likely that after a brief stay and perhaps employment with his friend Peter, the abbot of Celle, John endeavoured to join the archbishop's household with the support of a letter of Bernard of Clairvaux.[4] That letter, which recommended John on the basis of

---

1 On John's years as a student, see the chapter by Cédric Giraud and Constant Mews in this volume. See also Olga Weijers, "The Chronology of John of Salisbury's Studies in France (*Metalogicon* II.10)," in *The World of John of Salisbury*, pp. 109–116, and Katharine S.B. Keats-Rohan, "The Chronology of John of Salisbury's Studies in France: A Reading of *Metalogicon* II.10," *Studi medievali* 28 (1987), 193–203.

2 See Reginald Lane Poole, "John of Salisbury at the Papal Court" and "The Early Correspondence of John of Salisbury," in *Studies in Chronology and History* (Oxford, 1934), respectively pp. 248–258 and 259–286.

3 Avrom Saltman, *Theobald, Archbishop of Canterbury* (London, 1956), pp. 169–175.

4 *Sancti Bernardi opera*, ed. Jean Leclercq, Henri Rochais and C.H. Talbot, vol. 8, *Epistolae, II. Corpus epistolarum 181–310* (Rome, 1977), Letter 361, p. 307: "Testimonium enim bonum habet a bonis, quod non minus vita quam litteratura promeruit. Nec hoc didici ab illis, qui verba sicut verba iactare noverunt, sed a filiis meis qui me cum sunt, quorum verbis credo sicut crederem oculis meis. (...) Hoc quoque adicio ut eum vobis cum habeatis, qui scholas ibi regere non esset ei multa utilitas, tam propter paupertatem quam propter guerras terrae illius, et ego ei in hac parte melius providere possem, si videretur utilitati ipsius ista morositas deservire." After John was promoted to Chartres, Peter of Celle wrote to the archbishop of Canterbury that "your predecessor of holiest memory, Theobald, took [John] up from our lap and bosom (*de gremio et sinu nostro*) when he was needy and poor (*inopem and pauperem*)"; *The Letters of Peter of Celle*, ed. Julian Haseldine (Oxford, 2000), Letter 103, pp. 420–421.

hearsay in positive but tepid fashion, was nevertheless enough to bear fruit, and the new member of Archbishop Theobald's Canterbury household became over the years one of the shining stars of that hothouse of clerical talent. It is during his time in the service of the archbishop that John wrote most of his books, including the mammoth-sized *Policraticus*. His first letter collection, probably composed just after Theobald's death, consists of a mixture of personal letters and letters written as his master's secretary. John then associated himself to Thomas Becket in his newfound zeal for the liberty of the Church from 1163, and spent seven years in exile; even though he may have been of use to various people during that time,[5] and probably drafted letters for Becket,[6] he did not appear to have been actively involved in administrative tasks while in France. After the murder of December 1170 he looked for employment, and can be found mostly in Canterbury and Exeter, where he became treasurer in 1173 under his old friend bishop Bartholomew. In 1176, at the initiative of William White Hands, he was elected bishop of Chartres; he died in office there in 1180.

To understand the kind of ecclesiastical administrator John of Salisbury was, we shall describe his life as an *officialis* and a *curialis* and place it in the context of the development of lay and clerical administrations and courts, which is a crucial and well-studied feature of the period.[7] Such assessment has already been well made elsewhere; we shall present just the most salient

---

5   He wrote for instance to Henry the Liberal, count of Champagne, a letter which is a little treatise on the biblical canon, in which he described how he was head-hunted for the task. See *The Later Letters*, Letter 209, pp. 314–339. John described Henry's emissaries at p. 316: "quas [diuinarum litterarum propositis quaestionibus] cum michi Albericus Remensis, quem cognominant de porta Veneris, qua vulgo Valesia dicitur, nominee uestro, adhibitis aliquot litteratis uiris, proposuisset." On the context of such a request from a lay prince, see John F. Benton, "The Court of Champagne as a Literary Center," *Speculum* 36 (1961), 551–591.

6   Anne Duggan convincingly offered a list of Becket letters drafted by John on the basis of the presence of classical references. See "Authorship and Authenticity in the Becket Correspondence," in Brigitte Merta, Andrea Sommerlechner et H. Weigl, eds., *Vom Nutzen des Edierens. Akten des internationalen Kongresses zum 150-jährigen Bestehen des Instituts für Österreichische Geschichtsforschung Wien, 3.-5. Juni 2004* (Vienna-Munich, 2005), pp. 25–44, with the list of newly attributed letters at p. 44. More letters can be added because of similarities in the use of scriptural references, for instance Letters 151, 211 and 234 of the *The Correspondence of Thomas Becket Archbishop*, ed. Anne Duggan, 2 vols. (Oxford, 2000).

7   For the Plantagenet court, possibly the most structured lay court of the time, see Martin Aurell, "La cour Plantagenêt: entourage, savoir et civilité," in Martin Aurell, ed., *La Cour Plantagenêt (1154–1204). Actes du colloque tenu à Thouars du 30 avril au 2 mai 1999* (Poitiers, 2000), pp. 9–46; for Henry II's, see Nicholas Vincent, "The Court of Henry II," in Christopher Harper-Bill and Nicholas Vincent, eds., *Henry II: New Interpretations* (Woodbridge 2007), pp. 278–334.

aspects of the question.[8] More time will be spent on John's years as bishop of Chartres. They are the least studied part of his life, and have sometimes been described in rather dismissive terms. Here it will be argued that his episcopate is both more interesting and much better documented than has previously been thought.[9]

John's connection with the workings of the institutional Church was not limited to practical experience; his books and letters contain many reflective remarks on how the Church was run and should have been run, the two, as one would expect, being rather distinct in John's mind.

In the *Policraticus* most famously, and also in his letters, John harshly criticized some aspects of ecclesiastical life, and he was merciless about devious bishops, greedy archdeacons, sycophantic courtiers and lazy priests. As Frédérique Lachaud has shown, John belonged to an established tradition of criticism of the high-ranking clergy, especially the bishops. His denunciation of the follies of courtiers targeted the episcopal (and papal) courts as well as the secular ones.[10] The eighth book of the *Policraticus* spells out what comes across as a rather daring opinion, so much so that John felt the need to provide an extensive justification for it: that tyranny can be exerted by priests and prelates.[11] For John their tyranny was all the more dangerous and abhorrent

---

8   See for instance Cary J. Nederman, *John of Salisbury* (Tempe, Arizona, 2005), pp. 11–28, Christopher Brooke's introduction to *The Early Letters*, pp. xxv–xxviii. See also Klaus Guth, *Johannes von Salisbury (1115/20–1180): Studien zur Kirchen-, Kultur- und Sozialgeschichte Westeuropas im 12. Jahrhundert* (St. Ottilien, 1978), pp. 111–166.

9   I found out in June 2014, just before the manuscript of this book was sent off to the publisher, that Karen Bollerman and Cary Nederman had worked in parallel to on matters central to this chapter. Their contribution to this volume testifies to this, especially on the question of the relics brought to Chartres by John. See Karen Bollerman and Cary J. Nederman, "A Special Collection: John of Salisbury's Relics of Saint Thomas Becket and Other Holy Martyrs," *Mediavistik* 26 (2013), 163–181, and *eidem*, "'The Sunset Years': John of Salisbury as Bishop of Chartres and the emergent cult of St. Thomas Becket in France," forthcoming. Reassuringly, my learned colleagues have reached conclusions very close to my own.

10   Frédérique Lachaud, "La figure du clerc curial dans l'œuvre de Jean de Salisbury," in Murielle Gaude-Ferragu, Bruno Laurioux and Jacques Paviot, eds., *La Cour du prince. Cour de France, cours d'Europe (XIIIᵉ–XVᵉ siècles)* (Paris, 2011), pp. 301–320, esp. pp. 303–304. See also Thomas Head, "Postscript: The Ambiguous Bishop," in John S. Ott and Anna Trumbore Jones, eds., *The Bishop Reformed: Studies of Episcopal Power and Culture in the Central Middle Ages* (Aldershot, 2007), pp. 250–264; Thomas Head argues that bishops were opened to criticism because they had the impossible task of being both Mary and Martha.

11   *Policraticus* 8.7, ed. Webb, vol. 2, p. 349: "Michi uero indignari non debent sacerdotes, si et in eis fatear inueniri posse tirannos," developed in Chapter 8, which starts thus p. 358: "Ministros Dei tamen tirannos esse non abnego."

because it could wrap itself in the shroud of the divine Word.[12] He described many cases of greed, simony, dishonesty and incompetence among the clergy, and constantly reminded his reader that those vices and sins were worse in a cleric than in a layman, because the former had to lead their flock by example.[13] Everywhere he saw the root of bad practice and sinful desires in one particular vice, ambition. His portrayal of clerical ambition is particularly stern,[14] especially for those who dreamt of becoming bishop or archdeacon.[15]

The *Policraticus* was written during the very same years that John was at the centre of one of the largest courts in Europe, the household and administration of the archbishop of Canterbury. This juxtaposition of theoretical analysis and day-to-day *praxis* is unique because the *Policraticus* is peerless in its scope, length, and ambition. But many writers of the Plantagenet world of the second half of the 12th century also led double lives, as both practitioners and narrators of the courts; Walter Map, Gerald of Wales and Roger of Howden are probably the most famous. In John's case, thanks to the letters that he wrote at the

---

12   John draws a list of all possible clerical sins and crimes associate with biblical *exempla* that the culprits might dare use to vindicate themselves (7.19, pp. 175–177).

13   *Policraticus* 7.18 insists particularly on the criminal nature of clerical vices, especially in priests and bishops; John explained there that the people are more easily contaminated by their pastors' vices than by their virtues. But this theme runs through the book: "Palatia splendent sacerdotum et in manibus eorum Christi sordidatur Ecclesia." (ibid., 6.24, ed. Webb, vol. 2, p. 68). The central role of exemplarity in the idea churchmen had of themselves has been well studied; see for instance Caroline Walker Bynum, *'Docere verbo vel exemplo': An Aspect of Twelfth-Century Spirituality* (Missoula, Mont., 1979). Exemplarity was not a virtue limited to clerics. Princes were of course told, particularly in *specula* written for them, that their position made them examples and made virtue not just an private duty but a political and social one; see Michel Senellart, *Les Arts de gouverner, du 'regimen' médiéval au concept de gouvernement* (Paris, 1995). The same idea applied even more widely, as Frédérique Lachaud has shown for *officiales* in general. See Frédérique Lachaud, *L'Éthique du pouvoir au Moyen Âge. L'office dans la culture politique (Angleterre, vers 1150-vers 1330)* (Paris, 2010), pp. 157–167.

14   "Erubesce, Sydon, ait mare; et tu, clerice, quid sentis, cum laicus fere legis ignarus ambitionem tuam arguit et compescit?" (*Policraticus*, 7.19, ed. Webb, vol. 2, p. 180).

15   Ibid., ed. Webb, vol. 2, p. 179: "Nec tamen ambitione tanta episcopalis dignitas dumtaxat oppugnatur, eo quod iam summis et minimis eadem est dominandi praesidendi que libido. Qui enim aspirare non audet ad cathedram, pari auiditate et eisdem machinis praefecturas, archidiaconatus et alias aggreditur dignitates." On archdeacons' bad reputation, see Christopher N.L. Brooke, "The Archdeacon and the Norman Conquest," in Diana Greenway, Christopher Holdsworth and Janer Sayers, eds., *Tradition and Change: Essays in honour of Marjorie Chibnall* (Cambridge, 1985), pp. 1–19, revised in *Churches and Churchmen in Medieval Europe* (London, 1999), pp. 117–137.

time, on behalf of Theobald as well as for himself, and to the autobiographical insights scattered in his other works, it is possible to get some sense of his life as a courtier and an administrator. That is what the following pages of this chapter will endeavour to do.

John at the Service of Canterbury (1148–63)

The newly-appointed recruit of archbishop Theobald came back to England with an impeccable profile as a scholar. He was *magister Johannes*, and his Parisian (and possibly Chartrain) school years must have given him cachet, prestige, and great conversational skills. The French masters did not directly train him to be of use at court, although such a career path was becoming more common for the men turned out by the schools. One should beware of slightly anachronistic interpretations, though; it is only about a generation later, for men like Gerald of Wales, that new *magistri* started populating secular and ecclesiastical courts *en masse*.[16] John is a good case study: he was intellectually brilliant, had travelled extensively and had made friends in many places, but he was poor by the end of his years of study, and did not have an influential family network to support him. He had been taught more texts and concepts than probably any of his contemporaries, but not the minutiae of administration and court politics. The *Policraticus* demonstrates abundantly what use those concepts and texts were to the elaboration of his thoughts about courtly life and the duties of *officiales* and *curiales*. What will retain our attention here is what was expected of him at Canterbury, and how he met those expectations.

As Yves Sassier, who is otherwise more optimistic than me about John's legal knowledge, notes in this volume, there is no sign of law in the detailed description of his studies in the *Metalogicon*, nor any claims of formal legal education anywhere in his writings.[17] However, as Christopher Brooke rightly pointed out, his role at the court of Archbishop Theobald nevertheless had a strong juridical flavour.[18] That is obvious in the letters he drafted for the archbishop,

---

16 On this, see the seminal article by John Baldwin, "*Studium et Regnum*. The Penetration of University Personel into French and English Administration at the Turn of the Twelfth Century," *Revue des études islamiques* 44 (1976), 199–215.

17 See Sassier, "John of Salisbury and Law," 192.

18 Christopher N.L. Brooke, "John of Salisbury and his world," in *The World of John of Salisbury*, pp. 7–8.

which were sent at a time when the tide of appeals to the papacy was starting to swell and to change deeply the legal practices of the English Church.[19]

His position at Theobald's court was not well defined. He did not hold a precise title, and it is difficult to establish what prebends or properties he may have been granted. It may be that he never quite felt rewarded at the level that his service and devotion would have deserved; this is at least suggested in the letter – very likely drafted by him since it is in the early collection of his correspondence – that was sent in 1160 by the ailing Theobald to recommend John to the king.[20] To paraphrase Christopher Brooke's brilliant assessment of John's job description, John was not an administrator *per se*, nor was he a lawyer by training. He was brilliant at exposition, less so at organization; he became the archbishop's "most confidential secretary," a "personal adviser" who became essential at the end of his master's reign.[21] In Cary Nederman's words, John was appointed as a "jack of all trades."[22] It is telling that John, although he was in charge of his master's correspondence or at least of most of it, had very little to do with chancery work *stricto sensu*. We have already mentioned that he appeared in very few charters' witness lists, in contrast with other well-known members of the household;[23] Theobald had chancellors during John's time at Canterbury, early on a former monk of Bec, Elinandus, and, for the period 1152–1161, Philip, a secular cleric.[24]

The lack of title appears less significant if one keeps in mind Christopher Cheney's remark about 12th-century episcopal chanceries: "titles, unfortunately, throw very little light on functions."[25] The wealth of outstanding personalities at the Canterbury court under Theobald has often been noticed.[26] There John met

---

19   On this see for instance Charles Duggan, *Twelfth-Century Decretal Collections and their Importance in English History* (London, 1963) and, for the knowledge of canon law in England, Stephan Kuttner et Eleanor F. Rathbone, "Anglo-Norman Canonists of the Twelfth Century," *Traditio* 7 (1949/51), 279–358.

20   *The Early Letters*, Letter 126, p. 218: "Nunc autem eum uobis commendo prae ceteris qui in obsequio meo prae ceteris laborauit et minimum accepit de manu mea, cum sinceritate fidei et exhibitione operis meruerit plurimum."

21   Ibid., p. xxix.

22   Nederman, *John of Salisbury*, p. 14.

23   Roger of Pont-l'Évêque, for instance, can be found in many acts. See Saltman, *Theobald, Archbishop of Canterbury*, acts 55, 59, 165, 178, 252.

24   See C.R. Cheney, *English Bishops' Chanceries, 1100–1250* (Manchester, 1950), pp. 28–32. Cheney also made the very useful point that the word "chancery" can only be used in a loose sense, "to describe conveniently their secretarial and scribal arrangements" (ibid., p. vii).

25   Ibid., p. 27.

26   On Theobald's household see Saltman, *Theobald, Archbishop of Canterbury*, pp. 165–177, as well as Frank Barlow, *Thomas Becket* (London, 1986), pp. 30–40.

many of the friends and foes that would populate his life from then on, including, of course, Thomas Becket. Among these luminaries, many of whom would later on move up in the Church,[27] there was professional expertise: lawyers in particular stand out, well versed in either or both laws. First among them is master Vacarius, who was instrumental in introducing civil law to England, and who had arrived at Canterbury around 1143.[28] Herbert of Bosham gave a famous description of the group of *eruditi* who surrounded Theobald's successor, Thomas Becket. A biblical scholar and theologian himself, Herbert deplored the importance given to lawyers who specialised in secular law, and complained that such people, ignorant of Scripture, were none the less given faster promotion in the Church.[29] Willy nilly, Herbert confirmed there the well-established fact that legal matters were increasingly central to court life, in England and elsewhere, and legal experts needed and favoured. However, it is worth noticing that most of these men, at Thomas' court as well as at this predecessor's, did not have a precise title or assignment. This is revealing about what "Church administration" still was at the time: it was not yet the business of specialists, and many new chancery and legal practices were being slowly developed over decades.[30]

---

27 Thomas Becket first and foremost, but also Roger de Pont-l'Évêque, archbishop of York from 1154, two more archbishops and six bishops. For a list see Saltman, *Theobald, Archbishop of Canterbury*, p. 165 note 3.

28 On Vacarius and his significance, see Peter Stein, "Vacarius and the Civil Law," in Christopher N.L. Brooke, David E. Luscombe, Geoffrey H. Martin and Dorothy Owen, eds., *Church and Government in the Middle Ages. Essays presented to C.R. Cheney on his 70th Birthday* (Cambridge, 1976), pp. 119–137, and Francis de Zulueta and Peter Stein, *The Teaching of Roman Law in England around 1200* (London, 1990).

29 Herbert of Bosham, *Vita S. Thomae*, in *MB*, vol. 3, pp. 207–208: "Inter istos vero sacrae legis apocrisiarios taceo inpresentiarum illam quam ad saeculi jurgia secum simper habebat in forensic jure peritorum turbam, non quidem theologam, sed potius civicam quondam facundiam exercentes. (...) accidit ut (...) animarum constituantur pastores scripturarum ignari. (...) Nec quidem ob id dico quod sic fieri aut quod talis, videlicet, inops et mendicus et scripturarum ignarus, in episcopium sacerdotiumve eligi seu provehi debeat; sed quod saepe fieri sic contingat."

30 The *inspeximus*, for instance, appeared commonly in episcopal chanceries only from the 1170s; see Cheney, *English Bishops' Chanceries*, pp. 90–96. On the changing chancery practices at episcopal courts, see Julia Barrow, "From the Lease to the Certificate: The Evolution of Episcopal Acta in England and Wales (c.700-c.1250)," in Christoph Haidacher and Werner Köfler, eds., *Die Diplomatik der Bischofsurkunde vor 1250. La diplomatique épiscopale avant 1250* (Innsbruck, 1995), pp. 529–542, and Christopher N.L. Brooke, "English Episcopal Acta of the Twelfth and Thirteenth Centuries," in M.J. Franklin and Christopher Harper-Bill, eds., *Medieval Ecclesiastical Studies in Honour of Dorothy M. Owen* (Woodbridge, 1995), pp. 41–56.

In the 1150s Canterbury was still a perfect fit for John, who throughout his life was anything but a specialist.

His main contribution, as far as we can tell, was the letters he drafted for the archbishop, which make up about two-thirds of his earlier letter collection. Those letters have been hailed as the main source documenting the growing tide of appeals to Rome, and they contribute to England's having a special place in the development of canon law and particularly decretals in the second half of the 12th century.[31] But they have much more to offer to historians. John gave Theobald a strong voice, which could be affectionate or stern, and a style that is markedly more streamlined and less wordy than that of his own letters. There are other examples of 12th-century letters known to have been written on behalf of someone else, because they were included in the letter collections of the ghost writer.[32] The collaboration of John and Theobald stands out as the most sustained and the best documented. In general it seems that John refrained from the piled-on references, digressions, and private jokes that are constitutive of the style of his private letters; this demonstrates an awareness of the demands of his office and suggests that he was indeed a valuable and trustworthy subordinate.

Only one other side of John's duties at Canterbury is relatively well known, and that was his missions as an envoy to the papal court. His familiarity with Rome and the *curia* explains R.L. Poole's probably mistaken idea that John was employed there after he left the schools.[33] If the letter collection is to be believed, Theobald probably hired John at first as a diplomat, and his secretarial work took shape later.[34] John attended the council of Reims in 1148 with the archbishop, and claimed in a letter to have crossed the Alps ten times to

---

31   See Letters 99 and 100. For these letters as witnesses of an early use of Gratian in England, see for instance Z.N. Brooke, *The English Church and the Papacy from the Conquest to the Reign of John* (Cambridge, 1931), pp. 110–111; Charles Duggan, "Papal Judges Delegate and the Making of the 'New Law' in the Twelfth Century," in Thomas N. Bisson, ed., *Cultures of Power. Lordship, Status and Process in Twelfth-Century Europe* (Philadelphia, 1995), pp. 172–199, at p. 174; Duggan, *Thomas Becket*, p. 47; Richard H. Helmholz, *The Oxford History of the Laws of England*, vol. 1, *The Canon Law and Ecclesiastical Jurisdiction from 597 to the 1640s* (Oxford, 2004), p. 79. Most of these scholars see in these letters the sign that the *Decretum* was already well known in England in the late 1150s; it may be possible to reassess the question, since they are possibly the only available evidence of the kind.

32   A quick search through the *Patrologia Latina* shows letters written *in nomine cuiusdam* in the collections of Peter of Blois, Herbert de Bosham, Nicholas of Clairvaux and Stephen of Tournai.

33   See *supra* p. 105.

34   The earlier letters date from 1153–4.

visit the Curia. Of his early years of familiarity with papal matters he left a remarkable testimony, the *Historia pontificalis*, but unfortunately only a fragment of it remains; the narrative stops in the early 1150s. Later letters make clear that John made friends with influential members of the *curia*, first among them Nicholas Breakspear. Nicholas was made cardinal in 1149, at the time that he and John seem to have become friends. In 1154 he became the first and only English pope as Adrian IV.[35] John boasted of the closeness of his relationship with the pope of the *Metalogicon*, and in the *Policraticus* he noted in passing that he had spent once three months with Adrian.[36] It is the same lengthy visit in 1156 that provoked Henry II's anger and sent John into disgrace for a while,[37] but the very fact of that disgrace reveals that John was considered a serious political player; it seems that he was Theobald's representative to the new pope as well as the king's envoy on sensitive business.[38] It is clear from a much later letter sent during the exile years that John had expected to reap the fruits of his friendship with Adrian and had probably hoped to be made a cardinal.[39] The pope's premature death in 1159 put a final stop to such dreams; it also resulted in a schism in which Theobald and John got deeply involved, at a time when the archbishop's health had become very precarious.

---

35 For John's remembrance of the early times of that friendship, see Letter 52, *The Early Letters*, p. 90 and *Policraticus* 6.24, ed. Webb, vol. 2, p. 69. This reference, and the rest of our knowledge of John and Adrian's relationship, is based on Christopher Brooke, "Adrian IV and John of Salisbury," in Brenda Bolton and Anne Duggan, eds., *Adrian IV, the English Pope: Studies and Texts* (Aldershot, 2003), pp. 1–12.

36 See *Metalogicon*, p. 183. John wrote that his visit lasted for three months in the *Policraticus* 6.24, ed. Webb, vol. 2, p. 67: "Memini me causa uisitandi dominum Adrianum pontificem quartum, qui in me ulteriorem familiaritatem admiserat, profectum in Apuliam, mansique cum eo Beneuenti ferme tres menses."

37 See Giles Constable, "The Alleged Disgrace of John of Salisbury in 1159," *English Historical Review* 69 (1954), 67–76. John complained about it to Peter of Celle in Letter 19, pp. 31–32, and to the pope himself in Letter 30, p. 48, where he blamed Arnulf of Lisieux for pouring calumny in the king's ear.

38 In the *Metalogicon*, John wrote that Adrian had given him a ring for the king as a token of his "hereditary right" over Ireland (*Metalogicon* 4.42, p. 183). It is likely that that was not what Henry had hoped for, and the reason of his anger. See Anne Duggan, "*Totius christianitatis caput*: The Pope and the Princes," in *Adrian IV. The English Pope*, pp. 105–155.

39 *The Later Letters*, Letter 235, p. 434: "utriusque nostrum pater sanctissimus Adrianus, qui uos in sancta Romana fortissimam (ut spes est) columpnam plantauit ecclesia, me speciali quadam caritatis gratia prae ceteris conterraneis diligebat, et fortunae meae casus sortis suae euentibus connumerandos arbitrabatur." This letter was written to Walter, an Englishman whom Adrian had made bishop of Albano.

It is likely that John was given more autonomy and more work as Theobald's health declined; a high proportion of the letters written in the archbishop's name date from those final years. As early as 1156 the archbishop had mentioned to Pope Adrian IV a serious illness that had all but killed him the previous summer.[40] Allusions to his bad health continued over the next few years,[41] and eventually John was in a position where he could write to Becket, at the end of the *Policraticus*, that he was often acting in place of his master: "[Theobald] has charged me with the province, and he has forced on me the unbearable burden of all ecclesiastical affairs."[42] Indeed by 1159 he had completed the *Metalogicon* and the *Policraticus*, and probably devoted most of his time until his master's death in April 1161 to the affairs of Canterbury. John famously lamented in the prologue of the *Policraticus* that he had wasted twelve years trifling with courts and courtiers.[43] He probably wrote that in earnest, but his life as the close advisor and ghost-writer to the highest figure in the English Church was just as probably more than a mere day job. That he drafted both the old prelate's will and his farewell letter to the king, as well as the kind words chosen in the letter recommending John to the same king, testify enough to his deep involvement and acknowledged usefulness during Theobald's pontificate. Years later his friend Peter of Celle would write to Richard, then archbishop of Canterbury: "[Theobald] is indeed dead in the body but he still lives in his offspring (*in propagine*), and in John his most delightful memorial (*suauissimum memoriale*)."[44]

By the end, John almost certainly enjoyed the position of a *secretarius* as he defined it in the *Policraticus*: the closest and most influential advisor, a position he described there as full of rewards but also of pitfalls.[45] John stayed on at Canterbury after the death of his master, during the year of vacancy and under

---

40   *The Early Letters*, Letter 8, p. 14: "me gravis langor (...) aestate praterita adduxit ad portas mortis."

41   See for instance Letter 111, John to Peter of Celle: "de domini et patris mei diuturna et dubia infirmitate" (*The Early Letters*, p. 180).

42   *Metalogicon* 4.42, p. 184: "Siquidem pater meus et dominus, immo et tuus uenerabilis Theobaldus Cantuariensis archiepiscopus in aegritudinem incidit, ut incertum sit quid sperare quid timere oporteat. Negotiis more solito superesse non potest, iniunxit que mihi prouinciam duram, et importabile onus imposuit, omnium ecclesiasticorum sollicitudinem."

43   *Policraticus*, ed. Webb, vol. 1, p. 14: "Mirare magis quare non praecido aut rumpo funem, si alias solui non potest, qui me in curialibus nugis tamdiu tenuit et tenet adhuc tantae obnoxium seruituti. Iam enim fere annis duodecim nugatum esse taedet et paenitet me longe aliter institutum, et quasi sacratioris philosophiae lactatum uberibus ablactatum que decuerat ad philosophantium transisse coetum quam ad collegia nugatorum."

44   *The Letters of Peter of Celle*, Letter 103, pp. 420–421.

45   *Policraticus* 3.12, ed. Webb, vol. 1, pp. 210–211; see also Lachaud, "La figure du clerc curial," p. 305.

Thomas Becket, but his position changed. There is no evidence that he stayed in the first circle although the new archbishop did not spurn him.[46] He seems to have taken advantage of the lull in his career to collect his letters; he also wrote, probably at the request of the new archbishop, a *Life of Saint Anselm* that is not one of his best works. The circumstances of his departure for France in late 1163 and early 1164 are rather muddled. He may have been sent by Becket to prepare for a possible exile of the prelate, whose relationship with Henry II had already deeply and publicly soured. John also wrote that he himself had, again, fallen into disgrace with the king.[47] In any case John's visit soon turned into exile, and his formal employment as an administrator at Canterbury ended.

After the Murder

The years John spent in exile between 1163 and 1170 do not really belong in this chapter, given that John does not seem to have been formally employed anywhere.[48] What John did immediately after Becket's brutal and shocking death is not clear. Apart from the famous letter in which he described the murder, there is a gap in his correspondence. It must have been an unsettling time for him, so it is not surprising that he turned to what was closest to "home": not Salisbury but Exeter. John and the bishop of Salisbury, Jocelin de Bohun, had had a rather good relationship in the past and John said that he had tried to assuage Becket's wrath against the bishop in 1167.[49] However after the murder, and until 1172, the bishop was still suspended after the sentence pronounced against him by Becket for his participation in the coronation of Henry the Young King in June 1170. John was therefore unlikely to have wanted to go to Salisbury. On the other hand Exeter was a safe place to go and lick his wounds and think about his future. Frank Barlow has shown how John and his brothers had long and deep connections with the chapter of Exeter cathedral; his mother was still alive in 1170 and very probably living there.[50] John had been

---

46 On John's activities in 1161–3 see the precise outline in Nederman, *John of Salisbury*, pp. 28–29. He was for instance sent to collect the *pallium* for Becket in 1162. See William Fitzstephen, *Vita*, in *mb*, vol. 3, p. 36.

47 *The Later Letters*, Letter 136, pp. 12–13.

48 See *supra* p. 106.

49 See Letters 216 to the bishop of Coutances and 218 to Jocelin himself.

50 Frank Barlow, "John of Salisbury and his brothers," *Journal of Ecclesiastical History* 46 (1995), 95–109. On John's ailing mother and his visit to her as soon as he came back to England, see Letter 304, *The Later Letters*, p. 716. The fact that she lived in Exeter can be surmised from an earlier letter from John to his brother Richard (Letter 172, *The Later Letters*, p. 132).

associated with archbishop Theobald's support to Bishop Bartholomew's election in 1161.[51] His brothers, along with a local "Salisbury group," also favoured the new prelate.[52] One brother, Robert Fitzgille, had become archdeacon of Totnes when master Baldwin, the future archbishop of Canterbury, retired to a Cistercian monastery; he was also an intimate, as his physician, of bishop Bartholomew; he did well for himself and died a rich man.[53] During the early stages of his exile, John attempted to make his separate peace with the king, and seems to have asked Bartholomew to welcome him and his books in Exeter, maybe to recover his canonry.[54]

At Exeter he featured from 1171 on the witness lists of several of the bishop's charters.[55] Before 1173 he usually appeared relatively far down in the lists.[56] In 1173 he was made treasurer of Exeter. This boost to his status, and probably also to his income, may be deduced from the witness lists, where his name is mentioned higher up.[57] He accompanied bishop Bartholomew in his activities as an active papal delegate, often in tandem with Roger of Worcester; John himself was appointed judge at least once.[58] All this shows him once more in formal employment, but his services were not offered only to Exeter. He witnessed

---

51   See for instance the letter sent by John to Becket about the tensions that had arisen between king and archbishop about the election: Letter 128, *The Early Letters*, p. 222.

52   Barlow, "John of Salisbury and his brothers."

53   Ibid., pp. 100 and 109.

54   Letter 150, *The Later Letters*, p. 48: "Si uero michi Dominus redeundi uiam aperuerit, rescribite, si placet, an me redire oporteat libris et tota sarcina." In a letter sent in 1160–1 to Bartholomew, then archdeacon of Exeter, John sends greetings not just to his brothers but to others to whom he is also "bound by the ties of brotherly love," which seems to suggest that he was a member of the chapter (Letter 118, *The Early Letters*, p. 195).

55   The references are to the *English Episcopal Acta XI–XII: Exeter, 1046–1257*, ed. Frank Barlow (Oxford, 1995). His first appearance is probably no. 130, in which Richard of Ilchester, as archdeacon of Poitiers, restituted a church to Tavistock abbey; John, not named as master, is fifth on the list.

56   John was present as master John of Salisbury in third position on the list of no. 78, the notification of a decision taken by Bartholomew as judge-delegate about the tithes of Smisby, and no. 103, on the settlement of a dispute between the abbots of Evesham and Oseney, where he was fifth. He is the first witness in no. 142A, the confirmation in front of the bishop by William of Weston of a donation made by his father; John's promotion may signal the rather pedestrian nature of the act.

57   See, for instance no. 139, where he came first, or no. 81, about the settlement by Bartholomew of a dispute between the priories of Christchurch (Tynham) and Breamore, where he ranked second behind the dean of Chichester.

58   See nos. 78, 81, 142A, 103, 125, 130, 114, 139. On all this see Barlow, "John of Salisbury and his brothers," p. 104.

at least one decision taken in London in March 1176 by Roger of Worcester as judge-delegate, in which Bartholomew was not involved.[59] At the time, though, John was also in London with the bishop of Exeter.[60]

He also spent some of his time in his old haunts at Canterbury, where it is likely that he communed with the monks in their newfound devotion to Thomas Becket, in spite of the bitter correspondence he engaged in with them during the exile.[61] He does not appear in the witness lists of Richard of Dover's acts,[62] but he was asked to draft letters for the chapter, such as their long and florid epistle to the pope asking for Richard as their next archbishop.[63] It is probably at the request, or at least with the blessing, of the monks, that he wrote a short *Passio* of the new martyr and composed a "book of letters" relevant to the dispute which is known by a *florilegium* made from it around 1200.[64] Those letters have sometimes been understood to be a proto-collection of the Becket correspondence, but Anne Duggan has argued convincingly that they were more likely a choice of John's own letters.[65] At any rate John seems to have been part of the Canterbury scene again.

The reconciliation of Henry II with the Church after 1170 is a complex topic that has been often written about.[66] Tensions and compromises abounded, and John was involved in them. He had been vociferous about the people responsible for the murder, but he was also deeply involved in the campaign that supported Richard of Ilchester's promotion to one of England's richest and most prestigious bishoprics, Winchester. During the Becket conflict

---

59   *English Episcopal Acta XXXIII: Worcester, 1062–1185*, ed. Mary Cheney (Oxford, 2007), no. 212, March 1176. On John's ties with Worcester, see *infra* p. 128.

60   Ibid., no. 214.

61   See, for instance Letters 243, 244, 245, 247. On Becket's relations with his cathedral chapter, see Richard Southern, *The Monks of Canterbury and the Murder of Archbishop Becket*, William Urry Memorial Lectures, 1 (Canterbury, 1985).

62   *English Episcopal Acta II: Canterbury, 1162–1190*, ed. C.R. Cheney and Bridgett E.A. Jones (Oxford, 1986).

63   Letter 311, *The Later Letters*, pp. 760–767. He wrote a similar letter on behalf of Bartholomew, Letter 312, ibid., pp. 766–769, and another one in his own name to William White Hands, Letter 314, ibid., pp. 770–773.

64   Guy of Southwick's *florilegium* is in MS Oxford, St John's College 126, fols. 79r–91v.

65   See *The Correspondence of Thomas Becket*, vol. 1, pp. lxxxi–lxxxii.

66   See for instance Anne Duggan, *"Ne in dubium*. The Official Record of Henry II's Reconciliation at Avranches, 21 May 1172," *English Historical Review* 462 (2000), 643–658 and eadem, "Diplomacy, Status, and Conscience: Henry II's Penance for Becket's Murder," in Karl Borchardt and Enno Bünz, eds., *Forschungen zur Reichs-, Papst- und Landesgeschichte. Peter Herde zum 65. Geburtstag von Freunden, Schülern und Kollegen dargebracht*, 2 vols. (Stuttgart, 1998), vol. 1, pp. 265–290.

Richard had been one of the archbishop's enemies. He was a royal servant before anything else, and his hostile cohabitation as archdeacon at Poitiers with bishop John of Canterbury is an *exemplum* in conflicting principles and loyalties.[67] Richard was sent by Henry II to the Diet of Wutzburg in 1165, where he was suspected of having taken an oath of allegiance to the antipope Victor IV; in June 1166 he was excommunicated by Becket.

There were few stauncher supporters of the king against the exiled archbishop than the archdeacon of Poitiers; nonetheless John of Salisbury was instrumental in his elevation to Winchester a short three years after the murder. He wrote a series of letters to cardinals who had been favourable to Becket during the exile years to ask them to support the election of "that most devoted son of the Roman Church," Richard; he insisted that the canonical process had been respected, and that the pope should confirm the election.[68] He wrote other letters in the same spirit to Alexander III on behalf of Bartholomew and of the monks of Canterbury.[69] John's commitment to Richard's election did not pass unnoticed, and John can be found in a fair number of the acts of the newly elected bishop of Winchester.[70] John may just have been letting bygones be bygones. It is also possible that he was merely being pragmatic, as it was becoming clear that in many ways the English Church would remain the same, martyr or no martyr, and old practices of lay patronage and royal control were as lively as ever.[71]

John as Bishop of Chartres

Very little has been written about John's four years at the head of the diocese of Chartres, and it has been often assumed that this period is very poorly

---

67   On Richard, see Charles Duggan, "Richard of Ilchester, Royal servant and Bishop," *Transactions of the Royal Historical Society*, 5th Series 16 (1966), 1–21, and idem, "Bishop John and Archdeacon Richard of Poitiers," in Raymonde Foreville, ed., *Thomas Becket. Actes du colloque international de Sédières, 19–24 août 1973* (Paris, 1975), pp. 71–83.

68   Letter 316 to cardinals Albert and Theodwin, *The Later Letters*, p. 776. See also Letters 317 to Humbald of Ostia and 318 to the papal notary Gratian. On the role of these men in the dispute, see Anne Duggan, "Thomas Becket's Italian Network," in Frances Andrews, Christoph Egger et Constance M. Rousseau, eds., *Pope, Church and City: Essays in Honour of Brenda M. Bolton* (Leiden, 2004), pp. 177–201.

69   Letters 319, *The Later Letters*, pp. 780–783 and 320, ibid., pp. 782–785.

70   *English Episcopal Acta VIII: Winchester, 1070–1204*, ed. M.J. Franklin (Oxford, 1993). John can be found in no. 140, when Richard is still only bishop-elect and John first among the witnesses, no. 141, no. 166, and no. 171 (along with Bartholomew).

71   On this see Anne Duggan, "Henry II, the English Church and the Papacy, 1154–76," in *Henry II. New Interpretations*, pp. 154–183.

documented.[72] The archival resources that could have provided information from Chartres itself have twice almost been burned into oblivion, first in 1194 when the treasury cathedral burnt down along with most of the chapter's and bishops' archives,[73] and again on 26 May 1944 when the Bibliothèque Municipale and its manuscript collection were heavily bombed and burnt.[74] John's episcopate, in the rare occasions it has been assessed, was sometimes treated with slight disdain or even a tone of disappointment. Egbert Türk, on the rather thin basis of two letters by Peter of Celle and one by Peter of Blois saw in John's blunders and lack of ambition as a prelate a classic case of an intellectual unable to bring to actual life his ambitious theories.[75] Cary Nederman has offered a more balanced picture, weighing against the conclusions of Türk the more positive analysis given by Beryl Smalley of John's portrayal in the Chartres necrology.[76] Also more benevolent, but even vaguer, are the editors of his correspondence.[77]

Nederman also remarked that no "definitive evaluation" of John's term as a bishop could be made without an edition of his acts and charters. Although this chapter is certainly not the place for charter editing, it is in fact possible to gather much more evidence about John's actions as a prelate than has been previously done. It is reasonable to hope that this data will lead to a new outlook on the final years of John at Chartres.[78]

---

72   Jan van Laarhoven, in his edition of the *Entheticus*: "We have, alas, only very limited details of his episcopal activities, most of the scarce sources saying only that he was a good and conscientious shepherd to his people" (*Entheticus maior et minor*, vol. 2, p. 10). See also David Luscombe: "it may be doubted that John was bishop long enough for a resolute assessment to be made of his achievements" ("John of Salisbury in recent scholarship," in *The World of John of Salisbury*, p. 36).

73   See *Inventaire-sommaire des archives départementales antérieures à 1790. Archives ecclésiastiques. Série G*, vol. 1, ed. Lucien Merlet (Chartres, 1890), p. 2.

74   Currently, a project is being carried out at the Institut de Recherche et d'Histoire des Textes aiming at the restoration and digitalization of what remains of the Chartres manuscripts; it is led by Dominique Poirel et Claudia Rabel (see http://www.irht.cnrs.fr/recherche/projet-chartres).

75   Egbert Türk, Nugae curialium. Le règne d'Henri II Plantegenêt (1145–1189) et l'éthique politique (Geneva, 1977), pp. 92–93.

76   Nederman, *John of Salisbury*, pp. 38–39, quoting Beryl Smalley, *The Becket Conflict and the Schools: A Study of Intellectuals in Politics* (Oxford, 1973), pp. 107–108.

77   *The Later Letters*, p. xlvii: "In 1176 John entered his cathedral through the royal portal – all that now survives of Chartres Cathedral as John knew it – to end his days in suitable dignity and peace."

78   As for any detective work of the kind, the starting point here was Henri Stein, *Bibliographie générale des cartulaires français ou relatifs à l'histoire de France* (Paris, 1907). Not all references

John's elevation to Chartres was a result of patronage, and indirectly of his extended network within the ecclesiastical and lay elites of Northern France. During his years of exile, he often boasted of his connections at the highest level, while he was putting them at the service of Thomas Becket.[79] Among his correspondents was one of the brightest stars of the French Church, William White Hands.[80] William, the brother of the counts of Champagne and Blois and the brother-in-law of Louis VII, was bishop of Chartres from 1165 and archbishop of Sens from 1168; he stayed nominally in charge of the see of Chartres, where the canons sang his praise in their necrology in spite – or possibly because – of his pluralism which made him an absentee prelate.[81] Early in 1176 he became archbishop of Reims; the change of province made his position at Chartres untenable, and a new prelate had to be found quickly. John would be the chosen one.

What was Chartres in the late 1170s? From an ecclesiastical point of view it was a giant diocese of about 200 by 160 kilometres, bordered by the Seine to the north and the Loire to the south, very close to Paris on one side and neighbouring the Norman dioceses of Sées, Evreux and Rouen on the other;[82] it included Blois and Vendôme; as with most pre-1789 dioceses its exact borders are difficult to determine.[83] Even though John failed to become an English bishop, which might have been his ambition, it was no small achievement to reign over the see of Chartres. Fulbert and Ivo had distinguished themselves in the same

---

given by Stein for the diocese of Chartres have been explored here. Some refer to extracts of lost manuscripts collected in the 17th and 18th centuries; those would need to be investigated to establish a full inventory of John's surviving acts. See ibid., nos. 1402 (Saint-Robert de Fossard, a dependence of Josaphat), 1579 (Gohory), 1773 (La Brosse), 3343 (Saint-Chéron) and 3602 (Saint-Vincent-au-Bois).

79   See Julie Barrau, "Jean de Salisbury, intermédiaire entre Thomas Becket et la cour capétienne?," in Martin Aurell and Noël-Yves Tonnerre, eds., *Plantagenêts et Capétiens: confrontations et heritages* (Turnhout, 2006), pp. 505–516.

80   See *The Later Letters*, nos. 307, pp. 742–749 and 308, pp. 748–753.

81   See *Cartulaire de Notre-Dame de Chartres*, vol. 3, pp. 201–202.

82   See article "Chartres" in the *Dictionnaire d'histoire et de géographie ecclésiastiques*, vol. 12 (Paris, 1953). For a description of the delineations of the diocese, see *Cartulaire de Notre-Dame de Chartres*, vol. 1, pp. xlvi–l. Its abnormal size had been long noticed when a diocese of Blois was carved out of it in 1697; see Jules Gallerand, "L'érection de l'évêché de Blois (1697)," *Revue d'histoire de l'Église de France* 42 (1956), 175–228. In 1790 the map of dioceses was thoroughly changed to coincide with the new *départements* created by the Revolution.

83   See Jacques Dubois, "La carte des diocèses de France avant la Révolution," *Annales. Économies Sociétés Civilisations* 20 (1965), 680–691, who explains why it is difficult to establish precise maps. See the tentative maps on inserts between pp. 686 et 687.

office,[84] and his immediate predecessor was William White Hands, brother of the counts of Champagne and Chartres and brother-in-law of Louis VII, who had ruled mostly *in absentia* for twelve years. The less well-known Geoffrey of Lèves (1116–1149), scion of an influential Chartrain family, is also worth mentioning: he had such a high profile that he could step in when his metropolitan, the archbishop of Sens, was unavailable to consecrate abbots and fellow bishops.[85] Whatever the final verdict on the question of the schools of Chartres, intellectual interests were lively there, and the nearby cities of Orléans and Tours also had active schools, with a particular focus on the study of *dictamen* and classics.[86] In short, Chartres was no backwater.

In political terms, it was on the French side of the border between the Capetian and the Plantagenet *mouvances*. It also occupied a liminal position in the ecclesiastical province of Sens, as well as in the Blois-Champagne territories. In all respects, John's new diocese was on a border.[87] As Kathleen Thompson has shown about the nearby Perche, those frontier regions were

---

84   The latter, a towering and rather forbidding figure in the French Church, fought for episcopal autonomy against king and count. In reprisal, Theobald IV of Blois-Chartres sacked the episcopal palace when Ivo died in 1116. See André Chédeville, *Chartres et ses campagnes au Moyen Âge: XIᵉ au XIIIᵉ siècle* (Paris, 1973), pp. 266–267.

85   Lindy Grant, "Geoffrey of Lèves, Bishop of Chartres: 'Famous Wheeler and Dealer in Secular Business'," in Rolf Große, ed., *Suger en question. Regards croisés sur Saint-Denis* (Munich, 2004), pp. 45–56. Geoffrey consecrated the new bishop of Auxerre in 1136 and the new abbot of Morigny in 1144; Lindy Grant suggests that, although that remarkable role as vice-archbishop might be explained by the prelate's personal status, the see of Chartres certainly had a "special prestige" (ibid., p. 50).

86   See for instance Charles Vulliez, "L'apprentissage de la rédaction des documents diplomatiques à travers l'ars dictaminis' français (et spécialement ligérien) du XIIᵉ siècle," in Germano Gualdo, ed., *Cancelleria e cultura nel Medio Evo* (Vatican, 1990), pp. 77–95, and Richard Rouse, "Florilegia and Latin Classical Authors in Twelfth- and Thirteenth-Century Orleans," *Viator* 10 (1979), 131–160. Recently Patricia Stirnemann and Dominique Poirel have expressed doubts about the Orléans origins of the *Florilegium Gallicum* and the *Florilegium Angelicum*; they suggest that the latter might have come from the scriptorium of Montiéramey, and associate John of Salisbury himself with the former (in that case with what may appear like limited evidence). See Patricia Stirnemann and Dominique Poirel, "Nicolas de Montiéramey, Jean de Salisbury et deux florilèges d'auteurs antiques," *Revue d'histoire des textes*, nouvelle série 1 (2006), 173–188. On the use of the *Gallicum* by Thomas Becket and his entourage, see Anne Duggan, "Classical Quotations and Allusions in the Correspondence of Thomas Becket: An Investigation of Their Sources," *Viator* 32 (2001), 1–22.

87   On the borders of the Angevin Empire, see Daniel Power, *The Norman Frontier in the Twelfth and Early Thirteenth Centuries* (Cambridge, 2004).

rich both in dangers and opportunities.[88] The diocese of Chartres saw some of the tensest moments of the confrontation between the kings. Various meetings and battles took place in Fréteval, and the count of Vendôme, John, was a staunch supporter of Henry II throughout the first decades of his reign.[89] It is also clear that important ties existed between lay and ecclesiastical elites on both sides of what was, in many respects, an elusive border.[90] Many Normans and Bretons lived in Chartres, reinforcing the connections with Plantagenet continental lands.[91]

The relationships between bishops and their chapter could become spectacularly bad; in England, those of the monks of Christ Church, Canterbury, with Thomas Becket were icy and full of mutual bitterness[92]; with Archbishop Baldwin, about twenty years later, they turned into an open war partly about the remains and the booming cult of Baldwin's murdered predecessor.[93] In general, tensions and power struggles were common.[94] In Chartres the situation

---

88   Kahtleeen Thompson, *Power and Border Lordship in Medieval France. The County of the Perche, 1000–1226* (Woodbridge, 2002), pp. 86–114. She shows for instance how Rotrou of Perche could both have sided with the Young King in 1173–4 and re-establish fairly promptly afterwards a good and mutually profitable relationship with Henry II.

89   See Dominique Barthélémy, *La Société dans le comté de Vendôme de l'an mil au XIVᵉ siècle* (Paris, 1993), pp. 728–732.

90   On the borders of Normandy see Daniel Power, esp. his *The Norman Frontier*. An example of connections between Chartrain and Plantagenet territories is the long list of the possessions and priories of the abbey of Tiron across the Channel as confirmed by Alexander III in 1175 6 (*Cartulaire de l'abbaye de la Sainte-Trinité de Tiron*, ed. Lucien Merlet (Chartres, 1883), pp. 98–102).

91   See Chédeville, *Chartres et ses campagnes*, pp. 98–105.

92   See Southern, *The Monks of Canterbury*.

93   The fight is documented in detail, on the monks' side, by a colossal letter-collection gathered immediately after its (temporary) resolution. See *Epistolae Cantuarienses*, ed. William Stubbs (London, 1865).

94   On relationships between bishops and canons in England, see Everett U. Crosby, *Bishop and Chapter in 12th-Century England. A Study of the Mensa Episcopalis* (Cambridge, 1994), as well as Julia Barrow, "Cathedrals, Provosts and Prebends: A Comparison of Twelfth-Century German and English Practice," *Journal of Ecclesiastical History* 37 (1986), 536–564. No survey exists for the situation in France, and prosopographical studies have focused mostly on the late Middle Ages. There are case studies, such as Pierre-Clément Timbal, "Évêque de Paris et chapitre de Notre-Dame: la juridiction dans la cathédrale au Moyen Âge," *Revue d'histoire de l'Église de France* 50 (1964), 47–72, Joseph Avril, *Le Gouvernement des évêques et la vie religieuse dans le diocèse d'Angers (1148–1240)*, 2 vols. (Paris, 1985), and, relevant here but very dated, Louis Amiet, *Essai sur l'organisation du chapitre cathédral de Chartres du XIᵉ au XVIIIᵉ siècle* (Paris, 1922).

seemed by contrast irenic; John was given a resounding eulogy by the canons after he died, as we shall see. However, he arrived in a chapter used to a level of autonomy that the absentee bishop William White Hands could hardly have kept in check. The chapter was richly endowed and was in the process of getting back direct control of its domains, which had been unsatisfactorily entrusted to lay provosts.[95] The bishop, although less richly endowed, still had a considerable income at his disposal, mostly from lands in the south-western part of the diocese.[96] To some extent the chapter must also have supervised the schools. On a more colourful note, it is also known that some of its members were caught renting their houses to prostitutes and gamblers.[97] In the artificial cartulary of Notre-Dame of Chartres put together by Lucien Merlet and Eugène de Lépinois, one finds documents that are much more about the chapter than the bishops.[98] It shows that the canons were very jealous of their prerogatives[99]; of the six acts edited there that were produced during John's episcopate not one emanates from him.[100]

---

95 An initiative of bishop William, that transfer was confirmed by Alexander III in 1171; see *Cartulaire de Notre-Dame de Chartres*, vol. 1, no. 86, pp. 188–191. The pope took advantage of that opportunity to remind the canons of the utmost importance of being in residence, a topic that he had addressed two years earlier with the same audience and would go back to a few years later (ibid., nos. 77, p. 177 and 92, p. 199).

96 See Chédeville, *Chartres et ses campagnes*. A list of the bishop's property, although drawn much later (1300), nevertheless gives some idea of the extent and nature of that income: see *Cartulaire de Notre-Dame de Chartres*, vol. 2, no. 385, pp. 239–245 ("Hii sunt redditus episcopatus Carnotensis").

97 There is a letter from Urban III forbidding the rental of canonical houses to *joculatoribus, aleatoribus, cauponibus et mulieribus turpibus*; see *Inventaire-sommaire des archives départementales antérieures à 1790. Archives ecclésiastiques. Série G*, vol. 1, ed. Lucien Merlet (Chartres, 1890), p. 186.

98 *Cartulaire de Notre-Dame de Chartres*. Their main sources were the post-1194-fire chapter archives and from extracts of two copies of the so-called *Livre des privilèges de l'Église de Chartres* (BnF, MSS Lat. 10,094 and 10,095).

99 See for instance ibid., vol. 1, no. 80 pp. 179–180. It is the sentence pronounced against Hugh of Gallardon, who had two "men of Notre-Dame" upon whom he had no rights blinded and emasculated. Even though the maimed men received some form of compensation, it is obvious that the canons saw themselves as the main victims of the attack, and obtained the greater part of the fine.

100 Two of them are addressed to him, by Alexander III: no. 91, p. 198, which confirms the bishop's possession of the church of Saint-Georges in Vendôme, and no. 92, p. 199 to John and the chapter about the obligation of residence for anyone given an *honor Carnotensis ecclesie*.

Turning now to the circumstances of John's elevation to the see of Chartres, we find that the decision to make him William's successor is fairly well documented. Ralph Diceto has left the fullest account of the events.[101] On 22 July 1176, the canons of Chartres cathedral elected John; that was at the instigation of William White Hands and with the support of Louis VII. The explicit motive was his former companionship with the recent and glorious martyr, Thomas of Canterbury.[102] A distinguished delegation from the chapter – the dean, the chanter and the chancellor – crossed over to Canterbury to find their bishop-elect, carrying letters from the French king and Archbishop William, as well as their own, which was appropriately pompous.[103] John was ordained in the metropolitan church of Sens on 8 August by Maurice of Sully, bishop of Paris, and solemnly enthroned in his cathedral a week later, on the feast of the Assumption. His election is mentioned by chroniclers, for instance Roger of Howden, who also noted the Becket connection.[104] That he owed his mitre to his former master was not just acknowledged but proudly exhibited by John during his four years at Chartres: in his acts he decided to style himself "Johannes, divina dignatione et meritis sancti martyris Thome Carnotensis ecclesie minister humilis." Such an *intitulatio* would have been unusual enough to be highly noticeable.[105]

A letter of Celestine III in 1195 reveals that the canons of Chartres had a long-established habit of making any new bishop swear that he would respect the uses, customs, and privileges of the *Carnotensis ecclesia*.[106] It is highly likely that John had to jump through that particular hoop in August 1176, and that he

---

101   *Radulfi de Diceto decani Lundoniensis opera historica. The Historical Works of Master Ralph de Diceto Dean of London*, ed. William Stubbs, 2 vols. (London, 1876), vol. 1, pp. 410–412.

102   As Louis VII made clear in his letter of congratulations: "tum beati Thomae martyris consideratione, cujus familiaritatem meritis vestris meruistis adipisci, tum morum et scientiae vestrae contemplatione." See *Recueil des Historiens des Gaules et de la France*, vol. 16 (new ed., Paris, 1878), p. 163, repr. in PL 199, cols. 374–375.

103   Ibid.

104   *Chronica magistri Rogeri de Hovedene*, ed. William Stubbs, 4 vols. (London, 1868–71), vol. 2, p. 100: "Eodem anno magister Johannes Saresberiensis, quondam clericus et familiaris beati Thomae Cantuariensis martyris, factus est episcopus Carnotensis."

105   John's predecessors, for instance, chose much less noteworthy *intitulationes*: "Goslinus, Dei gratia, Carnotensis episcopus," "Robertus, Dei gratia, Carnotensis episcopus." This is also true of neighbouring prelates, such as Manasses of Orleans ("Manasses, Dei gratia, Aurelianensis ecclesie minister humilis") or Maurice of Sully, bishop of Paris ("Mauricius, Dei gratia, Parisiensis episcopus").

106   *Cartulaire de Notre-Dame de Chartres*, no. 125 p. 246: "frater noster episcopus Carnotensis, de antiqua et approbata consuetudine ecclesie vestre, vobis juramento tenetur astrictus ad antiquas et rationabiles et precipue privilegiatas ejusdem ecclesie consuetudines fideliter observandas." Apparently bishops had to swear not only once but twice.

was asked to do so by the dean of the chapter, Geoffrey of Berou, who had by then been in office for more than ten years and who would outlive John by two decades.[107] John must have shown some political skills to have left a good impression with those men.

To a large extent we know who they were. Some are mere names,[108] but others show a group solidly grounded in networks of kin and patronage. Archdeacons were supposed to be the bishop's men, not the chapter's. However, the archdeacons in place in 1176 were men whose status depended more on their long hold on their office and on their family connections than on the newcomer. The most senior of the six archdeacons was Milo of Lèves, brother of the late bishop Goscelin, who had been archdeacon since 1149;[109] Walter, a nephew of another former bishop, Robert the Breton, had been the archdeacon of Pinserais since 1164.[110] Possibly the best connected of all was the chancellor, Bouchard. His parents were Hugh of Puiset and Agnes of Blois; that made him the nephew of King Stephen and Theobald IV, count of Blois. His brothers were Hugh, bishop of Durham, and Evrard of Puiset, viscount of Chartres; Evrard appears as a mediator in one of John's acts.[111] Related to the highest aristocratic circles, Bouchard was also an ambitious man. He competed to become archdeacon of Orléans with Henry, count of Dreux, who later became bishop of Orléans; he went as far as travelling to the papal court to plead his cause, and eventually won. The story of his journey to Rome, as told by Helinand of Froidmont, shows him in a rather negative light.[112] Bouchard must have been a conspicuous presence in the chapter.

There is no evidence that John tried to change the personnel of the chapter during his four years at Chartres, but there are indications that he developed his own staff. One Robert *de Pignola* featured as the bishop's chaplain in a witness list.[113] More significantly, it seems that he had his own chancellor, distinct

---

107   See Lucien et René Merlet, *Les Dignitaires de l'Église Notre-Dame de Chartres* (*Archives du diocèse de Chartres*, V) (Chartres, 1900), p. 14.

108   For instance Richer the chanter (ibid., p. 34), Gilbert of Tardais the sub-dean (p. 52), and William of Beauvoir the *camerarius* (p. 87).

109   Ibid., pp. 128–129.

110   Ibid., pp. 162–163. He was possibly the "G. archidiaconus uester" described by Peter of Celle as his dear friend and relative. See *The Letters of Peter of Celle*, pp. 678–680.

111   *Cartulaire de Marmoutier pour le Dunois*, ed. Émile Mabille (Châteaudun, 1874), no. 189, p. 179: "mediante domino Ebrardo de Puteolo."

112   PL 112, col. 731.

113   *Marmoutier, Cartulaire Blésois*, ed. Charles Métais (Blois, 1889–91), p. 164: "Roberto de Pignola capellano nostro."

from the chapter's. Unfortunately that man, a certain Hugo, remains rather elusive.[114]

Such a context might have led to a very quiet and subdued episcopate. The reasons of John's death are not known – he was after all old but not very old, about 65 years old or so –but the fact that he died at Chartres after a short time in office might suggest a likely slow pace of business. The surviving evidence, which has been under-studied until now, tells another story altogether.

In the *Policraticus*, about two decades earlier, John had set high standards for prelates. If anything the reforming impulse had gathered impetus since then, and John attended the solemn call to reform that was the Third Lateran Council in 1179.[115] There he was part of a 59-strong delegation of French bishops, but he did not blend into anonymity, given that his forceful intervention about the excessive creation of new laws became a talking point.[116] That last Roman journey also reminds us how involved John had been since the days of Eugenius III in the growing importance of the popes in ecclesiastical and secular politics, as both the *Historia pontificalis* and many of his exile letters testify.

One well-known and crucial aspect of increased papal influence is the constantly burgeoning body of decretals issued by the pope in answer to questions, requests and appeals from the whole of Western Europe. Charles Duggan has shown the importance of these decretals, as well as the central place of

---

114   In his *Les Écoles de Chartres au Moyen Âge (du Vᵉ au XVIᵉ siècle)* (Paris, 1895), p. 284, A. Clerval tantalizingly alludes to a charter of John of Salisbury in which can be found "Hugo, capellanus et cancellarius Joannis episcopi," without giving any further reference. We have not been able to find this act.

115   For a detailed analysis of John's involvement in the council, see Jan van Laarhoven, "Non jam decreta, sed evangelium! Jean de Salisbury au Latran III," in Mario Fois, Vincenzo Monachino, Felix Litva, eds., *Dalla Chiesa antica alla chiesa moderna. Miscellanea per il Cinquantesimo della Facolta di Storia Ecclesiastica della Pontificia Universita Gregoriana* (Rome, 1983), pp. 107–119.

116   Peter the Chanter told of the episode in his *Verbum abbreviatum*, PL 205, col. 235: "...ait Joannes Carnotensis: Absit, inquit, nova condi, vel plurima veterum reintingi et innovari. (...) Timeamus ne dicat nobis Dominus : Bene irritum facitis praeceptum Dei, ut traditionem vestram servetis. Tales enim in vanum colunt me." The Gospel reference is to Mk 7:7–9: "in vanum autem me colunt, docentes doctrinas, et præcepta hominum. Relinquentes enim mandatum Dei, tenetis traditionem hominum, baptismata urceorum et calicum : et alia similia his facitis multa. Et dicebat illis : Bene irritum facitis præceptum Dei, ut traditionem vestram servetis."

England in their collection and diffusion.[117] John's uneasy feelings about the *noua condita* did not seem to apply to papal letters: he himself asked the pope for advice on the best way to fulfil his episcopal duties and received in response a long decretal from Alexander III.

Cum sacrosancta is an answer to a very detailed list of questions, which suggests that John took a full part in the "rush to consult the Apostolic See" of which Alexander III was a key protagonist.[118] John gathered his requests in one letter for the sake of convenience more than coherence, inasmuch as the thirteen items address diverse topics.[119] The initial paragraph looks into the status of judge delegates: the pope establishes their superior authority, as *uices* of the pope, over local bishops. Further on, some questions express the concerns of a diocesan bishop; for instance the last two enquire about whether ordinations should happen on feast days (the answer is no). On the sensitive matter of violent behaviour against clerics, Alexander III reiterates that women and other legal minors can be absolved by their diocesan bishops. Provisions are also made for the powerful and the delicate, who could not sustain the trip to the curia; details of their cases should be sent off to the Pope and instructions sent back. However, if such people used heir authority to induce other people to harm clerics they should be immediately sent off to the apostolic seat. This last topic might indicate that John had mellowed, or become more realistic, since his years of exile: then he had condemned any form of *acceptio personarum*, which means the acceptance that people should receive different legal treatments according to their standing in life.[120]

Some elements in the decretal were possibly more specific to Chartres, or maybe to the scholarly bishop's particular interests. There are two questions

---

117 See, among other things, Charles Duggan, *Twelfth-century Decretal Collections and Their Importance in English History* (London, 1963); idem, "Decretals of Alexander III to England," in Filippo Liotta, ed. *Miscellanea Rolando Bandinelli, Papa Alessandro III* (Sienna, 1986), pp. 87–151; idem, "Papal judges delegate and the making of the New Law in the twelfth century, "in Thomas Bisson, ed., *Cultures of Power: Lordship, Status, and Process in Twelfth-Century* Europe (Philadelphia, 1995), pp. 172–199.

118 The phrase is from Anne Duggan, in her recent analysis of Alexander III's legal legacy, "Master of the Decretals: A Reassessment of Alexander III's Contribution to Canon Law," in Peter D. Clarke and Anne J. Duggan, eds., *Pope Alexander III (1159–81). The Art of Survival* (Farnham, 2012), pp. 365–417.

119 For a short description of *Cum sacrosancta* see Duggan, ibid., p. 379.

120 John expressed his disgust at the widespread toleration of *acceptatio personarum* in three letters written in 1167 to three cardinals; see Letters 229, p. 402, 234, p. 430 and 235, p. 434. He also described Becket showing his perfection as prelate when he returned to Canterbury when he dismissed all forms of *acceptio personarum*; see Letter 304, p. 722.

about students and their masters (one about discipline). These two paragraphs did not find their way into later systematic decretal collections, possibly because the same issues are covered by *Sicut dignum*, sent to Bartholomew of Exeter in 1172, which appears just after *Cum sacrosancta* in the "Worcester collection."[121] The *Collectio Wigorniensis*, which features the earliest appearance (in full) of *Cum sacrosancta*, names the recipient as *Ioh(ann)is*, which shows that this bishop of Chartres was our John.[122] The collection was completed by 1181; the compiler must therefore have had an almost instant access to *Cum sacrosancta*, which would have been among the last items received before the *Wigorniensis* was organised by subjects.

John had been associated in the 1170s with the English prelates whose courts are known to have prompted the earliest English decretal collections: Roger of Worcester, Baldwin of Ford, who was Roger's successor and an old friend of John, Richard of Canterbury, in whose entourage we have already found our future bishop, and of course Bartholomew of Exeter.[123] Even though we cannot be sure how a copy of *Cum sacrosancta* reached Worcester from Chartres, it is quite likely that John was aware of the compilation being made there and took enough interest in it to volunteer a copy of the pope's letter himself. This hypothesis is made stronger by the fact that he knew one of the possible authors of the *Wigorniensis*, master Simon Lovell, and could have met the other one, master Silvester, who was at the service of Roger of Worcester.[124]

This interest not just in getting the pope's *responsa*,[125] but also in contributing to the very novel effort made in England towards collecting the new papal law does not sit very comfortably with John's outburst against the new law during the Lateran Council. Rather than resolving this contradiction in an artificial

---

121   Londres, British Library, MS Royal 10 A ii, fol. 51v.

122   Ibid., fol. 50v: "Ioh(ann)i carnot(ensi) ep(iscop)o." *Cum sacrosancta* covers fols. 50v–51v.

123   See Charles Duggan, "Decretals of Alexander III to England," in *Miscellanea Rolando Bandinelli*. On Roger of Worcester, see the very good study by Mary G. Cheney, *Roger Bishop of Worcester 1164–1179* (Oxford, 1980). On Bartholomew, see Adrian Morey, *Bartholomew of Exeter, Bishop and Canonist* (Cambridge, 1937). On John and Exeter, see *supra* p. 115.

124   In 1166–7 he wrote to his old friend Simon (*de tua dilectione (...) a multis diebus concepta fiducia*) to ask him to introduce favourably the bearer of the letter to bishop Roger. See Letter 198, pp. 284–287.

125   Another letter possibly addressed to John by Alexander III, which found its way into decretal collections, is *De cetero noveris*, addressed to a bishop of Chartres. See *Quinque libri decretalium Gregorii IX* (*Liber extra*), c.5, I, 36.

way, it may be better simply to see in John the conflicted opinions that men of his generation are famous for.[126]

Even though John's episcopate has been little documented so far, this is not, as has sometimes been supposed, due to a lack of surviving material. It has been possible to gather from various sources, mostly scattered, more than twenty different acts of John; a few more are alluded to in later sources but have stayed undiscovered to date.[127] Over a period of just four years, this places him among the active prelates of his generation. The bishops of Arras studied by Benoît-Michel Tock have averages of between 2.7 and 6 surviving acts per year in the second half of the 12th century[128]; John's is around 4.5.[129]

John's known actions as bishop of Chartres fall into three categories: as diocesan bishop, a role that, as one would expect, prompted the largest body of acts, as papal delegate, and also as an arbiter in his own right, outside his diocese and without papal delegation. This last category shows a man whose opinion and prestige were valued and called upon. His diocesan activities went from the mundane and petty to more ambitious, and possibly more politically dangerous, ventures. Protecting the rights of his Church against infringements was a core duty, and John seems to have been a satisfactory bishop in that respect, even though the powerful cathedral chapter took a large part of that task in their own hands as their charters and acts show. The canons found a like-minded man in John: in the necrology, after they had listed his personal

---

126 The word "dilemma" has been used twice in monograph titles about contemporary clerics, by John Cotts about Peter of Blois and Caroline Schriber about Arnulf of Lisieux. See John D. Cotts, *The Clerical dilemma. Peter of Blois and Literate Culture in the Twelfth Century* (Washington D.C., 2009), and Carolyn P. Schriber, *The Dilemma of Arnulf of Lisieux: New Ideas Versus Old Ideals* (Bloomington, 1990).

127 For instance the list of bishops made by the editors of the *Cartulaire de Notre-Dame de Chartres* in their introduction (p. xxxviii) gives under John's name "charte du prieuré de Chamars 1177." Saint-Martin de Chamars was a Marmoutier priory, set on the right bank of the Loir river outside Châteaudun. It is indeed very likely that John would have intervened in the priory business. The only standing candidate is an 1177 *convenientia* between Ursio of Fréteval and Marmoutier about "aquam Castriduni," which involved the prior of Chamars. John confirmed that agreement with his seal ("Diffinita etiam fuit apud Carnotum in presentia Johannis, Carnotensis episcopi, qui similiter eandem convenientiam confirmari fecit munimine sigilli sui."). See *Cartulaire de Marmoutier pour le Dunois*, no. 186, pp. 176–177.

128 Benoît Michel Tock, *Les Chartes des évêques d'Arras (1093–1203)* (Paris, 1991), p. xxvi.

129 This number is obtained by taking into account the same criteria as Tock's, and only includes acts of which John was the main issuer. There are at least ten more where he appears in a more minor role.

qualities and his penitential practices, the first action they described and praised was the "liberation" of a house belonging to the bishops from the oats the provost of Ballieul stored there.[130]

The new bishop also had to arbitrate internal disputes in Chartres, such as a disagreement between the nearby canons of Saint-Jean-en-Vallée and the church of L'Aumône, located *intra muros*, about the burials in the L'Aumône graveyard; this affair also required papal intervention.[131] Equally local was a conflict between the monks of Saint-Père of Chartres and the priests of the parish of Saint-Hilaire; we know of John's intervention through an act of his successor, Peter of Celle, transcribed in a 1236 *inspeximus*. It shows that the monks claimed that John had granted them, in writing, the oblations made to the parish church, to the priests' indignation and denial. A compromise was reached in this clash between venerable *consuetudo* and new written rights, but that again required papal intervention, through such luminaries as the bishop of Paris and the abbot of Sainte-Geneviève.[132]

The bulk of his surviving acts as diocesan prelate consists of confirmations of grants to various churches and monastic communities, or of confirmations of agreements resolving disputes. He used his authority to back up grants to churches. The recipients were sometimes long-established communities, such as Saint-Père de Chartres, which received an annual grant of grain from a knight called Gonherius,[133] but also flourishing Cistercian houses such as the Vaux-de-Cernay to which are given, in two different acts, a house near Saint-Arnoult by Guerri of Rochefort,[134] and land and tithes by a certain Adam and

130   *Cartulaire de Notre Dame de Chartres*, p. 202: "…qui domum episcopi ab avena, quam in ea preapositus Bailloli habebat, liberavit." That must be Ballieul-l'Evêque, about 4 kms from Chartres.

131   *Cartulaire de Saint Jean-en-Vallée de Chartres*, ed. René Merlet (Chartres, 1906), no. 102 (brief from Alexander III to John of Salisbury) and no. 103 (John's sentence), pp. 54–55. Saint-Jean, founded in the 1020s, had been transformed into a community of regular canons under the influence of Ivo of Chartres.

132   *Cartulaire de l'abbaye de Saint-Père de Chartres*, ed. Benjamin Guérard (Paris, 1840), vol. 2, no. 110, p. 689: "…cum ipsi monachi hoc privilegio felicis memorie J, quondam Carnotensis episcopi, probare niterentur, presbiteri vero eas sibi de consuetudine competere in contrarium allegarent (…). Dominus itaque papa utrique parti consulere intendens, venerabili fratri nostro M., Parisiensi episcopo, et…abbati sancte Genovefe, causam delegavit audiendam." The Parisian bishop and abbot were Maurice of Sully and Étienne of Tournai.

133   *Cartulaire de l'abbaye de Saint-Père de Chartres*, vol. 2, no. 48, p. 656.

134   *Cartulaire de l'abbaye Notre-Dame des Vaux-de-Cernay, de l'ordre de Cîteaux, au diocèse de Paris*, ed. Lucien Merlet et Auguste Moutié (Paris, 1857), vol. 1, no. 48, p. 65: "Johannes, divina dignatione et meritis sancti Thome (…) donationem et concessionem quam Guerri de Rupe Forti monachis de Sarneio dedit et concessit, scilicet domum quam Girebertus

his widowed sister Guiburc, a grant that was in fact more of a sale.[135] John also lent his weight to support new foundations, such as the community of Grandmontines at Les Moulineaux in the Rambouillet forest.[136] He bolstered that *donatio* with an unusual (for him, that is) amount of threats against potential greedy transgressors, which probably reflects the fragile nature of a recently created house.[137]

His support for monastic communities is also clear from when he arbitrated a dispute between the canons of Saint-Cloud, near Paris, and his own archdeacon of Dunois, Walter, about the church of Villemaur. The act itself has not survived, as far as we are aware, although the editors of *Gallia Christiana*, where we have found mention of it, wrote that it was in the cartulary of Saint-Avit (of Orléans).[138] The story seems plausible enough, though, given that the

---

Froeline de eo tenebat apud Sanctum Ernulfum et hospitem in ea manentem, libere et quiete tenendam et habendam, tam scripti quam sigilli nostri munimine confirmavimus." John reinforces by refering to it explicitly ("fidem litterarum Simonis de Rupe Forti secuti"), a previous confirmation by a layman, Simon of Rochefort, certainly a relative of the donor (also edited: ibid., no. 47, pp. 64–65).

135 Ibid., no. 46, pp. 63–64. The donors ("notificari volumus quod Adam de Capella et Guiburc soror ejus dederunt Deo ac monachis sancte Marie de Sarnaio, in perpetuam elemosinam, quicquid in terra de Proverleu possidebant") were given retribution by the monks ("Pro hac autem elemosina recepit predictus Adam cum uxore et filia, ex karitate monachorum, C libras parisienses minus C solidis, et Guiburc soror ejus cum liberis suis C libras ejusdem monete"), as had been established by earlier acts (see nos. 31 and 31 bis, pp. 48–51). The grant was repeated by Guiburc's sons in the 1180s, probably when they reached adulthood; the then bishop of Chartres refered to there is John (no. 67, pp. 83–84: "tempore predecessoris nostri Johannes episcopi").

136 *Recueil de Chartes et pièces relatives au prieuré des Moulineaux et à la châtellenie de Poigny*, ed. Auguste Moutié (Paris, 1846), no. 3, p. 3: "Johannes diuina dignatione et meritis sancti Thome (...) Ego J. carnotensis ecclesie minister humilis gratam habens et approbans donationem quam nobilis uir Joscelinus de Alneolo fecit fratribus de Grandi monte qui sunt in Molinello..."

137 Ibid.: "Statuens quod si quis huic pagine ausu temerario contraire (sic) presumpserit, indignationem omnipotentis dei, se noverit incursurum." On the early years of Notre-Dame des Moulineaux, later attached to the priory of Louye near Dourdan, see the *Recueil*, introduction, pp. xliv–liii.

138 *Gallia christiana*, col. 1147: "Anno 1178. qui episcopatus ejus secundus dicitur in chartulario sancti Aviti, ecclesiam de Villamauri canonicis S. Clodoaldi adjudicavit contra Wauterium archidiaconum Dunensem." This is corroborated by the fact that the archdeacon of Dunois was indeed a Walter; see René and Lucien Merlet, *Les Dignitaires de l'Église de Chartres*, p. 145. Walter is a witness in one of John's known acts; see *Cartulaire de Sainte-Croix d'Orléans (814–1300)*, ed. Eugène Jarry and Joseph Thillier (Paris, 1906), pp. 163–166.

FIGURE 1
Charter of John of Salisbury, Bishop of Chartres,
confirming the grant of a house to the abbey of the
Vaux-de-Cernay (1177).
COURTESY OF THE ARCHIVES DÉPARTEMENTALES DES
YVELINES, 45 H 30.

obituary of Saint-Cloud kept the memory of Odo, count of Blois and Chartres. He was praised for having given to the canons all he had in Dunois, including among other things Villemaur and its church.[139] It sounds likely that successive archdeacons of Dunois felt that Villemaur church was not Odo's to give, but John decided otherwise. How that affected his relationships with his archdeacon is anybody's guess. It certainly suggests a firmly established prelate.

It is the confirmation by John of an agreement between the chapter of Sainte-Croix d'Orléans and Hubert of Péronville (ibid., pp. 158–160): "Actum publice Carnoti, astantibus in presentia nostra Gaufredo decano, Gis[leberto subdecano], Burc[ardo] concellario (sic), Galterio Dunensi archidiacono." There is no trace of John's intervention in the Saint-Cloud case in the existing edition of the Saint-Avit cartulary, *Cartulaire du chapitre de Saint-Avit d'Orléans*, ed. G. Vignat (Orléans, 1886).

139   *Obituaires de la province de Sens*, vol. 1 (*Diocèses de Sens et de Paris*, part 2), ed. Auguste Molinier (Paris, 1902), p. 813: "Obiit Odo (...) qui dedit ecclesie Sancti Clodoaldi pro anima sua in pago Dunensi, absolutum ab omni consuetudine, quicquid habebat, in Villamauri cum ecclesia et in Chatonisvilla cum servis et ancillis."

Similarly, he seems to have taken a firm stance in a bitter dispute between the regular canons of Notre-Dame of Bourg-Moyen in Blois and the newly created community of secular canons at Saint-Sauveur in the same city. The former protested against the new school and the new cemetery that the brethren of Saint-Sauveur had created. They appealed to Alexander III with the support of the prestigious abbot of Sainte-Geneviève of Paris, Stephen of Tournai, who described the new canons in spiteful terms.[140] We know of John's involvement mostly through letters of Peter of Blois, who was typically emphatic in his praise.[141]

Collaboration with local lords is apparent. A certain Joscelin of Auneau was the donor in the act about Les Moulineaux; he also gives his blessing and support to the grant of Adam *de Capella* and his sister to the Vaux-de-Cernay.[142] He arbitrated a conflict between Marmoutier and one Walter Vittin, who had disposed too freely of the monks' lands in Notonville.[143] The involvement of Evrard of Puiset in the dispute, already noted, is interesting, since one of his ancestors had given half of Notonville to Marmoutier; this shows how persistent influence could linger even where direct property had been relinquished.[144] John seems to have been aware of this fluid situation and turned it to his advantage to reach a settlement.

There is more evidence that he was probably a dedicated and fastidious prelate. The territory of La Lande had been given to the Cistercian monastery of Fontaine-les-Blanches *ad opus grangiae* by a predecessor of

---

140 See *Lettres d'Étienne de Tournai*, ed. Jules Desilve (Paris, 1893), Letter 81, pp. 95–96 ("Oritur iuxta eos, et utinam non contra eos, nova quedam plantatio singularium seu secularium canonicorum: quam utrum Pater celestis plantaverit, necdum scimus"); and Letter 114, pp. 132–133 ("Novum sibi cimiterium, novos magistratus scolarum, novas occasiones venandi parrochianos alienos sibi concedi postulant.").

141 PL 207, col. 342: "Clerus Blesensis, coelestis arbitrii dispensatione proscriptus, vagus erat et profugus super terram, donec eis datus est episcopus animarum suarum, qui posset compati patientibus et ex longa experientia exsulandi sciret quam humanum sit exsulibus misereri."

142 See *Recueil de Chartes et pièces relatives au prieuré des Moulineaux*, no. 3, p. 3, and *Cartulaire de l'abbaye Notre-Dame des Vaux-de-Cernay*, no. 46, p. 63: "concedente Joscelino de Alneolo, de cujus feodo predicta elemosina extat."

143 *Cartulaire de Marmoutier pour le Dunois*, no. 189, p. 179: "contentio (...) super quasdam domos (sic) et vineas, quas idem G. apud nemus Nantovillae, sine assensum eorum, emerat et construxerat."

144 On this century-long process in Notonville, see the mostly archeological study by Philippe Racinet, "Une villa, un château, un prieuré: le site de Nottonville (Eure-et-Loir)," dans Élisabeth Magnou-Nortier, ed., *Aux sources de la gestion publique*, vol. 2, *L'invasio des villae ou la villa comme enjeu de pouvoir* (Lille, 1995), pp. 313–331.

John,[145] but a layman, Peter of Candes, still had rights over a church there ("ecclesia tua"). John warned Peter that his demands (he wanted mass to be celebrated in a way that was not the usual Cistercian fashion) were excessive, and enjoined him to be satisfied with the prayers that the monks said for him and his kin's salvation.[146] Apparently John expected some resistance, given that he also wrote to Bartholomew, archbishop of Tours, to ask him to press the same matter.[147]

The political dimension of a bishop's job is sometimes palpable. The nature of John's relationships with Henry II during his decade-long involvement in the public affairs of the "Plantagenet Empire" can be guessed even if it cannot be established with certainty. As Theobald's secretary he was well-placed to witness the collaboration but also the tensions between king and archbishop.[148] As Becket's *coexsul*, if he sometimes urged the embattled prelate to moderate the phrasing of his attacks upon Henry, he also firmly turned down schemes that might have brought him back the king's favour.[149] Diffidence and bitterness reached a climactic point with the murder in December 1170 and in the following months with what was perceived by John and his fellow mourners as leniency towards the men responsible for the murder.[150] Finally, as with many of the

---

145   On the complex relationship between La Lande and Fontaine-les-Blanches, see Giles Constable, *The Reformation of the Twelfth Century* (Cambridge, 1996), p. 221.

146   The letter, edited by Edmond Martène and Ursin Durand in *Thesaurus novus anecdotorum. Tomus primus* (Paris, 1717), col. 602, was reprinted in PL 199, col. 378: "Omnis eleemosyna tanto est Deo acceptior et largitori suo fructuosior, quanto ipsius industria commodior accipienti fuerit et utilior. Hinc est quod utilitati tuae providentes consulimus, et admonemus in Domino, ut in ecclesia tua de Landa monachos de Fontanis contra formam ordinis Cisterciensis missam celebrare non compellas. Sufficiat autem devotioni tuae officium divinum quod in ipsa abbatia pro tua et praedecessorum et successorum tuorum salute celebrare monachi statuerunt." The main source for this letter, and for the early history of Fontaine is quoted by Giles Constable (see above); it is the *Historia* of abbot Peregrinus, written c. 1200. For John's letter, see *Historia monasterii Mariae de Fontanis Albis*, in *Recueil des Chroniques de Touraine*, ed. André Salmon (Tours, 1854), p. 287.

147   Martène and Durand, ibid. Peter of Candes' troubled relationship with Fontaines-les-Landes made necessary the intervention of a papal legate, Henry of Albano, in 1182; see Stefan Weiss, *Die Urkunden der päpstlichen Legaten von Leo IX. bis zu Coelestin III. (1049–1198)* (Mainz, 1995), p. 274.

148   See Anne Duggan, "Henry II, the English Church and the Papacy, 1154–76," in *Henry II. New Interpretations*, pp. 154–183.

149   See for instance Letter 164, pp. 84–87, where he explained to his brother that the terms of the "peace" offered to him by the king were disgraceful.

150   The letter written by John early in 1171 in which he described the murder of a Christ-like Becket is justly famous. The indignation of Becket's friends is obvious in many letters, in John's collection and elsewhere. See for instance Letter 307 pp. 742–749, written on behalf of them all to William White Hands.

other *eruditi Thomae*, the English Church did not offer him any prestigious office after the death of his master; the hand of Henry II was probably felt there. However, once he had become bishop of Chartres *meritis sancti martyris Thome*, John began a new chapter in his relationship with the Plantagenets.

The county of Chartres was under Blois-Champagne domination, but the diocese also encompassed the county of Vendôme, in the affairs of which Henry was deeply involved. John, the count of Vendôme, had been since the 1150s a staunch supporter of the English king.[151] As in other parts of Western France, beyond the strict limits of Plantagenet territories, Henry was sometimes considered the right person to confirm or reinforce agreements, such as when in 1185 he confirmed the customs, servitudes, and respective right of the count of Vendôme and the Vendôme abbey of La Trinité.[152] It was therefore likely that the bishop of Chartres would have direct business with the king. John, count of Vendôme, had been excommunicated by our John early in his episcopate, for serious wrongs ("injurias, dampna, concussionemque"[153]) he had inflicted on the monks of La Trinité. Three years later, the sentence was lifted by John himself after the count had appealed to the papal legate, Peter cardinal of San Grisogono.[154] The motives for mercy are, as a matter of course, the heartfelt repentance of the count and the reparations he offered to the monks. But John insists very noticeably on the royal desire that the sinner should be forgiven. The physical presence of Henry and its purpose is made clear ("presente illustri Anglorum rege et pro eo intercedente"); his displeasure at the situation transcribed ("dominus rex Anglorum doleret illum tandiu excommunicari subjaceret"), as well as the pressure he put on the count, but also on the legate and the bishop ("regiam adjecit manum"); eventually it is because of the request of the king and the monks – in that order – that the excommunication is repealed ("ad preces domni regis Anglorum et abbatis et fratrum ecclesie prefate absolutus est").[155]

---

151   See Barthélémy, *La Société dans le comté de Vendôme*, pp. 728–732.

152   *Cartulaire de la Trinité de Vendôme*, ed. Charles Métais (Paris, 1894), vol. 2, no. 578, pp. 445–449. First among the witnesses featured "filio nostro Hugone Cestriensi electo:" Hugh of Nonant, who went into exile with Becket but reconciled with the king before 1170. In 1185 he had just been elected bishop of Chester.

153   Those terms were used in 1180, when John lifted his sentence, in order to recall the reasons of the excommunication. See ibid., no. 573, pp. 439–440.

154   Ibid. Even though John explicitly refered to the legate's intervention ("ad venerabilem patrem nostrum Petrum sancte Romane ecclesie, tituli sancti Grisogoni cardinalem, apostolice sedis legatum accessit."), Peter of Pavia did not issue an act himself, which must be the explanation for this affair in Weiss, *Die Urkunden der päpstlichen Legaten*, where the cardinal's activities in 1180 are described pp. 259–260.

155   Ibid.

The impression given by the pointed emphasis put on Henry II's intervention in that case is of a rather intense moment, and possibly a confrontation. This case also also shows that John was both aware of political necessities and anything but naïve about their implications for the *libertas ecclesie* he and his co-exiles had suffered for a decade earlier.

John was also involved, as bishop, in one of the major political upsets in 12th-century France: the communes. During the summer of 1180, the bourgeois of Châteauneuf in Tours took an oath, which was understood as a conspiracy by the canons of St-Martin.[156] The oath-takers were excommunicated by John of Salisbury, who had been sent there by Alexander III.[157] The culprits stood firm and the sentence was lifted in a matter of weeks by archdeacon Geoffrey, with John's accord.[158] Our bishop seems to have played a similar role much further from Chartres, against the protagonists of the commune of Meaux, which had been granted by Henry the Liberal.[159] According to Stephen of Tournai, John *bonae memoriae* excommunicated the *auctores* of the commune, again as papal delegate.[160]

Maybe it is now time to revisit the letters by Peter of Celle and Peter of Blois, from which a rather grim picture of John's time as a bishop has sometimes been drawn.[161] The abbot of Saint-Remi of Reims was, famously, John's oldest and dearest friend. In the late 1170s they had known each other for over three

156   On the whole affair see Hélène Noizet, *La Fabrique de la ville. Espaces et sociétés à Tours (IXᵉ–XIIIᵉ s.)* (Paris, 2007), pp. 267–268.

157   *Recueil des historiens des Gaules et de la France*, vol. 16, pp. 624–625, reprinted in PL 199, cols. 375–376. It is John's letter to the dean of Saint-Martin, notifying him of the excommunication (the thirty condemned men are named): "controversiam quae inter homines de Castro-Novo beati Martini et R. nobilem ecclesiae vestrae ecclesiae thesaurarium vertitur super quibusdam juramentis vel fidei praestatione quam occulte inter se dicuntur praedicti homines praestitisse in depressionem juris praedictae ecclesiae." He also announced that he was issuing his sentences "auctoritate apostolica."

158   Noizet, *La Fabrique de la ville*, p. 269.

159   On the Meaux events, see Mickaël Wilmart, "Les débuts de la commune de Meaux (1179–1184)," *Bulletin de la Société littéraire et historique de la Brie* 55 (2000), 108–130.

160   *Lettres d'Étienne de Tournai*, ed. Jules Desilve (Paris, 1893), Letter 80, pp. 94–95. In the same letter Stephen complained that the bishop of Meaux had not enforced the sentence and asked for direct papal intervention: "confirmatione excommunicationis communie Meldensis, quoniam episcopum eorum in executione sententie a bone memorie Io., Carnotensi episcopo, in prefatam communiam late negligentem experti sumus et mandate apostolici contemptorem."

161   See E. Türk, Nugae curialium, or Cotts, *The Clerical dilemma*, p. 166 ("Only John of Salisbury achieved episcopal rank (…), and his reign was riddled with problems with his cathedral chapter and a general lack of administrative effectiveness.").

decades, and both their letter collections testify to an intimate and often playful relationship; Peter also gave John material and moral support during his exile. In that light, it is certain that the three letters that the abbot wrote to his friend after his elevation are unusually critical and sombre.[162] He accused him first of neglect, reminding him that if the *episcopales sollicitudines* could justify John's silence, then the abbot of Saint-Remi could just as well use the same excuse.[163] He went on to repeat (anonymous) complaints about John that accused him of being flimsy, unreliable, temperamental, and under the influence of an unwise and greedy adviser.[164] Peter protested that he did not believe a word of it, but still asked John to prove them wrong ("rationes uellem habere quibus uanitates istas et insanias falsas possem refellere").

The second letter shows more moderation. Peter still found fault with the bishop, who seemed to have slighted a mutual friend, but tidings had reached Reims that John was behaving well and the abbot was ready to let his doubts subside.[165] The general tone of the letter is nonetheless quite dry. The last known letter is a straightforward dressing down. Apparently John had left a certain Hugh, canon of Saint-Remi and relative of Peter, "out in the cold" for almost a year, "outside [his] bolted door."[166] The unfortunate man eventually returned to Reims and complained. What this was really about is not easy to decipher, but it is clear that John had ignored a recommendation from his old friend. Peter suggested that the disappointing bishop could make up for his callousness by behaving more kindly to one of his own archdeacons; it is obvious though that the abbot of Saint-Remi did not have high hopes of that happening either. Thus ends the known correspondence between Peter and John.

All the existing evidence points towards a sour final few years in the relationship between the two friends. Whether the rather negative opinion the

---

162   *The Letters of Peter of Celle*, Letters 176, pp. 674–676, 177, pp. 676–678 and 178, pp. 678–680.

163   Ibid., Letter 176 p. 674: "Certe si episcopalium sollicitudinum allegationes negligentiam istam excipiunt meam eque consimili ratione defendunt. Esto. Nullum fuit tempus uaccum uel ueniendi uel scribendi, nunquid amandi, nunquid recordandi? Procul dubio quamlibet excusationem potest habere omnis actio, nullam dilectio."

164   Ibid., p. 678: "Hec et hec, inquiunt, facit episcopus, sic loquitur, sic mouetur, sic mutabilis est in promissis, sic instabilis in uerbis et consiliis suis, sic ingratus beneficiis, sic ad iram facilis, sic improuidus in disponendis iudiciis, sic totus pendet de uoluntate et consilio unius hominis, minus prudentis et multum cupidi."

165   Letter 177, p. 678: "Prosperum itaque et felicem statum in his que erga uos fiunt asseruit [Alexander, a friend of John] et ambages circumuolantes a corde nostro abegit."

166   Letter 178, p. 678: "Postulatio nostra apud uos pro Hugone cognato et amico nostro Remensi canonico ante fores uestras obseratas estatem et hiemem fecit, et ualde lassata et ieiuna ad sinum nostrum reuersa est."

abbot clearly formed of his friend's skills as a bishop should be taken at face value is another matter. During their entire relationship Peter of Celle had had the upper hand: he was a distinguished spiritual guide for many as well as a well-established and generous friend to John himself.[167] One can imagine that John's elevation suddenly disturbed the equilibrium of their relationship, when as late as 1173 he had addressed Peter as *domino suo unico*.[168] That idea is supported by the fact that Peter succeeded John at Chartres, where he died in 1182; he can therefore be suspected of harbouring episcopal ambitions for himself, which might have tainted his appraisal of John's success.

The case of Peter of Blois is even more complicated. Peter is a difficult figure to study, mostly because he is known mostly through his gigantic letter-collection, whose nature and posthumous success has been puzzling scholars for a long time.[169] His involvement with the affairs of Chartres is characteristically intricate. Peter was born in Blois, therefore in the diocese. He seems to have had links with various members of the chapters, and to have fostered a desire to become a canon there himself. He claimed to have been promised a place in the chapter by William White Hands, probably in the early 1170s,[170] and complained sourly when it did not materialize.[171] Richard Southern noticed that in a letter to bishop John Peter called himself *suus* [John's] *canonicus*,[172]

---

167   For a thorough assessment of Peter and his standing in the Church, see Julian Haseldine, "Understanding the Language of *Amicitia*. The Friendship Circle of Peter of Celle (c.1115–1183)," *Journal of Medieval History* 20 (1994), 237–260.

168   Letter 310, pp. 754–761.

169   In spite of its many shortcomings, the easiest entry point into the collection remains J.A. Giles' edition, reprinted in PL 207, cols. 1–560. Egbert Türk recently published a partial French translation with a bounty of introductions and notes: *Pierre de Blois: ambitions et remords sous les Plantegenêts* (Turnhout, 2006). On the collection, see Richard W. Southern, "Peter of Blois: A Twelfth-Century Humanist?," in *Medieval Humanism and Other Studies* (Oxford, 1970), pp. 105–134, Lena Wahlgren, *The Letter-Collections of Peter of Blois: Studies in the Manuscript Tradition* (Gothenburg, 1993), and Cotts, *The Clerical dilemma*, pp. 49–95 and 269–288.

170   PL 307, col. 381, to William: "Me ad obsequium suum plerique magnates promissionibus suis et donis alliciunt, sed vestra promissio, et nativi dulcedo aeris me fortius trahunt, et maxime praebendae Carnotensis desiderium, in quo mihi spem dedistis, et ideo uberes et certos redditus vestrae nudae pollicitationi posthabui."

171   PL 207, col. 221, "to a friend" (who made the plan fall through): "Cum dominus Senonensis me vocasset a scholari militia, et sub certa exspectatione tempestivi beneficii suae familiae ascripsisset, frequenti suggestione tua propositum revocavit, et sicut publice jactitasti, me illuso in spem meam alium introduxit."

172   PL 207, col. 217.

which is true, but described that letter as full of "effusive terms," which would show that John had given the *Blésois* his coveted prebend.[173] The text is in fact anything but friendly or sycophantic; Peter scolded the bishop for refusing to promote his own nephew Robert of Salisbury, in what the archdeacon saw as an ill-advised display of anti-nepotism.[174] But, as we have seen, Peter also expressed a profuse gratitude for John's support to the newly established secular canons of Saint-Sauveur of Blois in their conflict with neighbouring regular canons. Not only did Peter thank the bishop for his help,[175] but he also wrote a warm and scriptural eulogy of his actions to the dean and chapter of Saint-Sauveur, comparing him to two saviour figures of the book of Judges, Othniel and Ehud, sent by God to rescue his people and destroy is enemies.[176] Here as elsewhere, Peter of Blois is a difficult witness, because he was able to hold simultaneous opposite views about any topic; John was no exception.

John presented himself as Becket's man in his *intitulatio*. He owned his elevation to Chartres to his connection with the *neomartyrus*, as Louis VII's letter made clear.[177] It is therefore not surprising that he promoted the cult of Saint Thomas while at Chartres. Becket's death, prompt miracles, and canonisation resulted into almost immediate popularity, in England but also in the whole of

---

173 See Richard Southern, "The Necessity for Two Peters of Blois," in Lesley Smith and Benedicta Ward, eds., *Intellectual Life in the Middle Ages: Essays Presented to Margaret Gibson* (London, 1992), pp. 103–118, at p. 109 note 9. Southern overall very convincingly tears to pieces the theory, defended among others by Reto R. Bezzola and Peter Dronke, that there was one unique Peter of Blois at Chartres who was the author both of the letter collection and of a large poetical corpus. It is nonetheless a bit blurry about the minutiae of chapter life at Chartres, giving it for instance four archdeacons when there were six of them, or announcing a total of 76 canons with no reference and, as far we are aware, no sources backing such a precise number.

174 PL 207, cols. 217–218: "Scitis, quod Robertus Salebere caro et sanguis vester est (...). Nepoti vestro, dum honestus est, et ecclesiasticis idoneus beneficiis, minus aptum aut deteriorem, quaeso, non praeferitis extraneum, nec ab eo vestrae liberalitatis gratiam avertatis, in quo ista duo concurrunt, natura et meritum."

175 See *supra* p. 133.

176 PL 207, col. 240: "Legimus quod filiis Israel servientibus in tributo sub regibus Chusanrasathaim, Eglon, Moab et Amalech, suscitavit Dominus Othoniel, et Aiod qui jugum exactoris auferrent. Expressa siquidem pietatis imagine dominum Joannem episcopum Carnotensem misit Dominus pro salute nostra, ut reaedificentur muri terrenae nostrae Hierusalem, quatenus ecclesia Blesensis ruinis deformata veteribus in optatam redeat novitatem."

177 For the king's letter, see *supra* p. 124. *Neomartyrus* is used by Herbert of Bosham, see *Vita*, p. 524.

Europe.[178] Western France, especially once Henry II had made his peace with the Church over his responsibility in the death of his former chancellor, embraced the new cult with particular enthusiasm.[179] In 1174 a very dear friend of John of Salisbury, John of Canterbury, bishop of Poitiers, thanked Odo, the prior of Canterbury, for relics of the new saint that would soon find their way to Poitiers.[180] The martyr's friends lost no time in spreading the news of miracles and other signs of their dead master's sanctity. Our John, before he was sent for by the chapter of Chartres, described in a letter to the monks of Canterbury an assembly summoned at Bourges by Louis VII during which Pons, bishop of Clermont, presented to the king and magnates a lengthy list of miracles Thomas had accomplished for people from Auvergne.[181]

When he moved up to Chartres, John seems to have brought with him relics from Canterbury, which were likely to have been very welcome there.[182] The most common form of Becketian relic was the *aqua Thome*, water made holy and potent by a drop of the martyr's blood.[183] However, John had a value of higher item to offer his new chapter: a vial of actual blood. We know that from John's *obit* in the necrology of the cathedral chapter, where the canons

---

178   For the early cult, see for instance Anne Duggan, "A Becket Office at Stavelot: London, British Library, Additional MS 16,964," in Anne Duggan, Joan Greatrex and Brenda Bolton, eds., *Omnia disce. Medieval Studies in Memory of Leonard Boyle, O.P.* (Aldershot, 2005), pp. 161–182; Raymonde Foreville, "Le culte de saint Thomas Becket en France. Bilan provisoire des recherches," in Raymonde Foreville, ed., *Thomas Becket. Actes du colloque international de Sédières, 19–24 août 1973* (Paris, 1975), pp. 163–187.

179   See Raymonde Foreville, "La diffusion du culte de Thomas Becket dans la France de l'Ouest avant la fin du XIIᵉ siècle," *Cahiers de civilisation médiévale* 19 (1976), pp. 347–369.

180   Ibid., p. 355, quoted from William of Canterbury's miracle collection, MB, vol. 1, p. 438. The date of the completion of William's collection, sometimes see as mostly finished by 1174, has been now pushed forward by Marcus Bull and even further by Nicholas Vincent; see Nicholas Vincent, "William of Canterbury and Benedict of Peterborough: the manuscripts, date and context of the Becket miracle collection," in Edina Bozoky, ed., *Hagiographie, idéologie et politique au Moyen Âge en Occident. Actes du colloque international du Centre d'Études supérieures de Civilisation médiévale de Poitiers, 11–14 septembre 2008* (Turnhout, 2012), pp. 347–388.

181   *The Later Letters*, no. 323, pp. 794–799. The letter is known from William's collection; see MB, vol. 1, pp. 458–460. It is sent by John as "sacerdotum Christi minimus Johannes de Saresberia" to the prior and monks of Christ Church, Canterbury.

182   On John and relics, see the already mentioned recent article by Karen Bollerman and Cary J. Nederman, "A Special Collection." My contribution to the topic was written before the publication of that very thorough study.

183   On the *aqua Thome*, see Foreville, "La diffusion du culte de Thomas Becket dans la France de l'Ouest," pp. 354–355, and Kay Brainerd Slocum, *Liturgies in Honour of Thomas Becket* (Toronto, 2003), pp. 92–97.

announced proudly that they saw the blood in the *uasum* still fresh enough to drip.[184] This is confirmed by a letter that John sent to the archbishop and chapter of Canterbury between 1177 and 1179, in which he describes how a stonecutter who had mocked the saint and been struck half-dead was cured by water in which John had washed the phial (*philaterium*) in which he, John, had brought with him to Chartres.[185] His choice of words suggests that John had collected (*deposueram*) the holy blood at the very moment of the murder, rather than obtained it from the monks and prior, later guardians of the relics; it is a subtle way of reminding Christ Church of his close connection with the martyr.

John had mentioned earlier in the same letter the holiest relic that the cathedral held until then, the *camisia* of the Virgin, shirt in which, as he wrote, Mary was said to have given birth, and was central to the blooming marial worship and pilgrimage at Chartres.[186] Such detail was maybe a way of boasting to the Canterbury men of the spiritual endowment of his new see; it was also making clear that Becket could trump the Virgin herself when it came to healing apparently hopeless cases.[187]

---

184   *Cartulaire de Notre-Dame de Chartres*, vol. 3, p. 202: "Duo vasa preciosa eidem ecclesie contulit, in altero quorum sanguinem gloriosi martiris Thome, Cantuariensis archiepiscopi, videntibus nobis, adhuc stillantem, in altero reliquias sanctorum martirum Crispini et Crispiani posuit."

185   *The Later Letters*, no. 325, p. 804: "Praecepi igitur afferi philaterium in quo reposueram sanguinem beati Thomae, quem mecum Carnotum detuli, et aquam in qua philaterium lauaretur."

186   Ibid.: "Adductus est miser mutus, pectus tundens et oculos et manus erigens in caelum et ad capsam in qua est interula, id est camisia beatissimae Virginis qua utebatur quando peperit Saluatorem." The pilgrimage was the reason for the large ambulatory of the 12th-century cathedral. Its scope is clear in the collection of miracles compiled in the early 13th century and published by André Thomas, "Les miracles de Notre-Dame de Chartres, texte latin inédit," *Bibliothèque de l'École des chartes* 42 (1881), 505–550. The canons of Chartres probably looked at the success of the Becket pilgrimage with some envy. The author of the collection emphasizes with some relish that, after a miraculous vision granted to a cleric from London, Richard I developed a particular devotion for Our Lady of Chartres (pp. 528–531). Although in this collection Becket is shown a bit later as sometimes more potent a healer than the Virgin, he is also named, maybe with a hint of spite, in a list of grandees of this word who, explains the Chartrain author, cannot compete with the poor and the weak as the living manifestation of Christ and his *miracula*; there might be some added irony here, given that the martyr's name is associated in that list to "king Henry of England and his sons" (p. 547).

187   For a more complete survey of the question, see Marquis, "Antiquité du culte de saint Thomas de Cantorbéry dans l'église de Chartres," in *Pièces détachées pour servir à l'histoire du diocèse de Chartres, Archives du diocèse de Chartres*, ed. Charles Métais, vol. 3 (Chartres, 1899), pp. 277–286.

The phial of blood was not the only miracle-making relic in John's letter, since he mentioned a knife of the new saint, which he also washed in the water which cures miraculously the stonecutter.[188] The presence at Chartres of the knife is confirmed in two Chartrain collections of miracles of the Virgin. Their authors, despite their particular devotion to the Mary, admitted that the new martyr occasionally could solve and cure cases that even the Mother of God was unable to placate. The early 13th-century Latin collection describes the fate of a labourer who in July 1206, pushed by poverty, had harvested his oats on a feast day and found his scythe and flail glued to his hands. His friends tried to call out to the saint he had offended and local patron, saint Germanus, with no result, then brought it to Chartres to beg for Mary's help, to no avail. Only the knife of Saint Thomas (the phial of blood is mentioned but is not the operating relic here), when pressed on the unfortunate's hands, freed them from their undesirable appendices.[189] The French mid-13th-century version of the collection, written by Jean Le Marchant, adds that it was an "ancient" knife[190]; at no point it is suggested in the available sources that the knife was one of the tools of the martyrdom, and it seems much likelier that it was one of the archbishop's own knife.

It is certain that John did well by the Church of Chartres when he provided it with such distinguished remains of the recent martyr; it is actually possible that he gave to another church at Chartres, the monastery of Saint-Père, one further Becketian relic.[191] His other gifts of relics, also mentioned in the

---

188   Ibid.: "Hausit aquam in qua philaterium laueram et cultellum boni martiri, et illico pristinam recepit sanitatem."

189   Thomas, "Les miracles de Notre-Dame de Chartres," p. 549: "clamando ad Dominum et ejus gloriosam genitricem et sanctum Germanum et sanctum Leobinum et beatum Thomam martirem, de cujus sanguine portiuncula erat ibi et cultellus ipsius, et omnes sanctos Dei ut manifestaretur gratia Dei in homine illo. Apprehendit autem custos dictarum reliquiarum dictum cultellum et tetigit cum eo manum dextram persone mi[se]rabilis cui adheserat falcicula, ad cujus tactum soluti sunt digiti manus adherentis [fal]cicule (...) Similiter ad tactum ejusdem cultelli soluta est manus sinistra a manipulo."

190   *Miracles de Notre-Dame de Chartres de Jean le Marchant*, ed. Pierre Kuntsmann (Ottawa, 1973): "Et seint Tomas de Conteorbere,/De cui sanc ot illuec partie/Et son coustel d'anceserie."

191   An inscription placed on the tomb of John said that John had given a *capsula* of Thomas to Saint-Père. The lateness of the inscription makes it obviously problematic, but some of its phrases are taken directly from the medieval necrology of Saint-Josaphat, where John was buried. It is therefore difficult to decide what credit one should give it. Here is the text: "Hic jacet Domnus Joannes Salisburiensis, episcopus Carnotensis. Erat capellanus sancti Thome, archiep. Canturiensis (sic), cum ipse martyrium passus est apud Anglos, cujus capsulam dedit Sancti Petri Carnotensis. Obiit D. Joannes anno 1180, cui successit in

necrology, pale in comparison: one finds there saint Crispin and saint Crispinian, the companions of saint Gereon, and the Virgins of Cologne, none of which were to acquire a particularly important place in Chartrain worship and liturgy.[192] This rather plentiful bequeath is nonetheless a useful reminder that John, the sophisticated humanist, was very much a man of his times and had collected relics as many of his contemporaries did. The provenance of the relics of the 11,000 Virgins of Cologne is known, given that John had asked for them in a letter sent in 1166 to his friend master Gerard Pucelle, who was then at his spiritual perils living among schismatics in Cologne.[193] John asked in the same sentence for relics of the "kings," clearly the relics of the Magi sent in July 1164 from Milan by Rainald of Dassel; it is fascinating to see that in his relics hunt John had no qualm benefiting from the actions of Rainald whom he saw otherwise as an agent of Antichrist.[194] The necrology suggests that Gerald indulged him about the Virgins, but not about the Kings. The relics of the companions of saint Gereon, who were also Cologne saints, were probably a consolation prize sent by Gerard.

It is indeed a fitting closing point for this survey of John's short but unexpectedly active episcopal career to return to his canons' opinion of their English prelate, now put in the light of all the other evidence gathered here about his episcopate. The *obit* of the necrology draws the portrait of a good bishop by the standards of the time. John, it tells us, took the interests of his adoptive Church to heart. He protected its worldly possessions, and added to its spiritual (and material) wealth. He did so, most importantly, with the relics that have just been described. The necrology of Chartres gives little evidence of other gifts of relics; John's generosity must have stood out.

---

episcopatu Domnus Petrus Cellensis, abbas Sancti Remigii Rhemensis, vir eximius. Jacet in choro ubi epistola legitur." (M. Doublet de Boisthibault, "Deux inscriptions placées sur les tombes des deux évêques de Chartres," *Bulletin du Comité historique des arts et monuments. Archéologie et Beaux Arts* 3 (1852), 227–228).

192   *Cartulaire de Notre Dame de Chartres*, p. 202: "in altero [vaso] reliquias sanctorum martirum Crispini et Crispiniani posuit. Reliquias etiam gloriosas nobis contulit de Comitatu sancti Gereomi [sic] et de consortio Virginum Coloniensium." On the posterity of the cult of Saint Ursula's companions at Chartres, see Claudine Lautier, "Les vitraux de la cathédrale de Chartres. Reliques et images," *Bulletin Monumental* 161 (2003), 3–96 at pp. 46–47.

193   *The Later Letters*, no. 158, p. 70: "De cetero iam porrectas itero preces, quatinus de reliquiis regum et uirginum michi uestro aliquid transmittatis cum uestrarum testimonio litterarum."

194   The following year, John hailed Rainald's death as a sign sent by God; see Letter 225, *The Later Letters*, pp. 392–394.

Conclusion

Had he simply been an assiduous student in Paris, Archbishop Theobald's secretary, a partisan of Thomas Becket, and an ambitious cleric climbing the ladders of the ecclesiastical *cursus honorum*, John of Salisbury would not be the object of the present volume. The aspects of his life and career touched on by this chapter are common to many men of his generation. Combining the service of the grand and the great with literary pursuits which allowed for the venting of criticism and satire was not his monopoly: the names of Walter Map, Roger of Howden and Gerald of Wales come immediately to mind. Nonetheless, the ecclesiastical career of the author of the *Policraticus* proved both more successful (although bumpy) and more varied than most. It reveals a man who navigated lucidly and deftly the realities and the complexities of the political scene on which he progressed. Deep friendships, a cross-Channel life, a relative lack of specialisation – these elements were again shared with many of his contemporaries, but John seemed to have taken them to a higher degree than most. A polymath, he was also socially adaptable and certainly not shut away in an ivory tower. He could take remarkable risks – following Becket to the bitter end amounted to a career suicide in England – but he also looked after his own interests just like everybody else, and appeared to enjoy the social game. This man of letters clearly loved the company of his fellow men, and this may be the meeting point between the author and the professional cleric. Unlike others who were similarly in a position of observing the society they were fully part of, his outlook was never durably cynical or bitter. In his letters as in his treatises he could be angry, radical and severe at times, but he almost kept his faith in friendships and personal relationships. In his life and in his works John comes across as lucid, realistic and interested in many aspects of life, from the most mundane to the loftiest. That he was in his old days, thanks to his murdered saint of a master rather than to his literary merits, a popular and active bishop of Chartres should therefore come as no surprise.

PART 2

John of Salisbury as a Writer

∴

CHAPTER 4

John of Salisbury as a Writer

Ronald E. Pepin

"Otium sine litteris mors est et uiui hominis sepultura"
Policraticus, Prologue, cited from Seneca, *ep.* 82.3.

Modern scholars have almost universally hailed John of Salisbury with superlative praises for his Christian humanism, his vast knowledge, his sardonic wit and forthright candor. All of these qualities and many more are amply revealed in the extensive corpus of John's extant writings, a collection whose versatility embraced numerous genres: satirical and didactic verse; history; epistles; biography (hagiography); treatises on philosophy, education and political science.

John of Salisbury's honored place in academe, his presence in circles of medievalists and moralists, is surely not surprising, for besides his literary stature, interest in him is owing to a number of other biographical factors. For example, during John's student years in Paris from 1136–48, he attended lectures of the outstanding masters of the schools; his favorites proved to be controversial and condemned for their views: Peter Abelard, whom John referred to as the "Peripatetic of Le Pallet," and Gilbert de la Porrée, later bishop of Poitiers. As secretary to Archbishop Theobald of Canterbury, and also as his diplomatic envoy on the Continent, John came into contact with the leading ecclesiastical and political officials of the day. Later, in service to Thomas Becket, he was numbered among the *eruditi*, the "learned men" of the archbishop's household, among whom were notable literary figures and legal minds. His friends, acquaintances and adversaries comprise a roster of important historical personalities of the 12th century, from kings and princes to popes and prelates. He was recommended for a position by Bernard of Clairvaux, personal friend of Pope Adrian IV, "disgraced" enemy of King Henry II, loyal ally to Becket, resident guest of Peter of Celle, nominated to a bishopric (of Chartres) by King Louis VII of France. Through such contacts and experiences John developed a cosmopolitan outlook that is reflected in the quality of his writings.

Iocundissimus is the very first word of John's *Policraticus*. He employed this adjective, meaning "most pleasant" or "most enjoyable," to establish the tone of an encomium for literature that forms the prologue to his major work. As he commends the pleasure and profit (*fructus*) derived from such study, John relies on this adjective to underscore his point that no human activity is more

© KONINKLIJKE BRILL NV, LEIDEN, 2015 | DOI 10.1163/9789004282940_006

pleasant (*iocundior*) or more useful (*utilior*); he declares that reading and writing refresh the soul through their "sweet and wondrous pleasure" (*suauis et mira iocunditas*). This expressed devotion to reading and writing can serve as a key to understanding the man, the humanistic values he embraced, and the renown he has achieved.

John of Salisbury's enduring reputation depends chiefly on his writings, on his status as a man of letters. So it was in his own day, a period rightly celebrated for its classical renaissance. Even as a young man he was recommended for an administrative post on the basis of a meritorious way of life (*uita*) and literary learning (*litteratus*). At his death, the necrology of Chartres cathedral recorded that John had been a man "illuminated by rays of all knowledge" (*totius scientiae radiis illustratus*). These assessments are more than mere conventional compliments; they testify to wide learning acquired through reading. For John, "two currents flowed from the springs of ancient wisdom: pagan poets, philosophers, historians, with Cicero in the foreground; the Bible and the Fathers."[1] For him and for other educated men of the 12th century, these became part of the furniture of their minds and the foundation on which their writings rested.

His impressive acquaintance with classical literature and Sacred Scripture enabled John of Salisbury to establish an intellectual link between himself and his audience, for he wrote not only for literate men, but for literary men. Although John's major works were composed for Chancellor Thomas Becket, they were surely intended to circulate more widely. John himself identified some recipients: Peter of Celle received a copy of the *Policraticus*, as did Brito, a monk of Christ Church, Canterbury, who was an object of John's good-natured jibing in the *Entheticus maior*: "You will find Brito happy, if there is cheese around!"[2] Brito and a fellow-monk, Odo, who would one day become Abbot of Battle, are specifically mentioned as readers of the *Entheticus* when John advises his book: "Let these men be your companions; disclose all to them."[3] In fact, Odo and Brito are the only two names of actual contemporaries that occur in the poem, and significantly, both are hailed for their love of books. For John, such men were kindred spirits; they and the learned clerks in the household of Archbishop Theobald became his audience, an elite group of friends who would recognize his many allusions and unidentified quotations. As Professor Janet Martin's research has shown, the classical tradition became

---

1   Beryl Smalley, *The Becket Conflict and the Schools: A Study of Intellectuals in Politics in the Twelfth Century* (Totowa, NJ, 1973), p. 90.

2   *Entheticus*, l.1667, ed. Pepin, p. 188: "Invenies laetum/Britonem, si caseus adsit."

3   Ibid., l.1681, ed. Pepin, p. 188: "Hi tibi sint comites, illis tua cuncta revela."

for John and his circle a reinforcement of the sense of being a small group, and this was especially so in satirical passages.[4]

John of Salisbury's works are available now in multiple printed editions and translations. His original texts were all composed in Latin, a language in which he was expert and an acknowledged stylist of outstanding ability. Although he was English by birth, *"natione Anglus,"* according to his colleague, Herbert of Bosham, John had likely acquired a mastery of the literary language of the times early in his education, and surely before he went to Paris for studies. This view is supported by the fact that he was already composing competent elegiac verses in Latin during his time there, and serving as a tutor to young students as well.

For all intents and purposes, John was a lifelong writer. Amid the press of other duties in his manifold career as student, cleric and tutor, secretary to prelates, traveling emissary, holder of ecclesiastical benefices and, finally, bishop, he found time to commit his reflections and convictions to parchment in multiple genres. Perhaps this is why his works are fragmented: the satirical and didactic *Entheticus de dogmate philosophorum* seems to have been composed at various times from his student days onward to the mid-1150s; it ranges over themes from academe to court, from philosophical doctrines to political and social issues. The *Metalogicon*, perhaps his most coherent treatise, is a blend of biographical and educational information. The *Policraticus*, eight books in sections satirical, political and philosophical, was surely written over a period of time in which John's concentration was interrupted by administrative responsibilities. He acknowledged this himself in the *Prologue*: "Moreover, the unevenness of the books must be ascribed to various occupations by which I have been so distracted that at times I have scarcely been permitted to write anything."[5] His letters are separated into early, official correspondence, and later, more personal and polemical epistles. Even the two modern volumes of his *Letters* were issued years apart. It is no wonder, then, that internal coherence is sometimes hard to discover and defend in John's writings, and that a dean of John of Salisbury scholars could declare that, despite all his talents, "he lacked the capacity to write a book"![6]

---

4   Janet Martin, "John of Salisbury as Classical Scholar," in *The World of John of Salisbury*, p. 196. See also eadem, "Cicero's Jokes at the Court of Henry II of England: Roman Humor and the Princely Ideal," *Modern Language Quarterly* 51 (1990), 144–166, esp. p. 151.

5   *Policraticus*, Prologue, ed. Webb, vol. 1, p. 17: "Inaequalitas autem voluminum variis est occupationibus ascribenda, quibus in curia sic distractus sum ut vix aliquid scribere quandoque licuerit." Translations from Latin in this chapter are my own.

6   *The Early Letters*, p. xlv.

John invented titles for his major works that are derived from Greek roots. Scholars seem to agree that he did so not only to predict their content, but also to lend an air of authority to them. In an age of the rediscovery of ancient philosophical texts and commentaries, a time when Aristotle was hailed by John himself as "Philosopher *par excellence*,"[7] he surely must have felt that Greek-sounding names would enhance the dignity and appeal of his books. This practice was not uncommon among 12th-century authors, notably philosophers and schoolmasters, including Hugh of Saint-Victor and Saint Anselm. There is no evidence, however, to indicate that John of Salisbury had a command of Greek or had ever studied the language beyond an elementary level; like other scholars of his day, he read Latin translations of Greek works. Nevertheless, he bestowed the titles *Entheticus, Metalogicon* and *Policraticus* on his major literary pieces.

The *Metalogicon*, according to John, is so named because it undertakes the defense of logic, which for him embraces the entire trivium: grammar, rhetoric, dialectic. *Policraticus*, called "The Statesman's Book" by some translators, is subtitled *De nugis curialium et uestigiis philosophorum*, "On the Frivolities of Courtiers and the Footprints of Philosophers."[8] John applied the title *Entheticus* to two separate literary endeavors: a lengthy poem, *Entheticus de dogmate philosophorum*, and a shorter *Entheticus in Policraticum*, which serves as a preface to the major prose treatise. *Entheticus* is a puzzling neologism which has prompted a host of interpretations, solutions and confusions. Published translations of the longer poem have rendered it as "Summary" and "Introduction," akin to the German term *Einführung*, or "Indicator."[9] Clement C.J. Webb, a classical scholar and editor of the *Policraticus* and *Metalogicon*, commented on John's apparent intentions in imposing these names on his books, suggesting for the former "A book for the use of those governing states," and for the latter "An apology for logical knowledge." The title of the shorter *Entheticus*, he affirmed, means "introduction." As for the longer *Entheticus*, he admitted, "Indeed, I don't know."[10]

---

7   *Metalogicon* 2.16, p. 80: "excellenter philosophus appellatur."

8   John Dickinson, *The Statesman's Book* (New York, 1927); Joseph B. Pike, *Frivolities of Courtiers and Footprints of Philosophers* (Minneapolis, 1938).

9   Ronald E. Pepin, "John of Salisbury's *Entheticus*," *Allegorica* 9 (1987/8), 7–133, esp. p. 9; Jan van Laarhoven, *John of Salisbury's Entheticus maior and minor*, 3 vols. (Leiden, 1987), vol. 1, p. 104.

10   *Policraticus*, ed. Webb, vol. 1, p. xxii: "Quid dicere velit Entheticus, equidem nescio."

Entheticus de dogmate Philosophorum

The longer *Entheticus* (*maior*) is a satirical/didactic poem of 926 elegiac distichs (1852 lines). It has been called "difficult," "abstruse," and "enigmatic."[11] One scholar titled his examination of its puzzling verses "What Is The Entheticus?"; he concluded that, probably unfinished, it remains a "meandering, desultory and flawed" work.[12] Despite these and other criticisms leveled at John's poetic effort, there seems to be general agreement that the *Entheticus maior* is worthy of study for its insights into the development of the author's thoughts and convictions, which found full expression later in his prose works, and for its instructive, unrestrained cautions about 12th-century school, court, Church and cloister. In short, our understanding of many varied aspects of the culture of that momentous time would be weaker without the depictions and descriptions, the surveys, summaries, and even the sneers of this contentious poem. Its most recent editor was surely correct in declaring that "The value of the *Entheticus maior* for our historical knowledge is beyond dispute."[13]

The poem opens with a direct address of the book itself (*"Libelle"*), a literary device known as prosopopoeia, or personification of an abstract object. The *locus classicus* for this technique is Ovid's *Tristia*, the Roman poet's lament over his banishment from the City, also written in elegiac couplets. This figure of speech allowed John to shroud the identity of the real addressee of his verses, Thomas Becket, while assuming the innocent posture of an author merely conversing with his own "brain-child."[14] One recent assessment of this method suggests that it served a "pragmatic function of politeness" and permitted the author "greater frankness and simplicity of expression than consideration of rank might otherwise allow."[15]

The first part of the *Entheticus* concentrates on academic themes. It begins with a broad defense of the traditional curriculum, and specifically the place of logic in it, against educational innovators who denigrate the liberal arts and disparage wide reading of the classical *auctores* in favor of a facile, utilitarian course based on "natural eloquence." John has their brash spokesman declare

---

11   van Laarhoven, *John of Salisbury's Entheticus maior and minor*, preface, vol. 1, p. ix.

12   Rodney Thomson, "What is the *Entheticus*?," in *The World of John of Salisbury*, p. 300.

13   van Laarhoven, *John of Salisbury's Entheticus maior and minor*, vol. 1, p. 98.

14   Ibid., vol. 1, p. 48.

15   Jonathan M. Newman, "Satire between School and Court: The Ethical Interpretation of the *Artes* in John of Salisbury's *Entheticus in dogmata philosophorum*," *The Journal of Medieval Latin* 17 (2007), 125–142, esp. p. 127. The author views the use of prosopopoeia as a "thematic thread" in the *Entheticus*.

that "natural ability is the source of all [eloquence]" (*sit ab ingenio totum*), so there is no need for books and study, which are hindrances (*libri impediunt*), a form of torture (*tormenti genus est saepe uidere librum*). His advice: just be garrulous; away with writings! (*esto uerbosus, scripta repelle procul!*). In the *Metalogicon*, John would devote several Chapters (1. 6–8) to a refutation of the claim that "[p]recepts of eloquence are superfluous, since eloquence is present or absent in one by nature." (*Superflua sunt praecepta eloquentiae, quoniam ea naturaliter adest, aut abest*). Thus John enters the eternal fray between ancients and moderns, and roundly satirizes this new school of shallow learning along with its pompous advocate. These passages include a lengthy encomium on Philosophy, and the placement of Sacred Scripture, the "Queen of writings," (*scripturarum regina*), at the pinnacle of the curriculum and at the "summit of holy authority" (*arx imperii sacri*).

The second part of the *Entheticus maior* is truly a medley, whose unifying theme reflects the poem's subtitle, *De dogmate philosophorum*, but whose development is characterized by numerous digressions and topical intrusions. Indeed, it very much resembles a set of lecture notes with random explanations, comments and criticisms added. In these the poet reviews philosophical sects of classical antiquity, including Stoics, Epicureans, Peripatetics and Academics. John presents a balanced, if sketchy and selective, treatment in which he both commends and criticizes the doctrines of each, depending largely on their conformity to the Christian faith.

A major transition occurs when the author poses the rhetorical question, "But why do I survey the pagans whom error impelled?"[16] This line actually shifts the focus of the poem to the royal court and the manners of courtiers. In this dangerous setting, where "grace rarely abides and faith is scarce,"[17] the *Entheticus* will be unable to avoid the "jeering, mimicking and snorting" (*cachinnus, sanna, rhonchus*) of the wanton youths who populate the place, without the protection of a patron. The latter is identified as one who "cancels" unjust laws; this pun clearly alludes to Henry II's *cancellarius*, Thomas Becket. The verses that follow characterize the tyranny, oppression, injustice and lax morality of the king and officers of the court, all under pseudonyms, and the woeful state of the realm under their authority is detailed at length. Our poet fears that the chancellor, who pursues a stratagem of infiltration in order to recall the court from erroneous ways, might be striving in vain.

---

16   *Entheticus*, l.1269, ed. Pepin, p. 176: "Sed cur gentiles numero, quos error adegit?"
17   Ibid., l.1278, ed. Pepin, p. 177: "In qua rara manet gratia, rara fides."

The *Entheticus maior* concludes with a review of the perils and pitfalls of inns and hostels, and the unscrupulous hosts to be avoided as it journeys homeward. Even when the wayfarer arrives at Canterbury and enters the cloister there, it will find both trustworthy allies who revere literature and avaricious enemies who lie in wait to undermine the unwary. In the closing verses, John offers final counsels regarding good morals, and he commissions his book to win over the mind of its reader to him, to persuade the faithful to pray for him, and to fare well, living always by the law of God.

Given that the *Entheticus maior* shares an overall structure and numerous themes with the *Policraticus*, scholars in the past viewed the poem as an introduction to the prose work. This theory was advanced by Hans Liebeschütz and defended by Beryl Smalley; C.N.L. Brooke suggested that the poem was a draft introduction to the *Policraticus* that was "suppressed presumably because it was too caustic."[18] The latest editor of the *Entheticus maior* altered and enlarged these views in conjecturing that the poem in its present state is not a formal introduction, but "a large and partly elaborated draft of a great doctrinal poem."[19] To be sure, John had serious intentions in mind when he composed a lengthy poem that ranged over such topics as school and State, Church and court, philosophy and morals. These themes would be developed and vastly embellished in the *Policraticus*.

In matters of style and technicality, John was well acquainted with classical prosody, and he imitated the ancient satirists in his use of hexameters and pentameters, executing these flawlessly in his own poetry. His mastery of technical skills and his reliance on numerous poetic devices further attest to his wide reading and assimilation of the classical Latin poets. Like them, John adorned his verses with alliteration, assonance and repetition, as this example from the *Entheticus minor* (ll. 269–272) shows:

Nulla libris erit apta manus ferrugine tincta,
Nec nummata queunt corda vacare libris:
Non est eiusdem nummosque librosque probare;
Persequiturque libros grex, Epicure, tuus.[20]

---

18   *The Early Letters*, p. xlix; Hans Liebeschütz, *Medieval Humanism in the Life and Writings of John of Salisbury* (London, 1950), p. 21; Smalley, *The Becket Conflict*, p. 89.

19   van Laarhoven, *John of Salisbury's Entheticus maior and minor*, vol 1, p. 18.

20   *Entheticus maior*, vol. 1, p. 122: "No hand tinged with iron-rust will be suited to books,/Nor can moneyed-hearts have time for books:/It is not in one man's nature to approve money and books;/And your herd, Epicurus, persecutes books."

Moreover, the apostrophe in the last verse echoes Horace's *"Epicuri de grege porcus"* (*Epistles* 1. 4. 16). And as noted above, John adopted the prosopopoeia device from Ovid. Despite these classical adornments, John of Salisbury's poetry contains few flashes of genuine brilliance and verve, while sudden transitions and abrupt shifts often hamper the smooth flow of ideas. Overall, his poetic efforts, while impressive and important, do not rank among the finest or most familiar pieces produced in a prolific era of Latin verse.

The satirical verses of the *Entheticus maior*, however, compete with the best of an age that embraced the genre. John's biting mockery of educational innovators early in the poem and his scathing censure of courtiers and innkeepers near the end compare favorably in tenor and technique with 12th-century masterpieces, such as Bernard of Cluny's *De contemptu mundi* or Nigel of Canterbury's *Speculum stultorum*. Even the recurring laments for the decline of letters and the tavern scenes of Goliardic verses yield to John of Salisbury's caustic depictions of a shallow schoolmaster or a slanderous host. As one scholar asserted: "In satirical expression...he reaches here and there the pinnacle of 12th-century poetry."[21]

John's models were the great Roman satirists, whom he referred to as moralists, *"ethici."* The *Entheticus* contains many traceable echoes of Horace, Persius, Juvenal, and even Petronius, a rare author in John's day.[22] For example, John's satirical expression is often dependent on these sources, as when he ridicules one opponent as a "trifling lackey" (*tressis agaso*), a Horatian term, and another as a "hair-curler" (*ciniflo*), an insult borrowed from Persius. Besides vocabulary, our author adopts images from the ancient poets, as when he uses Juvenalian scenes to depict an informer dripping venomous gossip into his master's ear, or a pauper singing in a robber's face. John even conformed to Roman satirical tradition in his use, albeit restrained use, of obscenity. An instance is his suggestion that the royal court poses a threat to young boys "with hair not yet sprouting" (*non fruticante pilo*), a phrase indebted to Juvenal's satire (9) on sodomy.

These ancient practitioners of the genre provided him with exemplars of folly, as well as phrases and proper names. The latter, used as pseudonyms by our poet, afforded a protective measure against retribution, while at the same time they established a link between him and his educated audience.

---

21   Ibid., vol. 1, p. 95.

22   Janet Martin, "Uses of Tradition: Gellius, Petronius and John of Salisbury," *Viator* 10 (1979), 57–76; Ronald E. Pepin, "John of Salisbury's *Entheticus* and the Classical Tradition of Satire," *Florilegium* 3 (1981), 215–227.

The learned readers of John's *Entheticus maior* would undoubtedly recognize the sources of names bestowed on the reprobates that he paraded before them: Mato and Pedo (from Juvenal); Dinomaches and Polydamas (from Persius); Carinus and Baccara (from Martial). He borrowed several names from Petronius' *Satyricon*, including Quartilla the harlot, and Trimalchio, the host of a decadent banquet. The latter is also named in a clever letter to Peter of Celle (112), and in the *Policraticus* (8.7), John challenges his audience to come to Trimalchio's feast "if you can" (*si potes*). Professor Martin has reminded us that few allusions to the *Satyricon* appeared in England or on the Continent in John's time, and that his display of such "esoteric classical learning" confirms that his readers were likely a small group who could recognize them.

Dating the longer *Entheticus* has been problematic, chiefly owing to its rambling nature and disparate themes. While the earlier portions may have originated during John's school years, as the concentration on educational controversy and philosophical doctrines suggests, the latter parts can be placed in a more specific time frame based on internal evidence. The reference to Archbishop Theobald in the present tense, the allusion to the active role of the chancellor, and the mention of a "new court under a boy king,"[23] point clearly to the mid-1150s, probably 1155. Theobald died in April, 1161; Becket was appointed chancellor of the realm in December, 1154, or early January, 1155; Henry II must have seemed a mere "boy" when he ascended the throne of England at age twenty-one on 19 December 1154. Furthermore, the apologia that describes the activities of the poem's patron, the "defender of right," in his attempt to recall the royal courtiers from error and vice must have been written at the outset of Becket's tenure as chancellor, for such a stratagem of "*insinuatio*" could hardly have been undertaken later in his career. Perhaps, as has been suggested, the *Entheticus maior* was a parting gift to him as he set out for court.[24] At any rate, these passages in the poem are remarkable and historically important in that they actually apprise Becket that the aging primate of Canterbury, who had made him an archdeacon and helped to secure his appointment to the chancellorship, now hopes and prays that he will one day succeed him! These declarations are confirmed in John's *uita* of Becket, composed not long after his Archbishop's assassination in December, 1170, where John again claims that Theobald arranged for his promotion to chancellor

---

23   *Entheticus*, l.1463–1464, ed. Pepin, p. 182: "nova curia rege/sub puero."

24   Cary J. Nederman and Arlene Feldwick, "To the Court and Back Again: the Origins and Dating of the *Entheticus de dogmate philosophorum* of John of Salisbury," *The Journal of Medieval and Renaissance Studies* 21 (1991), 129–145, esp. p. 130.

because he was apprehensive about the new king's youth and the foolishness of his advisors.[25]

The *Entheticus maior* is an outspoken exhortation and a courageous censure of societal ills composed by an author of impressive learning and ample wit. It is an intriguing piece, yet also an enigmatic, frustrating one. Of course, its messages were clearer to John's contemporaries. Perhaps its harsh invective even reached the ears of powerful foes at court and led to his famous "disgrace" in 1156.

Metalogicon

The *Metalogicon* is a prose treatise in four books. John of Salisbury himself bestowed its title and declared its purpose to be the defense of logic.[26] A modern translator further defined its objectives in an expanded subtitle: "A 12th-Century Defense of the Verbal and Logical Arts of the Trivium."[27] Although the book is more coherent and less discursive than the *Entheticus maior*, there are notable affinities between the two, especially in their common academic themes, including harsh criticisms of educational foes; their concentration on philosophy and language arts; their extensive reliance on classical sources. Both were offered to the same patron, Thomas Becket, although more explicitly in the *Metalogicon* where internal evidence enables us to date its completion more precisely. In the closing chapter of the final book, John mentions not only that Archbishop Theobald, his lord "and yours also" (*et tuus*) is gravely ill, a fact that points to the late 1150s when John claims that he has assumed responsibility for ecclesiastical matters in all of England, but that the siege of Toulouse (September, 1159) was underway.

The Prologue to the *Metalogicon* is vitally important, not only for its author's clear expression of purpose and stated rationale for writing, but also for the excellent examples of his candor and convictions. It affords a brilliant illustration of John's graceful Latin style and his clever deployment of classical models. He begins with a generalization about the universality of detraction in human society and announces his own resignation to this reality. He acknowledges his inability to evade the "teeth" (*dentes*) of fellow-courtiers or to shield his

---

25   Ronald E. Pepin, trans. *Anselm & Becket: Two Canterbury Saints' Lives by John of Salisbury* (Toronto, 2009), p. 76.

26   *Metalogicon*. Prologue, p. 10: "Et quia logicae suscepit patrocinium, metalogicon inscriptus est liber."

27   Daniel D. McGarry, trans. *The Metalogicon of John of Salisbury: A Twelfth-Century Defense of the Verbal and Logical Arts of the Trivium* (Berkeley, 1962).

writings from their "bites" (*roderent*). After much provocation from the almost daily calumnies of a rival, and with friends urging him to respond, John at last decided to take up the battle, even though pressing administrative duties cause him to compose haphazardly. This admission of "*sermo tumultuarius*" is one of three instances in the Prologue where the author indulges in the artificial commonplace of self-deprecation,[28] confessing his natural dullness of mind, unreliable memory, and unpolished style, finally claiming to be ignorant of affairs and closing with another conventional feature: an appeal for the reader's prayers. John was likely guided in these topoi by Cicero's advice in *De inuentione* (1. 16. 22) that orators should display humility and submissiveness. Such rhetorical commonplaces abound in the writings of John of Salisbury, where they are used to enhance an argument, confirm a point, or conform to a tradition. He skillfully adapted rhetorical artifices and *sententiae* to his literary purposes in composing treatises, satirical verses and epistles. Perhaps most famous among myriad examples is John's revival of the metaphor "all the world's a stage" (*Policraticus* 3.8: *totus mundus...mimum uidetur implere*), which he attributes to Petronius.

Book One of the *Metalogicon* comprises twenty-five chapters. At the very outset, indeed in the opening sentence, John introduces an opponent characterized as a shameless disputant who assails the greatest gifts, reason and speech, that nature and grace bestow on human beings. Refusing to identify him explicitly out of reverence for his Christian name, John calls his adversary "Cornificius," a pseudonym that has sparked extensive speculation and an unavailing search for the actual person. Although John implies that Cornificius is a real individual, some critics have suggested that he was created by our author as an exemplar of the anti-classical educationists and opponents of logical studies whom he had already mocked in the longer *Entheticus*, and it is true that John puns mischievously on the name as he derides the foolishness that Cornificius "caws" (*cornicetur*).[29] However, the fact that John directs relentless accusations of a personal as well as professional nature against him supports the view that he really was a detested foe. Known as an outspoken critic, John of Salisbury nowhere else in his writings surpasses the vehemence

---

28   On the widespread use of the "affected modesty" topos in medieval literature, see Ernst R. Curtius, *European Literature and the Latin Middle Ages*, trans. Willard R. Trask (New York, 1963), pp. 83–85.

29   Studies directed specifically at identification of "Cornificius" and his school include Enrico Tacella, "Giovanni di Salisbury e i Cornificiani," *Sandalion* 3 (1980), 273–313; Rosemary Barton Tobin, "The Cornifician Motif in John of Salisbury's *Metalogicon*," *History of Education* 13 (1984), 1–6.

of his charges against "our" Cornificius, including bloatedness of belly, shame-lessness of speech, rapacity of hands, deformity of body, baseness of life, obscene lust, and many more disgusting physical and mental attributes.

Clearly, as a writer, John could compose acerbic invective in the style of Martial or Juvenal, both of whom are well known for their caustic characteriza-tions and vitriolic insults. Although John might be more closely identified with Horatian geniality, he sometimes revealed a capacity for Juvenalian bitterness, as in the depiction of "Cornificius" or that of "Lanvinus" (*Policraticus, Prol.*), his detractor mocked for grotesque features such as "swollen belly" (*turgidus uenter*); "puffy red face" (*tumida facies et rubicunda*); "insolent, insipid tongue" (*lingua procax insulsa*), or "Hircanus," the king who violated ancient customs. In the *Entheticus maior* (1301–40), John directs a litany of charges and accusa-tions of vicious behavior against this tyrant that rival any outburst in Juvenal's satires.

The primary thrust of John's denunciation of Cornificius and his "school" is against their hostility to the logical arts as represented in the trivium. After devoting the first six chapters to a description of Cornificius and his colleagues, their own inferior education, the notable teachers whom they defame, and their baseless contentions, he moves on to an encomium for eloquence and an extended definition of logic and liberal arts. This in turn leads to an explora-tion of the nature of grammar in particular, a brief survey of the great propo-nents of that subject, and a declaration of its immense value.

In Book Two, John returns to Cornificius, "mutilated and yet to be further mutilated,"[30] but still unsilenced and now indicted as an enemy of logic. Thus, the twenty chapters of this book concentrate on the dialectical arts and chas-tise "jugglers of verbal nonsense" (*nugidici uentilatores*), modern logicians who do not even adhere to the authoritative doctrines of Aristotle. In contrast to their sole, eternal preoccupation with logic, John insists on a balanced study of other disciplines in concert with dialectic.

Books Three and Four are basically a running commentary on the individual books of Aristotle's *Organon*. Indeed, a foremost historian of medieval philoso-phy has affirmed that "[l]e *Metalogicon* est, pour une bonne part, un résumé commenté de l'*Organon* aristotélicien."[31] The culmination of John's exposition is a discussion of reason and truth (Chapters 30–41). In the final Chapter (42), the author turns his attention to the present moment, "a time more to weep

---

30   *Metalogicon* 2, Prologue, p. 56: "Et si mutilus sit, sed amplius mutilandus Cornificius."
31   Édouard Jeauneau, "Jean de Salisbury et la lecture des philosophes," in *The World of John of Salisbury*, p. 103.

than to write," for "the whole world is subject to vanity."[32] As John associates himself with prominent personalities and momentous issues, the *Metalogicon* closes with commonly-known yet historically-important facts: the ongoing siege of Toulouse; the recent death of Pope Adrian IV, his countryman, and the schism that followed; the precarious health of Archbishop Theobald. John's assertions are illuminating and engaging: that no one was closer to the Pope's heart than he, not even his own mother; that the Pope delighted to dine with him, even sharing plate and cup; that his petitions secured from the Pope the grant of Ireland to his king; that Theobald has placed all responsibility for his See on his shoulders. Despite their hyperbole, these assertions ring true. Nowhere, save perhaps a rare exclamation in his letters, does John of Salisbury claim so much prestige or call such attention to himself. And yet, the last words of the *Metalogicon* constitute another appeal to "reader and listener" (*lector et auditor*) for prayers, that Christ might enlighten him, "a vain and wretched man," (*uanus et miser*) and make him a dutiful searcher, lover and worshipper of truth.

Entheticus in Policraticum

John of Salisbury composed a verse introduction of 306 lines to his *opus magnum* which bears considerable resemblance to the *Entheticus maior*, including its title and elegiac meter. He employs in it the same device of prosopopoeia, actually addressing his little book (*"libelle"*) more often than in the longer poem, and underscoring the image of the book as a traveller (to court, to Canterbury, etc.) more consistently. This piece is also commended to a patron, alluded to in the nearly-identical formula of the major poem as "[h]e who cancels the unjust laws of the realm."[33] Again the pun on *cancellat* clearly points to Becket. In this work, John returns to several key themes developed in the longer poem, and a reader will often note similarities of expression and sentiment in both. The ostensible purpose of the *Entheticus minor* is to introduce the *Policraticus*, as its title and placement in almost all the manuscripts suggest, and thus its composition must be dated before September, 1159, but probably not much before.

---

32   *Metalogicon* 4.42, p. 183: "Iam enim flere magis vacat quam scribere...quod mundus totus subjacet vanitati."

33   *Entheticus minor* l. 29, vol. 1, p. 233: "Hic est qui regni leges cancellat iniquas."

The shorter *Entheticus* is a more compact, more focused, "more refined" work than its longer counterpart, yet it exhibits "all the tricks and knacks of the professional 'classical' poet."[34] However, there are notable differences in content too. Politics and social issues dominate the *Entheticus minor*, while John's earlier emphasis on *dogmata philosophorum* and *scholae* disappear entirely; the Church finds only a small place in the poem, mainly in passages that dwell on Canterbury and the author's familiar friends there. Indeed, John practically abandons his use of pseudonyms in the shorter work, but replaces them, in part, with an intriguing menagerie, "a reigning ass, a converted wolf" (*regnat asellus, conuersus lupus*), a dozen animals in all, to personify the usual culprits. Yet, John does not neglect his favorite objects of criticism or spare his satire of fools and folly. In fact, this shorter *Entheticus* is filled with examples of *nugae*, the "trifles" or "frivolities" that would receive such extensive treatment in the *Policraticus*. In one concentrated passage (133–142), our poet locates *nugae* everywhere, repeating the term eight times to emphasize the reign of nonsense in all places and among all classes. Thus it is surely not surprising that Nigel of Canterbury, a monk of Christ Church, borrowed liberally from John's poem for his own verse introduction and prose text of his *Tractatus contra curiales*. Later, Richard de Bury quoted six lines from the *Entheticus minor* (without attribution) in his *Philobiblon* to support the claim that one cannot love both money and books.

Policraticus

In the autumn of 1159, John of Salisbury dispatched a copy of his *Policraticus* to Peter of Celle, appealing for his dear friend's approval and emendation for "a book on the frivolities of courtiers and footprints of philosophers."[35] He described the work as "unpolished" (*incultus*) and "garrulous" (*garrulus*), and many modern readers would hasten to agree, even if for John it was a disingenuous assessment. After all, his remark appears in a playful passage such as often characterized his correspondence with Peter, and one in which John jocularly charges another friend, Brito, with thievery (*"fur ille"*) for holding on to his copy so long. Yet, in evaluating verbal expression, *garrulus* has negative connotations; John had hurled this term disparagingly at his academic enemies

---

34   *Entheticus maior*, vol. 1, p. 67.
35   Letter 111, in *The Early Letters*, p. 182: "Edidi librum de curialium nugis et uestigiis philosophorum."

("*garrula turba*") in the longer *Entheticus*, while he cautioned his book to restrain a "*garrula lingua*" in the shorter one. Nevertheless, his *Policraticus*, in eight books comprising a quarter of a million words, is indeed garrulous and often so rambling and disjointed that it has been called a "mish-mash," and criticized for "obscurity, pretentiousness and lack of organization."[36] One scholar declared that "John packed his ideas into an untidy parcel, but the string seemed firm."[37] Indeed, some structure is evident in that the first three books concentrate on *nugae curialium*, the central ones on the art of right government, and the last two treat of *uestigiis philosophorum*. Within this general framework, however, a reader must contend with the author's penchant for digression, prolix style, extensive use of *exempla*, and "John's habit of proving everything twice by reference to both biblical and classical sources."[38]

Perhaps a single chapter of moderate length might illustrate these pervasive tendencies. In Chapter 1. 4, John embarks upon a survey of vain and frivolous pursuits that distract men (courtiers) from their duties and degrade their noble natures (*nobiliora ingenia*). First on the list is hunting (*uenatica*), and John immediately launches a series of *exempla* to demonstrate his claims. He balances negative examples of hunters who indulged in the sport for pleasure alone (Ganymede, Actaeon, Adonis), and those who sought to serve a common good (Hercules, Meleager, Aeneas). Twice he digresses from the classical exemplars: once to comment on the hunting hounds of Albania, and once to deride the excessive war-preparations of Emilians and Ligurians "if a tortoise threatens their territory" (*si finibus eorum testudo immineat*). He compares them with "our people" (*nostri*), who stir up more tumult and involve greater expense to declare war on wild beasts. John accuses hunters of lacking modesty, dignity, self-control and temperance.

Following these examples drawn from "the poets" (*poetae*), John sets forth a series of Scriptural *exempla* that includes Nimrod, who went from "stout hunter" (*robustus uenator*) to tyrant, and Esau, the hunter who sold his birthright for a mess of pottage. Into the story of Nimrod, who ruled in Babylon, John weaves an account of the tower of Babel, another instance of his attraction to detail and compulsion to digress. John reinforces his argument that men guided by wisdom and virtue do not indulge in this debased pastime of hunting by pointing out that no philosophers and sages of old (Socrates, Plato,

---

36   Michael Winterbottom, review of *Entheticus maior and minor* in *Journal of Ecclesiastical History* 39 (1988), 595–596, esp. p. 595.

37   Smalley, *The Becket Conflict*, p. 101.

38   Michael Wilks, "John of Salisbury and the Tyranny of Nonsense," in *The World of John of Salisbury*, p. 278; see also Liebeschütz, *Medieval Humanism*, pp. 116–117.

Aristotle, Seneca), no Christian fathers and saints (Augustine, Lawrence, Vincent) were troubled by this "madness" (*insania*).

As he concludes this discourse, John returns to "our own time," one in which mournful examples (*nostrorum temporum luctuosa exempla*) instruct us against this intemperate activity, he says, for we have seen that leaders and even kings have been struck down by divine wrath while engaged in the chase. This statement leads John to another digression, a review of restrictions placed on hunting and lands preserved for it, to the detriment of farmers and tenants who risk treason (*lesa maiestas*) if they hinder hunters. Finally, in keeping with his typically balanced manner, John acknowledges that hunting may be a lawful, useful occupation for those compelled to it by duty or necessity, but he disallows such bloody, filthy (*carnificium, sordes*) work for courtiers, noblemen, rulers and those in holy orders, because of their lofty positions. Thus, hunting for pleasure alone is banned as a trivial, frivolous pursuit; it is laudable only when guided by good judgement and moderation (*prudentia, moderatio*).

The foregoing summary of a chapter that comprises some twelve pages in a modern edition gives a sense of John of Salisbury's stylistic methods, but it does not do justice to his rhetorical skills and flourishes. An observant auditor will note how he maintains unity of theme amid the many digressions and *exempla* through judicious repetition of key terms. For example, he underscores the impropriety of hunting by linking it frequently to vanity (*uanitas*) and self-indulgent pleasure (*uoluptas*); the latter word appears more than a dozen times in the chapter. John also insists that hunting is "war on beasts" (*bellum bestiis*; *saeuire in bestiis*), and mocks it by the use of diminutives to describe the prey: "a little beast" (*bestiola*); "a timid little rabbit" (*lepusculus*). He interjects ironic exclamations: "You would think they captured the King of Cappadocia!" (*regem Capadocum captum credas*). He scorns hunters' jargon as "the liberal studies of the higher class in our times!" (*Haec sunt temporibus nostris liberalia nobilium studia*). He uses hyperbole: "the bees are scarcely permitted to roam freely" (*apibus uix naturali libertate uti permissum est*). And of course, John punctuates his text with allusions and quotations, mainly from poets, but also from historians and a naturalist, Pliny the Elder. Viewed positively, these features create in the *Policraticus* a kind of encyclopedia, or commonplace book, or a learned man's "philosophical memoir."[39]

The opening books of the *Policraticus* deride the manifold ways through which men, specifically courtiers, violate the rule of moderation through degrading pursuits and pastimes. John's censures range widely over such disparate

---

39   Cary J. Nederman, *John of Salisbury* (Tempe, Arizona, 2005), p. 51.

activities as hunting, gambling, acting, magic, omen and dream interpretation, all defined, exemplified and roundly denounced. Although these famous passages were "distinctly disappointing" to one translator in that they were "singularly devoid of contemporary flavor,"[40] they do offer extensive analysis of each vice, along with John's considered criticisms, generously supported by citation of authoritative sources. Moreover, there is the notable inclusion of a very personal example in Book 2. 28, where John describes an event of his boyhood, when a priest attempted to employ him as a medium in crystal gazing. One senses the author's relief in his admission that "I was judged useless" (*inutilis iudicatus sum*) for the purpose. And occasionally John lends his genial humor or glimpses of his own predilections to a learned discourse, as in his lengthy discussion of omens. There, among all the classical citations and examples from Roman history and mythology, and blended into the portentous sightings of birds and beasts, we discover John's loathing for toads: "I can't stand the sight of one!" (*Buffo. . .mihi tamen vel solo uisu molestus est*) and his preference for meeting a hare "on the table" (*commodior in mensa*) rather than on the road.

The proper order and governance of a Christian commonwealth becomes John's concentration in the central portion of the *Policraticus*. Books Four to Six constitute a *speculum regum*, a "mirror for princes." John begins by distinguishing between a tyrant and a true prince, affirming that the solc, or greatest, difference is that the latter submits to the law, rules his subjects according to its dictates, and believes himself to be their servant. Book Four describes in detail the responsibilities and virtues required of a prince. Books Five and Six are most famous for their development of an extended analogy between a commonwealth and the human body, which John claims to adopt from Plutarch, but which Hans Liebeschütz convincingly traced to Robert Pullen, one of John's teachers.[41] Commenting on *Deuteronomy* (17:14–20) in his *Sentences* (7.7), Pullen had likened the roles of kings and priests, *regnum et sacerdotium*, in governing a commonwealth to those of body and soul in a human being. He developed the theme by outlining the duties of judges, knights, peasants and other classes in society. John of Salisbury introduces the same topics in the same order as his former teacher, who later became a cardinal and served in the papal curia, where John was likely reacquainted with him.

This organic metaphor, in which our author likens the prince to the head, the king's council (*senatus*) to the heart, judges to the eyes and ears, soldiers to

---

40   John Dickinson, in *Policraticus* trans. Pike (foreword), p. vi.
41   Liebeschütz, *Medieval Humanism*, pp. 23–26.

the hands, and so on through all the classes of the commonwealth, expresses John's fundamental view of the state. He was fond of examples of this type, and in Book Six (24) he related a fable told to him by Pope Adrian IV about the rebellion of the members of the body against the voracious belly. From their subsequent deprivation they learned a salutary lesson about mutual cooperation, an ideal embraced by John of Salisbury, who was later credited with authorship of popular verses on this theme called *"De membris conspirantibus."*[42]

In a prologue to Book Seven, John again signals a thematic transition with the words "Having left the courtiers' hall" (*egressus aula curialium*), and at the end of Book Eight he sums up the overall purpose of his final books: to pass from frivolities to morally correct, serious matters, and to that which is fitting or beneficial for regulating one's life. For our author, this goal requires tracing the footsteps of philosophers, as his subtitle implies, and, broadly speaking, he does so, but with characteristic diversion and digression. For example, he devotes four Chapters (7. 9–12) to the subject of reading, and recommends that all writings should be read, even pagan (*gentiles*) authors, but with discretion. Typically, he supports his views with Scriptural and classical authority; in this case the latter is Seneca's advice to Lucilius, repeated in Macrobius' *Saturnalia*, to imitate bees in their discrimination and selectivity as they flit from flower to flower. Another interesting example is the discussion of various vices that occupies the last ten chapters of Book Seven. In an extended treatment of rampant societal hypocrisy, evidenced even among priests and prelates, John includes high praise for righteous monks (*claustrales*), with special commendation for virtuous Cistercians and Cluniacs, Carthusians and the "new order" (*noua professio*) of Grandmontines. These passages (7. 21–23) offer a sharp contrast to the harsh satire later directed at these orders by Nigel of Canterbury and Walter Map.

The final book of the *Policraticus* continues John's review of vices, culminating in a return to the subject of tyranny; one scholar labels this section a "treatise on tyranny."[43] Its twenty-five chapters are among his most expansive in the use of *exempla*, especially classical ones that illustrate vicious behavior, contrasting virtues, and the wretched ends to which all tyrants come. In one Chapter (11), John denounces lust as a vile vice excused only by lawful matrimony, and this leads to a lengthy digression on marriage which rehearses several classic arguments against that institution, such as those found in Saint

42   Ronald E. Pepin, "'On the Conspiracy of the Members', Attributed to John of Salisbury," *Allegorica* 12 (1991), 29–41.

43   Jan van Laarhoven, "Thou Shalt Not Slay a Tyrant! The So-Called Theory of John of Salisbury," in *The World of John of Salisbury*, p. 320.

Jerome's *Aduersus Iouinianum* and his purported source, Theophrastus. John even recounts the entire story of the Widow of Ephesus, verbatim, from Petronius. Needless to say, this chapter has been invoked by some literary historians, who place John of Salisbury near the top of their list of misogynists and misogamists.[44]

Life of Saint Anselm

John of Salisbury's *Life of Saint Anselm* was composed at the behest of Archbishop Becket to support the petition for his predecessor's canonization. It was included in the dossier presented to Pope Alexander III at the Council of Tours in May, 1163, requesting a declaration of sainthood for Anselm. The Pope, caught up in the swirl of pressing matters and overwhelmed by petitions, deferred action on Becket's nomination, and Saint Anselm's formal canonization was postponed for several centuries. John's *Life* fared not much better, for it remained little known and never mentioned, not even by the author himself. Although one 12th-century verse epitome has been identified,[45] the *Vita S. Anselmi* has survived in a single manuscript written by a monk of Canterbury in 1507.

John of Salisbury graced his hagiographical effort with commendable style and considerable rhetorical skill, but as fundamentally a canonization brief, the straightforward text offers few flourishes. In fact, the work is extensively dependent on the *Vita Anselmi* written more than half a century earlier by Eadmer, a monk and close friend of Anselm's. From this detailed, intimate biography John drew his accounts of the personal travails, virtues, visions and miracles of the saint. One scholar has even called John's *Vita* merely an abridgement of Eadmer's work.[46]

---

44 Vern L. Bullough, *The Subordinate Sex: A History of Attitudes Toward Women* (Baltimore, 1973), p. 186: "One of the most virulent assaults upon women was by John of Salisbury, who collected almost every possible example of troublesome women in history." See also Alcuin Blamires, *Women Defamed and Women Defended* (Oxford, 1992), p. 99; Katharina M. Wilson and Elizabeth M. Makowski, *Wykked Wyves and the Woes of Marriage* (Albany, NY, 1990), pp. 81–83.

45 Daniel J. Sheerin, "An Anonymous Verse Epitome of the Life of St. Anselm," *Analecta Bollandiana* 92 (1974), 109–124.

46 Alain Nadeau, "Notes on the Significance of John of Salisbury's 'Vita Anselmi'," in Frederick Van Fleteren and Joseph C. Schnaubelt, eds., *Twenty-Five Years (1969–1994) of Anselm Studies* (Lewiston, NY, 1996), p. 67.

To be sure, John's treatment of material that he derived from Eadmer is selective and significantly less detailed, amounting in some passages to mere paraphrase. However, he did not neglect to underscore Anselm's holiness by including Eadmer's examples of cures effected by the saint's cincture or by crumbs from his table; of fires and storms halted through his intercession. In fact, John's descriptions of visions and miracles attributed to Anselm are all sourced from Eadmer's *Vita*, save one that occurred after his work was completed. John was also guided by Eadmer's text in recording the saint's virtues, most notably his humility and charity. To illustrate these, John recounts charming anecdotes, such as Anselm's rescue of a hare that took shelter beneath his horse while fleeing from hounds. John borrowed liberally from Eadmer's *Vita Anselmi*, but in keeping with his narrower purpose, he presented information much more concisely, and certainly less intimately than the monastic author who had been Anselm's friend and chosen biographer.

John of Salisbury departed from Eadmer's style and substance in other ways too. Since his primary purpose was to secure papal canonization for the long-suffering Archbishop, he emphasized Anselm's sanctity in a manner that his predecessor had not. For example, from prologue to conclusion, John repeatedly referred to his subject as "blessed" (*beatus*) and "holy" (*sanctus*), whereas Eadmer called him simply "Anselm" or "Father Anselm." Moreover, John identified the saint as one whom God had summoned to dispel the darkness and to illuminate His Church, and throughout the *Vita* he employs epithets such as "apostolic man" (*uir apostolicus*), "servant of God" (*seruus Dei*), and "the Lord's anointed" (*christus Domini*) to reinforce his saintly status. Often, John attaches the adjective "true" (*uerus*) to these epithets; thus he hails Anselm as "true disciple of Christ" (*uerus discipulus Christi*) to emphasize his sanctity. Furthermore, in seven separate passages John places Anselm firmly in the company of legendary saints, comparing his charity to that of Saint Nicholas, his gift of prophecy to Saint Benedict's, and in three instances likening him to Saint Martin, patron of Tours. This was a clever choice on John's part, since the petition for Anselm's canonization was presented there. Also, John's pervasive use of Scriptural allusions and quotations served to affirm the holiness of Anselm, who became in his ministry "all things to all men" (1 Cor. 9:22) like Saint Paul, and who at his death "fell asleep in the Lord" (Acts 7:59) like Saint Stephen.

Although John of Salisbury's *Vita Anselmi* failed to secure immediate papal confirmation of sanctity, or a renowned place in hagiographic literature, we can still salute a worthy effort and be thankful that it has survived among his writings.

Historia Pontificalis

The *Historia pontificalis* is untitled in the single 13th-century manuscript (Berne, 367) in which it survives. The work is also unfinished, unattributed and undated. It was first printed, ascribed to John of Salisbury, and titled in the 19th century. Although the author states in a prologue that his book will address matters pertaining to papal history (*ad pontificalem historiam*), a point that he reiterates verbatim in Chapter 15, it is not a conventional history of the papacy. Rather, the *Historia pontificalis* is John's personal memoir of the papal court from 1148 to 1152, "enriched with learned allusions and digressions,"[47] including an embedded treatise on the teachings of Gilbert de la Porrée, his revered former teacher. The article by Clare Monagle in this volume treats of John's description of the trial of Gilbert in the *Historia pontificalis*.

The addressee of the *Historia pontificalis* is Peter of Celle, whom John salutes familiarly as *"Mi Petre,"* and "Dearest of friends" (*amicorum karissime*). The abbot of Saint-Remi was his closest friend, as their affectionate correspondence demonstrates; during John's lengthy exile from England (1163–70), he resided at Reims as Peter's guest. Probably owing to this circumstance of enforced leisure, John began to write the work in 1164, and he seems to have abandoned it as the strife of the Becket controversy wore him down and occupied more of his time as well. The text as we have it ends abruptly in the opening sentence of Chapter 46, confirming the sense that the book is incomplete, "a fragment."[48]

The *Historia pontificalis* is "well known for temperate and tentative judgements and for a remarkable density of convincing and amusing detail."[49] The character sketches of notable contemporaries are masterfully drawn by John, whose ability to punctuate a personal profile with telling actions and pointed dialogue is on full display. Moreover, as Roger Ray has convincingly demonstrated, they are "laced with humor," mostly at the expense of prelates, even cardinals and popes, as part of the author's effort to fill the narrative with verisimilar material.[50] For example, his concise portrait of Henry, Bishop of

---

47   *Historia pontificalis*, p. xix; see also Marjorie Chibnall, "John of Salisbury as a Historian," in *The World of John of Salisbury*, pp. 169–177.

48   Christopher Brooke, "Aspects of John of Salisbury's *Historia Pontificalis*," in Lesley Smith and Benedicta Ward, eds., *Intellectual Life in the Middle Ages* (London, 1992), p. 185.

49   Roger Ray, "Rhetorical Scepticism and Verisimilar Narrative in John of Salisbury's *Historia Pontificalis*," in Ernst Breisach, ed., *Classical Rhetoric & Medieval Historiography* (Kalamazoo, MI, 1985), p. 63.

50   Ibid., pp. 62 and 88–90.

Winchester, with his long beard and philosopher's gravity, making a spectacle of himself at the papal court while bustling about, like a Horatian Damasippus, to buy up old busts, is a masterpiece of ridicule. His account of an overwrought Pope Eugene III, drenched in tears and rushing down from his throne in the sight of all present [including John of Salisbury] to grovel before Count Hugh of Molise, so that his miter fell in the dust, forms a strange preface to John's claim to honor "so great a pontiff" (*honorem tanti pontificis*). Such tongue-in-cheek observations must have inspired J. Huizinga's characterization of John as "the man with the serious smile."[51]

John of Salisbury brought ample abilities and a skeptical attitude to his sole foray into formal history. These have been carefully traced and affirmed to be that which "set the *Historia pontificalis* apart from the average of medieval chronicles."[52] The work surely has historical value, for many facts and accounts would be lost without it, as would the insights and testimony of John himself to momentous movements and incidents of the mid-12th century. His eyewitness account of the trial of Gilbert de la Porrée at the Council of Reims is a balanced treatment, fair to Gilbert and to his adversary, Bernard of Clairvaux. The work is a "source of the first importance" for English ecclesiastical matters during the civil war and for information about the Second Crusade.[53] However, the internal virtues and the reputation of its scholarly author could not save the *Historia pontificalis* from centuries of oblivion. There is no mention of it among John's contemporaries, nor do other chroniclers of his day cite it. Perhaps the book remained "a private record for the interest and instruction of his friend Peter."[54] If so, it remains unacknowledged by Peter of Celle and unclaimed by John of Salisbury in any of their surviving works.

Life of Thomas Becket

John of Salisbury's *Life of Saint Thomas the Martyr* comprises a prologue and twenty-eight brief chapters, several consisting of only a sentence or two. The *uita* rapidly reviews the years of Becket's early life and service to Archbishop Theobald; his tenure as chancellor of England receives somewhat fuller treatment; his struggles and sufferings as Archbishop of Canterbury, culminating

---

51   Johan Huizinga, "John of Salisbury: A Pre-Gothic Mind," *Men and Ideas* (New York, 1970), p. 160.

52   Ray, "Rhetorical Scepicism," p. 92.

53   *Historia pontificalis*, p. xlii.

54   Ibid., p. xlvii.

in his assassination in the cathedral on 29 December 1170, dominate more than half the text. John's vivid, detailed description of the murder and its aftermath is an almost verbatim replication of a passage in a letter (Letter 305: *Ex insperato*) sent to John of Canterbury, Bishop of Poitiers, "perhaps only a few days later,"[55] and his *Life* was written not long afterward, surely in 1171. Thus, John's is the earliest account of the momentous event, and his *uita* of Becket should be dated among the first of fifteen surviving biographies from the 12th century, most produced within a dozen years of the saint's death, and foremost of three composed by his clerks (John of Salisbury, Herbert of Bosham, William FitzStephen). The preceding article in this volume by Karen Bollermann and Cary Nederman offers a comprehensive treatment of the relationship between John of Salisbury and Becket.

John's *Life* has been roundly criticized as "trite"; "a disappointment"; "superficial"; "derivative and impersonal."[56] Likely written in haste, perhaps to support a cause for the martyr's formal canonization, the *uita* is indeed short, sparse and sparing of John's acclaimed scholarship. The author's prologue acknowledges it to be "a concise and quite brief discourse."[57] The *Life* must not be underestimated, however, for in it the author's central themes of *libertas ecclesiae*, tyranny, and the malice of royal courtiers, the "beasts of the court" (*bestiae curiae*), receive ample practical illustration. Becket is specifically acknowledged a "champion of ecclesiastical freedom" (*assertor ecclesiae libertatis*). In fact, John's repeated comparisons of the Archbishop's tribulations to those of Christ, his emphasis on the martyr's "invincible constancy" (*uir inuictae constantiae*), and his frequent allusions to Scripture plainly underscore the sanctity of his subject. So does John of Salisbury's eyewitness account of the martyrdom.

William FitzStephen was present at Becket's murder, and he specifically named John of Salisbury as among his clerks who sought protection and had recourse to hiding places. This has led many to declare that John was not an eyewitness to the actions that he described. Others, and I among them, take FitzStephen at his word and believe that John took refuge under an altar or in some hidden corner of the darkening church where he was able to see the escalating violence, for his account of the savagery "retains the flavour of the

---

55 *The Later Letters*, p. xliv; see Frank Barlow, *Thomas Becket* (Berkeley, 1990), pp. 4–5.
56 See for example, *Historia pontificalis*, p. xxxiv; Michael Staunton, *The Lives of Thomas Becket* (Manchester, 2001), pp. 4, 7; Nederman, *John of Salisbury*, p. 80.
57 *Vita Thomae*, Prologue, ed. Robertson, vol. 2, p. 302: "succinctus et admodum brevis sermo."

event as no other document."[58] Indeed, it is a dramatic record of Becket's confrontation with his killers, his demeanor in death, and the outrage perpetrated on his body when one of them cruelly scattered his blood and brains on the pavement with a sword. This is not to deny that John might have consulted other witnesses to the horrific incident, or that he employed his considerable rhetorical skills in shaping it. In an illuminating essay, Richard C. Lounsbury has detailed how John patterned his description of the murder and mutilation after *exempla* in Lucan's *Pharsalia*, not to falsify his account, but to give it form and to promote its memory.[59]

John found models of presentation in Lucan, whom he considered not only a learned poet, but one whose "true narration" (*uera narratio*) of events placed him among historians as well. Thus, he turned to Lucan's account of the death of Pompey, that general's response to violent attack and the agony of death, the fury of his assassins, the mutilation of their victim, the hasty burial and lasting fame of the heroic sufferer. John skillfully adapted these *exempla* and their expressive diction to his own descriptions of Becket's confrontation with his assailants, his violent death at their hands and the aftermath of the murder in order to provide an appropriate moral and emotional context for an abominable reality. John of Salisbury's method, here and elsewhere in his writings, was to integrate relevant *exempla*, textual testimonies, to demonstrate a proof or moral quality through *similitudo*.

John's description of the fatal encounter remains a striking eyewitness account. We should recall that one of the assassins, William de Traci, later claimed (mistakenly) that he had severed the arm of John of Salisbury, and that Peter of Celle referred to John as one "stained by the precious blood of blessed Thomas."[60] These are not proofs positive, of course, but they lend credence to the view that a steadfast supporter, a man who refused a king to his face when Henry II proposed unacceptable terms for the restoration of his confiscated property, and endured long exile and penury, one who lauded *constantia* and *fidelitas*, would remain with his archbishop, albeit lurking in shadows, to the bitter end.

---

58   *The Later Letters*, p. xliv; Michael Staunton, *Thomas Becket and His Biographers* (Woodbridge, 2006), p. 19 also believes that John "was present in the cathedral on 29 December to witness the murder."

59   Richard C. Lounsbury, "The Case of the Erudite Eyewitness: Cicero, Lucan and John of Salisbury," *Allegorica* 11 (1990), 15–35.

60   *MB*, vol. 1, p. 134: "Willelmus...dixerit etiam se brachiam Joannis Saresberiensis praecidisse"; Peter of Celle, Letter 117, PL 202, col. 567: "Joannes pretioso sanguine beati Thomae pontificis et martyris intinctus."

John of Salisbury's *Life of Saint Thomas the Martyr*, for all its failed expectations in the judgement of modern scholars, enjoyed wide circulation inde-
pendently and as the preface to Alan of Tewkesbury's collection of Becket
correspondence. As a contribution to the hagiographical genre, the work was
influential in spreading the cult of Saint Thomas, and perhaps in helping to
secure his swift canonization. As importantly, the *Life* is a further expression of
John's constant defense of Church liberty and denunciation of tyranny through
commendation of saintly virtues and condemnation of vicious foes.

Epistulae

John of Salisbury's collected correspondence has been edited, translated into
English, and published in two volumes, styled "early" letters and "later" letters.
The first group belongs to John's years of service to Archbishop Theobald
(1153–61), and the second dates from the accession of Becket to the end of the
author's life (1163–80). While most of the epistles in the early collection were
written for Theobald as official documents dealing with ecclesiastical affairs,
there are 37 pieces directed to John's friends and associates in his own name.
The bulk of the letters from the later years are dominated by the Becket controversy, but many are personal missives. There are 325 epistles in all. John
invested in them his wit and wisdom, his vast learning, his impressive Latin
style. Thus they constitute the best illustration we have of his tastes and abilities. His personality emerges most in his letters, where we "hear his familiar
voice…for he lives in his writings as do few of his world."[61]
   A few examples must suffice, for a summary could not do justice to John of
Salisbury's epistolary skills, fluid expression or precise arguments. The most
attractive and entertaining feature of his personal correspondence is his evident good humor. John's letters to friends are laced with jests and puns, with
teasing remarks that established a genial tone and promoted a wholesome
camaraderie. These qualities characterize his best friendships, as with Peter of
Celle, who dedicated to him a treatise on breads mentioned in Sacred Scripture.
With masterful subtlety, John acknowledges his friend's ample generosity in
the past, his former kindness to one in poverty, his provision of daily bread.
Indeed, now he sends more bread, abundant bread, such delicious breads that
John could swallow them up, crumbs, crusts, and all! But a devourer of breads

---

61   Christopher Brooke, "John of Salisbury and His World," in *The World of John of Salisbury*,
      p. 20.

gets thirsty and choked by their dryness. In mercy, Peter should now provide wine, or beer will do. Anything to make him tipsy![62]

At another time Peter would thank John for letters that "filled my heart with joy, my mouth with laughter, for you have mingled jests with serious matter."[63] John's epistle (Letter 140) of congratulation to Nicholas, the newly-appointed archdeacon of Huntingdon, is another masterpiece of playful jibing, for he reminds his friend that he used to consider this "race of men" (*genus hominum*) as beyond salvation, and John thanks God that Nicholas now sees the light and has changed his baleful opinion of archdeacons! Sometimes John's anger and indignation flash forth, as when he slips into a letter (Letter 15) to Pope Adrian the "outrage" (*iniuria*) of Walkelin, an archdeacon who has named a bastard (*spurium*) borne by his hearth-mate (*focaria*) after the Pope; the concubine is pregnant again, and if she delivers a girl, the child will be called "Adriana." What a true friend of the Roman pontiff, who remembers him even in disgraceful acts!

The central theme of the second collection is "the tempest of the Becket dispute."[64] It is an important index to the personalities involved, to the strategies and intrigues of the participants, to the factual events and rumors that evolved during the lengthy conflict, which "plunged him [John] into politics up to the neck."[65] The letters testify to John of Salisbury's steadfast support for the Archbishop even as he claimed to upbraid him "more often and more harshly than any other mortal man"[66] for his overzealous provocation of the king; they are filled with John's sound counsel, founded on faith, philosophy and good sense.

John's epistles are also testaments to his forthright candor and courage in the defense of cherished principles, such as loyalty to the Pope, the primacy of Canterbury and Church liberty. He renews his devotion to these ideals again and again in his letters, as in the long epistle to a former Canterbury colleague, where he laments "the desolation of the Church in the kingdom of England" and twice calls its persecutor [Henry II] a "tyrant."[67] Moreover, John was adept

---

62   Letter 111, in *The Early Letters*, p. 57: "non abhorreo quicquid inebriare potest"; see Ronald E. Pepin, "*Amicitia Jocosa*: Peter of Celle and John of Salisbury," *Florilegium* 3 (1983), 140–156.

63   Peter of Celle, *ep.* 69, PL 202, col. 515: "cor meum jubilo, os meum impletum est risu. Miscuisti siquidem jocos seriis."

64   *The Later Letters*, p. xix.

65   Smalley, *The Becket Conflict*, p. 102.

66   Letter 150, in *The Later Letters*, p. 48: "saepius et asperius quam aliquis mortalium corripuerim dominum archiepiscopum."

67   Letter 187, in *The Later Letters*, p. 230: "...ecclesiae desolationem in regno Anglorum ingemiscimus...tirannus."

at developing his themes of distress and tribulation by using a "language of persecution" that has been clearly defined and traced in his letters.[68] He likened Becket's sufferings to those of Christ and accepted his own travails as a beneficial test of faith and spirit. Thus, in speaking of these letters, the Dean of Salisbury observed that "what emerges is the scholar, the diplomat and the man," and the characteristics of that man are "sanity and moderation, tolerance and readiness to reach a compromise, but in the last resort, inflexibility of principle."[69]

Keystones of Theme and Style

The foregoing survey and analysis of John's writings reveals his enduring values and recurring themes. First among these is moderation. For all his ardent advocacy of educational and ecclesiastical causes, for all his courageous candor and forthright expression, John of Salisbury adhered to this ideal in theory and in practice. From the invocation of moderation as "life's holy rule" (*uitae regula sancta*) in the *Entheticus maior* to his counsel of moderate action to participants in the Becket conflict, he evidenced his devotion to this virtue. With consistent, deliberate frequency in all his works, John insisted upon *modus, moderatio, modestia* and *frugalitas* as supreme guides of right living, leading to *ciuilitas*, his term for decent behavior in the society of men. Philosophically, he embraced a moderate skepticism as propounded by the Later Academy and pursued all his interests guided by it.[70] His definitions and denunciations of false educators, depraved courtiers, frivolity, tyranny and rashness are based on their excess and abandonment of moderation. His relentless exposition of serious matters and trifles, his *"seria et nugae,"* is fundamentally a contrast between moderate and immoderate behavior. The chapters by David Bloch and Christophe Grellard in this *Companion* provide ample analysis and discussion of John's skepticism, as does Professor Grellard's recent book (2013) on our author's place in the medieval renaissance of skepticism.

---

68 John McLoughlin, "The Language of Persecution: John of Salisbury and the Early Phase of the Becket Dispute (1163–66)," *Studies in Church History* 21 (1984), 73–87.

69 Sydney Evans, "John of Salisbury: A Man of Letters," *The Hatcher Review* 7 (1979), 3–18, esp. p. 18.

70 *Metalogicon*, Prologue, p. 11: "Academicus in his quae sunt dubitabilia sapienti"; *Policraticus*, Prologue, ed. Webb, vol. 1, p. 17: " nec Academicorum erubesco professionem qui in his quae sunt dubitabilia sapienti, ab eorum vestigiis non recedo."

Arguably, the word most associated with John of Salisbury in modern scholarship is "humanism." He has been identified as a humanist repeatedly in
books, articles and lectures, often as the foremost humanist of the Middle Ages
and a precursor of Renaissance humanism.[71] The earliest studies that so
defined John founded their judgement on his admiration for classical antiquity
and his vast knowledge of Roman authors: what is variously called Latin, literary or scholastic humanism. But since John embraced the fusion of classical
Latin literature and Christianity, and demonstrated his devotion to the traditions and texts of both, he is usually cited as a "Christian humanist." To be sure,
"humanism" is a term that lends itself to complex definition and interpretation, as insightful studies have illustrated, but none would seem to exclude
John from the ranks of its proponents. On the contrary, he "embodied the new
humanism that came to permeate 12th-century thought,"[72] and he "has come
to be known as the most eminent of the humanists."[73]

As a writer, John consistently reveals his theoretical and practical devotion to
humanism. He rarely misses an opportunity to impart moral principles and
good counsel for righteous behavior, and these are usually bolstered by citation
of authoritative sources. Thus, John repeatedly invokes Sacred Scripture and
Christian precepts, or adapts to his own intentions the *sententiae* of admired classical authors, or both. We observe the humanistic outlook in his epistles to friends
and acquaintances, especially those written during the Becket conflict; in his
major treatises; and in his satire, a genre whose purpose is to mock society's foibles
in order to correct them. In all his works, John evidences keen interest in human
affairs, including the human capacity to achieve fulfillment and earthly happiness through knowledge of the good (wisdom) and practice of the good (virtue).

Any list of John's stylistic propensities must be headed by his widespread
use of classical literature to underscore a point, almost any point. He employed
this practice in his personal correspondence and in his major works, where
quotations and allusions to Latin writers abound to a degree unparalleled

---

71   The literature on this subject is exhaustive and includes contributions from nearly every
     decade of the twentieth century and into the twenty-first. See, for example, Liebeschütz,
     Medieval Humanism; E.K. Tolan, "John of Salisbury and the Problem of Medieval
     Humanism," *Études d'histoire littéraire et doctrinale* 19 (1968), 189–199; Klaus Guth,
     "Hochmittelalterlicher Humanismus als Lebensform: ein Beitrag zum Standesethos des
     westeuropäischen Weltklerus nach Johannes von Salisbury," in *The World of John of
     Salisbury*, pp. 63–76; Glenn W. Olsen, "John of Salisbury's Humanism," *Gli Unamesimi
     Medievali*, ed. Claudio Leonardi (Florence, 1998), pp. 447–468.
72   J.J.N. McGurk, "John of Salisbury," *History Today* (January, 1975), 40–47, esp. p. 47.
73   M. Anthony Brown, "John of Salisbury," *Franciscan Studies* 19 (1959), 241–297, esp. p. 297.

among medieval authors. This salient feature of his writings, highlighted by Webb's extensive *Index auctorum*, led a generation of John of Salisbury scholars to hail him as "the best classical scholar of the age."[74] One early survey of his sources pronounced him "the greatest classicist of the Middle Ages."[75] Later studies, however, have resulted in a tempered assessment of his vaunted learning. Foremost among these is a dissertation and related articles by Janet Martin, who pioneered the investigation into John's exemplars and determined that his sources were often excerpts or compendia rather than complete texts.

Professor Martin's careful analysis of John's working methods reveals that he often preferred to consult *florilegia* rather than whole books, for the convenience of reference and also for their emphasis on morals.[76] For instance, his verbatim quotations from Suetonius in the *Policraticus* are often not taken directly from the Roman author's *De uita Caesarum*, but from Heiric of Auxerre's excerpts, even though the original text was readily accessible and popular in his day; there was likely a copy in Canterbury at Christ Church or St Augustine's Abbey library where John surely found many of the books he read and researched. In fact, John displays familiarity with Suetonius' work beyond that contained in Heiric's compilation, so one should not assume, as Professor Martin sensibly cautions, that he did not have given texts at his disposal when he preferred a *florilegium*. He used both, as one might expect of a busy administrator pressed for time, one who wrote in hours stolen from official duties. Thus, John read entire texts of some authors, such as his favorite ancient poets, but epitomes and extracts of other lengthy works, such as Aulus Gellius' *Noctes Atticae* and Frontinus' *Strategemata*.

One notable exception to John's practice of drawing citations from *florilegia*, and chiefly from manuscripts of English provenance, is Petronius' *Satyricon*. This book was apparently so appealing to him that he secured his own unabridged copy and exploited the text for themes, tales, verses, phrases and proper names: over twenty borrowings in all. Janet Martin's study of the textual tradition of this relatively rare work in the medieval period, and her analysis of John's references to it, illustrate his approach to sources.[77] Through her

---

74 Charles H. Haskins, *The Renaissance of the Twelfth Century* (Cambridge, MA, 1927), p. 225.

75 August C. Krey, "John of Salisbury's Knowledge of the Classics," *Transactions of the Wisconsin Academy of Sciences, Arts and Letters* 16 (1910), 948–987, esp. p. 948.

76 Janet Martin, "John of Salisbury as Classical Scholar," in *The World of John of Salisbury*, pp. 184–185.

77 Eadem, "Uses of Tradition: Gellius, Petronius and John of Salisbury," *Viator* 10 (1979), 57–76; see also eadem, "John of Salisbury's Manuscripts of Frontinus and of Gellius," *Journal of the Warburg and Courtauld Institutes* 40 (1977), 276–282.

efforts we are better able to glimpse John's classicizing humanism at work, and
to more fully appreciate his zest for assimilation and adaptation of classical
models. Moreover, she demonstrated convincingly that John treated sources
very casually, altering them at times to remedy corruptions or to make them
better conform to his arguments. In spite of these findings, Martin concluded
that he may "still be regarded as one of the most learned men of his time."[78]

Another important discovery from source studies is that John of Salisbury
not only manipulated them to suit his purposes, but on occasion invented
them, "cheating cheerfully," as one respected scholar put it.[79] The most noto-
rious instance of literary invention occurs in the *Policraticus*. In Books Five
and Six, John purports to exploit a manual of political theory composed by
Plutarch for the Roman emperor Trajan. He cites this source explicitly (5. 1) as
"a letter" (*epistola*) and later refers to it as "a little book" (*libellus*) whose title
is *Institutio Traiani*. However, John's definitive *extat*, "there exists," has not
only been called into question, but discredited outright and called "a fiction"
devised by our author to conceal the personal character of his political
views,[80] just as he employed pseudonyms so widely in satirical passages.
Although a case has been made for the existence of such a lost work by
Plutarch, prevailing scholarly opinion denies the authenticity of the *Institutio
Traiani* and accuses John of Salisbury of forgery. He was, it seems, not averse
to inventing sources. And, he practically admitted the practice in the prologue to the *Policraticus* when he cautioned the reader that "I do not promise
that all things written here are true, but whether true or false, they may serve
the needs of my readers."[81]

Also in the *Policraticus*, especially, we observe John's penchant for *exempla*,
illustrative tales used to reinforce a moral lesson. Indeed, Peter von Moos, the
leading guide to our understanding and appreciation of John's deployment of
such examples, noted that "half the text [is] taken up by literary *exempla*," a
fact observed by Liebeschütz, who asserted that the book is "dominated" by

---

78   Eadem, *John of Salisbury and the Classics*, PhD diss. (Harvard University, 1968), p. 198.

79   David Luscombe, "John of Salisbury in Recent Scholarship," in *The World of John of
      Salisbury*, p. 32.

80   Liebeschütz, *Medieval Humanism*, p. 24; a more detailed rejection of the authenticity of
      the *Institutio Traiani* is found in Hans Liebeschütz, "John of Salisbury and Pseudo-
      Plutarch," *Journal of the Warburg and Courtauld Institutes* 6 (1943), 33–39, and in Max
      Kerner, "Randbemerkungen zur *Institutio Traiani*," in *The World of John of Salisbury*,
      pp. 203–206.

81   *Policraticus*, Prologue, ed. Webb, vol. 1, p. 15: "...non omnia, quae hic scribuntur, uera esse
      promitto, sed siue uera seu falsa sint, legentium usibus inseruire."

them.[82] John of Salisbury was so attracted to this kind of illustration that he plundered classical, biblical and patristic sources for useful *exempla*, and sometimes applied them even as contradictory testimonies in his search for truth. His cautionary tales, anecdotes and *exempla* drawn from the pages of Valerius Maximus, Aulus Gellius, Frontinus, Macrobius and a host of other writers, teach, entertain and impress readers of the *Policraticus*, while securing the author's renown for scholarship.

John of Salisbury's works also attest to his affection for proverbial expressions and aphorisms, adopted from a wide range of ancient and contemporary sources. His writings are channels of transmission for wise and witty sayings, and many appear, sometimes credited to him, sometimes silently, in later works of literature. Such, for example, is "an unlettered king is like an ass wearing a crown,"[83] repeated in a number of 13th-century authors, including Helinand of Froidmont and Vincent of Beauvais. John so approved of the six keys of philosophy that he found in verses by "the old man of Chartres" (*senex Carnotensis*) that he commented at length on "a humble mind, zeal for learning, tranquil life, silent study, poverty, a foreign land," and then devoted a chapter to a seventh from Quintilian: "love for one's teacher."[84] He acknowledged our debt to the past with an aphorism, also attributed to Bernard of Chartres, that has enjoyed a long, independent life of its own and invited manifold commentaries too: "We are like dwarfs seated upon the shoulders of giants."[85]

John himself is the best example of reliance on the gigantic stature of predecessors to see farther and more clearly in the search for wisdom and truth. For him, Aristotle and Cicero were supreme authorities. Although the old claim that John was the first medieval writer to reveal an acquaintance with the entire *Organon* has been questioned, the extensive research of Cary J. Nederman has demonstrated Aristotle's influence on our author, especially in

---

82   Peter von Moos, "The Use of *Exempla* in the *Policraticus* of John of Salisbury," in *The World of John of Salisbury*, p. 209; Liebeschütz, *Medieval Humanism*, p. 68. A later and much fuller study by Professor von Moos is *Geschichte als Topik: Das rhetorische Exemplum von der Antike zur Neuzeit und die historiae im 'Policraticus' Johanns von Salisbury* (Hildesheim, 1988).

83   *Policraticus* 4.6, ed. Webb; vol. 1, p. 254: "rex illiteratus est quasi asinus coronatus."

84   Ibid. 7.13, ed. Webb, vol. 2, p. 145: "Mens humilis, studium quaerendi, uita quieta,/scrutinium tacitum, paupertas, terra aliena"; ibid. 7.14, vol. 2, p. 152: "...amor docentium."

85   *Metalogicon* 3.4, p. 116: "...nos esse quasi nanos gigantum umeris insidentes." For a delightfully-amusing history of this aphorism, see Robert K. Merton, *On the Shoulders of Giants: A Shandean Postscript* (New York, 1965). Several serious treatments have been published, including Édouard Jeauneau, "Nani gigantum humeris insidentes: essai d'interprétation de Bernard de Chartres," *Vivarium* 5 (1967), 79–99.

the *Metalogicon*, where John "draws more broadly on Aristotelian doctrine than has heretofore been suspected."[86] Professor Nederman confirmed that Aristotle is the most widely cited author in the book, and that in it John "gives freest reign [*sic*] to his sentiments about Aristotle."[87]

John derived principles of eloquence and morality from Cicero's *De oratore* and *De officiis*, books bequeathed by him to the cathedral at Chartres.[88] He modeled his style on Cicero and adhered to the moderate path of the Later Academy espoused by the Roman philosopher.[89] He based his own lucidity of expression, structure of sentences, and development of arguments on Ciceronian precedents. For example, John's combination of three themes relating to the characteristics of philosophers in the prologue to Book Seven of the *Policraticus* has been convincingly linked to Cicero's rhetorical plan in the final book of *De oratore*.[90] John seems to have consciously imitated Cicero's style in his letters as well as in his prose treatises. As Professor Nederman has observed, "John presents himself as a follower of Cicero in both language and method."[91]

John of Salisbury's definitions and diction are frequently adopted from Cicero, with and without attribution. Many terms that find prominent place in his works, such as *honestum* (moral correctness), *utile* (expediency), *frugalitas* (temperance) and *ciuilitas* (proper social behavior) bespeak a Ciceronian influence. When John mentions the Roman writer by name, something he does fifty times in the *Policraticus* alone, he often refers to him as "our Cicero," or he specifically acknowledges Cicero's authority in a formula such as "*Ciceronis auctoritas*," or by employing the emphatic adjective *ipse*, "Cicero himself," to stress his respected status.

Yet, in spite of his admiration for "great Aristotle" (*magnus Aristotilis*) and for "our Cicero" (*Cicero noster*), John, in typically blunt terms, could criticize even these intellectual giants: in the *Entheticus maior* (l. 875), he accused

---

86   Cary J. Nederman, "Knowledge, Virtue and the Path to Wisdom: The Unexamined Aristotelianism of John of Salisbury's *Metalogicon*," *Mediaeval Studies* 51 (1989), 268–288, esp. p. 270.

87   Ibid., p. 268.

88   Clement C.J. Webb, "Note on Books Bequeathed by John of Salisbury to the Cathedral Library of Chartres," *Medieval and Renaissance Studies* 1 (1941), 128–129.

89   Édouard Jeauneau, *Rethinking the School of Chartres*, trans. Claude Paul Desmarais (Toronto, 2009), p. 82; see also Birgir Munk Olsen, "L'humanisme de Jean de Salisbury, un Cicéronien au XIIe siècle," in Maurice de Gandillac and Édouard Jeauneau, eds., *Entretiens sur la Renaissance du XIIe siècle* (Paris, 1968), pp. 53–83.

90   Liebeschütz, *Medieval Humanism*, pp. 88–89.

91   Nederman, *John of Salisbury*, p. 53.

Aristotle of vainglory, and he repeated Saint Augustine's charge against Cicero that "All men marvel at his tongue, but not so his heart."[92]

John of Salisbury's qualities as a writer and character as a man have drawn students to him through the ages. Those who study his poems, letters and treatises discover in them the workings of a keen mind enriched by extensive reading and thoughtful reflection, and tempered by good sense. For many he has become *iocundissimus auctor, magister, amicus.*

---

92   *Entheticus maior*, l.1243, ed. Pepin, p. 1243: "Os hominis cuncti mirantur, non ita pectus."

CHAPTER 5

John of Salisbury and Classical Antiquity*

Laure Hermand-Schebat

Introduction: John of Salisbury and Classical Authors

After its rereading by the Church Fathers, classical, and thus pagan, Antiquity was sometimes clothed with not a small degree of prestige, sometimes suspect and condemned, especially when the theses it affirmed did not accord with Christian doctrine. The two positions might even coexist in one and the same author, to varying degrees. The fact that Jerome made abundant reference to classical authors, and in his own works imitated the style of Cicero, did not prevent him, in one of his letters, from proclaiming his renunciation of the pagan literature of Classical Antiquity. In Letter 22, the saint recounts the dream where God accuses him of being a Ciceronian (*Ciceronianus*) and not a Christian (*Christianus*); rebuked by God, he undertakes definitively to renounce profane literature.[1] He writes to Eustochium: "What has Horace to do with the Psalter, Virgil with the Gospels and Cicero with Paul? (...) We ought not to drink the cup of Christ and the cup of devils at the same time."[2] Jerome is

---

* English translation by David M.B. Richardson.
1 Jerome, *ep.* 22.30. On Jerome's dream and his cultural range see Pierre Courcelle, *Les Lettres grecques en Occident. De Macrobe à Cassiodore* (Paris, 1943), pp. 111–112; Pierre Antin, "Autour du songe de Jérôme," *Revue des Études Latines* 41 (1963), 350–357; Neil Adkin, "Some Notes on The Style of Jerome's Twenty-Second Letter," *Rivista di filologia e di istruzione classica* 112 (1984), 287–291; idem, "Notes on the Content of Jerome's 22nd Letter"; *Grazer Beiträge* 15 (1988), 177–186; Barbara Feichtinger, "Der Traum des Hieronymus: ein Psychogramm," *Vigiliæ Christianæ* 45 (1991), 54–77; Marcia L. Colish, *Medieval Foundations of the Western Intellectual Tradition, 400–1400* (New Haven, 1997), p. 23; Anne Fraïsse, "'Ciceronianus es, non Christianus', des rapports entre la culture classique et le christianisme," *Vita Latina* 154 (1999), 46–53; Ulrich Eigler, "La missione di trasmissione. Girolamo come mediatore di culture differenti," in Gianpaolo Urso, ed., *Integrazione Mescolanza Rifiuto. Incontri di popoli, lingue e culture in Europa dall'Antichità all'Umanesimo. Atti del Convegno Internazionale, Cividale del Friuli, 21–23 settembre 2000* (Rome, 2001), pp. 185–198. On medieval readings of Jerome's dream see Bernhard Bischoff, *Manuscripts and Libraries in the Age of Charlemagne*, trans. Michael M. Gorman (Cambridge, 1994), pp. 157–160. On links between pagan and Christian culture in Jerome see also Averil Cameron, *Christianity and the Rhetoric of Empire, The Development of Christian Discourse* (Berkeley, 1991), pp. 138–139, 178.
2 Jerome, *ep.* 22.29, ed. and trans. F.A. Wright, (Cambridge, Mass., 1933; repr. 1991), pp. 124–125: "Quid facit cum psalterio Horatius? cum evangeliis Maro? cum apostolo Cicero? (...) Simul bibere non debemus calicem Christi et calicem daemoniorum."

© KONINKLIJKE BRILL NV, LEIDEN, 2015 | DOI 10.1163/9789004282940_007

describing a true renunciation of pagan literature[3]: a renunciation that, while certainly formal when one thinks of the enormous influence of Latin rhetoric and literature on his work, was critical as a cultural project. Classical Antiquity remained in Jerome's eyes hard to reconcile with Christianity, and he was intensely aware of the conflict between the two cultures, pagan and Christian. Nevertheless, when attacked for having cited pagan authors in his works, he defended prudent use of Classical Antiquity in the service of Christian faith, invoking, among other examples, that of the apostle Paul citing a line of Menander.[4] It is in that same letter (70) that he uses the metaphor of the captive woman in Deuteronomy,[5] who cannot be wed until her head has been shaved and her nails cut:

> He had read in Deuteronomy the command given by the voice of the Lord that, when a captive woman had had her head shaved, her eyebrows and all her hair cut off, and her nails pared, she might then be taken to wife. Is it surprising that I too, because of the elegance of her style and the grace of her parts, desire to make that secular wisdom that is my captive and my handmaid a matron of the true Israel; or that, shaving off and cutting away all in her that is dead, whether this be idolatry, pleasure, error, or lust, I take her to myself clean and pure, and beget by her servants for the Lord of Sabaoth? My efforts promote the advantage of Christ's family, my so-called defilement with an alien increases the number of my fellow-servants.[6]

So Classical Antiquity must be shorn of its deceptive attractions in order to serve the truth of Christianity. And Jerome restricted the utility of classical

---

3   On the dream of Jerome as a dream of conversion see Jacqueline Amat, *Songes et visions. L'au-delà dans la littérature latine tardive*, (Paris, 1985), pp. 219–222.

4   Jerome, *ep.* 70.2.

5   Dt 21:10–13.

6   Jerome, *ep.* 70.2, ed. Jérôme Labourt (Paris, 1953), vol. 3, pp. 210–211. Adapted from the translation by W.H. Fremantle, Jerome, *Letters and Select Works* (Grand Rapids, Mich., 1892; repr. 1983), p. 149: "Legerat in Deuteronomio Domini uoce praeceptum mulieris captiuae radendum caput, supercilia, omnes pilos et ungues corporis amputandos, et sic eam habendam in coniugio. Quid ergo mirum, si et ego sapientiam saecularem propter eloquii uenustatem et membrorum pulchritudinem, de ancilla atque captiua Israhelitin facere cupio, si quidquid in ea mortuum est idololatriae, uoluptatis, erroris, libidinum, uel praecido, uel rado, et mixtus purissimo corpori uernaculos ex ea genero Domino sabaoth? Labor meus in familiam Christi proficit, stuprum in alienam auget numerum conseruorum."

texts to the stylistic domain: profane literature constituted a model "because of the elegance of its style and the grace of its parts" (*propter eloquii uenustatem et membrorum pulchritudinem*), but its content remained nonetheless fundamentally false and deceptive.

Other patristic authors endeavoured to define proper use of Classical Antiquity in broadening its utility. Augustine, in the second book of *De doctrina christiana*, compares texts from Classical Antiquity to the gold of the Egyptians used by the Hebrews in the Old Testament:[7]

> Any statements by those who are called philosophers, especially the Platonists, which happen to be true and consistent with our faith should not cause alarm, but be claimed for our own use, as it were from owners who have no right to them. Like the treasures of the ancient Egyptians, who possessed not only idols and heavy burdens which the people of Israel hated and shunned but also vessels and ornaments of silver and gold, and clothes, which on leaving Egypt the people of Israel, in order to make better use of them, surreptitiously claimed for themselves (they did this not on their own authority but at God's command, and the Egyptians in their ignorance actually gave them the things of which they had made poor use), similarly all the branches of pagan learning contain not only false and superstitious fantasies and burdensome studies that involve unnecessary effort, which each one of us must loathe and avoid as under Christ's guidance we abandon the company of pagans, but also studies for liberated minds which are more appropriate to the service of truth, and some very useful moral instruction, as well as the various truths about monotheism to be found in their writers. (...) As for their clothing -- which corresponds to human institutions, but those appropriate to human society, which in this life we cannot do without -- this may be accepted and kept for conversion to Christian purposes.[8]

---

7 Ex 3:21–22; 12:35–36.

8 Augustine, *De doctrina christiana* 2.40.60, ed. and trans. R.P.H. Green (Oxford, 1995), pp. 124–127: "Philosophi autem qui vocantur, si qua forte vera et fidei nostrae accomodata dixerunt, maxime Platonici, non solum formidanda non sunt sed ab eis etiam tamquam ab iniustis possessoribus in usum nostrum vindicanda. Sicut enim Aegyptii non solum idola habebant et onera gravia quae populus Israel detestaretur et fugeret sed etiam vasa atque ornamenta de auro et argento et vestem, quae ille populus exiens de Aegypto sibi potius tamquam ad usum meliorem clanculo vindicauit, non auctoritate propria sed praecepto Dei, ipsis Aegyptiis nescienter commodantibus ea quibus non bene utebantur, sic doctrinae omnes gentilium non solum simulata et superstitiosa figmenta gravesque sarcinas supervacanei laboris habent, quae unusquisque nostrum duce Christo de societate gentilium exiens debet

This passage occurs within a "long digression on the general principles of a 'baptized' classical culture, insofar as such a thing is possible."[9] The plunder taken from the Egyptians represents the "elements of cultural tradition that succeeding generations learn from their antecedents."[10] Augustine uses this image to talk of a conversion of pagan culture to Christian use: "the entire digression is thus a 'charter for a Christian culture', or rather for a traditional classical culture *in usum christianum conuersa*, insofar as that is possible and appropriate."[11] Augustine thus evokes the utility, for a Christianized classical culture, of the disciplines inherited from pagan antiquity, and in the rest of his digression he proceeds to enumerate and classify them. For him it is a question of giving them a different, Christian purpose. Augustine manifests a positive attitude to classical cultural tradition. The metaphor of *spolia Aegyptorum* became inscribed in the patristic tradition, which proceeded to put to work the concept of proper use (*usus iustus*).[12] In the writings of the Greek and Latin Fathers, a great number of images indicate the discriminating work required for a Christian appropriation of ancient culture:[13] notably, in Jerome, the image of the captive woman in Deuteronomy mentioned above.

John of Salisbury knew both the passage from Exodus telling of the plunder taken from the Egyptians and its patristic interpretation, as he evokes it briefly in the first chapter of the seventh book of the *Policraticus*:

---

abominari atque deuitare, sed etiam liberales disciplinas usui veritatis aptiores et quaedam morum praecepta utilissima continent, deque ipso uno deo colendo nonnulla vera inveniuntur apud eos (. . .) Vestem quoque illorum, id est hominum quidem instituta, sed tamen accomodata humanae societati qua in hac uita carere non possumus, accipere atque habere licuerit in usum convertenda christianum."

9   Luc Verheijen, "Le *De doctrina christiana* de saint Augustin. Un manuel d'herméneutique et d'expression chrétienne avec en II, 19(29)–42(63), une 'charte fondamentale pour une culture chrétienne'," *Augustiniana* 24 (1974), 10–20: the author provides a commentary on the image of the plunder taken from the Egyptians, and in a more general way analyses the digression in the second book of *De doctrina christiana* in order to bring out its salient points and its function. See also Georges Folliet, "Les dépouilles des Égyptiens," in Augustin, *Œuvres 11. Le magistère chrétien (De catechizandis rudibus. De doctrina christiana)*, trans. Gustave Combès and Jacques Farges (Paris, 1949), pp. 582–584.

10   Verheijen, "Le *De doctrina christiana*," p. 13.

11   Ibid., p. 13.

12   On the concept of "proper use" in the patristic tradition, and its employment by Augustine, see the note by Isabelle Bochet in Augustin, *Œuvres 11, 2. La doctrine chrétienne (De doctrina christiana)*, trans. M. Moreau (Paris, 1997), pp. 536–540.

13   Augustin, *Œuvres 11, 2. La doctrine chrétienne*, trans. M. Moreau, pp. 537–538. See also Christian Gnilka, *KRÊSIS. Die Methode der Kirchenväter im Umgang mit der antiken Kultur. I. Der Begriff des "rechten Gebrauchs"* (Basel, 1984), pp. 16–18.

...although the soul of the wise man does not refuse to learn even from the enemy, since the special people of God glitter in the golden clothing and silver ornaments of all the Egyptians.[14]

As in Augustine, gold, money, silver, clothing, and other finery taken by the Hebrews from the Egyptians signify nothing other than pagan knowledge, which must be rid of everything harmful or dangerous, and employed in the service of Christian truth.[15]

Situating himself within this patristic tradition, John of Salisbury does not tire in his praise of the benefits to be gained from reading classical texts, while also indicating the limits of pagan teaching, and recommending that pagan works be read with prudence and informed awareness. He devotes the tenth chapter of the seventh book of the *Policraticus* to this question: pagan teachings, once rid of their errors, need not frighten a Christian reader, and may even be of great use to him or her.[16] "Their gardens," he writes, "are full of flowers, perfumed, and laden with fruit."[17] This metaphor shows that ancient literature, for John, charms as much as it instructs, and offers the reader both pleasure and utility. Such a position is in principle founded on the unique nature of wisdom. Even if they were ignorant of the truth of Christ, the pagans may, unknown to themselves, have been penetrated by that wisdom, fundamentally indivisible, and may therefore pass on some portion of it, even to a Christian reader. In the same chapter of the *Policraticus*, wisdom is compared to a spring that not only irrigates the garden of delights that is the text of the Bible, but also flows as far as the gardens of the pagans:

Wisdom is a sort of spring from which rivers flow watering every land, filling not only the garden of delights of the Holy Scripture, but making

---

14   *Policraticus* 7.1, trans. Cary J. Nederman, (Cambridge, 1990), p. 149, ed. Webb, vol. 2,
      p. 133: "...licet et ab hoste doceri sapientis animus non detrectet, cum peculiaris popu-
      lus Dei auro argento uestibus et toto Egiptiorum ornatu resplendeat." Clement Webb
      cites in his note the medieval authors who commented on this passage after Augustine:
      Isidorus, in Chapter 16 of his *Questions on Exodus*, Rabanus Maurus, and Wilfred
      Strabo.

15   See Max Kerner, *Johannes von Salisbury und die logische Struktur seines* Policraticus
      (Wiesbaden, 1977), p. 28.

16   *Policraticus* 7.10, ed. Webb, vol. 2, p. 133: "...docere potest ut iugulatis erroribus gentilium
      dogmata nequaquam horreamus."

17   Ibid. 7.10, ed. Webb, vol. 2, p. 134: "Inde sunt floridi, redolentes et fructiferi gentium
      orti."

their way among the pagans so that they are not unknown even to the Ethiopians.[18]

So the writers of Classical Antiquity must not be rejected as sinners, or the reading of their works considered dangerous and ill-fated, but, as may be seen below, they must be read with the essential discerning criterion of Christian faith. Of those writers, the philosophers are of particular interest to John of Salisbury:

> That the genius of the philosophers of antiquity had abounded and that study was advanced by them is now not merely opinion but a judgment of which everyone in common is persuaded. For through study and prac-tice these geniuses prepared for themselves a path to matters which are by nature almost incomprehensible, and with their aid many discoveries were made known to posterity for which we rejoice and at which we marvel.[19]

In John's eyes, it is vital to read and study the ancient philosophers, as their works pass on a knowledge of the world that may be of profit to contemporary readers: the project of *Entheticus de dogmate philosophorum* is to discuss the philosophical teachings of Antiquity in order to collect the fruits of the philo-sophical work of the ancients, as John announces in the first lines of his poem:

> You will discuss the doctrines of the ancients and the fruit of the toil, Which Philosophy reaps from her studies.[20]

This project of study is immediately placed under the patronage of the Holy Spirit (ll. 3–6). It is a question, as a Christian, of garnering the fruits of ancient culture, using Christian faith as one's essential discerning criterion.

---

18   Ibid. 7.10, ed. Webb, vol. 2, p. 134: "Sapientia siquidem fons quidam est de quo egrediuntur flumina quae irrigant omnem terram, et non modo ortum deliciarum diuinae paginae replent sed etiam ad gentes pertranseunt ut nec etiam Ethiopibus omnino desint."

19   Ibid 7.1, (trans. Nederman p. 148), ed. Webb, vol. 2, pp. 93–94: "Antiquos quidem philoso-phos floruisse ingeniis, et studio profecisse, jam non celebris opinio est, sed omnibus in commune persuasa sententia. Ad res enim ex natura fere incomprehensibiles, studio et exercitatione uiam sibi fecit ingenium, et illorum beneficio plurima publicata sunt posteris, quibus gaudemus et miramur inuentis."

20   *Entheticus de dogmate philosophorum* ll.1–2, ed. and trans. van Laarhoven, vol. 1, p. 105: "Dogmata discuties veterum fructumque laboris,//quem capit ex studiis Philosophia suis."

If ancient philosophers occupy a privileged position, John continually recalls the value of liberal studies: the philosopher must also read the poets, the orators, and the historians. Thus, in the tradition of Quintilian, the *Metalogicon* develops an ardent defence of the liberal arts:

> That "Poetry is the cradle of philosophy" is axiomatic. Furthermore, our forefathers tell us that the liberal studies are so useful that one who has mastered them can, without a teacher, understand all books and everything written. Indeed, as Quintilian observes, "These studies harm, not those who pass through them, but only those who become bogged down in them."[21]

While John highlights poets in this passage, in another chapter of the *Metalogicon* he evokes the importance of grammar, foundation of the other liberal arts:[22]

> Grammar is "the science of speaking and writing correctly, the starting point of all liberal studies." Grammar is the cradle of all philosophy, and in a manner of speaking, the first nurse of the whole study of letters.[23]

He makes of this "science" not only the basis of all philosophy, but the prerequisite for any study of letters in general. This study of grammar does not embrace only the reading of the ancient grammarians, but also that of the poets, the orators, and the historians, in the form of examples and grammatical exercises.

---

21 *Metalogicon* 1.22. Translation adapted from *The Metalogicon of John of Salisbury. A Twelfth-Century Defense of the Verbal and Logical Arts of the Trivium*, trans. Daniel D. McGarry (Gloucester, Mass., 1971), p. 63, ed. Hall, pp. 49–50: "Poetas philosophorum cunas esse, celebre est. Disciplinas liberales tantae utilitatis esse tradit antiquitas, ut quicunque eas plene norint, libros omnes, et quaecunque scripta sunt, possint intelligere, etiam sine doctore. Ut enim ait Quintilianus, non nocent hae disciplinae per illas euntibus, sed circa illas haerentibus."

22 We refrain from developing here upon John's conceptions in respect of grammar, and refer instead to the rich analyses by Cédric Giraud and Constant Mews in the present volume, enlarged upon in the chapter entitled "John of Salisbury and the schools of the twelfth century," in particular the section concerning grammar ("John of Salisbury and grammar: a reading of *Metalogicon* I.13–25").

23 *Metalogicon* 1.13, p. 32: "Est enim grammatica scientia recte loquendi scribendique, et origo omnium liberalium disciplinarum. Eadem quoque est totius philosophiae cunabulum, et, ut ita dixerim, totius litteratorii studii altrix prima."

Yet, alongside these exhortations to read the texts of Classical Antiquity, John nevertheless constantly warns of the necessity for prudence in the reading of pagan texts. The reader is in absolute need of a discerning criterion; these texts are therefore reserved for a cultivated and informed public:

> But catholic books are safer and much more secure to read; pagan books offer more dangers to the simplest minds. Both are very useful to minds guided rather by faith. In fact, reading every book one by one makes you erudite; cautiously choosing the best makes you a good person.[24]

If pagan books present more dangers for less educated readers, John of Salisbury nonetheless vigorously affirms their utility, which he puts at the same level as that of Christian books. The quality needed for reading pagan texts without risk is expressed by the Latin adjective *fidelis* (*fidelioribus ingeniis*). The same adjective is used at the end of this chapter of the *Policraticus* to insist on the vigilance required by the reader of classical texts. John calls for a "prudent reader guided by faith" (*fidelis lector et prudens*).[25] Here, the adjective *fidelis* might be understood in the classic sense of "worthy of confidence, reliable," but it might also be more closely linked with the noun *fides* ("faith"), and indicate a reader informed by Christian faith.[26] The same expression can be found in the first chapter of the third book of the *Metalogicon* regarding the appropriate manner of reading Porphyry.[27] In John's eyes, the essential discerning criterion to be employed when reading ancient texts is Christian faith.

Classical Antiquity provides useful lessons for those who know how to use it in a prudent and informed fashion, but it is also fundamentally marked by non-fulfilment: pagan authors were unable to attain virtue because they lacked the gift of grace. "The ancients," John reminds us in the fifth book of the

---

24   *Policraticus* 7.10, ed. Webb, vol. 2, p. 133: "Ceterum libri catholici tutius leguntur et cautius; et gentiles simplicioribus periculosius patent: sed in utriusque fidelioribus ingeniis utilissimum est. Nam exquisita lectio singulorum, doctissimum; cauta electio meliorum, optimum facit."

25   Ibid. 7.10, ed. Webb, vol. 2, p. 134.

26   The adjective *fidelis* has this Christian sense from Late Antiquity onwards. In Tertullian it sometimes means someone of faith (*Apologeticum* 46.14), sometimes a baptized Christian as opposed to a catechumen (*De praescriptione haereticorum* 41.2). John of Salisbury uses it several times in the plural in the *Policraticus* and the *Metalogicon*, to indicate the community of believers. See for example *Policraticus* 7.21, ed. Webb, vol. 2, p. 198: "sanguinem Christi fidelibus ministrare"; *Metalogicon* 4.42, ed. Hall, p. 184: *fidelium precibus*.

27   *Metalogicon* 3.1, p. 104: *lector fidelis et prudens*.

Policraticus, "were ignorant of the saving truth."[28] The ancients were able only
to put on the garb of virtue; for virtue itself cannot be achieved without the
essentially Christian qualities of faith and charity:

> Let therefore the semblance of virtue be revered, provided it be under-
> stood that without faith and love there can be no substance of virtue.
> And if only we could find among us someone who could at least hold the
> semblance of virtue! *But who embraces the very self of virtue?* Who now
> clothes himself in even the shadow of the virtues in which we see that
> gentiles excelled, albeit, having no Christ, they did not attain the fruit of
> true blessedness?[29]

We must not deduce from this that the pagans did not possess any particular
virtue. John himself recalls "Socrates' self-mastery" (*continentiam Socratis*) and
"Cato's frugality" (*Catonis parcitatem*).[30] But they were unable to attain to virtue in its plenitude, and true wisdom incarnated in Christ. Human powers are
insufficient for virtue: it must be reinforced by the divine action of grace.
Drawing upon Augustine, John considers it to be impossible for humanity by
its own power to achieve wisdom or virtue; this is permitted only by grace in
action among the elect:

> Yet I do not follow the steps of Virgil or the gentiles to such a degree that
> I believe that anyone may attain to knowledge or virtue by the strength of
> his own will. I acknowledge that grace is operative in both the will and
> the accomplishments of the elect; I revere it as the way -- indeed, the only

---

28   *Policraticus* 5.11, ed. Webb, vol. 1, p. 333: "Unde et apud antiquos, etiam salutiferae veritatis
     ignaros, omne quod ex debito officii gratuitum esse oportet, si fiat ad pretium, in sordibus
     computatur." [For this reason, among all the ancients, even though they were ignorant of
     the truth of salvation, it was counted among the forms of sordid behaviour if one did for
     a price that which ought to be free on the basis of obligations of office. (trans. David M.B.
     Richardson based on Nederman, pp. 94–95)].

29   *Policraticus* 3.9 (adapted from the trans. by Joseph B. Pike, *Frivolities of Courtiers and
     Footprints of Philosophers. Being a Translation of the First, Second and Third Books and
     Selections from the Seventh and the Eighth Books of the* Policraticus *of John of Salisbury*
     (Minneapolis, 1938), pp. 178–179), ed. Keats-Rohan, pp. 197–198: "Sit ergo uenerabilis
     imago uirtutis, dum sine fide et dilectione substantia uirtutis esse non possit. Et utinam
     inueniatur in nobis qui uel uirtutis imaginem teneat. *Quis enim uirtutem amplectitur
     ipsam?* Quis etiam umbras uirtutum induit quibus uidemus floruisse gentiles, licet eis
     subtracto Christo uerae beatitudinis non apprehenderint fructum?"

30   *Policraticus* 3.9 (trans. Pike).

true way -- which leads to life and renders satisfaction to each one's good wishes.[31]

He stresses, besides, that it is on this precise point in respect of grace and its function on the road leading to virtue that he departs from Virgil,[32] and ceases to follow in his footsteps or in those of the pagans in general. This is when John has just cited the instructions given by the Sybil to Aeneas before he descends into Hell in Book six of the Aeneid;[33] and, even if, in an allegorical interpretation, he has already proposed that the Sybil should be seen as an image of divine providence, he recalls that it is alone and without any external intervention that Aeneas tears the golden bough from the tree of knowledge and the virtues. John's admiration for Classical Antiquity and his recourse to ancient texts cease when the latter contradict the dogma of the Christian religion. While recognizing the importance of Virgil and his teaching in respect of virtue, John cannot admit to the notion that humanity arrives at that state by its own devices, and he is therefore unable to follow the pagan author's reasoning to its conclusion.

Thus, in his reading of Classical Antiquity, John of Salisbury attempts to reconcile pagan teachings with Christian doctrine. This attempted reconciliation strongly permeates his entire philosophical approach, which, as Christophe Grellard has shown, "combines a Christian dimension with a clearly asserted ancient heritage."[34]

The Question of Greek

Although John certainly had available to him a rich and varied collection of Latin texts, the question has long been posed as to whether he knew Greek, and thus had access to the works of Plato and Aristotle in the original. Édouard Jeauneau affirms that "It is certain that John of Salisbury was ignorant of that

---

31   *Policraticus* 8.25 (trans. Nederman, *Policraticus*, pp. 227–228), ed. Webb, vol. 2, p. 421: "Non tamen eatenus Maronis aut gentium insisto uestigiis ut credam quempiam ad scientiam aut uirtutem propriis arbitrii sui uiribus peruenire. Fateor gratiam in electis operari et uelle et perficere; ipsam ueneror tamquam uiam immo reuera uiam quae sola ducit ad uitam et quemque boni uoti compotem facit."

32   On Virgil in the Middle Ages, see, e.g. Jean-Yves Tilliette, ed., *Lectures médiévales de Virgile* (Rome, 1985).

33   Virgil, *Aeneid* 6.136–144.

34   Christophe Grellard, "Jean de Salisbury, un cas médiéval de scepticisme," in *Freiburger Zeitschrift für Philosophie und Theologie* 54 (2007), 16–40, esp. p. 24.

language."[35] He probably had a rudimentary knowledge of it, permitting him to understand an etymology when the occasion demanded. And, as he mentions in the *Metalogicon*, he enjoyed the services of a translator on his journeys to Southern Italy.[36] We can therefore take it for granted that he read the Greek philosophers with the aid of Latin translations, or had some fragmentary knowledge through the intermediary of Latin.[37]

We know that John's teachers were ignorant of Greek, as he writes to John Sarrazin (Johannes Sarracenus) in Letter 194.[38] He addresses himself to Sarrazin for this very reason, to understand the Greek term *ousia*, which he had found in Ambrose, and its relation to the Latin terms *essentia, natura, genus,* and *substantia*, which he had read in Hilary of Poitiers. John Sarrazin, whose qualities as a philologist John of Salisbury appreciated, in fact knew Greek well, as he translated the *Celestial hierarchy* and the *Ecclesiastical hierarchy* of Pseudo-Dionysius, texts already translated in the 9th century by Johannes Scotus Eriugena. John of Salisbury knew this first translation, but nevertheless asks John Sarrazin to finish his.[39] Édouard Jeauneau has clearly shown that John of Salisbury's interest in Dionysius appears to have awoken quite late; this hypothesis would explain why he came to promote a new translation of Dionysian writings during the years 1166–7, when he had given so little space to them in his two works (*Policraticus* and *Metalogicon*) finished in 1159.[40]

---

35   Édouard Jeauneau, "Jean de Salisbury et la lecture des philosophes," in *The World of John of Salisbury*, pp. 77–108, esp. p. 96.

36   *Metalogicon* 1.15, p. 37: "Cum super hoc articulo multos conferentes et uaria sentientes audierim, non pigebit referre, nec forte audire displicebit, quod a Graeco interprete et qui Latinam linguam commode nouerat, dum in Apulia morarer accepi." [I have heard many persons arguing this point, and advocating diverse opinions on the question. Hence it will not be out of place to recount, nor will it perhaps be unwelcome to hear, what a Greek interpreter, who also knew the Latin language very well, told me when I was staying in Apulia.] (*The Metalogicon*, trans. Mc Garry, p. 44). See also *Metalogicon* 3.5, p. 119: *Graecus interpres natione Seueritanus* [a Greek interpreter, citizen of St Severino] and 4.2, p. 141: *interpres meus* [my intepreter].

37   Hans Liebeschütz, *Mediaeval Humanism in the Life and Writings of John of Salisbury* (London, 1950), p. 64; Kerner, *Johannes von Salisbury und die logische Struktur*, p. 78.

38   Letter 194, in *The Later Letters*, p. 272: "...obstaculum repperi quod nullus magistrorum nostrorum sufficit amouere quia Graecae linguae expertes sunt." [I recently came across a difficulty which none of our masters can remove since they are ignorant of Greek. (trans. Brooke)].

39   Ibid.: "Expecto a gratia uestra residuum Gerarchiae transferri." [I expect you in your kindness to translate the rest of the *De Hierarchia*. (trans. Brooke)].

40   Jeauneau, "Jean de Salisbury et la lecture des philosophes," pp. 97–102.

So John displays great interest in the Platonic tradition; but that interest very evidently extends to Plato himself. He describes him in the first book of the *Policraticus* as "prince of all philosophy,"[41] and in the seventh as "prince of philosophers."[42] At any event, John always thinks of Plato in association with Platonism, for it was essentially through the intermediary of Latin writers, from Cicero to Isidorus via Apuleius, Macrobius, and Augustine, that he knew the Greek philosopher's thought. "Apuleius, Augustine, and Isidorus," he writes in the second book of the *Metalogicon*, "report that Plato's merit lies in having brought philosophy to the height of perfection."[43] We know the importance of Plato and Platonism at the heart of the school of Chartres and in John's philosophical thinking. But John himself knew no more of Plato's works than did his contemporaries: his knowledge of Plato was in fact restricted to the *Timaeus*, in the partial translation by Calcidius.[44] He also quotes the *Phaedrus*, the *Laws*, and the *Republic*, works with which he was familiar from quotations in Cicero among others. For example, in the eighth chapter of the seventh book of the *Policraticus*, on virtue as the sole path of philosophy and sole means of attaining happiness,[45] he affirms that, if human eyes could see virtue, all humanity would turn towards it, quoting a passage from Plato's *Phaedrus*,[46] which he had read in Cicero's *De officiis* and perhaps his *De finibus*.[47] He may well have known other elements of Platonic philosophy from Apuleius' *De Platone et eius dogmate*,[48] and in references gleaned from Cicero and Macrobius.[49]

John equally had access to certain discourses by Gregory of Nazianzus. Rufinus had translated nine of them, and John had sight of the whole or a part of this Latin translation. In fact, for the *Policraticus*, all the quotations from

---

41   *Policraticus* 1.6, ed. Keats-Rohan, p. 47: "totius philosophiae princeps Plato."

42   Ibid. 7.6, ed. Webb, vol. 2, p. 111: "philosophorum princeps Plato."

43   *Metalogicon* 2.2, p. 58: "Tradunt ergo Apuleius, Augustinus, et Isidorus quod Plato philosophiam perfecisse laudatur."

44   John gives a résumé of it in his *Entheticus*, ll. 937–1088, ed. van Laarhoven, vol. 1, pp. 166–176, and in the *Policraticus* 7.5, ed. Webb, vol. 2, pp. 108–110. See Christophe Grellard, *Jean de Salisbury et la renaissance médiévale du scepticisme* (Paris, 2013), p. 32.

45   *Policraticus* 7.8, ed. Webb, vol. 2, p. 121: *ut ait Plato*.

46   Plato, *Phaedrus* 250d.

47   Cicero, *De officiis* 1.15; *De finibus* 2.52.

48   See in particular the multiple quotations in Chapter 5 of book 7, which appear to attest to direct knowledge of the work (Grellard, *Jean de Salisbury et la renaissance médiévale du scepticisme*, p. 32).

49   On indirect quotations from Plato in the Middle Ages see Michel Lemoine, "La tradition indirecte du Platon latin," in Roger Ellis, ed., *The Medieval Translator. Proceedings of the International Conference Held at Conques* (Turnhout, 1993), pp. 337–346.

Gregory of Nazianzus come from the same discourse, the *Apologeticus*. John quotes a passage from it in his prologue to the seventh book of the *Policraticus* with the mention *teste Gregorio Nazanzeno*.[50] Clement Webb in his notes identifies a quotation from a letter by Gregory of Nazianzus for this passage, but refers primarily to the Greek text, and fails to see the textual proximity between the *Policraticus* and Rufinus' translation. John perhaps also knew the translation made at his own time by Henry Aristippus, but this is not certain, and all his quotations are textually very close to the translation by Rufinus.

So the Ancient Greek material was transmitted through the intermediary of some Latin translations, either complete or partial, but above all via authors such as Cicero, Macrobius, Boethius, and Augustine who quoted Greek texts in Latin. Late Antiquity appears to have constituted an essential staging post between John of Salisbury and Classical Antiquity; if, as we have just seen, this is true for Greek texts, it will soon become clear that it applies to a large proportion of Classical Latin texts too. The indexes of John's classical sources presented at the end of modern editions of his works must therefore be read with caution, for the different classical works listed are certainly not all of the same status, and John did not read them all in the same form, but as complete or partial texts, extracts in anthologies, or quotations read in other authors. This distinction holds true even between works of one and the same author, as we shall see in the case of Cicero.

John of Salisbury, Reader of Aristotle

While John had a very restricted acquaintance with Plato, he read more works by Aristotle through the medium of Latin translations. He had wide knowledge of Aristotle's output of works of logic. John knew the *Logica uetus* (*Categories* and *On Interpretation*) via the translations and commentaries of Boethius. Of the texts belonging to the *Logica noua* (*Analytics*, *Topics*, and *On Sophistical Refutations*), he certainly knew the *Prior Analytics*, the *Topics*, and *On Sophistical Refutations*, which he read in Boethius' Latin translation, additionally aided by the same author's commentaries.[51] As for the *Posterior Analytics*, it has long been believed that he possessed the complete Latin translation produced by his contemporary James of Venice, and that he was

---

50   Kerner, *Johannes von Salisbury und die logische Struktur*, p. 79.

51   On this point, see Stan Ebbesen, "Jacques de Venise," in Max Lejbowicz, ed., *L'Islam en terres chrétiennes. Science et idéologie* (Villeneuve d'Ascq, 2009), pp. 115–132, esp. p. 28, and David Bloch, *John of Salisbury on Aristotelian Science* (Turnhout, 2012), pp. 27–28.

the first to use it.[52] One passage in the *Metalogicon* even provides reason for thinking that he had a second translation in front of him, as he compares two translations of a passage from the work,[53] probably that of James of Venice and a *translatio anonyma* that has come down to us in a manuscript of the beginning of the 13th century from the Capitular Library at Toledo.[54] But David Bloch has recently presented serious arguments suggesting that John's knowledge of the *Posterior Analytics* was not direct, and only partial, based on a collection of selected passages.[55]

For John of Salisbury, Aristotle is above all a logician. This is how John defines that view in the second book of the *Metalogicon*:

> Subsequently Aristotle perceived and explained the rules of the art [of logic], and he, "the Prince of the Peripatetics," is honored as its principal founder. While Aristotle shares the distinction of being an authority in other branches of learning, he has a monopoly of this one, which is his very own.[56]

In effect, John was aware only of the *Organon*, and, like his contemporaries, ignorant of the *Metaphysics* and the *Ethics*. But, as Cary Nederman has shown, he succeeded in gleaning from the *Organon* important aspects of Aristotle's moral and political doctrine, such as the doctrine of the just mean, aspects that he integrated into the social philosophy of the *Policraticus*.[57] It was probably also through Latin texts that he was able to perfect those few notions that he had of Aristotle's moral and political philosophy.[58]

---

52   Jeauneau, "Jean de Salisbury et la lecture des philosophes," pp. 103–104; Lorenzo Minio Paluello, "Iacobus Veneticus Grecus, Canonist and Translator of Aristotle," *Traditio* 8 (1952), 265–304. A recent elaboration can be found in Ebbesen, "Jacques de Venise."

53   *Metalogicon* 2.20, p. 96: "Gaudeant, inquit Aristotiles, species, monstra enim sunt (uel, secundum nouam translationem, cicadationes enim sunt); aut, si sunt, nichil ad ratio-nem." ["We may dispense with forms," says Aristotle "for they are representations (or, according to a new translation: chatter) and even if they did exist, they would have no bearing on our discussion."] (*The Metalogicon*, trans. Mc Garry, p. 135).

54   Kerner, *Johannes von Salisbury und die logische Struktur*, p. 80.

55   David Bloch, "James of Venice and the Posterior Analytics," *Cahiers de l'Institut du Moyen Âge Grec et Latin* 78 (2008), 37–50; idem, *John of Salisbury on Aristotelian Science*.

56   *Metalogicon* 2.2, (trans. McGarry, p. 77), ed. Hall, pp. 58–59: "Deinde Aristoteles artis [i.e. logicae] regulas deprehendit et tradidit. Hic est Peripatheticorum princeps, quem ars ista praecipuum laudat auctorem, et qui alias disciplinas communes habet cum auctoribus suis, sed hanc suo jure vindicans, a possessione illius exclusit ceteros."

57   Cary J. Nederman, *John of Salisbury* (Tempe, Arizona, 2005), p. 54.

58   Kerner, *Johannes von Salisbury und die logische Struktur*, p. 48.

If Aristotle's logic plays an essential role in the *Metalogicon*, John nonetheless refuses to give blind admiration to the philosopher from Stagira; in the context of his project to submit the received authority of ancient philosophical texts to the discernment of reason guided by divine revelation, he refuses to deify the philosopher and his writings:

> I do not claim that Aristotle is always correct in his views and teaching, as though everything he has written were sacrosanct. It has been proved, both by reason and by the authority of faith, that Aristotle has erred on several points.[59]

John develops similar arguments in Chapter 6 of Book 9 of the *Policraticus*, and in those verses of the *Entheticus* devoted to Aristotle.[60] While fulsomely praising Aristotle's qualities, among them subtlety (*subtilitas*) and oratorical restraint (*suauitas dicendi*), John also lists his errors (*errauit*) in the domains of cosmology and theology.

John of Salisbury and Philosophers

While John knew ancient philosophy principally through the intermediary of the patristic authors, he nevertheless had direct knowledge of Stoicism via Seneca. Already in Antiquity, the *Letters to Lucilius* had been divided into two volumes, which gave rise to two distinct manuscript traditions: letters 1 to 88 and 89 to 124.[61] The first volume was the more widely read in the Middle Ages; copies of letters 1 to 88 were more widely disseminated, and known by the end of the 12th century from Western Britain to Austria and Italy.[62] As Webb indicated in his *index auctorum* to the *Policraticus*, John knew only letters 1 to 88. The list of books left by John to Chartres Cathedral indicates that he also had in his possession a copy of the *Natural questions*,[63] but it is not likely that he

---

59   *Metalogicon* 4.27 (trans. McGarry, p. 244), ed. Hall, p. 164: "Nec tamen Aristotilem ubique bene aut sensisse, aut dixisse protestor, ut sacrosanctum sit quicquid scripsit. Nam in pluribus optinente ratione et auctoritate fidei, conuincitur errasse."

60   *Policraticus* 7.6, ed. Webb, vol. 2, pp. 111–114; *Entheticus de dogmate philosophorum* ll. 831–862, ed. van Laarhoven, pp. 158–161.

61   Leighton D. Reynolds, ed., *Texts and Transmission. A Survey of the Latin Classics* (Oxford, 1983), pp. 369–370.

62   Ibid., pp. 370, 374.

63   The list of works bears the mention "Senecam de naturalibus questionibus" (*Cartulaire de Notre-Dame de Chartres*, vol. 3, p. 202).

acquired it before 1159, the year he finished his two great works the *Policraticus* and the *Metalogicon*.[64] The catalogue of books present at Canterbury in about 1170 also mentions the apocryphal correspondence between Seneca and the apostle Paul,[65] a small collection certainly known to John, as he refers to the friendship between the two men, given credence by medieval authors, in the eighth book of the *Policraticus*.[66] He knew the *Controversies* of Seneca the Elder,[67] citing its judgement on Cicero, but confusing Seneca with his son, as was the habit of medieval authors and the first humanists.

Two of the main writers through whom John found access to Platonic and Neoplatonic philosophy were Macrobius and Boethius. Of the former, the Canterbury catalogue of about 1170 mentions no less than 11 manuscripts, to which must be added two volumes of glosses.[68] John knew the *Saturnales*[69] as well as the *Commentary on the Dream of Scipio*, which gave him access to Book 6 of Cicero's *De republica*. As regards Boethius, besides the translations of and commentaries on Aristotle's logic John knew the *Philosophiae consolatio* and *De trinitate*, to which should be added *De musica* and *De arithmetica*.[70]

John of Salisbury, Reader of Cicero

The Latin philosopher to whom John of Salisbury accords most importance, and to whom he refers in elaborating his own philosophical thinking, is quite

---

64   Grellard, *Jean de Salisbury et la renaissance médiévale du scepticisme*, p. 33.

65   Montague Rhodes James, *The Ancient Libraries of Canterbury and Dover. The Catalogue of the Libraries of Christ Church Priory and St Augustine's Abbey at Canterbury and of St. Martin's Priory at Dover* (Cambridge, 1903), p. 11: 178. "Epistole Senece ad Paulum."

66   *Policraticus* 8.13, ed. Webb, vol. 2, p. 318: "Michi tamen desipere uidentur qui quemcumque secuti non uenerantur eum quem et Apostoli familiaritatem meruisse constat et a doctissimo patre Ieronimo in sanctorum catalogo positum." [They appear to me to lack sense, those who, ready to follow any lead, show no veneration for him who, we are agreed, won the friendship of the Apostle Paul and who was given a place in the catalogue of saints by the learned Father Jerome.] (adapted from Pike, *Frivolities of Courtiers*, p. 376).

67   The Canterbury catalogue mentions as no. 230 a *Seneca de declamationibus* (James, *The Ancient Libraries*, p. 12).

68   James, *The Ancient Libraries*, pp. 8 (54–64), 9 (78–79).

69   See *Texts and Transmission*, p. 234.

70   The first two works appear in the Canterbury catalogue as nos. 80 to 87 (*The Ancient Libraries*, p. 9), the *De musica* as nos. 39 and 40 (ibid., p. 8). Four volumes besides (nos. 46, 47, 48, and 50) bear the title *Aristmetica* with no author named (ibid.); very probably one or more of them contained Boethius' *De Arithmetica*.

evidently Cicero.[71] Reiterating the judgement of Seneca the Elder in the *Controversies*,[72] John writes in the chapter of the *Entheticus* devoted to the Roman orator and philosopher:

> The Latin world held nothing greater than Cicero;
> Compared to his eloquence Greece was mute.
> Rome pits him and blandishes him against all the Greeks.[73]

This judgement on Cicero is again evident when, in the *Policraticus*, John cites his own espousal of the probabilism of the New Academy:

> I am the more ready to give ear to the school of the Academy because it deprives me of none of the things I know and in many matters renders me more cautious, being supported as it is by the authority of great men, since he in whom alone the Latin tongue finds whatever elegance it has to offset the arrogance of Greece turned to it in his old age, I mean of course Cicero, the originator of Roman style.[74]

The figure of Cicero and his philosophical thought are of the highest importance in John of Salisbury's oeuvre, but the number of Cicero's works of which he had direct knowledge was in the final analysis quite limited. At the same period, William of Malmesbury possessed a much more extensive Cicero collection. But John had an intimate knowledge of the few texts of Cicero he himself owned. He made a personal reading of them, and Cicero's ideas became his own. The *index auctorum* provided by Clement Webb for the *Policraticus*

---

71 On John of Salisbury and Cicero see Birger Munk Olsen, "L'humanisme de Jean de Salisbury, un cicéronien au XIIᵉ siècle," in Maurice de Gandillac and Édouard Jeauneau, eds., *Entretiens sur la Renaissance du XIIᵉ siècle* (Paris, 1968), pp. 53–83; Jean-Yves Tilliette, "Jean de Salisbury et Cicéron," *Helmantica* (*Chemins de la Reconnaissance*) 50 (1999), 697–710; Laure Schebat, "Pétrarque et Jean de Salisbury: aspects et enjeux de leur jugement sur Cicéron," *Cahiers de l'Humanisme* 3–4 (2002–3), 93–113.

72 Seneca the Elder, *Controversiae* 1.praef. 6.

73 *Entheticus de dogmate philosophorum* ll.1215–7, ed. van Laarhoven, vol. 1, p. 185: "Orbis nil habuit maius Cicerone Latinus,//cuius ad eloquium Graecia muta fuit.//Omnibus hunc Graecis opponit Roma vel effert."

74 *Policraticus* 2.22 (adapted from Pike, p. 107), ed. Keats-Rohan, pp. 126–127: "Eoque libentius Academicos audio quod eorum quae noui nichil auferunt, et in multis faciunt cautiorem, magnorum uirorum auctoritate suffulti, cum ad eos etiam in senectute transierit ille in quo Latinitas nostra solo inuenit quicquid insolenti Greciae eleganter opponit aut praefert, Ciceronem loquor, Romani auctorem eloquii."

suggests that John knew many texts by Cicero; but for many passages John in fact possessed another source, either a passage developing the same idea in another text by Cicero that we know for certain he knew, or an ancient or Late-Antique author who himself cited Cicero.

John did not read Cicero's speeches, texts that had a very restricted circulation in the Middle Ages. The references mentioned by Webb in his index consistently have an alternative source, sometimes another text by Cicero, sometimes another Latin author available at the time. Among works of rhetoric, John certainly knew *De inuentione* and the apocryphal *Ad Herennium*, two works that circulated widely during the Middle Ages. The bequest to Chartres Cathedral mentions a copy of *De oratore*, which John probably also knew.[75] He certainly had a good knowledge of Cicero's rhetoric, not only from *De inventione*, a schoolbook of the period, but also, from his years of study onwards, notably with Thierry of Chartres, from Boethius' glosses of the *Topics*.[76]

As regards the philosophical treatises, John had access to *De amicitia* and *De senectute*, mentioned in the catalogue of the library at Canterbury in about 1170.[77] From the bequest to Chartres Cathedral we know that John possessed at his death a copy of *De officiis*, a work that doubtless constituted his principle source of access to Cicero's philosophy: this is confirmed by an analysis of references.[78] As Christophe Grellard has shown, if knowledge of the *Tusculanes* is highly probable (although possibly partial, and limited to Books 1 and 2),[79] direct knowledge of *De natura deorum* and *De diuinatione* must be excluded.[80]

---

75 *Cartulaire de Notre-Dame de Chartres*, p. 202: "Tullium de officiis et de oratore." See *Texts and Transmission*, p. 107.

76 See John Ward, "Some Principles of Rhetorical Historiography in the Twelfth Century," in Ernst Breisach, ed., *Classical Rhetoric and Medieval Historiography* (Chicago, 1995), pp. 103–165; Grellard, *Jean de Salisbury et la renaissance médiévale du scepticisme*, pp. 33–34.

77 James, *The Ancient Libraries*, p. 9: *Tullius de senectute. Tullius de Amicitia.*

78 See on this point Frédérique Lachaud, *L'Éthique du pouvoir au Moyen Age. L'office dans la culture politique (Angleterre, vers 1150-vers 1330)* (Paris, 2010), pp. 179–186.

79 For example, Chapter 20 of book 4 of the *Metalogicon* is a collage of quotations from the first *Tusculan* (*Tusculanae disputationes* 1.38, 57, 66, 67, 70, 71).

80 Grellard, *Jean de Salisbury et la renaissance médiévale du scepticisme*, p. 230, note 47: "The summary of Cicero's positions in the *Entheticus* (ll. 1215–46, ed. van Laarhoven, vol. 1, p. 185) places the accent on questions of divine prescience and human liberty, but we need not necessarily assume direct knowledge of *De fato* or *De divinatione*. In fact, John appears to rely entirely on a summary provided by Augustine in *De ciuitate Dei* 5.9. The examples used in book 2 of the *Policraticus* and capable of being drawn from *De divinatione* may equally come from either Valerius Maximus or Saint Jerome. Lastly, the 'academic' solution to the problem of prescience in *Policraticus* 2.22 appears to rely on both Saint Augustine and Boethius, not to mention Abelard."

The question is more difficult for *De finibus* and the *Academica*. Mention of Epicurus' *kurias doxas* (Latinized to *kiriadoxa*) in the *Policraticus* may suggest very partial knowledge of the text,[81] perhaps through the medium of an anthology. In fact, for the other quotations from *De finibus* recorded by Webb, in each case there exists the possibility of another Latin author as John's source.[82] Christophe Grellard has very effectively demonstrated how unnecessary it is to suppose that John knew the *Academica*, even in the form of extracts. One might suppose, in fact, that, if he had known this text, he would have made enormous use of it in support of his own scepticism. But this is not the case. We must therefore conclude that he did not know it. He nevertheless mentions in the *Metalogicon* the dictum attributed by Cicero to Democritus, to the effect that truth is in the abyss.[83] John, however, does not mention Democritus, and talks of a well.[84] The same formula is to be found in the *Diuinarum institutionum* of Lactantius.[85] There is indeed a *Lactantium* among the books bequeathed by John, and it has recently been proposed that this should be identified with a manuscript containing the *Diuinarum institutionum*, produced in the entourage of Peter of Celle and dating from the end of the 1150s.[86] To conclude, John of Salisbury certainly knew at first hand *De inuentione*, *De oratore*, and *De officiis*, as well as the *Laelius* and the *Cato*, and part of the *Tusculanes*. The other philosophical works he knew only at second hand, from references in authors such as Augustine, Jerome, and Lactantius.

An interesting case of John's readings from Cicero is that of the correspondence, in particular the collection *Ad familiares*. Several apparent quotations derive in fact from Quintilian or Macrobius, and so turn out to be quotations at second hand. Thus, by his use of the expression *in epistolis sicut apparet* in the first book of the *Metalogicon*, John appears to refer directly to the letters of Cicero:

---

81   *Policraticus* 5.4, ed. Webb, vol. 1, p. 292. The source of this passage is Cicero, *De finibus* 2.7.20.

82   Grellard, *Jean de Salisbury et la renaissance médiévale du scepticisme*, p. 230, note 49. The citing of Crassus' anecdote (*De finibus* 5.92 in *Policraticus* 8.8, ed. Webb, vol. 2, p. 274) may come from Jerome or Ammianus Marcellinus, while the reference to the *indifferentia* (*Fin.* 3.53 in *Policraticus* 8.16, ed. Webb, vol. 2, p. 341) may be borrowed from Seneca (*Ep.* 82.10).

83   Cicero, *Academica* 1.44: *in profundo ueritatem esse*; 2.32.

84   *Metalogicon* 2.13, ed. Hall, p. 76: *in profundo putei*.

85   Lactantius, *Institutiones divinae* 3.28.12; 14.30.6.

86   Lynn Barker, "MS Bodl. Canon. Pat. Lat. 131 and a Lost Lactantius of John of Salisbury: Evidence in Search of a French Critic of Thomas Becket," *Albion* 22 (1990), 21–37.

But Marcus Tullius [Cicero] did not hate his son, of whom, as is evident in his letters, he insistently required the study of grammar. And Gaius Caesar wrote books *On Analogy* (...)[87]

But John read this information in Quintilian, and not directly from Cicero's letter, which, in any event, we know only from secondary quotations:

But it is only the superfluities of grammar that do any harm. I ask you, is Cicero a less great orator for having, as his letters show, demanded rigid correctness of speech from his son? Or was the vigour of Gaius Caesar's eloquence impaired by the publication of a treatise on Analogy?[88]

Similarly, a quotation from a letter in *Ad familiares*,[89] included in the third book of the *Policraticus*,[90] in fact comes from Macrobius,[91] despite John's

---

87   *Metalogicon* 1.21 (McGarry, p. 60), ed. Hall, p. 48: "At Marcus Tullius non oderat filium, a
      quo in epistolis sicut apparet grammaticam instantissime exigebat. Gaius Caesar de ana-
      logia libros edidit."

88   Quintilian, *De institutione oratoria* 1.7.34–5, ed. and trans. H.E. Butler (Cambridge, Mass.,
      1920; repr. 1989), pp. 144–145: "Sed nihil ex grammatice nocuerit, nisi quod supervacuum
      est. An ideo minor est M. Tullius orator, quod idem artis huius diligentissimus fuit et in
      filio (ut epistulis apparet [Cicero, *Epistularum fragmenta* 8.6]), recte loquendi asper quo-
      que exactor? aut vim C. Caesaris fregerunt editi de analogia libri?"

89   Cicero, *Ad familiares* 12.4.1, ed. David Shackleton Bailey (Stuttgart, 1988), p. 412: "Vellem
      Idibus Martiis me ad cenam invitasses; profecto reliquiarum nihil fuisset. Nunc me rel-
      iquiae vestrae exercent, et quidem praeter ceteros me." [I should like you to have invited
      me to your banquet on the Ides of March; there would have been no leavings. Now it is
      just your leavings that are worrying me, me indeed more than anybody else. (trans.
      W. Glynn Williams, Cicero, *The Letters to his Friends II* (Cambridge, Mass., 1929, repr. 1983),
      p. 529)].

90   *Policraticus* 3.14, ed. Keats-Rohan, p. 224: "Sed et in epistola ad Gaium Cassium uiolatorem
      dictatoris mordacius scripsit: Vellem Idibus Martiis me ad cenam inuitasses: profecto rel-
      iquiarum nichil fuisset. Nunc me reliquiae uestrae exercent." [But also to Caius Cassius
      who murdered the dictator, he wrote with much sarcasm: "I could wish you had asked me
      to your dinner on the Ides of March. Nothing, I assure, you, would have been left over. But,
      as things are, your leaving makes me feel anxious."].

91   Macrobius, *Saturnalia* 2.3.13, ed. Jacobus Willis (Stuttgart, 1970), p. 142: "Vigebat in eo exce-
      dens iocos et seria mordacitas, ut hoc est ex epistula ad C. Cassium dictatoris violatorem:
      'Vellem idibus Martiis me ad cenam invitasses, profecto reliquiarum nihil fuisset. Nunc me
      reliquiae vestrae exercent'. Idem Cicero de Pisone genero et de M. Lepido lepidissime cavil-
      latus est." [The vigor of his sarcasm could go beyond mere jesting, and express his
      deep feelings, as, for example, in his letter to Caius Cassius, one of the men who murdered

indication *in epistola ad Gaium Cassium*. Macrobius is equally the source of the suggestion of links between Cicero and the actors Roscius and Aesopus[92] in the eighth book of the *Policraticus*,[93] even though John, while copying Macrobius' text almost word for word, does not define his source, and once again adds the indication *ex epistulis quoque eius*.

There nevertheless remain in John's *Letters* several quotations from Cicero's correspondence that do not appear to derive from an intermediary source. An instance of evident textual affinity is to be found in Letter 172, written in 1166 to John's brother Richard:

> Are they not afraid that savagery will grow tame or (a saying which Cicero made his own) "that Caesar's spear will cool" or his sword grow blunt?[94]

---

the dictator, in which he said: "I could wish you had asked me to your dinner on the Ides of March. Nothing, I assure, you, would have been left over. But, as things are, your leaving makes me feel anxious." And he also made some witty jokes about his son-in-law Piso and about Marcus Lepidus. (Macrobius, *The Saturnalia*, trans. Percival Davies (New York, 1969), pp. 168–169)].

92 Macrobius, *Saturnalia* 3.14.11, ed. Willis, p. 198: "Ceterum histriones non inter turpes habitos Cicero testimonio est, quem nullus ignorat Roscio et Aesopo histrionibus tam familiariter usum ut res rationesque eorum sua sollertia tueretur, quod cum aliis multis tum ex epistulis quoque eius declaratur." [As for actors, we have the evidence of Cicero to show that they were not looked upon as being among the disreputable classes of society, since it is common knowledge that he was on such friendly terms with the actors Roscius and Aesopus that his professional skill was available to defend their interests and affairs, as it is clear from his letters and from many other sources. (Macrobius, *The Saturnalia*, trans. Davies p. 233).]

93 *Policraticus* 8.12, ed. Webb, vol. 2, p. 312: "Ceterum histriones non inter turpes habitos Cicero auctor est qui, sicut Furius Albinus refert, Roscio et Esopo familiariter usus est, adeo quidem ut res rationesque eorum sua sollertia tueretur; quod cum ex aliis multis, tum ex epistolis eius declaratur." [As for actors, Cicero testifies that they were not looked upon as being among the disreputable classes of society, Cicero who, as Furius Albinus says, was on such friendly terms with the actors Roscius and Aesopus that his professional skill was available to defend their interests and affairs, as it is clear from his letters and from many other sources].

94 Letter 172, in *The Later Letters*, pp. 132–133: "Nunquid timent ne feritas mansuescat aut (ut a Cicerone usurpatum est) 'ne refrigeat hasta Caesaris', aut gladius hebetetur?" Similarly, Letter 194 (*The Later Letters*, p. 270) repeats the expression *virtuti nuntium remittere* that occurs in a letter from Cicero to Cassius (Cicero, *Ad familiares* 15.16.3, ed. Shackleton Bailey, p. 573).

John here repeats an expression from a letter in the collection *Ad familiares*.[95] Other examples, also from John's letters, smack more of allusion than of quotation. Thus a passage from Letter 34, addressed to Peter of Celle after 1157,[96] evokes a piece of advice given by Cicero to his friend Porcius Cato.[97] At the beginning of Letter 192, dating from 1166 or 1167, John says that he remembers a letter from Cicero to Marcellus having as its theme the debt one has to others:[98] this letter too belongs to the fifteenth book of the collection *Ad familiares*.[99]

Some have thought that John of Salisbury, in common with many medieval authors, used one or more anthologies of the Roman orator's correspondence.[100] But this hypothesis seems improbable, for none of the anthologies of the 11th and 12th centuries contains substantial extracts from *Epistulae ad familiares*. The substantial work carried out by Birger Munk Olsen[101] on the subject reveals this unambiguously. Richard Rouse confirms the hypothesis:[102] the letters *Ad familiares* do not feature in either of the great anthologies of the school of Orléans (*Florilegium Gallicum, Florilegium Angelicum*). But the manuscript tradition attests to the separate circulation of the two halves of the

---

95 Cicero, *Ad familiares* 9.10.3, ed. Shackleton Bailey, p. 290: "Ego ceteroqui animo aequo fero. Unum vereor, ne hasta Caesaris refrixerit." [For myself anyhow I take it philosophically; my only fear is that Caesar's actions will have fallen flat. (trans. Glynn Williams, Cicero, *The Letters to his Friends II*, p. 217)].

96 Letter 34, *The Early Letters*, p. 60: "Hoc utique uobis ascribere fidelius ausim quam Porcio Catoni familiari suo Cicero pridem ascripserit." [I would venture at any rate to say this of you with more confidence than Cicero of old would have said it of his dear friend Porcius Cato].

97 Cicero, *Ad familiares* 15.4.1, ed. Shackleton Bailey, p. 552.

98 Letter 192, *The Later Letters*, pp. 262–263: "Ciceronem in epistola ad Marcellum scripsisse memini, quia sapientis iudicio refert plurimum cui quis obligetur, et honesti uiri grauatur animus quotiens eum aut rei familiaris angustia aut articulus temporis illi constituit debitorem, quem ratio honestatis et morum titulus coli prohibet uel amari. Et hoc quidem, ut arbitror, eleganter et uere dictum est." [I recall that Cicero wrote in his letter to Marcellus that in a wise man's judgement it is of the highest importance to whom one is indebted, and the mind of an honourable man is weighed down as often as lack of resources or a temporary crisis had made him a debtor to a man whom grounds of honour and manners forbid him to respect or love. And this, I think, was elegantly and truly said.].

99 Cicero, *Ad familiares* 15.11.2, ed. Shackleton Bailey, p. 565.

100 Carl Schaarschmidt, "Johannes Saresberiensis in seinem Verhältnis zur klassischen Litteratur," *Rheinisches Museum für Philologie* 14 (1859), 200–234, esp. p. 221.

101 Birger Munk Olsen, "Les classiques latins dans les florilèges médiévaux antérieurs au XIIIe siècle," *Revue d'Histoire des Textes* 9 (1979), 47–121 and 10 (1980), 115–164.

102 *Texts and Transmission*, p. 141.

collection. If the *Letters to Atticus* almost disappeared from circulation during
the Middle Ages (only a few quotations in anthologies are to be found), the *Ad
familiares* circulated more widely, although finally in rather restricted form.
The sixteen books of this latter collection feature in a manuscript of the first
half of the 9th century that ceased to circulate after the turn of the millennium.
But some manuscripts contain either Books 1 to 8 (family X) or Books 9 to 16
(family Y), or extracts from the collection. Several manuscripts of family Y,
comprising Books 9 to 16, circulated in the 12th and 13th centuries, one of these
being the collection of Wibald of Corvey.[103] So John of Salisbury certainly knew
the second half of the letters *Ad familiares*, as is shown by the examples previously cited, which contain only passages from Books 9 to 16 of the Cicero collection: he had consulted, or he possessed, a copy of family Y.

John of Salisbury and the Grammarians

The texts of two grammarians of Late Antiquity, Priscian and Donatus, circulated widely in the Middle Ages, and feature in the Canterbury catalogue
established in about 1170.[104] John of Salisbury used them in both the *Metalogicon*
and the *Policraticus*. He also used the commentary on Donatus by Servius, as
well as the *De nuptiis Philologiae et Mercurii* of Martianus Capella; five works
feature in the Canterbury catalogue under the latter author's name.[105] But he
used one ancient text just as much if not more: the *Institutio oratoria* of
Quintilian.

Even if he was not, strictly speaking, a grammarian, Quintilian constitutes
an essential reference for the *Metalogicon*, whose Book 1 sets out to be a defence
of "grammar," understood as the reading of ancient authors. John mentions
Quintilian in Chapter 19, after Donatus, Servius, and Priscian, the grammarians
in the strict sense of the term.[106] Comparing him with Seneca, in the eighth
book of the *Policraticus* John judges him to be more cultivated (*litteratiorem*),
and considers his style more refined and more elevated (*et acumine et grauitate dicendi*).[107] In the *Metalogicon* as in the *Policraticus*, quotations from the
Institutio oratoria are numerous, and derive from that work's twelve books.
However, John did not have available to him a complete text that was found at

---

103   Berlin, Staatsbibliothek Preussischer Kulturbesitz, lat. fol. 252.
104   James, *The Ancient Libraries*, pp. 7–8.
105   Ibid., pp. 8–9.
106   *Metalogicon* 1.19, p. 46.
107   *Policraticus* 8.13, ed. Webb, vol. 2, p. 321.

Saint-Gall, and restored to scholarship by Poggio Bacciolini in 1416. John read Quintilian's immense work in a text containing gaps. But these were not as numerous as those in the abbreviated version on which medieval references to Quintilian's work were based.[108] As Wim Verbaal has shown by comparing the passages quoted by John with the manuscripts of the abbreviated tradition, John had before him a more complete copy. Despite this, it appears difficult to conclude that he possessed an integral text.

John of Salisbury and the Historians

John did not know Caesar, Titus Livy, or Tacitus, but he was familiar with the *Epitome* of Florus,[109] which provides a summary of Livy's immense oeuvre. As for Sallust, called by John in the *Policraticus* the principal Latin historian,[110] John's quotations from him are so isolated and limited that it is difficult to tell whether he read him in the form of extracts or from a complete text. What is more, even though the Canterbury catalogue mentions eight manuscripts under Sallust's name,[111] it is impossible to know whether these were complete manuscripts, containing the *Catilina* and the *Jugurtha* (the *Historiae* belong to a separate manuscript tradition),[112] or *mutili* incorporating a long gap in the text of the *Jugurtha*.[113]

For the manner in which John read the three Latin historians Valerius Maximus, Suetonius, and Aulus Gellius, we have the invaluable work of Janet Martin. She added Petronius to these three for her study of the Latin classics in John's work. For his quotations from Valerius Maximus, at the beginning of his work on the *Policraticus* John used extracts compiled by Heiric of Auxerre in the 9th century, the *Collectanea*. John then abandoned these extracts in favour

---

108 "Medieval references to Quintilian's rhetorical oeuvre are all based on a summary, a collection of extracts derived in the final analysis from the manuals of the rhetoricians Fortunatianus and Julius Victor in the IVth century" (Wim Verbaal, *"Teste Quintiliano*: Jean de Salisbury et Quintilien. Un exemple de la crise des autorités au XIIᵉ siècle," in Perrine Galand et al., eds., *Quintilien ancien et moderne* (Turnhout, 2010), pp. 155–170, esp. p. 162. Trans. David M.B. Richardson).

109 Wim Verbaal, *"Teste Quintiliano,"* p. 164.

110 *Policraticus* 3.12, ed. Keats-Rohan, p. 211: *Crispo historicorum inter Latinos potissimo.*

111 James, *The Ancient Libraries*, p. 9 (nos. 94–101).

112 *Texts and Transmission*, pp. 347–349. John probably had no knowledge of this text, which, in any event, has come down to us only in fragmentary form.

113 Ibid., p. 341.

of a complete manuscript of Valerius Maximus' text.[114] John's textual quotations from Suetonius show that he did not possess a complete text, but a quite corrupt manuscript of the extracts compiled by Heiric of Auxerre under the dictation of his teacher Lupus Servatus.[115] Moreover, in many passages John reproduces the substance and not the words of Suetonius' text, which suggests the use of extracts and anthologies in addition to or in place of complete texts.[116] John also used an anthology for Aulus Gellius.[117] What is more, the extracts from *Noctes Atticae* present in John's work, and to this day not identified with any particular manuscript, were also used by William of Malmesbury in his *Polyhistor*.[118]

In respect of Petronius' *Satiricon*, a rare text in John's time, Janet Martin discovers a score of textual quotations, to which must be added several allusions.[119] She thinks John did not use an anthology, but three other forms of the tradition: short extracts from the tale, long extracts from the tale, and the *Cena Trimalchionis* passage.[120] Even if he borrowed from the library at Canterbury a large proportion of the texts that constitute sources for the *Policraticus*, John possessed a personal copy of Petronius; Janet Martin raises the hypothesis of one or more manuscripts acquired during the course of his studies in France.[121] Martin also studied the use John made of Frontinus' *Strategemata*,[122] and demonstrated that he used a manuscript close to a manuscript of the beginning of the 12th century, copied in part by William of Malmesbury (Oxford, Lincoln College, Lat. 100). John's manuscript was either the same as William's, or a copy of it. This link is explained by the fact that the two men used the Canterbury libraries, and so had access to the same manuscripts. Janet Martin has thus clearly demonstrated by her work that John had access to several classical authors in partial form, whether in anthologies or as short extracts. Such a precise study remains to be undertaken for a number of authors quoted by John, notably the poets, who had a substantial presence in medieval anthologies.

---

114   Janet Martin, "John of Salisbury and the Classics," *Harvard Studies in Classical Philology* 73 (1969), 319–321, esp. p. 319. This article is a résumé of her PhD in Medieval Latin, written in 1968 at Harvard.

115   Eadem, "Uses of tradition: Gellius, Petronius and John of Salisbury," *Viator* 10 (1979), 57–76, esp. p. 58.

116   Ibid., p. 59.

117   Ibid., p. 60.

118   Martin, "John of Salisbury and the Classics," p. 320.

119   Martin, "Uses of tradition," p. 69.

120   Ibid., p. 70.

121   Ibid., p. 71.

122   Janet Martin, "John of Salisbury's Manuscripts of Frontinus and Gellius," *Journal of the Warburg and Courtauld Institutes* 40 (1977), 1–26. See also *Texts and Transmission*, p. 172.

His Reading of the Poets

The most important poet for John of Salisbury was without doubt Virgil, whom he considered to be "the most learned of the poets,"[123] and whose *Bucolics*, *Georgics*, and *Aeneid* he read and quoted, sometimes at length. He relied, besides, equally on the commentary by Servius. Virgil's poems, and in particular the *Aeneid*, were invested with a philosophical meaning. In fact, for the school of Chartres Virgil was not only the poet *par excellence*; he was above all read through a systematically Platonist filter. In the tradition of Macrobius, Servius, and Fulgentius, whose work on Virgil's poems was directed at extricating the hidden meaning of the text (*integumenta Vergilii*), an allegorical reading of Virgil was developed at the beginning of the 12th century by Bernard Silvestris in his commentary on the Aeneid.[124] This author,[125] who is difficult to identify, and was long confused with Bernard of Chartres, explains in his prologue that Virgil was as much a philosopher as a poet (*in hoc opere et poeta et philosophus perhibetur esse Virgilius*), so that his verses, besides their elegance and literary qualities, contain examples encouraging the observance of moral rules. Bernard Silvestris then proposes a series of precise examples such as the love affair between Dido and Aeneas, designed to dissuade the reader from desiring what is forbidden. In similar fashion, John of Salisbury in his *Policraticus* considers Virgil's poetic fictions to bear a hidden philosophical truth[126]; among his borrowings from Bernard Silvestris is a rather fantastical etymology of Aeneas' name, the effect of which is to make the character into an allegory of the human soul.[127] Under the veil of fable,[128] the "Mantuan poet" succeeds in expressing the truth of all philosophy:

---

123   *Policraticus* 6.21, ed. Webb, vol. 2, p. 60, line 5: *poetarum doctissimus Maro*.

124   For this text see Bernardus Silvestris, *The Commentary of the First Six Books of the Aeneid of Vergil*, ed. Julian Ward Jones (Lincoln, Nebr., 1977).

125   On Bernard Silvestris see Peter Dronke, "Bernard Silvestris, Natura and Personification," *Journal of the Warburg and Courtauld Institutes* 43 (1980), 53–73; Brian Stock, *Myth and Science in the Twelfth Century. A Study of Bernard Silvester* (Princeton, 1972); Winthrop Wetherbee, *Platonism and Poetry in the Twelfth Century. The Literary Influence of the School of Chartres* (Princeton, 1972), pp. 104–125, 152–186.

126   See Seth Lerer, "John of Salisbury's Virgil," *Vivarium* 20 (1982), 24–39.

127   Max Kerner has demonstrated this parallel between John of Salisbury (*Policraticus* 8.24) and Bernard Silvestris (*Johannes von Salisbury und die logische Struktur*, pp. 40–41).

128   Regarding the veil of allegory, both the notion and the terms are particularly evident in the *Entheticus maior* in respect of Martianus Capella, a passage in which repeated use is made of the verb *tego*: *Entheticus de dogmate philosophorum* 186–198, ed. van Laarhoven, vol. 1, pp. 116–119. On this subject see Lerer, "John of Salisbury's Virgil," 31. On the technique of the *integumentum* at the heart of the school of Chartres see Édouard Jeauneau, "L'usage

You may be confronted by the Mantuan poet, who under the pretext of fiction expressed all the truths of philosophy.[129]

He develops similar arguments in Chapter 24 of Book 8 of the *Policraticus*, a chapter devoted to the Epicureans:

It is agreed by those who devote their activities to the investigation of the meaning of authors that Virgil has evinced his power in a double field by arraying the mysteries of philosophic moral perfection in the gossamer of poetic fancy.[130]

Relying on the commentary by Bernard of Chartres, John maintains that, in the first six books of his poem, Virgil describes the six ages of life, thus showing in the character of Aeneas the evolution of the human soul from birth to death:

If the words of the pagan may be employed by the Christian who believes that a nature divine and pleasing to God because of the grace inherent in it can belong to the elect alone (although I do not think that either the words or the thoughts of the pagans are to be shunned provided their errors are avoided), Virgil seems to have been by divine wisdom given a hint of this very fact: under the cloak of poetic imagination in his *Eneid* he subtly represents the six periods of life by the division of the work into six books. In these, in imitation of the *Odyssey*, he appears to have represented the origin and progress of man. The character he sets forth and develops he leads on and conducts down into the nether world.[131]

---

de l'*integumentum* à travers les gloses de Guillaume de Conches," in *Lectio philosophorum. Recherches sur l'école de Chartres* (Amsterdam, 1973), pp. 127–192; Francine Mora-Lebrun, "L'École de Chartres et la pratique de l'*integumentum*," in *L'Énéide médiévale et la naissance du roman* (Paris, 1994), pp. 89–108; Stock, *Myth and Science*, pp. 49–62.

129 *Policraticus* 6.22, (trans. Nederman, p. 130), ed. Webb, vol. 2, p. 63: "Procedat tibi poeta Mantuanus, qui sub imagine fabularum totius philosophiae exprimit ueritatem."

130 Ibid. 8.24 (trans. Pike, p. 404), ed. Webb, vol. 2, p. 417: "Constat enim apud eos qui mentem diligentius perscrutantur auctorum Maronem geminae doctrinae uires declarasse, dum uanitate figmenti poetici philosophicae uirtutis inuoluit archana."

131 Ibid. 8.24 (trans. Pike, p. 402) ed. Webb, vol. 2, p. 415: "Si uerbis gentilium uti licet Christiano, qui solis electis diuinum et Deo placens per inhabitantem gratiam esse credit ingenium, etsi nec uerba nec sensus credam gentilium fugiendos, dummodo uitentur errores, hoc ipsum diuina prudentia in Eneide sua sub inuolucro fictitii commenti, innuisse uisus est Maro, dum sex etatum gradus sex librorum distinctionibus prudenter expressit. Quibus conditionis humanae, dum Odisseam imitatur, ortum exprimere uisus est et processum, ipsumque, quem educit et prouehit, producit et deducit ad Manes."

John develops this analysis further, referring very precisely to the episodes of the first six books of the poem.[132] Seth Lerer has clearly shown how, in his allegorical reading of Virgil and his conception of *integumentum* and *inuolucrum*, John revisited the notions of Bernard of Chartres concerning the links between poetry and philosophy. As in the case of Cicero, John read the texts current to his period and thus also available to his contemporaries; but he read them on a deeper level, and his truly personal interpretation makes his position in respect of the classical texts original for his period.

Of the other epic Latin poets, John knew and quoted the *Pharsalia* of Lucan and the *Thebaid* of Statius. These two authors are included in the Canterbury catalogue composed in about 1170.[133] In the *Policraticus*, he associates Virgil with Lucan in characterizing the spirits of both poets as divine.[134] He moreover takes up Quintilian's judgement that Lucan's style makes him a model for imitation by orators rather than poets.[135] Thus in the eighth book of the *Policraticus* he calls him a "very serious poet" (*poeta grauissimus*), while not excluding the title of *orator*.

> This was intimated by a very serious poet, or if you prefer, according to Quintilian, give him the more proper name of orator; I do not object.[136]

Lastly, in the steps of Servius and Isidorus of Seville, he relates Lucan to the historians.[137] It is, in any case, partly in this respect that this poet interests him, as the *Pharsalis* gives him much information about Caesar and the First Civil War, allowing him to pose the question of tyrannicide among other things.

---

132 Ibid. 8.24, ed. Webb, vol. 2, pp. 415–417. On this subject, see Philippe Delhaye, "L'enseignement de la philosophie morale au XIIᵉ siècle," *Mediaeval studies* 11 (1949), 77–99, esp. p. 89, notes 13–17.

133 James, *The Ancient Libraries*, p. 10 (nos. 125–129 for Lucan and 130–135 for Statius).

134 *Policraticus* 2.2, ed. Keats-Rohan, p. 75: "signa quae Virgilius et Lucanus diuino comprehendunt ingenio." [the signs Virgil and Lucan understand with their divine intelligence].

135 Quintilian, *De institutione oratoria* 10.1.90, ed. and trans. H.E. Butler (Cambridge, Mass., 1922; repr. 1993), pp. 50–51: "Lucanus ardens et concitatus et sententiis clarissimus et, ut dicam quod sentio, magis oratoribus quam poetis imitandus." [Lucan is fiery and passionate and remarkable for the grandeur of his general reflexions, but, to be frank, I consider that he is more suitable for imitation by the orator than by the poet. (trans. Butler)].

136 *Policraticus* 8.23, ed. Webb, vol. 2, p. 404: "Innuit hoc poeta grauissimus aut, si iuxta Quintilianum rectius dicere malueris oratorem, non repugno."

137 Ibid. 2.19, ed. Keats-Rohan, p. 113: "...poeta doctissimus, si tamen poeta dicendus est qui uera narratione rerum ad historicos magis accedit." [a very learned poet, if you can call poet someone who, by his veracious narration of events, is closer to historians.] See Servius, *In Aeneidem* 1.382 and Isidorus, *Etymologiae* 8.7.10.

His knowledge of Ovid was quite wide, which is entirely normal for a 12th century typified by Ludwig Traube as *aetas Ouidiana*: Ovid's presence and influence increased considerably at this period, to the point that, by the end of the century, complete collections of his poems circulated widely, competing with separate editions of individual works.[138] So John knew the love poetry (*Amores, Remedia amoris, Ars amatoria*) and the poems of exile (*Tristia, Epistulae ex Ponto*), to which must be added the *Fasti*, the *Metamorphoses*, and the *Heroides*. Conforming to the medieval tradition of Ovid as *magister amoris*, John associates the poet with love, and in Book 3 of the *Policraticus* calls attention to the lightness of his verses.[139] He insists on the romantic levity of the poet's character in the judgement he pronounces a little later on in the same book of the *Policraticus*, a judgement he follows with a quotation from the *Ars amatoria*:

> So says the poet who filled not Rome but the world with his wanton love, the teacher of young women's seducers and lascivious lovers.[140]

But he is also interested in an ethical reading of the poetry, as in Book 7 of the *Policraticus*, where he praises in equal measure the elegance and the truth of Ovid's description of Envy (*Pallor*) in *Metamorphoses* (2. 775–782).[141]

Ethical preoccupations are precisely what John gleaned from his reading of Horace: "Horace takes pride in the fact that, for virtue's sake, he has reread Homer," he writes in the *Metalogicon*.[142] The works of Horace

---

138   *Texts and Transmission*, p. 258. On the circulation of Ovid's texts from the 9th to the 12th centuries, and in particular his presence in anthologies, see Birger Munk Olsen, "Ovide au Moyen Âge (du IXᵉ au XIIᵉ siècle)," in *La Réception de la littérature classique au Moyen Âge IXᵉ–XIIᵉ siècle). Choix d'articles publiés par des collègues à l'occasion de son soixantième anniversaire* (Copenhagen, 1995), pp. 71–94; idem, "Les classiques latins dans les florilèges médiévaux antérieurs au XIIIᵉ siècle," in *La Réception de la littérature classique*, pp. 145–273.

139   *Policraticus* 3.5, ed. Webb, vol. 1, p. 182: *Naso leuitatem uersificandi*. I choose here the edition by Webb, whose reading *leuitatem*, given by certain manuscripts, I find more satisfying than the *facilitatem* given by others and adopted by Keats-Rohan.

140   Ibid. 3.11, ed. Webb, vol. 1, p. 206: "Vnde ille qui non urbem sed orbem lasciuis impleuit amoribus, sollicitatorem puellarum et impudicum instruens amatorem, ait."

141   Ibid. 7.24, ed. Webb; vol. 2, p. 212: "Pestem hanc, licet poetici nube figmenti, Naso depinxit eleganter quidem et uere." [This plague, although under the veil of poetic fiction, Ovid described with as much elegance as truth.]

142   *Metalogicon* 1.22 (trans. McGarry, p. 63) ed. Hall, p. 49, line 23: "Gloriatur Horatius se uirtutis causa relegisse Homerum."

available to him included the *Satires*, the *Epistles*, and the *Ars poetica*. He probably had no knowledge of the *Odes*.[143] The only quotation from the latter collection in the *Metalogicon* derives from Priscian[144]; another in the *Policraticus* is from Augustine's *De musica*.[145] Other instances comprise proverbial formulae that John could have read elsewhere. The Canterbury catalogue, moreover, mentions eight volumes with Horace as author's name.[146] John also quotes extracts from the *Satires* of Persius and Juvenal, two authors that also feature in the Canterbury catalogue.[147] Of the comic poets, John does not appear to have known Plautus, but quotes several lines from the comedies of Terence, an author with several entries in the Canterbury catalogue.[148]

In respect of all these poets, a systematic textual study of the quotations, and of textual variants in particular, ought to permit a better understanding of the form in which John read Latin poets other than Virgil, and perhaps allow us to identify the anthologies or *excerpta* that he consulted. Lastly, there is no call to suppose that he had even a partial knowledge of Catullus. The mention of the author's name (*Catulli*) in the *Metalogicon*, and the reference to a line containing the term *litterator*, are from Martianus Capella.[149]

Conclusion: A Dwarf on the Shoulders of Giants?

With some exceptions, John did not have much broader access to ancient texts than that enjoyed by his contemporaries. Upon close examination of his reading of these texts, however, it appears that, as in the case of biblical and patristic texts, he studied and meditated upon them at length in order to gain mastery of them. He constantly draws upon ancient references in support of his own thoughts. In effect, he endows Classical Antiquity with immense prestige. John invokes the majesty of Antiquity with its associated great names in Chapter 4 of Book 3 of the *Metalogicon*, a chapter devoted to the *Peri hermeneias* (*De interpretatione*) of Aristotle:

---

143 Kerner, *Johannes von Salisbury und die logische Struktur*, p. 29.
144 *Metalogicon* 4.42, p. 183.
145 *Policraticus* 8.15, ed. Webb, vol. 2, p. 336.
146 James, *The Ancient Libraries*, p. 10 (nos. 117–124).
147 Ibid., p. 10 (nos. 136–138 for Juvenal and 141–149 for Persius).
148 Ibid., p. 9 (nos. 88–92).
149 *Metalogicon* 1.24, p. 55.

> Besides, reverence is to be shown to the words of the ancient authors, both in careful and assiduous use and because they convey a certain majesty derived from the great names of antiquity.[150]

The respect in which he holds the texts of Classical Antiquity can be understood only from the perspective of his use of them on his own account, as witnessed by the term *utendi*.

It is a matter, not of setting Classical Antiquity on a pedestal, but of entering into contact with the texts in a spirit of everyday familiarity, and respect marked with affection:

> They dress the interpretations of the ancient authors up in almost everyday clothing, which becomes in a way even more resplendent when brightened by the distinction of antiquity's gravity. Accordingly, the words of the ancient authors should not be lost or forgotten, especially those that give their full opinions and have wide applicability. Such words preserve scientific knowledge in its entirety, and contain tremendous hidden as well as apparent power.[151]

John always positions himself within the perspective of personal use of the texts read: he exhorts his own readers to retain in particular those passages that can easily be applied to numerous ends (*quae commode possunt ad multa transferri*). The study of Classical Antiquity permits us, besides, to ensure a continuity of knowledge (*integritatem scientiae*), and the transmission of the accumulated knowledge of the ancients to our contemporaries.

Certain formulations used by John might suggest that he is asserting a superiority of the ancients over the moderns. He thus affirms in the same chapter:

---

150   Ibid. 3.4, p. 116: "Praeterea reuerentia exhibenda est uerbis auctorum, cum cultu et assiduitate utendi, tum quia quandam a magnis nominibus antiquitatis, praeferunt maiestatem." Translation adapted from Peter Godman, *The Silent Masters: Latin Literature and Its Censors in the High Middle Ages* (Princeton, 2000), p. 170.

151   Ibid. 3.4 (trans. adapted from McGarry, p. 168), p. 117: "Vestiunt enim sensus auctorum, quasi cultu cotidiano, qui quodam modo festiuior est, cum antiquitatis grauitate clarius insignitur. Sunt ergo memoriter tenenda uerba auctorum, sed ea maxime quae plenas sententias explent, et quae commode possunt ad multa transferri. Nam et haec integritatem scientiae seruant, et praeter hoc a se ipsis tam latentis quam patentis energiae habent plurimum."

While the sense of the words that were used by the ancients and those that are used by moderns may be the same, their greater age has made the former more venerable.[152]

It is in any event in this sense that the Spanish humanist Luis Vives understood the famous description, attributed to Bernard of Chartres, of the moderns as dwarfs perched on the shoulders of the giants that are the ancients.[153] In his *De disciplinis* Vives in fact rebels against that image, and claims the same stature for ancients and moderns.[154] In John of Salisbury, however, although the moderns are of smaller stature than the ancients, once they are perched on the latters' shoulders they can see further than them:

> Our own generation enjoys the legacy bequeathed to it by that which preceded it. We frequently know more, not because we have moved ahead by our own natural ability, but because we are supported by the strength of others, and possess riches that we have inherited from our forefathers. Bernard of Chartres used to compare us to dwarfs perched on the shoulders of giants. He pointed out that we see more and farther than our predecessors, not because we have keener vision or greater height, but because we are lifted up and borne aloft on their gigantic stature.[155]

---

152   Ibid. (trans. McGarry, p. 166) ed. Hall, p. 116: "Licet itaque modernorum et veterum sit sensus idem, venerabilior est vetustas."

153   On this image, its origins, and its influence, see George Sarton, "Standing on the Shoulders of Giants," *Isis* 24 (1935–6), 107–109; R.E. Ockenden, "Standing on the Shoulders of Giants," *Isis* 25 (1936), 451–452; Raymond Klibansky, "Standing on the Shoulders of Giants," *Isis* 26 (1936), 147–149; Joseph de Ghellinck, "Nani et gigantes," *Archivium Latinitatis Medii Aevi (Bulletin du Cange)* 18 (1945), 25–29; August Buck, "Aus der Vorgeschichte der 'Querelle des Anciens et des Modernes'," *Bibliothèque d'Humanisme et de Renaissance. Travaux et documents* 20 (1958), pp. 527–541; Robert King Merton, *On the Shoulders of Giants* (New York, 1965); Édouard Jeauneau, "'Nani gigantum humeris insidentes', essai d'interprétation de Bernard de Chartres," *Vivarium* 5 (1967), 79–99; idem, "Nains et géants," in *Entretiens sur la Renaissance du XIIᵉ siècle*, pp. 21–52; Luigi Spina, "Nains et géants: une dialectique antique," *L'Information littéraire* 56 (2004), 28–33.

154   Juan Luis Vives, *De disciplinis* 1.5, in *Opera omnia* (Valencia, 1785), vol. 6, p. 39: "Non est ita, neque nos sumus nani, nec illi homines gigantes, sed omnes ejusdem staturae"[No, we are not dwarfs, they are not giants, but we are all the same size].

155   *Metalogicon* 3.4, (trans. McGarry, p. 167) ed. Hall, p. 116: "Fruitur tamen aetas nostra beneficio praecedentis, et saepe plura nouit non suo quidem praecedens ingenio, sed innitens uiribus alienis, et opulenta doctrina patrum. Dicebat Bernardus Carnotensis nos esse quasi nanos gigantum umeris insidentes, ut possimus plura eis et remotiora uidere, non

The moderns are the inheritors of a past tradition. But that tradition by no means condemns them to permanent inferiority; on the contrary, it constitutes a formidable springboard for the development of contemporary knowledge. This is a dynamic conception of tradition authorizing progress,[156] a trait that might be qualified as humanist.

In his relationship to ancient authors, John of Salisbury occupies an entirely original position in the Middle Ages. While medieval authors often considered their counterparts in Classical Antiquity as an external, intangible authority, as prestigious guarantors of their own discourse, John in his works practiced a real appropriation of the ancient texts, not unlike the concept of "innutrition" that would be developed by Renaissance writers in their reception of Petrarch.[157] In Chapter 10 of Book 7 of the *Policraticus*, with reference to Seneca and Macrobius, John develops the image of bees[158] to describe the imitation of the ancients[159]:

> As we read in the book entitled *Saturnalia* and in the epistles of Seneca to Lucilius, we ought in some sort to imitate the bees who wander about and cull flowers, then arrange what they brought in, distribute it in combs and, by a mixing process and by their own peculiar ability, change the various pollens into one flavour. Whatever we have acquired by our various reading, let us also turn to virtue's purpose.[160]

---

utique proprii uisus acumine, aut eminentia corporis, sed quia in altum subuehimur et extollimur magnitudine gigantea."

156   Godman, *The Silent Masters*, p. 171.

157   On the imitation of the ancients in the Renaissance see Francesco Bausi, "Poésie et imitation au Quattrocento," in Perrine Galand-Hallyn and Fernand Hallyn, eds., *Poétiques de la Renaissance: le modèle italien, le monde franco-bourguignon et leur héritage en France au XVIᵉ siècle* (Geneva, 2001), pp. 438–462; Thomas M. Greene, *The Light in Troy. Imitation and Discovery in Renaissance Poetry* (New Haven, 1982); Martin L. McLaughlin, *Literary Imitation in the Italian Renaissance: the Theory and Practice of Literary Imitation from Dante to Bembo* (Oxford, 1995). On innutrition in Joachim du Bellay, see Jean Vignes, "De l'autorité à l'innutrition: Sébillet de Du Bellay, lecteurs de Cicéron," in Jean-Pierre Néraudau, ed., *L'Autorité de Cicéron de l'Antiquité au XVIIIᵉ siècle. Actes de la Table Ronde organisée par le Centre de recherches sur les classicismes antiques et modernes. Université de Reims. 11 décembre 1991* (Caen, 1993), pp. 79–92.

158   On this image and its influence see Jürgen von Stackelberg, "Das Bienengleichnis. Ein Beitrag zur Geschichte der literarischen *Imitatio*," *Romanische Forschungen* 68 (1956), 271–293 (esp. pp. 279–280 on John of Salisbury).

159   Seneca, *Ep.* 84.3–7; Macrobius, *Saturnalia* 1. praef. 3–7.

160   *Policraticus* 7.10, ed. Webb, vol. 2, p. 133: "Vt enim in libro Saturnalium et in epistolis Senecae ad Lucilium legitur, apes quodammodo debemus imitari, quae uagantur et flores carpunt, deinde quicquid adtulere disponunt et per fauos diuidunt et succum uarium in

The accent here is on transformation (*mutant, conuertamus*), as witness also the image of digestion developed later on in the same chapter.[161] For John, the reading of Classical Antiquity must result in the production of something new and personal: his reading of ancient authors involves creativity. This should be compared with the attitude of the Church Fathers to the use of ancient pagan texts; for them, these texts were to be used in the service of Christian doctrine, to which they remained strictly subordinate. John's position was that ancient authors and their texts were a source of inspiration, a support and a stimulus for the development of his own thinking. As Wim Verbaal affirms: for John, "use of a classical authority is nuanced and diverse, and adapted to the needs of the author."[162] John himself, in his prologue to the first book of the *Policraticus*, evokes the appropriation of ancient texts as a process that allows him to write his own work:

> For the most part, the material that is utilised comes from elsewhere, except when I make my own that which is said commonly and rightly, so that I sometimes express ideas by means of my own abridgement, while at other times I express them faithfully and authoritatively in the words of others.[163]

It is a matter of making someone else's words his own. In this passage, John outlines a dialectic of the self and the other that permits a dynamic and personal relationship with the authors of Antiquity. Thanks to this living relationship with classical texts, a kind of dialogue with Classical Antiquity arises across space and time:

> Although pleasurable in many ways, the pursuit of letters is especially fruitful because it excludes all annoyances stemming from differences of time and place, it draws friends into each other's presence, and it

---

unum saporem mixtura quadam et proprietate spiritus sui mutant. Nos quoque, quicquid diuersa lectione quaesiuimus, conuertamus in usum uirtutis."

161   Ibid. 7.10, ed. Webb, vol. 2.

162   Verbaal, "Teste Quintiliano," p. 168: "l'emploi d'une autorité classique se nuance, se diversifie, s'adapte selon les besoins de l'auteur."

163   *Policraticus*, 1 prol. (trans. Nederman, p. 6) ed. Keats-Rohan, p. 24: "Haec quoque ipsa, quibus plerumque utor, aliena sunt, nisi quia quicquid ubique bene dictum est facio meum, et illud nunc meis ad compendium, nunc ad fidem et auctoritatem alienis exprimo uerbis."

abolishes the situation in which things worth knowing are not experienced.[164]

Literature, inasmuch as it comprises both reading and writing, permits this tie of friendship between great men of different epochs, and in this way acquires its fundamental function of transmission: it abolishes time and forgetting.

---

164   Ibid. 1 prol. (trans. Nederman, p. 3) ed. Keats-Rohan, p. 21: "Iocundissimus cum in multis, tum in eo maxime est litterarum fructus, quod omnium interstitiorum loci et temporis exclusa molestia, amicorum sibi inuicem praesentiam exhibent et res scitu dignas aboleri non patiuntur."

CHAPTER 6

John of Salisbury and the Writing of History

Clare Monagle

...the records of the chronicles are valuable for establishing and abolishing customs, for strengthening or destroying privileges; and nothing, after the grace and law of God, teaches the living more surely and soundly than knowledge of the deeds of the departed.[1]

John of Salisbury made this statement regarding the utility of historical writing in the Prologue of his *Historia pontificalis*. Its purpose, he declared, was pedagogical. The role of the chronicle was to record the way humans managed themselves, their status, and their property at a given time. This record could then be a source to later generations for understanding the constellations of laws, duties, and customs that contributed to their present reality. This claim for this particular use of history was unusual for its time. In the *Historia pontificalis*, unlike many of his contemporaries, John of Salisbury was not interested in recounting supernatural signs and wonders that bore God's presence in the world.[2] Nor was he concerned with ecclesiastical history in the Eusebian mode, in which the unfolding of human time saw the repeated figurings of the Old and New Testaments.[3] Rather, John was interested in the negotiations of the world. In this work, he repeatedly described conflict between important men (and very occasionally women) over issues of primacy, whether it was primacy of orthodoxy, in land-holding, or in ecclesiastical status. He depicted a cast of frail egos attempting to strengthen their position in the world and the attempts of the Pope to manage those egos.

---

1 *Historia pontificalis*, pp. 3–4: "Valet etiam noticia cronicorum ad statuendas uel euacuandas prescriptiones et priuilegia roboranda uel infirmanda; nichilque post gratiam et legem Dei uiuentes rectius et ualidius instruit quam si gesta cognouerint decessorum."

2 Much recent work has been done on the presence and use of the supernatural in Anglo-Norman historiography by Jeffrey Jerome Cohen, see his *Of Giants: Sex, Monsters, and the Middle Ages* (Minneapolis, 1999) and *Hybridity, Identity and Monstrosity in Medieval Britain: On Difficult Middles* (New York, 2006). Most recently, see Carl S. Watkins, *History and The Supernatural in Medieval England* (Cambridge, 2007).

3 On the influence of Eusebius, see Michael I. Allen, "Universal History 300–1000: Origins and Western Developments," in Deborah Mauskopf Deliyannis, ed., *Historiography in the Middle Ages* (Leiden, 2003), pp. 17–42.

The *Historia pontificalis* has received little attention in the historiography of medieval historical writing. Scholars have tended to spend more time with the livelier of his contemporary Anglo-Norman chroniclers, such as Gerald of Wales and Geoffrey of Monmouth. These historians offer a dazzling array of monsters, demons, and mythical heroes for the consideration of scholars, enabling rich insights into not only the medieval imaginary, but also the clearly evident ideological uses of the past in the 12th century. The *Historia pontificalis* has also received relatively little focus when compared to John of Salisbury's more famous works, the *Metalogicon*, his educational treatise, and his *Policraticus*, his epochal work of political theory. These works, both fundamental to our understanding of intellectual life in the 12th century and both brimming with crucial historical and theoretical detail, have tended to overshadow the more modest, and less finished, *Historia pontificalis*.

While the oversight, on both counts, is understandable, it is also a shame. The *Historia pontificalis* offers a revealing exploration of the day-to-day administrative life of the Papacy in the period 1148–52, the period of time that John spent at the papal court as an emissary of Archbishop Theobald of Canterbury. It describes the pope, Eugenius III, engaged in various activities, such as negotiating with nobles who have requested a divorce, or responding to threats of schism from the English Church, or overseeing the Council of Reims. The account is revealing because, in its exploration of the conflicts of men, and also the efforts of the Pope to broker solutions to those conflicts, John offers a reading of how the minutiae of life in the world relates to the higher spiritual realities of Christian life. As he tells us, he aims "to relate noteworthy matters, so that the invisible things of God may be clearly seen by the things that are done, and men may by examples of reward and punishment be made more zealous in the fear of God and pursuit of justice."[4] This quote has the appearance of a standard Pauline formulary, one that reduces the minutiae of the world to epiphenomena of divine presence. But what we see in the *Historia pontificalis* is the presentation of genuine interest in the detail of the human data that reveal the "invisible things." The noteworthy matters in the *Historia pontificalis*, as depicted by John, are moments of competing political conflict in Christendom. John seems to be asking how God's invisible things can be seen within the self-interested posturing of the political actors in his story. In spite then, of the absence of dragons or fabled kings in this work of history, John's *Historia pontificalis* deserves another look.

---

4 *Historia pontificalis*, Prologue, p. 3: "Horum uero omnium uniformis intentio est, scitu digna referre, ut per ea que facta sunt conspiciantur inuisibilia Dei, et quasi propositis exemplis premii uel pene, reddant homines in timore Domini et cultu iustitie cautiores."

Famously, John was the courtier *par excellence* of the 12th century. From his relatively humble origins in Old Sarum, he used his excellent education in the schools of Paris as the basis for a distinguished career in the service of the English Church. He wrote at length about his experiences as a student in his *Metalogicon,* which also encompassed his meditations on educational theory. In the *Policraticus* he theorized the political, famously contributing the organic metaphor that made an analogy between the human body and the political community. In these works, both written in the 1150s, John of Salisbury moved from the particular to the general. That is, he always combined literary registers, between precise *exempla* and overarching theoretical speculation. Consequently, both the *Metalogicon* and the *Policraticus* are filled with fascinating historical details, as well as informed by deeply held philosophical positions. As a courtier, John had the anecdotes, which he combined with his proto-scholastic vision of a world unified by God. In the *Historia pontificalis,* written after the aforementioned texts, we see another exploration of the particular by John of Salisbury.[5] As he narrates the events of the papal court between 1148 and 1152, depicting moments of strife and mess in a temporal frame, he is implicitly meditating on the larger issues of power, meaning and governance. John of Salisbury's extraordinary 12th-century foundation as schoolman, theorist and courtier meant that his vision of history, however filled with the detritus of administrative life, was informed by a complicated understanding of human motivation and culpability. The purpose of this essay, in which I will consider some select parts of the text, is to show just how John's depiction of events in time in the *Historia pontificalis* were underscored by his more famous preoccupations with ideas and with the political.

The Prologue

Cary Nederman has written on John's use of *exempla* in the *Policraticus* that "John's *exempla* are meant to help the reader bridge the gap between abstract moral discourse, on the one hand, and the actual conditions in which human beings find themselves, on the other."[6] All of his writings are characterized by the regular use of lively examples that give vivacity and energy to his prose. In the *Metalogicon,* John's oft-quoted statement that we are "dwarfs perched on the shoulders of giants...we see more and farther than our predecessors, not because

---

5   Chibnall dates the work in the late 1160s, see Chibnall, "Introduction," *Historia Pontificalis,*
     pp. 25–30.
6   Cary J. Nederman, "Editor's Introduction," in *Policraticus,* trans. Nederman, p. xii.

we have keener vision or greater height, but because we are lifted up and borne aloft on their gigantic stature," in which he articulated his notion of the cumulative learning of the moderns based on the achievements of the past, actually emerges as part of John's larger account of the career of Bernard of Chartres.[7] In this instance, the example of Bernard is used to demonstrate humble and morally fortified pedagogy in practice. John's works, then, always attempt to move between the abstract and the particular. The Prologue to the *Historia pontificalis*, in which he sets out his guiding principles for the following work, allows some insight into his authorial convictions about the relationship between God and events in the world. That is, his Prologue gives us a sense of the theoretical framework that lies behind John's discussion of examples in the rest of the text. And it also allows us insights into John's understanding of what comes between the world and God, the human language that shapes deeds in time into historical narrative.

He begins with an intellectual genealogy of sorts, listing the biblical and patristic sources that recount the Christian past, supplying what Christopher Brooke has called "a hasty history of history."[8] He cites the Book of Chronicles, the Gospels, the Acts of the Apostles, Eusebius, Cassiodorus, Orosius, Isidore and Bede. He then mentions two contemporary authors, Hugh of Saint-Victor and Sigebert of Gembloux as the immediate predecessors in his endeavor. This genealogical unfolding of history's history was a standard beginning in medieval historical writing.[9] John's beginning, thus, does not seem to constitute a departure from the standard tropes of medieval historiography. Where he does depart in his Prologue, however, is in his statement of what impelled him to write his own work. Here John departs abruptly from the sweeping typological historical writing of his self-described antecedent. After noting that Sigebert of Gembloux's chronicle terminated in 1148, John declares that "[f]rom that time, however, there is not a single chronicle that I can discover; though I have found in church archives notes of memorable events which could be of help to any future writers who may appear."[10] From the very big picture of the universal

---

7   *Metalogicon*, p. 116: "Dicebat Bernadus Carnotensis nos esse quasi nanos gigantum umeris insidentes, ut possimus plura eis et remotiora uidere, non utique proprii uisus acumine, aut eminentia corporis, sed quia in altum subuehimur et extollimur magnitudine gigantea." Trans. McGarry, p. 167.

8   Christopher Brooke, "Aspects of John of Salisbury's *Historia Pontificalis*," in Leslie M. Smith and Benedicta Ward, eds., *Intellectual Life in the Middle Ages: Essays Presented to Margaret Gibson* (London, 1992), pp. 185–195, esp. p. 185.

9   Antonia Gransden, *Legends, Traditions and History in Medieval England* (London, 1992), pp. 125–152.

10   *Historia pontificalis*, p. 2: "Verum exinde cronicum alicuius librum non potui repperire, licet aliquas rerum memorabilium subnotationes in archiuis ecclesiarum inuenerim, que possint si qui forte scripturi sunt eorum diligentiam adiuuare."

histories of the Bible and Eusebius, John locates himself in church archives, pondering notes of memorable events. John is also moved to write in order to correct certain prejudices in Sigebert's chronicle. John noted of his predecessor's work that "[f]or although he was anxious to handle great events in many kingdoms, he gave more space and care to those which concerned his Germans. Out of zeal for them, probably, he inserted some things in his chronicle which seem contrary to the privileges of the Roman Church and the traditions of the Holy Fathers."[11]

John thus locates himself in the archive, attempting to remedy the account of Sigebert due to its bias towards "his Germans," and which did not accord adequate respect to the papacy. It is tempting then, as has so often been done with John of Salisbury, to read his historical practice as proto-modern. He refers to the archive, after all, he challenges the slant of other historians. Yet, as Roger Ray has shown, this would be to take John's claims too literally.[12] For, what we have in John's statements about his own historical method is a rhetorical performance of verisimilitude. Historical writing was, after all, considered part of the rhetorical arts at this time. As a skilled rhetorician, trained in the art of persuasive speech, John's account of his historical method must be understood not as an unmediated account of his work practice, but as a mode of persuasive speech aimed at convincing his readers of the likeliness of his account. John was, in the *Metalogicon* and the *Policraticus*, a determined exponent of the role of effective rhetoric in human affairs. That is, in both works, he stressed the importance of morally grounded persuasive speech as the foundation of society. And persuasive speech, the art of rhetoric, aimed not at finding the Truth, but in generating probable logic, in playing around with a hypothesis, rather than in proving an ultimate thesis.

John's insistence on the necessity of rhetoric as the foundation of society was pronounced for its time. While all schoolmen were trained in rhetoric, as part of their grounding in the liberal arts, John was singular in his articulation of the relationship between rhetoric and effective governance and administration. In the *Metalogicon*, John wrote, "[d]eprived of their gift of speech men would degenerate to the condition of brute animals, and cities would seem like corrals for livestock, rather than communities composed of human beings

---

11   Ibid., p. 3: "Fuit tamen sollicitus multorum percurrere momenta regnorum, set in hiis amplius et diligentius studuit immorari, que ad suos Teutones pertinere noscuntur. Quorum etiam fauore cronicis suis nonnulla inseruisse uisus est, que videntur ecclesie Romane priuilegiis obuiare, et sanctorum traditionibus patrum."

12   Roger Ray, "Rhetorical Skepticism and Verisimilar Narrative in John of Salisbury's *Historia Pontificalis*," in Ernst Breisach, ed., *Classical Rhetoric and Medieval Historiography* (Kalamazoo, 1985), p. 66.

united by a common bond for the purpose of living in society, serving one another, and cooperating as friends."[13] It was the art of rhetoric, John argued, that nurtured and polished language and enabled civilisation. John would of course, then, have been well aware that history writing was a branch of rhetoric. Consequently, as a historian his aim would have been to narrate and to persuade as is appropriate to rhetoric, rather than to demonstrate a proof, or to establish facts in the manner of dialectic. Thus when John situates himself in the archive, humbly finding gaps in the extant records, he was laying out a tableau of his own plausibility. That is, if we read his Prologue as a piece of rhetoric, John's assertion of his historical method is far more likely to constitute a writerly performance of authority, than to articulate a likely practice.

This is important, because in recognizing the rhetorical strategies within the Prologue, we are given a glimpse into the notions of plausibility and verisimilitude that John thought likely to be effective. John says "[i]n what I am going to relate I shall, by the help of God, write nothing but what I myself have seen and heard and know to be true, or have on good authority from the testimony or writings of reliable men."[14] John's statement here locates authority in eyewitness and in testimony, it assures the reader of his proximity and access to the events under discussion. As a scholar, John was, first and foremost, interested in the use of language to build political communities and maintain peace. His statement that he will only deal with events that he has witnessed himself, or experienced through the words of trusted people, itself testifies to that conviction of civilizations built in words. That is, in claiming the epistemological reliability of witness, he was more broadly asserting that the communities of men could adequately represent the past in human speech. As a rhetorician aiming at the presentation of plausibility, John's Prologue thus suggests that the use of the idea of the archive, the criticism of other historians, and, the idea of the witness, all had purchase in that regard.

The Prologue to the *Historia pontificalis* is consequently quite unusual. It combines the large frame of universal history with John's very particular articulation of his evidentiary basis. Movement between the two registers seems abrupt. For example, John tells us of his biblical predecessors, the writers of the gospels, that

---

13   *Metalogicon*, pp. 13–14: "Brutescent homines si concessi dote priuentur eloquii, ipsaeque urbes uidebuntur potius pecorum quasi saepta quam coetus hominum nexu quodam societatus feoderatus, ut participatione officiorum et amica inuicem uicissitudine eodem iure uiuat." Trans. McGarry, p. 11.

14   *Historia pontificalis*, Prologue, p. 4: "In hiis autem que dicturus sum nichil auctore Deo scribam, nisi quod uisu et auditu uerum esse cognouero, uel quod probabilium uirorum scriptis fuerit et auctoritate subnixum."

"the holy evangelists take up the story, teaching what God as man performed in man for man; and flying on swift wings to the four corners of the earth, spread the word which saves the souls of the faithful and unites the Church without spot or stain to Christ."[15] The evangelists narrated the story of salvation in the world, John's historical antecedents made nothing less than ultimate truth the subject of their writings. Then John tells us that he will continue the work of Sigebert, who finished his chronicle with "the council of Reims, celebrated in the year of our lord 1148, in the time of Louis king of the Franks, when Conrad was reigning in Germany."[16] We move swiftly from sweeping biblical history, to his concrete world of competing kings and councils, with the relationship between the two registers left unexplained. With his emphasis on archives and evidence, John seemed to be drawing a sharp line between the historians of the past who dealt in the enormity of sacred history, and his own focus on the detail of the here and now. The juxtaposition between the past and present, expressed in this way, inaugurates the *realpolitik* of John's account. His time, apparently is not the time for sacred history. It is the time for sifting through the nitty-gritty of events, and for considering how Christian leadership can best occur in a murky world of mixed allegiances. In this, as Nederman has written, the *Historia pontificalis*

> ...is a work that merits a place alongside the rest of his major texts, even though it lacks some of the final polish of the *Metalogicon* or *Policraticus*. John takes his greatly vaunted union of philosophical wisdom and practical reason into a world that he knows all too well, the realm of the ecclesiastical court.[17]

The Trial of Gilbert of Poitiers

One of the largest sections of the *Historia pontificalis* is that which concerns the trial of Gilbert of Poitiers, which took place just after the official business

---

15   Ibid., Prologue, p. 1: "Quem locum sancti euuangeliste excipiunt, edocentes quid in homine et pro homine gesserit Deus homo, et alis pernicibus in quatuor mundi climata euolantes, uerbum seminant quod animas credentium saluat, et Christo iungit ecclesiam non habentem maculam neque rugam."

16   Ibid., Prologue, p. 2: "eam produxit usque ad concilium Remense, quod tempore iam dicti Ludouici regis Francorum celebratum est, Conrado regante in Alemannia, anno dominice incarnationis M°C°XLVIII°."

17   Cary J. Nederman, *John of Salisbury* (Tempe, Arizona, 2005), p. 79.

of the Council of Reims in 1148. This case was overseen by Pope Eugenius III, and present at the gathering was a large group of cardinals, bishops and Parisian masters. The pope was responding to accusations of heresy that had been brought to his attention by Bernard of Clairvaux. Acting on the reports of two of Gilbert's archdeacons, Bernard charged Gilbert with promulgating four heretical propositions; that the divine essence is not God; that the properties of the persons are not the persons themselves; that persons (in the theological sense) are not predicated in any proposition; that the divine nature did not become flesh.[18] At this trial, Bernard argued that Gilbert's attempt to impose standard grammatical categories on the three persons of the Trinity had undermined the integrity of Trinitarian doctrine. Bernard's point was that the forms of linguistic analysis used by the schools to analyze created things in the world were not applicable to divine beings. Taking place eight years after his successful condemnation of Abelard, once again Bernard used the adversarial structure of a trial to impose a polemical split between monastery and school, and also between himself and the cardinals who were present at the case. Gilbert, however, was no easy target. He was a scholar and cleric of reputation and age, unburdened by the threat of scandal that always accompanied Abelard. Gilbert was fortified in faith and learning, a man of moral and intellectual strength. Gilbert's clash with Bernard loomed less of an adversarial joust than Abelard's, and more of a genuine contest of equally venerable figures and ideas.[19]

John's long and involved discussion of Gilbert's trial enabled him to explore a number of the issues foreshadowed in his Prologue. Here we have an explicit discussion about the efficacy and utility of human language, taking place between two of the most eminent men of the day, and arbitrated by the Pope. Although the language might be abstract, the context of a trial makes the stakes of such discussion clear. The use of theological language always ran the risk of heretical error, and had the potential to impugn the reputation of the speaker or writer. At the trial of Gilbert of Poitiers, then, theory met practice, inasmuch as the theological was intersecting with the juridical and the political. John's Prologue explored how the universal might intersect with the local, to consider the relationship between macro- and microcosm. Gilbert's

---

18   Otto of Freising, *Gesta Friderici I. Imperatoris*, ed. G. Waitz (Hanover, 1978), 52, p. 75: "Quod videlicet assereret divinam essentiam non esse Deum. Quod proprietates personarum non essent ipsae personae. Quod theologicae personae in nulla predicarentur propositione. Quod divina natura non esset incarnata." The translation is paraphrased from C. Mierow, trans., *The Deeds of Frederick Barbarossa* (New York, 1953), p. 88.

19   On the trial itself, see Clare Monagle, "The Trial of Ideas: Two Tellings of the Trial of Gilbert of Poitiers," *Viator* 35 (2004), pp. 113–129.

trial encouraged the discussion of these issues at length. How adequately could human language explain the Divine persons? How ought the flawed motivations and behaviours of the protagonists be understood in relationship to their higher ideals and aspirations? How could the Pope effectively manage the conflict between these protagonists, reconciling difference and restoring harmony? All of these questions went to the heart of John's larger question about how humans are to understand the difference between ineffable and perfect God, and their inherited world of chaos, conflict and diversity.

John's account of the trial began "Master Gilbert, bishop of Poitiers, the most learned man of our day, was summoned to the court to answer the bishop of Clairvaux – a man of the greatest eloquence and highest repute."[20] This beginning introduced the problem of human understanding to the forefront, the fact that two such men were unable to agree was already suggestive of the problems endemic to human communication. John knew both men personally, he knew of that which he spoke in terms of their eminence of reputation. John had been one of Gilbert's students, and was famously an advocate of the schools and their educational methods in his *Metalogicon*.[21] He was also sufficiently well acquainted with Bernard that the famous Abbot had written a generic testimonial for John in 1147 or 1148 – around the time of the trial – which helped him to secure a position with the archbishop of Canterbury.[22] For a career bureaucrat like John, the trial would have tested his loyalties. As a scholar, John understood and sympathized with the project of the schoolmen. That is, he understood the interest of men such as Abelard and Gilbert in constructing a framework of abstractions generated through reason, which could form the basis of an architectonic theology. But as a chronicler of the bureaucratic, the corporate and the political, John was actively involved in the machinations of governance and administration in the world. John's career had been based on the application of his education in the liberal arts to the practice of administration. The content of the trial then, in which the ideas of the schools were transported outside of their usual environment and their implications challenged, in many ways mimicked the content of John's many other writings.

---

20   *Historia pontificalis* 8, p. 15: "Euocatus apparebat in curia uir etate nostra litteratissimus magister Gislebertus episcopus Pictauorum, responsurus clarissime opinionis et eloquentissimo uiro abbati Clarevallensi..."

21   John described his education in Paris in *Metalogicon* 2. 9. For more details see Katharine S.B. Keats-Rohan, "John of Salisbury and Education in Twelfth-Century Paris from the Account of his *Metalogicon*," *History of the Universities* 6 (1986), 1–45.

22   On this, see Christopher Brooke, "John of Salisbury and his World," in *The World of John of Salisbury*, p. 8.

That is, John had often written about the possibilities and pitfalls of human speech in the world of deeds and administration, bringing his high rhetorical theory down to the level of action. This trial, similarly, placed the high theology of Gilbert of Poitiers in the larger context of the Papal council.

Gilbert was a scholar deeply concerned with the problem of talking humanly about God, with the paradox of using limited earthly language to speak of ineffable divine things. His response to this problem was a grammatical one. Following Priscian, students studying grammar in the schools were taught that a *nomen* (name) signified substance and quality. A noun signified the thing in itself (substance), but also always signified the thing by which it came into being (quality). Nouns, therefore, were composed of both the *id quod est* (that which is) and the *id quo est* (that by which it is). This grammatical rule applied to composite beings in the world, which could be understood in the nominative, as concrete things, and in the ablative as shaped by something outside of themselves, an essential quality informing the concrete being. When it came to speaking about God, however, this distinction became problematic. Could the same rule be applied to the *nomen Dei* (God)? Did the application of the rule to God mean that he was both said to be, and to be informed by a quality independent from himself? In relation to the Trinity, this distinction became even thornier. Could the *nomina* Father, Son, and Holy Spirit be said to be individual things? And could those things be said to be created by a quality or qualities outside of themselves? The application of the substance/quality distinction to the Trinity undermined the radical unity of God; it had the capacity to fracture the mysterious one-ness of the Trinity. This was the charge leveled against Gilbert at Reims: that his application of grammatical categories to the sacred being of the Trinity had resulted in a heretical splintering of God's simplicity. It was contended that in applying grammatical analysis to the Trinity he had actually created a quaternity, the three persons of the Trinity plus the quality informing those persons, that quality by which they could be understood to be divine. Häring has argued that in Gilbert's thought the substance/quality distinction was "transformed from a logical principle of speech and law of philosophical disputation into a formula expressing what may be called the metaphysical constitution of concrete, composite beings, both material and spiritual."[23] This was, indeed, the broader charge of the trial: that Gilbert had transferred a grammatical distinction to the realm of the metaphysical and in so doing allowed human grammatical rules to define transcendent beings.[24]

---

23   Nikolaus Häring, "The Case of Gilbert de la Porrée Bishop of Poitiers," *Mediaeval Studies* 3 (1951), 1–40, esp. p. 5.

24   For a deeper analysis of the thought of Gilbert of Poitiers, see Lauge Olaf Nielsen's *Theology and Philosophy in the Twelfth Century* (Leiden, 1982). Marcia Colish also treats the theology of Gilbert of Poitiers in her two volume work, *Peter Lombard* (Leiden, 1994).

Gilbert's use of the distinction between *id quod est* and *id quo est* was initially deployed in relation to concrete things in the world, as he attempted to find a way through the debates around universals that had bedevilled the schools in the first decades of the twelfth century. It was when, however, he was accused of applying these insights to theology that the criticisms began.

Hence John's interest in the trial: at stake was the limit of language. The question of the trial was how to understand the names that bear divinity to us. As a scholar, he was fascinated by the efficacy of language in the making of society. Like other observers of the trial, he was fascinated by what the outcome would be, at what sort of limits might be placed around the theology of divine names. But he was also interested in the internal politics of the event of the trial. That is, he speculated on the motivations of the protagonists, as well as reported the intrigues of the event. In so doing, his account of the trial works in two registers. He dwells in the complicated ideas of the schools, working through the minutiae of Gilbert's theology and its implications for understanding the possibilities of speech. He also, however, reads the trial as a piece of politics in the world. He narrates the world of competing loyalties, human contingency and administrative compromise. This is the world that runs through all his writings, and is the place in which he lives, the world of human affairs and competing interests. We see this in his comparison of the protagonists of the trial, Gilbert and Bernard of Clairvaux. John notes that Bernard was an exceptional biblical scholar, and he was "so saturated in the Holy Scriptures that he could fully expound every subject in the words of the prophets and the apostles. For he had made their speech his own, and could hardly converse or preach or write a letter except in the language of scripture."[25] Bernard's talents as a preacher are without doubt, but John tells us that he "had little knowledge of secular learning [*saeculares litteras*] in which the Bishop [Gilbert], it is believed, had no equal in our own day."[26] Each figure is exemplary and, according to John, astonishingly learned. Yet they are in conflict in the world, negotiating the fraught space of the trial.

John makes this worldly context clear by beginning his account of the trial with the story of a secret meeting convened by Bernard to which he summoned his supporters. John speculates as to why these men were happy to accede to Bernard's will, declaring that "I cannot say whether they acted out of zeal for

---

25   *Historia pontificalis* 12, pp. 26–27: "adeo diuinis exercitatus in litteris ut omnem materiam uerbis propheticis et apostolicis decentissime explicaret. Sua namque fecerat uniuersa et uix nisi uerbis autenticis nec in sermone communi nec in exhortationibus nec in epistolis conscribendis loqui nouerat."

26   Ibid. 12, p. 27: "Seculares uero litteras minus nouerat, in quibus, ut creditur, episcopum nemo nostri temporis precedebat."

the faith, or jealousy of his [Gilbert's] fame and merit, or a desire to propitiate the abbot, whose influence was then at its height and whose counsel was most weighty in the affairs of Church and State alike."[27] After casting aspersions on the motivations of those involved, John then describes the secret meeting in which the Abbot, and his camp, plotted to ambush Gilbert during the trial, which was to start in the following days. At the meeting, Bernard suggested that a *symbolum fidei* ought to be drafted, with which Gilbert could be confronted at the trial. John then records a furious response from the cardinalate upon hearing of this meeting, he writes that "they were very wrath with the abbot and those who had assembled at his request: they agreed among themselves to support the cause of the bishop of Poitiers, saying that the abbot had attacked master Peter [Abelard] in exactly the same way."[28] The story told by John, then, is one where the trial of Gilbert's ideas is overtaken by the posturing and politics taking place between Bernard and the Curia. We see this again, when John states that "[the Cardinals] suspected, or made a show of suspecting, that the abbot wished to win the English and Gallic parts of the Church to his side and induce them to follow him; so that the papacy should be powerless to pronounce any sound judgment in opposition to them – especially at that time and in that place – or clear master Gilbert if the Church in England and Gaul were against him without provoking sedition."[29] The trial then becomes a power struggle between different branches of the Church, with the English and Gallic Churches attempting to bypass the authority of Rome. The effect of John's account of this skullduggery is a lively, yet depressing tableau, in which a good man's reputation lies on the line as a result of the self-interested actions of others.

After elaborating the pre-trial machinations, John then narrates the trial itself and records that Gilbert "joined conflict with confidence, and though many men questioned him searchingly he supported his answers with such

---

27   Ibid. 8, p. 16: "Incertum habeo an zelo fidei, an emulatione nominis clarioris et meriti, an ut sic promererentur abbatem, cuius tunc summa erat auctoritas, cuius consilio tam sacerdotium quam regnum pre ceteris agebatur."

28   Ibid. 9, pp. 19–20: "Quod cum ad cardinalium audientiam peruenisset, supra modum indignati sunt aduersus abbatem et illos qui prece eius conuenerant: condixerunt ergo fouere causam domini Pictauensis, dicentes quod / abbas arte simili magistrum Petrum aggressus erat."

29   Ibid. 9, p. 20: "Suspicabantur enim aut se suspicari simulabant quod abbas in partem suam allicere, et post se trahere uellet Gallicanam et Anglicanem ecclesiam, contra quarum subscriptiones salubriter nichil diffinire posset apostolica sedes, in eo presertim loco et tempore constituta, nec magistrum Gislebertum posset sine seditione absoluere condempnantibus illis."

sound arguments and authorities that he could not be tripped up verbally."[30]
The characterization of Gilbert is in sharp contrast with the garrulous and
aggressive Bernard. Gilbert, in this telling, speaks only when spoken to, and is
fortified by years of erudition and the vast armory of sources that he was able
to call upon with his memory. Gilbert proves, at the trial, that the problematic
ideas charged to were actually taken from a student's workbook, rather than
from his work itself. The Pope does suggest that Gilbert should slightly modify
certain parts of his treatise on Boethius' *De trinitate* for the purpose of clarity.
Gilbert readily assents to this, and John tells us that Gilbert "was acquitted of
the charge and stigma of his opponents."[31] The result, according to John, is a
victory for Gilbert, and a humbling defeat for Bernard. Of the two men, John
writes that "[b]oth were keenly intelligent and gifted interpreters of scripture:
but the abbot was more experienced and effective in transacting business."[32]
And this, to some degree, is Bernard's undoing at the trial. In John's telling, he
overplays his hand and is exposed to the wrath of the cardinals. Gilbert's quiet
solidity and focus is depicted in sharp juxtaposition with Bernard's busy-ness.
Gilbert, with his worldly ideas, is somewhat sanctified. The saintly Abbot, on
the other hand, is brought down to earth in this depiction of his power plays
and struggle for supremacy.

John's account of the trial, then, clearly privileges the figure of Gilbert over
Bernard.[33] This was in spite of the allegiance that John owed Bernard, who had
been his patron. The reason for John's support of Gilbert becomes clear in his
theological excursus that follows the account of the trial. In this section John
explores Gilbert's theology, and outlines its integrity and efficacy. John writes of
Gilbert's thought that "[h]e made use of every branch of learning as occasion
demanded, knowing that all were consistent with each other, and mutually illuminating."[34] Gilbert's ideas are praised for their integrated qualities, in that he
understands how different branches of knowledge relate to the whole. In his

---

30   Ibid. 10, p. 21: "Episcopus uero fretus auxilio et consilio cardinalium conflictum adiit con-
      fidenter, et de pluribus et a pluribus interrogatus, sic auctoritatibus et rationibus response
      muniebat, ut capi non potuerit in sermone."

31   Ibid. 11, p. 25: "Sed et hiis episcopus annuens absolutus est ab aduersariorum impetitione
      et nota."

32   Ibid. 12, p. 27: "Uterque ingenio perspicax et scripturis inuestigandis deditus, sed abbas
      negociis expediendis exercitatior et efficatior."

33   I have explored John's support for Gilbert in more depth in Clare Monagle, "Contested
      Knowledges: John of Salisbury's Metalogicon and Historia Pontificalis," *Parergon* 21.1,
      (2004), 1–17.

34   Ibid. 12, p. 27: "Utebatur, prout res exigebat, omnium adminiculo disciplinarum, in singu-
      lis quippe sciens auxiliis mutuis uniuersa constare."

discussion of Gilbert's thought, paraphrasing the Bishop, John writes "lest devotion should be dumb, words may be used figuratively, either to stimulate our devotion, or to teach our children, or to confound and destroy our enemies."[35] In his hands, Gilbert's abstract theology was transformed into a defense of theological language for pastoral, pedagogical and polemical purposes. In Gilbert, John constructs a figure of moral integrity who, like himself, deploys language for constructive purposes. Gilbert is, in many ways, the hero of the *Historia pontificalis*, providing rhetorical ballast among the earthly politics of the various protagonists.

The Second Crusade

John's section on the Second Crusade reprises many of the themes we have seen in his Prologue, and in his account of Gilbert's trial. The famously disastrous crusade, in John's telling, was the result of the "misfortunes that befell the Christians through the deceit of the Byzantine Emperor and the forces of the Turks, their army was weakened by the jealousy of princes and the wrangling of priests."[36] The Crusade becomes a farcical tale of errors, a shambolic exercise in incompetency. The account begins with the arrival of Louis and Eleanor in Antioch in 1149, where they were entertained by the Queen's uncle, Raymond of Antioch. John's account does not shirk gossip, he quickly reports the rumour of a scandalous relationship between uncle and niece, noting that "the attentions paid by the prince to queen, and his constant, indeed almost continuous, conversation with her, aroused the king's suspicions."[37] John inaugurates his crusade account not with an account of battle or a theological justification for the warfare, but with the petty intrigues of marital discord playing out in the transported court. John tells us that the queen wished to remain in Antioch with Raymond after the King's departure, and sought Louis's permission to do so. Louis is advised by one of his secretaries to refuse the Queen's application. This secretary, a eunuch called Terricus Gualerancius, suggested to Louis that "it would be a lasting shame to the kingdom of the Franks if in addition to all the other disasters it was reported that the king had been deserted by his wife,

---

35   Ibid. 13, p. 36: "Sed ne deuotio muta sit, translatis utitur uerbis uel ad se excitandam, uel ut instruat paruulos suos, uel ut confundat et conterat inimicos."

36   Ibid. 24, p. 54: "Preter incomoda que dolo Constantinopolitani imperatoris et Turcorum uiribus acciderant Christianis, exercitum eorum debilitabat inuidia principum et contentio sacerdotum."

37   Ibid. 23, p. 52: "...familiaritas principis ad reginam et assidua fere sine intermissione colloquia regi suspicionem dederunt."

or robbed of her."[38] This is the murky world of the court, which was fuelled by anxiety about gossip, shame and reputation. John's rhetorical effect, here, is to deploy these recognizable courtly themes in order to divest the events of the crusade from their lofty rhetorical frame. Instead he gives us his own mildly satirical rendering of the events, from the French side.

John then goes on to describe the remainder of the events from the perspective of the Frankish army. He attempts no large overview of the events, or an account of military strategy or ideology. Instead, he delights in highlighting moments of petty selfishness or incompetence on the part of the protagonists. For example, he noted that the "Germans declined to have anything to do with the Franks in shipping their baggage across the Hellespont, and went to the length of refusing a request to wait for the king, who was following a few days' journey behind, saying that the Franks were nothing to them."[39] In implicit contrast with the ideal of a united Christendom that so often infused crusading ideology, John details a world of competing affiliations and identifications. The Germans cannot be relied upon to help their fellow Frankish Christian warriors, the Crusade is a world where the divisions between kingdoms are played out again in the East. This is not the sacramental renewal of holy war, but rather the divisive repetition of old wounds and grudges.

The Crusade also suffers from poor leadership on the part of self-proclaimed papal legates, Arnulf bishop of Lisieux and Godfrey bishop of Langres. John claims that they used this title illegitimately, having never received such an assignment from the Pope. John describes how these men were in constant disagreement, incapable of uniting for the shared cause. He declared that "[w]hatever one recommended the other decried; both were smooth-tongued, both extravagant, both (it is said) mischief-makers, devoid of the fear of God... Few if any have brought more harm on the Christian army and whole community."[40] But John is also pained to point out that the legitimate papal legates, Theodwin bishop of Porto and Guy, cardinal priest of Saint Chrysogonus, were "decent men, but far from equal to such high office."[41] As an example of their

---

38 Ibid. 23, p. 53: "...tum quia regno Francorum perpetuum opprobrium imminebat si inter cetera infortunia rex diceretur spoliatus coniuge uel relictus."

39 Ibid. 24, p. 54: "Teutones enim Francorum in rebus trans Hellespontum gerendis usque adeo dedignati sunt habere consortium, ut rogati regem qui eos prosequebatur aliquo dierum itinere interiecto noluerint expectare, respondentes nichil sibi cum Francis..."

40 Ibid. 24, pp. 54–55: "Quicquid predicabat unus alter depredicabat, ambo facundi, ambo sumptuosi, ambo (ut creditur) discordie incentores et expertes timoris Domini...Exercitui et publice rei Christianorum rarus aut nullus fuit hiis perniciosior."

41 Ibid. 24, p. 55: "uiri quidem boni sed tanto officio minus idonei."

inadequacy to the task, John describes how "Theodwin, differing from the Franks in language and customs, was regarded as a Barbarian. As for Guy, he had scant knowledge of French."[42] The problem, according to John, is that of the Tower of Babel, it is linguistic. In the case of Arnulf and Geoffrey, they are smooth-tongued but unable to forge consensus due to their own selfish desires. In the case of Theodwin and Guy, they were good men but their language was inadequate to the task of communicating. Here, through this vignette, John refrains one of his most common themes, the necessity that eloquence in language be underpinned by an appropriately fortified moral *habitus*.[43] Arnulf and Geoffrey are eloquent, but immoral. Theodwin and Guy are moral, but lack fluency. As such, in John's rendering, the Crusade was doomed.

John's final vignette in his account of the Crusade concerns the decision of Kings Louis and Conrad to abandon their attack on Damascus. John is quite sure that had they stayed the course, they "would have occupied it [Damascus] (as the best authorities believe) if they had persevered for fifteen days."[44] John then narrates how the Kings were let down by their soldiers, who refused to continue to siege the city, instead wishing to return home. John describes these conversations in detail, noting that "King Conrad approved their counsel; the bishop of Langres resisted it."[45] The difficult decision about abandoning the siege was, according to John, made through fractious debate. The King of France, at the end, is convinced that he should follow Conrad's lead as a mark of consideration and respect, and the account then records that "In the end he gave way, and all returned home."[46] So went the final deed of the French King, the account ends with a moment of acquiescence on the part of Louis. He concedes the siege, according to John, with resignation. John's final sentence here is short, and to the point, "*Sic itaque flexus est, et omnes ad sua redierunt.*" After the various deceptions, negotiations and miscommunications that have gone into the Crusade, all narrated in long sentences with complicated construction, John then provides this pithy summation. This sentence, in its pith, conveys John's authorial resignation at the ways in which the complicated affairs of men so often become mired in difference and confusion. This messy world

---

42   Ibid. 24, p. 55: "Tadewinus enim moribus et lingua dissonans Francis barbarus habebatur. Guido uero linguam Francorum tenuiter nouerat..."

43   On the concept of *habitus* see Cary J. Nederman, "Nature, Ethics, and the Doctrine of 'Habitus': Aristotelian Moral Psychology in the Twelfth Century," *Traditio* 45 (1989–90), 87–110.

44   *Historia pontificalis* 25, p. 57: "Ante urbem castra metati sunt, eamque essent (ut proculdubio creditur) habituri, si perstitissent diebus quindecim."

45   Ibid. 25, p. 58: "Rex Conradus approbauit consilium; dissuasit episcopus Lingonensis."

46   Ibid. 25, p. 58: "Sic itaque flexus est, et omnes ad sua redierunt."

of the Crusade, in John's depiction, stands in sharp juxtaposition with the ideals of unity that undergird its theology.

Conclusion

It is thought that John wrote the *Historia pontificalis* while in exile in Reims, as a result of his support for Thomas Becket. John stayed there between 1164 and 1170, taking refuge with his friend Peter of Celle, who was then abbot of Saint-Remi.[47] This period afforded John much time for writing and reflection, as his extensive letter collection from that time attests. At this time John was necessarily in the grip of the implications of the conflict between King and Archbishop of Canterbury. After all, his circumstances depended upon the dispute, and any improvement of his lot could only come with its resolution. John was himself, at that time, caught up in the deeds of men, subject to their strife and egotistical whims. It is not surprising, then, that so much of the *Historia pontificalis* details the world of competing loyalties, kingdoms and languages in which humans live. This is not a world of heroes, of epic success or failure, or of saints and sinners. Even the Second Crusade, a disaster that afforded significant loss of life, resources and pride, is written as a bumbling story of buffoons and avarice. This seems to be a long way from John's statement in his Prologue, when he loftily declares that he writes "to relate noteworthy matters, so that the invisible things of God may be clearly seen by the things that are done, and men may by examples of reward and punishment be made more zealous in the fear of God and pursuit of justice."[48]

These ambitious words seem incongruous next to the clumsy antics of the human actors who inhabit the *Historia pontificalis*. How can the invisible things of God be found amongst the marital spat between Eleanor and Louis, or in the dislike evinced by the Cardinals for Bernard of Clairvaux, to take just two examples from the text. John's answer, I would argue, is in the exemplarity of these frail figures of foible and pride. The *Historia pontificalis* is not concerned with the Truth in some modernist historical sense, but with pedagogical verisimilitude. That is, as in the *Policraticus* and the *Metalogicon*, John deploys *exempla* in order to vivify theory. Read this way, the depictions of human actors in the *Metalogicon* function as literary devices that domesticate

---

47   For an extended discussion of John's biography, see the introduction to this volume.

48   Ibid., Prologue, p. 3: "Horum uero omnium uniformis intentio est, scitu digna referre, ut per ea que facta sunt conspiciantur inuisibilia Dei, et quasi propositis exemplis premii uel pene, reddant homines in timore Domini et cultu iustitie cautiores."

the historical past, bringing the reader into a recognizable world of likeliness. In so doing, these frail humans enable John to explore his key theme of the possibilities and impossibilities of human speech. Speech, on the one hand, makes communication possible and guarantees the civilization that John holds so dear. On the other hand, the world of governance is exemplified by miscommunication, competing dialects and acts of mendacity. These negative qualities of human discourse, as depicted in the *Historia pontificalis*, guarantee the strife and confusion in the world that is a mark of the perennial contingency of human language after the fall. This is the antinomy that informs all of John's writing, that which exists between language as God-given, and yet also the most evident mark of man's post-lapsarian location in time.

Some readers may find the gap between the lofty language of the prologue and the workaday deeds of the text's characters to be a failing of the work, as a sign of John's failure to master the historical form. This assessment, however, misses the point. When read sympathetically, John's exploration of deeds in time can offer a vista upon the attempt of one intellectual to match the high theory of his time with the quotidian details of his working life. That is, how can the dialectical theology and high rhetoric in which the author was so famously trained by brought to bear upon the world of concrete things? Successful or not, John's attempt to match theory and practice gives us a sense of how he attempted to manage the things of the world within the intellectual and spiritual frames in which he had been inculcated.

PART 3

John of Salisbury and the Intellectual World of the 12th Century

∴

CHAPTER 7

John of Salisbury and Law*

Yves Sassier

Since the highly laudatory judgement delivered in the mid 19th century by Friedrich Carl von Savigny,[1] studies devoted to John of Salisbury have regularly underlined the extent and exceptional quality, for his period, of the legal knowledge displayed by this great humanist, both in his major work, the *Policraticus*, and in his correspondence.[2] John either read or perused the *Digest*, the *Institutes*, and the *Code* of Justinian, his knowledge of the latter work extending even to the *tres libri* (Books 10 to 12), whose availability was still limited in the 1150s. He makes many allusions to the *Novels*, and his analyses, by virtue of the definitions included in them or the vocabulary used, bear witness to the influence of certain teachers of the school of Bologna or their disciples. John of Salisbury must, therefore, also have consulted one or more of the many glossed manuscripts or the smaller number of *Summae* written in the first half of the 12th century. His correspondence, in particular that part of it where he writes in the name of Archbishop Theobald of Canterbury, whose secretary he was, is scattered with allusions to canonical sources, some of them suggesting to some specialists that John may have had available to him a manuscript of the *Decretum* of Gratian.[3] His command of legal vocabulary in these letters is astonishingly precise, and leaves no room for doubt as to his familiarity with the rules of argument applied before ecclesiastical courts, notably those surrounding the procedure of the appeal to Rome, then in full process of proliferation. Walter Ullmann in the 1940s revealed the influence of the legal philosophy of this future bishop of Chartres, and of the legal propositions with which his

---

* English translation by David M.B. Richardson.

1 Friedrich Carl von Savigny, *Geschichte des römischen Rechtes im Mittelalter* (Heidelberg, 1850), esp. vol. 4, pp. 432–433.

2 See especially the point of view expressed by C.N.L. Brooke in *The Early Letters*, pp. xx–xxi, and *The Later Letters*, pp. xii–xiii. See also Max Kerner, "Römisches und Kirchliches Recht im *Policraticus*," in *The World of John of Salisbury*, pp. 365–379. Idem, "Johannes von Salisbury und das gelehrte Recht," in Peter Landau and Jörg Müller, eds., *Proceedings of the Ninth International Congress of Medieval Law, Monumenta juris canonici, series C, subsidia 10* (Vatican, 1997), pp. 503–521.

3 *The Early Letters*, no. 99, p. 153 and note 1; no. 100, p. 157 and note 5; no. 131, p. 230 and note 9. However, it appears to us difficult to be so positive. John never mentions Gratian by name, and circulation of the *Decretum* remained very limited in the 1150s.

Policraticus abounds, on certain Italian jurists of the Late Middle Ages[4]; later works by the same great 20th-century historian abundantly underline the debt owed to John by one Lucas de Penna.[5] Christopher Brooke for his part, in considering the legal content of the *Early Letters* of John of Salisbury, did not hesitate to see in him a "professional lawyer."[6]

Of course, as the specialists do not fail to stress, the distance between John of Salisbury and the *iurisperiti* of his time remains no less great. The chronology of his studies, while certainly somewhat uncertain, does not appear capable of encompassing a long period of "scholastic" apprenticeship in academic law. Only quite late on, after some 12 years (1136–47) of training and instruction in the arts and theology at Paris and Chartres, followed by a brief visit to his friend Peter of Celle in 1148, then two years (1148–50) in the entourage of Archbishop Theobald of Canterbury, was he able to travel to Italy and frequent the Roman curia for three years. Historians make of this "Roman" period an important moment for the acquisition of solid practical knowledge in the fields of law and Church administration, but they do not venture so far as to think that John was able to pursue legal training to any degree of depth, either at Rome or at Bologna, as there is nothing to indicate anything of the kind. It is, however, certain that, between 1148 and 1150 and after 1153, he knew canon lawyers of repute such as Bartholomew of Exeter and Gerard Pucelle, and encountered in the entourage of Archbishop Theobald the glossator Vacarius, probably a disciple of Martinus, one of the "four doctors of Bologna." Contrary to what has long been supposed, John of Salisbury could not have read Vacarius' *Liber pauperum*, a commentary on the *Digest* and the *Code* of Justinian, as the most recent studies date this work to the 1180s,[7] and John's own interpretations can

---

4   Walter Ullmann, "The Influence of John of Salisbury on Medieval Italian Jurists," *English Historical Review* 59 (1944), 384–393; republished in idem, *The Church and the Law in the Earlier Middle Ages: Selected Essays* (London, 1975).

5   Walter Ullmann, *The Medieval Idea of Law, as Presented by Lucas de Penna: A Study in Fourteenth-Century Legal Scholarship* (London, 1946), esp. pp. 31–33 and 169–170; idem, "John of Salisbury's *Policraticus* in the Later Middle Ages," in Karl Hauck and Hubert Mordek, eds., *Geschichtsschreibung und geistiges Leben im Mittelalter: Festschrift für H. Löwe zum 65 Geburtstag* (Cologne, 1978), pp. 528–529.

6   Christopher Brooke, "John of Salisbury and his World," in *The World of John of Salisbury*, pp. 1–20, esp. p. 7.

7   On Vacarius, see Richard W. Southern, "Master Vacarius and the Beginning of an English Academic Tradition," in Jonathan J.G. Alexander and Margaret T. Gibson, *Medieval Learning and Literature: Essays Presented to R.W. Hunt* (Oxford, 1976), pp. 257–286; Peter Stein, "The Vacarian School," *Journal of Legal History* 13 (1992), 23–31 (proposes the 1180s for the writing of the *Liber Pauperum*); Leonard E. Boyle, "The Beginnings of Legal Studies at Oxford," *Viator*

scarcely be said to follow the line of Vacarius' glosses. But nothing prevents us from thinking that he may have received practical advice from the Italian master, in respect of Roman law as well as the discipline of canon law, in which Vacarius also excelled. John may also have conversed and even debated with him questions regarding the interpretation and scope of certain texts of Justinian, and, finally, have gained knowledge of the *Summae* and glossed manuscripts the master had at his disposition, not to mention Vacarius' own annotations. One of the manuscripts John appears to have had knowledge of is a *summa* of the *Code*, known as *Summa Trecensis*, which legal historians have attributed in turn to Irnerius, Rogerius, Martinus, and, most lately, a Provencal jurist by the name of Geraud.[8]

Truth be told, identification of the sources of inspiration of the future bishop of Chartres is sometimes uncertain and perilous, as is shown by the very legitimate hesitations of the specialists listed in the studies by Max Kerner and Georg Miczka; in respect of the extracts taken from glosses and *Summae*, of which there are not many in John's oeuvre, the fact that he modifies the extracts and fills them with extra propositions sometimes makes it difficult to recognize with entire certainty the source used. A characteristic example of the liberty he employs in the matter of quotations is provided by the definition of *aequitas* proposed by him in *Policraticus* 4. 2 as follows (we underline those terms that do not feature in any other definition of *aequitas* emanating from a previous or contemporary glossator): "Porro aequitas, ut iuris periti asserunt, rerum conuenientia est, quae cuncta coequiparat <u>ratione</u> et imparibus causis paria iura desiderat, <u>in omnes aequabilis, tribuens unicuique quod suum</u> est."[9]

---

14 (1983), 107–121 (proposes a date towards the end of the 1170s). A synthesis of these positions may be found in Jason Taliadoros, *Law and Theology in Twelfth-Century England. The Works of Master Vacarius (c.1110/1120-c.1200)* (Turnhout, 2006), pp. 31–35. See also Peter Landau, "The Origins of Legal Science in England in the Twelfth Century: Lincoln, Oxford and the Career of Vacarius," in Martin Brett and Kathleen B. Cushing, *Readers, Texts and Compilers in the Earlier Middle Ages: Studies in Medieval Canon Law in Honour of Linda Fowler-Magerl* (Aldershot, 2009), pp. 165–182. A sole *mention* of Vacarius by John of Salisbury in the *Policraticus*, ed. Webb, vol. 2, pp. 398–399. The *Liber Pauperum* has been edited by Francis de Zulueta (London, 1927).

8 André Gouron, "L'auteur et la patrie de la *Summa Trecensis,*" *Jus commune* 12 (1984), 1–38; article reprinted in *Études sur la diffusion des doctrines juridiques médiévales* (London, 1987), III. On John of Salisbury's knowledge of Roman law and of the *Summa codicis Trecensis*, see the study by Max Kerner, "Römisches und Kirchliches Recht im *Policraticus,*" (*supra* note 2), and esp. Georg Miczka, "Johannes von Salisbury und die *Summa Trecensis,*" in *The World of John of Salisbury*, pp. 381–399.

9 *Policraticus* 4.2, ed. Webb, vol. 1, p. 237.

As Webb and many others have indicated, Cicero provides the inspiration for the two central elements here: *rerum conuenientia...*, *que in paribus causis paria iura desiderat.* But it is the glossators – Martinus, followed by others such as the authors of the *Summa Institutionum "Iustiniani est in hoc opere"* and the *Summa Trecensis* – who fashioned the definition by assembling these elements. Georg Miczka is of the opinion, and, it seems to us, justly so, that John's contemporary source is none other than the *Summa Codicis Trecensis*, which contains the following formula (we underline the expressions adopted by John): "aequitas enim est rerum conuenientia que cuncta coequiparat et in paribus causis paria iura desiderat, que plurimum prodest ei qui minimum potest." The formula "plurimum prodest ei qui minimum potest" is a Latin version of a reply by Socrates to Thrasymachus, his interlocutor in Plato's *Republic.* To this interlocutor who had claimed that the just is what profits the strongest (*plurimum prodest ei qui plurimum potest*), Socrates had suggested the inverse proposition: the art of governing (and thus that of promoting the just) profits the subject to which it applies, which is to say the weakest. The echo of this discussion, and the Latin translation of Socrates' reply, reached the intellectuals of the 12th century thanks to a relation of the episode, accompanied by a definition of justice, in a commentary by Chalcidius on Plato's *Timaeus.* This definition was relayed to the 12th century not only by a commentator on Chalcidius, as Georg Miczka has pointed out,[10] but also by certain glossators, including not only the author of the *Summa Codicis Trecensis*, who alone associated equity and justice in this way in one and the same definition,[11] but also, in the 1170s, Placentinus, who would modify the wording and the meaning in his *Summa institutionum* (1.1): "Iustitia est secundum Platonem uirtus quae plurimum potest in his (sic) qui minimum possunt" (which is most efficacious in respect of those who have the least power). There is no doubt that John of Salisbury was aware of the debate between Thrasymachus and Socrates; he had read Chalcidius' commentary, and was, we know, the pupil of one of the most brilliant commentators on Chalcidius' work, William of Conches. In this same Chapter 2, John himself uses the expression derived from Socrates' response; affirming that the prince is "the servant of equity (...), the shield of the infirm blocking the spear of the wicked in defence of the innocent," he adds that the prince's office is "most useful to those who are most powerless."[12]

---

10   Miczka, "Johannes von Salisbury und die *Summa Trecensis*," p. 385 and note 18.

11   It is this unusual association that prompts Georg Micza to see *Summa Trecensis* as John's source.

12   *Policraticus* 4.2, ed. Webb, vol. 1, p. 249: "officium quoque ejus illis qui minimum possunt, plurimum prodest."

John's modification, in a passage on equity very probably borrowed from *Summa Trecensis*, aims to replace this definition of justice drawn from Plato with another, itself very ancient and rehabilitated in the 12th century, notably by Abelard[13]: *tribuens unicuique quod suum est*. This example among many others[14] shows clearly that the future bishop of Chartres did not consider himself bound by the texts he used; he adapted them as he thought fit, doubtless, in the case discussed here, desiring to restore a more common and more legalistic definition of *iustitia*, one that he derived from Cicero as well as Ulpian.

A more thoroughgoing account is required of such manifest familiarity with the law on the part of a lettered non-jurist. It might, perhaps, be appropriate to this end to divide our investigation into several distinct propositions, inspired in part by a remark of C.N.L. Brooke, enlarged upon by Max Kerner. Apart from practical use of the rules of law, to be found principally in John's letters, we find in the *Policraticus* numerous passages of a juridical nature, most often derived from the law of Justinian. These are introduced in support of an ethical discussion addressed to the prince[15] and, more generally, to all those bearing a responsibility in the functioning of the *res publica*. We shall turn our attention first to John's eminently philosophical and ethical examination of the law and of that hierarchy of norms that the prince is absolutely obliged to respect and safeguard in the exercise of his function: a reflection that had to give rise to the question of reconciling such a requirement with certain maxims of Roman law affirming the prince's omnipotence, both in the matter of legislation and with regard to laws. We shall go on to evoke John's constant concern to submit the actions of the prince's administrators, and, more generally, those acts that punctuate the life of the human community (*res publica* or Church), to precise

---

13   Abelard, *Theologia christiana* 2.49, ed. Eloi Marie Buytaert (Turnhout, 1959), p. 152: "Recte ciuitas est appelandus, ubi par aequitatis censura unicuique quod suum est seruat." It should be noted that Abelard, John's teacher, himself associated what is classically given as the definition of justice with the notion of equity. Another definition of justice, this one inspired by Cicero, is to be found in Abelard's *Dialogus inter Philosophum, Judeum et Christianum*, ed. Rudolf Thomas (Stuttgart, 1970), p. 118: "Justitia virtus est communi utilitati servata suam cuique tribuens dignitatem."

14   See, above, the passage on definitions of the law (ed. Webb, vol. 1, p. 237) proposed on the basis of propositions by Chrysippus, Demosthenes, and Papinianus included in book 1 of the *Digest*. John gives a faithful rendering of Chrysippus' definition, but entirely distorts those of the other two.

15   Besides Kerner's article, "Römisches und Kirchliches Recht im *Policraticus*," see by the same author *Johannes von Salisbury und die Logische Struktur seines Policraticus* (Wiesbaden, 1977), p. 149 sqq., where he effectively stresses the importance of the law in John of Salisbury's political discourse.

rules that quite frequently find their origin and expression in those texts of the
Roman law that John knows remarkably well, and which he regards as constituting a living law applicable to his time. As we have just now established, however, John also has a practical vision of the law, and we shall soon see that he
applies his knowledge to very concrete situations such as the trial before the
ecclesiastical court, a context into which his correspondence so frequently
gives us access; this quite apart from the conception he has of good procedure
in secular courts, a conception he is keen on sharing with his contemporaries.

Reflection on the Rule of Law at the Heart of the Discourse
on Power

The *Policraticus* distils a vision of legality that, while firmly rooted both in the
tradition of ancient philosophy and in the theological conception of politics
that had triumphed many centuries earlier, is highly original because it is articulated with uncommon power, and also because it uses the resources made
available by the nascent science of jurisprudence, while retaining a critical and
autonomous approach to it. When undertaking to distinguish the prince from
the tyrant, which he does on two occasions in his *Policraticus*, John chooses the
criterion of legality, very common in Antiquity but scarcely used since. First, in
Chapter 1 of Book 4, he opens with a sentence that, while its translation may be
subject to debate, clearly formulates the principle of legality: "the main difference between the tyrant and the prince is that the latter obeys the law, and
rules his people, of whom he considers himself the minister, by the power of
the law (...)."[16] Four books further on (8.17), John resumes this same distinction

---

16   *Policraticus* 4.1, ed. Webb, vol. 1, p. 235: "Est ergo tiranni et principis haec differentia sola
     uel maxima quod hic legi obtemperat et eius arbitrio populum regit cuius se credit min-
     istrum." The translation adopted here is the one most commonly proposed by specialists;
     it relates the relative pronoun *eius* to the antecedent *legi*, and the pronoun *cuius* to the
     antecedent *populus*; but other translations are possible. That given by Nicolas de Araujo,
     "Le prince comme ministre de Dieu sur terre; la définition du prince chez Jean de Salisbury
     (*Policraticus*, IV.1)," *Le Moyen Âge* 112 (2006), 63–76, sees *eius* as alluding to the deity: "(...)
     and rules his people by the will of Him (God) whose minister he considers himself to be."
     A third translation, whose validity we defend in "Le prince, ministre de la loi? (Jean de
     Salisbury, *Policraticus*, IV, 1–2)," in Hervé Oudart, Jean-Michel Picard and Joëlle
     Quaghebeur, eds., *Le Prince, son peuple et le bien commun, de l'Antiquité tardive à la fin du
     Moyen Âge* (Rennes, 2013), pp. 125–144, would relate the two pronouns *eius* and *cuius* to
     one and the same antecedent, *legi*: "(...) and rules his people by virtue of the force of the
     law whose minister he considers himself to be."

and criterion in the definition he gives of the tyrant: "the tyrant is one who oppresses his people with violent domination, while a prince governs by the laws. For law," he adds, "is the gift of God, the model of equity, the norm of justice, the image of the divine will (...). The prince fights for the laws and for the liberty of the people; the tyrant thinks of nothing but of disposing of the laws and reducing his people to servitude."[17] To derive his primacy from the law, and to rule his people by the law, making himself the servant of the laws (4.1: *legibus deuotione promptissima famulatur*)[18] and imposing respect for the laws on his people; this is then the criterion distinguishing the prince from the tyrant. John was certainly not the first medieval thinker to formulate the principle of legality. To take only one previous example, that of Isidore of Seville, the prince's respect for the laws, although not serving as a distinguishing criterion between king and tyrant, lay at the heart of this Spanish bishop's thinking on royalty,[19] and at the heart, too, of a theory of legality that occupies the entire preamble of the *Liber iudicum*, composed in the Visigoth kingdom shortly after Isidore's death.[20] But, quite apart from dusting off the principle of legality as the criterion for distinguishing between a good ruler and a tyrant, it will be a peculiarity of John of Salisbury's argument that he takes account of current knowledge of the texts of Justinian, and of the use made of those texts by the 12th-century glossators, texts contradictory in appearance, some of them reinforcing John's proposition, others having the contrary effect of weakening it. His own knowledge of Justinian sources allows him, at the end of Chapter 1 of Book 4, to cite the great Roman text proclaiming the supremacy of the law over the prince, the *Digna uox* constitution promulgated in 429 by the emperors Theodosius II and Valentinian III (C. 1.14.4): "A voice worthy of the majesty of one who rules is that of the prince proclaiming himself to be bound by the laws, because the authority of the prince depends on the authority of law. To submit the principate to the laws is in truth a greater thing than to exercise

---

17 *Policraticus* 8.17, ed. Webb, vol. 2, p. 345: "Est ergo tyrannus, ut eum philosophi depinxerunt, qui uiolenta dominatione populum premit, sicut qui legibus regit princeps est. Porro lex donum Dei est, aequitatis forma, norma iustitiae, diuinae uoluntatis imago, salutis custodia, unio et consolidatio populorum, regula officiorum, exclusio et exterminatio uitiorum, uiolentiae et totius iniuriae poena. [...] Princeps pugnat pro legibus et populi libertate; tyrannus nihil actum putat, nisi leges euacuet, et populum deuocet in seruitutem."

18 Ibid. 4.1, ed. Webb, vol. 1, p. 237; see also ibid. 3.14, ed. Webb, vol. 1, p. 232: "Utique qui a Deo potestatem accipit, legibus seruit et iustitiae et iuris famulus est. Qui uero eam usurpat, iura deprimit et uoluntati suae leges summittit."

19 Isidore of Seville, *Sententiae* 3.51.1 and 2.

20 *Leges Visigothorum antiquiores*, t. 1, ed. Karl Zeumer (Hanover, 1894), p. 46.

imperium, so that the prince may be convinced that nothing is allowed him that departs from the equity of justice."[21]

But John also knew the other two texts from Justinian's corpus – they are in the *Digest* – which tend remarkably to diminish the scope of *Digna uox*: these are Ulpian's two remarks where he proclaims, first, that "the prince is not bound by laws" (D. 1.3.31: *princeps legibus solutus est*), and then that "what the prince has decided has the force of law" (D. 1.4.1: *Quod principi placuit legis habet uigorem*). John also knew certain elements of the argument proposed by some glossators in their efforts to reconcile these three texts, notably the two words that take on the quality of antonyms in this context: *necessitas* and *uoluntas,* employed by those same glossators to distinguish the obligation imposed on the people, *ex necessitate,* to obey the laws, and that imposed on the prince to comply *ex uoluntate sua*: on the one hand, as Thomas Aquinas would write in the following century, the "coactive" force of the law that binds the people, matched with sanctions, and, on the other, its "directive" force, to which the prince submits on his own initiative. Did John discuss this theme with Vacarius, whose *Liber pauperum* would soon include several glosses on *Digna uox* and the *Princeps legibus solutus* opposing the *necessitas* imposed on the people to the *uoluntas* allowed the prince? Was John himself inspired by a passage in the *Summa Trecensis* evoking, much less clearly than Vacarius would, the prince's submission *ex uoluntate* to the law?[22] The fact remains that in *Policraticus* 4. 6 we see John applying the two antonyms to Christ, whom he proposes as a model to the prince in having "accomplished all the justice inherent in the law, having submitted to it *non necessitate sed uoluntate,* because his will resided in the law." It would therefore seem that John is by no means ignorant of the sense of the opposition of the two terms, and that he no doubt knows that *Digna uox* is interpreted by some – Vacarius[23] – as suggesting to all princes that they

21 *Policraticus* 4.1, ed. Webb, vol. 1, p. 237: "Digna siquidem uox est, ut ait imperator, maiestate regnantis, se legibus alligatum principem profiteri. Quia de iuris auctoritate principis pendet auctoritas; et reuera maius imperio est, submittere legibus principatum, ut nihil sibi princeps licere opinetur, quod a iustitiae aequitate discordet." John's text follows that of the code of Justinian as far as *ut nihil sibi princeps*...which is of his own invention.

22 *Summa Trecensis,* ed. Herman Fitting (Berlin, 1894), p. 15: "Set tamen cui imperari non potest, ut pari et imperatori, hortando seu sui exemplum prebendo id agit, ut ex voluntate se supponat legitime necessitati."

23 Vacarius, *Liber pauperum,* ed. Francis de Zulueta (London, 1927), 1.8, p. 13: "Observare autem leges debent tam ceteri quam imperator. Sed ipse ex propria voluntate, ceteri ex necessitate." Ibid., p. 15: D.1.3.31: "Legis solutus, scilicet ut legibus vivat sponte, non necessitate ei subjectus." Ibid., p. 16: C.1.14.4, *"Digna vox"*: "Quo manifestius vigor et auctoritas legum pareat, principatum legibus subicit imperator, non precipiendo sed suadendo, et

submit *non necessitate sed uoluntate* to the *leges*. Finally, he either suspects or knows that there are those in the entourage of princes who do not hesitate to use Ulpian's remark in the sense of completely liberating the prince with regard to this rule: John denounces this abuse, notably in Chapter 7 of the same Book 4, where, after an allusion, taken from the prologue to the *Decretum* of Ivo of Chartres,[24] to those universal precepts (expressed by him in the very terms used by Augustine and also Gratian in defining natural law)[25] from which no man may absolve himself with impunity, he raises the tone against those in royal entourages who proclaim "that the prince is not subject to the law and that what pleases him has the vigour of law not only when he legislates justly, in accord with equity, but no matter how he does it." "The king," he says, "whom they thus liberate from the ties of the law: let them, if they dare, make him an outlaw *(extra legem)*."[26] We must be wary of deducing from this that John declines to recognize the capacity of a *potestas* to "legislate justly, in accord with equity," to promulgate rules.[27] In Book 2 (c. 25) he even presents us with a prince whose function is to make laws and to derogate from and abrogate them, and who, moreover, has the monopoly in interpreting a rule of law.[28] Using a constitution of Constantine featuring in the *Code* of Justinian

---

quod suadet commendando, sui quoque exemplum dando." Commentary on the *Legibus alligatum* of *Digna vox:* "Legibus alligatum, scilicet ut legibus vivat sponte, eis non necessitate subjectus."

24 Kerner, "Römisches und Kirchliches Recht im *Policraticus*," pp. 374–375.

25 *Policraticus* 4.7, ed. Webb, vol. 1, p. 259: "Sunt autem precepta quaedam perpetuam habentia necessitatem, apud omnes gentes legitima et quae omnino impune solis non possunt. Ante legem, sub lege, sub gratia, omnes lex una contringit: quod tibi non uis fieri, alii ne feceris, et quod tibi uis fieri faciendum, hoc facias alii."

26 Ibid. 4.7, ed. Webb, vol. 1, p. 259.

27 Still taking his inspiration from Ivo of Chartres, he then distinguishes those rules meriting *perpetuam praeceptionem aut prohibitionem*, which cannot be abandoned at the prince's will or whim *(libito)*, from those that are *mobilia*, for which *dispensatio uerborum* is permissible, so that, however, by virtue of the preservation of the balance between the honest and the useful *(compensatione honestatis aut utilitatis)*, the spirit of the law *(mens legis)* is preserved intact (vol. 1, p. 259, ll. 19–24). It is legitimate to ask whether John is here restricting the *potestates* to the realm of interpretation of the laws (this would be the "hidden" meaning of the expression *dispensatio verborum*; the word *dispensatio,* which can mean "softening" of the rule, is also capable of being interpreted in the sense of "dispensation," the theory of which was just then being elaborated by canonists; one asks oneself whether this is the case here), a function for which contemporary glossators (Géraud, Rogerius) also required that *mens earum (legum) servetur.*

28 *Policraticus* 2.26, ed. Webb, vol. 1, p. 139: "Equidem dici solet, et uerum est, quia in manu principis est, ut possit mitius iudicare quam leges, cum et qui legem tulit, derogandae, vel

(1. 14), in this instance John distances himself from the *Summa Trecensis*, which favours the intervention of a judge.[29] But the attack launched in 4. 7, along with other allusions gleaned from here and there[30] in the *Policraticus*, show the reservations he had in respect of Ulpian's words, which he judged to be dangerous because they were likely to be of use in justifying tyrannical abuses of power. While refraining from a frontal attack on such an interpretation, in Chapter 2 of Book 4 John would seek to demonstrate that the *uoluntas* of the prince is only apparent, not the equivalent of a "whim," and that it is in reality strictly subject to the supreme principle of equity, comparable to the will of God: as he writes at the end of his quotation from *Digna uox,* the prince can be assured "that nothing is permitted him that departs from *aequitas iustitiae.*"

Immediately after this sentence, the final one of Chapter 1 of Book 4, John opens the following chapter by giving a series of definitions designed to explain the sense of this expression "equity of justice," and the constraint it imposes on the prince. The "equity of justice" is none other than divine law disseminating *iustitia Dei* to humanity. *Cuius (Dei) iustitia iustitia in aeuum est et lex eius aequitas*: "The justice of God is justice for eternity, and his law is equity." John's words join with those of Martinus in identifying *aequitas* with God. But Martinus also qualified it as *fons iustitiae*, while the canonist Gratian called it *mater iustitiae.* No expression of this kind is to be found in John of Salisbury, who, as we were able to note in the very first pages of this study,[31] immediately gives another definition of *aequitas*, no doubt inspired by the *Summa Trecensis* and the glossators, but to which he also applies the classic definition of justice: *tribuens unicuique quod suum est.* John thus departs from the glossators, whose discourse on equity and justice sought to draw a pronounced distinction: making the former a primordial concept, an objective reality inscribed in the

---

abrogandae illius, habeat potestatem. [...] Interpositam inter ius et aequitatem interpretationem, soli principi et oportet, et licet inspicere. Ubi aliud ius suadet, aliud aequitas, quae in publica utilitate uersatur, principis quaerenda est interpretatio, quae generalis est, et necessaria. Ubi de scripto, et sententia dubitatur, mens est inquirenda auctoris."

29   *Summa codicis Trecensis*, 1.14.5–6. See what we say of this *infra.*

30   See for example *Policraticus* 4.4, ed. Webb, vol. 1, p. 244: "At ne ipsum principem usquequaque solutum legibus opineris..." Ibid. 7.20, ed. Webb, vol. 2, p. 186: "Cum enim sibi conciliauerint gratiam potestatum, de iure patere sibi asserunt uniuersa eo quod princeps (ut dicunt) legibus non subicitur et quod principi placet legis habet uigorem..." On his reservations in respect of Ulpian (and perhaps also on a more general attitude of distrust as regards blind reliance on Roman law), see *The Early Letters*, p. 241, Letter 133: "Quod si quis de solo nititur Ulpiano immo de opinione Ulpiani, Deo propitio erudietur, ne de spiritu proprio nequam sit aduersus eum qui superbos humiliat et exaltat humiles."

31   *Supra,*, pp. 195–196.

world's natural order and originating from the divine will alone, and the latter a reality concerned with the sphere of human activity, deriving from the intervention of a human will. In the words of the author of the *Summa Codicis Trecensis*, "What is equitable does not become just unless it is voluntary."[32] In John of Salisbury, what Ennio Cortese calls "the subjective moment of the norm" is absent.[33] Certainly, John immediately represents law as the interpreter of equity, in a way personifying it by declaring that it is to this interpreter that "a will for equity and justice made itself known"; in our opinion, however, this "will for equity and justice" can only be the divine will, as, indeed, is implied by the definition of the law immediately given by John. This definition, once again, has its origin in Book 1 of the *Digest*, which records three definitions, deriving from the Roman jurisconsult Papinianus, the orator Demosthenes, and finally Chrysippus, leader of the Stoa.[34] The *Digest* gives pre-eminence to that of Papinianus, who, taking his inspiration from Demosthenes, emphasizes the actions of the community or its representatives as the mode by which law comes into being: the law is *commune praeceptum, uirorum prudentium consultum, communis rei publicae spontio* (Demosthenes: *decretum uero prudentium hominum* [...], *communis spontio ciuitatis*). John prioritizes the definition given by the stoic Chrysippus, who emphasizes the universality of a law of nature,

---

32   *Summa Codicis Trecensis*, ed. Fitting, p. 3: "Quicquid enim aequum ita demum justum si est voluntarium." See also G. Miczka, "Johannes von Salisbury und die *Summa Trecensis*," pp. 383–384.

33   Ennio Cortese, *La norma giuridica. Spunti teorici nel diritto comune classico*, 2 vols. (Milan, 1962–4), vol. 2, p. 39 sqq.

34   "Lex vero ejus interpres est utpote cui aequitatis et justitiae uoluntas innotuit. Unde et eam omnium rerum et divinarum et humanarum compotem esse Crisippus asseruit ideoque praestare omnibus bonis et malis et tam rerum quam hominum principem et ducem esse. Cui Papinianus, uir quidem juris experimentissimus, et Demostenes, orator praepotens, uidentur suffragari et omnium hominum subicere obedientiam, eo quod lex omnis inventio quidem est et donum Dei, dogma sapientium, correctio uoluntariorum excessuum, civitatis compositio, et totius criminis fuga, secundum quam decet vivere omnes qui in policae rei universitate uersantur." Order in the *Digest*: Papinianus' definition in D. 1.3.1: "Lex est commune praeceptum, virorum prudentium consultum, delictorum quae sponte vel ignorantia contrahuntur coercitio, communis rei publicae spontio." Then Demosthenes' definition in D. 1.3.2: "Lex est cui omnes obtemperare convenit; tum ob alia multa; tum vel maxime eo, quod omnis lex inventum ac munus Dei est; decretum vero prudentium, coercitio eorum quae sponte vel involuntarie delinquantur, communis spontio cvitatis ad cujus praescriptum omnes qui in ea republica sunt, vitam instituere debent." Lastly, Chryssipus' definition of the law in D. 1.3.2: "Lex est omnium divinarum et humanarum rerum regina. Oportet autem eam esse praesidem et bonis et malis, et principem et ducem esse..."

queen of all things divine and human, directing humans in common with all other beings. He then mentions Papinianus and Demosthenes, but takes nothing from the former and only a few words from the latter, and above all the following definition: "all law is an invention and gift of God" (Latin translation of Demosthenes: ...*omnis lex inuentum ac munus Dei est*); he adopts neither the elements of these two definitions that signify the communitarian and contractual (*communis sponsio*) origin of the law, nor the notion of it as deriving from a deliberative and thus dialectical project on the part of guardians of the *prudentia* that presides over its creation. In John's eyes, law as a gift of God can only be *dogma sapientium*, and *compositio ciuitatis*: it depends on the truth revealed to those who possess *sapientia*, who formulate it, and, in a way, relay it to other humans[35]; it "assembles" the city, and "puts [it] in order" (the main meanings of *componere*, from which *compositio* derives). It is precisely these characteristics, and this desire to fuse together divine and human law, or, at the very least, make the second the direct extension of the first, that is found at the end of the *Policraticus*, in the definition in Book 8 already evoked above: law is the "gift of God [divine law], image of divine will [human law], guarantor of salvation [...], the union and consolidation of peoples."

In short, John takes the *Digest*'s definitions as his starting point, but changes their wording in order to liberate the law in its fundamental aspect from any voluntarist intervention, to free it from the autonomous will of a human legislator; the voluntarist vision gives way to a theological vision of law's origin, in which the human mediator – the one who necessarily translates divine *aequitas* (the definition in Book 8 makes law the *forma aequitatis*) into words – is reduced to the role of telling to the people, in the manner of Moses the initial "legislator," or Gideon the arbiter of the law's application, the rule whose *auctor* is none other than God.[36] The two definitions, of an equity that subsumes justice and of the law as interpreter of divine will, serve the same end here: to assert that the will of the human legislator is a captive will, totally subjugated to this objective principle of equity, coming directly from God.

This definition of law is followed by an analysis of the particular situation of the prince in his relationship to the law. Here again borrowing the vocabulary of the glossators, John begins by saying that all the prince's subjects are constrained by obligation (*necessitate*) to observe the law. Then he comes to the prince, and

---

35   John recalls in the *Metalogicon* (4.13) that the ancients related *prudentia* and *scientia* to knowledge of the sensible world, and intellection or *sapientia* to that of the spiritual world and divine things. A classic distinction taken up by Lactantius, Augustine, Jerome, Isidore of Seville, etc., and which John too makes his own.

36   On Gideon see *Policraticus* 8.22, ed. Webb, vol. 2, p. 387.

to Ulpian's famous maxim *princeps legibus solutus est*, John's intention here being to give his own interpretation, endeavouring, it seems, to exclude the glossators' *ex uoluntate*, or at least to limit its scope. In substance, he writes that the prince is said to be exempt from the laws because what must guide him in his function, and does indeed guide him if he is truly a prince, is not fear of punishment, but his sole duty of cultivating equity through love of justice, and administering *utilitas rei publicae*, which implies the effacement of his personal will – his private will – in the general interest. Here John introduces what seems to be an allusion to submission *ex uoluntate*, derived from the glossators: "But who, when it comes to public affairs, can speak of the will of the prince (*de principis uoluntate*), when, in this domain, he is permitted to desire nothing except that of which he is persuaded by law or equity, or which is implied by considerations of general utility?"[37] Thus in public affairs the will of the prince has to be subordinated to *lex, aequitas*, and *utilitas communis*, and it is on this basis that it possesses what John calls "the force of judgement" (*uim judicii*), and that, he goes on, "what pleases him in such matters has the force of law, inasmuch as his ruling does not depart from the spirit of equity (*ab aequitatis mente*)." Such a ruling is bound to be, "as a consequence of painstaking contemplation, the image of equity," which is to say the image of the command of God.

"To desire nothing except that of which he is persuaded by law or equity": this form of words could not of course amount to downright denial of the prince's normative prerogative. It embodies a possibility of choice between the terms of human law and the principle of equity: the verb *persuadere* is not used by mere chance. We know that John, who was doubtless not ignorant of a debate among the glossators of his time as to the potential conflict between positive law and equity,[38] has already, prior to Book 4, replied to the following question: what is to be done when there is reason to wonder whether the law

---

37   Ed. Webb, vol. 1, p. 238: "Princeps tamen legis nexibus dicitur absolutus, non quia ei iniqua liceant, sed quia is esse debet qui, non timore poenae sed amore iustitiae aequitatem colat, rei publicae procuret utilitatem, et in omnibus aliorum commoda priuatae praeferat uoluntati. Sed quis in negotiis publicis loquetur de principis uoluntate, cum in eis nil sibi uelle liceat nisi quod lex aut aequitas persuadet aut ratio communis utilitatis inducit?"

38   On this debate see Jacques Krynen, "Le problème et la querelle de l'interprétation de la loi en France, avant la Révolution (Essai de rétrospective médiévale et moderne)," *Revue historique de droit français et étranger* 86 (2008), 161–197, and, more particularly, for the 12th to 13th centuries, pp. 164–170, as well as the major contributions (Eduard Maurits Meijers, Marguerite Boulet-Sautel, Ennio Cortese, Philippe Godding, etc.) cited in notes 11 to 18 of the same article.

actually conforms with the principle of equity? Here again we have Roman law, perhaps also John's reading of a gloss of his time influenced by Bulgarus, one of the *quatuor doctores*, supplying John with the appropriate reply, to be found, we have already noted, in another passage of the *Policraticus* (2. 25). There he writes with the utmost clarity, relying on a constitution of Constantine (C. 1.14.1) and very probably also a gloss on this passage or on an unknown *Summa*,[39] that "where the law proposes one solution and equity another, in a matter of public utility, the prince must be required to provide the interpretation that is general and necessary," that is to say the interpretation that generates a solution that is general and binding on everyone, first of all on the judges charged with its implementation.

The principle of equity may, in short, oblige the prince to modify or abrogate a legal rule that contradicts that principle. In the name of equity, the prince may change or modify the law. As, however, equity is none other than the cosmic harmony willed by God, the will that animates the prince in his function as legislator is a subordinate one, and what John of Salisbury intends should prevail throughout this Book 4 is a hierarchy of norms – by the way entirely classic in respect of the Christian vision of the rule of law – by which the prince is made subject to divine law.[40] John writes: "The sanction of all the laws has no sense *si non diuinae legis imaginem gerat* ['if that sanction does not assume the image of divine law', that is to say does not strive to implement and imitate it], and any princely constitution is useless if it does not accord with the discipline of the Church."[41] Here, as he stated clearly in Chapter 7 of Book 4, relying on the prologue to the *Decretum* of Ivo of Chartres, John seeks to distinguish at the heart of the law governing human societies a hard, unalterable core, and at the same time a part of the law that may develop so long as it does not challenge the authority of that hard core comprising divine commandments, evangelical doctrine, and the canons of the great founding councils; so long, that is, as it remains in harmony with Christian principles: *conueniens et consonans christianitati*, as Hincmar of Reims had said three centuries earlier. Within this

---

39   See on this point the analysis by George Miczka, "Johannes von Salisbury und die *Summa Trecensis*," p. 396.

40   On the philosophical aspect of this demonstration by John, see Christophe Grellard, "*Le prince est sujet de la loi de justice*: Loi de Dieu, lois des hommes chez Jean de Salisbury," in Silvère Menegaldo and Bernard Ribémont, eds., *Le Roi fontaine de justice. Pouvoir justicier et pouvoir royal au Moyen Âge et à la Renaissance* (Paris, 2012), pp. 85–102.

41   *Policraticus* 4.6, ed. Webb, vol. 1, p. 251: "omnium legum inanis est censura si non diuine legis imaginem gerat, et inutilis est constitutio principis, si non est ecclesiasticae disciplinae conformis. Quod et christianissimum non latuit principem, qui legibus indixit ne dedignentur sacros canones imitari."

vision of the source of the law and the normative hierarchy resides, of course, the postulate, not to be discussed here, of another dependency binding the prince to those who see themselves as the direct interpreters of the divine will: the ministers of the divine cult, who are the soul of the *corpus rei publicae* of which the prince is the head; the prince is their minister, as John emphasizes in the very first lines of the following chapter.[42]

Finally, it should be emphasized that the hierarchy of norms revealed to us here by John of Salisbury is no more than a hierarchy submitting human law to those rules of which he will later write that they "draw their eternal validity from the word of God expressed in the Scriptures and in the Law,"[43] and, within human law, conforming secular law to the law of the Church. It is not a hierarchy of the sources of each of these two branches of human law. A sign that John's approach is more that of a theologian and moralist than of a real jurist is that we will not find here the essential element represented, in the discourse of glossators, by the question of the hierarchy between the law of the prince and custom, then much debated, notably on the basis of a passage by the jurisconsult Julian featuring in the *Digest*. John was aware of certain Roman texts on custom. A passage in Book 7, where he calls to mind the places where an *inuetera consuetudo, etiam si rationi aduersetur aut legi*, may persist shows that he is not ignorant of the constitution of Constantine (C.8.52.2) affirming that ancient custom "has no force enabling it to prevail *aut rationem aut legem*," and that he knows the criteria (antiquity, conformity to reason and to *ius*) according to which a customary rule can be qualified as good or bad. In a letter evoking the conflict between King Henry II of England and those denouncing the *Constitutions of Clarendon*, the future Bishop of Chartres develops these criteria and applies them to the relations between the king and the Church, declaring that the king ought to demand of the Churches in his kingdom only

> ...those customs that are not inimical to divine laws, do not dishonour the priesthood, imply no peril to souls, and do not compromise the liberty of his mother the Church, from whose hand he received the sword with a view to protect it and to ward off from it all offences against the law.[44]

---

42   See the passage in book 5 where, defining the prince as "head" of the *corpus rei publicae*, he presents him as *subiectus Deo et his qui uices illius agunt in terris* (ed. Webb, vol. 1, pp. 282–283). See also ibid. 4.3, ed. Webb, vol. 1, p. 239.

43   *The Later Letters*, p. 348, Letter 213.

44   Ibid., p. 140, Letter 174. "(...) consuetudines quae non sunt diuinis legibus inimicae, quae bonis moribus non aduersantur, quae sacerdotium non deshonestant, quae periculum non ingerunt animarum, quae matris ecclesiae, de cuius manu suscepit gladium ad ipsam tuendam et iniurias propulsandas, non subruunt libertatem."

All we can know, however, is that he requires of custom that same conformity in respect of divine laws that he demands of secular laws, and that the question of the formal sources of human law does not really interest him. Notably, John does not here concern himself with stressing the role of the prince legislator in examining and suppressing customs contrary to divine law and accepted practice; such an observation would perhaps be self-evident: he does not deny the prince the right to decide whether the rule of law conforms to the principle of equity. The question would in any event be left, a century later, to Guibert of Tournai, who would cite two passages... from the *Policraticus*![45] What is most important to John is no doubt to mitigate Ulpian's two maxims by demanding that the prince should absolutely respect the superior principle of equity; indeed, from the moment that any human law is truly – and John does not use the expression – the *aequitas constituta* of the glossators, that is to say faithful to that superior principle, John requires the prince to show that law absolute respect.

The Law of Justinian, a Model for the Monarchs of the 12th Century

John of Salisbury's distrust of Ulpian's formulae, and his requirement that equity should be guarantor of the conformity of law with the lessons of *ratio* and the Scriptures, did not prevent him from casting an admiring eye over the whole of the Justinian *Corpus*, whose rigour and perfection, to his eyes revelatory of the most accomplished of civilisations, aroused in him unfeigned fascination. To John, Trajan was without doubt a model of ethical perfection; but the great Christian emperors – Constantine, Theodosius, Arcadius, Justinian – were also examples to follow, indeed instructors (*possunt instruere*) for every Christian prince, and the first of their lessons worthy of retention was this act of theirs ensuring that "the most holy laws (*sacratissime leges*) that constrain the lives of everyone were known and applied by everyone."[46] Max Kerner and Jacques Krynen have stressed how, all through the *Policraticus*, John does not cease to call upon the princes of his time to apply effectively a great number of imperial constitutions contained in the *Code* and the *Novels*.[47] Whether it was a matter

---

45 *Le traité "Eruditio regum et principum" de Guibert de Tournai*, ed. A. De Poorter (Louvain, 1914), p. 48 sqq.

46 *Policraticus* 4.6, ed. Webb, vol. 1, p. 253.

47 Kerner, "Römisches und Kirchliches Recht"; Jacques Krynen, "*Princeps pugnat pro legibus*...Un aspect du *Policraticus*," in Jacques Krynen, ed., *Droit romain, jus civile et droit français, Études d'histoire du droit et des idées politiques*, 3 (1999), 89–99.

of protecting the Church and the status of its members, or combatting the exactions of royal agents and suppressing venal justices, he did not cease to call in example this arsenal of Roman legal texts, often going so far, framing them with biblical texts, as to suggest that a profound harmony existed between these laws and the precepts of Holy Scripture. In every domain, it seems that it was his manifest desire to restrict the "legislative" action of the prince to the recollection of pre-formulated norms, and the mere reactivation or conservation of ancient laws whose perfection, as John saw it, made them apt to defy time.

Protecting the Church and the status of its members? When faced with a monarch who – and this is already palpable in John's *Early Letters* – claimed to exercise strong authority over the English Church, it was good policy to rely more on the first book of Justinian's *Codex* than on conciliar canons or pontifical decretals; it was therefore to the Roman emperors themselves that John returned in order, by their example, to indicate the limit that should not be crossed by a prince of the 12th century a little too inclined to consider himself *legibus solutus*, stating that:

> We can draw from divine law many arguments in favour of the respect due to the Church; but, in order that a rival power should not have the audacity to contravene that principle, the laws of princes [the Roman emperors] treat the matter generously and benevolently, venerating and supporting the Christian faith and confirming the privileges of ministers of the Church and sacred places.[48]

Accordingly, in *Policraticus* 5.5, John calls to mind the punishments facing those who render themselves guilty of attacks on the rights and privileges of the Church and its ministers, citing to this end nearly word for word the two constitutions *Si quis in hoc genum* (C. 1.3.10) and *Si ecclesiae uenerabilis* (C. 1.3.13) suppressing such felonies.[49] Between these two, he cites the constitution *Placet Clementiae nostrae* (C. 1.13.17) exempting clerics from proceedings under common law and from secular jurisdiction. Two books further on (7.20), in reproducing two of Justinian's *Novels* (Auth. 1, 5.6 and 9.6), he recalls the rules for ordaining bishops and acceding to ecclesiastical functions; then he calls attention to clerical privilege, citing the "authentic" *Omnes qui ubique sunt* (C. 1.3.31).[50] John then justifies his recourse to imperial law rather than to the fathers of the Church normally used by canonists, saying that, while the

---

48   *Policraticus* 5.5, ed. Webb, vol. 1, pp. 296–297.
49   Ibid. 5.5, ed. Webb, vol. 1, p. 297.
50   Ibid. 5.5, ed. Webb, vol. 1, p. 297.

teachings of the latter are more substantial in these matters, unlike the precepts of the Christian emperors they are complicated to the point that "their value is lost."[51]

Combatting the abuses of royal officials? John of Salisbury was fully aware of the quite widespread scourge represented in his time by the venality of the prince's agents, extending from the highest echelons of those holding the reins of government in the provinces to ordinary tax officials. He develops this aspect at great length in Chapter 16 of Book 5.[52] Again borrowing from the solutions offered by Roman public law, John's purpose here embraces both prevention and sanction. The first category, that of prevention, comprises elements already mentioned in Chapter 12: the oath to be required of an officer of the law, upon taking up his duties, to deliver his judgements *cum ueritate et legum obserua-tione*, and the placing of the books of the Bible in front of the judge's chair before every trial, "so that the presence of God himself should fill the entire court, and inspire all those present with fear and respect before the holy scriptures..."[53]: here again John draws his inspiration from a passage of the *Codex* (C. 3.1.14 and 3.1.14.1), without citing it in full. Also under the heading of prevention comes, in Chapter 15, the description of the duties of governors (*praesides prouinciarum*) and other officers of the law towards their officials and those accountable to them. John here adopts the essential part of his opinion from certain passages of the *Digest* concerning the proper behaviour of holders of public office, calling on governors and other officials to take care to protect the weak against the abuses of the powerful (D. 1.18.6), not to burden the inhabitants of their province with the costs of their accommodation (D. 1.16.4), to ensure that their province enjoys peace and tranquillity while dealing ruthlessly with the wicked (D. 1.18.13), to be readily available without being on terms of too great familiarity with their officials (D. 1.18.19), and to ensure that all acts deriving from their office remain free of monetary charge (D. 1.16.6.3).[54]

Under the heading of sanctions, in Chapter 16 of Book 5 the future bishop of Chartres turns his attention to the punishment of the venality of royal agents[55];

---

51   On all the above see Jacques Krynen, "Sur la leçon de législation ecclésiastique du *Policraticus*," in Giles Constable and Michel Rouche, eds., *Auctoritas. Mélanges offerts au professeur O Guillot* (Paris, 2006), pp. 497–502.

52   *Policraticus* 5.16, ed. Webb, vol. 1, p. 349 sqq. On this point, see John of Salisbury's thinking and that of his contemporaries and subsequent generations regarding affairs in England, in Frédérique Lachaud, *L'Éthique du pouvoir au Moyen Âge. L'office dans la culture politique (Angleterre, vers 1150-vers 1330)* (Paris, 2010), p. 590 sqq.

53   *Policraticus* 5.12, ed. Webb, vol. 1, p. 334.

54   Ibid. 5.15, ed. Webb, vol. 1 p. 344 sqq.

55   Ibid. 5.16, ed. Webb, vol. 1, p. 349 sqq.

he calls urgently for a stricter application of the laws, evoking the Julian laws on the misappropriation of public funds, reproduced in Book 9 of the *Codex*, and also broadly recalled in Book 48, Chapter 11 of the *Digest*. He writes:

> Liable under the *lex Julia repetundarum* is anyone who, charged with any *potestas* whatsoever, has accepted money with a view to judging or not judging, deciding or not deciding, calling for testimony or not calling for testimony; in short, with a view to doing something more or something less than is required by his office.

And John, borrowing from the *Digest* (D. 48.11.7 and 8), goes on to insist on the detail of the law's dispositions, using the very precise legal vocabulary provided him by his source: mobile goods appropriated to the officer's profit to be excluded from usucaption, sales and leases extorted at too high or too low a price to be annulled, etc. ...Then come other dispositions transcribed word for word from the *Codex*: one obliging an ex-governor who has committed misconduct in his province to return there under close guard in order to restore fourfold the goods taken by his servants, soldiers, and subordinates, and those taken by himself (C. 9.27.1); another exhorting judges to "remove their hands from money and goods that are not theirs," and not to make the judgements they deliver "an occasion to amass booty" (C. 9.27.3); another, finally, ordering all concerned to denounce such misdeeds and bring evidence before the court (C. 9.27.4). John concludes: "May our contemporaries listen to these rules, for I scarcely dare to hope that they might observe them." In other parts of the *Policraticus* John praises the Romans' actions in support of moral discipline; he recalls the substance of the great Republican sumptuary laws (8. 8),[56] also mentioning (3. 14)[57] the imperial laws curbing sexual deviations. We talked before of this "hard, inalterable kernel of the law" that the prince is duty-bound to safeguard in his own legislation: we might very legitimately ask whether the future bishop of Chartres was not tempted, on occasion, by the notion of in some sense assimilating to this immutable core the emperors' *sacratissimae leges* whose application he was recommending. At the very least, as we have already stressed, he sets them as models to be followed by a prince, no doubt authorized to adapt them to the context of place and time, but reminded of the respect due to their *mens*, their spirit or intention. Here we see confirmed a strong vision of *auctoritas ueterum legum*, eminently comparable to the one that Hincmar of Reims was able to defend three centuries earlier.

---

56 Ibid. 8.8, ed. Webb, vol.2, p. 277 sqq. See Krynen, *"Princeps pugnat pro legibus,"* p. 95.

57 Ibid. 3.14, ed. Webb, vol. 1, p. 220 sqq., with the constitution *Cum uir nubit* (C. 9.9.31) cited in full.

The Perspective of a Practitioner of the Law and of Judicial Procedure?

As secretary to Archbishop Theobald, John was very often called upon to write up the many missives by his master devoted to legal cases dealt with in both the diocese and the ecclesiastic province of Canterbury. Many of these communications were addressed by the archbishop to the popes of the period, the majority to Adrian IV, some to Alexander III, often concerning appeals to Rome, whose use had not ceased to intensify since the end of the 1140s. As a general rule, they contain a summary of the case and of the course of the judicial stage preceding the appeal. It is highly probable that, when writing like this in the archbishop's name, in the majority of cases John did not do so from dictation, but relied on a dossier of documents, the judge's report, and perhaps in some instances also his own account as a witness of the attitudes and statements of the parties to the case. The question of his involvement in the hearings he mentions remains unresolved. Although no source says so in so many words, it is easy to imagine that this intimate counsellor, very close to the archbishop whose ear he had, and, what is more, entrusted with relations with the Apostolic See, had to intervene actively in the most delicate of cases. The legal vocabulary he uses thus very probably comes from his own knowledge of the law applicable to the situations brought to the judge's attention, and from his own knowledge of process law. A number of these cases concern disputes about the custodianship of churches, sometimes aggravated by a violent act of dispossession by one of the parties. John's accounts of these matters shows that he was perfectly well-informed as to the terminology applicable in such cases. When the occasion demands, his references to forcible dispossession or – and it comes to the same thing under Roman law – dispossession carried out in the absence of any authorizing judgement (*uiolenter spoliatos, uiolenter et sine iudicio destitutus, absque iudicio spoliatam*, etc.),[58] and to the applicability (or non-applicability) of restitution prior to *iudicium petitorium* are very precise.[59] Letter 72, distinguishing *iudicium possessorium* from *iudicium petitorium,* and also instancing the *exceptio rei iudicatae* available under Roman law to anyone who has already been prosecuted and judged a first time for the same offence, bears effective witness to John's mastery of this terminology. Other letters, touching on clerical discipline (Letter 100), on the highly complex question of the legal nature of *sponsalia* and the constitutive element of marriage, much debated in the mid 12th century (Letter 131), and on the prohibition of remarriage for

58   Examples: *The Early Letters*, nos. 2, 53, 65, 66, 68, 72, etc.
59   Examples: ibid., nos. 78, 102.

women previously married to clerics (Letter 99), tell us of the diverse elements of canon law John had to know in order to exercise his function in the entourage of Archbishop Theobald. Certain of the letters have no doubt been capable of giving rise to the hypothesis that John had a copy of Gratian's *Decretum* in his possession, but none allows us to think that, at any moment during the decade he spent in the entourage of Thomas Becket's predecessor, he had in his hands the *Paucapalea* (c. 1150), one of the first and most notable critical commentaries on Gratian's work.

In conclusion, however, we will return to the *Policraticus*, and to Book 5, where, describing the different parts of the *corpus rei publicae*, John sets about using his understanding of the rules of process law to try to inculcate them into those who constitute the prince's ears, tongue, and eyes: the governors and provincial judges, whom he reproaches with being not only venal but also *scientiae legis ignaros*.[60] There is to be found in John of Salisbury, repeated many times in several of the later chapters of Book 5, a kind of cry of repulsion against all those who dishonour their function, notably those who sell their judgement, whether just or unjust, sell the justice that is the *princeps et regina* of the office whose servants they are: "What is just has no need of payment, for justice must be done for its own sake, and it is iniquitous to sell what is owed," he says; "To sell justice is iniquitous, and selling injustice smacks of perversion in iniquity." "He alone sells justice who does not possess it, for, before the deal is even concluded, justice has abandoned the miserable seller."

In short, an acerbic analysis of the behaviour of the judges of his time, with no quarter given, and an uncompromising account that explains John's desire to remind governors and other judges of the duties attached to their functions, the need for the judge to have a *religio* of his office, in other words a scrupulous vision and awareness of the duties imposed on him by it: to have a knowledge of the law, a will to do what is right, the strength to execute it, and a rigorous awareness, too, of his responsibility before God. John's ambition is to guide the judge in his function, to teach him down to the most technical detail what it is fitting for him to do and what he must be careful to avoid doing. Chapters 13 and 14, while not constituting a coherent and comprehensive *ordo iudiciorum* properly speaking, contain a certain number of rules of procedure inspired by Book 2 of the *Code*, Book 48 of the *Digest*, and *Novel* 124 *De litigantibus*.

John begins with an injunction to the judge to hear from the prosecutor (or the plaintiff), at the moment of the *litis contestatio*, a *sacramentum calumpniae* guaranteeing the sincerity of the accusation and the absence of ill-will, and to receive as well from the defendant (or the accused) an analogous oath declaring

---

60   *Policraticus* 5.11, ed. Webb, vol. 1, pp. 331–332.

that he defends his cause persuaded of its validity in law, and without bad faith. Any refusal to take the oath will be met by sanctions: if on the part of the prosecutor by the loss of his right to pursue the case; if on the part of the defendant by a sentence of condemnation; refusal amounting to admission of fault.[61] Here John cites or draws inspiration from *Code* 2.58.2 and 6, and *Novel* 124.

There follow long discussions of the advocates' oath obliging them also to respect the truth and to be faithful in their conduct of the legal argument, then advice to the judge in respect of guaranteeing a fair trial, stressing the need to rebalance by the application of equity any apparent inequalities associated with the prestige or the quality of the advice of one of the advocates. Lastly, after setting out very precise deontological rules attached to the function of advocate, and stating the rule whereby the advocate's affirmation engages his client unless the latter contests it immediately, John recalls the *lex Remmia*, by the terms of which a false accusation implies for its author, after the acquittal of the accused, a punishment analogous to that to which the latter would have been liable.[62] Many of the rules stated here are drawn from or inspired by *Code* 2.6.5 to 6.7, or borrowed from title 48.16.1 of the *Digest*. John stresses *en passant* that a proceeding should not last more than three years, a period laid down by the Justinian texts.

Lastly comes advice devoted to means of proof, to the superiority of *testes* (witnesses summoned to the court) over *testimonium* (evidence reported to the court), indicated in two rescripts of the emperor Hadrian; to the not negligible role that may be played by presumption (it was by means of presumption, he explains, that the "judgement of Solomon" was resolved), and to the crucial importance of the stage of the trial when witnesses are heard by the judge, whose powers of discretion must be very broadly conceived. In effect, John explains, adopting the very terms of a rescript addressed by Hadrian to one of his governors, "it is by a decision of your own understanding" (*ex sententia animi tui*) that you have to decide what you believe or what you consider to be insufficiently proven.[63] Here again we have the man of experience, witness of and perhaps actor in the practices applying in Church courts, and conscious of the judicial negligence that was rife in his time, relying on an entire arsenal of texts originating in Roman law in order to express his concerns. His aim is perhaps not so much to confine civil or criminal proceedings at any cost within the body of rules for the functioning of ecclesiastical courts, provided progressively during the course of the 12th century by specialists in canon law,

---

61   Ibid. 5.13, ed. Webb, vol. 1, pp. 339–340.
62   Ibid. 5.13, ed. Webb, vol. 1, pp. 340–341.
63   Ibid. 5.14, ed. Webb, vol. 1, pp. 342–343.

as to give a moral basis to the judicial function, and to plead for a more rational and egalitarian system of justice, delivered without distinction of person, without either undue haste or excessive delay, with respect for the dignity of others, and in the spirit of truth; in sum, to remind the judge that he is duty-bound to ensure that the justice he administers is the image of divine truth.

The centrality of the law in the service of a *res publica* where the most perfect harmony reigns between the different organs and functions that animate it: there is in John of Salisbury's work the conviction that the *disciplina officialium* that is the guarantor of that harmony cannot be realized except in full recognition of the sovereign function of the law. It is the tool of the prince in the sense that it is by laws that he must rule his people; at the same time, it is, or at least comes near to being, the *causa finalis* of his function, in the sense that law in accordance with equity is the reflection of divine will, and that the prince who orientates his *regimen* to the strict application of such a law promotes the reign of divine law on earth. Behind John's conception of the centrality of law is the discovery of the Justinian texts; there is above all that fascination with Roman law insofar as – and this nuance stands out from a reading of his remarks regarding Ulpian's contribution – it does not encourage the excess of tyranny, and proves to be an authentic reflection of *lex diuina*[64]; a Roman law "that provides this highly knowledgeable man with an unshakeable historical reference to a society pacified under the authority of a prince *qui legibus regit, ...qui pugnat pro legibus.*"[65] What, in effect, would be John's attitude to the law without his encounter with Justinian?

---

64 As Julie Barrau strongly emphasized in the course of a conference given on 13 February 2013 in the context of the *Atelier Jean de Salisbury* (Université de Paris-Sorbonne, Université Paris-Panthéon-Sorbonne and Université de Lorraine) on *Jean de Salisbury et le droit canon*, this demand for the absolute primacy of divine law in every decision by the prince, and indeed the Pope, constantly recurs in John's correspondence, and it tends to become more radical – notably to turn to distrust in principle of any rule, either ancient or modern – in the context of the struggle between archbishop Thomas Becket and Henry II and in the final years of John's life. See, among other texts (*The Later Letters*, nos. 174, 213, 217, 225, 233, 273, 281), that of Peter the Chanter (*Verbum abbreviatum*, PL 205, col. 235), also cited by J. Barrau, relating John's attitude at Lateran Council III (1179): "(...) ait Joannes Carnotensis: Absit, inquit, noua condi, uel plurima veterum reintigi et innouari. (...) Timeamus ne dicat nobis Dominus: 'bene irritum facitis praeceptum Dei, ut traditionem uestram seruetis.Tales enim in uanum colunt me'" (Mc, 7.7-9). See also Julie Barrau, "La *conversio* de Jean de Salisbury: la Bible au service de Thomas Becket," *Cahiers de Civilisation Médiévale* 50 (2007), 229–244.

65 Krynen, "*Princeps pugnat pro legibus...*," p. 96.

CHAPTER 8

John of Salisbury's Political Theory

Cary J. Nederman

John of Salisbury is commonly and with some good reason regarded to be the first systematic political theorist of the Latin Middle Ages, a claim grounded mainly on his authorship of the magisterial *Policraticus* (started in perhaps 1156 or 1157 and substantially completed by late 1159).[1] Of course, the *Policraticus* is far more than a work of political theory in the sense of a treatise that concentrates wholly on normative questions about the nature of justice, authority, good government, political order and the like. In it, John addresses a wide range of topics that go well beyond what we might ordinarily expect political theorists to discuss – concerns as far-flung as astrology and spirit-conjuring, theology, popular entertainment, and the teachings of the classical schools of philosophy. Yet the core of the *Policraticus* is essentially political in bearing, after the fashion that John conceived politics, namely, as the manner in which rulers and their agents used their offices for the promotion of public goods and goals shared by all members of a community. Inevitably, this central focus led John to analyze and appraise theoretical principles and problems that would be familiar to any political theorist who flourished either before or after his time. The *Policraticus* is perhaps best described as the philosophical distillation of the experiences and wisdom of one of the most learned courtier-bureaucrats of 12th-century Europe. Although the meaning of the title *Policraticus* – a pseudo-Greek neologism, like the titles of some of his other writings – has been debated, it seems to have been invented by John in order to

---

1 The standard Latin critical edition of the *Policraticus* is that of Clement C.J. Webb, 2 vols. (Oxford, 1909). (Katharine Keats-Rohan's critical text of Books I–IV of the *Policraticus* in CCCM [Turnhout, 1993] will be not be employed here, since the promise of a companion volume containing Books V–VIII, which form the focus of the present chapter, has not thus far been fulfilled.) There are multiple partial English translations: John Dickinson, trans., *The Statesman's Book of John of Salisbury* (New York, 1927); Joseph B. Pike, trans., *Frivolities of Courtiers and Footprints of Philosophers* (Minneapolis, 1938); and Cary J. Nederman, trans., *Policraticus: Of the Frivolities of Courtiers and the Footprints of Philosophers* (Cambridge, 1990). In the present chapter, I make use of all of these translations, although with occasional modifications as warranted by the Latin text. In subsequent citations of the *Policraticus*, the book and chapter numbers are given, followed by the volume and page number(s) in the Webb edition and by the name of the translator and page number(s) in the English version.

© KONINKLIJKE BRILL NV, LEIDEN, 2015 | DOI 10.1163/9789004282940_010

convey the implication of classical learning and erudition as well as to capture the political content of the work.[2]

The tacit classicism of the title suggests an important question regarding how we are to situate the work historically and intellectually. On the one hand, a certain group of scholars has tended to view the fundamental ideas of the *Policraticus* as relatively unrelated to their time and place, steeped in the wisdom of the ancients instead of the immediate political milieu.[3] On the other hand, some literature on John's political theory has concentrated primarily on its commentary upon problems of political ethics arising from contemporary events and prominent personalities, most especially the politics of the court.[4] Both positions have some merit. After all, John held the classical tradition as he knew it in very high esteem, as evidenced by the famous remark in the *Metalogicon* (which he attributes to Bernard of Chartres) that modern thinkers occupy the position of mere "dwarfs perched on the shoulders of giants" from days long gone.[5] Yet John also was a deeply engaged servant of the Church, who not only rubbed shoulders with, but closely advised, some of the leading ecclesio-political figures of his age, and he first undertook to compose the *Policraticus* at a moment of particular professional and personal turmoil and despair which could not but have tinged its contents.[6] Perhaps it is most reasonable to characterize John's political theory as an effort to remold key elements of the classical philosophical tradition with which he was familiar to suit the political realities of 12th-century Christian Europe. His theoretical framework is neither anachronistically tilted toward the ancient past nor merely pragmatically engaged with the contemporary scene, but rather represents an attempt to apply ideas derived from the "giants" of former days to the pressing political concerns of his time. John of Salisbury's political theory constitutes a synthesis of classical learning and current politics, of the pagan past and the medieval Christian present.

The *Policraticus* depends heavily upon authoritative sources as a means for extending and enhancing its arguments. John believed that the case for a specific

---

2   See *Policraticus*, ed. Keats-Rohan, pp. viii–ix.

3   For example, Joseph Canning, *A History of Medieval Political Thought 300–1450*, 2nd ed. (London, 2005), pp. 110–114; Janet Coleman, *A History of Political Thought: From the Middle Ages to the Renaissance* (Oxford, 2000), p. 53.

4   For instance, Egbert Türk, *Nugae Curialium: Le règne d'Henri II Plantegenêt (1145–1189) et l'éthique politique* (Geneva, 1977), pp. 68–84; Frédérique Lachaud, *L'Éthique du pouvoir au Moyen Âge: L'office dans la culture politique (Angleterre, vers 1150-vers 1330)* (Paris, 2010).

5   *Metalogicon* 3. 4, p. 116: "...nanos gigantum umeris insidentes..."

6   See Cary J. Nederman, *John of Salisbury* (Tempe, Arizona, 2005), pp. 20–25.

claim was strengthened not only by rational demonstration but also by the antiquity and the eminence of the authorities one could adduce in support of it. John's most important authority, both quantitatively and qualitatively, is Scripture. While his careful and often subtle use of biblical imagery and texts reveals a thorough knowledge of both Testaments, he manifests a clear preference throughout the *Policraticus* for the Old Testament, especially the books of the prophets and of wisdom. At times, the *Policraticus* even engages in biblical commentary. Much of Book 4, for instance, is taken up with exegesis of a passage from Deuteronomy, by means of which John demonstrates the salient features of the good ruler. John is also conversant with the Fathers of the Latin Church and other early Christian authors. The *Policraticus* displays a particular fondness for Augustine and Jerome, and for the historical writings of Orosius, but there are few available writers of the patristic age whom John fails to cite.

By contrast, the political writings of the most prominent classical philosophers (such as Plato, Aristotle, and Cicero) were almost entirely unknown during John's time. This created something of a dilemma for him, since the postulation of innovative concepts unsupported by long-standing tradition lacked authority in medieval Europe. His solution is one that was not uncommon during the Middle Ages: he created a bogus authority – in essence, he perpetrated a forgery – in order to legitimize ideas that were otherwise original to him. Specifically, the *Policraticus* purports to adapt a work called the "Instruction of Trajan," said to be a letter composed by the Roman imperial writer Plutarch.[7] John attributes to this treatise many of the most significant and insightful features of his political theory, especially the claim that the political system can be analyzed in detail as an organism or living body whose parts are mutually devoted to and dependent upon one another. The framework for the whole of Books 5 and 6 is allegedly lifted from the "Instruction of Trajan." Yet there is no independent evidence for the existence of such a work as described by John, whether by Plutarch or by or some later Plutarchian imitator. And when subsequent authors cite the "Instruction of Trajan," it is always on the basis of the report of the *Policraticus*. Hence, scholars now usually conclude that the "Instruction of Trajan" was actually a convenient fiction fashioned by John as a cloak for that intellectual novelty commonly despised in his day.[8]

---

7   *Policraticus* 5. 1–3, ed. Webb, vol. 1, pp. 281–289.

8   Hans Liebeschütz is the scholar most closely associated with this development; see his classic "John of Salisbury and Pseudo-Plutarch," *Journal of the Warburg and Courtauld Institutes* 6 (1943), 33–39. Max Kerner is perhaps the leading dissenter, his arguments for a pre-existing text given in "Randbemerkungen zur *Institutio Traiani*," in *The World of John of Salisbury*, pp. 203–206. Without rehearsing the debate, the position pioneered by Liebeschütz continues to be convincing.

Courtly Conduct

John tells us repeatedly that he was a creature of the court, his daily activities shaped by the myriad demands imposed by diplomacy, correspondence, and legal dispute. John regarded the world of the court with a jaundiced eye, as fraught with intrigue and flattery, vice and corruption.[9] In turn, these circumstances are reflected in the text of the *Policraticus*, especially its first three books. Books 1 and 2 examine the "frivolities of courtiers," ranging from feasting and drinking to hunting and gambling, the performing arts, and occultism. John's examination of such frivolities, while an interesting and useful source for courtly conduct in his time, commands our immediate attention less than does Book 3, the main aim of which is to disparage the efforts of flatterers to manipulate the actions of their superiors. In John's view, flattery, which predominates among courtly modes of speech, detracts from good government by leading the ruler and his counselors and servants down the path to vice. John says that flattery is always "accompanied by deception, fraud, betrayal, [and] the infamy of lying."[10] John's standard of speech is free and open debate, sincere in seeking after the honorable and the virtuous course of conduct. In his view, one should "prefer to be criticized by anyone whomsoever rather than be praised by one who...flatters; for no critic need be feared by the lover of truth."[11] Flattery is inimical to the kind of rational discourse oriented toward truth that he believes must accompany any government whose goal is truly to seek the common good and justice for the governed.

Adapting Cicero's concept in *De amicitia* of false friendship based on "profit" and "lucrative results," John treats flattery as the quintessential courtly vice, according to which the flatterer seeks his own good without reference to the good of others. John explains that "since men...love not their friends but themselves in each instance, it is necessary to have the garb of pretense in order to be pleasing."[12] Such costumes – which John consistently compares to the masks and tricks of actors on the stage[13] – constitute the relationship built on flattery.

---

9   See *Policraticus*, Prologue, ed. Webb, vol. 1, pp. 12–18.

10   Ibid. 3.5, ed. Webb, vol. 1, p. 184, trans. Pike, p. 165: "...omnis adulatio comites habet dolum et fraudem proditionemque et notam mendacii..."

11   *Policraticus* 3.14, ed. Webb, vol. 1, p. 231, trans. Pike, p. 210: "...potius a quolibet reprehendi quam siue ab errante siue ab adulante laudari. Nullus enim reprehensor formidandus est amatori ueritatis."

12   *Policraticus* 3.7, ed. Webb, vol. 1, p. 189, trans. Pike, p. 170: "...cum ad homines uentum sit, qui non amicos sed seipsos in singulis amant, multiplicitatis fucus ut placeat necessarius est."

13   On John's employment of this trope, see Donnalee Dox, *The Idea of the Theater in Latin Christian Thought: Augustine to the Fourteenth Century* (Ann Arbor, 2004), pp. 87–92.

By contrast, John upholds friendship as the antithesis of flattery. Real friendship, however, may only flourish "if utility ceases" and "one cherishes friendship on account of its own virtues." John agrees with Cicero that such friendship for its own sake is "rare," commenting (perhaps somewhat hyperbolically) that it occurs amongst only "three or four pairs of friends" amid "the multitude and variety of persons" – a direct reference to *De amicitia* 4. 15.[14] What forms the foundation of friendship? John declares that cultivation of "benevolence toward everyone...is the fount of friendship and the first step toward charity." Such benevolence is entirely distinct from flattery because it proceeds by "untrammeled honor, observant duty, the path of virtue, the acceptance of service, and the sincerity of words. And it is aided by fidelity, namely, constancy of speech and deed, and by truth, which is the foundation of all duties and goods."[15] Honor and virtue are the keys to the existence of real friendship. Thus, as to the question of whether "there can be friendship or charity among bad men," John sides with Cicero (*De amicitia* 18. 65): "It cannot exist except among good men." Whatever similarities seem to create a harmonious bond amongst evil men, he insists, are only faint imitations of the true bond of friendship that arises between persons fully inculcated in virtue.[16] Real reciprocity is found only among people who share virtuous characteristics.[17]

Why is the possession of virtue among friends the chief characteristic of friendship? Since the goal of virtue is the realization of the good of others, only virtue assures that friends will be truly oriented toward each other's good first and foremost, rather than their own advantage. Perhaps as importantly, at least in the context of John's immediate concern with courtly flattery, virtue stands

---

14   *Policraticus* 3.7, ed. Webb, vol. 1, pp. 189–190, trans. Pike, p. 171: "...si cesset utilitas, rarus aut nullus est qui propter se uirtutem amicitiae colat. In tot circulis seculorum, in tanto etatum lapsu, in tanta multitudine et differentia personarum uix, ut ait Lellius, tria inueniuntur aut quattuor paria in amore."

15   Ibid. 3.5, ed. Webb, vol. 1, p. 182, trans. Pike, p. 163: "Est equidem omnium captanda beniuolentia quae fons amicitiae et primus caritatis progressus est; sed honestate incolumi, officiorum studiis, uirtutis uia, obsequiorum fructu, integritate sermonis. Assit et fides dictorum scilicet factorumque constantia, et ueritas quae officiorum et bonorum omnium est fundamentum."

16   Ibid. 3.12, ed. Webb, vol. 1, p. 211, trans. Pike, p. 193: "Si tamen inter malos caritas aut amicitia esse potest, hoc etenim quaesitum est. Sed tandem placuit eam nisi in bonis esse non posse."

17   For an examination of John's application of these lessons in his own life, see Cary J. Nederman, "Textual Communities of Learning and Friendship Circles in the Twelfth Century: An Examination of John of Salisbury's Correspondence," in John N. Crossley and Constant J. Mews, eds., *Communities of Learning: Networks and the Shaping of Intellectual Identity in Europe, 1100–1450* (Turnhout, 2011), pp. 75–85.

in close and irrevocable connection to truth. Since virtue requires knowledge of the good, which is grounded in truth, as John says above, the bond of friendship must rest on the commitment of the friends to seek and respect the truth. As a general precept of his thought, John emphasized that open and free debate and criticism formed a crucial quality of the public spheres of the court and of the school. Individuals should be protected in their liberty to engage in conscientious, constructive reproval of the morals of others and to challenge ideas that do not meet up to rational evaluation. (John's concept of liberty in this regard will be elucidated more fully below.) Likewise, people should be prepared to listen to and consider seriously such honest criticism when it is rendered. This quality seems particularly necessary in the case of friendship, which is guided by truthfulness. "If a friend makes a mistake he is to be instructed," John insists, "If he should instruct, he is to be listened to."[18] "Truth is stern," but the virtuous man wishes to know when he has gone astray, and the true friend provides this knowledge unflinchingly: "Better the chastisement of a friend than the fraudulent kissing-up (*oscula*) of a flatterer."[19] It is in this sense that friendship is a bond of faith or trust (*fides*), because friends can be trusted to shun pretense and to speak the truth in all matters for the sake of one another.[20]

It should be obvious, then, why John introduces a normative standard of friendship into his discussion of courtly flattery. "Under the guise of friendship" the flatterer does extreme harm, specifically, "he blocks the ears of listeners lest they hear the truth." In support of this, John quotes from *De amicitia* 26. 90 to the effect that the man who refuses to listen to the truth endangers his own well-being.[21] The flatterer covers over the faults of those whom he flatters, which is ultimately detrimental to the good of the flattered; the friend speaks the truth openly and desires to correct his fellow friend with patience and good will.[22] Flattery betokens a slavish cast of mind, whereas friendship is grounded in true intellectual liberty and the honest give-and-take entailed thereby.[23] Consequently, "those who are vulgar and base flatterers are not admitted...among friends,"[24]

---

18   *Policraticus* 3.14, ed. Webb, vol. 1, p. 231, trans. Pike, p. 210: "...amicus autem si errat, docendus; si doceat, audiendus."

19   Ibid. 3.6, ed. Webb, vol. 1, p. 185, trans. Pike, p. 167: "Meliora siquidem sunt...amici uerbera quam fraudulenta oscula blandientis."

20   Ibid. 3.6, ed. Webb, vol. 1, pp. 185–186.

21   Ibid. 3.4, ed. Webb, vol. 1, p. 177, trans. Pike, p. 159: "...sub amantis specie...auditorum aures obturat ne audiant uerum..."

22   Ibid. 3.4, ed. Webb, vol. 1, p. 180.

23   Ibid. 3.4, ed. Webb, vol. 1, p. 178.

24   Ibid. 3.5, ed. Webb, vol. 1, p. 180, trans. Pike, p. 162: "Sunt tamen qui uulgares et adulationes plebeias non admittant...cum amicorum..."

since such flattery is sure to undermine the trust that friends possess in one another's virtue and truthfulness. In sum, friendship and flattery are wholly incommensurable ways of living with one's fellow human beings. No person should ever imagine that he serves the interests of his friend by lies, deceptions, or duplicitous conduct; this is the supreme example of failing to live up to the moral code imbedded in friendship, on John's Ciceronian understanding of it.

John clearly believes that the ethical stringency of friendship would be the guiding principle applied in a well-ordered court. Such a court would be free of flattery and its members would concern themselves with their various duties in such a way as to promote the common good and justice. It would be a court characterized by free and open criticism of ideas and conduct, without rancor and with the greatest degree of mutual trust. John fully realizes, however, that the chances for creating such a court are minimal at best. The image of the "court of friends" should perhaps be conceived instead as a regulative ideal for him – like the king whom he will describe in later books of the *Policraticus* – rather than a blueprint which he aspires to apply precisely and rigorously. In particular, the honorable courtier needs to know how to distinguish between people like himself – true friends – and those who take on the pretense of friendship for the sake of self-interest, and how to treat each. This is the central message of Book 3. John cites the dictum, derived from *De amicitia* 16. 59, that "one is to live among enemies as though among friends, and to live among friends as if in the midst of enemies."[25] In other words, John believes that it is necessary to treat those of whom one is distrustful at court with a veneer of affection until one can establish their true intentions. If they prove to measure up to the standard of friendship, they can be admitted into one's circle of friends; thereafter, they are to be treated with honesty and valued for their own sake, which may mean that they will be subjected to open critical scrutiny when their words and deeds are unseemly. This is an irony of friendship for John: one of the features of a truly friendly bond is the readiness on the part of both parties to apply unsparing criticism to the other when such is appropriate and necessary. One friend so loves another that he will not shrink from the moral duty of correction.

The most extreme enemy of the friendly (that is, virtuous and truth-seeking) courtier is the tyrant, the nemesis of religion and morality whose spectre is raised throughout the *Policraticus*. Interestingly, John closes Book 3 with advice about how to cope with a manifest tyrant within the confines of court. Friendly acts of criticism and correction will, of course, be ineffectual with a

---

25   Ibid. 3.12, ed. Webb, vol. 1, p. 215, trans. Pike p. 196: "Philosophus sic inter hostes uiuendum censuit tamquam inter amicos, et inter amicos ac si in mediis hostibus uiueretur…"

tyrant, since tyranny reflects the extreme of self-interest and self-aggrandizement. Therefore, the courtier must adopt an entirely different strategy, namely, to engage in precisely that form of flattery that would otherwise be forbidden to him. The state of the tyrant's moral character is so corrupt that the only way to survive at court is to cloak oneself in deceit. John's general prohibition on mendacity is not absolute, therefore. Indeed, the *Policraticus* from beginning to end countenances what John terms at one point "pious deception."[26] In the case of the tyrant, the *Policraticus* explicitly legitimizes the use of the weapons of deceit – flattery among them – in order to combat the grave endangerment to social and political order. After his relentless attack on flattery throughout Book 3, he introduces an exception:

> In the secular literature, there is caution that one is to live one way with a friend and another with a tyrant. It is not permitted to flatter a friend, but it is permitted to flatter the ears of a tyrant. For in fact, the man whom it is permitted to flatter, it is permitted to slay. Furthermore, it is not only permitted, but equitable and just, to slay tyrants.[27]

Leaving aside the vexed issue of John of Salisbury's theory of tyrannicide, to be discussed below, the relevant point of this passage is that the rules of civilized society do not apply in the case of the tyrant, whom John likens to a traitor and a public criminal. Since the tyrant behaves by violence and fraud, purely according to his own will, he is utterly incapable of experiencing friendship. Thus, deceitful flattery is legitimated for John in the case of the tyrannical head of state, precisely because of the grievous harm that he commits. Deception ceases to be a sin or an evil when directed to the defense of humanity against tyranny. The ethical courtier has little choice but to fight the enemy with the tools of the enemy. John seems to suggest, indeed, that just as one may have a duty (both to God and to one's fellows) to kill a tyrant, one has a duty to deceive him with flattery if by that sleight further harm is deflected. Thus, Book 3 of the

---

26   See Cary J. Nederman and Tsae Lan Lee Dow, "The Road to Heaven is Paved with Pious Deceptions: Medieval Speech Ethics and Deliberative Democracy," in Benedetto Fontana, Cary J. Nederman, and Gary Remer, eds., *Talking Democracy: Historical Perspectives on Rhetoric and Democracy* (University Park, PA, 2004), pp. 187–211, at pp. 199–203.

27   *Policraticus* 3.15, ed. Webb, vol. 1, p. 232, trans. Nederman, p. 25: "Vnde et in secularibus litteris cautum est quia aliter cum amico, aliter uiuendum est cum tiranno. Amico utique adulari non licet, sed aures tiranni mulcere licitum est. Ei namque licet audulari, quem licet occidere. Porro tirannum occidere non modo licitum est sed aequum et iustum." In this passage, John adapts the language of Cicero, *De officiis* 3.6.32.

Policraticus represents John of Salisbury's attempt (within the overarching agenda of his book) to draw lessons derived from Cicero into the salient context of the court. The exigencies of the court require both a rigid adherence to the moral code of friendship and a readiness to recognize the limitations of that code in practice.

Secular Government: Tyranny vs. Kingship

The foregoing mention of the tyrant leads us directly into the heart of John's conception of the organization of earthly government. Lacking access to classical discussions of varying constitutional systems, John largely takes for granted that the only legitimate regime is the rule of a single man – a principality – who is answerable to God alone. The nature of the prince's office is, in turn, wholly dependent upon the personal character of the incumbent himself. Good men, whose wills are pious and just, are kings; evil men, desirous of their own interests and ready to trample upon their subjects, are tyrants. The terms used for these two types are thus normative by definition: a king rules for the sake of his people, loves God, and demonstrates the moral and spiritual traits appropriate to his position, such as respect for and deference to the Church and its ministers; a tyrant loves only himself, displays ambition and self-seeking behavior, and thereby denigrates not only his subjects, but also the clergy and pious causes. It is noteworthy that John's treatment of secular government in the *Policraticus*, while it does not stint attention upon kingship, perhaps inclines more toward the critical analysis and condemnation of tyranny and its foundations. Perhaps this is not surprising, given John's apparent belief in the vast corruption of courtly life discussed above.

Tyranny for John is not, at least in the first instance, a wholly political concept or category. He identifies in the *Policraticus* several species of tyrant: the private tyrant, the ecclesiastical tyrant, and the public or royal tyrant.[28] According to John, anyone who employs the power he possesses to impose his own will arbitrarily upon another person may be classified as a tyrant. John explicitly admits that his notion of tyranny deviates considerably from the ordinary usage of that term:

> Although it is not possible for all men to get hold of rulership or kingdoms, still men are either rarely or never immune from tyranny. It is said that the tyrant is one who oppresses a people by forceful domination; but

---

28   Ibid. 8.17, ed. Webb, vol. 2, pp. 346–347, trans. Nederman, pp. 191–192.

it is not solely over a people that he exercises his tyranny, but he can do so from the lowest position. For if not over a people, still he will lord over (*dominatur*) whomever he can...Who is it who does not wish to come before some other one if he might be subdued?[29]

What especially distinguishes John's concept of tyranny is the universality of its application. Any immoderate use of power, any attempt to exceed the proper bounds of liberty, qualifies as a case of tyranny, regardless of whether it occurs within the household, the manor, the shire, the parish, the monastery or the kingdom. Tyranny is the peculiar vice of those who use to excess any power with which they are endowed, and who thus further their own interests at the expense of the liberty of others.

But what motivates the tyrant to impose himself upon whomever he can? According to John, the answer stems from the deep-seated desire among human beings to seek pleasure and to gratify themselves sensually, that is, to live in the manner of Epicureans.[30] As John remarks, "They who wish to do their own will are to be rated as Epicureans; for when actions become the slave of lust, affection changes to passion."[31] The vices of Epicureanism spring from "the well of passion," which leads men to suppose that they "can do with impunity" whatever they wish and "can to a certain degree be just like God" – not in imitation of divine goodness, but in the belief that their wills can supplant God's own. Thus, Epicureanism promotes pride and ambition, leading to "a passion for power and honors" that constitutes the root of tyranny.[32] The psychology of Epicurean

---

29   Ibid. 7.17, ed. Webb, vol. 2, pp. 161–162, trans. Nederman, p. 163: "Et, licet omnes occupare non possint principatus et regna, a tirannide tamen omnino immunis est aut nullus aut rarus. Dicitur autem quia tirannus est qui uiolenta dominatione populum premit; sed tamen non modo in populo sed in quantauis paucitate potest quisque suam tirannidem exercere. Nam etsi non populo, tamen quatenus quisque potest dominatur...Quis est qui sic subditum tractet sicut se uellet tractari si subderetur?" In this passage, John adapts the language of Cicero, *De officiis* 3. 6. 32.
30   On John's views concerning Epicureanism, and its relation to tyranny, see Cary J. Nederman and Karen Bollermann, "'The Extravagance of the Senses': Epicureanism, Priestly Tyranny, and the Becket Problem in John of Salisbury's *Policraticus*," *Studies in Medieval and Renaissance History*, 3rd series 8 (2011), 1–25.
31   *Policraticus* 8.24, ed. Webb, vol. 2, p. 412, trans. Pike, p. 399: "Illos quoque Epicureorum nomine censendos arbitror qui suam uolunt in omnibus implere uoluntatem. Nam, cum res libidini seruiunt, in uoluptatem transit affectus."
32   Ibid. 7.17, ed. Webb, vol. 2, pp. 160–161, trans. Nederman, pp. 162–163: "Hic autem puteus cupiditatis est...homo, propriae cognitionis ignarus et debitae subiectionis detrectans iugum, fictitiam quandam affectat libertatem ut possit uiuere sine metu et impune quod

pleasure thus frames John's entire theory of tyranny – public as well as private and ecclesiastical.

Despite the generic character of tyranny, John focuses most of his attention in the *Policraticus* on the public tyrant. In perhaps his most famous discussion of the theme, John posits a definition of the tyrant in terms explicitly derived from traditional sources such as Saint Gregory the Great and Isidore of Seville: "A tyrant, as depicted by the philosophers, is one who oppresses the people by rulership based on force...The tyrant thinks nothing done unless he brings the law to nought and reduces the people to slavery."[33] The tyrant is the enemy of law and justice; he compels his subjects to act as he would have them, regardless of their own wills. The *Policraticus* equates tyranny with the denial of any meaningful liberty to those whom the tyrant rules. Yet the *Policraticus* introduces important clarifications of and elaborations upon this position which modify its significance, specifically, the postulate that all men seek to acquire and maintain their own liberty. That is, they aim to make their own independent choices. According to John, "Liberty judges freely in accordance with individual judgment."[34] The *Policraticus* insists that such liberty is the absolute prerequisite for the acquisition of virtue: the morally good man must be free to choose for himself the correct course of conduct as the circumstances dictate.[35] This is not to say that the free man will always make the right decision; but no morally defensible choice whatsoever is possible in the absence of liberty.[36]

Yet, at the same time, liberty necessarily involves a measure of obedience, in the sense that it is connected to the pursuit of virtue and the (self-imposed) obligation to strive to perform good deeds. In other words, liberty is not coextensive with doing whatever one wishes or desires; liberty is not license. John fears that men are too often ignorant of the distinction between the two: they do not know that liberty is a matter of self-control, limitation and moderation, whereas license entails no such restraint. The person who confuses liberty with license "affects a kind of fictitious liberty, so that he can live without fear

---

uoluerit facere et quodammodo iam esse sicut Deus; non tamen quod diuinam uelit imitari bonitatem, sed Deum dando impunitatem malis ad suam uult malitiam inclinari. De radice ergo superbiae surrepit ambitio, potentiae scilicet cupiditas et honoris..."

33   Ibid. 8.17, ed. Webb, vol. 2, p. 345, trans. Dickinson p. 335: "Est ergo tirannus, ut eum philosophi depinxerunt, qui uiolenta dominatione populum premit...tirannus nil actum putat nisi leges euacuet et populum deuocet in seruitutem."

34   Ibid. 7.25, ed. Webb, vol. 2, p. 217, trans. Dickinson, p. 323: "Libertas ergo de singulis pro arbitrio iudicat..."

35   See ibid. 1.5, ed. Webb, vol. 1, p. 37 and 7.25, ed. Webb, vol. 1, pp. 217–218.

36   Thus, John asks at *Policraticus* 8.9, ed. Webb, vol. 2, p. 281, "...etenim quid opus est libertate si uolentibus luxu perire non licet?"

and do with impunity whatever pleases him, and somehow be just like God; not, however, that he wishes to imitate divine goodness, but rather to incline God to favor his evil will by granting him immunity from punishment."[37] License is a sort of self-deification in which a man fails to distinguish between the arbitrary pursuit of desires and the divinely granted freedom to make moral choices. The man of license wishes to conform God's will to his own, thereby equating whatever he chooses with what God had ordained. On "the pretext of liberty,"[38] license releases men from their duties and inverts their proper relationship with God.

To enjoy liberty, one must have the conditions that permit its efficacious exercise. Slavery, as one might surmise, renders liberty impossible because it denies to men the power to will anything at all according to their own discretion. The slave is unfree because he is in the power of another. So power is a concept intimately associated with liberty: To have true liberty one must have the power to put free determinations into action. John's concern is that those men who confuse liberty with license are incapable of knowing what limit to place on the quest for power; their pursuit of unbounded liberty is simultaneously ambition for the power through which their license can be realized and their wills gratified. Ambition is understood by John in a classical rather than a modern sense; it is an excessive grasping for the power to realize one's own desires, a function of a (false) Epicurean conception of pleasure. License (ignorance of the true nature of liberty) requires ambition, and ambition (if realized) in turn produces tyranny.[39] The *Policraticus* thereby redefines the tyrant as one whose license is rendered efficacious by means of the acquisition of power: "When such a man does attain to power, he exalts himself into a tyrant, and, spurning equity, does not scruple in the sight of God to oppress the equals of his nature and rank."[40] In other words, the tyrant is someone who, lacking discretion in his decisions, chooses anything he desires in the name of (false) freedom and possesses the power to realize his will. Tyranny is the practical consequence of license.

---

37 Ibid. 7.17, ed. Webb, vol. 2, p. 161, trans. Dickinson, p. 282: "...fictitiam quandam affectat libertatem ut possit uiuere sine metu et impune quod uoluerit facere et quodammodo iam esse sicut Deus; non tamen quod diuinam uelit imitari bonitatem, sed Deum dando impunitatem malis ad suam uult malitiam inclinari."

38 Ibid. 7.25, ed. Webb, vol. 2, p. 219, trans. Dickinson, p. 324: "...imagine libertatis..."

39 See ibid. 7.17, ed. Webb, vol. 2, p. 162, trans. Dickinson, p. 283.

40 Ibid. 7.17, ed. Webb, vol. 2, p. 161, trans. Dickinson, p. 282: "Cum uero potentiam nactus est, erigitur in tirannidem et aequitate contempta naturae et conditionis consortes inspiciente Deo deprimere non ueretur."

This also gives us a clue to the triadic relationship between tyranny, enslavement and liberty. Insofar as tyranny is understood as the excessive application of power, that power must be used over someone else; it entails compelling another person to conform to one's own desires or wishes regardless of his own determinations. Any instance of the employment of power in accordance with license must simultaneously be the denial of freedom to at least one other individual. The surfeit of liberty is only coherent in a relational context, where there is a concomitant deficit in liberty elsewhere. Consequently, tyranny is not only vicious in itself, but is also dangerous because it denies the possibility of virtue to those enslaved by it. Since virtue is necessarily voluntary – free choice in accordance with right – slavish (hence involuntary) action can by definition never be virtuous. When John describes slavery as "the image of death" or "the yoke of vice,"[41] he means to convey that the slave has lost all possibility of living a truly virtuous or faithful life. Even if his behavior is to all external standards good, the slave will never attain virtue, insofar as he has not acted freely in accordance with his own circumstantial determinations.

By contrast, the situation in which there is no tyranny will be a condition in which there is no slavery, that is, in which liberty exists in perfect equilibrium. In the absence of tyrants, each person would be free to act virtuously without hindrance or interference from any of his virtuous fellows. Capturing the spirit of the New Academic moderate skepticism of Cicero that he embraces, John proclaims that "it is part of the best and wisest man to give a free reign to liberty and to accept with patience freely spoken words, whatever they may be. Nor does he oppose himself to its works so long as these do not involve the casting away of virtue."[42] Minor faults and errors will be tolerated in the name of defending the liberty of individuals to form, and to behave in accordance with, their own discretionary judgments. Only severe threats to religion or good morals would be deemed worthy of correction and punishment in the genuinely free community. Is it any wonder that John so effusively praises tolerance as a quality of the well-ordered society?[43] Toleration alone is regarded by the *Policraticus* as the touchstone of the harmonious pursuit of liberty. In a tolerant community, neither tyrants nor slaves can subsist at any level.

---

41   These phrases appear, for instance, in *Policraticus* 7.17, ed. Webb, vol. 2, p. 161 and 8.13, vol. 2, p. 323.

42   Ibid. 7.25, ed. Webb, vol. 2, p. 219, trans. Dickinson, p. 324: "Viri tamen optimi et sapientissimi est habenas laxare libertati et quaelibet dicta eius patienter excipere. Sed nec operibus se opponit, dum uirtutis iacturam non incurrat."

43   See Cary J. Nederman, *Worlds of Difference: European Discourses of Toleration, c.1100-c.1550* (University Park, PA, 2000), pp. 39–52.

Admittedly, John is not sanguine about the realization of a temporal polity founded on the twin principles of liberty and toleration. He regards licentiousness, ambition and their offspring, tyranny, to be far too widespread to be easily rooted out. But the *Policraticus* does give some consideration to the prerequisites for the free and tolerant society. In particular, John holds that it pertains to the prince, the supreme public power in the realm, to ensure the liberty of those over whom he reigns. This is why the problem of liberty is especially important when considering the nature of government. John in fact considers the legitimacy of rulership to turn on the existence of liberty in the community at large. By definition, "the prince fights for the laws and liberty of the people."[44] In view of John's stipulation that good laws were "introduced for the sake of liberty,"[45] we may conclude that the preservation of the liberty of subjects is the prime function of kingship. No liberty is possible where the temporal community is disordered: because the prince assures that his subjects "have peace and practice justice and abstain from falsehood and perjury," only through his rule will they "enjoy liberty and peace in such fullness that nothing can in the least disturb them."[46] The intimate relationship between a people and its royal head arises from an organization of society in which each is free to choose his own course of action in accordance with the dictates of right. Under such a harmonious order, none need fear enslavement and those who desire more than their proper sphere of liberty – in sum, who attempt to tyrannize – will be kept in check.

As a consequence, the prince occupies a very special and sensitive place in the network of liberty. If the ruler is good, he will respect the freedom of his subjects and will eradicate threats to it; if he is evil, then the distribution of liberty among members of the community will become unbalanced. The connection here between royal virtue and public liberty is clearly mediated through John's Aristotelian definition of virtue itself as a mean between excess and deficiency.[47] When applied to the king, this notion of virtue leads John to conclude that the ruler must neither allow his subjects too much liberty nor control them too closely. Rather, the hallmark of good rule is moderation: "With how much

---

44   *Policraticus* 8.17, ed. Webb, vol. 2, p. 345, trans. Dickinson, p. 335: "Princeps pugnat pro legibus et populi libertate..."

45   Ibid. 7.25, ed. Webb, vol. 2, p. 218, trans. Dickinson, p. 323: "Quae fauore libertatis sunt introducta..."

46   Ibid. 4.11, ed. Webb, vol. 1, p. 274, trans. Dickinson, p. 54: "...dum pacem diligunt et iustitiam colunt et periuriis abstinent, tantae libertatis et pacis gaudio perfruuntur, quod nichil est omnino quod uel in minimo quietem eorum concutiat."

47   See ibid. 3.3, ed. Webb, vol. 1, p. 176.

care should the prince moderate his acts, now with the strictness of justice, and now with the leniency of mercy, to the end that he may make his subjects all be of one mind in one house, and thus as it were out of discordant dispositions bring to pass one great perfect harmony?"[48] The prince must exercise his own moral liberty to make determinations as circumstances dictate so as to promote mutual respect and charity among his subjects. This requires that the ruler never overlook or encourage moral error within the community, yet also never punish those evils (stemming from the bad choices that free persons sometimes make) that do not endanger public order or religious orthodoxy. On the one hand, the king should suppress those "flagrant outrages" which "it is not permissible to tolerate or which cannot be tolerated in good conscience."[49] Yet, on the other hand, the *Policraticus* objects to the ruler "who is too ready to fault his subjects, and take revenge on them for their faults."[50] Like all other good men, the prince is expected to use his power moderately in accordance with the nature of virtue. But unlike anyone else within his society, the ruler's failure to conform to the dictates of the virtuous mean will necessarily result in disorder and loss of liberty for the rest of the community.

We are thereby led to conclude from the account of the *Policraticus* that political disorder and lack of freedom are the inevitable consequences of the immoderate conduct of government. If the ruler seeks for himself excessive domination, if he attempts to use his power to enslave the community, then he is a public tyrant. That is, the public tyrant is a person of tyrannical character whose ambition for the supreme governmental office has been fulfilled. What renders him a public tyrant is strictly speaking neither his moral qualities nor the power he possesses, but the conjunction and combination of the two. The result of public tyranny is the disruption of the properly ordered community in the face of demands for the slavish obedience of subjects. There can be no liberty among members of the polity when a tyrant rules. A public tyrant claims a monopoly of discretionary authority over all those under his control, so that the maintenance of his full license requires the absence of true freedom on the part of any other. The *Policraticus* insists that "as long as all, collectively and

---

48   Ibid. 4.8, ed. Webb, vol. 1, p. 264, trans. Dickinson, p. 39: "quanta sollicitudine oportet principem moderari nunc rigore iustitiae, nunc remissione clementiae, ut subditos faciat quasi unanimes esse in domo et quasi discordantium in ministerio pacis et caritatis operibus unam faciat perfectam et maximam armoniam?"

49   Ibid. 6.26, ed. Webb, vol. 2, p. 78, trans. Dickinson, p. 265: "Vitia enim flagitiis leuiora sunt; et sunt nonnulla quae non ferri licet aut quae fideliter ferri non possunt."

50   Ibid. 4.9, ed. Webb, vol. 1, p. 267, trans. Dickinson, p. 43: "...qui in subiectorum culpis nimis pronus est ad uindictam..."

individually, are borne along at the will of a single head, they are deprived of their own free will."[51] Nor does John believe that the victim of the public tyrant ought "to make a virtue of necessity by uniting consent and necessity and by gracefully embracing that which is incumbent upon him." To pretend that one wishes what one has not freely chosen is to preserve the semblance of liberty only, without retaining "any measure of real and pure liberty."[52] John instead advocates positive measures to protect the community from its tyrant – in the last instance, tyrannicide, as we shall see below. Since public tyranny creates an enslaved populace, and inevitably destroys the possibility of virtue, the legitimate ruler is never free to abrogate the legitimate liberty of subjects. Only when private citizens themselves become tyrants is the royal power of correction and punishment properly employed. By contrast, the good government of the king, typified by rule in accordance with the virtuous mean, is regarded by the *Policraticus* to be the sole guarantee that moral goodness shall predominate within a society.

The Body Politic

John has been widely celebrated for his watershed contribution to the tradition of thought that models political organization along organic lines.[53] Although it enjoyed a long history prior to John's lifetime, and was commonly employed throughout the Middle Ages, the organic metaphor was articulated in Books 5 and 6 of the *Policraticus* in unprecedented detail and scope (albeit allegedly derived from the Plutarchian "Instruction of Trajan" discussed above). John begins with the simple observation that the commonwealth may be likened to a "body endowed with life."[54] The differentiation of the offices of political society can thus be represented in a manner analogous to the distinction of the parts of the human anatomy. Like all bodies, the commonwealth is animated by a soul

---

51   Ibid. 3.10, ed. Webb, vol. 1, p. 203, trans. Pike, p. 184: "Dum enim omnes unius praesidentis uoluntate feruntur, uniuersi et singuli suo priuantur arbitrio."

52   Ibid. 3.10, ed. Webb, vol. 1, pp. 203–204, trans. Pike, p. 184: "in eoque libertatis seruatur umbra, si se quisque quod praecipitur simulate uoluisse, facitque, immo uidetur facere de necessitate uirtutem, dum necessitate iungit consensum, et quod incumbit gratanter amplectitur. Hic porro nullae sunt partes uerae aut ingenuae libertatis..."

53   The still-standard work on the topic is Tilman Struve, *Die Entwicklung der Organologischen Staatsauffassung im Mittelalter* (Stuttgart, 1978), which should now be supplemented by Gianluca Briguglia, *Il corpo vivente dello Stato: Una metafora politica* (Milan, 2006).

54   *Policraticus* 5.2, ed. Webb, vol. 1, p. 282, trans. Dickinson, p. 64: "...corpus quoddam quod diuini muneris beneficio animatur."

which guides its activities; John asserts that the place of the soul belongs to "those who preside over the practice of religion."[55] Note that the clerical soul of the polity is not, strictly speaking, a "member of the republic," just as the eternal soul of man is not coextensive with the mortal physical organism that it "quickens and regulates."[56] Thus, the soul enjoys a somewhat anomalous place in relation to the body.[57] Properly speaking, John's body politic is a physical entity ruled by the prince who occupies the place of the head. At the heart of the republic lies the senate, composed of the counselors whose wisdom the ruler consults. The senses correspond to the royal judges and local agents who exercise jurisdiction in the king's name. The financial officers constitute the stomach and intestines of the body, while the two hands are formed by the tax collector and the soldier respectively. Finally, John compares the feet to the artisans and peasants "who raise, sustain and move forward the weight of the entire body."[58] Each of these parts of the organism, according to the *Policraticus*, has its own definite functions and tasks which are fixed by its location within the overall scheme of the body. The sum and substance of Books 5 and 6 constitutes a thorough and extensive analysis of the responsibilities attached to all of these offices in turn.

We should not be tempted to suppose that the entire point of John's organic depiction of the community was merely to justify hierarchy and division within society. To the contrary, the body politic is invoked in the *Policraticus* as the expression of a principle of cooperative harmony through which otherwise disparate individuals and interests are reconciled and bound together. This is a theme that runs throughout John's writings: he recurrently stresses "reciprocity" as the salient characteristic of natural and social systems.[59] In the case of the *Policraticus*, John insists that "there can be no faithful and firm cohesion where there is not an enduring union of wills and as it were a cementing together of souls. If this is lacking, it is in vain that the works of men are in harmony, since hollow pretence will develop into open injury, unless the real spirit of helpfulness is present."[60] All the parts of the body, in other words,

---

55   Ibid. 5.2, ed. Webb, vol. 1, p. 282, trans. Dickinson, p. 64: "Illos uero, qui religionis cultui praesunt, quasi animam corporis suspicere et uenerari oportet."
56   Ibid. 5.2, ed. Webb, vol. 1, p. 283, trans. Dickinson, p. 65: "...et in corpore humano ab anima uegetatur caput et regitur."
57   See Cary J. Nederman and Catherine Campbell, "Priests, Kings and Tyrants: Spiritual and Temporal Power in John of Salisbury's *Policraticus*," *Speculum* 66 (1991), 572–590.
58   *Policraticus* 5.2, ed. Webb, vol. 1, p. 283, trans. Dickinson, p. 65: "...qui totius corporis erigunt sustinent et promouent molem."
59   See, for example, Letter 111 (*The Early Letters*, p. 181).
60   *Policraticus* 5.7, ed. Webb, vol. 1, p. 309, trans. Dickinson, p. 95: "...coherentia fidelis et firma esse non potest, ubi non est tenax unio uoluntatum et quasi ipsarum animarum conglutinatio.

must be truly dedicated to a common or public welfare which supersedes the aggregate private goods within the polity. The ruler and magistrates are advised to attend "to the common utility of all,"[61] the lesser parts are counseled "in all things [to] observe constant reference to the public unity,"[62] and in general "all the members" are expected to "provide watchfully for the common advantage of all."[63] John praises ancient Carthage for promoting a spirit of cooperation in which "all labored together in common, and none idled."[64] John claims that the unity of the body politic can only be established and maintained by means of a joint commitment to a public good which benefits every part without distinction, so that "each and all are as it were members of one another by a sort of reciprocity, and each regards his own interest as best served by that which he knows to be most advantageous for the others."[65] John's political body is one in which, beyond all social differentiation, "mutual charity would reign everywhere,"[66] because all wills are attuned to the same precept of an enduring common purpose which encompasses the true interests of the whole. Unity follows from cooperation, and cooperation stems from the existence of a good shared by the entire community and each of its members.

A question remains, however, about what constitutes the substance of the common good of the body politic. How is the public welfare to be realized? In the physical organism, the joint purpose is achieved by the maintenance of the health of the whole body.[67] Analogously, John contends that the "health" of the body politic, the public welfare, is coextensive with the dissemination of justice throughout the organs and members. John's actual definition of the

---

Quae si defuerit, hominum frustra sibi congruunt opera, cum dolus in perniciem pergat sine affectu proficiendi."

61   Ibid. 6.24, ed. Webb, vol. 2, p. 73, trans. Dickinson, p. 257: "...omnium utilitatem attende."
62   Ibid. 6.20, ed. Webb, vol. 2, p. 59, trans. Dickinson, p. 243: "...ad publicam utilitatem omnia referantur."
63   Ibid. 6.24, ed. Webb, vol. 2, p. 71, trans. Dickinson, p. 256: "Omnia denique membra publicis inuigilant commodis..."
64   Ibid. 6.22, ed. Webb, vol. 2, p. 62, trans. Dickinson, p. 62: "Omnium namque laborem communem agnosces et neminem otiari..." John's source for this account of Carthage is Virgil, *Aeneid* 1. 420–436.
65   *Policraticus* 5.20, ed. Webb, vol. 2, p. 59, trans. Dickinson, p. 244: "...ut singula sint quasi aliorum ad inuicem membra et in eo sibi quisque maxime credat esse consultum in quo aliis utilius nouerit esse prospectum."
66   Ibid. 6.29, ed. Webb, vol. 2, p. 86, trans. Dickinson, p. 276: "...regnante undique mutua caritate..."
67   See Takashi Shogimen and Cary J. Nederman, "The Best Medicine? Medical Education, Practice and Metaphor in John of Salisbury's *Policraticus* and *Metalogicon*," *Viator: Medieval and Renaissance Studies* 42 (2011), 55–74.

common good in terms of justice is simultaneously imbedded in a recognition of a correlative obligation on the part of all members of the commonwealth: "So long as the duties (*officia*) of each individual are performed with an eye to the advantage of the whole, as long, that is, as justice is practiced, the sweetness of honey pervades the allotted sphere of all."[68] Every organ of the body must conduct itself according to the dictates of justice if the polity is to exist as a corporate unity. All other public goods flow from the presence of justice in the corporate totality, and none of the collateral benefits of human society are possible in the absence of that equity which is the product of the just will.

It may still be unclear why John would make justice the touchstone of the political organism's common good. The answer has much to do with the very manner in which John defines justice. Following Cicero's definition in *De officiis* 1. 7. 23, the *Policraticus* asserts, "It is agreed that justice consists chiefly of not doing harm and of prohibiting out of duty to humanity those who seek to do harm. When you do harm, you assent to injury. And when you do not impede those who seek to do harm, you then serve injustice."[69] The essence of justice pertains to a responsibility toward others; this responsibility is not simply constituted by a negative obligation to refrain from the commission of injury, but also entails a positive duty to protect others from harm as well. To behave in accordance with justice requires one both to ensure that one's own acts do not threaten the good of others and to attend to the injurious actions that other people may commit. Justice is thus inherently productive of social cooperation, whereas injustice necessarily tends to human disharmony and social disintegration. Nor does John believe that justice is a virtue the cultivation of which is best left to a few individuals. Rather, he contends that justice is rooted in the Christian teaching of the golden rule: "Justice…in all things does to others that which it desires to have others do to it."[70] Any truly faithful Christian is as a consequence obliged to perform just deeds. Yet John's defense of justice as a generalized virtue is not limited solely to a theological context. In line with his effusive praise of Trajan, whom he regards as the most virtuous of pagan rulers, John also propounds a secular conception of moral psychology

---

68   *Policraticus* 5.22, ed. Webb, vol. 2, p. 63, trans. Dickinson, p. 247: "…dum sic coluntur officia singulorum ut uniuersitati prospiciatur, dum iustitia colitur, fines omnium mellea dulcedo perfundit."

69   Ibid. 4.12, ed. Webb, vol. 1, p. 277, trans. Dickinson, p. 59: "In eo autem maxime constat iustitia, si non noceas et ex officio humanitatis prohibeas nocentes. Cum uero noces, accedis ad iniuriam. Cum nocentes non impedis, iniustitiae famularis."

70   Ibid. 4.12, ed. Webb, vol. 1, p. 277, trans. Dickinson, p. 58: "…iustitia…usquequaque faciens alii quod faciendorum uellet ab alio fieri sibi ipsi."

through which John can explain how justice may be acquired by every human soul. According to John, justice is like all other virtues in the sense that it is an ingrained disposition (*habitus*) which is created by assiduous practice.[71] Hence, it is possible for any person to become just by fashioning and shaping one's character in a rigorous manner. In short, justice in its temporal aspect is treated by John as a moral quality for which all persons are equally suited.

John's approach to justice has important repercussions for his theory of the body politic. Since the exercise of justice is the salient characteristic of a polity oriented toward the common good, justice must determine the manner in which each of the bodily members performs its functions. This is obvious in the case of the king, who is regarded to be the chief purveyor of justice. The royal will must unfailingly perform just acts and promote universal equity through the promulgation of law, as addressed above in the discussion of kingship. Yet John's emphasis on the justice of the head by no means precludes the other members of the body from playing a significant role in the actualization of a just polity. It is the dissemination of responsibility for justice that leads John to declare that "every magistrate is but the slave of justice."[72] Unjust men ought to be excluded from among the advisors who form the heart, since the king must be guided only by those who place the safety of the commonwealth above their own profit.[73] Likewise, the senses, composing judicial officials, are expected to be diligent in "the administration of justice among the provincials."[74] No less than the king himself, such magistrates "are bound to justice by their profession or by an oath."[75] We must consequently apply to these public servants the same rigorous standards regarding the performance of justice that were imposed upon the prince. Nor are the hands exempted from a duty to realize a just community. John describes the unarmed hand of the tax collector as "that which administers justice,"[76] while he reserves for the warrior's armed hand the authority to render just determinations effectual. Soldiers "execute

---

71   On this theme in John's work generally, see Cary N. Nederman, "Nature, Ethics and the Doctrine of *Habitus*: Aristotelian Moral Psychology in the Twelfth Century," *Traditio* 45 (1989/90), 87–110 at pp. 98–103.

72   *Policraticus* 5.11, ed. Webb, vol. 1, p. 333, trans. Dickinson, p. 126: "Omnis etenim magistratus iustitiae famulus est."

73   See ibid. 5.9, ed. Webb, vol. 1, pp. 321–322.

74   Ibid. 5.11, ed. Webb, vol. 1, p. 330, trans. Dickinson, p. 123: "…in iure reddendo prouincialibus praesidet."

75   Ibid. 5.17, ed. Webb, vol. 1, p. 367, trans. Dickinson, p. 166: "…iudicibus…qui professione aut sacramento iustitiae obligati sunt…"

76   Ibid. 6.26, ed. Webb, vol. 2, p. 79, trans. Dickinson, p. 166: "…eruantur abscidantur et procul eiciantur…"

the judgment that is committed to them to execute...in accordance with equity and the public utility...As it is for judges to pronounce judgment, so it so for these to perform their office by executing it."[77] Even the feet are accorded a measure of obligation towards fostering the dictates of justice. The proper health of the body requires that the "lower [members] respond faithfully...to the just (*iure*) demands of their superiors."[78] The obedience of the feet is limited to the performance of their functions consistent with the precept of rectitude that forms the common good. By implication at least, the feet ought to refuse what is unjustly asked of them by the rest of the body.

The effect of John's argument is the wide diffusion of responsibility for the maintenance of justice: all members of the body politic are ultimately charged with guarding and protecting the common good. This represents an important innovation in medieval political thought. John's predecessors (and indeed, many of his successors) had tended to attribute the duty for the promotion of justice wholly to the monarch. The *Policraticus*, on the other hand, describes a commonwealth in which the greater and lesser parts cooperate in the dissemination of justice within the total community; none is exempt. From head to toe, the political organism must be disposed to the performance of justice if it is to survive. John's version of the organic metaphor thus represents a thorough account of how the organs and limbs necessary to the body are coordinated when each member is fully attuned to the practice of justice.

The Theory of Tyrannicide

A considerable proportion of John's reputation as a political theorist rests on his apparent (and controversial) advocacy of the legitimacy of political violence, in the form of his doctrine of tyrannicide. The ascription of a theory of tyrannicide to John rests primarily on two pieces of evidence. The first is his insistence (in the context of his discussion of courtly flattery, addressed above) that it is lawful, right and just to take the life of a tyrant. The second consideration stems from his extensive citation of historical cases of tyrants who, by virtue of their tyrannical conduct, met with painful or violent ends. One might doubt that such evidence could actually amount to a full and proper theory.

---

77   Ibid. 6.8, ed. Webb, vol. 2, p. 23, trans. Dickinson, pp. 199–200: "...faciant in eis iudicium conscriptum ...ex aequitate et publica utilitate...sicut iudicum dictare iudicium, ita et istorum faciendo exercere officium est."

78   Ibid. 6.20, ed. Webb, vol. 2, p. 59, trans. Dickinson, p. 244: "...inferiora superioribus pari iure respondeant..."

This is an old suspicion. The pre-humanist Coluccio Salutati had expressed misgivings about John's "theory" in the 14th century: "The learned John of Salisbury...[who] declares that it is right to kill a tyrant and tries to prove this by a multitude of illustrations, seems to me to reach no such result. His illustrations prove, not that the murder of tyrants is right, but that it is frequent."[79] More recently, scholars have renewed the challenge to the interpretation of John's writing as a theoretical source of the view that tyrants ought to be slain. For instance, Jan van Laarhoven declares of tyrannicide that "John does not have such a theory. John has a praxis...and he draws only one conclusion: tyrants come to a miserable end."[80] For van Laarhoven, we ought to drop all discussion of tyrannicide and speak instead of John's "tyrannology," that is, his account of how tyrants actually live and die.[81] Even if John makes the additional moral judgment that tyrants deserve the end they get, we are still not to impute to the *Policraticus* a theoretical defense of the justifiability of slaying a tyrant. Van Laarhoven represents a statement of pronounced skepticism about John's adherence to a doctrine of tyrannicide.

Before we dismiss John completely as a genuine theorist of tyrannicide, however, we ought perhaps to examine whether there is any validity in this interpretation of his conception of tyranny. A careful appraisal indicates that there is still some wisdom in a reading of John's doctrine of tyrannicide that connects his discussions of tyrant slaying to the political ideas contained in the remainder of the *Policraticus*. When we view the doctrine of tyrannicide as a feature or logical consequence of John's political thought as a whole, it becomes clear that he did mean for his readers to conclude that – at least under fixed conditions – it is right and proper to employ force against a tyrant. More specifically, we may locate the theoretical root of tyrannicide in John's unique application of the organic metaphor to depict the political community. John's treatment of tyrannicide suggests that he meant for the doctrine not to stand on its own, but to be seen as a direct and inescapable corollary of his understanding of the polity as an animate entity. It is this aspect of John's argument that for better or worse ultimately vindicates his reputation as a theoritician of political violence.

The first intimation of a connection between John's discussion of tyrannicide and his conception of the body politic appears in Book 3 of the *Policraticus*.

---

79   Coluccio Salutati, "De Tyranno," in Ephraim Emerton, ed., *Humanism and Tyranny: Studies in the Italian Trecento* (Cambridge, MA, 1925), p. 90.

80   Jan van Laarhoven, "Thou Shall *Not* Slay a Tyrant! The So-called Theory of John of Salisbury," in *The World of John of Salisbury*, pp. 319–341, at p. 328.

81   Ibid., p. 329.

As already noted, John's reference to the doctrine of tyrannicide occurs there within the context of his treatment of flattery. This may seem an odd place to assert the legitimacy of slaying the tyrant. John's immediate purpose in invoking the idea is, as we have seen, to demonstrate that while flattery is ordinarily evil, it is not always so. John believes that to flatter a tyrant is to protect oneself and one's community from the wrath and vengefulness that might guide the tyrannical ruler's reaction to honest advice. If through flattery and dissimulation one may turn a tyrant away from an evil policy, or at least mitigate the effects of such evil, then one has a clear obligation to do so, according to John. After all, John regarded the tyrant to be evil incarnate, the *imago prauitatis*, to whom no respect or subservience is owed by the good man. Hence, one must employ for the sake of the whole polity those means to which one has access, including flattery, in order to deflect the debilitating and sinful consequences of tyrannical rule.

As part of his "proof" for the validity of this claim, John cites tyrannicide as part of the argument from Book 3 quoted above. On initial consideration of this passage, it does not seem to constitute much of a defense of tyrannicide. Rather, as van Laarhoven has correctly pointed out, what John actually presents is a syllogism of which the principle of the propriety of tyrannicide is the minor premise (the major premise is that whoever may be slain may be flattered).[82] The conclusion of the syllogism is that one may flatter a tyrant – precisely what we would expect in the context of the section in which the argument appears. To suppress the syllogistic character of John's remarks is to distort seriously the significance of his reference to the legitimacy of slaying a tyrant. Rather, tyrannicide appears merely to be assumed for the sake of justifying the use of flattery upon the tyrant. But we ought not to neglect the fact that John does attempt to give some foundation to the minor premise of his syllogism in the same section of Book 3. He goes on to explain that the tyrant whom one may flatter is the usurper, the servant not of God but of his own will.[83] To be a usurper, in this sense, is not merely to ascend to the throne by illegitimate means; it is rather to exercise power in accordance with arbitrary will and caprice. This reflects John's emphasis throughout the *Policraticus* upon the characteristic viciousness of the tyrant, who necessarily misuses whatever power he employs, since all authority is from God and therefore good. In consequence, "Respect for the right and the just is either not sufficiently present or else wholly wanting from the face of tyrants."[84] John's assertion is obviously unproblematic in the case of

---

82   Ibid., p. 320.
83   *Policraticus* 3.15, ed. Webb, vol. 1, p. 232.
84   Ibid. 8.17, ed. Webb, vol. 2, p. 347, trans. Dickinson, p. 338: "Ergo respectus honesti et iusti minimus aut nullus est in facie tirannorum..."

so-called private and ecclesiastical tyrants who assail justice and right and must consequently be punished either by the prince or the Church. Such non-public tyrants are, of course, restrained within the confines of human and divine laws and institutions. Indeed, it is in order to deter those who prefer their own will to the public good that law is promulgated and enforced by rulers. By contrast, the public tyrant poses a special difficulty: Who may impose upon the vicious ruler the law which it is his duty to proclaim and execute over the whole community?

John evinces a clear awareness of the dimensions of this problem in Book 3. He suggests that we might fruitfully reconceptualize tyranny on the order of the "crime of *majesté*," that is, treasonous behavior against a superior. Under the law pertaining to *majesté*, John remarks, "it is permissible for all to prosecute those charged with the crime of majesty."[85] In stating this, John merely repeats the customary legal precept that anyone (even a woman or a serf) may lay and testify to the charge of treason.[86] But John imparts to this concept new force by adding the proviso that public tyranny ought to be understood as the ultimate treason, a crime against the very body of justice (*corpus iustitiae*). When viewed from this perspective, John argues, "Not only do tyrants commit a crime against the public, but, if it is possible, more than the public."[87] In other words, since justice is ultimately a divinely endowed or inspired gift to a political community, to offend against justice itself (the crime of the tyrant) is to attack God's will as well as to assault the body politic. This imputes to everyone concerned with the performance of justice the authority to act against, to prosecute, the tyrant by the appropriate means. Fear of retribution cannot excuse hesitation: "Truly there will be no one to avenge a public enemy," since the tyrant is the friend of none nor does he enjoy any just claim on loyalty. In short, the public tyrant must be opposed by all who can do so. Indeed, John describes the removal of the tyrant in terms of a duty, an obligation: "Whoever does not prosecute [the tyrant] sins against himself and against the whole body of the secular republic (*in totum rei publicae mundanae corpus*)."[88] So John does not regard tyrannicide as a matter of choice for the individual; it is

---

85   Ibid. 3.15, ed. Webb, vol. 1, p. 233, trans. Pike, p. 212: "...crimen maiestatis omnes persecutores admittit..."

86   For a more thorough discussion of *majesté*, see ibid. 6. 25, ed. Webb, vol. 2, pp. 75–77.

87   Ibid. 3.15, ed. Webb, vol. 1, p. 233, trans. Pike, p. 212: "Tirannis ergo non modo publicum crimen sed, si fieri posset, plus quam publicum est."

88   Ibid. 3.15, ed. Webb, vol. 1, p. 233, trans. Pike, p. 212: "Certe hostem publicum nemo ulciscitur, et quisquis eum non persequitur, in seipsum et in totum rei publicae mundanae corpus delinquit."

instead an obligation which is incumbent upon every member of the community. In turn, those who renounce their duty are complicit in tyranny. This is the sense in which recalcitrant individuals commit a crime against themselves as well as the polity: they affront justice (and thereby God) by refusing to do what right demands of them.

John's argument in the third book of the *Policraticus* goes no further. In particular, he does not articulate any theoretical foundation for the obligation to oppose tyranny that he imputes to all members of the community. But by referring to the corporate "body" of the secular state, and by associating it with the *corpus iustitiae*, John directs his reader's attention to the fifth and sixth books of the *Policraticus*, wherein he presents his theory of the body politic in terms of the organic metaphor. The implication is clear: if we seek to understand why every person in the polity is obliged to oppose the tyrant even to the point of slaying the oppressor, then we must turn to the organic conception of the secular community. In turn, John's refusal to equate the performance of justice with the specialized activity of the monarch has profound implications for his doctrine of tyrannicide. Viewed in the light of his presentation of the organic metaphor, John contends that since cooperation between the parts of the body is achieved through the disposition of each member toward the practice of justice in the whole, the organs and limbs have an obligation to resist the disease of injustice when it threatens to infect the organism. Ordinarily, the enforcement of justice is achieved through the application of the laws within which the path of equity is found, insofar as tyrants are normally of the private variety. In such cases, the head and members act in concert to render just judgment and its execution. But on some occasions the ruler may be tainted by injustice, revealing himself to possess the moral characteristics of the tyrant instead of the true king. At such times, it becomes impossible to impose the law upon the ruler, because he is himself its source and final judge. Thus, extralegal remedies need to be introduced.

Recognition of a cogent theoretical foundation for John's doctrine of tyrannicide does not, however, resolve all outstanding interpretive difficulties. It might reasonably be asked whether John has consistently or coherently applied this theory in the more substantial discussion of tyranny and tyrannicide contained within seven chapters of Book 8. Scholars have long pointed out that the purpose of this section was not really to demonstrate the legitimacy of tyrannicide.[89] Rather, John's aim was to show that all tyrants come to a bad end, and do so at the behest of God Himself. Tyrants may be slain in battle, or

---

89   See Richard H. and Mary A. Rouse, "John of Salisbury and the Doctrine of Tyrannicide,"
       Speculum 42 (1967), 693–709 at pp. 703–704, 709.

struck down by natural disaster, or even die at an old age in bed – but every tyrant can expect punishment of the most horrific sort administered directly by the divine will, whether solely in the afterlife or in this life as well.[90] In consequence, John regards the killing of a tyrant by one of his subjects to number among several possible fates which may accord with the plan of God's justice. "Wickedness is always punished by the Lord," the *Policraticus* proclaims, "but sometimes it is His own, and at other times it is a human hand, which He employs as a weapon with which to impose punishment upon the unrighteous."[91] Ultimately, John maintains, the way in which the tyrant meets his bad end depends upon the determination of God, although repentance and prayer may hasten the implementation of divine judgment.

The sovereignty of the divine will raises the question of whether any theory of tyrannicide is meaningful when men are viewed merely as God's instruments. How can there be room left for independent human discretion when all legitimate cases of tyrannicide are seen to be directed by and subject to a divine plan? We must take care not to interpret John's remarks about the instrumentality of human action too literally. The *Policraticus* manifests a highly developed conception of man's liberty and free will, as we have seen. John would seem to believe that God works through human hands when men freely accede to the divine will and serve it accordingly. To understand this perspective, we must acknowledge the dual significance of justice in John's thought. On the one hand, the performance of justice by each member of the political body is vital to the maintenance of the stable reciprocal structure from which all the material and secular benefits of communal life flow. Yet, on the other hand, justice in John's account retains an ultimate spiritual significance. While just deeds have their reward on earth, they are also steps on the path to otherworldly salvation. Thus, John advocates what one might term the "unity of justice": Those whose wills are just shall be "translated from riches to riches, from delights to delights, from things temporal to things eternal."[92] In other words, justice constitutes both the key to happiness in the present world and the assurance (insofar as true justice is inseparable from faith) of eternal beatitude. The common good shared by members of the political organism is therefore not, broadly speaking, ultimately distinct from the religious goals of the body of Christian believers.

---

90   *Policraticus* 8.21, ed. Webb, vol. 2, pp. 379–381.
91   Ibid. 8.21, ed. Webb, vol. 2, p. 379, trans. Dickinson, p. 375: "Punitur autem malitia semper a Domino; sed interdum suo, interdum quasi hominis utitur telo in penam impiorum."
92   Ibid. 4.10, ed. Webb, vol. 1, p. 268, trans. Dickinson, p. 47: "...de diuitiis ad diuitias, de deliciis ad delicias, de gloria ad gloriam principes transferantur, de temporalibus ad eterna?"

The inescapable conclusion of the fundamental unity of justice is that the man who performs just deeds in the context of the Christian republic additionally reserves his place in heaven. This would seem to be the sense in which John remarks that God sometimes employs a human hand in eliminating tyrants: the man who commits tyrannicide does the bidding of God by imitating the divine will in the practice of justice. The secular obligation that members of the body politic acquire to serve the dictates of justice is paralleled by their divinely-ordained duty to live in accordance with God's righteous law. When viewed in this manner, John's survey of the final disposition of various tyrants may be regarded as a casebook filled with illustrations of, generally speaking, how divine retribution is the end of tyranny and, more specifically, how parts of the political organism that do their duty according to the requirements of temporal justice also fulfill their responsibilities to God. Where the third book of the *Policraticus* had defended the justifiability of tyrannicide in mainly secular terms, John's return in Book 8 to the theme of slaying the tyrant makes explicit reference to the theological context of this theory. The convergence between justice in the polity and divine justice does not negate, but rather reaffirms, his theory of tyrannicide.

That John intended his audience to draw a connection between the secular organic metaphor and his theologically-informed treatment of the bad ends of tyrants is clear from the text of Book 8. At the beginning of his discussion of tyranny, he refers the reader to his previous survey of "the duties of the prince and of the different members of the commonwealth." Review of that passage, John contends, renders it "easier to make known here, and in fewer words, the opposite characteristics of the tyrant."[93] John envisages the qualities of the well-ordered body politic to be the reverse image of the characteristics of the polity ruled by the tyrant. A society which allows a tyrant free reign and affords no resistance to his dictates resembles nothing so much as a deformed and monstrous creature. John refers in this regard to "the commonwealth of the ungodly" which "has also its head and members, and strives to correspond, as it were, to the civil institutions of a legitimate commonwealth. The tyrant who is its head is the likeness of the devil; its soul consists of heretical, schismatic and sacrilegious priests...; its heart of unrighteous counselors is like a senate of iniquity; its eyes, ears, tongue and unarmed hand are unjust judges, lawyers and officials; its armed hand consists of soldiers of violence whom Cicero calls brigands; its feet are those in the humbler walks of life who go against the

---

93   Ibid. 8.17, ed. Webb, vol. 2, p. 345, trans. Dickinson, p. 335: "...superius dictum est et quae principis sint officia aut rei publicae membra diligenter expositum. Vnde facilius et paucioribus poterunt innotescere quae e regione dicenda sunt de tiranno."

precepts of the Lord and His lawful institutions."[94] The irreligious polity thus inverts all of the features of the political body ordered according to justice. Licentious self-interest pervades the deformed body; the mutual and reciprocal service typical of the well-arranged organism is replaced by the Epicurean gratification of personal pleasures and passions. If the perverted body coheres at all – if, in other words, it does not merely disintegrate from internal conflict – then it does so only because of the superior coercive force of its tyrannical head. In such a monstrosity there can be no truly shared or unifying principle of communal organization.

Hence John expresses confidence that the slaying of a tyrant is legitimate, so long as the act has been performed "without loss of religion or honor... tyrants ought to be removed from our midst."[95] Certainly, one way of ridding the republic of a tyrant is for its members "to pray devoutly that the scourge with which they are afflicted may be turned aside from them."[96] The reason that this approach is considered preferable is that human judgment, while it may approximate divine justice, is nevertheless potentially fallible in a way that God's will is not. But should the perpetuation of the tyrant's rule endanger the communal welfare, justice (in both its earthly and heavenly aspects) dictates that he be slain. As noted before, the tyrant has in such circumstances become a "public enemy," an outlaw, who may be killed without hesitation or remorse. Exactly as the outlaw rebels against the just laws of his land, so the tyrant may be understood as "a rebel against God," preferring his own patrimony to divine justice.[97] To the extent that this equation is valid, so too is John's conclusion: "If it is lawful to kill a condemned enemy, then it is [lawful] to kill a tyrant."[98] The tyrant is indeed an enemy on perhaps a grander

---

94   Ibid. 8.17, ed. Webb, vol.2, pp. 348–349, trans. Dickinson, p. 339: "Habet enim et res publica impiorum caput et membra sua, et quasi ciuilibus institutis legittimae rei publicae nititur esse conformis. Caput ergo eius tirannus est imago diaboli; anima heretici scismatici sacrilegi sacerdotes et, ut uerbo Plutarchi utar, praefecti religionis, impugnantes legem Domini; cor consiliarii impii, quasi senatus iniquitatis; oculi, aures, lingua, manus inermis, iudices et leges, officiales iniusti; manus armata, milites uiolenti, quos Cicero latrones appellat; pedes qui in ipsis humilioribus negotiis praeceptis Domini et legittimis institutis aduersantur."

95   Ibid. 8.20, vol. 2, p. 378, trans. Dickinson, p. 373: "Non quod tirannos de medio tollendos esse non credam sed sine religionis honestatisque dispendio."

96   Ibid. 8.20, ed. Webb, vol. 2, p. 378, trans. Dickinson, p. 373: "...deuotis precibus flagellum quo affliguntur auertant."

97   Ibid. 8.22, ed. Webb, vol. 2, p. 398, trans. Dickinson, p. 395: "...in Deum...insurgere."

98   Ibid. 8.19, ed. Webb, vol. 2, p. 371, trans. Dickinson, p. 364: "Sicut ergo dampnatum hostem licet occidere, sic tirannum."

scale; his offense is not against one or a few laws, but against the very idea of law as a manifestation of justice. In sum, toleration of the tyrant must ultimately be tempered according to the extent of his harmfulness to the political organism. John is thus quite consistent in advocating patience where possible, but tyrannicide when necessary. Nor need one fear divine retribution; God surely confirms and even rewards the just determinations of human beings in such matters. When humans will what is truly just, they reveal themselves to be created in the divine image and are at one with their holy master.

It is noteworthy that the way in which tyrannicide must occur has to be strictly consistent with the reason for which it is practiced, namely, in accordance with justice in the community and the will of God.[99] John insists that the theory thereby specifies the conduct (or range of conduct) acceptable in carrying out the deed. In order to achieve a just goal, in other words, one can only use a just means. Justice is a measuring stick against which may be judged the rectitude of various particular instances of tyrant-slaying. Thus, John asserts that oaths or bonds of fealty claim priority over the duty to slay a tyrannical ruler: "None should undertake the death of a tyrant who is bound to him by an oath or an obligation of fealty."[100] The reason is that such pledges are private covenants vouchsafed before God himself and do not depend upon other considerations for their performance. One is as bound to keep a sworn promise to a wicked man as to a good one. This is the only principle of promise consistent with justice, and it is one John's contemporaries would well have understood. Similar considerations of justice lead John to proscribe the use of poison as a method of slaying the tyrant. It is on this point that the distance between John's theoretical defense of tyrannicide and his historical examples is most apparent. In his litany of the ends of Roman emperors, John mentions several tyrants who died by the poisoner's art.[101] Initially, he passes such information to his reader without additional comment. But he later judges poison to conflict with the terms under which tyrannicide is justly committed: "As for the use of poison, although I see it sometimes wrongfully adopted by infidels, I do not read that it is ever

---

99   John's quintessential example of tyrannicide performed justly and piously is the biblical Judith's murder of the tyrant Holofernes. See Karen Bollermann and Cary J. Nederman, "The Sword in Her Hand: Judith as Anglo-Saxon Warrior and John of Salisbury's Tyrant Slayer," in Gianluca Briguglia and Thomas Ricklin, eds., *Thinking Politics in the Vernacular from the Middle Ages to the Renaissance* (Fribourg, 2011), pp. 23–41.

100 *Policraticus* 8.20, ed. Webb, vol. 2, p. 378, trans. Dickinson, pp. 372–373: "...ne quis illius moliatur interitum cui fidei aut sacramenti religione tenetur astrictus."

101 Ibid. 8.19, ed. Webb, vol. 2, p. 366.

permitted by any law."[102] John's argument is not that the poisoning of tyrants is unprecedented, but that it is unjust. John's refusal to sanction poison as a just method of tyrannicide points to his view that the theory itself dictates not only the worthiness of the end, but also the range of means which might appropriately be employed to fulfill the goal. The rectitude of methods for the accomplishment of tyrannicide cannot be determined merely by a study of previous cases. The requirements of justice are discovered solely through philosophical and religious reflection.

We would, however, be unjustified in asserting that the conception of tyrannicide in the *Policraticus* was merely theoretical, in the sense that it lacked any practical import. John's references to the historical practice of tyrannicide, and his discussion of the relationship between ends and means, suggest his approval of actual opposition to tyranny. Perhaps more significantly, the theory itself stipulates the penalties for the refusal to do one's duty: not only does recalcitrance do serious harm to the body politic and to the justice for which it stands, but it is also an implicit affront to God. To accede to the rule of a tyrant, and thereby to participate in the "commonwealth of the ungodly," is the mark of a weak, sinful and impious people; to seek the tyrant's removal is a sign of righteousness and virtue among the populace. By fashioning his account of tyrannicide in terms of virtue, and by specifying the consequences of declining to act on one's obligation, John makes abundantly clear his confidence that tyrants will be slain in the future as they have been in the past. The function of John's remarks in the *Policraticus* was not to incite individuals to commit any particular act of tyrannicide, but rather to articulate the theoretical premises of such behavior through the demonstration of a duty to slay a tyrant when circumstances dictate. Nor would someone familiar with the general tenor of John's career and thought expect a different conclusion. As in so many facets of John's intellectual life, theory and practice ultimately merge. John could not abide dry scholastic exercises any more than the complete absence of philosophical reflection. For him philosophy was only really valuable as a guide to a virtuous and honorable life, as an instrument rather than an end in itself.[103] The case of the doctrine of tyrannicide is illustrative of this general intellectual orientation. Theory is necessary if one is to know how to treat a tyrant consistent with the precepts of justice. But theory is barren except insofar as it eventually intersects with and enriches practice. John of Salisbury's doctrine of tyrannicide is neither mere philosophical fancy nor a vague warning to tyrants.

---

102   Ibid. 8.20, ed. Webb, vol. 2, p. 378, trans. Dickinson, p. 373: "Sed nec ueneni, licet uideam ab infidelibus aliquando usurpatam, ullo umquam iure indultam lego licentiam."

103   On this point more generally, see Nederman, *John of Salisbury*, pp. 41–43, 86.

It is instead a challenge to members of the body politic to perform their duty to God and commonwealth when the situation requires it.

Conclusion

What we find reflected in the *Policraticus*, then, is a bold and often innovative (despite its author's wishes) attempt to weave together the still relatively embryonic European knowledge of ancient philosophy with pressing concerns about secular and religous in the early stages of discovering and articulating their foundations and legitimating principles. The *Policraticus* has sometimes been criticized for its general "messiness," in the sense that it fails to conform to classical norms of philosophical argumentation. But, as scholars rightly point out, its *sui generis* character reflects the simple fact that John of Salisbury lacked a clear model or precedent in the ancient tradition of political theorizing on which to base his own efforts.[104] Indeed, as we have seen, John's very invention of one such source – the pseudo-Plutarchian "Instruction of Trajan" – suggests precisely the dilemma in which he found himself. Thus, the fact that John was able to resuscitate so many of the key themes of classical political thought on the basis of such fragmentary evidence must be held to his credit. From another perspective, however, one might speculate that, should John have enjoyed access to one or more of the major political writings of pagan antiquity, he might have been more constrained and less creative in his analysis of the events and institutions of his time. Lacking such a pre-existing archetype, John was relatively unencumbered in molding the "giants" of the past to the problems of 12th-century politics. The feature of John's political theory that some may regard as its primary weakness – its unsystematic quality in comparison with the philosophical rigor of the major Greco-Roman thinkers – perhaps proves after all to be among the greatest strengths of the *Policraticus*.

---

104   Suggested by both David Luscombe, "The Twelfth Century Renaissance," in J.H. Burns, ed., *The Cambridge History of Medieval Political Thought, c.300-c.1450* (Cambridge, 1988), p. 326 and Canning, *A History of Medieval Political Thought*, p. 111.

CHAPTER 9

John of Salisbury on Science and Knowledge

David Bloch

Introduction and Background

Knowledge is by nature uncertain. This is something that John of Salisbury strongly believes, and it has profound consequences for his general views on science and knowledge.[1] John considers himself an Academic skeptic and as such certain knowledge is unobtainable,[2] except by the intervention by God.[3] On the other hand, John of Salisbury is apparently the first thinker of the 12th century to incorporate the newly rediscovered Aristotelian *Organon* in his views on knowledge, science and education. The *Metalogicon* is particularly concerned with adopting Aristotle's theories, most of which seem to be considered – by Aristotle as well as by John – the foundation of science, knowledge and education. But Aristotle himself was not a skeptic, so John faced a difficult task, to combine his skepticism with an Aristotelian theory of science and knowledge.[4]

The 12th Century and Aristotle

If one looks at the works of some of John's contemporaries, or near contemporaries, they are at first glance strikingly different. First, in some works, for instance Hugh of Saint-Victor's *Didascalicon*,[5] Aristotle is not at all prominent. In the writings of some of John's most cherished teachers, like Abelard and

---

1   *Metalogicon* 1, prologus, p. 11. See also *Policraticus* 7. 1, ed. Webb, pp. 93–95.
2   *Metalogicon* 1, prologus, p. 11, 2. 13, p. 76, 2. 20, pp. 91–92, 3, prologus, p. 102; *Policraticus* ed. Keats-Rohan, 1, prologus, pp. 25–26, 2. 22, p. 122; *Policraticus*, ed. Webb, 7, prologus, p. 93. On John's skepticism, see Christophe Grellard, "Jean de Salisbury. Un cas médiéval de scepticisme," *Freiburger Zeitschrift für Philosophie und Theologie* 54 (2007), 16–40, and, in particular, idem, *Jean de Salisbury et la renaissance médiévale du scepticisme* (Paris, 2013).
3   *Metalogicon* 4. 37, pp. 176–177, 4. 39, pp. 178–179.
4   For a comprehensive presentation of the argument set forth in this article, see David Bloch, *John of Salisbury on Aristotelian Science* (Turnhout, 2012).
5   *Hugonis de Sancto Victore Didascalicon de studio legendi*, ed. Charles Henry Buttimer (Washington, 1939).

Gilbert of Poitiers, Aristotle may be important, but it is *not* for his *logica noua*. In fact, the texts of this "new logic" play no role as is clear, for instance, in Abelard's great handbook of dialectic,[6] which is dominated by the "old logic."[7] Second, Academic skepticism finds no place in their works either, although they would have known the position from Cicero and Augustine. John of Salisbury is virtually unique among 12th-century thinkers in discussing the entire *Organon* and in adopting a skeptical stance.[8]

Scholars of the early 12th century knew Aristotle's *Categories* and *De interpretatione*, but the Philosopher was considered a major authority despite this limited access to his works. Most of the remaining parts of the *Corpus Aristotelicum* were translated in the second quarter of the century, but only logic became influential in the course of the century, and even then not all the works were popular. The *Sophistical Refutations* was read and used with care already in the second quarter of the century. The *Prior Analytics* and the *Topics* were certainly known, but the extent of their influence is still uncertain. The *Posterior Analytics* was little read. Adam of Balsham "Paruipontanus" knew the *Topics* when he wrote his *Ars disserendi* in the 1130s,[9] and Thierry of Chartres' *Heptateuchon*, compiled in the 1140s and containing no excerpts from the *Posterior Analytics*, constitutes the first real evidence that the "new logic" was part of the scholarly discussions.[10] A number of anonymous commentaries on the *Sophistical Refutations*, all of which are difficult to date but certainly written at some time between 1140 and 1200, suggest more than casual knowledge of the new Aristotle, but the depth is difficult to determine. We are not familiar with thorough discussions of the new Aristotelian texts in

---

6   *Petrus Abaelardus: Dialectica, First Complete Edition of the Parisian Manuscript with an Introduction*, ed. Lambert Marie De Rijk, second edition (Assen, 1970, first edition 1956).

7   On the "old logic" (*logica vetus*), see Sten Ebbesen, "Ancient Scholastic Logic as the Source of Medieval Scholastic Logic," in Norman Kretzmann, Anthony Kenny, and Jan Pinborg, eds., *The Cambridge History of Later Medieval Philosophy: From the Rediscovery of Aristotle to the Disintegration of Scholasticism, 1100–1600* (Cambridge, 1982).

8   On medieval skepticism and its rarity, see Henrik Lagerlund, "A History of Skepticism in the Middle Ages," in Henrik Lagerlund, ed., *Rethinking the History of Skepticism: The Missing Medieval Background* (Leiden, 2010), pp. 1–28.

9   Adam of Balsham, *Twelfth Century Logic: Texts and Studies, I: Adam Balsamiensis Parvipontani, Ars disserendi (Dialectica Alexandri)*, ed. Lorenzo Minio-Paluello (Rome, 1956).

10   Gillian Rosemary Evans, "The Uncompleted *Heptateuch* of Thierry of Chartres," *History of Universities* 3 (1983), 1–13; Charles Burnett, "The Contents and Affiliation of the Scientific Manuscripts Written at, or Brought to, Chartres in the Time of John of Salisbury," in *The World of John of Salisbury*, pp. 127–160; Bloch, *John of Salisbury on Aristotelian Science*, appendix 2.

the 1130s and 1140s. John of Salisbury has in fact the most explicit 12th-century treatment of these works that were to become so influential in the 13th century.[11]

Aristotle's views on knowledge (Greek ἐπιστήμη, Latin *scientia*) are set forth primarily in the *Posterior Analytics*. In this text, he deals with real knowledge, that is, the one based on premises that are "true, primary, immediate, and better known than, prior to, and causes of the conclusion."[12] This kind of knowledge he calls "demonstrative" (Greek ἀποδεικτική, Latin *demonstratiua*), and it is based on the formal deductions (Greek συλλογισμοί, Latin *syllogismi*) that are analyzed in *Prior Analytics*. Such knowledge must be universal, that is, it can not be about particulars; it must be absolutely and necessarily true in the sense that it can never have been, be or become false; the knowing subject must be absolutely certain and convinced that it is true;[13] and it must state an essential relationship between subject and predicate. These are only some of the very strict demands that an Aristotelian theory of knowledge must, and can, fulfill. It is obvious that a consistent Academic skeptic could never accept this.

The demands of dialectic as described in Aristotle's *Topics* are less strict. Dialectic is based on "generally accepted premises/opinions" (Greek ἔνδοξα, Latin *probabilia*), and it produces probable knowledge. It does not provide ἐπιστήμη/*scientia* proper, but the result is not pseudo-knowledge either, the latter being described and analyzed in the *Sophistical Refutations*. Dialectic is, one might say, the more Socratic method, since it is characterized by being essentially a dialogue or discussion. This means that in all cases one has to accept and use, or refute, the propositions put forward by the opponent, either a real opponent or one that has been mentally constructed in order to have an internal dialogue. The immediate goal is to win the argument, but, if the discussion has been properly conducted, the participants will also have progressed

---

11   Robert Pasnau, "Science and Certainty," in Robert Pasnau and Christina van Dyke, eds., *The Cambridge History of Medieval Philosophy*, 2 vols. (Cambridge, 2010), vol. 1, pp. 357–368.

12   Aristotle, *Analytica Priora*, trans. Iacobi, ed. Lorenzo Minio-Paluello and Bernard Dod (Bruges, 1968), 1. 2, 71b19-23, p. 7: "Si igitur est scire ut posuimus, necesse est et demonstrativam scientiam ex verisque esse et primis et immediatis et notioribus et prioribus et causis conclusionis; sic enim erunt et principia propria ei quod demonstratur."

13   For a discussion of certainty as an attribute of Aristotelian knowledge, see Sten Ebbesen, David Bloch, Jakob Leth Fink, Heine Hansen and Ana María Mora-Márquez, *History of Philosophy in Reverse. Reading Aristotle through the Lenses of Scholars from the Twelfth to the Sixteenth Centuries* (Copenhagen, 2014), pp. 148–165, and David Bloch, "Aristotle on the Exactness or Certainty of Knowledge in *Posterior Analytics* I.27," in a forthcoming volume edited by Börje Bydén & Christina Thomsen Thörnqvist on the reception of Aristotle's works in the Middle Ages.

towards a higher degree of knowledge. Aristotle's *Topics* is to a large extent a guide to those who are to participate in such discussions. Finally, dialectic seems also to have a more basic philosophical function in analyses of scientific principles. Just as a modern science cannot treat its own principles, so Aristotelian demonstration cannot treat demonstrative principles. In order to do this, the philosopher, or scientist, has to use dialectic to ask the relevant questions concerning the principles, at least to make clear where the problems might be.[14]

John of Salisbury and Aristotle

John's *Metalogicon* is the work in which he describes and analyzes the entire *Organon*. Aristotle's *Categories* (*Metalogicon* 3. 2–3) and *De interpretatione* (*Metalogicon* 3. 4), along with Porphyry's *Isagoge* (*Metalogicon* 3. 1), are introductory. They are the fundamentals that have to be learned before one proceeds to the real tools and methods by which one can hope to obtain knowledge. These tools are, according to John, found in *Prior* and *Posterior Analytics*, *Topics* and *Sophistical Refutations*. He announces at the outset (*Metalogicon* 3.5) that he prefers the *Topics*, and later he states that the *Elenchi* must be preferred over the two *Analytics* (*Metalogicon* 4. 24). This is a curious reversal of the roles that scholars have normally attributed to these texts throughout history. Aristotle states at the beginning of *Prior Analytics* that demonstration is the goal of the whole inquiry (*APr.* 1.1, 24a1-2). The Greek commentary tradition called it the "goal" (τέλος) of logic (Philoponus, *In APo.* 3.1-2). And the Latins somehow gained access to this tradition, as is clear from a number of anonymous 12th-century commentaries,[15] and John himself refers to Burgundio of Pisa for the claim that Aristotle earned the honorary title *the* Philosopher because of his theory of demonstration (*Metalogicon* 4. 7).

The first relevant question for the interpreter to ask is, therefore, how well John knows Aristotle's *Organon*. John will make some basic claims that appear

---

14   *Top.* 1. 2, 101a25-b5. However, the precise meaning of this is disputed in modern literature. See Terence Irwin, *Aristotle's First Principles* (Oxford, 1988).

15   See, in particular, Anonymus Aurelianensis I (Sten Ebbesen, "Anonymi Aurelianensis I *Commentarium in Sophisticos elenchos*, Edition and Introduction," *Cahiers de l'Institut du Moyen Âge grec et latin* 34 (1979), iv–xlviii, 1–200), Anonymus Aurelianesis II (Sten Ebbesen, "Anonymus Aurelianensis II, Aristotle, Alexander, Porphyry and Boethius. Ancient Scholasticism and 12th Century Western Europe," *Cahiers de l'Institut du Moyen Âge Grec et Latin* 16 (1976) 1–128), Anonymus Aurelianensis III (edition by C.T. Thörnqvist forthcoming) and Anonymus Cantabrigiensis (edition by Ebbesen forthcoming).

almost anti-Aristotelian, for instance that demonstrative science is not generally useful and that knowledge is by nature uncertain, and these claims are not
compatible with Aristotle's views. One might well suspect that John was somehow influenced by what he had learned about the individual texts.

Clearly he knows some of the texts from the *Organon* very well. Not surprisingly he is able to discuss the *Categories* and the *De interpretatione* carefully, but these texts had been in use for a long time already when John
studied. However, he also provides us with a thorough summary of the *Topics*
and brief but reasonably accurate ones of the *Prior Analytics* and the
Sophistical Refutations. There are no reasons to suspect that he did not know
these work well.

The *Posterior Analytics*, is treated very differently.[16] Contrary to what he
does in the case of the other Aristotelian texts, John does not summarize the
Posterior Analytics. First he has a description of the reasons why this text is
almost useless, although the reasons that he gives are generally not correct
(*Metalogicon* 4. 6). Then follows a chapter which claims, in apparent contrast
to the preceding one, that Aristotle's discovery of demonstrative theory was an
exceptional achievement and the reason he gained his honorary title, the
Philosopher (*Metalogicon* 4. 7). In the next chapter John sets forth the functions and sources of demonstration (*Metalogicon* 4. 8), before he plunges into
a string of chapters with topics more or less distantly relevant to the theory
of demonstration such as sensation, imagination, opinion, prudence, science,
wisdom, reason, understanding and the soul (*Metalogicon* 4. 9–21). In the
entire *Metalogicon*, there is actually no treatment of the *Posterior Analytics* as
such, only general descriptions and analyses of demonstration and demonstrative theory. His main interest is clearly the nature of principles and how
one obtains them. John's views on this issue are similar to Aristotle's as found
in *Posterior Analytics* 2. 19, where one *perceives* something, stores it in one's
memory, in time gains *experience* through a collection of memories, and finally
one somehow obtains universal principles through some kind of mental act
(νοῦς/*intellectus*). But, if one does not accept that one can obtain demonstrative principles in the Aristotelian sense, this process is the foundation not only
of demonstration but also of dialectic. As such John considers it an important
part of science and knowledge.

---

16   For substantial treatments of John's knowledge, or lack of knowledge, of the *Posterior
      Analytics*, see David Bloch, "John of Salisbury, the *Quadrivium* and Demonstrative
      Science," *Classica & Mediaevalia* 60 (2009), 335–345, and, in particular, Bloch, *John
      of Salisbury on Aristotelian Science*. It seems clear to me that John did not know this
      text well.

The second question to be asked is what kind of use he makes of his Aristotelian knowledge. To find the answer to this question is, at least to some extent, to examine John's theory of science and knowledge.

John would claim that he holds Aristotelian views on science and knowledge. He accepts the methods and results of the *Topics*, and he sees no true opposition between his views on demonstrative science and Aristotle's. Despite the fact that John values the *Topics* and Aristotelian dialectic above the rest of logic, the modern interpreter will find many of his views on science and knowledge in the chapters concerned with demonstration.

According to John, the basic process of obtaining the principles (perception, memory, experience, intuition) contains an inherent difficulty that Aristotle did not consider. For it is strange that this process should provide the necessary principles for demonstration, since it is built on sense perception. For a skeptic like John sensations and perceptions are naturally uncertain, and no indisputable knowledge can be based on them.[17] It is true that this is the process that humans go through to obtain the most basic principles of knowledge, but they do not have the characteristics that Aristotle assigns to them.

As a consequence, the deductions that the scholar or scientist puts forward will also suffer. The chain of reasoning may, and should, be valid, but there is no guarantee as regards the contents of the individual propositions. The value of these all depend upon whether or not they contain truths or falsehoods, and this cannot be established with absolute certainty.

Still, even though one cannot have absolutely certain knowledge that is based on chains of reasoning through necessary arguments, one can at least try to come as close as possible to this ideal:

> One must have prior knowledge of the principles, and from these one must gather the sequence of truths by coherent reasoning based on necessity; and one must progress by working very hard to place the argument on solid ground, so to speak, in order that the lack of necessity would not result in the appearance of a gap in the argument, a gap, which would jeopardize the otherwise resulting demonstrative knowledge. Certainly, not every science/knowledge is demonstrative, but only those that are based on true, primary and immediate principles. For just as not every deduction is a demonstration but every

---

17   Although it must be admitted that he does sometimes accept certain perceptions. See *Policraticus* 7. 7, ed. Webb, vol. 2, pp. 114–117.

demonstration is a deduction, so also knowledge/science comprises the demonstrative but not conversely.[18]

Necessary deductions are deductions that allow of no exception or contrary conclusion. This is the essential nature of demonstrative deductions, and only through these does one truly have knowledge. But whereas these deductions are apparently a realizable goal for Aristotle, they are not so for John, at least not without divine intervention. Instead he proposes that one continuously strive *towards* true knowledge, all the time acknowledging that one will never fully reach it. One must keep working on the weak points in the argument, fortify it and emend it so that no "gaps" (*hiatus*) are left. This also means that one must always remember that the argument is not complete, or certain, and as such it is in a sense un-Aristotelian and un-demonstrative. The results of this kind of demonstration is one kind of science (or knowledge), but it is not science/knowledge *per se* (see further below).

In making this suggestion on behalf of demonstrative science, John seems actually to have made it serviceable even beyond the scientific discipline, in which he has claimed it has its proper function, namely mathematics. In short, he seems to have made it a *dialectical* procedure. This also makes sense of the claim that he makes elsewhere, that dialectic is of great value in demonstrations.[19] One of the major differences between demonstration and dialectic was thought to be that demonstrations needed no opponent with whom to debate, whereas dialectic was always a conversation (even when it took place in one's own soul). Demonstrative argument had the advantage that it would never contain premises and principles that were only there to test the person involved, or as a result of incompetence on the part of one of the parties of the discussion. On the other hand, its reliance on principles that could not be questioned made it weak in the eyes of a skeptic. Thus, in chapter six of Book four of the *Metalogicon* John informs us that demonstration (in the strong, Aristotelian sense of the word) is generally almost useless, since very few branches of scholarship will benefit from it. The mathematicians are actually

---

18   *Metalogicon* 4. 8, p. 146: "Necesse enim est disciplinarum praenosse principia, et ex his ex necessitate verorum sequelam colligere consertis rationibus, et ut sic dixerim calcatius urgendo nequis quasi ex defectu necessitatis videatur hiatus, qui demonstrativae scientiae praeiudicium afferat. Non utique omnis scientia demonstrativa est, sed illa dumtaxat quae ex veris et primis est et immediatis. Nam sicut non omnis syllogismus demonstratio, sed omnis demonstratio syllogismus est, sic demonstrativam scientia inconvertibiliter ambit."

19   Ibid. 3. 5, p. 119.

the only scholars for whom it is really useful, and even among them it is pretty much used only by the geometers. This, John continues, makes it even more irrelevant, since geometry is not a discipline that is well cultivated among the Latins. He is well aware that it is important among the Arabs, Egyptians and in other foreign places, but not so among us, he says.

According to John, dialectic could help demonstration to overcome its weak spots, and he would have found Aristotelian support in *Topics* 1. 2 and *Sophistical Refutations* 2. The passage from the *Topics* informs us that dialectic can be used "philosophically" to test the principles, and the *Elenchi* passage states that demonstration and dialectic are both "discussions" (*disputationes*, which is Boethius' translation of the Greek τὸ διαλέγεσθαι). Other authors of the 12th century noted that this was a strange way to characterize demonstration, but in general there seems to have been a tendency to regard demonstration and dialectic as disciplines that are much closer to each other than Aristotle would allow.[20]

The Conceptual Apparatus of Human Beings

Our limited capacity for obtaining knowledge has been established by God, but these very faculties are also gifts from God. Through them we can learn as much about truth as we are meant and entitled to.

Perception (*sensus*) is particularly important, since it is the most basic one. Our knowledge in general depends on it. The perceptions are stored in our memory (*memoria*), which, according to Augustine and others, is a treasure house or store house of images that can be manipulated and used by imagination (*imaginatio*). This conceptual apparatus (perception, memory, imagination) is common to man and many animals, but there are other faculties and abilities that are found only in man. The first and most important ones are reason (*ratio*) and speech (*sermo*). These are used in forming opinion (*opinio*), faith (*fides*), knowledge (*scientia*), and intuitive understanding (*intellectus*), and these all combine to provide man with the possibility of obtaining wisdom (*sapientia*). John does not describe exactly how one goes through these different stages to reach wisdom, but he informs us that wisdom must here be taken in both a practical and a theoretical sense, that is, striving for and recognizing truth and virtue, and doing what is good. It is simply the goal of

---

20   Niels Jørgen Green-Pedersen, *The Tradition of the Topics in the Middle Ages: The Commentaries on Aristotle's and Boethius' Topics* (Munich, 1984), pp. 213–214; Bloch, *John of Salisbury on Aristotelian Science.*

philosophy.[21] This he would have learned from major authorities such as Augustine and Boethius,[22] and it was apparently a common view in the first half of the 12th century.[23] Some would even claim that wisdom *is* philosophy,[24] but others would take a more Aristotelian approach and say that wisdom is a combination of understanding the principles and understanding what follows from these principles.[25]

Whereas the above Augustinian and Boethian views would be natural for John's contemporaries, such a conception of knowledge and wisdom, a conception that is found scattered particularly throughout Books 1 and 4 of the *Metalogicon*, might seem difficult to combine with John's skeptical and Aristotelian dialectical views. No matter whether wisdom is stable knowledge of both practical and theoretical subjects, or solid understanding of principles and what results from these, it would seem to be unobtainable if one subscribes to John's skepticism. In subscribing to this traditional view of wisdom, and accepting its reality, he seems to be keeping double books. On the one hand, he stands alone with his Academic skepticism, which he has combined with his views on Aristotelian dialectic. On the other hand, he is firmly rooted in 12th-century views.

Logic: The Tool of Science and Knowledge

Reason is the starting point of knowledge and wisdom. Speech is also necessary, since "unspoken wisdom" is not actually real wisdom, as John would have learned from Cicero.[26] Reason and speech are necessary conditions, then, but they are not by themselves sufficient. Their main function is rather to make the tools, the "arts" (*artes*), needed for progress towards opinion, faith, knowledge, prudence, virtue and, in the end, wisdom.

The entire *Metalogicon* testifies to the fact that logic is the most important tool. Human beings can advance towards knowledge and wisdom without logic, but they are not as efficient and successful as they will be if they master this branch of learning.

---

21   *Metalogicon* 2. 1, pp. 56–57.
22   Augustine, *Confessiones* 3. 4. 8; Boethius, *De topicis differentiis* 2. 6.
23   Hugh of Saint-Victor, *Didascalicon* 2. 1.
24   William of Conches, *Glosae in Boetium* 1 pr. 1, ed. Lodi Nauta (Turnhout, 1999), p. 29.
25   Anonymus Aurelianensis II, *De paralogismis*, ed. Ebbesen, p. 31. See Aristotle, *EN* VI.7.
26   *Metalogicon* 1. 1, pp. 12–13. See Cicero, *De inventione* 1. 1. 1; *De oratore* 2. 1. 5, 2. 2. 6, 2. 11. 48; *De officiis* 1. 16. 50.

The two main functions of logic are "discovery" (*inuentio*) and "judgement" (*iudicium*). This definition has un-Aristotelian, Ciceronian roots and was widely used by 12th-century scholars. Even with the advent of Aristotle's *Organon* it did not disappear, but the two conceptions of logic, the strict Aristotelian and the rhetorically influenced Ciceronian, were combined.[27] Discovery is the process of finding the right kind of arguments in a given context. Judgement is the process of evaluating the arguments and assigning each of them their proper place in the chain of arguments. In addition, John informs us,[28] knowledge of how to make divisions, definitions, and inferences also falls under logic. Thus,

> it is very easy to talk about "definition," "arguments," "genus" and the like. But it is much more difficult to find them in each of the branches [of knowledge] and thus to make the art [of logic] perform its duty.[29]

Logic must be applied in all branches of knowledge; for it will help one find the constitutive elements of the branch in question.

Into the overall framework of logic John incorporates the Aristotelian branches of logic: demonstration, dialectic, and sophistry. They all contribute to one's grasp of discovery and judgement. In fact, they constitute the way by which one puts the discovery/judgement distinction into practice. The recently discovered Aristotle is thus seen through the eyes of the old logic, and the result is a powerful tool that will elicit as much knowledge as possible from the individual branches of science.

Furthermore,

> all things have a way of contributing to each other, so that one will become more proficient in any proposed branch of learning to the extent that he has mastered neighbouring and related branches.[30]

And a few chapters later he says that

> the systems[31] of all branches [of learning] are interrelated, and each attains its perfection only through the others. Few are those, if there

---

27   See Bloch, *John of Salisbury on Aristotelian Science.*

28   *Metalogicon* 2. 5, p. 61.

29   Ibid. 2. 9, p. 70: "Sic de definitione aut argumentis aut genere et similibus loqui facillimum est, sed eadem ad artis explendum officium in singulis facultatibus invenire longe difficilius."

30   Ibid. 3. 5, p. 119: "Siquidem sibi invicem universa contribuunt, eoque in proposita facultate quisque expeditior est, quo in vicina et cohaerente instructior fuerit."

31   Perhaps one should rather use "principles" to translate *rationes*, as McGarry does (see *Metalogicon*, trans. McGarry, p. 204).

are any at all, that can achieve the highest point without assistance from another.[32]

Aristotle divides the sciences (Gr. ἐπιστῆμαι, Lat. *scientiae*) into the theoretical, the practical, and the productive, all with a number of sub-branches.[33] He clearly believes that they are all autonomous and related only in a few cases.[34] There is no suggestion in Aristotle that a person who has mastered mathematics will *eo ipso* also be on his way to understanding natural science, metaphysics, ethics, or any other branch of learning; on the contrary, this would be a case of wrongly mixing different sciences.

In contrast, John would apparently claim that there is some sort of connection between the branches of sciences, and the accumulation of knowledge in one branch gradually increases knowledge in neighbouring ones, thereby providing the person with overall knowledge and understanding of the world.[35] This is also the point about mastering not only dialectical but also demonstrative and sophistic method. For even though dialectic is, according to him, the one that is most useful and applicable in most areas, demonstration is still the best method in mathematics – and therefore needed for full scientific understanding – and sophistry may not *per se* provide knowledge, but it does sharpen the tools of dialectic and demonstration. Mastery of sophistic logic enables one to see when the argument is flawed, how it is flawed, and to some extent how (if possible) it can be corrected by dialectic or demonstration. One could say that, according to John, demonstration establishes valid arguments with necessary and true premises; dialectic both examines, establishes, and demolishes valid (and sophistic) arguments in general; sophistry tries to establish invalid (but somehow persuasive) arguments and/or arguments that are for some reason or other unacceptable (but somehow persuasive), and it tries to demolish valid and/or acceptable ones. Different sciences demand different methods: dialectic is used for most branches of learning, in combination with sophistry, to establish knowledge as far as possible. Demonstration is used for mathematics in particular, but it may also contribute more generally

---

32   *Metalogicon* 4. 1, p. 140: "Nam disciplinarum omnium connexae sunt rationes, et quaelibet sui perfectionem ab aliis mutuatur. Vix est quae sine alterius adminiculo, si tamen omnino aliqua est, quae ad summum possit ascendere."

33   Arist., *Metaph.* 6. 1–4, 1025b1–1028a6. See also *Top.* 6. 6, 145a13-18; *EN.* 6. 2, 1138b35–1139b13.

34   So e.g. geometry in relation to optics and arithmetic in relation to harmonics, optics and harmonics being subordinate to geometry and arithmetic respectively; see *APo.* 1. 7, 75b12-17; 1. 9, 76a22-25; 1. 13, 78b35-39.

35   See also *Historia pontificalis* 12, p. 27, on a similar view attributed to Gilbert of Poitiers. There are also tendencies in Abelard: see *Dialectica* 3. 1, pp. 286–287.

to scientific rigour.[36] The final result is a mixture of different, but interrelated kinds of knowledge. The structure of the *Metalogicon* is an example. For in the very first prologue, John states that he will not restrict himself to logic but also include ethics, because "all things that are read or written are useless, except in so far as they contribute some kind of help to life."[37] John is an advocate of a particular kind of unity of the sciences, and on the theoretical level demonstration is incorporated.

We need a solid foundation in science, and this is provided by God.[38] For God himself cannot, of course, be questioned as a first principle.[39] Also, in a famous passage from the *Policraticus*, John mentions a large number of philosophical problems that cannot easily be solved, but there are no problems involving first principles.[40] Thus, John exhibits the clear features of a scholar standing at the beginning of the Aristotelian tradition with the necessary tensions between competing, if not contrary, views: on the one hand, he prefers probable science and skepticism, and he would never question the fact that there are certain first principles provided by God, which are two views that are difficult to reconcile but certainly belong primarily in a non-Aristotelian context;[41] on the other hand, he wants to incorporate Aristotle's treatises within this framework, as is particularly clear in the case of the *Topics*.

The basis of obtaining knowledge is the seven liberal arts. One would think that both trivium and quadrivium would be crucial if John was to live up to his views on the unity of the sciences, but this seems not to be the case. John's knowledge of the quadrivium is less than impressive. We know from the famous Chapter ten of Book two of the Metalogicon that he learned some of the basics from Hardewin the German, and he apparently reviewed what he learned with Richard the Bishop, but, whereas his other studies were very thorough, he never delved deeper into the mysteries of the quadrivium. Admittedly, it was only a few scholars of the 12th century who studied the quadrivium

---

36   *Metalogicon* 2. 3, p. 60.

37   Ibid. 1, prologus, p. 11: "omnia quae leguntur aut scribuntur inutilia esse nisi quatenus afferunt aliquod adminiculum vitae."

38   On certainty as regards the principles, see, in particular, *Policraticus* 3. 1, p. 174, 7. 7, pp. 114–117; and Luigi Cazzola Palazzo, "Il valore filosofico della probabilità nel pensiero di Giovanni di Salisbury," *Atti della Accademia delle Scienze di Torino, Classe di Scienze Morali, Storiche e Filologiche* 92 (1957–8), 96–142, pp. 125–134.

39   *Policraticus*, ed. Keats-Rohan, 2. 26, pp. 143–144, 3.1, pp. 174–175.

40   Ibid. 7. 2, ed. Webb, vol. 2, pp. 98–99. The principles discussed in ibid. 7. 7, vol. 2, p. 115, which, according to John, cannot be disputed, are solely geometrical ones.

41   On the tension involved in combining such views, see Palazzo, "Il valore filosofico della probabilità nel pensiero di Giovanni di Salisbury," pp. 127–128.

thoroughly, but considering John's strong views on the unity of science and his access to great teachers in Paris and Chartres, it does seem a little odd that he never tried to progress beyond an elementary level. More importantly, his lack of knowledge seems partly to have distorted his views on Aristotelian science, since these views contribute crucially to his conception of the *Posterior Analytics* and demonstrative science as basically useless subjects except in mathematics.[42]

Trivium, on the other hand, is very important. The first one needs to learn is grammar, which is the foundation of all subsequent studies, Then follows logic proper, and naturally the student should complete his knowledge of the trivium by studying rhetoric.[43] When the student has carefully studied the disciplines of the trivium he masters "discovery" and "judgement" as well as the methods of division, definition, and inference.[44] All of this is relatively unproblematic. One simply has to learn these skills and methods and then one will master the necessary basis of knowledge. This is to be done primarily by using the Aristotelian writings.[45]

The principles of knowledge and the basic methods did not cause as great problems as one would have expected, then, and John will focus instead on the *use* of these principles, and of the methods (demonstration and, in particular, dialectic) to be used in obtaining knowledge. In general he wants to proceed from what may reasonably be called a quasi-Aristotelian demonstrative procedure with substantial dialectical elements:

1.   In all branches of science it holds that principles must be recognized before the investigation proper can take place.

---

42   On John's views on, and knowledge of, the quadrivium, see David Bloch, "John of Salisbury, the *Quadrivium* and Demonstrative Science," *Classica & Mediaevalia* 60 (2009), 335–345. For a more optimistic view on John's knowledge and use of the quadrivium, see Gillian Rosemary Evans, "John of Salisbury and Boethius on Arithmetic," in *The World of John of Salisbury*, pp. 161–167.

43   *Metalogicon* 1. 12–13, pp. 31–33; 2. 3, pp. 59–60. See also ibid. 2. 10, pp. 70–73.

44   Ibid. 2. 6, pp. 63–66.

45   The order of study that John would apparently prefer is: *Isagoge, Categories, On Interpretation, Topics, Prior Analytics, Posterior Analytics, Sophistical Refutations.* To moderns it is somewhat surprising that the *Topics* is placed before the *Prior Analytics*, but the 12th century probably learned about this possibility from the Greek commentaries, as can be seen in an anonymous Latin commentary on the *Prior Analytics*, probably dating from 1160–80: Orléans, Bibliothèque Municipale 283, p. 178a–b. In any case, this ordering of the works fits John's general views perfectly. On the order of study, see also Hugh of Saint-Victor's *Didascalicon* praefatio, pp. 1–3.

2. From these principles one must deduce one's conclusions, and they must follow by necessity from the principles; that is, the deductions must be formally valid.

3. But extreme care is demanded of these two procedures; every effort must be made to ensure that no gaps (*hiatus*) can be found in the investigation. That is, one must be able to follow the individual steps of the argument, and they must all be clear and immediately convincing. Otherwise the argument cannot be seen as *per se* necessary.[46]

This description of research method is in accordance with the descriptions above. Before using one's tools for research, one must fully realize the principles on which the science in question is based, and from these principles one deduces the conclusions. According to Aristotle, the foundation cannot be disputed or be in any way uncertain, as long as one stays within the boundaries of the science in question. But John thinks that the researcher should continually work to strengthen the argument and fill in the gaps, which means that a truly demonstrative argument is impossible, according to him. This is, of course, in complete accordance with his general skeptical outlook, and in many ways the procedure is more practical than Aristotle's. However, by viewing demonstration in this light, John has more or less abolished the ideal demonstration. Demonstration does *not* allow the expansion of its syllogisms by new middle terms. This is something that the Greek commentators knew well from a passage in the *Posterior Analytics*, and among the Latins a statement to this effect is later found in the *Auctoritates Aristotelis*,[47] but John seems not to have used this Aristotelian

---

46 *Metalogicon* 4. 8, p. 146: "Sed ad hanc disciplinam quis idoneus est? Profecto et siquis in aliquo, eam in multis nullus perfecte assequitur. Necesse enim est disciplinarum praenosse principia, et ex his ex necessitate uerorum sequelam colligere consertis rationibus, et ut sic dixerim calcatius urgendo nequis quasi ex defectu necessitatis uideatur hiatus, qui demonstrativae scientiae praeiudicium afferat." ("Who, then, are qualified to handle this discipline [*scil.* demonstration]? True, there are some who master it in some areas, but no one does so completely in many areas. For one must (1) have prior knowledge of the principles, (2) and from these one must gather the sequence of truths by coherent reasoning based on necessity; (3) and one must progress by working very hard to place the argument on solid ground, so to speak, in order that the lack of necessity would not result in the appearance of a gap in the argument, a gap, which would jeopardize the otherwise resulting demonstrative knowledge.")

47 *Auctoritates Aristotelis* (*super primum librum Posteriorum Aristotelis*) no. 62, ed. Jacqueline Hamesse (Leuven, 1974), p. 316: "Demonstrationes non augentur per media, sed in post assumpto et in latus."

passage.[48] Thus, according to John, dialectic is the only science that truly remains potent. While on the other hand, the proper Aristotelian science of demonstration is reduced to a basic description of method that may be applied in all areas of research as an ideal that dialectic may strive for as far as possible. That is, one should try as hard as possible to make the principles of one's deductions necessary, while at the same time knowing that the attempt will never be completely successful. Many 12th-century authors had problems distinguishing demonstration clearly from dialectic, so John was not alone in his general understanding.[49]

These are all complicated matters, and they are difficult to handle in both the original Aristotelian form and in John's modified version. The process of learning itself, on the other hand, is very simple, according to John: you read, you learn, you meditate (or think hard), you apply yourself actively to the process![50] These are the primary tools in the exercise of philosophy in general and virtue in particular, the latter being the goal of philosophy,[51] and they should lead to scientific knowledge.[52] The procedure involved John explains as follows:

> "Reading" examines the matter that is put forth in written works and is immediately at hand; "learning" also most often engages with written works, and sometimes it moves on to non-written material that has been hidden away in the archives of memory or to those things that stand out in the understanding of a given subject. "Meditation," however, proceeds further to the unknown things, and often rises itself all the way to the incomprehensible things, and explores not only the clearly manifested

---

48   Arist., *APo.* 1. 12, 78a14-21; Themistius, *Paraphr. APo.* 26. 33–27. 8, in *Ioannis Philoponi in Aristotelis Analytica posteriora commentaria, cum Anonymo in librum II*, Commentaria in Aristotelem Graeca XIII.3, ed. Maximilian Wallies (Berlin, 1909). See *Aristotle's Prior and Posterior Analytics. A Revised Text with Introduction and Commentary*, ed. W.D. Ross (Oxford, 1949), p. 550 (*ad loc.*): "The advancement of a science, says A., is not achieved by interpolating new middle terms. This is because the existing body of scientific knowledge must already have based all its results on a knowledge of the *immediate* premises from which they spring; otherwise it would not be science."

49   On this, see Bloch, *John of Salisbury on Aristotelian Science*, pp. 132–141.

50   See, in particular, *Metalogicon* 1. 23, pp. 50–51. And for John's illustration of part of the practice as seen in his description of Bernard of Chartres' teaching, see ibid. 1. 24, pp. 51–55, and above 1. 1. 1.

51   Ibid. 1. 23, p. 50: "Praecipua autem sunt ad totius philosophiae et virtutis exercitium."

52   Ibid. 1. 23, p. 50: "At lectio, doctrina et meditatio scientiam pariunt" = "Reading, learning and meditation give birth to scientific knowledge/understanding."

things, but also the hidden ones. The fourth element in the process is applying oneself to the work...[53]

That is, the researcher (or student) *reads* the basic texts, or is *taught* by the teacher reading the texts aloud.[54] The texts should be carefully selected among the authoritative and well-established ones; for reading at random does not make a philosopher.[55] At the reading-stage he is merely supposed to obtain a solid foundation provided by the authoritative authors and texts. At this stage, the process does not involve much interpretation and analysis.[56] Next, the researcher *learns* from the texts, not only while reading, but also afterwards when he remembers what he has read. At this stage, a more critical approach is taken in the attempt to understand the subject and where the problems are. Furthermore, the researcher may use not only the text(s) in front of him, but also works that he has previously read. At the third stage, he ponders the contents of the texts carefully (that is: he *meditates*) in order to understand the subjects fully, and sometimes he even obtains fruits that were not easily extracted from the texts themselves. Thus, the researcher continues to analyse the contents at an even deeper level, and in particular he is now allowed to move beyond the texts and use his own mind, even though the texts and authorities will always be the foundation. The final part of the process consists in *applying oneself* actively to the work in accordance with the knowledge that has been obtained through the preceding three steps. This is the final stage at which one's knowledge is structured and put to practical, that is, ethical, use. By use of an older distinction found for instance in Cicero, Victorinus, and Augustine who are the primary sources, this stage is called wisdom (*sapientia*). Wisdom is thus distinguished from knowledge (*scientia*) by being on a higher level than knowledge, or rather by being a higher form of knowledge.[57] Sometimes it is virtue itself (and then *scientia* is the road to

---

53   Ibid. 1. 23, p. 50: "Lectio vero scriptorum praeiacentem habet materiam, doctrina et scriptis plerumque incumbit, et interdum ad non scripta progreditur, quae tamen in archivis memoriae recondita sunt aut in praesentis rei intelligentia eminent. At meditatio etiam ad ignota protenditur, et usque ad incomprehensibilia saepe se ipsam erigit, et tam manifesta rerum quam abdita rimatur. Quartum operis scilicet assiduitas..." Generally on these concepts, see, in particular, ibid. 1. 23–24, pp. 50–55.

54   On the ambiguity of "reading" (*lectio*), see ibid. 1. 24, p. 51, see Quint., *Inst. orat.* 2. 5. 4.

55   *Policraticus* 7. 9, ed. Webb, vol. 2, p. 128.

56   See also *Metalogicon* 3. 1, pp. 103–105.

57   See Abelard, *Dialectica* 4. 1, p. 469.

virtue),[58] sometimes the grasp of eternal things and the goal of philosophy (and then knowledge is concerned with temporal and sensible things).[59] Since this final part of the process is primarily *practical*, it is not strictly speaking part of the theory of obtaining knowledge.[60]

On the surface, this theory of how to obtain knowledge is not surprising, and it relies on good authorities. It even seems to be based in part on Aristotle, since inductive processes are basic in the theories of both Aristotle and John.[61] But it is not basically as Aristotelian as one might have expected.

First, John's conception of knowledge as being of sensible and temporal things rather than having eternal and stable objects is actually very un-Aristotelian. According to Aristotle, knowledge is concerned with that which cannot be otherwise.[62] Of course, this is not to say that there are no eternal and stable objects according to John, but these are not the object of knowledge (*scientia*).

---

58   *Policraticus*, ed. Keats-Rohan, 3. 1, p. 174: "Praecedit ergo scientia virtutis cultum, quia nemo potest fideliter appetere quod ignorat." ("Knowledge precedes the cultivation of virtue, for no one can reliably strive for something that he does not know.")

59   *Metalogicon* 1. 6, 1. 7, 4. 13, pp. 23, 24, 151–152, with the references in Hall's (or Webb's) edition, and *Policraticus* 5. 9, ed. Webb, vol. 1, p. 319. For a 12th-century discussion of *sapientia*, see Anonymus Aurelianensis I, *Commentarium in Sophisticos elenchos, ad SE*. 1, 165a21 (ed. Ebbesen), pp. 32–33. Note also that, since wisdom is primarily virtue, which is directed towards action, unspoken wisdom is not actually true wisdom: see *Metalogicon* 1. 1, p. 13. On the other hand, John is also aware that wisdom is often thought of as pure contemplation: *Metalogicon* 4. 19, pp. 156–157. On the difficult concept of wisdom (*sapientia*), see also Hugh of Saint-Victor, *Didascalicon*, 1. 2, pp. 6–7, 1. 4, pp. 10–11, 1. 8, pp. 15–16.

60   For a brief description of "study" (*studium*) that is in accordance with this procedure, see *Metalogicon* 1. 11, p. 30. The origin of this is Cicero, *De oratore* 1. 5. 18. This text was not easily available in the Middle Ages, but John seems to have owned a copy: See, e.g. Birger Munk Olsen, "L'humanisme de Jean de Salisbury: un Ciceronien au XIIᵉ siècle," in Maurice de Gandillac and Édouard Jeauneau, eds., *Entretiens sur la Renaissance du XIIᵉ siècle* (Paris, 1968), pp. 53–69, p. 54 and p. 68, note 6; Enrico Tacchella, "Giovanni di Salisbury e i Cornificiani," *Sandalion*, 3 (1980), 273–313 (p. 288 with note 61). It should, however, be noted that more recent scholarship has shown that even the works of Cicero was not so well known to John as he would sometimes have us believe. See Rodney M. Thomson, *William of Malmesbury* (Woodbridge, 1987, repr. 2003), pp. 9–12 with notes 39, 53–54.

61   For John's views on induction, see, e.g. *Metalogicon* 4. 9–11, pp. 147–150; *Policraticus* 2. 18, ed. Keats-Rohan, pp. 106–111. It should be noted that John seems to stress *lectio*, *doctrina* and *meditatio*, while making only little of the central role of induction. Both *lectio/doctrina/meditatio* and induction are described as relevant for obtaining knowledge, but the further progress from the results of induction is unclear in John's work. He seems to be caught between a traditional "religious" procedure and a traditional "philosophical" procedure at a time where the latter was beginning to dominate epistemology.

62   *APo.* 1. 8, 75b21–36.

Second, the procedure of obtaining knowledge through *lectio, doctrina,* and *meditatio* was not an original contribution made by John. It was the way that one was supposed to read the authoritative religious texts, and it is found in similar form in Hugh of Saint-Victor's *Didascalicon* and many other authors.[63] There is also evidence that the procedure, or one very similar, was used in the study of the arts.[64] Furthermore, it clearly worked as a prototype of the much more refined scholastic form of study and research that came to dominate in the thirteenth century. Thus, it is a clear and unproblematic part of a 12th-century tradition.

But this is actually somewhat strange. For one would have expected a new direction in theories of science as a result of the availability of the *Ars noua*. Apparently, Hugh did not have access to it when he wrote the *Didascalicon* in the 1120s. John did have such access in the 1150s, but still the procedure is basically the same as the one found in *Didascalicon*. Aristotle has invaded the basic methods and principles (and even here they are still far from completely Aristotelian), but concerning the concept of knowledge, and the understanding of the process of obtaining knowledge, there are only minor differences between Hugh and John.

Perhaps all this is not actually very surprising, since John is after all our first source concerning the new Aristotle, but it is contrary to the impression that one gets from the *Metalogicon*: that John conducts analyses and provides us with a thoroughly Aristotelian theory.[65] In this work, descriptions and analyses of Aristotle's works occupy most of Books 3 and 4, and the Aristotelian theories are clearly meant to provide a foundation for studies. However, despite what has often been assumed,[66] there is no doubt that John was no less a 12th-century scholar than were Abelard, Thierry of Chartres, William of Conches and the rest of his illustrious teachers.

---

63   Hugh of Saint-Victor, *Didascalicon,* praefatio, pp. 2–3.

64   *Adelard of Bath, Conversations with his Nephew: On the Same and the Different, Questions on Natural Science, and On Birds*, ed. and trans. Charles Burnett, with Italo Ronca, Pedro Mantas España, and Baudoin Van den Abeele (Cambridge, 1998), pp. 4–6; *Guillelmi de Conchis Glosae super Platonem*, ed. Édouard Jeauneau (Turnhout, 2006), pp. 15–16. Furthermore, Cicero, *De inventione*, 1. 25. 36 played a part in the conception of study.

65   Cary Nederman, "Knowledge, Virtue and the Path to Wisdom: The Unexamined Aristotelianism of John of Salisbury's *Metalogicon,*" *Mediaeval Studies* 51 (1989), 268–286, presents this view in its strongest form.

66   See, e.g. Charles Burnett, "John of Salisbury and Aristotle," *Didascalia* 2 (1996), 19–32, p. 21; Brian Hendley, "John of Salisbury's Defense of the *Trivium,*" in *Arts libéraux et philosophie au Moyen Âge: Actes du quatrième congrès international de philosophie médiévale, Université de Montréal, Canada, 27 août – 2 septembre 1967* (Paris, 1969), pp. 753–762. Both view John of Salisbury as a step ahead towards the 13th century.

CHAPTER 10

Qui Recta Quae Docet Sequitur, Uere Philosophus Est

The Ethics of John of Salisbury

Sigbjørn Sønnesyn

Illa autem quae ceteris philosophiae partibus praeminet ethicam dico, sine qua nec philosophi subsistit nomen, collati decoris gratia, omnes alias antecedit.[1]

That part of philosophy that towers above the others I call ethics, which surpasses all others on account of her accumulation of beauty. Without her, neither will the name of philosophy subsist.

John of Salisbury always stayed close to moral considerations, regardless of his theme and topic – no learning was worth the time and effort, he said, unless in some way it contributed to a better way of living.[2] As the quotation at the head of this essay shows, ethics enjoyed pride of place within John's hierarchy of the disciplines of knowledge and wisdom. Still, John never wrote what we may term a moral treatise, in which he might set out the structure and substance of his moral thought. In John's preserved writings we see the application rather than the pure essence of his ethics. Yet, John's repeated reference to the various parts of philosophy and to the position of ethics in relation to the other parts has created an expectation on the part of modern critics of an implicit system of ethics, itself a part of the system of philosophy as a whole.[3] Such expectations of finding philosophy and its parts to be ordered systems are amplified by the characteristics of the modern practice of philosophy. This is perhaps reflected in some of the most celebrated recent attempts at reconstructing an ethical system from the various statements scattered across John's collected

---

1 *Metalogicon* 1.24, p. 52. The author wishes to thank C. Stephen Jaeger, Thomas J. Ball, and the editors of this volume for helpful advice and significant suggestions of improvement.

2 See, e.g. ibid., prol., p. 11: "omnia quae leguntur aut scribuntur inutilia [sunt] nisi quatenus afferunt aliquod adminiculum uitae."

3 John's own notion of the practice of philosophy is admirably studied in C. Stephen Jaeger, "John of Salisbury, a Philosopher of the Long Eleventh Century," in Thomas F.X. Noble and John Van Engen, eds., *European Transformations: The Long Twelfth Century* (Notre Dame, 2012), pp. 499–520.

© KONINKLIJKE BRILL NV, LEIDEN, 2015 | DOI 10.1163/9789004282940_012

oeuvre, where John's anticipation of distinctly modern ideas is highlighted. John's classical humanism has for a long time been seen as his perhaps most notable defining quality,[4] and more recent studies have added great depth to this view by documenting the Aristotelian and Skeptical conceptual schemes at the heart of John's ethics.[5]

In what follows I seek to offer a somewhat different perspective. While drawing on the valuable contributions to our understanding of John's ethics offered by the recent attempts to describe John's moral thought in a more systematic form based on its constituent parts and their central sources and inspirations, this present study will present John's ethics in terms of its main aspirations and ultimate aims rather than of its material contents. John's celebrated appropriation of classical ethics should, it will be argued, be seen as subordinated to the fundamental perceptions of human life and its purpose drawn from patristic thought, Saint Augustine in particular. That is to say, the classical conceptual schemes constituting the expression of John's moral thought – and hence most modern expositions of the same – should not be seen as forming a self-enclosed system of moral philosophy, but rather as an attempt to appropriate the rich resources of classical philosophy to advance the Augustinian conception of the Christian life.

John's Ethics: Problems in Contemporary Research

The centre of focus in recent research on John of Salisbury has been on what made John's thought unique, perhaps somewhat to the detriment of the study of what made his thought a unity. This emphasis may be understandable if seen in the light of the interpretation it was designed to oppose. For a long time, ethics in John of Salisbury was often presented as something more akin

---

4 See primarily Hans Liebeschütz, *Medieval Humanism in the Life and Writings of John of Salisbury* (London, 1950). See also Klaus Guth, "Hochmittelalterlicher Humanismus als Lebensform: ein Beitrag zum Standsethos des westeuropäischen Weltklerus nach Johannes von Salisbury," in *The World of John of Salisbury*, pp. 63–76. For a critique of this view, see in particular C. Stephen Jaeger, "Pessimism in the Twelfth-Century 'Renaissance',' *Speculum* 78 (2003), 1151–83, and Glen W. Olsen, "John of Salisbury's Humanism," in Claudio Leonardi, ed., *Gli Umanesimi Medievali: atti del II. Congresso dell' internationales Mittelateinerkomitee, Firenze, Certosa dell Galluzzo, 11–15 settembre 1993* (Florence, 1998), pp. 447–468.

5 See in particular Cary J. Nederman, "Beyond Stoicism and Aristotelianism: John of Salisbury's Skepticism and Twelfth-Century Moral Philosophy," in Istvan P. Bejczy and Richard G. Newhauser, eds., *Virtue and Ethics in the Twelfth Century* (Leiden, 2005), pp. 175–195.

to a system of classical quotations and allusions rather than a coherent body of philosophical thought in the traditional understanding of the term; an expression of a literary rather than philosophical culture. Such an under-standing has now largely been discredited, following the publication of a number of studies arguing that John was an innovative and accomplished thinker in his own right, and that his impressive knowledge of classical thought and writing was put to a creative and original use.[6] In particular, it has been argued that John adapted recognizably Aristotelian doctrines into a framework inspired by the skeptic philosophy of the New Academy, thus creating an original synthesis escaping the constricting dichotomy of Stoic/Christian ethics of interiority and Aristotelian teleological virtue ethics. On this reading, the defining characteristics and core values of the ethics of John of Salisbury are twofold: firstly, he departs from most other moral theo-rists of the day, who drew their inspiration mainly from Stoicism and Cicero, in presenting the Aristotelian doctrine of the mean as the crucial element of his definition of virtue.[7] That is to say, virtue is conceived of as consisting in finding the golden mean between the vices of the deficient and the exces-sive: courage is the mean between cowardice and rashness, justice the mean between permissiveness and severity, temperance between self-denial and self-indulgence.[8] Moderation, acting according to the mean, is thus the main characteristic of acting virtuously across the spectrum of individual

---

6   See, e.g. Cary J. Nederman and J. Brückman, "Aristotelianism in John of Salisbury's 'Policraticus'," *Journal of the History of Philosophy* 21 (1983), 203–229, *passim*.

7   I refer here primarily to Nederman, "Beyond Stoicism and Aristotelianism," although others have described John's relations to skeptical thought in other ways; see Christophe Grellard, "Jean de Salisbury. Un cas médiéval de scepticisme," *Freiburger Zeitschrift für Philosophie und Theologie* 54 (2007), 16–40. Nederman's claims do, of course, take into account the palpable fact that the major moral treatises of Aristotle were unknown to John except to the extent to which they had been mediated through secondary, mainly Roman sources. Even though I follow Nederman's lead in referring to the definite statements of Aristotelian ethics in works that were unknown to John, I also remain aware, as Nederman is also, that the ideas had reached John in mediated rather than direct form. In addition to the studies quoted else-where in this chapter, see also Cary J. Nederman, "The Meaning of 'Aristotelianism' in Medieval Moral and Political Thought," *Journal of the History of Ideas* 57 (1996), 563–585, and idem, "Nature, Ethics, and the Doctrine of 'Habitus': Aristotelian Moral Psychology in the Twelfth Century," *Traditio* 45 (1989–90), 87–110. See also the concise list of Aristotelian works available to John in Klaus Guth, *Johannes von Salisbury: Studien zur Kirchen-, Kultur- und Sozialgeschichte Westeuropas im 12. Jahrhundert* (St. Ottilien, 1978), pp. 64–66.

8   Most fully treated in Cary J. Nederman, "The Aristotelian Doctrine of the Mean and John of Salisbury's Concept of Liberty," *Vivarium* 24 (1986), 128–142.

virtues. Secondly, John advocates an extended liberty of the intellect, emphasizing to a remarkable degree the freedom each individual should possess by right in relation to assenting to or dissenting from truth claims.[9] Moderation and the liberty required to act moderately, then, are the two pillars on which John's moral philosophy is said to rest.[10]

It has been demonstrated beyond all doubt that these elements are present in John's texts and thought in abundance. Nevertheless, I will argue that these two principles cannot on their own carry the full weight of the moral thought of John of Salisbury. We consequently need to supplement our account of the basic principles of his ethics. But on what grounds do I find this account of John's ethics to be in need of supplementation?

My main objection to highlighting moderation and liberty as the core principles of John's ethics is that these principles as they appear in John's writings seem entirely formal, while John's ethics as a whole have a clear substantial content to which these formal considerations are subordinated. Let us start with the ideal of moderation according to the mean. If acting virtuously can be summed up as acting with moderation according to the mean, this would seem to entail that the mean between opposing vices in every case should be able to provide action with sufficient direction to attain virtuous moderation. But in order to provide such direction for the would-be virtuous agent, the mean would have to be known to that agent at the time of acting. However, neither John nor his presumed model Aristotle provide a doctrine of the mean that comes close to providing such knowledge – on the contrary, in order to determine what the mean between two opposing vices in a given moral predicament is, one must already be virtuous. For the virtuous mean between two vicious extremes is not identifiable through a stable algorithm; it cannot be found through mere calculation of the mathematical mean between two end points, nor is it the same for all moral agents or in all moral situation.[11] The mean, in the moral sense

---

9   See previous note, and Nederman, "Beyond Stoicism and Aristotelianism," pp. 184–194; Cary J. Nederman, "Aristotelianism and John of Salisbury's Letters," *Viator* 18 (1987), 161–173.

10   Thus most explicitly and most recently stated in Nederman, "Beyond Stoicism and Aristotelianism," pp. 176–177: "This moral doctrine has a specific, albeit chastened, content built around the promotion of two paramount values: first, that individuals enjoy a right, and perhaps a duty, to individual liberty in judging for themselves in matters of right and wrong (…), and second, that the yardstick of human action should be 'modest moderation." See p. 195 of the same article.

11   Aristotle, *Nicomachean Ethics* 1106a-b; see Nederman, "Aristotelian Concept of the Mean," pp. 135–136.

introduced by Aristotle, is relative to persons and circumstances.[12] It consists in striking the right and appropriate balance, not finding the mathematical mean, and as such it is the result of a moral judgement rather than of the application of a system of rules. It is a substantive judgment for which the formal description of virtue as the mean between opposing vices is entirely insufficient as a guide. If the mean depends on persons and circumstances, it is powerless and blind as a guide for how to exercise proper discretion in particular situations. The mean is not something one brings to particular situations in order to analyse them and find the right course of action; it is the outcome rather than the starting point of moral reasoning. This sort of moral reasoning is what John, following authoritative models of classical philosophy, calls moderation; moderation *finds* the mean. Making the mean a core principle in ethics therefore seems to invite the danger of putting the cart before the horse; moderation can hardly start out from the point it seeks to find. The only way to escape circularity here seems to be to make moderation dependent on some more profound principle capable of supplying the moral agent with a sound basis for making moral judgements.

The concept of liberty cannot supply such a basis. If we accept that the doctrine of the mean in some way or other plays a significant role within John's ethical system – as we must – then the exercise of liberty, too, must be moderated to strike a balance between the excessive and the deficient. Liberty may be abused, and needs to be exercised within the bounds of wisdom, justice, and temperance, and with courage that dares to act, but does not act rashly. Liberty, then, on John's account must be moderated according to some principle extrinsic to itself. Thus, it seems that both the doctrine of the mean and the concept of liberty require some extrinsic principle in order to function according to their intended purpose, and that neither can function as a principle for the other.

We need not go far or search widely to find a principle within John's thought capable of fulfilling this function; John explicitly tells us what this principle is, and in so doing he firmly anchors his ethics within a long and variegated tradition of thought:

> That towards which all rational beings reach is true happiness (*uera beatitudo*). For there is no one who does not want to be happy; but not all follow one and the same way towards that which they desire. One way is nevertheless set out for all, but as a king's highway that splits into a

---

12   *Policraticus* 1.4, ed. Keats-Rohan, pp. 39–40, and *Policraticus* 8.12, ed. Webb, vol. 2, p. 316.

multitude of paths. This way is virtue; for no one may proceed towards happiness unless by way of virtue.[13]

Virtue, then, is not only defined as the mean that avoids vicious extremes; it is also and fundamentally the mode of life that enables human beings to attain their deepest desire and ultimate end. Virtue and happiness constitute the good for human beings, but in different ways and to different degrees:

> Virtue, then, is the service of happiness, happiness the reward of virtue. These two are the supreme goods (*summa bona*), the former of the journey, the latter of the homeland. For nothing is more excellent than virtue while the exile sojourns absent from the Lord; nothing is better than happiness when the citizen reigns and rejoices with the Lord. These, indeed, surpass all other things because virtue encompasses everything that should be done, happiness everything that should be desired. But happiness is superior to virtue because in all things, that for the sake of which something is done (*propter quod aliquid*) surpasses that which is done for the sake of something else (*quod propter aliquid*). For one is not happy in order to act rightly; on the contrary one acts rightly in order to be happy.[14]

The last point here is crucial for our present concerns. Happiness, *beatitudo*, *felicitas*, is the overarching aim of all human endeavour, and the final end of all virtue, of all individual virtues. As such, it is also the standard by reference to which virtue is measured. Here, then, we find John appearing to identify the sort of unifying and defining standard by which virtue may be moderated

---

13   *Policraticus* 7.8, ed. Webb, vol. 2, p. 118: "Illud autem quo omnium rationabilium uergit intentio uera beatitudo est. Nemo etenim est qui non uelit esse beatus; sed ad hoc quod desiderant non una uia omnes incedunt. Vna tamen est omnibus uia proposita sed quasi strata regia scinditur in semitas multas. Haec autem uirtus est; nam nisi per uirtutem nemo ad beatitudinem pergit." All translations from the *Policraticus* are my own.

14   Ibid. 7.8. ed. Webb, vol. 2, p. 118: "Virtus ergo felicitatis meritum est, felicitas uirtutis praemium. Et haec quidem bona sunt summa, alterum uiae, alterum patriae. Nichil enim uirtute praestantius, dum exul peregrinatur a Domino, nichil felicitate melius, dum ciuis regnat et gaudet cum Domino. Sunt autem haec omnibus aliis praestantiora quia uirtus omnia agenda, felicitas omnia optanda complectitur. Felicitas tamen uirtuti praestat quia in omnibus praestantius est propter quod aliquid quam quod propter aliquid. Non enim felix est ut recte agat, sed recte agit ut feliciter uiuat." See Augustine, *De doctrina Christiana* 1.4.9.

without collapsing into circularity.[15] But this raises the questions of what John means by "happiness" here, and to what extent John's concept of happiness is capable of fulfilling the function of being a standard and a supreme point of reference for virtue. If we are to follow John's own advice in what we should consider the keystone of his moral thought, we need to analyse in some detail his notion of happiness, its sources, its substantial contents, and its conceptual structure.

The Definition and Role of Happiness in John's Ethics

We may begin compiling an account of John's concept of happiness by noting that on this question, just as throughout his collected oeuvre, John aligned himself with the mainstream current of moral thought from Socrates until his own time. The notion that the ultimate goal of human life is to attain happiness is the cornerstone of the mode of ethical philosophy characterizing Socrates, Plato, and Aristotle; Cicero, Seneca, and Boethius; Augustine, Anselm, and Abelard.[16] Despite the obvious differences between these thinkers, they would all agree on the formal structure of ethics as directed towards the study of the supreme good for human beings, and of how this good could be attained. John explicitly and repeatedly draws from and embeds his own thought in

---

15   It is perhaps worthy of remark that Nederman, in arguing for the primacy of moderation and intellectual liberty in John's ethics claims that John's thought lacks the teleological dimension found in Aristotelian ethics. The passages quoted here should be enough to show that such a dimension is heavily present in John's thought.

16   The literature here is more than massive, and a bibliographical note can do no more than to arbitrarily scratch the surface. A superb overview of this tradition of moral thought can be found in Terence Irwin, *The Development of Ethics: A Historical and Critical Study, Volume 1: From Socrates to the Reformation* (Oxford, 2007). The late classical and early Christian thinkers are admirably treated in Ragnar Holte, *Béatitude et sagesse: saint Augustin et le problème de la fin de l'homme dans la philosophie ancienne* (Paris, 1962), while Étienne Gilson, *Introduction à l'étude de saint Augustin* (Paris, 1969), pp. 1–10 is still fundamental. For Boethius, see John Marenbon, *Boethius* (Oxford, 2003), pp. 102–112. For Saint Anselm, see Sigbjørn Sønnesyn, "'Ut sine fine amet Summam Essentiam': The Eudaemonist Ethics of St Anselm," *Mediaeval Studies* 70 (2008), 1–29, and Bernd Goebel, "'Beatitudo Cum Iustitia'. Anselm von Canterbury über Gerechtigkeit, Freiheit und das Verhältnis von Gerechtigkeit und Glück," in Jörg Disse and Bernd Goebel, eds., *Gott und die Frage nach dem Glück: Anthropologische und etische Perspektiven* (Frankfurt am Main, 2010), pp. 60–120. Abelard discusses the highest good for instance in his *Collationes* 2.68, ed. John Marenbon and Giovanni Orlandi (Oxford, 2001), pp. 84–87; see John Marenbon, *The Philosophy of Peter Abelard* (Cambridge, 1997).

such a tradition of moral philosophy, and uses the structural and substantive elements shared by this tradition as a basis for combining the insights of thinkers in other respects far removed from one another.

In order to bring out the complexity and depth of John's concept of happiness I will here focus on three central and deeply interrelated features that John drew from philosophical tradition: a teleological view of human nature; the notion that the *telos* of humanity was happiness; and a notion of the kind of happiness that was specific to human nature.[17]

John's ethics are deeply embedded in a teleological mode of thought. The essence of this kind of moral thinking is the idea that all things seek their own fulfilment, that is, that all things have an end or goal towards which they remain orientated, and towards which they strain to progress. This goal – *telos*, in Latin *finis* – is an indispensible part of the definition of a thing, and corresponds to the final cause within the widely diffused Aristotelian scheme of fourfold causality.[18] *Finis* in this sense usually appears in John's writings in the context of rational action directed at some purpose. He may speak of victory as the *finis* of battle[19]; that persuasion through speaking is the *finis* of the orator, curing by medicine of the doctor, and of the adulator to deceive by soothing talk;[20] that wisdom is the *finis* of philosophy;[21] and that certitude is the *finis* of reason.[22] Common to all these examples is the notion of the *finis* as the fulfilment of some purposeful activity, and the idea that these activities to a large extent are defined by the ends at which they aim. As we have seen above, John envisions happiness as the end of human life as such in very much the same way as he sees persuasive speaking as the end of the orator. Being human, however, can hardly be said to be a purposeful activity like public oratory, medicine, adulation, or philosophy. So how do John and his models justify the transposition from rational, purposeful activity to other modes of being and acting?

---

17   See Irwin, *The Development of Ethics*, p. 5.

18   For the Aristotelian formulation of this notion of causality, see, among myriad accounts, the condensed exposition in Jonathan Barnes, *Aristotle: A Very Short Introduction* (Oxford, 2000), pp. 83–91, and the fuller treatment in T.H. Irwin, *Aristotle's First Principles* (Oxford, 1998), pp. 95–97 and *passim*. Although John of course never had direct access to Aristotle's most mature and morally salient formulations of this doctrine, the conceptual scheme itself was available to him in numerous ways; of which Calcidius's commentary on Plato's *Timaeus* and Boethius's *Consolatio Philosophiae* are among the most important.

19   See John of Salisbury, Letter 145, in *The Later Letters*, p. 38: "Et quia finis pugnae uictoria est..."

20   *Policraticus* 3.10, ed. Keats-Rohan, p. 204: "Sicut enim finis oratoris est persuasisse dictione, medici curasse medicina, sic adulatoriae finis est suauiloquio decepisse."

21   *Policraticus* 5.9, ed. Webb, vol. 1, p. 319: "philosophiae finis sapientia est."

22   *Metalogicon* 2.20, p. 90: "ratio cognitionis certitudinis finem quaerat aut teneat."

Here, the Aristotelian influence on the tradition of teleological ethics comes particularly to the fore. The teleological mode of thought was invoked to explain the workings of nature as much as the actions of rational beings. The term *natura* could be applied universally to everything that exists in and of itself, as opposed to that which existed by art;[23] or it could be used more specifically, in the truest sense of the word, to what made each kind of thing the kind of thing that it is.[24] That is to say, each species of substance, be it a daffodil, fire, a halibut, or a human being, partook in a nature, an essence, which conferred a certain mode of being, a certain potential of innate capacities and properties, and an impulse towards realizing this potential by developing the innate capacities as fully as possible.[25] Natures were on this mode of thought regarded as teleological, in that each kind of thing was ordered towards reaching its own perfection by the full development of the innate potential inherent in its nature. The *finis* of each nature, then, constituted the full realization of the mode of being and acting constituting the characteristics of that nature.[26]

The concept of nature plays a major role in the thought of John of Salisbury, but as so often the terminological unity of usage is analogical rather than univocal. The term occurs several hundred times in each of John's major works, and his usage extends over a wide range of meanings the interrelationship of which is highly complex. Still, for our present purposes, what we need is merely to show that John held a notion of nature like the one sketched out above; a full analysis of John's concept of nature as such, although interesting, would be beyond the present scope.[27] From this perspective, a highly illuminating example is found in the 8th Chapter of the first book of the *Metalogicon*. This is, of course, arguably among John's works the one that wears its Aristotelianism most conspicuously. This first book deals with a view of learning as a development of a shared human potential rather than something you either possess in

---

23   For John, human *artes* were based on nature, and constituted a development of rather than an alternative to it; See, e.g. *Metalogicon* 1.11, p. 30.

24   Concise expositions of the concept of nature in the high middle ages are easily available in Edith Dudley Sylla, "Creation and Nature," in A.S. McGrade, ed., *The Cambridge Companion to Medieval Philosophy* (Cambridge, 2003), pp. 171–195, here pp. 176–177; and Gyula Klima, "Natures: the Problem of Universals," in ibid., pp. 196–207, *passim*.

25   See Irwin, *The Development of Ethics*, pp. 134–139.

26   Again, John never had direct access to Aristotle's mature formulations of this mode of thought, but it was available to him through various intermediaries, for instance Boethius, *Consolatio Philosophiae* 3.10–11.

27   An interesting analysis of John's notion of nature in a wider sense can be found in Barbara Hebling-Gloor, *Natur und Aberglaube im Policraticus des Johannes von Salisbury* (Zurich, 1956).

full or not at all based on purely innate qualities, and in this context the concept of human nature becomes a contentious question. In *Metalogicon* 1.8, John argues that human nature, although bountifully endowed with potential, is in need of both God's grace and human endeavour in order to realize this potential. John provides the following, slightly hesitant definition:

> For nature, as some people have it, -- although it is hard to define -- is a certain generative force (*uis quaedam genitiua*) implanted in all things, by which they can act or be acted upon. It is called generative, moreover, because all things acquire a nature in the course of being generated, and because for each thing its nature is the principle of its existence. For any one thing gets from its components its aptitude for this or for that, whether these components are known by the name of parts, or befall at the origin of matter and form, as in simple things that do not admit to the accumulation of parts, or the notion of composition only enters through the decree of divine goodness.[28]

This definition, the formulation of which appears to be John's own, shows a concept of nature as the principle that makes any given thing come into existence, and confers a definite form of existence, a definite kind of "thingness," on it. It is through its nature that a thing of any kind acquires the aptitudes and capabilities that belong to its kind, and it is through its nature that it is impelled to act according to these aptitudes and powers. But nature is not conceived along the mechanistic lines more familiar to the modern mind, and its causality is certainly not restricted to efficient causation alone. Nature needed to be developed, and directed towards its proper end. John exemplifies this through a reminder of the way in which Socrates curbed his natural wantonness through assiduous practice of virtue.[29] He proceeds to stress that every human being needs to work at developing the potential naturally given to them, those with only limited talents as much as the prodigiously gifted. "Nature is always

---

28   *Metalogicon* 1.8, p. 25: "Est autem natura ut quibusdam placet, licet eam sit definire difficile, uis quaedam genitiua rebus omnibus insita ex qua facere uel pati possunt. Genitiua autem dicitur, eo quod ipsam res quaeque contrahat a causa suae generaionis, et ab eo quod cuique est principium existendi. Res enim quaelibet a componentibus contrahit unde ad hoc apta sit uel ad illud, siue componentia partium nomine censeantur, siue accedant ad originem materiae et formae ut in simplicibus quae coaceruationem partium non admittunt, siue ratio componendi ad solius diuinae bonitatis decretum accedat." My own translation.
29   Ibid. 1.8, p. 26.

beneficial, but so far it never or rarely attains the highest summit (*culmen*) without application."[30] There is, then, in John's notion of nature a *culmen* towards which it should reach and develop. And John's insistence that Socrates defined and perfected his dissolute character through "the castigation of philosophy and the exercise of virtue" shows that this teleological concept of human nature played a core role in what John had defined as the key task and province of ethics.[31]

This view of nature reinforces the requirement of a definite conception of the end towards which one should develop – as John's example of Socrates's excessive love of women shows, the given and innate was no dependable guide for what qualities should be perfected, and what qualities should be contained. So far we have seen that John subscribed to a teleological structure in ethical thought, and that the role of ethics was to realize the *finis* embedded and innate in human nature. These are abstract considerations detailing the structure rather than the substantial content of John's ethics; and this content is of course an indispensible part of our account of John's moral thought. Yet these abstract structures are necessary for fully to grasp the substantial content of John's account of the *finis* of human nature, *beatitudo*, happiness. But while John's implicit endorsement of teleological naturalism highlights his affinity for Aristotelian thought, his thinking about the substantial content of the natural *finis* of human beings betrays profound reliance of what we for the sake of convenience may call Augustinian Neo-Platonism.

Of course, in classical and patristic thought it was precisely the substantive content of the notion of the highest good for human beings that distinguished the various schools of philosophy from each other. The basic teleological structure of moral thought was shared across the spectrum of different philosophical directions, and the various accounts of the precise definition of the highest good for human beings, being the most central philosophical question of all, became the source of all significant differences between philosophical schools. This is as evident in the basic structure of Cicero's *De finibus bonorum et malorum* as it is in Augustine's presentation of the various schools of classical philosophy in *De ciuitate Dei*, Book 8. While it is perhaps doubtful that John read *De finibus*, he certainly studied *De ciuitate Dei* intently; and the eighth book of that work forms the backbone for John's own discussion of the history of philosophy in *Policraticus* 7.

---

30   Ibid. 1.8, p. 27: "Prodest utique natura, sed eatenus aut numquam aut raro ut sine studio culmen optineat."

31   Ibid. 1.8, p. 26: "naturae tamen intemperantiam, castigatione philosophiae et uirtutis exercitatione repressit..."

We may confidently assert, then, that John knew the full importance and the full consequences of giving a substantive definition of happiness.

When John claims that all rational beings reach for happiness, he is not merely making a statement of psychological motivation, a purely subjective teleology ordered towards whatever each individual considers most conducive to their own happiness. On the contrary, the end that all rational beings desire and act to realize is dictated by their nature, and consists in the full realization and perfection of the aptitudes and qualities characterizing that nature. In the Aristotelian form, this notion culminates in an analogical rather than substantial unity of definition: the *telos* of each species of thing, which we call happiness in rational creatures, is specific to each nature, and the different manifestations of such ultimate goods possess no substantial similarity, only purely formal definitions. The highest good for human beings has very little in common with the *telos* of ants or water, apart from the formal definition as that which completes and perfects a nature. Within the various classical schools of moral philosophy there is comparatively little effort to find a supreme good transcending genera and species; the full realization of human nature alone is at the heart of ethics.

Considering John's reputation as perhaps the quintessential 12th-century humanist, we might expect something like this mode of thought to govern John's account as well. What John in fact offers, however, has a somewhat different emphasis. While we should be wary of overemphasizing the differences between Aristotelian and Augustinian/Neo-Platonist notions of happiness, there is in John's thought a strong stress on the unity of the highest good for all created things, and how the transcendence of this good renders the human soul incapable, through its own terrestrial, material nature, to attain happiness face to face with God, that goes beyond Aristotelianism.[32]

John's most profound thinking on human happiness is not presented in one comprehensive treatise; it is found scattered throughout his various works. There are, however, some passages where we find this problem given explicit treatment, and the cumulative effect of these passages, combined with the traditions of thought John invokes to make his own arguments, provides a

---

32 I do not mean by this to neglect or downplay the significant influences John's thought betrays from Aristotelian thought as well as from other thinkers, like Boethius or Abelard. While all of these are vital to John's discussion of happiness as well as for his moral thought in general, I am here merely emphasizing the singular importance of Augustinian thinking on John's substantive definition of happiness. Augustine's influence on Boethius and Abelard should also be kept in mind.

comprehensively Augustinian view of what comprises the ultimate happiness and highest good for human beings. We have already made our acquaintance with a part of one of these passages above, *Policraticus* 7.8, where John discusses the relative positions of happiness and virtue. In this same passage, John goes on to provide some additional glimpses of his notion of happiness as the enjoyment of the highest good.

It may initially seem as though John makes mutually exclusive or at least contradictory claims about the nature of happiness during the course of this chapter of the *Policraticus*, however. At various points in his discussion, he appears to identify virtue, happiness, and God as the highest good. Now, one defining characteristic of the highest good in the traditions of thought available to John was that it was single, indivisible, and simple. The highest good must be self-sufficient, embracing the plenitude of goodness that leaves nothing to be desired apart from itself.[33] Positing three very different entities as the highest good within a few lines of each other, as John does in *Policraticus* 7.8, ostensibly militates forcefully against this idea. We have, however, already seen that the contradiction implicit in calling both virtue and happiness the highest good is only apparent; virtue is the highest good in the order of human acts on earth, but happiness is the highest good in a more simple and fundamental sense, as the attainment of the full perfection of human nature as it could and should be. In the same way, the tension between John's statement that "happiness is the one and single supreme good of all" and his insistence a few paragraphs bellow that God is *summe bonus et summum bonum*, supremely good and the supreme good, may be resolved.[34] In his discussion of the various schools of classical philosophy in the first parts of *Policraticus* 7, John follows closely the Augustinian presentation of the same material in *De ciuitate Dei*, Book 8. This fact is overwhelmingly clear simply from the source apparatus of Webb's edition, but it becomes still clearer when one compares the congruency in overall mode of argument and of substance in the Augustinian and the Sarisberiensian accounts. Within the Augustinian tradition, the apparent opposition between identifying the supreme good as happiness and as God is resolved by specifying that God is the supreme good in the most simple and fundamental sense, while happiness consists in the human enjoyment of God according to the capabilities inherent in human nature.

---

33   See for instance Aristotle, *Nicomachean Ethics*, 1097a15–b21. In texts available to John, this question was addressed for instance Boethius (e.g. *Consolatio Philosophiae* 3.2) and Anselm of Canterbury (e.g. *Monologion* 17).

34   Compare *Policraticus* 7.8, ed. Webb, vol. 2, 561c (p. 320) with 563b (p. 323).

The enjoyment of God, *Deo frui*, is of course a fundamental idea of Augustine's metaphysics and theology.[35] In *De doctrina Christiana*, for instance, Augustine states that goods enjoyed for their own sake are better than goods used to attain other goods.[36] Enjoyment, *frui*, is therefore raised above use, *uti*, and the enjoyment of the highest good is raised above the secondary, instrumental, and derivative goodness of the things we use in order to attain what is supremely good and enjoyed only for its own sake.[37] Now, in Augustine's theology, only God is enjoyed purely for his own sake, and consequently God is the one, single, simple and supreme good. As we have seen, John subscribes to this view. Combining insights from Plato, Augustine, and Boethius, John claims that

> the philosopher, whose intention is directed towards becoming wise, is according to (Plato) one who loves God, and, suppressing vices, applies his soul to intelligible things (*rebus agnoscendis*) so that from the understanding of these things he may proceed to true happiness. For these things (sc. *res agnoscendae*) make a man happy if the chains of vice are unbound, and as though through ascending stages of contemplation he is given to look into the lucid and unfailing fount of good.[38]

Happiness, by this account, means ultimately the beatific vision of God, as the outcome of progressive liberation from vice and contemplative ascent from sensible things to the transcendent truth.

---

35   See, e.g. Oliver O'Donovan, "'Usus' and 'Fruitio' in Augustine, 'De Doctrina Christiana' 1," *Journal of Theological Studies* 33 (1982), 361–397, John M. Rist, *Augustine: Ancient Thought Baptized* (Cambridge, 1994), pp. 164–166, and, old but far from dated, Étienne Gilson, *The Christian Philosophy of Saint Augustine* (London, 1961), pp. 165–169.

36   See Augustine, *De doctrina Christiana* 1.3.7, ed. R.P.H. Green (Oxford, 1995), p. 14: "Res ergo aliae sunt quibus fruendum est, aliae quibus utendum, aliae quae fruuntur et utuntur. Illae quibus fruendum est nos beatos faciunt; istis quibus utendum est tendentes ad beatitudinem adiuvamur et quasi adminiculamur."

37   See *De doctrina Christiana* 1.4.8, ed. Green, p. 14: "Frui est enim amore inhaerere alicui rei propter se ipsam," with 1.5.10, ed. Green, p. 16: "Res igitur quibus fruendum est, pater et filius et spiritus sanctus, eademque trinitas, una quaedam summa res communisque omnibus fruentibus ea, si tamen res et non rerum omnium causa, si tamen et causa."

38   *Policraticus* 7.8, ed. Webb, vol. 2, p. 120: "Philosophus autem, cuius intentio dirigitur illuc ut sapiat, eodem auctore amator Dei est, et uitia subigens rebus agnoscendis applicat animum ut his agnitis ad ueram beatitudinem possit accedere. Haec autem hominem beatum faciunt si et uitiorum soluantur uinculis, et quasi quibusdam gradibus contemplationis lucidum et indeficientem fontem boni detur inuisere."

John states explicitly on several occasions that this beatific vision also constitutes the full perfection and realization of human aptitudes and potential,
again drawing on Platonic, Neo-Platonic, and Christian resources in making
his point. He twice quotes with approval Plato's anticipation of Christian theology in the Timaeus: "He (sc. Plato) (…) affirms that divine goodness is the
end (*finis*) of all things. (…) So consequently he made all things similar to himself, so that the nature of each thing should be capable of happiness (*capax
beatitudinis*)."[39] Although this phrase is lifted verbatim from Chalcidius's Latin
translation of the *Timaeus*, John may very well have found it in Abelard's theological works, where the exact same extract occurs repeatedly and in this same
context.[40] The notion that human nature was capable of happiness, indeed
created specifically to be capable of God's happiness, is widespread in the
mainstream of theological thought to which John frequently professes and
displays his allegiance. John's repeated invocation of this idea is therefore
both significant and revealing. Whenever he discusses the substance of true
happiness, the happiness by reference to which the life of virtue is called happiness, he aligns himself with the tradition of Augustinian Neo-Platonism that
defines the beginning and the end of ethics as the beatific vision of God in the
full perfection and realization of human nature.[41]

As we have seen above, John's view of human nature entails that only specific potentials and aptitudes are to be developed, while others should be contained and made subordinate to the higher elements of what constitutes the
human person. John's identification of the parts of human nature that should
be perfected is therefore essential to a comprehensive picture of John's notion
of human happiness. Such identification is provided for instance in the first
chapter of the third book of the *Policraticus*. This chapter deals with the definition of what John calls *salus uniuersalis et publica*, public and universal welfare.[42] Augustine is once again the model for John's account here. John begins
by defining that *salus* as the good condition of life (*incolumitas uitae*), a definition that on its own is singularly unhelpful, but which serves as the point of
departure of a line of reasoning that ultimately touches the heart of John's

---

39   Ibid. 2.12, ed. Keats-Rohan, p. 91: "Ille (…) finem omnium diuinam astruit bonitatem. (…)
     Itaque consequenter cuncta sui similia, prout natura cuiusque beatitudinis capax esse
     poterat, effici uoluit."
40   See, e.g. Peter Abelard, *Theologia Scholarium* 3.30, ed. Eligius-Marie Buytaert and Constant
     J. Mews (Turnhout,1987), p. 512.
41   Gilson, *Christian Philosophy of Saint Augustine*, pp. 3–10 remains an engaging and enlight-
     ening account of this core part of Augustine's thought.
42   *Policraticus* 3.1, ed. Keats-Rohan, pp. 172–175.

moral anthropology. The good condition of human life pertains primarily to the highest part of the human person, that is, the soul. The soul is the principle of life and unity for the whole body-soul compound, the rational and spiritual part that turns corruptible matter into a living organism.[43] But the soul, in turn, is itself animated by God as its principle and end: Just as, for the body, living means to be quickened and moved by the soul, and acquiesce to the soul through the disposition of (bodily) movements and to become as one with it through a certain necessity of obeisance; so too the soul lives by this, that it in its own way is quickened and truly moved by God, obeying Him with submissive devotion and acquiescing to Him in all things. To the extent it fails to do this, to that extent it also fails to live.[44]

In the same way as those parts of the body over which the body loses control will wither and die, so too will the soul wither unless it is completely filled and animated by God. Here there is a strong correlation between inner completeness and outer perfection of life: "God occupies the whole soul that lives perfectly, possesses it, rules over it, and lives in it entirely."[45] Of course, John reminds us, we do not really talk of the soul as having parts, as it participates more fully in God's simplicity than does the body. We may still use the term in a figurative sense to talk about the virtues, which, while not adding anything quantitative or truly divisible to the soul, extends and deepens it to make it reach more fully for its supreme good.[46] When the Holy Spirit infuses itself into these "parts" of the soul, the life of the soul is made firm and perfected.[47] Reaching his definition, John states that "this seems to me to be the well-being of life, when the mind, animated by the

---

43   Ibid. 3.1, ed. Keats-Rohan, p. 173: "Caro siquidem uiuit ab anima, cum aliunde corpori uita esse non possit, quod semper inertiae suae torpore quiescit, nisi spiritualis naturae beneficio moueatur."

44   Ibid.: "Sicut ergo corpori uiuere est uegetari moueri ab anima et dispositione sui motibus animae adquiescere et ei quadam obediendi necessitate concordare, sic et anima ex eo uiuit quod suo modo uegetatur et uere mouetur a Deo et ei subiecta deuotione obtemperat et in omnibus adquiescit. Si quo minus, et eo minus uiuit."

45   Ibid.: "Deus animam perfecte uiuentem totam occupat, totam possidet, regnat et uiget in tota."

46   Ibid.: "Partium expers [anima] est simplicisque naturae, et totius duplicitatis ignara. Partes tamen quas potuit, sibi a distributore bonorum uendicauit. Quas, inquis? Virtutes utique, quibus uiget et operatur et sui experimentum facit. Si non ergo multiplicitate partium et quantitatis quadam distensione crescit, ratione tamen et intellectu, appetitu boni, auersione mali, manente simplicitatis natura dilatatur."

47   Ibid.: "Cum uero partes istas spiritus implet – Deus enim spiritus est – solida et perfecta est uita animae."

Spirit, is enlightened for the knowledge of things, and enkindled for the love of good and the practice of virtue."[48]

Again, then, we see the beatific vision of God as the *finis* of human life and endeavour, and the prize for which the virtuous life is both a preparation and a prelibation. It is this composite notion of happiness as the *finis* of human nature, I would argue, that constitutes the backbone and the focal point of the ethics of John of Salisbury. As such, it also provides the framework within which John's treatment of the concept of virtue must be seen.

This patristic heritage, however, carries with it its own set of problems and paradoxes, and one such paradox must be treated before we move on to describing John's account of the virtuous life. The role of grace in John's account of the human moral agent brings the patristic heritage even more clearly into focus, and highlights John's divergence from classical variants of teleological naturalism. For while, on for instance the Aristotelian account, natures are capable of attaining fulfilment and perfection by their own natural powers, John's account of human nature is predicated on the principle that the natural powers of human beings are radically insufficient for the realization of the human *finis*. Grace, John repeatedly states, is always and everywhere necessary for the full realization of the specifically human aptitudes and potentials. Reason is a prodigious gift, capable of sublime achievements; but even reason, *qua* gift, is dead where grace is absent.[49] Before we move on to study John's account of the moral life, the life of virtue, we must address the issue of the extent to which the role John prescribes for grace leaves any room at all for human liberty and human endeavour.

Grace and the Limits of Human Endeavour

The concept of grace in John's thought, and the role it plays in his lines of argument, has received comparatively little attention in recent scholarship. It may even be said that an insistence on the absolute primacy of grace goes against the grain of the modern perception of John as a moderate humanist defending the potential of human reason and creativity. Let us therefore begin by looking

---

48   Ibid. 3.1, ed. Keats-Rohan, p. 174: "Et haec michi uidetur uera et unica incolumitas uitae, cum mens uiuificante Spiritu ad rerum notitiam illustratur, et accenditur ad amorem honestatis et cultum uirtutis."

49   E.g. ibid. 3.1, ed. Keats-Rohan, p. 175: "Non tamen corruptae naturae aduersus gratiam magnifico fimbrias aut falerias erigo, quasi ipsa aliquid boni habeat quod non acceperit, cum certum sit quia sine ea nichil possumus facere."

in some detail at how John discusses grace in his various works, to see the extent to which John is committed to the paramount role of grace in successful human agency.

Although John's most detailed treatments of grace are found in his prose works, it may be useful to start by quoting from the at once more poignant and more economical formulations found the *Entheticus maior*. John states his view plainly and unconditionally: "without grace the forces of nature will strive in vain/and all its efforts towards good will be void (...). She precedes and rules the mind, she exhorts the affections, she also promotes the uses of our labours, watches over the tongue and does not permit it to be guilty, she uplifts affection, directs reason, composes actions, unlocks secrets, teaches truths."[50] This deep, all-embracing, all-penetrating notion of grace that we find distilled in the *Entheticus* is discussed, in more detail but with less economy, in John's major prose works. In the *Metalogicon*, grace acts as the foundation for learning, and the life-giving factor that fructifies the mind as it strives for wisdom. There is no shortcut to learning, as the Cornificians claimed; only hard work will suffice. Reading, learning, and meditation are the pillars supporting the house of knowledge. Grammar – that is, learning to read the staple texts of school learning – thus becomes an inescapable starting point for the would-be savant; but even this basic discipline is sterile in the absence of grace:

> It is accordingly evident that grammar, which is the basis and root of scientific knowledge, implants, as it were the seed (of virtue) in nature's furrow after grace has readied the ground. This seed, provided again that cooperating grace is present, increases in substance and strength until it becomes solid virtue, and it grows in manifold respects until it fructifies in good work, wherefore men are called and actually are good. At the same time, it is grace alone which makes a man good. For grace brings about both the willing and the doing of good.[51]

---

50   *Entheticus maior*, ll.225–226 and 230–234, p. 120. Latin text, p. 121: "hac sine naturae vires frustrantur, et eius/ad bona conatus omnis inanis erit (...). Haec mentem praevenit atque regit/haec monet affectus, operum quoque promovet usus,/linguam custodit, nec sinit esse ream,/erigit affectum, rationem dirigit, actus/componit, reserat abdita, vera docet." See also van Laarhoven's insightful commentary in vol. 2, pp. 280–282.

51   *Metalogicon* 1.23, pp. 50–51: "Vnde constat quod grammatica quae istorum fundamentum est et radix, quodam modo sementem iacit in sulcis naturae, gratia tamen praeeunte, quae si ei cooperatrix quoque affuerit, in solidae uirtutis robur coalescit, et crescit multipliciter ut boni operis fructum faciat, unde boni uiri nominantur et sunt. Sola tamen gratia quae et uelle bonum et perficere operatur (...)." Trans. McGarry, p. 65.

Grace, then, is vital for all intellectual work, in an intimate and pervasive way. It provides the basis – readies the ground – and provides the principle and actuality of growth. Again, John makes clear that philosophy as a human activity depends on the gift of grace from its beginning to its end, saturating it throughout. As we have seen, John claims that the human being is fully alive to the extent that the soul rules the body, and to the extent that the Holy Spirit rules the soul. Now, while all other created things are filled by the Spirit on account of their nature, the mode in which the spirit of God fills and fulfils rational creatures is through grace.[52] "They exist, then, because Truth is in them. They are enlightened, because Wisdom is in them. They love the good, because the Fount of goodness and love is in them. For all human or angelic virtue is a certain vestige of divinity somehow impressed on rational creature. The indwelling Holy Spirit impresses sanctity on the soul, and scatters its rivulets widely, revealing the gifts of diverse graces."[53]

This mode of thought and this form of expression is thoroughly Augustinian. Augustine often defined grace as the operation of the Holy Spirit in the human being,[54] and here we find John relying on the same idea. John here identifies grace with the freely given gifts of the Holy Spirit. John's line of argument here serves to underpin his insistence, as we have seen, that grace is necessary for all human activity. If the soul, as the ruler of the body, only lives to the extent that it is filled by the Holy Spirit, and the Holy Spirit operates in rational creatures through grace, it follows that grace is a sine qua non of all human endeavour, just as John insists.

Whenever he speaks about grace, then, John appears wholeheartedly to embrace the Augustinian notion of grace without the reservations and qualifications that would leave space for a separate sphere of individual agency and judgement. Grace provides that initial spark that allows human nature to quicken and start growing, and anticipates and carries all human striving towards goodness and truth to completion. No part of the healthy soul is closed to the Spirit of God, John says.[55] All this, however, appears to uncover an unacknowledged and unresolved tension in John's thinking. His statements on

---

52   *Policraticus* 3.1, ed. Keats-Rohan, p. 174: "cum sit in omnibus per naturam, sola inhabitat rationabilia per gratiam."

53   Ibid. 3.1, ed. Keats-Rohan, p. 174: "Sunt ergo, quia in eis ueritas est. Illustrantur, quia in eis sapientia est. Bonum diligunt, quia in eis fons bonitatis et caritatis est. Omnis etenim uirtus angelica uel humana quoddam diuinitatis uestigium est rationali creaturae quodammodo impressum. Spiritus Sanctus inhabitans imprimit animae sanctitatem eiusdemque riuulos multiphariam spargit, diuersarum exerens carismata gratiarum."

54   See Richard Cross, "Weakness and Grace," in Robert Pasnau with Christina van Dyke, eds., *The Cambridge History of Medieval Philosophy*, 2 vols. (Cambridge, 2010), vol. 1, p. 450.

55   See *Policraticus* 3.1, ed. Keats-Rohan, p. 173: "Nullus ei angulus exceptus est."

grace and its all-encompassing role seem to undermine his own emphasis on human liberty. Is John, then, inherently inconsistent, or can we find some way, some perspective, to resolve this tension?

The problem of human freedom and its apparent negation in divine grace was acknowledged in the tradition of thought within which I would like to place John of Salisbury.[56] The basis for the possibility of human freedom within the paradigm of grace within this tradition of thought rests on a strong claim for the true purpose of freedom, which in turn is bound to the purpose of human life in the first place.[57] By developing the specifically human faculties and potentials through the inculcation of the virtues, human beings may ultimately attain the very perfection for which these faculties were created: the beatific vision of God. However, while human beings must direct all their striving towards this ultimate end in order to have the possibility of attaining it, the innate powers of human nature are radically insufficient to reach their appointed end unaided.[58] Only through the free gift of grace can human nature be raised to the beatific vision. Within this paradigm, human freedom means primarily this potential to participate according to their proper measure in their own salvation, and salvation is ultimately the sole and single purpose for freedom.

If by modern standards, then, the Augustinian freedom is curiously circumscribed, it is not so when seen from within the tradition of Augustinian thought. Using freedom to pursue ends other than that perfect end for which it was created is an abuse rather than a true exercise of the freedom of the will. The full and entirely free commitment of the individual is an integral part of the Augustinian model of free human agency, and to that extent human will remains free. The striving towards God as the true *telos* of human life must be grounded in one's own volition, it cannot be coerced. On this view, the will is free to give its consent to any end, any perceived good it wills; but it is constrained by the fact that choosing its own ends will strangle it, while choosing the divinely given end will truly liberate it.[59] This mode of thought thus creates the somewhat paradoxical situation where it is only through freely surrendering one's own will in order to follow the will of God that human beings truly exercise their freedom. Trying to use the divinely given freedom for one's own ends means losing true freedom. It is arguably this paradox that, unless treated

---

56   This acknowledgement is clearly indicated by the number of works arguing against an actual conflict between freedom and grace.

57   See, e.g. Anselm of Canterbury, *De veritate* 5, ed. F.S. Schmitt, 6 vols. (Edinburgh, 1946–61), vol. 1, pp. 181–183.

58   See particularly Augustine's anti-Pelagian writings, for instance *De natura et gratia* 4.

59   See, e.g. Rist, *Augustine*, pp. 133–134.

precisely as a paradoxical mystery, creates the apparent conflict between free will and grace that Augustine and his followers strove to resolve.

Now, as we have seen, John embraced the Augustinian notion of the ultimate *telos* and highest good for human beings. The conclusion to the discussion about the human soul and human agency in *Policraticus* 3.1, from which I quoted earlier, is that the good life for human beings is found "when the mind is enlightened by the life-giving spirit to the knowledge of things, and is enkindled for the love of good and the cultivation of virtue."[60] The ultimate perfection of human beings is both a moral and an intellectual perfection, but some initial knowledge is necessary for the cultivation of virtue to find direction.[61] Here, John seems to envision some independent room for human powers after all, when he claims that such knowledge is found in two ways: either, by using reason to discover what lies within the scope of human intellect, or being illuminated by grace to learn what is beyond this scope.[62] Human nature, human reason, human endeavour is not powerless and pointless, but efficacious within the larger scheme of salvation. But John takes care to clarify that he does not mean to separate the spheres of nature and grace after all. "Yet I do not boastfully raise the smoke and mirrors of corrupt nature against grace, as though nature had any good that it had not been given, when it is certain that we can do nothing without grace."[63] Human reason is efficacious and good, but only within the framework of grace – there is no opposition, no competition.

John's insistence that human beings retain their freedom to act of their own volition, and indeed have an obligation to exercise this potential, can be seen for instance in his debunking of those who use various methods of divination and soothsaying to predict the future. John maintains that the future is not determined, but remains open to and in need of human agency and human responsibility.[64] While some would claim that God's providence and prescience necessary entails a form of determinism, John strenuously denies this, drawing on Boethius and Anselm to bolster his views.[65] Even if God, who is outside of time, knows in his timeless and unchanging way how individual human beings will act, this

---

60 *Policraticus* 3.1, ed. Keats-Rohan, p. 174: "cum mens uiuificante Spiritu ad rerum notitiam illustratur, et accenditur ad amorem honestatis et cultum uirtutis."

61 Ibid.

62 Ibid.: "aut rationis exercitio quod sciri potest intellectus inuenit aut quod absconditum est reuelans gratia oculis ingerens patefecit."

63 See above, note 48.

64 *Policraticus* 2.20, ed. Keats-Rohan, pp. 118–119.

65 As stated by both Webb and Keats-Rohan in their respective apparatuses: "In capitulis sequentibus Augustini et Boethii sequitur Noster"; see Webb, vol. 1, p. 113 with Keats-Rohan, p. 118.

does not impose any causal necessity on the actions of these individuals, John claims.[66] Human freedom remains; but left to its own devices it is bound to fall short of the ideals and goods it is created to realize. "In this alone is free will effective for man, that it is sufficient for him to do works of iniquity, but not for good, unless he arises anticipated and aided by grace."[67] The predicament of the human agent, then, is such that his actions are not pre-determined, and hence open to his free choice, but unless he surrenders his will to God's and cooperates with grace, it will not bring him any closer to what he truly desires.

John proceeds to emphasise this in the crucial eight and last book of the *Policraticus*. The theme of the synergetic effects of human obedience and divine grace forms a powerful undercurrent throughout the chapters of the closing book of the *Policraticus*, drawing heavily on a mode of thought that we also find in the theological heavyweights of John's own time and milieu. In particular, John's terminology and lines of argument here invoke the theology of free will and grace found in Saint Anselm and Saint Bernard. It is significant, though hardly surprising, that we find this mode of thought strongly present in crucial parts of the *Policraticus*.

The theological presence makes itself felt both in terminology and in argument. The terminological parallels, few but revealing, provide further grounds for ascribing basic tendencies in John's argument to theological influences. In *Policraticus* 8.5, for instance, we find John taking as given the characteristically Anselmian specification of the two inclinations of the will: "The authority of Sacred Scripture marks out two inclinations of the will to have existed in man from the beginning: that is, the desire for what is just (*iustum*), and the desire for what is useful (*commodum*)."[68] Textually, John is clearly drawing on Hugh

---

66   *Policraticus* 2.20, ed. Keats-Rohan, p. 118.

67   Ibid., p. 119: "In eo tamen solo adhuc ei liberum uiget arbitrium ut sibi ad opus iniquitatis sufficiat, etsi ad bonum non nisi a gratia praeuentus et adiutus assurgat."

68   Ibid. 8.5, ed. Webb, vol. 2, pp. 243–244: "Duos quidem affectus in homine ab initio extitisse sacrae Scripturae designat auctoritas, appetitum scilicet iusti et commodi appetitum." In his apparatus, Webb notes the absence in the Bible of such a formulation, and refers instead to what he finds to be a parallel in Augustine. The dichotomy in Augustine, however, is not identical with the one in play in John; and the combination of *affectus* and *commodum* is almost exclusively found in Anselm or texts clearly drawing on him. See in particular Anselm of Canterbury, *De casu Diaboli* 12, ed. Schmitt, vol. 1, pp. 251–255, and *De concordia praescientiae et praedestinationis et gratiae Dei cum libero arbitrio* 3.11, ed. Schmitt, vol. 2, pp. 278–284. For Anselm's moral psychology see in particular Bernd Goebel, *Rectitudo, Wahrheit und Freiheit bei Anselm von Canterbury: eine philosophische Untersuchung seines Denkansatzes* (Münster, 2001) and Goebel, "*Beatitudo cum iustitia*"; see Sønnesyn, "*Ut sine fine amet summam essentiam*." Cf. Hugh of Saint-Victor, *De sacramentis Christiane fidei* 1.7, ed. Rainer Berndt SJ (Frankfurt, 2008), p. 174.

of Saint-Victor's *De Sacramentis* 1.7 here, but the conceptual framework was proposed by Anselm. While this tradition of the Anselmian argument deserves closer scrutiny than would be appropriate here, it must at present suffice to say that the explicit invocation of Anselmian moral psychology here should help us bring into focus the strong undercurrent of this mode of thought in John's own formulations. John's tyrant resembles the Devil, whose fall in Anselm's account of it is caused by his excessive desire for his own *commodum* at the cost of his desire for the justice of God for its own sake.[69] In *Policraticus* 8, John repeats his assertion from earlier in the work that the tyrant, the antithesis of the good man and good citizen John wants to portray, is made a slave by his own falling away from the will of God, and his own refusal of assistance offered by the Spirit of God.[70] Returning to the phrase from the second letter to the Corinthians, *Ubi Spiritus Dei, ibi libertas*, which John frequently quoted, he argues that if this is so, then there is no state more servile than that of the one whom the Spirit does not stir.[71] The parallels both to the Anselmian account of the fall of the Devil and to John's own discussion of the workings of the Spirit in man are significant. Humility, obedience, and an uncompromising choice of the justice of God over one's own benefit continues to guide the discussion of the good and deficient citizen in the closing chapters of Book 8. John speaks of the *uires obedientia cum gratia*,[72] the powers of obedience with grace, that enable human beings to attain true happiness, *uera beatitudo*.[73] The fact that we find these ideas stressed so emphatically in these closing chapters of the *Policraticus*, placing the political and moral discussions of the middle books firmly within the framework of human agency in obedience and grace presented in the earlier books, shows that John wanted to highlight the symbiotic relationship between true freedom and divine grace in human agency in its ideal form. This does not mean that grace depended on human free choice in the same way as human free choice depended on grace. Grace was always the

---

69   Anselm of Canterbury, *De casu Diaboli* 12–14.

70   *Policraticus* 8.16, ed. Webb, vol. 2, p. 344: "Tu naturae gratiae et gloriae distingue libertatem, et inuenies nullam earum de uanitate contingere, nec tibi conditio magis seruilis occurret quam tiranni."

71   Ibid.: "Si enim ubi Spiritus Domini ibi libertas, miserrima profecto seruitute deprimitur quem spiritus nequam exagitat."

72   Ibid. 8.25, ed. Webb, vol. 2, p. 422: "Porro iocundus timor, qui in dilectionis reuerentiam cadit, non nouit otiari aut praescriptam sibi praeuicari legem, sed timoris foras mitti aculeos et ex amore facit bona, sponte sua adherens iustitiae; et quasi uiribus obedientiae cum gratia quodammodo uiolenter nititur adquirere uitam qui per inobedientiam ex leuitate arbitrii cucurrit in mortem."

73   Ibid.: "Timor innocentiam parit, iustitiam benefaciendi mandatorum obediantia promouet, rectoque calle ad ueram beatitudinem iustus perducitur."

primary agent, always already there to anticipate, assist, and amplify human actions far beyond what these actions were capable of attaining on their own accord. John, justly famous for his classical humanism, in no way tries to obliterate a notion of humanity's vast potential, or the necessity and fruitfulness of human endeavour; but he situates this endeavour firmly within the framework of divine grace. The life of virtue, then, is important, and human beings are capable of directing and furthering their own moral development – but only if the moral life is an integrated part of Christian life as a whole. It is firmly within the parameters of a full Christian life, then, that we need to situate his account of virtue and the virtues.

Virtue and the Virtues in John of Salisbury

Research over the last decades, particularly the pioneering work of Cary Nederman, has succeeded in establishing a strong presence in John's thought of a doctrine of virtue and the virtues first elaborated by Aristotle, but reaching John mainly through intermediaries like Cicero, Boethius, and others.[74] If my argument so far is tenable – and provided John's thought is internally consistent and coherent – this doctrine of the virtues must be anchored in the account of happiness sketched out above. It will be apparent from the structure of my argument so far that I hold this to be the case. Let us nevertheless defer asking and answering this question until we have given an outline of the doctrine or doctrines of virtue available to John, and how this intellectual heritage is visible in his own thought. We should once again remember that John left no comprehensive and condensed definition of virtue behind in his writings, and we are consequently dependent upon piecing together disparate and dispersed statements to form a full picture of his understanding of this concept. A brief glance at classical and Christian definitions prior to John may help us in selecting relevant statements from his own works.

When Socrates redirected philosophy from the study of nature to the study of ethics, that is, the study and development of human *mores*, the locus of ethics, for Socrates himself as well as for his pupils and the schools they instituted,

---

74   In addition to the articles referred to above, see also Cary J. Nederman, "Nature, Sin and the Origins of Society: The Ciceronian Tradition in Medieval Political Thought," *Journal of the History of Ideas* 49 (1988), 3–26, and idem, "Knowledge, Virtue and the Path to Wisdom: The Unexamined Aristotelianism of John of Salisbury's *Metalogicon*," *Mediaeval Studies* 51 (1989), 268–286.

was the human soul.[75] The development of human *mores*, habits of character, meant developing various facets or faculties of the human soul in order to realize its full potential. This realization could not be achieved through monadic actions, as though momentarily springing to life in a single action only to disappear from the soul once the action ceased. On the contrary, the soul was perfected to the extent that it developed stable habits, stable propensities to act in a certain way.[76] Aristotle made the definitive elaboration of this notion in his account of *hexeis*, habits of character.[77] Such habits dispose those who embody them to act in a certain way. Those habits that dispose human beings to act well and in accordance with the *telos* of human life were called virtues, *aretê*, while habits hindering such modes of action are called vices. The rational soul, as the locus of human agency, had to act in accordance with the virtues in order to fulfil its potential, and the virtues were nothing more than the habits of the soul disposing it to act in a certain way. Virtues were inculcated through assiduous repetition until they became habitual, that is, until they became inherent parts of the soul. In Aristotle's ethics, they were inextricably bound to, and had their ultimate purpose in, the highest good, that is, happiness: "Happiness (eudaimonia) is an activity (energeia) of the soul according to virtue (kath'aretên)."[78] The virtues dispose the soul to act, and happiness is the activity of the soul disposed in the best way.

As Cary Nederman has shown, Cicero adopted this notion of virtue and helped make it a staple of Latin moral terminology and conceptual basis. Cicero speaks of virtue (*uirtus*) as a habit of the rational soul (*habitus animi*) and in harmony with nature and reason.[79] Virtue denotes those qualities that make a man good, and allows him to attain the highest good for human beings. Crucial for our present concerns, moreover, Cicero carefully emphasises the crucial role of a clear notion of the highest good in order to arrive at a definite content of the life of virtue; virtue without some highest good with which to justify it and give it substance is blind.[80]

---

75   See John of Salisbury, *Policraticus* 7.2, ed. Webb, vol. 2, p. 105: "Et primus quidem Socrates uniuersam philosophiam ad corrigendos componendosque mores flexisse memoratur, cum ante illud omnes phisicis, id est rebus naturalibus, perscrutandis maximam operam dederint." This quotation, as indeed the extended argument in which it occurs, is quoted directly from or based upon Augustine, *De ciuitate Dei*, book 8.

76   See, e.g. Irwin, *The Development of Ethics*, pp. 25–27 and 155–157.

77   See ibid., pp. 153–197.

78   Aristotle, *Nicomachean Ethics* 1098a16–18.

79   Cicero, *De inventione*, 2.159, ed. Eduard Stroebel (Leipzig, 1915), p. 148.

80   Cicero, *De finibus bonorum et malorum* 5.6.15, ed. L.D. Reynolds (Oxford, 1997), p. 178.

This Ciceronian view is set up as an alternative to the Stoic doctrine, which Cicero seeks to refute. For the Stoics, a virtue itself was the highest good; there was no separate highest good over and above virtue.[81] For them, then, virtue did not set human beings on the course for happiness; it constituted it. Cicero rejected this view; so did Augustine and the Fathers of the Church. For Augustine, happiness in its fullest form was not attainable for human beings in their terrestrial existence, but only in the afterlife.[82] Furthermore, happiness was not attainable by human endeavour alone, but only through the aid of divine grace.[83] In some ways this widened the gap between virtue and happiness, in so far as the life of virtue could not reach complete and lasting happiness, but only act as a necessary stage on the journey towards happiness, providing fleeting glimpses of what true happiness would be like. Nevertheless, virtue was still for Augustine a necessary and inescapable part of the good human life, and aligned towards happiness as its ultimate end and justification.[84]

From what we have already seen from John's account of happiness as the ultimate end of human moral life, his account of the virtues seem to tap into the traditional debate in an intimate way. John's claim quoted above that *mores* are habits of character from which flows the repetition of individual acts illustrates his acceptance of the Aristotelian view of virtues as stable habits of character, deeply ingrained into the soul. It is significant in this context that he goes on to identify virtue and vice as the two categories into which the various *mores* can be separated, and that he uses the four cardinal virtues as concrete examples of virtuous *mores*. John's usage of the term *mos* here should not, therefore, lead us to doubt that he is drawing from the doctrine of virtues as stable habits of character. The notion that virtues and vices may be comprised by the general term *mores* saturates the immediate intellectual milieus of John's life and work. It occurs in the moral teaching of Anselm of Canterbury,[85] and it forms the opening discussion of Abelard's unfinished moral treatise *Scito te ipsum*.[86] Its recurrence in John's writings, then, may be seen as an

---

81   See the third book of Cicero's *De finibus*.

82   See, e.g. Rist, *Augustine*, pp. 48–53.

83   See, e.g. Gilson, *Christian Philosophy of Saint Augustine*, pp. 152–153.

84   For Augustine on Roman and Christian virtue and virtues, see in particular T.H. Irwin, "Splendid Vices? Augustine For and Against the Pagan Virtues," *Medieval Philosophy and Theology* 8 (1999), 105–127.

85   Most clearly in Anselm of Canterbury, *Liber Anselmi de humanis moribus* 133–134, ed. Richard W. Southern and F.S. Schmitt (Oxford, 1969), p. 89.

86   See Peter Abelard, *Scito te ipsum*, ed. David E. Luscombe (Oxford, 1971), p. 2.

illustration of John's immersion into a living tradition, a Christian redevelopment of the classical doctrine of virtues as stable habits.

We have also seen above that the virtues as John perceives them are fundamentally teleological in character, that is, that their purpose is to realize the highest good for human beings. This highest good transcends the life of virtue itself; virtue is for the sake of happiness, and not vice versa, and true happiness is the prize to be hoped for beyond terrestrial existence. The virtues, then, are not in any way to be considered instruments geared towards some hedonistic conception of happiness – John rejects the interpretations of Epicureanism that posit pleasure as the highest good.[87] The life of virtue provides the partial but genuine happiness attainable in this life, but only if it is chosen for the sake of the transcendent highest good for human nature, the beatific and loving vision of God. This is also evident in John's treatment of what the Romans, in this following the Platonic rather than the Aristotelian tradition, identified as the cardinal virtues: justice (*iustitia*), prudence (*prudentia*), fortitude (*fortitudo*), and temperance (*temperantia*).[88] All these cardinal virtues regulate the life of virtue in relation to the supreme good in their own specific way. Prudence was the virtue dealing with finding this supreme good and how it could be attained; fortitude ensured the perseverance and strength to attain it; justice governed the relationship to God and fellow men; and temperance contained the other virtues within their proper measure. Human nature, raised above other animate creatures on account of the faculty of reason, reached its perfection in the attainment of the purpose of reason, the beatific vision of Truth. Prudence, then, held a key place even among the cardinal virtues:

> Prudence consists entirely in insight into the truth, together with a certain skill in investigating the latter; whereas justice embraces the truth and fortitude defends it, while temperance moderates the activities of the aforesaid virtues. Thus it is indubitable that prudence is the root of all the virtues. If this root is severed, then the other virtues will wither and die of thirst, even as branches do when they are cut off from their natural source of sustenance. For who can embrace or practice something of which he is ignorant? Truth is the subject matter of prudence, as well as the fountain-head of all the virtues. One who comprehends

---

87　John's fullest discussion of this is found in *Policraticus* 7.15, ed. Webb, vol. 2, 671b–673a. (pp. 153–157).

88　See, e.g. Irwin, *The Development of Ethics*, pp. 83–84.

truth is wise, one who loves it good, "one who orders his life in accordance with it happy."[89]

Wisdom, virtue, and happiness are here defined as a way of life to be practiced rather than as some thing to be possessed. Virtue is a disposition to act
well, but it is only possessed to the extent it issues in action; this is repeatedly emphasised in John's works. One particularly interesting statement to
this effect is found in the crucial seventh book of the *Policraticus*. In 7.11,
John argues that the true meaning of philosophy, and the end, rule, and perfection of all human endeavour is the love (*caritas*) of God and the divine.[90]
Caritas is an active principle acting on, developing, perfecting those who
embody it, and consequently it becomes a principle of activity for them.[91]
The distinction between the truly wise, the true philosophers, and those
who merely seem wise and wear the disguise of philosophy, is not contained
in what they say, but in how they translate their statements into living
embodiment: "also the vain imitator of the philosopher may intermittently
teach what is right; but who follows the right that he teaches, he is truly a
philosopher."[92] John goes on, in the next chapter, to emphasise once again
that virtue is not found in words, but in action, in a way of life. Those who
claim that philosophy and virtue are purely a matter of words are wrong, he
says: "For the commendation of virtue consists in action, and virtue insepa-
rably accompanies wisdom."[93]

   As Pierre Hadot and others have underlined, the definition of philosophy
as a way of life rather than as a body of doctrine was firmly rooted in the
main schools of philosophy of the classical world, and was carried through

---

89   *Metalogicon* 2.1, p. 57: "Prudentia uero tota consistit in perspicientia ueri, et quadam
     sollertia illud examinandi. Porro iustitia illud amplectitur, fortitudo tuetur, temperantia
     uirtutum praecedentium exercitia moderatur. Vnde liquet prudentiam uirtutum omnium
     esse radicem, quae si praecidatur, ceterae uelut rami naturae beneficio destituti marcida
     quadam ariditate euanescunt. Quis enim amplectetur aut colet quod ignorat? At ueritas
     materia est prudentiae et uirtutum fons, quam plene nouerit, sapiens est, qui amauerit,
     bonus, et beatus qui tenuerit eam." Trans. McGarry, pp. 74–75.
90   See *Policraticus* 7.11, ed. Webb, vol. 2, p. 135.
91   Ibid. 7.11, ed. Webb, vol. 2, p. 136: "Haec est itaque uera et immutabilis philosophantium
     regula ut sic in omnibus legendis aut discendis, agendis aut omittendis quisque uersetur
     ut proficiat caritati."
92   Ibid.: "Sed recta dumtaxat interdum docet uanus philosophi imitator; sed qui recta
     quae docet sequitur, uere philosophus est."
93   Ibid. 7.12, ed. Webb, vol. 2, p. 136: "Nam uirtutis commendatio consistit ab opere, et sapi-
     entiam uirtus inseparabiliter comitatur."

into the middle ages in many ways and by many different carriers.[94] John is therefore again entirely in line with the practice of philosophy evident in the texts and traditions available to him. In many ways, this definition of philosophy may help explain why he does not come across as particularly concerned with originality and individual creativity in philosophy. John does not regard the task of the philosopher to be to add pieces of doctrine to an existing body, or alternatively to develop a new body of doctrines. Rather, the task of the philosopher, which is the task he sets out to perform himself, is to initiate others into the practice of philosophy as a way of life, and to cultivate that way of life himself. John's own practice is thus very much of a piece with the mode of thought he defends in his writings. The purpose of ethics is not to construct a reified system of thought abstracted from the nitty-gritty of human life, but to cultivate that life in the best possible way. The fruits of John's thought and writings are not primarily to be found in books, but in lives.[95]

If my reading of John so far has any merit, it should also be able to incorporate the doctrine of moderation according to the mean and John's preoccupation with liberty within the scheme I have sketched out so far. The evidence adduced to substantiate the claim that these elements form important parts of John's ethics is very strong, and I have no desire to throw any doubt upon their pervasive presence in John's thought and works. There is, I would argue, nothing in what I have argued so far that excludes the presence of the doctrine of the mean or the importance of liberty from John's ethics. If we regard ethics as primarily about a way of life through which the potential of human nature is actualized through the development of specifically human aptitudes, then liberty becomes an invaluable and indeed irreplaceable prerequisite for morality; not for its own sake, as a value or a good in itself, but as a necessary condition for the intrinsic activity which alone could develop human beings according their natural *finis*. Freedom, to John, cannot be freedom to choose one's own ends, one's own ultimate good, nor can it perform the part of an ultimate good itself; John is perfectly clear as to the nature of the highest good for human beings is, and in order for this good to be attained, freedom must be exercised with moderation. The value of freedom is derivative from its relation to the highest good, and freedom is consequently only truly valuable and necessary for

---

94   See, e.g. Pierre Hadot, *Philosophy as a Way of Life: Spiritual Exercises from Socrates to Foucault*, trans. Michael Chase, ed. with an introduction Arnold I. Devinson (Oxford, 1995).

95   See above, note 15.

human beings to the extent it is conducive to the realization of humanity's natural *finis* and *summum bonum*.

The same qualification must also be made for the doctrine of the mean. To say that the mean is the good between two opposing evils is not, of course, the same as saying that whatever is found between two opposing evils is the good. The mean is valuable only inasmuch as it prevents the over- or under-shooting of the target. This is a staple feature of classical and patristic thought on the virtues. Justice, unless tempered by clemency, runs the danger of col-lapsing into cruel severity; but unless bolstered by courage and decisiveness it runs the danger of permitting evil. In both cases, the deficiency of justice is a deviation from the good of justice – the end justice is intended to serve. Only by reference to this end may the mean between cruelty and permissive-ness be found. The same applies to the other virtues as well; the mean between cowardice and rashness is not found in a consideration of circum-stances alone; it is reached through a moral judgement evaluating circum-stances in the light of the good. Evaluating circumstances in the light of the good, moreover, is the task of prudence. Prudence sees the truth, and finds the ways to its attainment. All virtues, taken in isolation from each other and abstracted from the ultimate end they should serve, may lead to evil; but it is only by realigning them to the *summum bonum* that they may regain their virtuous character. Moderation, then, is not so much about finding a point of balance between two extremes as it is about calibrating the aim to avoid missing the target. If we raise the doctrine of the mean to a principle in itself, we render it blind and capricious; it is only through subordinating it to an overriding vision of the good that we give the notion of moderation meaning.[96]

This is perhaps most strikingly illustrated in John's works by his account of the only case in which the good does not reside in the mean. In the course of identifying the end of philosophy and the overarching aim of human life with loving God above all, John makes it clear that when it comes to humanity's ultimate end, there is to be no limits, no moderation, no aiming for the mean between two opposing evils. The order of charity is ordered towards inordinate abandon of restraint when it comes to loving the highest good:

---

96   It follows from this that there is no necessary opposition between the reading of John's ethics presented here, and an emphasis on the skeptical elements of his thought; see Christophe Grellard's incisive account of John's ethics as both Christian and skeptic in Grellard, "Un cas médiéval de scepticisme."

[Philosophy]⁹⁷ herself indeed contains the knowledge of all things, and, governor (*moderatrix*) of all, she constitutes the proper measure and limits of all human acts, words, and thoughts. But there is one thing for which not even she knows how to ordain limits; there is one thing for which she prescribes as its proper measure that it should be without measure. Whatever she does or says is directed towards that which has no limits for those who philosophize rightly; for her substance consists in this, that on this point she should not in any way reach her limit. For if, as Plato says, a philosopher is one who loves God, what else is philosophy but love of the divine? This is certainly what she does not want to be terminated, lest she also be ended, which is not for the good. For what is circumscribed, ceases to be; and if the love of God is extinguished, the name of philosophy vanishes. Thus also the Wisdom of God, while he prescribed for many things their measure, ordered that God be loved without measure; unless this measure will be prescribed for charity, that God be loved without limit to love.⁹⁸

Moderation according to the mean, then, is clearly subordinate to the teleological, eudaemonist naturalism I have sketched out above. The proper measure of the mean is only to be found by reference to that which itself has no proper measure, no termination. We see, then, how the features that distinguish John's ethics from the moral thought of his contemporaries and predecessors may be absorbed into a basic structure of thought that John shared with tradition as well as with his contemporaries, and indeed arguably remain unintelligible if isolated from this basis structure. The Aristotelian elements within John's ethics are perhaps the most immediately striking features of his

---

97 I have chosen to translate the "*ipsa*" of the original quotation with "philosophy," even though it is glossed as "*sapientia*" in Webb's apparatus, and translated thus in Cary J. Nederman, *John of Salisbury, Policraticus: Of the Frivolities of Courtiers and the Footprints of Philosophers* (Cambridge, 1990), p. 160. The reference of "*ipsa*" is not given in John's text, but the overall tenor of John's argument here is more towards the process of seeking and loving wisdom rather than the possession of it. Furthermore, similar formulations are used of philosophy elsewhere in John's works, but not of wisdom.

98 *Policraticus* 7.11, ed. Webb, vol. 2, p. 136: "Ipsa siquidem rerum omnium continet disciplinam et omnium moderatrix uniuersis humanae uitae actibus et uerbis et cogitationibus modum et terminos ipsa constituit. Est tamen cui nec ipsa nouit terminum praefinire; est cui in eo praescribit modum ut non habeat modum. Quicquid agit aut loquitur, illus tendit quod apud recte philosophantes non habet terminum; nam et eius substantia in eo consistit ut illud nequaquam terminetur."

thought; but these elements are given their justification and substance through their subordination to notions of happiness and human fulfilment sustaining the Augustinian tradition. John's moral thought, then, arguably forms an exemplification of his own doctrinal statements: he aims to utilize the works of human reason to the fullest, but in order to allow these works to attain their perfection he humbly – moderately! – leaves them open to the fructifying work of grace.

CHAPTER 11

John of Salisbury and Theology*

Christophe Grellard

There is no theology as such to be found in John of Salisbury.[1] His literary out-put contains no work of theology: he left neither a spiritual treatise, after the manner of the writings of his friend Peter of Celle, nor a treatise of scholastic theology, even though he studied this discipline for at least six years at the schools of Paris. In many ways, despite his solid scholastic training, John appears to have been a stranger both to the practices inherent to scholastic culture and to the new themes engendered by it. He adopts in their stead the *topos* of the monk as the true philosopher, of the cloister as the setting for knowledge of the divine,[2] thus seeming to belong to the often-evoked opposition between cloister and schools.[3] Yet he speaks with undeniable respect of his theological teachers, in particular Gilbert of Poitiers, in both the *Metalogicon* and the *Historia pontificalis*. How is this to be explained? We may certainly suppose that his career as an ecclesiastical administrator after 1148 scarcely left him time any longer to concern himself with purely speculative questions of theology. We may also, although in a more audacious and perhaps somewhat facile vein, invoke a certain cast of mind. Undeniably, as will be seen, John of Salisbury reveals himself to be a partisan of the return to the biblical text. When, in our search for clues as to John's literary tastes, we examine a list of the books he left to Chartres Cathedral, we find mainly biblical commentaries.[4] The more directly speculative items are, on the one hand, the works of Pseudo-Dionysius in the new translation by John Sarrazin, and, on the other, Lanfranc's treatise

---

* English translation by David M.B. Richardson.
1 Unless I am mistaken, there exists no study of the theology of John of Salisbury. Some elements of his ecclesiology may be found in Georg Miczka, *Das Bild der Kirche bei Johannes von Salisbury* (Bonn, 1970).
2 John of Salisbury, *Policraticus* 7.21, ed. Webb, vol. 1, p. 200: "Cum uero philosophos imitari nostro tempore (quo uirtus exinanita est, et Astream relictis hominibus ad celos constat redi-isse) sit arduum, uita claustralium uirtutem philosophorum incomparabiliter antecedit aut, quod melius crediderim, rectissime et tutissime philosophantur."
3 See for example Peter of Celle, *De disciplina claustrali*, ep. dedic., c. 5 in *Pierre de Celle, L'École du cloître*, ed. Gérard de Martel (Paris, 1977), p. 100. On this same opposition: Marie-Dominique Chenu, *La Théologie au XIIe siècle* (Paris, 1957), Chapter 10, pp. 225–250.
4 *Cartulaire de Notre-Dame de Chartres*, pp. 201–202, cited in Clement Webb, *John of Salisbury* (London, 1932), pp. 165–169.

© KONINKLIJKE BRILL NV, LEIDEN, 2015 | DOI 10.1163/9789004282940_013

against Béranger, which, while no doubt marking the beginning of the epoch of scholastic theology, was, by the second half of the 12th century, no longer at the cutting edge of developments in the discipline. I should like, however, without prejudice, to examine a third alternative: that John of Salisbury's relationship to theology can be understood only in the context of the academic scepticism that he openly espoused, and which defined the structure of his entire philosophical oeuvre.[5] In a perspective that, in spirit, was no great distance from that of Lactantius, John of Salisbury espoused a form of sceptical fideism that was inimical to the idea of a rational examination of the nature of the divine, and emphasized the practical dimension of the divine cult. These two elements, the rejection of the speculative and the primacy of the political, are what constitute John's attitude with respect to theology. In order to clarify this conception of theology, I shall begin by examining John of Salisbury's theological training. I shall then endeavour to identify the traces of scholastic theology in his work, so as to relate them to his scepticism. Lastly, with particular reference to the *Policraticus*, I will demonstrate what constitutes a political theology.

John of Salisbury's Theological Training

John of Salisbury's years of study are quite well documented, thanks in particular to the "autobiographical" chapter of the *Metalogicon*.[6] It is possible to identify three principal places of study prior to the writing of his principal works: Paris, Montier-la-Celle, and Canterbury.

Paris

It is the first of these locations that is the best known, as it is the explicit subject of the above-mentioned chapter in the *Metalogicon*. There, John of Salisbury gives a brief description of his three theology teachers Gilbert of Poitiers, Robert Pullen, and Simon of Poissy, and the part played by theology in his curriculum:

---

5 I defend this hypothesis at more length in Christophe Grellard, *Jean de Salisbury et la renaissance médiévale du scepticisme* (Paris, 2013).

6 See *Metalogicon* 2.10, pp. 70–73. On John's period as a student in France, see Olga Weijers, "The Chronology of John of Salisbury's Studies in France (*Metalogicon* II, 10)," in *The World of John of Salisbury*, pp. 109–125; Katherine S.B. Keats-Rohan, "The Chronology of John of Salisbury's Studies in France: A Reading of *Metalogicon*, II.10," *Studi medievali* 28 (1987), pp. 193–203; David Bloch, *John of Salisbury on Aristotelian Science* (Turnhout, 2012). On autobiography in John of Salisbury, see Georg Misch, *Geschichte der Autobiographie, 3. Das Mittelalter, 2, Das Hochmittelalter im Angang*, 2 (Frankfurt-am-Main), 1962, pp. 1157–1295.

At the end of three years I returned and sought out Master Gilbert, whose disciple I became in dialectical and theological subjects. But all too soon Gilbert was transferred. His successor was Robert Pullen, a man commendable alike for his virtue and his knowledge. Next, Simon of Poissy, a dependable lecturer but rather dull in disputes, took me as his student. The last-mentioned two only instructed me in theology.[7]

We may assume that these studies took place between 1141 and 1147. As can be seen, John says nothing about their content, inasmuch as the distinction between "divine sciences" and theology does not appear to indicate a separation between classical training in exegesis and a more dogmatic approach, as witness the genre of *Sentences* that was developing at that time. "Divine sciences" are in point of fact related to Gilbert of Poitiers, and it is evident from the *Historia pontificalis* that John was familiar with Gilbert's speculative oeuvre (in particular the commentary on *De trinitate*), and not only his exegetical output. The succession of John's theology teachers appears to have been as follows: from 1141 to 1142 (date of his accession to the diocese of Poitiers) he studied logic and theology under Gilbert's direction; from 1142 to 1144 (date of the latter's departure for Rome) he studied with Robert Pullen; lastly, from 1144 to 1147, he was a pupil of Simon of Poissy. So it was with the latter, of whom we sadly know nothing, that he studied the longest.[8] The attributes given to Simon, "a dependable lecturer but rather dull in disputes," suggest teaching of a somewhat classical bent. The impression is reinforced if this is the same Simon presented as an adversary of the Cornificians in Chapter 5 of Book I of the *Metalogicon*.[9]

Leaving aside this Simon, is it possible to arrive at a more precise identification of the influence on John of the teachings of Gilbert and Robert? In Gilbert's case, as already mentioned we have a summary of the doctrines developed in the commentary on *De trinitate*, occupying a large portion of the *Historia pontificalis*. It is possible to identify at least one aspect that bears signs of the influence of Gilbert of Poitiers. Glossing the third chapter of the *Trinity*, John

---

7 *Metalogicon*, trans. Daniel McGarry (Berkeley, 1962), p. 99, ed. Hall and Keats-Rohan, p. 72: "Reuersus itaque in fine triennii repperi magistrum Gillebertum, ipsum que audiui in logicis et in diuinis, sed nimis cito subtractus est. Successit Rodbertus Pullus, quem uita pariter et scientia commendabant. Deinde me excepit Simon Pexiacensis, fidus lector, sed obtusior disputator. Sed hos duos in solis theologicis habui praeceptores."

8 *L'Histoire littéraire de la France*, 14 (1817), pp. 6–7, attributes to him a work whose *incipit* is *Quare inspicit*, but which is otherwise unknown. See supra, the contribution by Cédric Giraud and Constant Mews, pp. 46 and 61.

9 *Metalogicon* 1.5, p. 21.

introduces some thoughts on the understanding that belongs principally to God and to a small number of men, and which alone is capable of attaining certainty: "And as opinion wavers and vacillates in its delusions, so understanding, which belongs only to God and at most very few men, embraces things which are true and enduring."[10]

Such a position very clearly originating with Boethius, while not exposed so precisely in the *Trinity*, can however be found in Gilbert, in his prologue to the *Hebdomades*,[11] and it resonates with the hierarchy of the faculties given such prominence by John of Salisbury in his *Metalogicon* and *Policraticus*.[12] In its strictest sense, *intellectus* is the direct apprehension of intelligible realities, and produces wisdom, the crown of human speculative activity, while reason, which produces science or knowledge, remains turned towards the sensible, temporal world.[13] It is, accordingly, thanks to this faculty of intellectual intuition that the human spirit penetrates the divine causes of things. At the same time, John's remark is very general, and is reminiscent as much of Abelard as of Gilbert, both of whom rely on Boethius.[14] It is therefore difficult to speak of an enormous theological influence from Gilbert of Poitiers in this respect. It therefore appears that Gilbert's doctrinal influence on John is relatively slight. John probably admired and respected his former teacher but he did not borrow many theses from his teaching. We may assume that his turn of mind was too different.

The case of Robert Pullen is a little different. It has been acknowledged since Liebeschütz that the politico-theological themes developed in Pullen's *Sentences* are one of the sources of the *Institutio Traiani* elaborated by John in Book 5 of the *Policraticus*.[15] If a general influence is not to be excluded, we might still have questions as to the extent of such a connection, inasmuch as

---

10   *Historia pontificalis*, ed. Chibnall, p. 32: "Et sicut opinio in uanis fluctuat et uacillat, sic intelligentia, que solius Dei est et admodum paucorum hominum, uera comprehendit et certa."

11   Gilbert de Poitiers, *The Commentaries on Boethius by Gilbert de la Porrée*, ed. Nikolaus H. Häring (Toronto, 1966), p. 185.

12   *Metalogicon* 4.18, p. 156; *Policraticus*, 2.18, ed. Keats-Rohan, pp. 107–110. On this question see Grellard, *Jean de Salisbury et la renaissance médiévale du scepticisme*, pp. 60–62.

13   This distinction between knowledge and wisdom, taken from Cicero, is passed down by Augustine, and forms the determining principle for all his œuvre. See for example *Contra Academicos* 1.19–22, and *De Trinitate* 12.21–24.

14   See Pierre Abélard, *De intellectibus*, ed. and (Fr.) trans. Pierre Morin (Paris, 1997), p. 40; Boèce, *Consolatio philosophiae*, ed. Claudio Moresceni and (Fr.) trans. Éric Vanpeteghem (Paris, 2008), 5 pr. 4.30–2, pr. 5.12.

15   See Hans Liebeschütz, *Medieval Humanism in the Life and Writings of John of Salisbury* (London, 1950, repr. 1980), pp. 23–26.

Robert Pullen scarcely goes beyond a few stock assertions concerning the two swords and the metaphor of the body politic. However this may be, as the *Sentences* appear to reflect Pullen's teaching very broadly[16] we might equally consider the possibility of further parallels. In fact there appears to be scarcely one theme that allows of such a possibility, and that one is the theme of divine prescience. Nevertheless, as Pullen's position closely follows that of Boethius on this point (God knows all things inasmuch as they are present to his sight, and his providence is co-eternal with his being),[17] it is difficult to tell whether John of Salisbury was influenced by his English master or directly by the Roman senator Boethius, with whose works, in common with all philosophers and theologians of his time, he was eminently familiar.[18] On the other hand, there is perhaps another important way in which Robert Pullen influenced John: as a vector of transmission of the theology of Abelard. Certainly a dialogue with that theology constantly recurs in Pullen's *Sentences*. Now, as will become evident, John of Salisbury knew several of Abelard's arguments, notably on virtue, although he only very briefly followed courses in logic under the master himself: and, by his own confession, without understanding a great deal of the subject matter.[19] In the final analysis, then, doubtless not too much should be made of the influence of Robert Pullen. It is no doubt in his sermons that the most precise points of convergence with John of Salisbury might be discovered: in criticism of worldly activities such as hunting and games, in injunctions to cultivate the virtues and find God within oneself, and in contempt for the world.[20] It is nevertheless difficult to tell the degree to which these themes, in fact adopted by John, may or may not have originated from Robert, as they belong more broadly to a conception of philosophy, developed in the monasteries, to which John was initiated by his friend Peter of Celle.

Montier-la-Celle

John's second *alma mater*, more uncertain this time, is Montier-la-Celle. We may suppose that John, short of resources, approached Peter of Celle in 1147, the latter having been elected Abbot of La Celle in 1145.[21] A letter by John of

---

16   See Francis Courtney, *Cardinal Robert Pullen. An English Theologian of the Twelfth Century* (Rome, 1954).

17   Robert Pullen, *Sententiarum libri octo*, PL 186, cols. 708–714.

18   On *aetas boetianna*, see Chenu, *La Théologie*, pp. 142–158.

19   *Metalogicon* 2.10, pp. 70–71: "Ibi ad pedes eius prima artis huius rudimenta accepi, et pro modulo ingenioli mei quicquid excidebat ab ore eius tota mentis auiditate excipiebam."

20   See Courtney, *Cardinal Robert Pullen*, pp. 32–53.

21   See Christopher Brooke's clarification in *The Early Letters*, pp. xvi–xvii.

Salisbury mentions the help Peter had given him at a time of financial difficulties, and Peter of Celle speaks of John as *clericus noster*. It was at this moment, then, that John tasted that monastic calm for which he appears always to have retained a certain nostalgia. It is also to Peter that John turns when he wishes to obtain a tract by Bernard of Clairvaux or Hugh of Saint-Victor. Thus, on the material as well as the spiritual plain, Peter of Celle appears to be the vector by which John made contact with monastic philosophy. It is perhaps because of the time he spent at La Celle that John takes up the classic identification of monks as the true philosophers. It is nevertheless by their virtue, and not by their aptitude for speculation, that they are philosophers.[22] This is perhaps one of the sources of John's frequently reaffirmed conviction that there is a primacy of ethics in philosophy, and that ethics is crowned by grace and charity. It is nevertheless difficult to identify real similarities between the work of John of Salisbury on the one part and that of Peter of Celle and, more broadly, monastic authors such as Bernard of Clairvaux, on the other. The parallels are more thematic in nature than stylistic or literary. In fact, one would be hard put to it to describe John's language as mystical, or even poetic. There is also a general absence of a theory of ecstasy or contemplation in his work.

The first level of influence can no doubt be found in the methods of *lectio* and *meditatio*. Although a real insistence on this dual approach can certainly be found in Peter of Celle,[23] John of Salisbury returns more directly to a double source in Bernard of Chartres and Hugh of Saint-Victor.[24] *Lectio* – which has a double sense, at the same time private reading (termed *praelectio*) and public lecture – provides the mind with the material needed for philosophical practice. This *lectio* may be reinforced by *doctrina*, which establishes points of comparison between what is read and what is stored in the memory. Straightaway, then, texts produced by *auctores* are placed at the core of the philosophical approach: on the one hand, authors must be examined who are authoritative by virtue of their style and their thought, and their particular meaning abstracted, and, on the other hand, acquaintance must be made with the different literary genres in order to abstract their speculative dimension and the lessons that they contain. Reading, public or private, is meaningful only if it is linked to something else: bridges must be built, points of contact established

---

22   See for example *Policraticus* 7.21, ed. Webb, vol. 2, p. 200: "Cum uero philosophos imitari nostro tempore (quo uirtus exinanita est, et Astream relictis hominibus ad celos constat rediisse) sit arduum, uita claustralium uirtutem philosophorum incomparabiliter antecedit aut, quod melius crediderim, rectissime et tutissime philosophatur."

23   Pierre de Celle, *De disciplina claustrali*, p. 234.

24   See *Metalogicon* 1.24, pp. 51–55; *Policraticus* 7.13, ed. Webb, vol. 2, pp. 145–152.

between the genres, so as to create a dialogue between them. But it is the personal process of *meditatio* that allows us (in rather Augustinian vein) to pass beyond these external masters that are books, in order to examine the data acquired, appropriate it, and truly convert it into knowledge.[25] The influence of Augustine's theory of divine illumination can in fact be detected time and time again in John of Salisbury's writings, notably in the *Entheticus* and the *Policraticus*.[26] However, knowledge thus gained must in turn confront an external test in the context of *collatio*. The equivocal nature of the term is manifest in John, notably where he is reporting Bernard's teaching method. As has been pointed out elsewhere,[27] *collatio* has a monastic origin, and refers first of all to the monastic spiritual exercise of sharing in common, the reading of the *Conferences* or "conventual" reading that closes the day under the Rule of Benedict (Chapter 42). Bernard adapted this form of *collatio* for the use of the pupils in his school. The day ended with readings of immediate relevance to religious questions, to which might equally be added literary texts recommended for purposes of imitation.[28] In the same chapter, however, the sense of the term varies to indicate sharing, confrontation, and discussion.[29] It then becomes a "working procedure between students, taking the form of collective emulation in seeking or expressing the truth."[30] It is principally this sense of *collatio* that John adopts on his own account to stress that truth emerges from

---

25 *Metalogicon* 1.23, pp. 50–51.

26 *Entheticus maior*, ll. 641–52, ed. van Laarhoven, p. 147; *Policraticus* 3.1, ed. Keats-Rohan, pp. 172–175.

27 Gérard Paré, Adrien Brunet, Pierre Tremblay, *La Renaissance du XIIe siècle* (Paris, 1933), p. 122; Jacques Châtillon, "Les écoles de Chartres et de Saint-Victor," in *La scuola nell'Occidente Latino nell'alto medio evo* (Spoleto, 1972), pp. 795–839, esp. pp. 822–823.

28 *Metalogicon* 1.24, p. 53: "Sed quia nec scolam nec diem aliquam decet esse religionis expertem, ea proponebatur materia quae fidem aedificaret et mores, et unde qui conuenerant quasi collatione quadam animarentur ad bonum. Nouissimus autem huius declinationis immo philosophicae collationis articulus pietatis uestigia praeferebat, et animas defunctorum commendabat, deuota oblatione psalmi qui in paenitentialibus sextus est, et oratione Dominica Redemptori suo. Quibus autem indicebantur praeexercitamina puerorum in prosis aut poematibus imitandis, poetas aut oratores proponebat et eorum iubebat uestigia imitari, ostendens iuncturas dictionum, et elegantes sermonum clausulas."

29 *Metalogicon* 1.24, p. 54: "Et quia in toto praeexercitamine erudiendorum nihil utilius est quam ei quod fieri ex arte oportet assuescere, prosas et poemata cotidie scriptitabant, et se mutuis exercebant collationibus, quo quidem exercitio nihil utilius ad eloquentiam, nihil expeditius ad scientiam, et plurimum confert ad uitam, si tamen hanc sedulitatem regat caritas, si in profectu litteratorio seruetur humilitas."

30 Paré, Brunet, Tremblay, *La Renaissance du XIIe siècle*, p. 123.

confrontation and from comparison of opinions.[31] This is in effect the dialectic exercise of disputation, of confronting probable arguments with the purpose, as has been seen, of approaching the truth:

> A good intellect readily assents to what is true, and rejects what is false. Such mental capacity is originally a gift of nature, and is fostered by our inborn reason. It rapidly waxes in strength as a combined result and expeditiously when it is founded on the essential principles of the art of logic and its rules. Although one may sometimes profitably exercise his reason alone, just as he does with a partner, still mutual discussion is evidently more profitable than solitary meditation. Iron is sharpened by iron, and one's mind is more cogently and effectively stimulated by the sound of the words of another, particularly if the other person is wise or modest.[32]

But the principal monastic influence is perhaps to be found on another level: it is in his steadfast and complete adherence to Augustinian positions that John of Salisbury still associates himself more with monastic philosophy than with that of the schools. Augustine is in fact a constant and universal presence in John of Salisbury's thinking. The clearest passage in this regard is no doubt the beginning of Book 3 (Chapters 1 and 2). This text emphasizing the importance of self-knowledge belongs precisely in the tradition called by Gilson "Christian Socratism," of which Bernard of Clairvaux was one of the principal representatives.[33] For John of Salisbury, revisiting

---

31   It is the term used for the trial opposing Pythagoras to his pupil in Chapter 12 of book 5 of the *Policraticus*. On this text see Christophe Grellard, "Doxographie et anecdotes. L'écriture sceptique de Jean de Salisbury," in François Lecercle and Guillaume Navaud, eds., *Anecdotes philosophiques et théologiques de l'Antiquité aux Lumières* (Paris, 2012), pp. 101–104. Elsewhere, *collatio* is presented as the sceptical method in Chapter 8 of book 7, ed. Webb, vol. 2, p. 122.

32   *Metalogicon* 3.10, trans. Mc Garry, ed. Hall and Keats-Rohan, pp. 137–138: "Ingenium uero bonum est, quod uero facile adquiescit, et falsum aspernatur. Hoc autem primum a natura oritur per fomitem innatae rationis, deinde affectione boni, et usu uiuacius conualescit. Vsus quidem exercitium roborat paritque facultatem probandi et examinandi ueri, facilius tamen et expeditius, si artis praeceptorumque compendio solidetur. Sed licet nunc ad se nunc ad alterum contingat utiliter exerceri, collatio meditatione uidetur utilior. Vt enim ferrum ferro acuitur, sic ad uocem alterius contingit animum colloquentis acutius et efficacius excitari."

33   Étienne Gilson, *The Spirit of Mediaeval Philosophy*, trans. A.H.C. Downes (London, 1991), pp. 209–228: "Self-knowledge and Christian Socratism."

the Socratic injunction is in the first instance an opportunity to remind his readers both of the intellectualist dimension of ethics, founded on knowledge, and of the necessity of a recourse to grace in implementing those same ethics:

> This seems to me the only real safeguard of life: that the mind, by the life-giving power of the spirit, be illuminated for the acquisition of knowledge and be inspired with the love of honor and zeal for virtue. Therefore knowledge precedes the cultivation of virtue, for no one can truly seek that of which he is ignorant; nor can evil be effectively shunned unless it be known. Further, the treasures of knowledge are disclosed to us in two ways; first, by the use of reason understanding discovers what is capable of being known; second, revealing grace discloses what has been hidden by presenting it to our eyes. It is then through nature or through grace that each one can arrive at the recognition and knowledge of truth of those things that are indispensable. What is more remarkable, every one of us carries in his heart a book of knowledge, opened by the exercise of reason. In this are portrayed not only the forms of all visible things and nature in general; the invisible things of the Fabricator of all things are also written down by the very hand of God. (...) Therefore the recognition of truth and the cultivation of virtue is the general and universal safeguard of the individual, of the state, and of rational nature; while its contrary is ignorance and her hateful and hostile offspring, vice. Ignorance is indeed fittingly called the mother of vice, for she is never so barren as not to produce a useless crop of hateful things. The moralist remarks: No incense to the gods avails to plant a mite of wisdom in the brain of fools. Recognition connotes certitude and applies either to learning or to faith. Let the rule of faith be deferred however, as it will be discussed in its own time and place. Learning then involves knowledge of self, which cannot be attained if it fails to measure its own strength or if it be ignorant of the strength of others.[34]

---

34   *Policraticus* 3.1, trans. Pike, pp. 154–155, ed. Keats-Rohan, pp. 174–175: "Et haec michi uidetur uera et unica incolumitas uitae, cum mens uiuificante Spiritu ad rerum notitiam illustratur, et accenditur ad amorem honestatis et cultum uirtutis. Praecedit ergo scientia uirtutis cultum quia nemo potest fideliter appetere quod ignorat, et malum nisi cognitum sit utiliter non cauetur. Porro scientiae thesaurus nobis duobus modis exponitur cum aut rationis exercitio quod sciri potest intellectus inuenit aut quod absconditum est reuelans gratia oculis ingerens patefecit. Sic utique aut per naturam aut per gratiam ad ueritatis agnitionem et scientiam eorum quae necessaria sunt unusquisque potest accedere. Quodque magis mirere quilibet quasi quendam librum sciendorum officio rationis apertum gerit in corde. In quo non modo uisibilium species rerumque omnium natura depingitur, sed ipsius opificis omnium inuisibilia Dei digito conscribuntur. (...) Agnitio quidem

Without putting in question the subordination of the material to the spiritual, John stresses the importance of harmony between soul and body in view of the integrity of human life. Taking up a thoroughly Augustinian schema, he asserts a hierarchy passing from body to soul and from soul to God.[35] The soul thus lives fully when it is governed by God, just as a person lives fully when the soul holds the body in submission. To live in God is to discover oneself as a rational creature, a vestige of the divine, illuminated by truth with a light that makes possible true love of God. The practice of virtue therefore depends on the prior acquisition of a *scientia*, which is to say knowledge of the good and the true, while the precedence of knowledge over virtue follows from the impossibility of searching for something of which one is ignorant. Two things make possible the acquisition of this knowledge (also termed *agnitio ueritatis*): reason and grace, which together provide the individual with a form of certitude. Everyone carries in his or her heart a book of knowledge, a book that can be opened by the exercise of reason, and which contains all the forms of sensible things. This is therefore a Platonic type of innatism, proposing the thesis of the contemplation of self as a condition for the recognition of truth and the practice of virtue. But all *scientia* presupposes *notitia sui*: an evaluation of one's own capacities, a conducement to humility, and a restraint on the pride of reason. Thus, not without a certain ambivalence, John suggests that knowledge of self, passing as it does through evaluation of one's own capacities and the capacities of others, tends to become reassigned to knowledge of the other and of the world. The first task of anyone aspiring to wisdom is in effect to situate himself precisely in the world. Absence of this reasoned detour via the external world leads to the loss of self and the impossibility of knowledge.[36] The main thing is therefore to determine accurately one's place in the universe and one's own relationship to God. This is the sense very appositely created by the following juxtaposition of the Delphic oracle cited after Juvenal, with a text of Persius by

---

certitudinem habet, et uel in scientia uel in fide consistit. Sed fidei regula paulisper differatur, quoniam eam tempus et locus suus expectat. Ceterum scientia sui notitiam habet. Quod euenire non potest si non metiatur uires suas, si ignorat alienas."

35   Elsewhere, John attributes the schema to Socrates; see *Entheticus maior*, ll.797–800, ed. van Laarhoven, p. 157: "Nam carni mundus, servitque caro rationi, / quae pars est animi participata Deo. / Omnia sic laeto Socrati famulantur, eique, / quem vis nulla potest laedere, mundus obit." On John's Socraticism see Christophe Grellard, "Le socratisme de Jean de Salisbury," in Suzel Mayer, ed., *Réception philosophique de la figure de Socrate, Diagonale φ* 2 (2008), 35–59.

36   On this point, see the critique of the wise man who seeks to know the unknowable: *Policraticus* 7.1, ed. Webb, vol. 2, pp. 93–95.

way of explication and interpretation, in a perspective of John's own where classical texts are engaged in a mutually illuminative dialogue:

> The first task of man aspiring to wisdom is the consideration of what he himself is: what is within him, what without, what below, what above, what opposite, what before, and what after? (...). While he who does not know himself, what of profit does he know? (...). There is an oracle of Apollo which is thought to have come down from the skies; *noti seliton*, that is, know thyself. With this in mind, the moralist writes: Learn, puny beings, to know the cause of things; Why we are born and what our lives should be (...). Such contemplation bears fourfold fruit: benefit to self, affection for neighbor, scorn for the world, and love of God.[37]

Knowledge of the self is thus first of all knowledge of one's limits. There is quite evidently here a dialectic of elevation and abasement that leads from a correct estimation of one's worth to the love of God. Thus recognition of one's own insignificance must lead to love of one's neighbour. This love must nevertheless be limited by knowledge of the baseness of the world, and in this way reattached to the love of God. As a good Augustinian, John of Salisbury relates every form of love to the love of God. The world cannot be loved for itself, but only as a stage leading towards the love of God.[38] The themes developed in this text echo certain passages from Bernard's *De consideratione*. Reflection must lead to an examination of who we are and where we come from, so that we may discover in ourselves humility and the fear of God.[39] But, beyond the

---

37   *Policraticus* 3.2, trans. Pike, pp. 155–157, ed. Keats-Rohan, pp. 175–176: "Est ergo primum hominis sapientiam affectantis quid ipse sit, quid intra se quid extra, quid infra quid supra, quid contra, quid ante uel postea sit contemplari. (...). Verum qui se ipsum ignorat, quid utiliter nouit? (...). Oraculum Apollinis est descendisse de caelo creditur: Notiseliton, id est, Scito te ipsum. Non nesciuit hoc ethicus dicens: Discite et, o, miseri, causas cognoscite rerum / quid sumus aut quidnam uicturi gignimur (...). Haec etenim contemplatio quadripartitum parit fructum, uilitatem sui, caritatem proximi, contemptum mundi, amorem Dei." John quotes Juvenal, *Satires*, 11, 27; Persius, *Satires*, 3, 66–72.
38   For a perspective on the theme *contemptus mundi* see Robert Bultot, *Christianisme et valeurs humaines. A. La doctrine du mépris du monde en Occident, de S. Ambroise à Innocent II* (Leuven, 1964), t. 4, vols. 1 and 2. Unless I am mistaken, only these two volumes, devoted to the 11th century, have been published. There is, however, an article by the same author on the spread of the theme of contempt of the world in the schools: Robert Bultot, "Grammatica, ethica et contemptus mundi aux XIIe et XIIIe siècles," in *Arts libéraux et philosophie au Moyen Âge. Actes du quatrième Congrès international de philosophie médiévale* (Montreal, 1969), pp. 815–827.
39   See esp. Bernard de Clairvaux, *De consideratione* 1.5, 2.3–5 and 9–10, 5.1.

probable influence of Bernard, John of Salisbury is securely anchored in a certain Augustinian tradition.

Canterbury

From 1148, John of Salisbury was curial clerk in the entourage of Theobald of Canterbury. While this arrangement has received little academic attention, it is probable that the circle of learned clerks assembled around the bishop made up a milieu that encouraged intellectual emulation. Something of the kind emerges from correspondence where John of Salisbury, in writing to fellow clerics, frequently provides a short philosophical exposé by way of *captatio beneuolentiae* before addressing the practical matter in hand. Similarly, depending upon his correspondent, he does not hesitate to have recourse to his technique of the *exemplum*.[40] We may therefore wonder whether he was, in some way or another, able to pursue his theological training during his time at Canterbury. On this point, the most important consideration is no doubt the contact he was able to have with Vacarius, and the law training he received from him.[41] If Vacarius is better known for his body of work in civil law, the *Summa matrimonio* of which he was the author nevertheless indicates a good knowledge of canon law, and his controversy with Hugo Speroni shows that he was a good theologian.[42] Moreover, besides Vacarius, several canon lawyers (such as Gerard Pucelle) frequented the episcopal court. Then, while at Canterbury, John had access to two relatively well-stocked libraries, those of Christ Church and St Augustine's Abbey. If we can trust the catalogue of 1170 to give us an idea of what was available to John, we must recognize that theological "novelties" have scant representation there. The most recent author is Hugh of Saint-Victor.[43] On the other hand, the "classics," Boethius, Augustine, Ambrose, are well represented. It would appear that the context of the time allowed little scope for the speculative theology of the schools, even supposing

40   See Grellard, *Jean de Salisbury et la renaissance médiévale du scepticisme*, pp. 131–151.
41   On Vacarius, see Jason Taliadoros, *Law and Theology in Twelfth-Century England. The Works of Master Vacarius (c.1115/20–c.1200)* (Turnhout, 2006). On John of Salisbury's connection to the law, see in this volume Yves Sassier and, on the canon law in particular, see Jacques Krynen, "Sur la leçon de législation ecclésiastique du *Policraticus*," in Giles Constable and Michel Rouche, eds., *Auctoritas. Mélanges offerts au professeur Olivier Guillot* (Paris, 2006), pp. 497–502.
42   See Ilirano da Milano, *L'eresia di Ugo Speroni nella confutazione del maestro Vacario* (Vatican, 1945).
43   See Montague Rhodes James, *The Ancient Libraries of Canterbury and Dover. The Catalogue of the Libraries of Christ Church Priory and St Augustine's Abbey at Canterbury and of St. Martin's Priory at Dover* (Cambridge, 1903), pp. 35–36 and 41.

that John had any desire to pursue it. Finally, John carried out several missions to southern Italy at this period. We know that, in this particular context, he probably came in contact with still-unpublished fragments of the parts of the *Organon* that were not yet available in Latin.[44] Here too, he probably met the translators of Aristotle, Burgundio of Pisa and perhaps James of Venice. We may therefore wonder whether, on this occasion, he did not also come in contact with certain aspects of Greek theology. It is very probably at this time that he met John Sarrazin, with whom he would remain in contact, and whom he encouraged to retranslate Pseudo-Dionysius.

Up to now, we have primarily considered the scholastic dimension of John's theology, as the training he received appeared to concentrate primarily on that discipline. The works left by him to the library at Chartres nevertheless attest to an interest in another aspect of theology: biblical exegesis. In this legacy are in effect to be found the commentary of Hugh of Saint-Victor on *Jeremiah*, that of Origen on *Joshua* and of Peter Lombard on the *Psalms*, and a gloss on the books of *Kings*. In general, John has rather a historian's relationship to the Bible: he peruses it for historic *exempla* that he can reuse in the parts of his oeuvre devoted to ethics and politics. This is striking in his letters, where he presents lists of biblical names associated with particular situations to serve as *exempla*, advice to determine the conduct to adopt in this or that situation. For instance, he cites Lot's situation at Sodom, associated with Joseph's at the court of the pharaoh and Daniel's in Babylon, as an example to those, like Gerard Pucelle, who are inclined to seek the company of schismatics.[45] He nevertheless occasionally indulges in the practice of exegesis. In a very classical perspective, outlines of a theory of exegesis founded on distinguishing the four senses of the Scriptures are to be found in the *Policraticus*.

> For although on the face of it the written word lends itself to one meaning only, manifold mysteries lie hidden within, and from the same source allegory often edifies faith and character in various ways. Mystical interpretation leads upward in manifold ways, so that it provides the letter not only with words but with reality itself.[46]

---

44 On this point see Bloch, *John of Salisbury on Aristotelian Science*, pp. 34–43.

45 Julie Barrau, *Bible, lettres et politique. L'Écriture au service des hommes à l'époque de Thomas Becket* (Paris, 2013), pp. 183–188.

46 *Policraticus* 7.12, trans. Pike, p. 264, ed. Webb, vol. 2, p. 144: "Licet enim ad unum tantummodo sensum accommodata sit superficies litterae, multiplicitas misteriorum intrinsecus latet et ab eadem re saepe allegoria fidem, tropologia mores uariis modis edificet; anagoge quoque multipliciter sursum ducit ut litteram non modo uerbis sed rebus ipsis instituat."

As Julie Barrau points out, this represents a quite widely-held *doxa*, notwith-standing the fact that lists proposing three categories and those proposing four competed at the time. John of Salisbury rarely instances these debates. He contents himself with mentioning Ticonius' list reported by Augustine, which proposes seven mystic senses. Exegetical theory thus appears to be of little interest to John, who frequently confines himself to distinguishing more broadly between the letter and the spirit.[47] Predominantly, he uses the Bible tropologically, as a reservoir of examples permitting us to understand how past events reported in the Bible indicate how we should act. Nevertheless, he sometimes ventures a more mystical or spiritual reading founded on analogy, as, for example, when he compares the angels sent to Sodom to the scriptures, and the blinded Sodomites to bad readers who seek to force the text.[48]

So it can be seen that John of Salisbury received a solid theological training during the period before he wrote his two principal works, the *Policraticus* and the *Metalogicon*. Such a training required legitimation, as Henry the Liberal thought fit to question him on the Bible.[49] It is nevertheless difficult to identify precisely the impact that scholastic theology may have had on John's own speculative approach. In many respects, as was the case in the realm of logic, John appears to display a certain conservatism, a reticence towards the novelties of whose development he takes note. Such a conservatism would explain his predilection for monastic theology, but it could scarcely be said to facilitate an understanding of the substantial use he makes of canon law: which is why we must now examine the practice of explication by scepticism.

From Scholastic Theology to Sceptical Fideism

John of Salisbury openly professes scepticism on many occasions in the *Metalogicon* and the *Policraticus*, asserting the mode of philosophy practised by the Academy, on the model of Cicero. John presents the sceptical attitude both as a prudential reaction in face of the fallibility of human reason, and as

---

47   For example *Policraticus* 1.6, ed. Keats-Rohan, p. 47. On the pre-eminence of this distinc-
      tion in the medieval attitude (and the nuanced approach we should employ when consid-
      ering the importance given to the four senses), see Gilbert Dahan, *L'Exégèse chrétienne de
      la Bible en Occident médiéval, XIIe–XIVe siècle* (Paris, 1999); Luisa Valente, "Une séman-
      tique particulière: la pluralité des sens dans les Saintes Écritures (XIIe siècle)," in Sten
      Ebbesen, ed., *Sprachtheorien in Spätantike und Mittelalter* (Tubingen, 1995), pp. 12–32.
48   *Policraticus* 7.13, ed. Webb, vol. 2, pp. 147–148.
49   Letter 209, in *The Later Letters*, pp. 315–339.

implementation of the key concept of moderation. As the hypothesis has been expressed elsewhere that this scepticism is fundamental to John's entire approach, at least at the methodological level, it is apposite to ask whether such a stance had consequences for his conception of theology. I should like to maintain here that such a scepticism is precisely one of the reasons for his lack of interest in, even his opposition to the theology of the schools. The fact is, this scepticism developed in the context of Christianity, and within a frame-work broadly inspired by Augustine (explicitly) and Lactantius (implicitly).[50] Both are perceived as promoting a Christian scepticism that seeks to shake the confidence that reason has in itself, in order to make way for faith as a mode of access to truth. This being the case, the renewal of scepticism by John of Salisbury, by very virtue of its patristic origin, is indissociable from a form of fideism. I shall therefore begin by recalling John's own conception of the links between scepticism and religion, before going on to examine the persistence, in a sceptical context, of certain traits of scholastic theology, and to identify the impact of a form of negative theology on his approach to the divine.

Scepticism and Theology

What place can faith and its objects have in a sceptical philosophy? John of Salisbury concedes in the *Policraticus* that radical scepticism, characterized by the fact of doubting everything, is foreign both to knowledge and to faith, because, notwithstanding their differences, both knowledge and faith pro-cure a form of certainty, "for they who are in doubt about everything for the reason that they have no criterion are as far from faith as they are from knowledge."[51]

For all that faith procures only an indirect vision of divine realities, it is nonetheless exclusive of doubt. This being so, John of Salisbury finds himself obliged to dismiss the radical forms of scepticism, for he wishes to preserve a place for faith. Accordingly, in Chapter 2 of Book 7 he reprises a set of more or

---

50 On the place of Lactantius in John of Salisbury see Grellard, *Jean de Salisbury et la renais-sance médiévale du scepticisme*, p. 35. On the identification of the *Lactantius* left by John of Salisbury to Chartres Cathedral see Lynn Barker, "MS Bodl. Canon. Pat. Lat. 131 and a Lost Lactantius of John of Salisbury: Evidence in Search of a French Critic of Thomas Becket," *Albion* 22 (1990), 21–37.

51 *Policraticus* 7.2, trans. Pike, p. 219, ed. Webb, vol. 2, p. 96: "Nam qui de omnibus dubitant, eo quod nichil habent certum, tam a fide quam a scientia alieni sunt."

less classic arguments in order to refute the radical sceptic's claim to be a philosopher. What is the implication of such a critique of such a form of scepticism? The same critique is taken up from a different perspective in Chapter 7
of Book 7. Adopting an architectonic conception of knowledge (relying on a
dual, geometric and architectural model), where the recognition of indubita-
ble principles, serving as foundations, is a condition for success in identifying,
by a transfer of confidence, other, less certain forms of knowledge, John identifies three types of principle, or three sources of authority: sensation, reason,
and religion. There is no good reason to doubt our immediate perceptions
(snow is white, fire warms), any more than we must doubt mathematical
truths, which constitute the paradigm of rational truths. And, similarly, there is
a set of principles of religion that are beyond all possible doubt, even if they
may not possess the same certainty as rational truths. Those principles are the
existence of God and the identification of certain of his properties: power, wisdom, and goodness: "in fact he who questions whether God exists and whether
he is powerful, wise, and good is not merely irreligious; he is lacking in faith
and deserves to be taught his lesson by punishment."[52]

As soon as we touch upon irreligion and perfidy, we leave the domain of
philosophical debate to enter that of judicial constraint. The assertion of indu-
bitable religious principles is justified a little further on in the text:

> We are by no means discussing here those questions which pertain to the
> domain of religion, since there too certain postulates are made which, in
> order that faith may be more meritorious, transcend the experience of
> reason. These, though reason may not impel, must be a concession to
> piety. That belief should be accorded sacraments where reason fails is but
> what Christ has deserved of us by his many benefits and great miracles.
> Not to believe in Him is just as impious as it is perverse to dissent stub-
> bornly from what is probable.[53]

---

52   Ibid., 7.7, trans. Pike, p. 236, ed. Webb, vol. 2, p. 115: "Qui uero an Deus sit deducit in quaes-
      tionem et an idem potens sapiens sit an bonus, non modo irreligiosus sed perfidus est, et
      pena docente dignus est instrui."

53   Ibid., 7.7, trans. Pike, p. 237, ed. Webb, vol. 2, pp. 115–116: "Hic tamen nequaquam agitur de
      his quae ad cultum religionis pertinent, quoniam et ibi nonnulla quodammodo petuntur
      quae, ut fides amplius mereatur, experientiam rationis excedunt; sed haec ipsa, etsi ratio
      non urgeat, debentur pietati. Vt enim sacramentis, ubi ratio deficit, adhibeatur fides, mul-
      tis beneficiis magnis que miraculis promeruit Christus cui non credi impium est, sicut a
      probabilibus dissentire pertinaciter est proteruum." See below analyses of the relation-
      ship between theology and politics, and remarks on Chapter 3 of book 5 of the *Policraticus*.

These principles are beyond reason in order that faith might be meritorious, but they have nevertheless been rendered more credible and more easily perceivable by the miracles and teaching of Christ. The Incarnation is explicitly presented as the definitive refutation of an Epicurean atheism that is associated with upholding chance against providence. This conviction that faith is situated beyond all doubt, and that scepticism cannot begin until a point beyond where the principles of faith take hold, will constantly be reaffirmed, notably in the correspondence.[54]

So the scepticism that John of Salisbury wishes to promote has to accommodate a set of objects that are beyond all reasonable doubt, and which serve as point of departure for the subsequent examination of phenomena. According to John, if all things were in fact equally unknowable then no search for the truth would be possible. Now, his Ciceronian scepticism depends upon this *inquisitio ueritatis*. In defending the certainty of the principles of sensation, reason, and faith, John's purpose is at one and the same time to dismiss universal scepticism and to make possible a local scepticism. John considers that first form of scepticism to have been refuted both by Cicero and by the Fathers of the Church, Augustine chief of all. And it is to the perspective opened up by them that he claims to subscribe: one must, on occasion, know how to be a sceptic according to a different form of scepticism:

> However Cicero, on his own testimony, passed over to those who express doubt on all philosophic questions. Even our Augustine does not assail them, since he himself somewhat frequently employs Academic moderation in his works and propounds many matters as ambiguous which would not seem to be in question to another arguing with greater confidence and just as safely. To me, however, no one seems to speak with greater safety who is circumspect in language just to guard himself from slipping into error.[55]

Here, to be a sceptic means to accept a contentious debate founded on the confrontation of probable arguments, with the aim of having the truth emerge. And such a debate is legitimate in respect of all subjects that cannot manifestly

---

54   For example John of Salisbury, Letter 281, *The Later Letters*, p. 616.

55   *Policraticus* 7.2, trans. Pike, p. 221, ed. Webb, vol. 2, p. 98: "Verumtamen ad illos qui de singulis dubitant quae sapienti faciunt quaestionem, Cicero seipso teste transiuit; nec eos noster Augustinus persequitur, cum et ipse in operibus suis Achademico temperamento utatur frequentius et sub ambiguitate proponat multa quae alii confidentius nec magis temerarie disputanti non uiderentur habere quaestionem. Michi tamen non uidetur quisquam eo loqui securius qui ita circumspectus est in uerbo ne prolabi possit ad falsa."

be resolved by the authority of the senses, reason, or faith. Now, the domain thus opened up to scepticism is much broader than one might expect, and includes a certain number of theological questions. John in effect proposes a catalogue of questions susceptible to being put in doubt:

> Those things are of doubtful validity for the man of wisdom which are supported by the authority of neither faith, sense, nor apparent reason, and which in their main points lean toward either side. Such are questions concerning providence, concerning the substance, quantity, power, efficacy, and the origin of the soul; fate and adaptability of nature; chance and free will (...); use, beginning, and end of virtues and vices; whether everyone who possesses one virtue possesses all; whether all sins are equal and to be punished equally (...); whether angels possess no form of their own or what sort of bodies they do have; and what are the things it is pious to ask of God himself, who is beyond the comprehension of the whole of rational nature and is exalted above all that can by grasped by the mind.[56]

Of all these questions, the ones belonging (either partly or entirely) to the domain of theology are those relative to providence, the status of the soul, contingency and necessity, virtue and sin, and the nature of angels. John is more ambiguous when it comes to the status of a rational inquiry into divinity. Inasmuch as the theme is absolutely beyond all rational inquiry, it is only by humble petition that some slight apprehension of divinity is at all possible. The introduction of the probable into the domain of theology is not in itself new; it is the approach that Abelard goes so far as to demand in respect of a question such as the Trinity. John of Salisbury nevertheless explicitly places such a recourse to the probable within the prerogative of the academic method, flouting the criticisms that Bernard had addressed to Abelard.[57] An examination of the precise nature of this sceptical approach to theology is thus called for.

---

56   Ibid., 7.2, trans. Pike, pp. 221–222, ed. Webb, pp. 98–99: "Sunt autem dubitabilia sapienti quae nec fidei nec sensus aut rationis manifestae persuadet auctoritas et quae suis in utramque partem nituntur firmamentis. Talia quidem sunt quae quaeruntur de prouidentia, de substantia quantitate uiribus efficacia et origine animae, de fato et facilitate naturae, casu et libero arbitrio, (...). De usu et fine ortu que uirtutum et uitiorum, an omnes uirtutes habeat qui unam habet, an omnia sint peccata aequalia et aequaliter punienda. (...) An angeli omnino sua non habeant aut qualia habeant corpora, et quae pie quaeruntur de ipso Deo qui totius naturae rationalis excedit inuestigationem et super omnia, quae mente possunt concipi, exaltatur."

57   See Christophe Grellard, "Scepticisme et incroyance. La querelle entre Pierre Abélard et Guillaume de Saint-Thierry sur le statut de la foi," *Cîteaux* 63 (2012), 245–262.

Scholastic Theology and Academic Scepticism

Certain of the subjects open to the doubts of the wise are to be found in John of Salisbury's oeuvre, where the pros and cons of each instance are confronted sceptically. Two at least of these subjects assuredly belong to theology: providence (and prescience), and the status of angels. It will become clear that John gives no great attention to the second of these. To the first, however, he devotes a substantial inquiry in the second book of the *Policraticus*.

John covers the question of divine prescience during the course of his critique of divination, in Chapters 20 to 22 of Book 2 of the *Policraticus*. On the one hand, this discussion turns on the relationship between the necessity of divine prescience and the possibility of human freedom, and, on the other, the problem of divine fallibility and its relationship to the mutability and contingency of the sensible. In Chapter 20, responding to astrologers who introduce a concept of strict necessity under the pretext of respect for divine power, John, reprising the position developed by Boethius in the fifth book of the *Consolation of Philosophy*, maintains that divine knowledge does not (any more than human knowledge) modify the nature of things. He nevertheless feels obliged, at the end of the chapter, to introduce quite explicitly a thesis that allows space to be preserved for human freedom, when he maintains that there are unrealized instances of the possible.[58] It is this thesis that John goes on to discuss in Chapter 21, where he poses a question that echoes Abelard's reflections on divine immutability: can God know what he does not know? If there are unrealized possibles, this signifies that God can know what he does not know, and by extension not know what he knows, which casts doubt on divine immutability. John contents himself with reformulating the problem: how can God know in immutable fashion things that are mutable? And, relying on Boethius, he reaffirms the immutability of divine knowledge.[59] God, in effect, knows all things in one sole, simple and eternal gaze. All the terms knowledge, prescience, providence, and predestination relate to one sole thing in God, which is to say simple and eternal divine essence, for which all things are present. In this way, John maintains that God has an infallible knowledge that cannot increase. Nevertheless, and John believes by this means to dismiss at one stroke both Stoics and Epicureans, he maintains at the same time that God has liberated the series of contingent things from all

---

58 *Policraticus* 2.20, ed. Keats-Rohan, p. 119.

59 On the positions of Boethius and Abelard regarding divine prescience see John Marenbon, *Le Temps, l'éternité et la prescience de Boèce à Thomas d'Aquin* (Paris, 2005).

constraints of necessity.[60] Thus Chapter 21 develops a classically Boethian position, where the immutability of divine knowledge does not put in question the mutability of created things:

> God's knowledge therefore remains everywhere intact and immovable, and if there be any variability in anything it is a mutability due not so much to the One who knows as to the thing known. For what God's knowledge comprises is subject to change, but that knowledge itself knows naught of such changes and compasses and holds within its one sole and indivisible ken the totality of all that can be expressed in words or ascertained by any sense whatsoever. To such a degree does it comprehend under a single form and without motion that for it neither past nor future exists, just as it comprehends the local without location, the growing without beginning, the departing without end, the fluctuating without change, the temporal without mutability and motion. Nor is this surprising in the state of eternity, except that all that is there is marvelous, since even with us contemplation grasps to a certain extent the abstract idea of movement and of rapidity.[61]

Knowledge, in effect, causes no necessity in its object. Thus God has a uniform apprehension of mutable events, without that putting in doubt the contingency of created things. It is this thesis that sets off the discussion in Chapter 22, where John examines an objection already considered by Abelard, notably in the *Theologia scholarium*: if a thing happens other than God has foreseen, then he is in error.[62] But, if God can foresee possibles that will not happen, either he is in error or these possibles are impossible, and, in this case, from the possible follows the impossible, and this is normally rejected. It is necessary to

---

60   *Policraticus* 2.21, ed. Keats-Rohan, p. 124.

61   Ibid., 2.21, trans. Pike, p. 102, ed. Keats-Rohan, p. 121: "Manet itaque usquequaque immobilis integritas scientiae Dei, et si quid uarietatis alicui inest, non tam scientis quam scitorum mutabilitas est. Licet enim quae scientia Dei complectitur mutabilitati subiaceant, ipsa tamen alterationis uices ignorat, et uno singulari aspectu et indiuiduo omnium quae dici aut quocumque sensu excogitari possunt uniuersitatem claudit et continet, adeo equidem sine motu ut localia sine loco, nascentia sine initio, decedentia sine fine, fluctuantia sine alteratione, temporalia sine mutabilitate aut mora, sic uniformiter comprehendat ut ei nec praeterita transeant nec futura succedant. Nec mirum hoc in aeternitatis statu, nisi quia quicquid ibi est mirabile est, cum et in nobis mutabilium motum et festinantium cursum aliquatenus quiescens comprehendat aspectus." See also ibid., p. 125.

62   Pierre Abélard, *Theologia scholarium* 3.112, ed. Eloi-Marie Buytaert and Constant Mews (Turnhout, 1987), p. 546.

linger at more length over this chapter, for it permits a slightly better under-standing of John's conception of the links between scepticism and theology. John in fact begins by arguing in favour of the first element of Abelard's alter-native, maintaining initially that irrationality must be preferred to perfidy, and then emphasizing that there is no consensus of the wise to maintain that from the possible follows the impossible. On this occasion, John invokes the Academicians and the theory of the probable in order to submit this affirma-tion to critical examination, and to doubt:

> I am the more ready to give ear to the school of the Academy because it deprives me of none of the things I know and in many matters renders me cautious, being supported as it is by the authority of great men, since he in whom alone the Latin tongue finds whatever elegance it has to off-set the arrogance of Greece turned to it in his old age. I mean of course Cicero, the originator of Roman style, whose work *De natura deorum* proves that he favored this school toward the end of his life.[63]

Having recalled this, John seeks to defend at one and the same time the propo-sitions that God cannot be in error and that a thing foreseen may fail to hap-pen. Although he appears to know Abelard's logical solution, he adopts a different approach. Perhaps drawing inspiration from Boethius' distinction between *prouidentia* and *praeuidentia*, John adjudges both that *prouisa* may fail to happen and that certain things may not be *praeuisa*. Thus, indirectly and perhaps involuntarily, John rediscovers the thesis attributed by Cicero to Carneades in *De fato* (no doubt known to John indirectly through Augustine), that the gods have no knowledge of voluntary (or contingent) future events, but only of those that are necessary.[64] Meanwhile, however, John has to con-sider another objection: if certain things foreseen have not come to be, this signifies that what is is capable of not being, and that what has been is capable of not having been. He gives a dual response to this objection. Firstly, he

---

63   *Policraticus* 2.22, trans. Pike, p. 107, ed. Keats-Rohan, pp. 126–127: "Malo cum Academicis, si tamen alia uia non pateat, de singulis dubitare quam perniciosa simulatione scientiae quod ignotum uel absconditum est temere diffinire, praesertim in quo assertioni meae fere totus aduersabitur mundus. Eo que libentius Academicos audio quod eorum quae noui nichil auferunt, et in multis faciunt cautiorem, magnorum uirorum auctoritate suf-fulti, cum ad eos etiam in senectute transierit ille in quo Latinitas nostra solo inuenit quicquid insolenti Graeciae eleganter opponit aut praefert, Ciceronem loquor, Romani auctorem eloquii quem ad eos quasi in calce uitae diuertisse liber De Natura Deorum inscriptus docet."

64   Cicero *De fato* 7.13–14. See Saint Augustine, *De ciuitate Dei* 5.9.

reprises Boethius' theory of divine knowledge: by virtue of his eternal nature, God is not subject to temporal determinations, but is outside time. His gaze apprehends things outside their temporal determinations, in the eternal present.[65] Nevertheless, while such a solution permits a defence of divine infallibility, it also carries with it the implication of divine omniscience, so that nothing can escape from God. In response to such a thesis, John cites some passages of the scriptures (Is 9:10; the Passion) that attest that God is capable of not foreseeing everything, or of leaving certain things undetermined. John accordingly proceeds to reaffirm his thesis: contingency escapes from divine anticipation, so that providence is capable of not having foreseen an event. More precisely, John maintains two theses: first, *cum multis*, he maintains that, if something is foreseen by God, it will happen, and, if it does not happen, it has not been foreseen; secondly, *probabiliter*, he also maintains a thesis that is not incompatible with the first, to the effect that, if a thing is capable of not happening (if it is contingent), it is capable of not having been foreseen:

> I do agree with many others that if God has foreseen any event it will come to pass; if it does not come to pass, he has not foreseen it. Hence, on credible grounds it is inferred, at least, that if there is the possibility of its not coming to pass, there is even the possibility that it has not been foreseen. Truth itself knows what will truly follow upon what, and natural reason weighs fully and perfectly the rational connection. The Academy of the ancients makes to human beings the concession that whatever seems probable to each, that he has full right to defend.[66]

Even if he does not claim it, John of Salisbury appears desirous of making Cicero's position on divine prescience his own. No doubt conscious of the boldness involved in defending a thesis that has been rejected by Augustine as impious, not to say atheistic, John takes care to specify that he has no wish to limit divine power, but claims the right accorded by the Academicians to seek out the probable. The entire chapter is in fact infused by a recurring appeal to scepticism in affirmation of that right. The question of prescience is in effect

---

65   *Policraticus* 2.22, ed. Keats-Rohan, p. 128.

66   Ibid., 2.22, trans. Pike, p. 114, ed. Keats-Rohan, pp. 133–134: "Hoc autem cum multis sentio quia, si quid Deus praeuidit, eueniet, et si non euenerit, non praeuidit. Vnde probabiliter ad minus colligitur quia, si potest non euenire, potest etiam non fuisse praeuisum. Quid enim ex quo ueraciter consequatur, ipsa ueritas nouit, iuncturam que rationum plene et perfecte primitiua ratio pensat. Hanc autem humano generi indulget Academia antiqua licentiam ut, quicquid unicuique probabile occurrit, suo iure defendat."

one of those problems upon which humanity cannot achieve knowledge of the truth, which is known to God alone. The search for the probable is therefore legitimate if it is accompanied by recognition of our own ignorance, and leads us to honour the majesty of God.[67] This particular domain is therefore one where rational search for a solution reveals the limits of reason, and encourages humility in face of divine truth. As such, it will be seen to exemplify John's conception of the relationship between scepticism and theology. What should in fact be concluded from such a chapter? In the first place, if John appears to have some knowledge of contemporary debates on prescience, and in particular the theses proposed by Abelard, he largely skirts around the logical dimension of those debates. At no time does he take up Abelard's logical analyses, or even those of William of Conches or Boethius. His theological culture remains very classical, and resistant of any desire to import into theology too large a dose of logic: he refers in preference to Augustine, and to the epistemological rather than the logical contributions of Boethius. Nevertheless, if he takes up the *locus classicus* of Philosophy's response in the *Consolation*, based on the eternal and simple nature of divine knowledge, he departs from it when he discreetly reintroduces quite a heterodox position taken from Cicero. But the essential for John is to show that this type of debate can only reveal the limits of reason, and encourage the practice of religion. The prime role of scepticism is to allow such a position.

Scepticism and Negative Theology

The opening up of certain theological questions to sceptical doubt, with a view to arriving at a probable solution, must not conceal the fact that, essentially, theological problems are founded, on the one hand, on the principles given by the authority of revelation, and, on the other, on an attitude of humility towards God. It is without doubt in this last point that John of Salisbury moves away from any scholastic or pre-scholastic approach to theology, to come closer to a more monastic style, more or less explicitly influenced by Neoplatonism (and Augustinism in particular), and oriented towards contemplation and the love of God. This is what appears, especially, at the end of the *Metalogicon*. From Chapter 30 of Book 4 onwards, John's reflections on the links between reason and truth progressively depart from the domain of epistemology to join that of theology, where it is God, inasmuch as he is a measure of what is true, who becomes their principal object. In this entire set of chapters, John endeavours

---

67   *Policraticus* 2.22, ed. Keats-Rohan, p. 133.

to found the epistemological argument (what truth is available to humanity?) on an ontological approach of a distinctly Neoplatonic kind, with reference to a certain number of explicit sources, headed by Augustine, but including Hilary of Poitiers, Bernard of Chartres, and Gilbert de la Porrée, together with Plato, Apuleius, and Boethius.

Within the framework of this Neoplatonically-inspired theology, John of Salisbury adopts as his own a model founded on (divine) perfection, and on the degradation of that perfection at the lower levels, the levels of the angels and of humanity, who can only imitate divine perfection. God is reason *par excellence*, the *ratio prima* or *ratio primitiua*, both because He is knowledge of all things, and because this knowledge is infallible. Accordingly, He is perfectly stable and perfectly solid, and this epistemic stability finds justification from an ontological standpoint: God alone is the perfectly immutable being. This superposition of the epistemological and ontological levels emerges in John's conception of truth, which is a property not only of our judgements but also of things. In this perspective, God alone is absolutely the truth, inasmuch as He is original truth. All truths of secondary order are only imitations of this first truth, and the degree of truth of each thing depends on that thing's proximity to the divine principle:

> Original truth is found in the divine majesty. There is also another truth, which consists in an image or likeness of the divinity. The truth of anything is directly dependent on the degree in which it faithfully reflects the likeness of God. The more deficient anything is in this respect, the more it fades into falsity and nothingness.[68]

It follows that neither being nor truth in its full sense can be found at the level of sensible things. The degradation of the principle nevertheless occurs progressively, and, before arriving at the corporeal creature that is man, John reserves a place for the angels, who occupy an intermediary position between God and humanity. His analyses rely largely on Augustinian theory as developed, in particular, in the *City of God*.[69] The angels, who are spiritual creatures, are free from the ties of the body, and enjoy a vision of things in God. For this double reason, their knowledge is always true, and, although not universal,

---

68   *Metalogicon* 4.39, trans. McGarry, p. 267, ed. Hall and Keats-Rohan, p. 179: "Est autem pri-
      maeua ueritas, in maiestate diuina; alia uero est quae in diuinitatis consistit imagine, id
      est in imitatione. Omnis enim res tanto uerior est, quanto imaginem Dei fidelius exprimit,
      et quanto ab ea magis deficit, tanto falsior euanescit."

69   See Saint Augustine, *De ciuitate Dei* 11.29.

perfect in its nature. Like Augustine, then, John considers the angelic vision to be infallible but incomplete. Humanity, at the lowest level of rational creatures, is marked by its imperfection. The cause of human imperfection is dual. It is due both to the ties of the body and to original sin. These two causal factors condemn humanity to error. Human knowledge is accordingly a degraded image of the higher epistemic levels, and human reason can only imperfectly imitate the reason of the angels and, *a fortiori*, that of God. John of Salisbury's theory of truth is thus based on the idea, apposite for a Christian philosopher, that God is truth.[70] This thesis lay at the foundation of Augustine's theory of illumination, and it is the same with John. Already in the *Entheticus*, he maintains that human reason is an image of divine reason, and that it is thus capable of grasping divine truth interiorly, by turning on itself: a condition of divine teaching. And this teaching is made possible by the diffusion of divine light in the soul. This light fulfils the same role as physical light in the faculty of perception.[71] Thus, without God, humanity is blind. This is the same epistemology that John was to develop some years later in the final part of Book 4 of the *Metalogicon*, but this time embedded in an explicitly sceptical and Platonic perspective (as, for John, scepticism and Platonism are broadly linked). As can be seen, if John of Salisbury adopts the elements of a theology inspired by Neoplatonism and principally Augustinism, it is primarily due to the epistemological implications of such a theology; and what John retains of it is at the same time the desire for truth that is proper to every person, and the feeble part given to every person in that same truth:

> Truth is both the light of the mind and the subject matter of reason. God and angels see truth directly, God beholding universal truth, and the angels particular truths. But man, no matter how perfect, glimpses the truth only in part, and to a definitely limited degree. However, the more perfect a man is, the more ardently he desires to comprehend the truth.

---

70 See for example *Metalogicon* 4.39, ed. Hall and Keats-Rohan, p. 179: "Porro haec in Deo unum quia Ratio et Verbum aeternum de se dicit: ego sum veritas." John quotes John 14:6, which is the basis for Augustine's theory of illumination. See Saint Augustine, *De magistro* 38.

71 *Entheticus maior*, ll.629–40, ed. van Laarhoven, p. 147: "Est hominis ratio summae rationis imago, / quae capit interius vera docente Deo. / Ut data lux oculis tam se quam cetera monstrat, / quae sub luce patent et sine luce latent, / claraque fit nubes concepto lumine solis, / cum dependantes flatus abegit aquas, / subdita sic ratio formam summae rationis / sordibus expulsis induit, inde micat. / Tunc mens tota nitet, et vero lumine plena / res falsa abigit, et bona vera colit. / Sicut nemo potest aliquid nisi luce videre, / sic hominis ratio caeca fit absque Deo."

> For truth is the basis of certitude, in which reason's investigations flour-
> ish and thrive.[72]

What we in fact see in these chapters is a movement from the ontological and theological justification of error and human impotence to a form of fideistic scepticism. But on this point, again, John merely reprises and radicalizes a schema of Augustinian type. The theory of truth founded on the classic identification between God and the truth, and on the intellect's capacity to apprehend such a truth, leads to the position that all knowledge presupposes divine illumination. To this classical point of view is added the theory of imitation and degradation, of Neoplatonic (perhaps Dionysian) inspiration, so that the further one departs from the principle the more inevitable falsehood becomes. This conception of truth permits John to account for humanity's incapacity fully to apprehend the truth, as humanity no longer shares God's nature.

The final chapters of the *Metalogicon* (Chapters 40 and 41) in fact pursue this inquiry into the incapacity of humanity to gain access to the truth. John identifies eight obstacles to knowledge of the true, all coming down to the frailty of a humanity marked by sin, and the disproportion between our intelligence and the supernatural phenomena we seek to apprehend:

> The human heart is so seduced that it but rarely succeeds in attaining
> knowledge of the truth. The many impediments to understanding include
> invincible ignorance of such things as the mysteries of the Holy Trinity,
> which reason cannot explain; the frailty of man's condition; the brevity of
> human life; the neglect of what is useful and corresponding concern with
> what is unprofitable; the perplexing conflict of probable opinions; sin,
> which makes one unworthy of seeing the light; and finally the great mul-
> titude and vast expanse of subjects to be investigated.[73]

---

72 *Metalogicon* 4.39, trans. McGarry, p. 267, ed. Hall and Keats-Rohan, p. 178: "Veritas autem
    lux mentis est et materia rationis. Hanc Deus uniuersaliter, angelus particulariter intue-
    tur. Homo autem etiam perfectissimus pro parte modica uidet, sed quo perfectior, eo
    amplius appetit. Haec est soliditas certitudinis, in qua rationis uiget examen."

73 Ibid. 4.40, trans. McGarry, pp. 268–277, ed. Hall and Keats-Rohan, pp. 179–180: "Sed quia
    multa sunt quae praepediunt intelligentiam, utpote inuincibilis ignorantia eorum, quae
    ratione expediri non possunt, sicut sunt Sanctae Trinitatis arcana, et item fragilitas condi-
    cionis, uita breuis, utilium negligentia, occupatio inutilis, probabilium conflictus opinio-
    num, culpa quae lucem demeretur, et tandem numerositas, et immensitas inuestigabilium,
    adeo obductum est cor humanum, ut ad ueri notitiam raro possit accedere."

From these eight obstacles John draws several conclusions. The first is to do with the vanity of pagan philosophies, characterized by a descent into worldly dissipation. To this vanity must be opposed the contemplation of self, which alone allows us to establish within ourselves the cult of the divine. This contemplation of self falls within the Augustinian perspective of the reformation of God's image obscured by sin. At this juncture, John's criticism of philosophers relies very broadly on the theme of *uanitas*, drawn by him from the Sapiential Books, which frame his reflections. John's sceptical fideism in fact depends largely on the convergence he believes to discover between Neoplatonic theology and the Sapiential Books, chiefly Ecclesiastes. He cites convergence between philosophy and the scriptures in order to affirm the vanity of the senses:

> All that is vain, is, precisely because of its emptiness, illusory. After deluding minds, which it dupes by it false pretensions, it vanishes like a phantasm of the imagination. Because of this ephemeral nature of what is transitory and perishable, Ecclesiastes, in his discourse concerning all earthly things, declares: "Everything under the sun is vain." He does so in such forceful and impressive language, and with such authoritative probability, that his saying has become commonplace among all peoples, and has passed into all languages. Penetrating the minds of all who have ears to hear, it shakes their souls to their very depths.[74]

But it is above all in Chapter 41 that John goes on to make enormous use of these Sapiential Books to promote a sort of negative theology. It is in effect the second conclusion derived from his eight cognitive obstacles: that it is impossible for humanity fully to know what God is. It is the disproportion between the immensity of God and the frailty of the human intellect that prevents this type of knowledge. Thus, in criticizing those who claim, by means of reason, to say what God is, and in particular to elucidate the mystery of the Trinity, John criticizes the very possibility of scholastic theology. Such a critique converges with a critique of the pride of philosophers who claim to know all the laws of

---

74   Ibid. 4.35, trans. McGarry, p. 258, ed. Hall and Keats-Rohan, pp. 172–173: "Omnia uero uana quatenus uana sunt fallunt, et cum falsitate deceptas mentes illuserint, uelut phantasmata euanescunt. Vnde ob hanc rerum euanescentium disparentiam, omnia quae sub sole sunt uana esse in contione uniuersorum qui uersantur in mundo proclamat Ecclesiastes, tanta quidem maiestate uerbi, tanta probabilitate sententiae, ut ad omnes nationes et linguas uox illa pertranseat, et omnium qui aures audiendi habent, corda penetrando concutiat."

the sensible world. And this double critique has as its aim the establishment of limits to reason in the face of faith, by emphasizing the unknowable dimension of God's being:

> As Augustine observes in his book *On order*, our best knowledge of God is of a negative nature. If a person who is ignorant of natures and morals and reasons, and who is a puppet of his passions, and an addict to perishable things, or who perhaps lives chastely although he is ignorant of the various branches of knowledge, imagines that he can find God by processes of investigation and argumentative reasoning conducted by the faculties of his own unaided mind, he is doubtless making the greatest possible of all mistakes. Augustine remarks elsewhere: What we realize that we do not know God constitutes our truest wisdom concerning Him. He also says: No small part of our knowledge of God consists in knowing what He is not, as it is absolutely impossible to know what He is.[75]

Certainly, this is not a form of negative theology in any precise sense. John contents himself with citing three occasions where Augustine affirms our ignorance in respect of God. John's aim here is to demonstrate the limits of raison when it comes to knowledge of divine truth, in order to promote the role of faith. It is at this level that scepticism and fideism come together; hence John's final conclusion, the substitution of the useful for the true. It is principally in this context that quotations from the Sapiential Books are called in evidence, and at this level too that they are brought into alignment with John's sceptical positions in respect of knowledge. The chapter's structure is in fact very clear. It begins by quoting Ecclesiastes 3:22 to warn against seeking truths that exceed our capacities.[76] The quotation is exemplified by means of theological inquiries into the Trinity, related by John to the beatific vision. A second

---

75 Ibid. 4.40, trans. McGarry, p .271, ed. Hall and Keats-Rohan, p. 181: "Vt autem ait Augustinus in libro de ordine, Deus melius nesciendo scitur, quem siquis ignarus naturarum, et morum rationum que, cupiditatum ue seruus, et rebus pereuntibus inhians aut forte caste uiuens, et disciplinarum nescius, ingenii uiribus quaerendo et disputando inuenire confidit, procul dubio tantum errabit, quantum errari plurimum potest. Alibi quoque. Ignorantia Dei, eius uerissima sapientia est. Et item. Non est parua scientia de Deo scire quid non sit Deus, quia quid sit omnino sciri non potest."

76 Ibid. 4.41, p. 182: "Altiora inquit te ne quaesieris, et fortiora te ne scrutatus fueris. Ecce temeritatem eorum cohibet, qui deificae Trinitatis arcana, et ea quorum uisio in uita aeterna promittitur, irreuerenti uerbositate discutiunt. Vnde et si scientia uideatur augeri, deuotio certe minuitur."

quotation from Ecclesiastes (3:24) then allows him to introduce the idea of futile questions, inquiry into which must be limited.[77] This point is then exemplified by reference to the audacity of philosophers, denounced by John (following Augustine and Lactantius) in the *Policraticus*. He reinforces this critique of philosophers with another quotation from Ecclesiastes (8:17).[78] Then he again cites Ecclesiastes 3:22, which opposes divine prescriptions to the examination of God's works. If such an examination is to be legitimate, it must be limited, and subordinated to divine law.[79] It is at this point that John goes on to introduce the superiority of the useful to the true for a humanity typified by inadequacy. In fact, returning to the key elements of his scepticism, he recalls that knowledge depends on perception, which is fallible. This fallibility prevents us from recognizing the useful, so that God, in order to supply that inadequacy, has made known his law. Once truth has made itself inaccessible, all that remains for humanity is a practical substitute for the truth, which is the useful, known by virtue of God's law. It is explicitly in correction of error, frequent in both sensation and reason, that faith, and the law that faith enables us to recognize, must intervene, "since not only man's senses, but even his reason frequently err, the law of God has made faith the primary and fundamental prerequisite for understanding of the truth."[80]

This having been said, the final word in respect of John of Salisbury's sceptical theology is very clearly indicated in the final lines of the same Chapter 41:

> We know that our knowledge flows ultimately from our senses, which are frequently misled, and that faltering human infirmity is at a loss to know what is expedient. Accordingly, God in His mercy, has given us a law, to

---

77   Ibid. 4.41, p. 182: "In superuacuis inquit rebus noli scrutari multipliciter. Et in pluribus eius operibus non eris curiosus. Multos enim supplantauit suspicio eorum, et in uanitate detinuit sensus eorum."

78   Ibid. 4.41, p. 182: "Hic quoque illorum audaciam reprimit, qui sollicitantur de omnibus et uolunt de uniuersis reddere rationem, cum constet auctoritate Salomonis in Ecclesiaste quod nec minimae rei quae sub caelo est nedum caelestium aut supra caelestium, plenam possit homo reddere rationem."

79   Ibid. 4.41, p. 182: "Quae praecepit Deus cogita illa semper, et in pluribus operibus eius non eris curiosus. Quia enim de radice sensuum, qui frequenter falluntur, scientia manat, et decepta infirmitas quid expediat parum nouit, data est per clementiam Dei lex quae utilium scientiam aperiret, et indicaret de Deo quantum sciri licet, aut quantum expedit quaerere."

80   Ibid. 4.41, trans. McGarry, p. 273, ed. Hall and Keats-Rohan, p. 182: "Et quia tam sensus quam ratio humana frequenter errat, ad intelligentiam ueritatis primum fundamentum locauit in fide."

make evident what is useful, to disclose how much we may know about Him, and to indicate how far we may go in our inquiries concerning Him.[81]

When sceptical arguments have demonstrated the fallibility of reason and perception, and their inability to arrive at the truth in a trustworthy manner, then, in order to succeed in apprehending that truth, humanity is left with faith alone. Faith, nevertheless, reveals only in a mirror, and partially. It is accordingly utility made manifest by God's law that truly permits us to orientate ourselves safely, and to act correctly. In the final analysis, John of Salisbury's sceptical theology is a political theology.

The Political Theology of John of Salisbury

For John of Salisbury, politics, in the shape of action to lead a community towards a common good and make justice reign, must depend on divine law, of which the prince guided by the priests is the servant. The conception of society promoted by John of Salisbury is thus profoundly theologico-political, inasmuch as it is rooted in a certain concept of faith and of the law.

In its broadest sense, faith is not immediately a religious notion: it is simply the confidence one is able to accord someone or something. John recalls for the occasion the etymology proposed by the Stoics, according to which faith derives from the fact of doing what one says.[82] This idea of confidence, or contract, nevertheless equally provides the point of departure for the religious notion of *fides*. Faith is a kind of contract by which one gives one's confidence to invisible truths revealed by grace:

> If, nevertheless, we posit as a certainty something that is not in all respects certain, then we approach the domain of faith which Aristotle defines as exceedingly strong opinion. Faith is, indeed, most necessary in human affairs, as well as in religion. Without faith, no contracts could be concluded,

---

81 Ibid. 4.41, trans. McGarry, pp. 272–273, ed. Hall and Keats-Rohan, p. 182: "Quia enim de radice sensuum, qui frequenter falluntur, scientia manat, et decepta infirmitas quid expediat parum nouit, data est per clementiam Dei lex quae utilium scientiam aperiret, et indicaret de Deo quantum sciri licet, aut quantum expedit quaerere."

82 *Policraticus* 3.6, ed. Keats-Rohan, p. 186: "Non manet fides incolumis ubi aliud agitur et aliud simulatur, praesertim animo et uoluntate nocendi. Dicitur enim fides, si sequimur Stoicos, eo quod fiat quod dictum est."

nor could any business be transacted. And without faith, where would be the basis for the divine reward of human merit?[83]

Faith is therefore that which permits a contractual relationship to be established between God and humanity by the mediation of religion, which is the affair of priests. This is the idea that is developed in Chapters 3 and 4 of Book 5 of the *Policraticus*, devoted to presenting the soul of the body politic, which is to say the priesthood.

In the context of presenting the structure of the republic according to the apocryphal *Institutes of Trajan*, which he attributes to Plutarch, John employs a corporeal, or rather organic metaphor, making the republic the analogue of a living body.[84] Now, if the prince is the head of this body, the function of soul falls to those who implant God's cult in the heart of the citizens, and preside over the practice of that cult:

> Those things which establish and implant in us the practice of religion, and transmit to us the worship of God (here I do not follow Plutarch, who says "of the Gods") fill the place of the soul in the body of the commonwealth. And therefore those who preside over the practice of religion should be looked up to and venerated as the soul of the body. For who doubts that the ministers of God's holiness are His representatives?[85]

---

83   *Metalogicon* 4.13, trans. McGarry, p. 223, ed. Hall and Keats-Rohan, p. 151: "Si autem quod non usquequaque certum est, pro certo statuatur, fit accessus ad fidem, quam Aristotiles definit esse uehementem opinionem; fides autem tam in humanis quam in diuinis rebus maxime necessaria est, cum nec contractus sine ea celebrari inter homines possent aut aliqua exerceri commercia. Inter Deum quoque et homines meritorum praemiorum que nequit esse commercium, fide subtracta."

84   John of Salisbury relates this model to Plutarch's *Institutio Traiani*. See *Policraticus* 5.1, ed. Webb, vol. 1, pp. 281–282. It has been quite widely accepted since the contribution of Hans Liebeschütz that the *Institutio Traiani* is a fake created by John himself. See Hans Liebeschütz, "John of Salisbury and Pseudo-Plutarch," *Journal of Warburg and Courtauld Institutes* 6 (1943), 33–39. The contrary point of view is nevertheless defended by Saverio Desideri, *La institutio Trajani* (Genoa, 1958), and more recently by Charles Brucker, in his introduction to *Le Policratique de Jean de Salisbury. Livre V, traduction de Denis Foulechat; édition critique et commentée des textes français et latin avec une introduction par Charles Brucker* (Paris, 2006). See in the present volume the analysis by Laure Hermand.

85   *Policraticus* 5.2, trans. J. Dickinson, p. 64, ed. Webb, vol. 1, p. 282: "Ea uero quae cultum religionis in nobis instituunt et informant et Dei (ne secundum Plutarcum deorum dicam) cerimonias tradunt, uicem animae in corpore rei publicae obtinent. Illos uero, qui religionis cultui praesunt, quasi animam corporis suspicere et uenerari oportet. Quis enim sanctitatis ministros Dei ipsius uicarios esse ambigit?"

This immediately implies a privileged status for religion and priests. That status is reinforced by the republic's first principle, which the prince must strive to promote: the honour due to God.[86] Nevertheless, this injunction to honour God is not so much the postulate of a Christian thinker as a principle of conservation necessary to every human society. John justifies its status as the first principle of the republic at the end of a reflection on what constitutes the unity of a community. On this point, John insists, there is convergence between pagans and Christians. Yet it is not self-evident to humanity that the honour rendered God is a political imperative. Governments are therefore obliged to put stratagems in place to promote the love of God.[87]

That our love for God is not immediate is a result of the very nature of God and the frailty of the human condition. The cult maintained by priests must therefore find a set of sensible stimuli designed to render the invisible visible and strengthen the contract between God and humanity. Now, if God's presence manifests itself indirectly and partially in his creation, as also by the Incarnation, nevertheless "the plenitude of his presence is never complete":

> Yet the angels, who already participate in the blessedness which is reserved for us in the future, are adored when seen of me, because in them a certain actual presence of the Deity is visible. Thus too in the face of the Saviour something of Deity shone forth, when he made a scourge of cords and drove the buyers and sellers from the temple, thus showing that all transaction of business is to be banished from the house of prayer. But in other men, although the presence of the Deity may be felt near at hand, His fulness is never actually present, and yet cannot wholly be concealed.[88]

---

86   Ibid. 5.3, ed. Webb, vol. 1, p. 284: "In summa ergo quattuor sunt quae nititur rei publicae principibus inculcare: reuerentiam Dei, cultum sui, disciplinam officialium et potestatum, affectum et protectionem subditorum. Deum ergo in primis asserit honorandum."

87   Ibid. 5.3, ed. Webb, vol. 1, p. 284: "Magnorum quoque uirorum strategemmatibus et strategemmaticis utitur, quae, si per singula inserantur, tediosa erunt lectori et pro parte a fidei nostrae sinceritate recedent. Ceterum, quia sancti patres et principum leges illius deducta tamen perfidia uidentur inherere uestigiis, doctrinam eius sermone catholico et succincto, adiectis ex parte strategemmaticis eius, attingamus."

88   Ibid. 5.3, trans. J. Dickinson, p. 71, ed. Webb, vol. 1, pp. 288–289: "[A]ngeli, iam futurae beatitudinis nostrae participes, uisi adorantur ab hominibus eo quod in eis uisa est quaedam praesentia deitatis, cum tamen creaturam a creatura adorari omnino non liceat. Sic etiam in facie Saluatoris aliquid deitatis resplenduit, quando de funiculis facto flagello uendentes et ementes eiecit de templo, docens omnem negotiationem exterminandam esse a domo orationis. In aliis uero etsi assit diuinitatis praesentia, plenitudo eius in praesenti nequaquam adest sed usquequaque latere non potest."

Reinvesting an emanationist model, John envisages a process of gradual diffusion of the divine presence, with its effect becoming progressively exhausted in such a way that, if divinity manifests itself fully to the degrees immediately adjacent to it (those of the angels), it can no longer be fully perceived at the lower levels. Each level nevertheless participates more or less in the deity by the intermediary of the level one stage higher. The conclusion that John draws is that something improperly perceived and thus improperly known cannot be correctly honoured. Faith, understood as an affective phenomenon, must therefore be reinforced by a set of mediations available to the senses. This is the function of the cult and of works, which constitute the second manner of honouring God. The prime purpose of the cult is to make the divine visible and to channel works, which are the external manifestation of faith. Works are in effect one of the forms of charity, and evidence of our love for God. It is nevertheless necessary that these evidences of love should be correctly addressed to their recipient. This is the function of the cult presided over by priests. Thus, as human frailty after the Fall renders individual faith insufficient in itself, because too uncertain in its relationship to its object, it is necessary to add to it an external dimension:

> But the worship which consists in the display of external works requires a medium; Inasmuch asas no bodily approach to the spirit is accessible to us, as was plainly taught by Him who, in the case of the woman of Samaria, said for the instruction of the Church: God is a spirit, and they that would worship Him must worship in spirit and in truth. In order, however, to provide a way whereby the weakness of our humility may ascend to His throne, and have some ground for merit, He who endowed us with senses has wished to be worshipped with the senses; and He who will glorify both soul and body demands the faithful service of both. He also desires to be worshipped with the body to the end that the tardiness of unfaithfulness or negligence may have nought wherewith to excuse itself.[89]

---

89   Ibid. 5.3, trans. Dickinson, p. 72, ed. Webb, vol. 1, p. 289: "Ille autem cultus qui in exterioris operis exhibitione consistit, medio indiget, eo quod ad spiritum corporalis nobis non patet accessus; quod et illum planum est docuisse, qui in Samaritana Ecclesiam instruens ait: Spiritus est Deus, et eos qui uolunt adorare, in spiritu et ueritate oportet adorare. Ut tamen ad thronum illius quocumque modo materiam meritorum, sensualiter coli uoluit qui sensum dedit; et qui animam glorificabit et carnem, utriusque fidelem expetit famulatum. Se quoque uoluit etiam corporaliter honorari ut quantauis tarditas infidelitatis aut negligentiae excusationem non habeat."

It is therefore concomitant of faith that it should be publicly taken in charge by a third party that will serve as an intermediary with God, and provide a corporeal substitute for the spiritual union with God. The cult, inasmuch as it provides our faith with a set of sensible intermediaries, accordingly allows the frailties inherent in our nature, weighed down as it is by the burden of sin and the body, to be palliated. It is therefore necessary to render God a double homage, at the same time of the spirit and of the senses:

> His point of departure is from reverence for supernatural beings; ours is from God, who is to be loved by all men alike and worshipped with all their heart, and all their soul, and all their strength. The proof of love is the works which it shows forth; and though He can be loved for Himself and directly, after the manner of one who pours out his soul to his beloved without the need of any medium, nevertheless, for external worship the intervention of something intermediate is necessary, since no one has ever seen God.[90]

The rites and religious practices put in place in the context of the cult are first of all justified by the carnal nature of humanity, as palliatives to its corporeality. Scepticism, in bringing to the fore the cognitive limits of sense and reason, is theologically justified by original sin, and, in turn, becomes the foundation of a normative conception of society, where the law of God and the cult that accompanies it serve to moderate the ethical and political effects of humanity's cognitive deficiencies.[91]

---

90   Ibid. 5.3, trans. Dickinson, pp. 67–68, ed. Webb, vol. 1, pp. 284–285: "Porro ei initium a reuerentia numinum est, nobis a Deo, qui ab omnibus generaliter amandus est et colendus ex toto corde, ex tota anima, ex omnibus uiribus suis. Probatio uero dilectionis exhibitio operis est; et, licet per se ipsum possit amari, tamquam qui citra opem medii se infundat amanti, tamen ad cultum exteriorem alicuius medietatis interuentus necessarius est, eo quod Deum nemo uiderit umquam."

91   I deal at length with John's political theology in the triptych "Le sacré et le profane. Le statut des laïcs dans la Respublica de Jean de Salisbury," in Patrick Demouy, ed., Les Laïcs dans les villes de la France du Nord au XIIe siècle (Turnhout, 2008), pp. 167–187; "La religion comme technique de gouvernement chez Jean de Salisbury," Cahiers de civilisation médiévale 53 (2010), 237–254, and "Le roi est sujet de la loi de justice. Loi des dieux, loi des hommes chez Jean de Salisbury," in Jean-Patrice Boudet, Silvère Menegaldo and Bernard Ribémont, ed., Le Roi fontaine de justice: pouvoir justicier et pouvoir royal au Moyen Âge et à la Renaissance (Paris, 2012), pp. 85–103.

Conclusion

John of Salisbury is undoubtedly one of the most interesting representatives of the Christian sceptical tradition from Lactantius to Petrarch. His conception of action and speculation is rooted in experience of the contingency of the world and the solidity of faith in God, beyond the limits of a fallen human nature. It is therefore scarcely surprising that, despite his years of study in Paris, John remained a stranger to the nascent scholastic movement, which in a sense relied on a conviction that human reason has the means to elevate itself to a form, admittedly imperfect, of knowledge of the divine. For John, on the contrary, the reason of philosophers is definitely incapable of apprehending with precision the truth that has turned its back on them as punishment for their pride. There indeed remains room open for probability-based inquiry, concerning certain questions of scholastic theology. Essentially, however, owing to the decay of reason, the only resource left to humanity is to rely on faith in God and in his law that was given to humanity in palliation of its fall from grace. The final word of John of Salisbury's scepticism therefore consists in following the law of God and the injunctions of those entrusted with its keeping, that is to say the priests. The necessary consequence of John of Salisbury's theological scepticism is thus the uneasy cohabitation of politics and theology in medieval and modern Europe.

PART 4

John of Salisbury and his Readers

∵

CHAPTER 12

Filiation and Context

The Medieval Afterlife of the Policraticus

Frédérique Lachaud

Historians of political thought have long shown an interest in the reception of the *Policraticus* in the later Middle Ages. Besides being a seemingly inexhaustible source of stories and anecdotes, and an essential intermediary in the perception of ancient philosophy, this work developed some key topics, such as the nature of the body politic or tyranny and tyrannicide, which would be taken up and discussed well into the 15th century. Walter Ullmann, Amnon Linder, Max Kerner and Thomas Elsmann have traced how knowledge of this great text was disseminated; they have also established a list of manuscripts, and mapped their geographical diffusion.[1] Others scholars have highlighted the debt to John of Salisbury of a number of thinkers, from Helinand of Froidmont and Vincent of Beauvais to Christine of Pisan. All these demonstrate the importance of the *Policraticus* in later medieval political thought.

Given the magnitude of what amounts to a cultural phenomenon, retracing the diffusion of the *Policraticus* is central both to studies on John of Salisbury and to intellectual history in general. Yet such an approach must be sensitive to the different contexts in which the *Policraticus* was received: in most cases, what was truly significant was the way particular ideas taken from it were used and adapted by its readers for their own specific

---

[1] Walter Ullmann, "The Influence of John of Salisbury on Medieval Italian Jurists," *The English Historical Review* 59 (1944), 384–392; idem, "John of Salisbury's *Policraticus* in the Later Middle Ages," in *Geschichtsschreibung und geistiges Leben im Mittelalter: Festschrift für Heinz Löwe zum 65. Geburstag* (Cologne, 1978), pp. 519–545, repr. in *Jurisprudence in the Middle Ages. Collected Studies* (London, 1980); Amnon Linder, "John of Salisbury's *Policraticus* in Thirteenth-Century England: the Evidence of MS Cambridge Corpus Christi College 469," *Journal of the Warburg and Courtauld Institutes* 40 (1977), 276–282; idem, "The Knowledge of John of Salisbury in the Late Middle Ages," *Studi medievali*, 3rd series 18 (1977), 315–366; Max Kerner, "Johannes von Salisbury im späteren Mittelalter," in Jürgen Miethke, ed., *Das Publikum politischer Theorie im 14. Jarhundert* (Munich, 1992), pp. 25–47; Thomas Elsmann, *Untersuchungen zur Rezeption der Institutio Traiani. Ein Beitrag zur Nachwirkung antiker und pseudoantiker Topoi im Mittelalter und in der Frühen Neuzeit* (Stuttgart, 1994). I wish to thank Michael Lobban for his suggestions and corrections.

purposes.[2] The rationale behind the use of the *Policraticus* by authors active in Canterbury in the generation following that of John of Salisbury was different from the purposes of a Cistercian author such as Helinand of Froidmont in early 13th-century France. Even more so, this may be said about the use of the *Policraticus* by Italian jurists in the 14th and 15th centuries, or in the context of the political and military difficulties of the Valois kings in the first half of the 15th century.

Nor should this influence be seen as even for the reception of the *Policraticus* was often fragmentary and tentative. It was diffused in different forms, ranging from the full text through to short extracts – in particular the *Institutio Traiani* –[3] or summaries.[4] Whole sections or short passages were quoted. There were also broad adaptations of the text; in a few cases, borrowings were so significant as to produce imitations of John of Salisbury's work. In tracing the influence of John of Salisbury, one also needs to bear in mind the numerous non-attributed quotations, or borrowings from the *Policraticus* that do not acknowledge their source. Although John's name clearly appears in some early manuscripts of the text,[5] few of its late medieval readers identified him. Lucas de Penna mistook *Policraticus* for the name of the author of the book.[6] Coluccio Salutati mentioned John of Salisbury, but in an erroneous form ("Johannes de Saberiis").[7] In his *Speculum morale*, the Franciscan Vital du Four (†1327) – obviously

---

2 There is also the issue of the genre which the *Policraticus* belongs to. In early modern France, for instance, the fact that the *Policraticus* did not fit any recognised genre baffled scholars: see Alain Cullière, *"Les Vanitez de la cour*, de Mézeray,"* in Venceslasz Bubenicek and Roger Marchal, eds., *Gouvernement des hommes, gouvernement des âmes. Mélanges de langue et littérature françaises offerts au Professeur Charles Brucker* (Nancy, 2007), pp. 453–467, esp. p. 453 and note 3.

3 See the list compiled by Elsmann, *Untersuchungen zur Rezeption der Institutio Traiani,* pp. 249–275.

4 e.g. Bibliothèque nationale de Luxembourg 60 (first third of the 13th century). I wish to thank Cédric Giraud and Thomas Falmagne for this information.

5 It appears for instance in London, British Library, Royal 13 D. IV, fol.161r: *Explicit Policraticus Iohannis de Saresbiri*. The manuscript dates from the abbacy of Simon, abbot of St Albans (1167–83). In the 14th century, it was purchased by Richard of Bury, and was returned to St Albans only after the death of the bishop of Durham in 1345: Christopher R. Cheney, "Richard de Bury, Borrower of Books," *Speculum* 46 (1973), 325–328, esp. p. 328.

6 Walter Ullmann, *The Medieval Idea of Law as Represented by Lucas de Penna. A Study in Fourteenth-Century Legal Scholarship* (London, 1946), p. 31 and note 5. Guglielmo da Pastrengo also knew the *Policraticus*, but not the name of its author (ibid.).

7 *Tractatus de Tyranno von Coluccio Salutati*, ed. Francesco Ercole (Berlin, 1914), p. xxx: "Aliud enim est occisum aliquem esse, aliud iure cesum; ut michi visus sit vir eruditissimus Johannes de Saberiis, qui libro, quem, nescio quam ob rem, dicimus Policratum. . ."

unaware of the identity of John of Salisbury – described Augustine reading the *Policraticus*, a scene Beryl Smalley found "engaging."[8] By contrast, Denis Foulechat wrote a few lines about John of Salisbury in the preface to his translation of the work made in 1372 and even referred to him as a "vaillant docteur."[9]

Sometimes, John of Salisbury's text appeared under the title *"De nugis philosophorum."* In his *Breuiloquium*, for instance, John of Wales quotes this title on twenty-two occasions – clearly referring to John of Salisbury's work – but he attributes these passages to a "Caecilius Balbus," whose name is given in *Policraticus* 3.14.[10] Mentions of the *Nugae curialium* usually also refer to the *Policraticus*. Moreover, medieval readers sometimes distinguished the *Institutio Traiani* from the *Policraticus*, and the attribution of that section of the treatise to Plutarch was widely accepted.[11] As for *"Policraticus,"* this title baffled many. Denis Foulechat considered its possible meanings at some length.[12] Coluccio Salutati admitted his uncertainty when it came to the meaning

---

8   Beryl Smalley, *English Friars and Antiquity in the Early Fourteenth Century* (Oxford, 1960), pp. 241–242.

9   Denis Foulechat, *Le Policratique de Jean de Salisbury (1372), Livres I–III*, ed. Charles Brucker (Geneva, 1994), p. 87.

10   *Policraticus* 3.14, ed. Webb, vol.1, pp. 222–223. In 1855, Eduard Wölfflin thought it possible to reconstruct the work of this Balbus, on the basis of the fragments quoted by John of Salisbury, as well as from other texts: *Caecilii Balbi De nugis philosophorum quae supersunt*, ed. Eduard Wölfflin (Basel, 1855). However, as early as 1861, this was questioned by August Reifferscheid, "Zwei litterarhistorische Phantasmata: I. Der Grammatiker Petronius. II. Caecilius Balbus De nugis philosophorum," *Rheinisches Museum für Philologie*, neue Folge 16 (1861), 1–26. Eduard Wölfflin's reply is on pp. 615–618. The debate was revived by Joseph Scheibmaier, *De sententiis quas dicunt Caecilii Balbi* (Munich, 1879). On this matter, see Webb in his edition of the *Policraticus*, vol.1, p. 222, note 1; Leighton Durham Reynolds, ed., *Texts and Transmission: A Survey of the Latin Classics* (Oxford, 1983), p. 329; Georg Wissowa, ed., *Paulys Real-Encyclopädie der classischen Altertumswissenschaft*, t. 5 (Stuttgart, 1897), cols. 1196–8; Hubert Cancik and Helmuth Schneider, eds., *Der neue Pauly. Enzyklopädie der Antike, Altertum*, t. 2 (Stuttgart-Weimar, 1997), col. 894. Specialists have usually followed Reifferscheid's position, although the whole issue probably needs addressing afresh.

11   This is for instance the case with Guibert of Tournai in his *De modo addiscendi* (c. 1262). In the epistle to Michel of Lille that opens his treatise, Guibert states that he is going to provide him with the *De instructione Trajani* by Plutarch, as well as with *Johannem Policraticum*. It is not quite clear, however, whether the latter refers to the title of the work, or to the name of its author (A. de Poorter, "Un traité de pédagogie médiévale: le *De modo addiscendi* de Guibert de Tournai O.F.M., notes et extraits," *Revue néo-scolastique de philosophie* 24 (1922), 195–228, esp. p. 207).

12   Foulechat, *Le Policratique de Jean de Salisbury (1372), Livres I–III*, pp. 87–88.

of this title.[13] Finally, there were also some false attributions to John of Salisbury of works which shared similarities with the *Policraticus*. The short treatise *De septem septenis* was sometimes attributed to John.[14] It was also assumed that he had written the anonymous poem *Dialogus linguae et uentris*, also known as *De membris conspirantibus*, after the Frères de la Vie commune printed an edition of the *Policraticus* in Brussels c. 1480 in which the text was followed by an edition of the poem.[15]

In what follows, we will address the question of the circulation of the *Policraticus* in 12th- and 13th-century England, before turning to its influence in 13th-century France. At first sight this distinction may seem artificial in a cultural world that was largely common to Northern France and England, but it is justified by the thematic and textual shift that took place in the reading of the *Policraticus* when the text became widely known on the Continent: some topics seem to have lost their relevance (such as the issue of clerical life) in favour of a new focus on the definition of knowledge or on the body politic. Meanwhile, the *Policraticus* was also used in the context of new types of texts, such as the *specula* written for the French royal court and books for preachers. The last section will focus on the enlargement of the readership of the *Policraticus* in the later Middle Ages, also with a special emphasis on its French component.

---

13   See supra note 7. Also in a letter to Pietro Corsini, cardinal of Porto: "...*De nugis curia-lium et vestigiis philosophorum* quem librum nescio qua ratione *Policraticum* vocant." Giuseppe di Stefano, *La Découverte de Plutarque en Occident: aspects de la vie intellec-tuelle en Avignon au XIVe siècle* (Turin, 1968), pp. 132–133. Readers of the *Policraticus* in the early modern period still hesitated about this. Cullière, "Les Vanitez de la cour," p. 453 and note 2. For some Renaissance authors, "Poli-" was a prefix expressing diversity. For instance, Joseph Scaliger: "P. Pitheous [Pierre Pithou] m'exposa ce mot de Policraticus, disant que c'était pour ce qu'il contenait beaucoup de choses." (quoted ibid.)

14   PL 199, cols. 945–64; see Richard Sharpe, *A Handlist of the Latin Writers of Great Britain and Ireland before 1540* (Turnhout, 1997), p. 370.

15   The poem is on fols. 247–49. See Sharpe, *A Handlist*, p. 370, Ernst Philip Goldschmidt, *Medieval Texts and Their First Appearance in Print* (London, 1943), pp. 59 and 68 and Ronald E. Pepin, "'On the Conspiracy of the Members', Attributed to John of Salisbury," *Allegorica. A Journal of Medieval and Renaissance Literature* 12 (1991) 29–41. Beryl Smalley also mentions the mistaken attribution by the Franciscan John Lathbury (d.1362) of a *De corde sive musica amoris* to John of Salisbury (Smalley, *English Friars and Antiquity*, p. 230).

Knowledge of the *Policraticus* in England in the 12th and 13th Centuries

The *Entheticus minor* mentions three initial addressees in England for the *Policraticus*:[16] these are William Brito, sub-prior of Canterbury,[17] Odo, prior of Canterbury and later abbot of Battle (†1200),[18] and Thomas Becket, to whom the text is dedicated, but who may not have received his copy before the end of the autumn 1159.[19] In any case, the *Policraticus* circulated rapidly among the friends of John of Salisbury and Thomas Becket. The fact that a copy – or copies – of the text was kept in Canterbury may explain its influence on Peter of Blois (c. 1130/1212), who was secretary to the archbishop, and who seems to have been the first writer to make extensive use of the *Policraticus*.[20] In some of his letters to John of Salisbury,[21] he expressed his admiration for the latter's character and work,[22] although nothing may confirm absolutely the hypothesis of a friendship between the two men.[23] At the end of Letter 22, which he sent to John in 1169 or 1170, Peter bestows the highest praise on the

---

16 *Entheticus minor*, ll. 191–2 (vol. 1, p. 243). The *Policraticus* was also sent to Peter of Celle in 1159: see infra.

17 He may have had the text copied in full, according to Letter 111 of John of Salisbury to Peter of Celle: *The Early Letters*, pp. 180–182.

18 Oxford, Bodleian Library, lat. misc. c. 16, was given by Abbot Richard († 1235), the successor of Odo, to Battle Abbey. The manuscript may have been in the possession of Odo himself (Linder, "The Knowledge of John of Salisbury," p. 320).

19 Letter 111 of John of Salisbury to Peter of Celle, which accompanied the *Policraticus*, mentions that Thomas Becket has not received the book yet. A literal interpretation of the letter implies that Peter ought to return the manuscript with his annotations before John sends the *Policraticus* to the archbishop: *The Early Letters*, p. 182.

20 On Peter of Blois: Ethel Cardwell Higonnet, "Spiritual Ideas in the Letters of Peter of Blois," *Speculum*, 50 (1975), 218–244; John D. Cotts, "Peter of Blois and the Problem of the 'Court' in the Late Twelfth Century," in John Gillingham, ed., *Anglo-Norman Studies 27. Proceedings of the Battle Conference 2004* (Woodbridge, 2005), pp. 68–84; idem, "Monks and Mediocrities in the Shadow of Thomas Becket: Peter of Blois on Episcopal Duty," *Haskins Society Journal* 10 (2001), 143–161; idem, *The Clerical Dilemma. Peter of Blois and Literate Culture in the Twelfth Century* (Washington, D.C., 2009); Egbert Türk, *Pierre de Blois. Ambitions et remords sous les Plantegenêts* (Turnhout, 2006).

21 PL 207, Letters 22, 49, 70, 114, 130, 158, 218.

22 The admiration he feels for the person of John of Salisbury is expressed in Letter 130: the life, the company (*conversatio*) and the words (*verba*) of John of Salisbury, his exemplarity also, are all underlined (PL 207, col. 385).

23 On the relationship between the two men, see Cotts, *The Clerical Dilemma*, pp. 21–33.

Policraticus – or rather the book on the *"nugae curialium"* that he had just finished reading – expressing admiration both for its culture (*optima forma eruditionis est*) and form (*artificiosam sententiarum uarietatem*).[24] His letters are in fact replete with passages taken from the work of John of Salisbury; their extensive diffusion contributed significantly to the transmission of knowledge of the *Policraticus* down to a late period.[25]

For instance Peter does not scruple to use John of Salisbury's work when he tries to justify his own strategy as a writer. In Letter 92, sent to Reginald, bishop of Bath, he fights the accusation of plagiarism thrown at him by "your Cornificius," a name that recalls *Metalogicon* 1.1-6.[26] The whole letter is a defence of his method of writing: to some extent, it rests on borrowings from authors whom he puts himself on a par with,[27] and it is striking to observe that the way Peter of Blois conceives of his work matches what John of Salisbury writes on his own manner of writing.[28] Ironically it was the very accusation of plagiarism that led Peter of Blois to borrow largely from the *Policraticus* for his defence – and without acknowledging his source.[29]

---

24   PL 207, col. 82. John D. Cotts has identified in this letter a diplomatic stand close to that of John of Salisbury: Cotts, *The Clerical Dilemma*, pp. 182–185. Letter 114 also contains a praise of John of Salisbury's style, though this seems less sincere. Peter explains that he has been asked to produce a *uita* of Thomas Becket, and probably wishes to dispose of this matter under the pretext that an excellent account of the life of the saint already exists: he has just discovered this text, and (rightly) suspects John of Salisbury of having written it: PL 207, cols. 342–3. The letter is commented on in Türk, *Ambitions et remords*, pp. 200–201.

25   About 250 manuscripts of the collections of Peter of Blois's letters have been identified, the first collection dating from about 1184. On this, see Lena Wahlgren, *The Letter Collections of Peter of Blois* (Göteborg, 1993), p. 63 (she mentions that the quotation of Jerome in Letter 79 may have been known to Peter through John of Salisbury).

26   PL 207, col. 290.

27   On this point see Cotts, *The Clerical Dilemma*, pp. 97–98.

28   Cf. *Policraticus* 7.10, ed. Webb, vol. 2, p. 133. John D. Cotts has stressed the fact that Letter 92 is a rhetorical exercise quite similar to those practiced by John of Salisbury or Peter of Celle: Cotts, *The Clerical Dilemma*, p. 93.

29   For instance, he repeats the anecdote from *Policraticus* 6.15 about Caesar, who could dictate four letters at the same time: PL 207, col. 290; cf. *Policraticus* 6.15, ed. Webb, vol. 2, p. 41. The quotation from Ovid's *Metamorphoses* 11, ll. 266, 268 is also found in *Policraticus* 7.24. See Cotts, *The Clerical Dilemma*, pp. 93 and 97. The use of the metaphor of dwarves sitting on the shoulders of giants also echoes *Metalogicon* 3.4, though this image may have been a commonplace at the time. On this point, see esp. Édouard Jeauneau, "'Nani gigantum humeris insidentes'. Essai d'interprétation de Bernard de Chartres," *Vivarium* 5 (1967), 74–99.

Peter of Blois also borrowed from John of Salisbury's work when setting out his conception of pedagogy and teaching. In Letter 101 he puts together an ideal programme for the education of the nephews of the archdeacon of Nantes, drawing on the *Policraticus*, but obliterating the context of the passages he quotes. Where John of Salisbury lists (in *Policraticus* 7) the questions that the sceptical philosopher may consider, Peter compiles them into an actual teaching programme.[30] He also finds in the *Policraticus* the names of Roman historians whose work he recommends for moral edification and the progress of liberal science: Trogus Pompeius, Flavius Josephus, Suetonius, Hegesippus, Quintus Curtius, Tacitus and Titus Livius.[31] In the *Policraticus*, however, these names illustrate a passage in praise of tyrannicide, and John completes the list in a mischievous way with two fictitious authorities, "Serenus and Tranquillus," whom Peter wisely leaves out of his own compilation.[32] Without doubt he knew the passage well, but chose not to quote the considerations of John of Salisbury on tyrannicide.

Peter draws extensively on John of Salisbury when discussing military matters, but the way he recasts the passages John dedicated to these matters may suggest that here he was quoting from memory, rather than attempting to dissimulate plagiarism.[33] He is also close to the *Policraticus* when dealing with hunting as an

---

30   PL 207, cols. 312–3. *Policraticus* 7.2, ed. Webb, vol. 2, p. 98. On this matter, see Philippe Delhaye, "Un témoignage frauduleux de Pierre de Blois sur la pédagogie du XIIᵉ siècle," *Recherches de théologie ancienne et médiévale* 14 (1947), 329–331, esp. pp. 329–330.

31   PL 207, col. 314.

32   *Policraticus* 8.18, ed. Webb, vol. 2, pp. 363–364. See Cotts, *The Clerical Dilemma*, pp. 112–114.

33   See Delhaye, "Un témoignage frauduleux," p. 331 (on Letter 101). In Letter 94, where he criticizes the lack of military discipline of his contemporaries, Peter models his text on *Policraticus* 6.2, 3, 4 and 10 (PL 207, cols. 293–7). When detailing the duties of combatants, he quotes the *Policraticus*, regretting that the knights of his day are far from observing the rules of their order. Instead of fighting the enemies of Christ, they give themselves over to a life of debauchery, an echo of *Policraticus* 6.6 where John of Salisbury laments the absence of military discipline in England. Peter then reproduces what John writes about Publius Cornelius Scipio Nasica who ordered that a fleet be constructed outside the navigating season, so that his soldiers would not be idle, an anecdote that draws upon Book 4 of Frontinus's *Strategemata*. He also reproduces the story about Octavian giving a strict military discipline to his adoptive sons, but attributes it to Trajan, who would have thus reinforced the discipline of his army. As for the anecdote on the military training of Pompeius, Peter quotes it more or less literally. Further on, when discussing the reasons for Rome's domination, he takes his inspiration from the *Policraticus*, but abbreviates the corresponding passage. The section on rustic combatants, who are tougher than those who are used to soft living, almost certainly comes from John of Salisbury, rather than from Vegetius. This may equally be the case with the image of the Roman youth,

activity unworthy of clerics. He reprimanded Walter, bishop of Rochester, for his passion for the hunt in Letter 56, which was probably written in 1176. In this letter, several passages come from *Policraticus* 1.4: the fact that the Scriptures never refer to good hunters, hunting as a noxious art practiced by the Thebans – a wicked nation – and the figures of Alcides and Meleager.[34] There are also noticeable similarities, for instance, in John of Salisbury's and Peter of Blois's considerations on law, notably in their attacks on those who are hostile to the use of Church law.[35] Like John of Salisbury, Peter of Blois expresses concern about the lack of control on administrators, and the exactions for which they are responsible. Letter 95, sent to Henry II, denounces the oppression of the subjects of the king, and compares royal servants with locusts, an echo of *Policraticus* 6.1.[36]

Their discussion of the place of clerics in courts also share common features. The curial cleric (and that other topic which is linked to it, the bad shepherd) had been a popular topic with Church reformers since Petrus Damianus, and this was a key theme for both John of Salisbury and Peter of Blois. It is central in Letter 5 sent to Geoffrey of Bocland,[37] and above all in Letter 14

---

who wash away the sweat accumulated in running or exercising in the camp in the Tiber, far from the enerving waters of the fountain of Salmacis (after Ovid's *Metamorphoses* 4, ll. 285–7). Peter of Blois also mentions the discipline of Biblical armies, as the *Policraticus* does. He repeats the anecdote about Scipio Africanus, who reproached a soldier for his ornate shield. Finally, he follows John of Salisbury in his disapproval of the combatants of his own day, who come back from war without wound or scar, adding that they rush to join the drinking contest.

34   PL 207, cols. 169–71. Letter 61, sent to Reginald, later bishop of Bath, repeats the same attacks (PL 207, cols. 181–4). There hunting is described as a "futile activity fashionable in the circles of the court," and one which is unsuitable for someone who strives to attain sainthood. Pagan kings and princes devoted themselves to falconry in order to find solace; Peter borrows from the *Policraticus* the example of Ulysses, who introduced the art of falconry into Greece as a consolation for those who had lost parents under the walls of Troy – but who refused to teach this art to his own son. Even more so than Letter 56, Letter 61 repeats word for word whole sections taken from the *Policraticus*, in particular *Policraticus* 1.4.

35   See Letter 158, PL 207, col. 453. The letter refers to a conflict between Christ Church and Saint Augustine.

36   Some key passages from Letter 95 reproduce textually *Policraticus* 3.10, 5.5, 6 and 12 and 6.1: PL 207, cols. 297–302.

37   In Letter 5 sent in 1203 to Geoffrey of Bocland, archdeacon of Norfolk, where he praises his retirement from court (*The Later Letters of Peter of Blois*, pp. 30–37). He also criticizes the world of the court, which he describes as being both hell and a labyrinth: his correspondent has escaped from the fire of curial worries, from a fateful labyrinth or from the bowels of hell, and, like a new Joseph, has been able to flee the temptations of the court (ibid., p. 31). The image of the labyrinth is peculiar to Peter of Blois.

which Peter wrote in 1183 or 1184 to the staff of the king's chapel: the minstrels, mimes and actors whose presence in courts is criticized by John of Salisbury are also mentioned here.[38] These similarities should come as no surprise, since both writers lived in the same circles and shared the same concerns. Nonetheless, Peter of Blois had a more moderate and more pro-royal point of view than John of Salisbury. This means that he was more mellow in his criticism of royal govenment and of curial clerics, and there is no real equivalent in his letters of the scathing irony of his predecessor. He also defended, with some *pro domo* arguments, the office of archdeacon, which John of Salisbury had attacked.[39]

Another writer who moved in Canterbury circles in the last decades of the 12th century, and who borrowed extensively from John of Salisbury, was Nigel Longchamp, a monk of Christ Church (c. 1135–98?).[40] The *Policraticus* was not among the books which Nigel left on his death,[41] but there is no doubt that he must have had access to a copy of the book when writing his *Tractatus contra*

---

38   Peter of Blois revised this text, perhaps in 1193, giving it a more critical tone. The two
      versions of the letter are edited in Wahlgren, *The Letter Collections of Peter of Blois*,
      pp. 140–165. See also Cotts, *The Clerical Dilemma*, p. 157 and idem, "Peter of Blois and the
      problem of the 'court'," pp. 78–79.

39   Cotts, *The Clerical Dilemma*, p. 165. In his *Canon episcopalis* (c. 1196–7), a treatise on the
      duties of the bishop, Peter of Blois condemns harshly the prelate who neglects his duty, in
      a manner that recalls the concerns of John of Salisbury on this subject (PL 207, cols.
      1097–1112).

40   Nigel Longchamp was a monk of Christ Church in 1170: according to Boutemy, he may
      have been in Canterbury already in 1163 or 1164, and he is perhaps the same "master
      Nigellus" to whom John of Salisbury wrote in 1168 (André Boutemy, *Nigellus de Longchamp
      dit Wireker*, 1: *Introduction, Tractatus contra curiales et officiales clericos* (Paris, 1959), p.
      24): *The Later Letters*, no. 284 (p. 624). In the conflict between Henry II and the arch-
      bishop, Nigel was a supporter of Thomas Becket, but not a familiar (Boutemy, *Nigellus de
      Longchamp*, p. 16). He is the author of the *Speculum stultorum*, a successful satirical poem
      that may date from the late 1170s or the early 1180s. The poem follows the adventures of
      the ass Brunellus, and this is the pretext for Nigel to review the different estates of society;
      the satirical tone of the work may echo the attacks of John of Salisbury against ambitious
      clerics and monks, but there does not seem to be any direct borrowing from the
      Policraticus. The same may be said about some passages where Nigel attacks Forest Law,
      which places animals above humans, an argument also found in John of Salisbury's criti-
      cism of Forest Law: *Speculum stultorum*, ed. John H. Morzley and Robert R. Raymo
      (Berkeley, 1960), p. 88, ll. 2565–70.

41   Montague Rhodes James, *The Ancient Libraries of Canterbury and Dover. The Catalogue
      of the Libraries of Christ Church Priory and St Augustine's Abbey at Canterbury and of
      St. Martin's Priory at Dover* (Cambridge, 1903), nos. 1084–91.

curiales et officiales clericos.[42] The two main arguments of Nigel's treatise, which he completed in 1193 and dedicated to Richard I's chancellor, William Longchamp, are the corruption of the English clergy and the necessity for William, as prelate and legate of the pope, to abandon the chancellorship, and more generally his participation in lay matters. The beginning of the text distinguishes between statesman and churchman (symbolised by Martha and Mary) and depicts the trials of court and government. Nigel then satirizes the flatterers who crowd the entourage of the great. The whole work betrays the influence of the *Policraticus* – about a quarter of the *Tractatus* derives directly from it –[43] but the most substantial extracts appear in the parts of the treatise that deal with false and ambitious clerics. Nigel borrows from *Policraticus* 7.18 and 19 the hypocritical objections of ambitious churchmen who pretend not to have the requisite qualities for the promotion they are seeking.[44] He also reproduces some sections from *Policraticus* 7.21, in particular the image (after Mt 7:15) of the hypocrite who is a lamb on the outside, but a wolf, or a fox, on the inside.[45] However, he does not follow the order of his model; neither does he always quote the *Policraticus* literally, preferring to adapt the text in a skilful way. Here and there also, some original feature spices up the *Tractatus*, such as the picture of the hypocrites who push themselves forward by lamenting the state of morals with the powerful: Nigel blames them for handling too easily the accusation of tyranny against princes.[46] In the section of the *Tractatus* about clerics who appeal to the prince, so as to achieve their career ambitions, quotations from the Novels (1.6 and 123) and the Code (1.3.30) are in fact borrowed from *Policraticus* 7.20. There are also similarities in the commentaries that follow these quotations, but Nigel skips what he probably sees as secondary considerations.[47] He reproduces, however, what John of

---

42   André Boutemy analyses all the borrowings made from the *Policraticus* in the introduction to his *Nigellus de Longchamp*.

43   Boutemy, *Nigellus of Longchamp*, pp. 123–130. The verse preface reuses some themes and expressions found in the *Entheticus minor*. This poem is copied in two manuscripts; in the 15th-century manuscript, it is preceded by the *Entheticus*, a fact that suggests the similarity of the two poems in the minds of medieval readers (London, British Library, Cotton Julius A VII, fols. 55–65). Both poems are addressed to the book which is about to go on a journey to find its dedicatee; the suspicion of the court is also a theme shared by both texts.

44   Nigel uses the image of the body, whose sick head makes the members vacillate, but he applies it to the Church, not to the civil *res publica* (ibid., p. 192).

45   Ibid., p. 170; Cf. *Policraticus* 7.21, ed. Webb, vol. 2, pp. 191–192.

46   Ibid., p. 171.

47   Ibid., p. 174; cf. *Policraticus* 7.20, ed. Webb, vol. 2, p. 186. John of Salisbury follows this passage with a diatribe against those who even refuse to listen to what the princes say on the subject. This is not picked up by Nigel.

Salisbury writes about the abuse that consists in saying that what pleases the prince has the force of law, a position he identifies in ambitious clerics who want to manipulate temporal power, against the law of the Church, so that they may accumulate benefices.[48] More than three decades after the publication of the *Policraticus* it was the debate on the personality and action of William Longchamp that led to a new reading of this work.

Although their positions on the vocation of curial clerics or the Becket conflict were not identical, John of Salisbury, Peter of Blois and Nigel Longchamp belonged to the same narrow world: Peter of Blois knew John of Salisbury, and this was perhaps the case of Nigel Longchamp as well. The borrowings made from the *Policraticus* by Peter of Blois and Nigel Longchamp are also proof of the intellectual esteem in which John of Salisbury's work was held in Canterbury. It is nevertheless noticeable that apart from the general criticism of officers, they do not take up the passages of the *Policraticus* that bear on power: what is of interest to them is mainly the role of clerics in the contemporary Church and in the world.

By contrast, the interest in topics we would consider as "political," to use an anachronistic category, is one of the main features of Gerald of Wales's treatise on the government of princes. Gerald probably wrote the first part of *De principis instructione* early on in his career,[49] but the finishing touches to this work are likely to have been made during the expedition of Prince Louis. At the time – probably before the defeat of Louis on the battlefield at Lincoln in May 1217 – he seems to have placed all his hopes for a reform of the kingdom on a renewal of royal government under Capetian rule. *De principis instructione* is the

---

48   Here also, Nigel only copies the most important passages the *Policraticus* dedicates to this theme, dropping the considerations he deems to be secondary. Nigel does not reproduce what John of Salisbury writes about the civil laws being praised by those who misappropriate temporal power for their own purposes; nor does he use the image of the laws that are similar to the cobweb, catching small insects, not large animals. He copies in full the diatribe of John against those who encourage princes to intervene in the granting of benefices, and who praise tyrants who have thus acted in the past. He also quotes John's lament on the way those who denounce these abuses are accused of being public enemies. He reproduces, albeit in a different order, the pretexts brought forward by those who wish to short-circuit canon law in the matter of elections. In both works, this is followed by a long list of examples, but in a slightly different order. He finally quotes nearly word for word two stories given by John of Salisbury about the confusion of some corrupt clerics, and here he mentions explicitly his source, "John, bishop of Chartres."

49   Alongside a clerical cursus, where he felt that his ambitions were thwarted, Gerald of Wales was active in the service of the king. On his career and his work, see Robert Bartlett, *Gerald of Wales 1146–1223* (Oxford, 1982).

expression of a position deeply hostile to Angevin kingship, and Gerald's text may reflect ideas fashionable in some circles at the end of John's reign. Similarities between this work and the *Policraticus* have been suggested. Yet we may discount the hypothesis of a direct connection between *De principis instructione* 1.6 and *Policraticus* 4.8,[50] since both writers follow the same passage from Aulus Gellius, which they probably knew through some anthology.[51] The metaphor of the body, so central in the *Policraticus*, appears in Gerald's text in the guise of the prince physician of the *regnum*,[52] and as a way to express the link between the prince/head and the subjects/members;[53] but its place in the *De principis instructione* is minor. Gerald's discussion of the relationship between the prince and the law also recalls John of Salisbury's text:[54] both authors insist on the necessity for the prince to model his laws on those of ancient Rome and to have them enforced,[55] although there is no actual textual similarity beyond the same quotations from Roman law. Two other points raise the question of a possible influence of the *Policraticus* on the *De principis instructione*. The first is the maxim of the illiterate prince who is like a crowned ass:[56] but one may conjecture that it was commonplace around 1200. The other is the passage Gerald dedicates to tyrannicide, which he seems to praise:[57]

---

50   Linder, "The Knowledge of John of Salisbury," p. 324 and note 57.

51   *Noctes Atticae* 1.26; Janet Martin, "John of Salisbury as Classical Scholar," in *The World of John of Salisbury*, pp. 179–201, esp. p. 195 and eadem, "John of Salisbury's Manuscripts of Frontinus and of Gellius," *Journal of the Warburg and Courtauld Institutes* 40 (1977), 1–26, esp. p. 16.

52   *De principis instructione* 1.10, *De principis justicia*, in *Giraldi Cambrensis opera*, vol. 8, ed. George F. Warner (London, 1891), pp. 34–35.

53   Ibid., 1.19, p. 105.

54   In the second chapter, *De principis mansuetudine*, Gerald develops the principle of the self-limitation of the power of the prince, who deliberately chooses to subject himself to the laws (ibid., pp. 9–10).

55   The subject of Chapter 20 is the law-giving prince; Gerald praises the imperial laws that impose the respect of Christian religion and a number of interdictions, especially about the observance of religious feasts (ibid., 1.20, p. 115 sq.).

56   Ibid., p. 5.

57   Ibid., 1.16, p. 56. A witness of the popularity of the *Policraticus* in the early 13th century has recently been uncovered by Ilya Dines ("The Earliest Use of John of Salisbury's *Policraticus*: Third Family Bestiaries," *Viator* 44 (2013), 107–118). A group of Anglo-Latin bestiaries (the so-called "third-family" group), were compiled at Lincoln Cathedral c. 1210 by the theologian William de Montibus, or by persons close to him. Two manuscripts containing bestiaries of the third family also include abstracts from the *Policraticus* (Oxford, Bodleian Library, Douce 88; Wesminster Abbey 22: ibid., p. 113), and the text of the bestiaries itself refers to several passages in John of Salisbury's text, in particular about hypocrisy, hunting, and the social organisation of bees.

there is however no direct quotation from the *Policraticus* in this section of the *De principis instructione*. If some of Gerald's theses are similar to the positions held by John of Salisbury – to the extent that one feels he may have had at least an indirect access to his work – he never quotes the *Policraticus*. It is tempting to think that the reforming ideas of the *Policraticus* did exert an influence at the time, but this is a statement which must be made with the greatest of caution, pending further research.[58]

The same may be said of the influence of the *Policraticus* on *Bracton*.[59] This extensive treatise on common law is associated with Judge Henry of Bratton (†1268), but it was probably compiled in the 1220s and 1230s under the instructions of Judge Martin of Pateshull or his successor William Raleigh, being revised around 1250.[60] Its author probably wished to adapt civil law to contemporary English law,[61] and to encourage a general reform of the judicial courts: he likened the English legal system to a sick man – the consequence of confusions on doctrine and principles – and this patient had to be healed through the proper instruction of new recruits.[62] As Hermann Kantorowicz has shown, the knowledge of law that the author of *Bracton* demonstrates, as well as his complete mastery of Latin, enabled him to write in a competent way on technical matters, but also to compose passionate speeches on moral, religious and political subjects.[63]

Some sections from *Bracton* bring the *Policraticus* to mind: the passages on delegating royal power to righteous persons,[64] and on right judgement[65] recall

---

58   The question of the influence of the *Policraticus* on Ralph Niger and Walter Map needs a more thorough examination. Ralph Niger and John of Salisbury knew each other, and "John bishop of Chartres" is mentioned at the beginning of Ralph's commentary on the Books of Kings III–IV (Lincoln Cathedral 26, fol. 1r): "Huius uero audacie mee incentores habui venerabiles Johannem Carnotensem episcopum et magistrum meum Gerardum puellam dictum qui hoc mihi non minus licere quam expedire persuaserunt."

59   *Bracton on the Laws and Customs of England*, ed. George E. Woodbine, trans. Samuel E. Thorne, 4 vols. (Cambridge, Mass., 1968–77).

60   See the seminal study by Frederick Bernays Wiener, "Bracton. A Tangled Web of Legal Mysteries That Defied Solution for More Than Seven Centuries," *The George Mason Law Review* 2 (1978), 129–165.

61   Hermann Kantorowicz, *Bractonian Problems. Being the Ninth Lecture on the David Murray Foundation in the University of Glasgow prepared, but not delivered* (Glasgow, 1941), p. 77.

62   Paul R. Hyams, *Kings, Lords and Peasants in Medieval England: the Common Law of Villeinage in the Twelfth and Thirteenth Centuries* (Oxford, 1980), pp. 85–86.

63   Kantorowicz, *Bractonian Problems*, p. 78.

64   *Bracton*, vol. 2, pp. 306–307. As noted by Thorne in the critical apparatus of his edition of *Bracton*, the formulation of this advice recalls *Policraticus* 4. 3 and 8 and *Policraticus* 5.11 and 16.

65   *Bracton*, vol. 2, pp. 302–303 and 306–307.

the prescriptions of John of Salisbury on these matters.[66] It is difficult, however, to decide to what extent these are actual borrowings: both works tap the same sources, and comment on the same passages from the Scriptures, such as Exod.18 on delegation of power. In a similar way, the definition of tyranny in *Bracton*[67] reminds one of *Policraticus* 8.17: however the classical definition of the tyrant who oppresses the people had by then entered the common political vocabulary. Similarly the reflections on the obedience owed to the king and his representatives by the people echo *Policraticus* 5.4,[68] but they also follow scriptural sources. More relevant perhaps in this context is *Bracton*'s position on the relationship between the king and the law. Some sections of the treatise seem to indicate that there cannot be any limitation to the king's power, while others favour a limited power. It has been suggested that the latter would reflect the opposition of the author of *Bracton* to some judgements given *per uoluntatem regis* between 1232 and 1234, for which Peter des Roches was responsible.[69] This may well be the case, but the apparent contradictions of Roman law maxims on the relationship between the king and the law were already the subject of much debate in the 12th century, and probably helped to shape political ideas in late 12th- and early 13th-century England. They are at the heart of what John of Salisbury writes on power in his commentary of *Digna uox* in *Policraticus* 4.1: if the king is the living law, he ought also to subject himself to the laws. As such, although a direct connection between the two texts may be difficult to prove, *Bracton* fits into an intellectual tradition that John of Salisbury contributed to establish.

This continuity is patent in some of the texts relating to the baronial movement of 1258–65. Several occurrences even suggest that the *Policraticus* may have exerted a direct influence at the time. The letter sent by the barons to Pope Alexander IV in order to justify the expulsion of the Poitevins in July 1258 picks up the definition of the *res publica* in *Policraticus* 5.2.[70] The *Carmen de bello Lewensi* also seems to betray the influence of John of Salisbury's ideas. This 968 line-long text was written after the baronial victory of Lewes by an

---

66   *Policraticus* 5.6 (ed. Webb, vol. 1, p. 302) and 8, 17 (vol. 2, p. 357).

67   *Bracton*, vol. 2, p. 305.

68   Ibid., vol. 2, p. 359.

69   David A. Carpenter, "Justice and Jurisdiction under King John and King Henry III," in *The Reign of Henry III* (London, 1996), pp. 17–43.

70   Matthew Paris, *Chronica majora*, ed. Henry Richards Luard, 7 vols. (1872–83), vol. 6, addimenta, no. 205, pp. 402–403.

anonymous supporter of Simon of Montfort.[71] It does not quote the *Policraticus* literally, but many sections are close to the text of John of Salisbury. For instance, it criticises the heir to the throne, the Lord Edward – whom the author suspects of wanting to act without subjecting himself to the laws – in terms that recall the *Policraticus*: "whatever he likes he says is lawful, and he thinks that he is released from law, as though he were greater than the King. For every king is ruled by the laws which he makes..."[72] Also targeted is the king who deems his will to be lawful, and who believes he can dispense with the laws (ll. 443–58). Further on, the *Carmen* contrasts the positions of Henry III[73] and of the barons in the shape of fictitious speeches. The first defends his conception of unlimited power, especially when it comes to the nomination of officers.[74] The reforming discourse, on the other hand, denounces the corruption of justice, and stresses that the bounds meted to royal power, far from diminishing it, result instead in an amplification of royal virtue: resisting the law is for the king an act of self-destruction. The law remains, while the king falls.[75] All these assertions are reminiscent of some key-passages of the *Policraticus* on the relationship between the king and the law. One may find another echo of the ideas of John of Salisbury in the analogy between the kingdom and a human body, and the interdependence between the whole and the parts in the kingdom.[76] John Maddicott has suggested that the *Carmen de bello Lewensi* was a product of the culture of English schools in the

---

71   It has survived in a single manuscript, from the abbey of Reading (London, British Library Harley 978, fols. 107r-114r). The text is edited in C.L. Kingsford, *The Song of Lewes* (Oxford, 1890), with a substantial critical apparatus. For the history and composition of this manuscript, see Andrew Taylor, *Textual Situations: Three Medieval Manuscripts and their Readers* (Philadelphia, 2002), pp. 5 and 83–136. Andrew Taylor argues that the manuscript "was for the most part the work of professional scriveners in Oxford," but that it probably reflected the personal tastes of a monk at the Abbey of Reading, William of Winchester, who may have resided in Oxford in 1264 or 1265. The central part of the manuscript, which contains the *Carmen de Bello Lewensi*, was probably written no later than 1265 (ibid., pp. 84–85).

72   *The Song of Lewes*, ll. 443–5, p. 15: "Quicquid libet, licitum dicit, et a lege/Se putat explicitum, quasi maior rege./Nam rex omnis regitur legibus quas legit..." (trans. C.L. Kingsford)

73   Ibid., ll. 489–504, 515–6 and 521–4.

74   Ibid., ll. 502–3.

75   Esp. ibid., ll. 673–4, 693–700, 848–9, 871–2.

76   Ibid., ll. 783–6 and 827–8. The analogy with the human body is used as a rhetorical argument (the members must obey the head) in a speech of the London aldermen in 1271. This was directed at the people of London, who wanted to see Walter Hervi elected to the mayoralty (*De antiquis legibus liber. Cronica maiorum et vicecomitum Londoniarum*, ed. Thomas Stapleton (London, 1846), p. 150).

mid-13th century: this would therefore be valuable evidence of the knowledge of the *Policraticus* in the schools.[77]

The imperatives of prosody may explain why they are no direct quotations from the *Policraticus* in the *Carmen*. The text known as the *De tyranno et principe*, which was probably compiled between 1265 and 1272, is a different case altogether.[78] The first section – with the heading *De tyranno et principe* – rests entirely on three passages from *Policraticus* 8.17. The tyrant oppresses his people by the means of violent domination, while the prince governs according to the laws; the prince fights for the laws and the freedom of his people, while the tyrant's unique desire is to destroy the laws and to subject his people. The prince is the image of divinity, but the tyrant is the image of the strength of the Enemy, and of Luciferian wickedness. The origin of the tyrant is iniquity, and out of this poisonous root an evil and deadly tree germinates and grows. Indeed, if iniquity and injustice, that kill charity, did not give birth to tyranny, secure peace and perpetual tranquillity would reign forever.

The second section, rubricated *Quod tyranni sunt ministri Dei*, also borrows from *Policraticus* 8.18. Tyrants are the servants of God, since in his wrath He has given kings to men, some good, others evil: they are the instrument of the punishment of evil subjects, and it is through them that good subjects may be corrected and tried. Furthermore, any power is good since it derives from God, and if tyranny is an abuse of the power conferred on man by God, it does however contain some elements whose use may be beneficial. The universal nature of tyranny, which is one of the most powerful arguments of the *Policraticus*, is also reproduced. Following these two sections there are about twenty short portraits of Roman emperors, of good and bad princes – who are all reduced to complete nothingness by death. Then we find some general reflections on kingship and tyranny, inspired by Isidore's *Etymologies* and the *Policraticus*: in ancient Greece, the term "tyrant" referred to kings, and this did not necessarily have a derogatory significance. It was only later that the term acquired a negative meaning, and that it was used to refer to the worst kings, those whose excessive and cruel domination oppresses the people. The text ends with some reflections on the link between tyranny and the fate of Rome, taken from *Policraticus* 2 and 3.

---

77   John Robert Maddicott, *Simon de Montfort* (Cambridge, 1994), pp. 355–356.

78   Cambridge, Corpus Christi College 469, fols. 158v-66v. The text is edited in Frédérique Lachaud, *"De tyranno et principe* (Cambridge, Corpus Christi College, ms. 469): un pamphlet 'britannique' contre la tyrannie d'Henri III?," in Jean-Philippe Genet, dir., *Les Îles Britanniques: espaces et identités, Cahiers de Recherches Médiévales et Humanistes. A Journal of Medieval and Humanistic Studies* 19 (2010), 87–104, at pp. 96–104.

What is the significance of *De tyranno et principe*? Amnon Linder suggested that it was a pamphlet whose positions would reflect those of the reforming barons.[79] However, this is perhaps mistaking the nature of this text, which is preceded by a compilation of general notions of a spiritual, moral and political order: the section on tyranny, which acts as a transition with the two chronicles that follow in the manuscript, is the counterpart of the definition of the prince given in the first section of the work. More convincing is the idea also put forward by Linder that *De tyranno et principe* is a product of monastic culture. In any case, its existence challenges the view that the *Policraticus* was not widely known in 13th-century England.[80] Scholastic as well as monastic culture gave it some place, and it may have irrigated political discourse.[81]

At this point, we may pause to examine the case of John of Wales (†c. 1285). His work clearly betrays the influence of the *Policraticus*, though it is not certain whether he first read the text in England or in France.[82] John of Wales was

---

79 Amnon Linder, "John of Salisbury's *Policraticus* in 13th-Century England: The Evidence of MS Cambridge Corpus Christi College 469," *Journal of the Warburg and Courtauld Institutes* 40 (1977), 276–282.

80 See the comment by Ullmann, "John of Salisbury's *Policraticus* in the Later Middle Ages," p. 523.

81 In particular, the question of the possible influence of the *Policraticus* on the work of the Franciscan friar Thomas Docking, regent master at Oxford from 1260 to 1265, deserves to be studied in depth. On this point, see Beryl Smalley, "Some Latin Commentaries on the Sapiential Books in the Late Thirteenth and Early Fourteenth Centuries," *Archives d'histoire littéraire et doctrinale du Moyen Âge* 18 (1951), 103–128, esp. p. 113.

82 On the borrowings from the *Policraticus* by John of Wales, see Frédérique Lachaud, "De la satire politique au 'miroir': Jean de Galles et la lecture du *Policraticus* de John of Salisbury au XIIIᵉ siècle," in Cédric Giraud and Martin Morard, eds., *Universitas scolarium. Mélanges offerts à Jacques Verger par ses anciens étudiants* (Paris, 2011), pp. 385–407. For the biography and work of John of Wales: Jenny Swanson, *John of Wales. A Study of the Works and Ideas of a Thirteenth-Century Friar* (Cambridge, 1989) and William A. Pantin, "John of Wales and Medieval Humanism," in John A. Watt, John B. Morrall and Francis X. Martin, eds., *Medieval Studies Presented to Aubrey Gwynn, S.J.* (Dublin, 1961), pp. 297–319. The edition used here is Venice, 1496, repr. in Lyon in 1511: *Summa Johannis Valensis de Regimine Vite Humane seu Margarita Doctorum ad Omne Propositum*. Jenny Swanson suggested that the first two loquia of the series were written in the 1260s and 1270s; according to William A. Pantin, however, all the *loquia* must date from the Parisian period of John of Wales. The references to Helinand of Froidmont in the *Breviloquium* seem to argue in favour of a composition of the *loquia* in France, but one cannot exclude the fact that John of Wales had read the *Policraticus* before moving to Paris. See also Smalley, "Some Latin Commentaries," pp. 113–114 about the quotations from the *Policraticus* in the biblical commentaries of the Parisian master Nicholas Gorran.

lector to the Franciscans in Oxford before settling in Paris around 1270; he was
regent master in theology there from 1281 to 1283. His vast output includes four
treatises called *loquia*, whose purpose was to help writing sermons and to feed
moral and spiritual discussions. In the *Breuiloquium de uirtutibus antiquorum
principum et philosophorum*, the presentation of philosophical schools clearly
betrays the influence of John of Salisbury. A tenth of the text at least comes
from the *Policraticus*, in the form of direct or abbreviated quotations, as well
as paraphrases. Nevertheless John of Wales does not follow the order of his
model,[83] and in some places, he weaves together passages taken from different parts of the *Policraticus* into a continuous text.[84] Moreover some of John
of Salisbury's fundamental ideas are ignored. For instance, Chapter 2 of the
section on justice stresses the importance of giving just laws, but leaves aside
the issue of the relationship between the prince and the law. The other major
treatise of John of Wales, the *Communiloquium siue Summa collationum*, demonstrates deeper knowledge of the *Policraticus*, and it explicitly mentions the
name of John of Salisbury.[85] The work is divided into seven parts uneven in
length. John of Salisbury's influence is particularly obvious in the first two.[86]
The first part is a description of the "constitution" of the *res publica*, which is
compared with a body. This in turn is broken up into ten "distinctions," which
deal with the *res publica* in general, and with the prince and the main offices
of administration and justice. It is the longest section of the text; it is also the
closest to Books 5 and 6 of the *Policraticus*. The second part, entitled *De colli-
gatione membrorum adinuicem*, presents the different links that unite the

---

83   For instance, John of Wales illustrates Chapter 1.1, *De iustitia in possidenda*, with some
      exempla drawn from *Policraticus* 3.14, on the necessity to combat flattery; the sections of
      this chapter on moderation, fortitude and patience in exercising power distantly echo
      Policraticus 4.8.
84   For example, the passage of the *Breviloquium* about the education of Augustus's children
      (*Summa Johannis Valensis*, fol. 205r) was put together from two differents sections of
      Policraticus 6.4.
85   *Communiloquium* 1.8.7. (ibid., fol. 48v).
86   In the rest of his book, John of Wales gets further away from his model. According to its
      title, the third part of the *Communiloquium* is dedicated to the instruction of men about
      "what is in common to all." In fact, John of Wales draws a series of distinctions according
      to gender, age, the differences created by nobility, riches, "quality of life" (an expression
      which refers to sin and penance), estate (married people, widows and widowers, virgins),
      events or fortune, and "complexion" (illness and good health). The fourth part deals with
      the body of the ecclesiastical *res publica*, the fifth with the instruction of schoolmen –
      disciples and doctors – the sixth with the instruction of the religious. The work ends with
      an *ars moriendi*, a preparation to death.

members of the body: in particular respect and the desire to serve the common good bind the body together.

The original feature of the *Communiloquium* is that it borrows John of Salisbury's ideas but fits them into categories used in contemporary preaching *summae*: John of Wales adapts his knowledge of the *Policraticus* to a structure that profoundly alters the text and the spirit of his model. Dropping the ironic style of John of Salisbury and leaving out his acerbic comments on society and the exercise of power, he reorganises his borrowings into a didactic text whose tone is much more neutral than that of its source. For instance, in *Communiloquium* 1.9, *De informatione militum*, which betrays the influence of *Policraticus* 6, John of Wales omits everything that could distract the reader from the main topic of the duties of the combatant, such as John of Salisbury's observations on the fatal consequences of the bad choice and lack of preparation of combatants.[87] He also systematically leaves out John of Salisbury's comments that refer to the reality of the mid-12th century (for instance his attacks on the carelessness of the English nobility, particularly visible when faced with aggressive neighbours) and modifies the order of the text in order to adapt it to the new framework of preaching *ad status*.

The use of the metaphor of the body politic by John of Wales is also revealing of the mutation undergone by the text of John of Salisbury. *Communiloquium* 1.1 takes up the definition of the *res publica* as a body, as well as the specific analogy between the human body and the different parts of the *res publica*. The following nine distinctions unravel the significance of the members. If the whole demonstration is inspired by the *Policraticus*, it also clearly shares its general outline with manuals for preachers. For instance, when he writes about the feet of the body in 1.10, John of Wales reuses the general plan of John of Salisbury's work, and part of his text. He explains how magistrates ought to

---

87 In Chapter 5, the way he reworks the section of the *Policraticus* on the causes of Roman victories is characteristic: whereas John of Salisbury emphasizes the causes of the military superiority of Rome with a series of questions that are as many criticisms of contemporary morals, John of Wales merely lists them, and then explains that these are the reasons why the Romans always vanquished their adversaries (*Summa Johannis Valensis*, fol. 51v; cf. *Policraticus* 6.2, ed. Webb, vol. 2, p. 9). In Chapter 7, which rests to some extent on *Policraticus* 6.8, John of Wales dwells on the fact that combatants ought to defend the Church, and he draws a list of punishments meted by the ancients to those who did not fulfil their function properly. In particular, the figure of the braggart soldier ought to act as a foil to the proper soldier. However, the demonstration of John of Salisbury, who attacked with a sharp wit the temptation of vanity in warriors, before giving the justification for their office, is shortened in favour of a more direct teaching on the duties of the *militia*.

take care of, direct and sustain, the feet, by referring specifically to "Plutarch." While John of Salisbury, however, evokes the multitude of the feet, which make the body of the *res publica* look like a centipede, John of Wales uses Hugh of Saint-Victor's classification of mechanical arts: this enables him to review summarily the main activities of the *populus inferior*, and the spiritual duties attached to them (1.10.2).[88] The section on the feet has an obvious moral and spiritual content; above all, John of Wales's purpose is to teach the virtue of obedience. But this is very different from the aim pursued by John of Salisbury, who stresses the interconnection between the members, as well as the necessity for the feet, or workers, to support the whole of the body politic through their efforts, in view of the common good. The contrast drawn by John of Salisbury between one's own duties and those of others, as well as his passionate defence of the notion of obligation, have been left aside in favour of a general discussion of the moral and spiritual duties of the different estates of Christian society, seen from the point of view of predication. All should strive to fulfil their own function and remain in their station.

In his discussion of the body politic, John of Wales also introduces a number of significant elements that do not appear in the text of John of Salisbury. This is particularly the case with his discussion of the place of the Church in this scheme. In the *Policraticus*, the priests are part of the body politic, where they hold the place of the soul. Instead John of Wales chooses to dedicate a separate part of his work to the discussion of what he calls the *res publica ecclesiastica*: the fourth part of the *Communiloquium* is an examination of the body of the Church, which John of Wales distinguishes carefully from the "civil body." Instead of a Pauline reading of the Church as the body of the faithful, it is the Church as an institution which is under consideration here.[89]

Finally, one should consider the position of John of Wales on tyrannicide, which is perhaps not as clear-cut as has been stated.[90] In *Communiloquium* 1.3.20 he argues that it is not a sin to kill the tyrant, but a just and equitable act,

---

88   These are *lanificium, armatura, navigatio, agricultura, uenatio, medicina* and *theatrica*.

89   In the ecclesiastical *res publica*, the pope is the equivalent of the prince in the civil *res publica*. For John of Wales, the metaphor of the body may apply to the members of the ecclesiastical body. In the way the pope is the head of the Church, the bishop holds the place of the head in his diocese. The archdeacons, who command over the subdeacons and "levites," are the ears and eyes. The judges and preachers (*oratores*) are the equivalent of the mouth. The canons (whose role is to elect and advise the bishop) are similar to the heart. The officials and deans, whose duty it is to protect the Church, are the hands of the ecclesiastical body. Parish priests and clerics who reside in churches are the feet. All contribute to the harmony of the ecclesiastical *res publica*.

90   Swanson, *John of Wales*, p. 82.

an argument he claims to have found at the end of *Policraticus* 3. It is also with good reason that justice is armed against the one who disarms the laws, John of Wales writes. One should follow Cicero's prescription that any relationship with the tyrant should be discontinued: such men ought to be removed from human society, like the sick members in the body, since they are harmful to others members. The fact that John of Wales does not reproduce the multiple and ambiguous warnings sent by John of Salisbury to the would-be destroyers of tyrants may create the impression that he supported tyrannicide, but the assertion according to which it is not a sin to kill the tyrant is presented as a warning found in "secular letters" – which is in fact what John of Salisbury also writes – and not as the personal position of the author.

The wide circulation of some of John of Wales's writings – there are at least 140 manuscripts of the *Communiloquium*, 150 of the *Breuiloquium*, on top of translations and summaries –[91] may have contributed significantly to the diffusion of some of John of Salisbury's ideas. Nevertheless, in John of Wales's work, a simplified text has replaced the vivid and caustic irony of the *Policraticus*,[92] as well as the discursive ampleness of the 12th-century treatise. Allusions to the reality of John of Salisbury's day have gone,[93] but John of Wales also abstains from criticizing openly the behaviour or morals of his time. These transformations may have conditioned the survival of the *Policraticus* in the context of preaching literature.

Reading the *Policraticus* in 13th-Century France

John of Salisbury sent a copy of the *Policraticus* to Peter of Celle at the end of the summer 1159.[94] This was perhaps a first step towards the diffusion of his work on the Continent. John's exile may also have contributed to the circulation

---

91 Ibid., pp. 232–256.

92 This is for instance the case with the passages where he deals with the vices of the *curiales*: the argument of John of Salisbury is toned down, and inserted into a classification inspired by one of the most popular septenaries of vices.

93 On this, see Smalley, *English Friars and Antiquity*, pp. 54–55.

94 On the friendship of John of Salisbury and Peter of Celle, see John D. Cotts, "Monks and Clerks in Search of the *Beata Schola*: Peter of Celle's Warning to John of Salisbury Reconsidered," in Sally N. Vaughn and Jay Rubinstein, eds., *Teaching and Learning in Northern Europe* (Turnhout, 2006), pp. 255–277. Also *The Letters of Peter of Celle*, ed. Julian Haseldine (Oxford, 2001), appendix 8, pp. 712–718. Letter 70 of Peter of Celle probably refers to the collection of letters of John of Salisbury, and not to the *Policraticus*, and may be dated from c. 1161 or 1162 (ibid., p. 717).

of the book in France, and the bishop of Chartres's legacy to his Church included a copy of the *Policraticus*. In France, however, major borrowings from this work do not seem to predate the early 13th century: this must lead to a cautious assessment of the conditions of the circulation of the *Policraticus* in France in the second half of the 12th century. Other factors may have contributed to create a favourable environment for its diffusion, such as the attractiveness of Parisian schools, the contacts between English and French elites – in particular during the crisis of the end of John's reign – or the expansion of a specific Cistercian culture.[95]

Helinand of Froidmont is the first witness of this influence. The success of his lyrical work probably gave Helinand entry to the court of Philip Augustus, but around 1185 he decided to join the Cistercian order. His familiarity with John of Salisbury's text is clear in a sermon he pronounced towards the end of his life, during the Albigensian crusade.[96] He takes up the passages John of Salisbury dedicates to the issue of the legitimacy of the combatant, and stresses the significance of choosing the soldier well, and of the soldier's oath, whether the soldier is spiritual or "corporal." The combatant also ought to defend the *res publica* and justice, and Helinand reminds his listeners of the combatant's duties by borrowing some passages from *Policraticus* 6.5 to 10. He also exposes at length the vices of officials, compared with locusts, and does this by quoting extensively from *Policraticus* 6.1.[97]

In fact, Helinand had already put John of Salisbury's work to good use in his *Chronicon*, which was probably brought to completion at Froidmont in

95   It was probably the copy left by John of Salisbury to Chartres which was borrowed from the Cathedral library by canon Landolfo Colonna in 1303: Lynn K. Barker, "MS Bodl. Canon. Pat. Lat. 131 and a Lost Lactantius of John of Salisbury: Evidence in Search of a French Critic of Thomas Becket," *Albion* 22 (1990), 21–37, esp. p. 25. A copy of the *Policraticus* was kept in some Cistercian houses in the late 12th century, including the abbeys of Pontigny and Signy. MS Bibliothèque Municipale of Charleville-Mézières 151, dating from the years 1170–80, originates from the abbey of Signy (diocese of Reims), a daughter of Igny. MS 60 of the Bibliothèque de l'Université de Médecine of Montpellier comes from the abbey of Pontigny, the second foundation of Cîteaux. It dates from the late 12th century or the early 13th. The presence of the *Policraticus* in Pontigny may be connected with Becket's stay in this house. But other witnesses build up a picture of the *Policraticus* circulating widely among Cistercian houses: such are MS 60 of the Bibliothèque nationale de Luxembourg (from Orval) and perhaps Cambridge, Corpus Christi College 69.

96   PL 212, *sermo* 25, cols. 685–92. See Edmé Renno Smits, "Helinand of Froidmont and the A-Text of Seneca's Tragedies," *Mnemosyne* 36 (1983), 324–358, esp. p. 341, note 69.

97   PL 212, col. 690; see *Policraticus* 6.1, ed. Webb, vol. 2, p. 5.

the early 1210s.[98] There he demonstrates his familiarity with different sections of the *Policraticus*,[99] in a way that suggests he had access either to the whole of the work or a long summary. He also seems to have been aware of the identity of its author.[100] The longest extracts are in 11.38, in a section called *Lex de rege constituendo*. As in *Policraticus* 4, Dt 17 provides the connecting thread for Chapter 38, and justifies the title of the section.[101] The commentary on

---

98   Philippe Delhaye, "La morale politique de Hélinand de Froidmont," in *Littérature et religion. Mélanges offerts à M. le Chanoine Joseph Coppin à l'occasion de son quatre-vingtième anniversaire* (Lille, 1966), pp. 107–117. For Smits, the wide range of authorities used by Helinand of Froidmont would rather reflect Parisian culture: "Helinand of Froidmont and the A-Text of Seneca's Tragedies," p. 339.

99   As will be seen infra, Helinand of Froidmont knows *Policraticus* 4 to 6, including the "Instruction of Trajan." He is also familiar with other sections: the one where John of Salisbury evokes Ulysses and hunting (*Chronicon* 13.11), the passage where he attacks divination (ibid., 10.72) and the one where he unravels the significance of the golden bough (ibid., 8.71).

100   On this point, see Peter Molnár, "De la morale à la science politique. La transformation du miroir des princes au milieu du XIIIe siècle," in Paolo Odorico, ed., *L'Éducation au gouvernement et à la vie. La tradition des "règles de vie" de l'Antiquité au Moyen Âge. Actes du colloque international, Pise, 18 et 19 mars 2005* (Paris, 2009), pp. 181–204. For a long time the chronicle of Helinand of Froidmont was thought to have survived exclusively in the compilations of Vincent of Beauvais. Today, two witnesses of the work are known: Vatican Library, Reg. Lat. 535, which includes Books 1 to 18, and London, British Library, Cotton Claudius B IX (Books 1 to 16). Books 19 to 44 are lost; Books 45 to 69 are known through the 1669 edition by Bertrand Tissier, but no manuscript of this section is known.

101   Jacques Krynen, "Du bon usage des '*Leges*'. Le droit savant dans le *De bono regimine principis* d'Hélinand de Froidmont (1210)," in Angela De Benedictis, ed., *Specula Principum* (Frankfurt am Main, 1999), pp. 159–170, esp. p. 159, note 1. Specialists disagree about the intentions of Helinand of Froidmont. For some, Helinand may have written a mirror of princes that was inserted later in his chronicle by breaking up the chronological continuity of the text. See Krynen, "Du bon usage des '*Leges*'" and John W. Baldwin, *The Government of Philip Augustus. Foundations of French Royal Power in the Middle Ages* (Berkeley, 1986), p. 571. According to Peter Molnár, Brother Guérin was the addressee of this treatise (Molnár, "De la morale à la science politique," p. 186 note 16). However, studies by Marinus M. Woesthuis, Edmé Renno Smits and Eric Saak favour the idea of a digression in the chronicle: Marinus M. Woesthuis, "*Nunc ad Historiam Revertamur*: History and Preaching in Helinand of Froidmont," *Sacris Eruditi. Jaarboek voor Gosdienst-Weterschepper* 34 (1994), 313–333; idem, "Vincent of Beauvais and Helinand of Froidmont," in Serge Lusignan and Monique Paulmier-Foucart eds., coll. Marie-Christine Duchenne, *Lector et compilator. Vincent de Beauvais, frère prêcheur, un intellectuel et son milieu au XIIIe siècle* (Nancy, 1997), pp. 233–247; Erik L. Saak, "The Limits of Knowledge: Hélinand de Froidmont's Chronicon," in Peter Binkley, ed., *Pre-Modern Encyclopaedic Texts. Proceedings of the Second COMERS Confress, Groningen, 1–4 July 1996* (Leyde, 1997), pp. 289–302; Edmé Renno Smits,

Dt 17 proper includes lengthy quotations from *Policraticus* 4.[102] Next come passages on the moderation of the prince – which are all drawn from *Policraticus* 4.11 – a section on the love of the *res publica* (*Policraticus* 4.11), the letter from Plutarch to Trajan (*Policraticus* 5.3), and finally the analogy between the *res publica* and a natural body (*Policraticus* 5.2).[103] Helinand closely follows *Policraticus* 5, and gives the four principles necessary to a prince: the reverence due to God, his own education, the *disciplina* of the officers and the powerful, and the protection of his subjects.[104]

The next section is a commentary on the relationship between the king, justice and law: it takes Dt 16 for its departure point (*iuste quod iustum est*

"Editing the Chronicon of Helinand de Froidmont: the Marginal Notes," *Sacris eruditi. Jaarboek voor Gosdienst-Weterschepper* 32 (1991), 269–289. For an examination of the structure of the *Chronicon*, see Monique Paulmier-Foucart, "Hélinand de Froidmont. Pour éclairer les dix-huit premiers livres inédits de sa chronique. Édition des titres des chapitres et des notations marginales d'après le manuscrit du Vatican, Reg. lat. 535," *Spicae. Cahiers de l'atelier Vincent de Beauvais* 4 (1986), 81–254.

102   In his commentary on Dt 17:15–17 Helinand of Froidmont quotes largely from *Policraticus* 4.4 and 5. For his commentary on Dt 17:18, he borrows passages from *Policraticus* 4.6 and 5.9. For Dt 17:19, *Policraticus* 4.4 and 7 are quoted. For Dt 17:20, Helinand quotes *Policraticus* 4.8 and *Policraticus* 5.7 and 8. Dt 17:20 is illustrated by *Policraticus* 4.9. It is at this point that Helinand inserts a long digression that rests on *Policraticus* 4.10 and 12. In fact, the commentary of "Aquilinius" (Caius Aquilius Gallus, a jurisconsult of the 1st century B.C.) on the action of *dolus*, quoted by Helinand, is in *Policraticus* 4.12. Ecclus. 31, *qui potuit transgredi et non est transgressus*, is commented with a passage drawn from *Policraticus* 4.10.

103   Vatican Library, Reg. Lat. 535, p. 286: "Est autem res publica, ut Plutarco placet, corpus quoddam quod diuini muneris beneficio animatur. Et nutu summe equitatis agitur, et regitur quodam moderamine rationis. Que ad religionem pertinent uicem anime obtinent. Qui religionis cultui presunt quasi corporis anima suscipendi sunt. Augustus Cesar eo usque sacrorum pontificibus subiectus fuit, donec et ipse necui omnino subesset, uestalis creatus est pontifex. Princeps caput est huius corporis, uni subiectus Deo et his qui uices Dei agunt in terris. Maior est enim qui benedicit quam qui benedicitur et penes quem est conferende dignitatis auctoritas eum cui confertur dignitas honoris priuilegio antecedit. Unde et eum deponere potest sicut Samuel Saul. Ejus est enim nolle cuius est uelle, et eius est auferre, qui de iure conferre potest. Cordis locum senatus obtinet, oculorum aurium et lingue officia sibi uendicant iudices et presides prouinciarum. Officiales et milites manibus coaptantur, qui semper asistunt principi, lateribus assimilantur. Questores et commentarienses, non illi qui carceribus presunt, sed comites rerum priuatarum, uentris et intestinorum ferunt ymaginem. Pedes agricole sunt."

104   After *Policraticus* 5 (3, 4, 5, 7, 9, 10, 15, 16).

persequeris). This part is more technical,[105] but still draws heavily on *Policraticus* 5.16. The passage on the illicit receipt of gifts, the misappropriation of public funds and the corruption and avidity of officers also rests largely on *Policraticus* 5.1, 15 and 17. The analysis of the relationship between the prince and the law refers to *Policraticus* 5.1. The passages on the love of justice, moderation and equity, the knowledge of the judge, and the officers of justice, are all inspired by the text of John of Salisbury, although the influence of Peter the Chanter is also perceptible there. The last sections of the text are not organised according to any clear order: Helinand emulates John of Salisbury in his discussion of soldiers' duties, by explaining that the oath makes the combatant. Like John, he emphasizes that the dubbing ceremony must take place in a church. He then reverts to the judicial function of the king, who is the image of equity; this means that he can shed blood without sinning. The prince who does not control his officers is responsible for their exactions, and he ought to show his love for his subjects. The last section disputes the maxim according to which what pleases the prince has the force of law; and laws are similar to a cobweb, capturing small insects but letting large ones get through.

Overall more than three-quarters of 11.38 of Helinand's *Chronicon* rely on the *Policraticus*, in particular on Books 4 to 6. But the long and subtle reflections of John of Salisbury on the body politic, on the duties of combatants, or on corruption have been reduced to a number of short sentences.[106] In the past, Helinand of Froidmont's reliance on the *Policraticus* led a number of critics to charge him with plagiarism.[107] Studies undertaken since the 1990s clarify his project: in particular, the notion that the *Chronicon* set out to be a compilation of available knowledge, with study and education in sight, may justify the numerous borrowings from John of Salisbury's text. This does not imply that the *Chronicon* was in any way neutral, since Helinand's purpose was to put together a compilation aimed at the love of God, and to create textual weaponry in order to combat doctrinal errors.[108] This means that he did not scruple to fight what he saw as preconceived ideas and false opinions. The polemical

---

105   The legal reflections of Helinand of Froidmont are analysed by Jacques Krynen, "Du bon usage des *'Leges'*." Peter Molnár stresses, however, that some sections attributed to Helinand are already found in the *Policraticus* ("De la morale à la science politique," p. 192 note 40). Nevertheless, one may follow some of Krynen's conclusions, for instance when he states that Helinand did not find the definitions of the *aequitas rudis* and of the *aequitas constituta* in the *Policraticus* (Krynen, "Du bon usage des *'Leges'*," p. 168).

106   See Molnár, "De la morale à la science politique," pp. 187, 189–190.

107   Hans Hublocher, *Helinand von Froidmont und sein Verhältnis zu Johannes von Salisbury. Ein Beitrag zur Geschichte des Plagiates in der mittelalterlichen Literatur* (Regensburg, 1913).

108   Saak, "The Limits of Knowledge," p. 299.

dimension of his work accounts for the criticisms he addresses to some *aucto-ritates*,[109] including the *Policraticus*. For instance, he rejects the position of John of Salisbury on the wealth of princes. For John, possessing treasures is licit, as the example of Solomon suggests. Relying on Augustine, Helinand defends the opposite view, and explains that Solomon sinned by accumulating too much wealth.[110]

The same critical stand comes forth into view in a passage where Helinand discusses the interpretation of the golden bough given in *Policraticus* 8.25. In this chapter, John constructs a theory of knowledge based on original sin and grace: man has tasted from the tree of the Garden of Eden and has strayed from truth, virtue and life. In order to regain these, he must find the tree of science, and cut from it truth (by the way of knowledge), virtue (by the way of action), and life (by the way of joy). Only he who puts in front of him the bough of vir-tue cut from the tree of knowledge may return to God. It is here that John of Salisbury introduces some considerations on Virgil, *Eneid* 6: instructed by the Sibyll, Eneas was able to enter the Elysean Fields of the blessed after making an offering of the bough of Proserpina, whose name suggests the life that pro-gresses and elevates man out of vice. Chapter 25 ends with the recognition of the role of Grace, which has planted the tree of knowledge and the wood of life in the Church.[111] Helinand reuses the image of the golden bough in *Chronicon* 8.71: Eneas gave a golden bough to Cerberus and was thus able to escape from him.[112] For Helinand however this simply means that one may appease hatred through gifts, and win back lost favour through riches. He even regards John of Salisbury's interpretation of the golden bough as incongruous: neither Pluto

---

109 Ibid., p. 293; Smits, "Helinand of Froidmont and the A-Text of Seneca's Tragedies," p. 339 note 66 on the criticism of Peter Comestor or Peter Lombard by Helinand. These criti-cisms appear in the margins, for instance *Auctor contra Iohannem*, p. 282 of the manu-script of the Vatican Library for an attack on the positions of John of Salisbury.

110 Vatican Library, Reg. Lat. 535, pp. 282–283: "Quid hic dicunt qui domino prohibente argen-tum et aurum sibi thesaurizant, questum ex calumpnia facientes, et querentes habundan-tiam singularem de multorum inopia, de rapinis diuitias, beatitudinem de calamitate, si quis obicit copiam Salomonis. Principem non prohibet lex locupletem fieri sed auarum. Sed nec obiciende sunt diuitie non concupite, et ab ipso domino promisse et date. Hec Iohannes. Augustinus tamen dicit Salomonem in multiplicatione auri et argenti, sicut in uxorum peccasse, unde apparet eum non solum ex promissione divina sed etiam ex pro-pria concupiscencia tantas acquisisse diuitias. Ille igitur opes credende sunt a Deo Salomoni et promisse et date, que illi dono clabantur a ceteris regibus. Illas autem uitiose habuit in quarum multiplicatione laborauit..."

111 Ed. Webb, vol. 2, pp. 419–422.

112 Vatican Library, Reg. Lat. 535, pp. 197–198.

nor Proserpine may bestow virtues or science – that is to say the science that is useful and leads to salvation.[113] Further on, Helinand returns to the passage where John of Salisbury explains that when one cuts from the tree the bough of science and virtue, another grows immediately in its place, since where they are exerted science and virtues always grow. On the outside, this image may seem very positive, Helinand writes, but in reality it is violent and disharmonious.[114] It is only in a very convoluted way, unwisely, and even criminally, that one may suggest that the prophecies of the Sibyll express divine advice or wisdom.[115]

Helinand of Froidmont stands out among the authors who borrowed from the *Policraticus* in the 12th and 13th centuries for the critical attitude he adopts towards his model. Although he seems to have had access to most and perhaps to the whole of the *Policraticus*, his adaptation of the treatise's positions is relatively short. But in spite of this, his abbreviated version of some key-passages of the *Policraticus* played a significant role in the diffusion of John of Salisbury's ideas. In particular, Helinand seems to have been the principal mediator between John of Salisbury and the work undertaken by the Dominican Vincent of Beauvais. In his *Speculum historiale*, completed in 1244, Vincent makes extensive use of Helinand's work, and reuses the passages of *Chronicon* 11.38 that quote John of Salisbury, although he does not seem to know the name of the author of the *Policraticus*.[116] These passages appear again in the *Speculum doctrinale*, and in the *De morali principis institutione*, a treatise completed shortly before Vincent's death in 1264.[117]

---

113 Ibid., p. 197: "Carnotensis autem aliam interpretationem ponit de ramo aureo: sed ut mihi uidetur incongruam. Nam eam ad uirtutes et scientiam intorquet. Absit autem ut Pluto uel Proserpina uirtutes aut scientiam dare credantur; scientiam dico utilem et salutarem."

114 Ibid., p. 197: "Fauorabilis uidetur huius interpretatio sed uiolenta magis est, et sibi ipsi inconsonans."

115 Ibid., p. 198: "Inconuenientissime immo et insipientissime et scelerissime et sceleratissime huiusmodi uaticinia ad Dei consilium uel sapientiam referuntur in quibus per artem magicam ueritas a mendacio queritur, uita a mortis, lux a tenebris, honestas et iusticia a nequam spiritibus et immundis."

116 The text of Helinand's "treatise" is edited in PL 212, cols. 735–46 and 771–1082, as well as other fragments from the *Chronicon* in the revised version of Vincent de Beauvais's *Speculum historiale* 29. Several sections from Helinand's chronicle are also reproduced in the *De morali principis institutione* (ed. Robert J. Schneider, Turnhout, 1995) and in the *Speculum doctrinale* 7 (ed. Douai, 1624). On this matter, see esp. Molnár, "De la morale à la science politique," pp. 193–204. On the wider connection between the two authors, see also Monique Paulmier-Foucart, "Écrire l'histoire au XIIIe siècle. Vincent de Beauvais et Hélinand de Froidmont," *Annales de l'Est* 33 (1981), 49–70.

117 The passages where Helinand of Froidmont quotes the *Policraticus* and which are taken up in the *De morali principis institutione* are listed in the edition by Schneider, pp. 170–171.

Vincent considerably abbreviated Helinand's text, while making it more accessible by dividing it into rubricated chapters; he may also have deliberately omitted a number of reflections that alluded to the superiority of the spiritual power or weakened the dynastic principle.[118] Vincent's work in turn influenced the *De eruditione principum* of the Dominican William Peyraut, who relies on him entirely for his knowledge of the *Policraticus*.

This does not necessarily mean that Helinand's and then Vincent's work imposed an authorized and shortened version of the *Policraticus*: already in the late 1250s and in the 1260s, if not before, it was circulating in France in its entirety, and was being drawn on by other writers. One such writer was the Franciscan Guibert of Tournai, who taught in Paris, and whose *Eruditio regum et principum*, completed in 1259, relies heavily on the *Policraticus*. Indeed, the whole of his treatise is organized around the sentence from *Policraticus* 5.3: "Regibus igitur atque principibus IIII[or] mihi videntur necessaria ad salutem: Dei reverentia, sui diligentia, disciplina debita potestatum et officialium, affectus et protectio subditorum."[119] Guibert handles a number of topics, and there the influence of John of Salisbury's text is clear: these include entertainment and especially hunting, the *curiales* and their vices, the control of officers, justice and the equity of the prince. While these borrowings perhaps reflect Guibert's knowledge of Vincent of Beauvais's *Speculum doctrinale*,[120] he certainly also had direct access to the *Policraticus* when he wrote the *Eruditio*.[121] The section of the first epistle that bears on the reverence due to God comes

---

118   This is what Molnár seems to suggest, "De la morale à la science politique," pp. 194–197, about the absence of the end of Helinand' interpretation of Dt 17:11 (iuxta legem eius sequeris sententiam eorum nec declinabis ad dextram vel ad sinistram) and of the sentence "maior est enim qui benedicit quam qui benedicitur." In the same article, Peter Molnár offers a complete analysis of the borrowings from the *Policraticus* in the *Speculum doctrinale* and the *De morali principis institutione*.

119   *Le traité* Eruditio regum et principum *de Guibert de Tournai O.F.M. (étude et texte inédit)*, ed. A. de Poorter (Louvain, 1914), p. 6.

120   See the remarks of Charles Munier in his introduction to *De l'Institution morale du prince* (Paris, 2010), p. 51.

121   Although Guibert does not mention the title of the *Policraticus* in the *Eruditio* and does not seem to know the name of its author, he does quote it clearly in his *Erudimentum doctrinae*, a pedagogic treatise he compiled a few years later, around 1262: A. de Poorter, "Un traité de pédagogie médiévale: le *De modo addiscendi* de Guibert de Tournai, O.F.M. Notes et extraits," *Revue néo-scolastique de philosophie* 24 (1922), 195–228, esp. p. 206 for the date. *De modo addiscendi* 4.26, ed. Enrico Bonifacio (Turin, 1953), p. 243: "Requiritur etiam paupertas in censu, prout sapiens quidam, Bernardus scilicet Carnotensis, ut dicitur in Polycratico Ioannis Saresberiensis, cum interrogaretur de forma et modo addiscendi: Mens, inquit, humilis, studium quaerendi, uita quieta/Scrutinium tacitum, paupertas,

from *Policraticus* 4 and 8. The passage on entertainment and hunting is reproduced from *Policraticus* 1.4 and 5, and from Book 4, although it does not follow
the order of John of Salisbury's text.[122] Guibert of Tournai also uses the organic
metaphor, but this is in order to assimilate the prince and those who follow a
religious rule into a sort of body.[123]

Guibert's borrowings pertain to a complex process of rewriting. For instance,
he analyses at length the meaning of the terms used in *Policraticus* 5.3. The
expression *disciplina...potestatum et officialium* is the pretext for some very
personal reflections on the real exercise of power in the kingdom, for instance
in towns, and enables Guibert to justify the intervention of Louis IX in some
sectors of political life, such as legislation. The method he sets out at the beginning of his treatise clarifies the approach he takes when modelling some of his
text on the *Policraticus*: he will handpick from his predecessors' works, taking
notes, but he will consider them as guides, not as masters.[124]

The political topics discussed in the *Policraticus* inspired authors from
Helinand of Froidmont to Guibert of Tournai, although they abbreviated and
adulterated the essential passages of John of Salisbury's work on these matters.
If there was a rupture in the influence of the *Policraticus* on political thought,
this was due to the impact of the rediscovery of Aristotle's ethical and political
work. Some of Thomas Aquinas's or Giles of Rome's reflections can still be situated within the framework provided by the *Policraticus*, such as the analogy
between the *res publica* and the natural body, or the distinction between king
and tyrant. But they did not reuse the *Policraticus* literally and the influence of
John of Salisbury on their thought seems secondary. For instance, although

---

terra aliena,/Haec reserare solent multis obscura legendi." (cf. *Policraticus* 7.13). References
to the *Policraticus* are also found in 1.2 (ibid., pp. 63–64) and 2.9, where Guibert quotes the
letter of Plutarch to Trajan (ibid., pp. 93–94).

122   About half of the text of Chapter 1 in the first part of the treatise duplicates the passages
on hunting and games in *Policraticus* 1.4 and 5. Nevertheless the text of Guibert of Tournai
offers a number of original features. It is mainly a commentary of Dt 17:16: here Guibert,
who has just condemned those who keep large followings, replies to the objection according to which hunting implies keeping a large number of horses. For Guibert, hunting is a
childish activity that does not suit the prince. Jerome allows fishing for the monks, but
forbids hunting. Like John of Salisbury, Guibert laments the fact that the art of hunting
survives among the nobility, and then criticizes the noisy triumph of hunters.

123   *Le traité* Eruditio regum et principum *de Guibert de Tournai*, p. 30.

124   Ibid., pp. 199–200. The deep influence of the *Policraticus* on John of Wales and Guibert de
Tournai argues for a favourable reception of John of Salisbury's work in the Franciscan
order. However, the uses which those two Franciscan writers put the *Policraticus* to were
quite dissimilar.

one may see some echo of the concerns expressed in the *Policraticus* in the section of the *Summa theologiae*[125] where Aquinas offers an analysis of the maxim "the prince is not bound by the laws," the vocabulary he uses is different from that of John of Salisbury. In Aquinas's view, the prince exerts coercive power and nobody can pass a judgment against him if he acts against the law; the law's coercive power is entirely dependent on the authority of the sovereign. It is when it comes to directive power that the sovereign is subject to law, but only of his own free will. Aquinas is probably closer to the *Policraticus* when discussing tyrannicide in his *De Regno* (a treatise written for the young king of Cyprus), where a whole section is devoted to this matter.[126] Here Aquinas approves of the intervention of public authority to depose the tyrant, but rejects the individual act of tyrannicide:[127] however, in the *Summa theologiae* IIa IIae 42.2, he seems to defend resorting to sedition against a tyrannical ruler, provided the effects of this action are no worse than tyranny itself. On the death of the king of Cyprus, Thomas stopped writing the *De regno*, probably at 2.4. Several decades later it was another Dominican, Ptolemy of Lucca, who completed this work. He refers explicitly to the *Policraticus*, for instance in 2.7, about the analogy between the human body and any kingdom, city, camp or association.[128] In 4.23, he explains that a proper political organization is similar to a well laid-out body, in which organic forces have a perfect vigour.[129] The reference to "Plutarch" and to the organic metaphor also appears in 3.24: but he compares the counsellors to the eyes in the body, instead of the heart. Both Aquinas and Ptolemy of Lucca knew the *Policraticus*; but compared with other sources, especially Aristotle, it seems to have exerted only a distant influence on their thought.

Giles of Rome adopts a relatively similar stand in his *De regimine principum*, completed about 1279, probably in response to an order from the French royal

---

125   *Summa theologiae* Ia IIae, qu. 96, art. 5.

126   *De regno* 1.5 and 6: *De regimine principum ad regem Cypri*, ed. Joseph Mathis (Turin, 1924), pp. 7–10.

127   *De regno* 1.6: ibid., p. 9. In 1.12 of *De regno*, about royal virtue, he is close to *Policraticus* 8.17: the king does in his kingdom what God does in the world (ibid., p. 18).

128   Ibid., p. 31: "Amplius autem, quodlibet regnum, sive civitas, sive castrum, sive quodcumque collegium assimilatur humano corpori, sicut ipse Philosophus tradit, et hoc idem in *Policratico* scribitur: unde comparatur ibidem commune aerarium regis stomacho, ut sicut in stomacho recipiuntur ubi et diffunduntur ad membra, ita et aerarium regis repletur thesauro pecuniarum, et communicatur atque diffunditur pro necessitatibus subditorum et regni."

129   Ibid., p. 108.

court. In this work, which has a strong Aristotelian outlook,[130] the influence of the *Policraticus* is limited to the use of the organic metaphor: this appears above all in the discussion of the two main forms of justice according to Aristotle, commutative justice and distributive justice. In 1.2.11, Giles of Rome explains that any kingdom or congregation is comparable to a natural body (*cuidam corpori naturali*).[131] Such a body is composed of different elements linked together and mutually ordered: in a similar way, one may observe that any kingdom or congregation is made of persons linked together and ordered towards a single aim. If one may express it *figuraliter*, in the members of this body there is so to speak a double justice, commutative and distributive. Metaphorically, the members are mutually ordained: this is commutative justice. The body members are different from each other, and they all fulfil different functions in the body. Without this commutative justice, the city or kingdom could not last. As for the order of the members according to the heart, this refers to distributive justice: the heart helps the vital spirit flow in the body and the different members move according to their proportions and dignity. In a similar way, the king or duke ought to distribute goods and honours by considering the virtue and dignity of the citizens. Here the organic metaphor enhances the mutual obligations of the members as well as their connection with the person of the king. This tension is already present in the *Policraticus*, but in Giles of Rome's work, the metaphor helps to assert the superiority of royal power. It sits awkwardly with the Aristotelian notions of commutative and distributive justice, and one feels that Giles of Rome only paid lip service to a well-known image.

At least fifteen surviving manuscripts of the full text of the *Policraticus* date from the century and a half after its completion.[132] This suggests that it probably

---

130 *De regimine principum* is usually considered as a commentary on Aristotle's work, but some of the references to Aristotle are fictitious, and the Aristotelian outlook may be a form of rhetorical device. On this, see Matthew Kempshall, "The Rhetoric of Giles of Rome's *De Regimine Principum*," in Frédérique Lachaud and Lydwine Scordia, eds., *Le Prince au miroir de la littérature politique de l'Antiquité aux Lumières* (Rouen, 2007), pp. 161–190.

131 Giles of Rome, *De regimine principum* 1.2.11 (ed. Rome, 1607), pp. 76–79.

132 For the 12th century: Montpellier, Bibliothèque de la Faculté de Médecine 60 (Pontigny); Charleville-Mézières, Bibliothèque Municipale 151 (Signy); Soissons, Bibliothèque Municipale 4 (this may be the copy John of Salisbury left to Chartres, according to Patricia Stirnemann, Atelier Jean de Salisbury, 15 February 2013); Oxford, Bodleian Library, Barlow 6 (Malmesbury); Oxford, Bodleian Library, lat. misc. c. 16 (Battle); London, British Library, Royal 13 D IV (St Albans); Cambridge, Corpus Christi College 46 (the copy owned by Thomas Becket?). For the 13th century: London, British Library, Royal 12 F VIII (Rochester); Oxford, Bodleian Library, Barlow 48 (Cirencester?); Oxford, Bodleian Library, Auctarium F I 8; London, British Library, Royal 13 E. V; Troyes, Bibliothèque Municipale 787; Rouen, Bibliothèque Municipale 926 (Jumièges).

circulated quite extensively: yet it seems to have fitted uneasily into the new conceptual framework provided by scholastic writing on one hand, the genre of the Capetian "mirror of princes" on the other. John of Salisbury's style contrasts sharply with the expression of authors active in the schools, by its difficulty, and by its learned and convoluted aspect. The satirical and ironic tone of the work, its in-house character as well lost some of their importance. This was also the case, in the 13th century, with some of the topics treated in the *Policraticus*, such as the vocation of secular clerics serving the courts. Above all, while scholasticism created concepts, the *Policraticus* still belonged to the field of moral criticism and reform.

The Inflections of the Later Middle Ages

In the 14th and 15th centuries the circulation of the *Policraticus* widened: the number of copies was multiplied, and it reached a new readership, including circles of jurists.[133] In parallel, it also circulated beyond France and England: in the Iberian Peninsula,[134] in Italy, in Germany, in Poland and as far as Iceland.[135] A testimony to this phenomenon, as well as to the uneven access to the text of John of Salisbury, can be seen in the prologue that Denis Foulechat wrote for his translation of the *Policraticus*: before being asked to do this work, he says, he had known of it, but somehow had never been able to read it in full.[136]

---

133   Amnon Linder suggests at least 24 new copies for the 14th century, 38 for the 15th ("The Knowledge of John of Salisbury," p. 336). For the widening readership of the *Policraticus*, see the studies mentioned in note 1.

134   See Ullmann, "John of Salisbury's *Policraticus* in the later Middle Ages," p. 524. It has been suggested that the *Policraticus* may have influenced the 15th-century Portuguese chronicle of Fernão Lopes: Maria da Conceição Camps, "A presença do *Policraticus* de João de Salisbúria na *Crónica de D. João I* de Fernão Lopes," *Mediævalia. Textos e Estudos* 22 (2003), 121–156. Unfortunately it does not seem possible to prove that Fernão Lopes had a direct knowledge of the *Policraticus*, although there are clear similarities between his work and that of John of Salisbury in the exposition of some key political principles.

135   See Linder, "The Knowledge of John of Salisbury," pp. 338–345. The *Policraticus* was copied in Kraków in 1435–6; this manuscript was the exemplar for several copies made in the second half of the 15th century, for the benefit of some masters of the University: Ryszard Palacz, "Les manuscrits du *Policraticon* de Jean de Salisbury en Pologne," *Mediaevalia philosophica polonorum* 10 (1961), 55–58. Zenon Kaluza has shown that the *Policraticus* did not influence the late 12th-century *Chronica Polonorum* of Vincent of Kraków, contrary to previous assumptions (forthcoming article).

136   Foulechat, *Le Policratique de Jean de Salisbury* (1372), *Livres I–III*, p. 86.

The themes and some passages from the *Policraticus* also went on circulating through the intermediary of Vincent of Beauvais and John of Wales: some writers, such as the Pseudo-Burley, William Worcester or the author of the *De regimine principum* addressed to Henry VI seem to have known the *Policraticus* only through these works.[137]

From the late 14th century, better knowledge of the ancient texts that had inspired John of Salisbury led to a different understanding of the *Policraticus*. In works dealing with war and the discipline of combatants, for instance, quotations from the *Policraticus* were completed and rendered more precise by reading Vegetius, Frontinus and Valerius Maximus, so that it becomes difficult to pinpoint the influence of the *Policraticus*.[138] The rediscovery of most of Plutarch's works from the 14th century onwards (his treatise on anger, which was given the title *De patientia* in *Policraticus* 4.8, was already known of in the 12th century[139]) generated greater interest in the *Institutio Traiani*, which in turn probably stimulated renewed curiosity regarding the treatises of Plutarch.[140]

The wider circulation of the *Policraticus*, and of topics associated with it, may explain why it was seen as a prerequisite for political writing. This accounts for the necessity felt by many to defend or reject the positions of John of

---

137   According to Ullmann, the *Boke of Noblesse* mentions the *Policraticus* (Ullmann, "John of Salisbury's *Policraticus* in the Later Middle Ages," p. 525). The work now attributed to William Worcester includes sections on officers, the common good etc. It mentions the *Communiloquium* of John of Wales, for instance about the common good (*The Boke of Noblesse Adressed to King Edward the Fourth on his Invasion of France*, with an introduction by John Gough Nichols (London, 1860), pp. 56–58), but it does not seem to refer to the text of John of Salisbury. In a similar way, the *Tractatus de regimine principum* dedicated to Henry VI probably before 1450 quotes the *Communiloquium* 1.4 (prologus) of John of Wales on judges being the eyes of the body politic, but not the *Policraticus* (*Four English Political Tracts of the Later Middle Ages*, ed. Jean-Philippe Genet (London, 1977), p. 126 and note 384).

138   The text was made more accessible thanks to the glossed translation of Valerius Maximus by Simon of Hesdin and Nicolas of Gonesse (between 1375 and 1401), as well as through several commentaries, in particular in the circles of Italian post-glossators. This means that it is sometimes impossible to distinguish the influence of the *Policraticus* from that of the authorities it drew on. This is particularly the case with Christine of Pisan: see *Le Livre du corps de policie*, ed. Angus J. Kennedy (Paris, 1998), p. xxvii.

139   Di Stefano, *La Découverte de Plutarque en Occident*, p. 23.

140   Marianne Pade, "Translations of Plutarch in the Fourteenth and Fifteenth centuries," in Peter Andersen, ed., *Pratiques de traduction au Moyen Âge. Medieval Translation Practices* (Copenhagen, 2004), pp. 52–64; Giuseppe Di Stefano, "La découverte de Plutarque en France au début du XVe siècle. Traduction du *De remediis irae* ajoutée par Nicolas de Gonesse à sa traduction de Valère-Maxime," *Romania* 86 (1965), 463–519.

Salisbury,[141] whose statements on tyrannicide, for instance, could sow confusion in people's minds. It is imperative however to stress the multifarious nature of this reception, and not simplify the analysis of this process: even more so than in the previous period, the use and reading of the *Policraticus* narrowly reflect the needs of the milieus that received the work.

The Circulation of the *Policraticus* in the 14th and 15th Centuries (Outside France)

Amnon Linder has stressed the shift of the production of new copies of John of Salisbury's work from England to France in the later Middle Ages.[142] This does not mean that the *Policraticus* did not circulate in England. Richard of Bury (1287–1345) refers to *Policraticus* 4 in his *Philobiblon* 14 when he praises learning, in particular the connection between power and learning,[143] and he owned a copy of the text.[144] The Benedictine Ranulph Higden (†1364) echoes the prologue of *Policraticus* 5 in the prologue of his *Polychronicon*.[145] The *Policraticus* was equally well known among the mendicants, in particular in the group of "classicizing" mendicants studied by Beryl Smalley, who were anxious to integrate classical culture in their works. It is mentioned by the Dominican friars Thomas Waleys (*fl.* 1318–49) in his *De modo et forma praedicandi*, probably written in Avignon,[146] and Robert Holcot (*c.* 1290–1349) – who may have collaborated with Richard of Bury on the *Philobiblon* –[147] in his commentary

---

141   See for instance the first prologue written by Denis Foulechat for his translation of the *Policraticus* (*Le Policratique de Jean de Salisbury* (1372), *Livres I–III*, p. 86).

142   Linder, "The Knowledge of John of Salisbury," p. 336.

143   *The Philobiblon of Richard de Bury, Bishop of Durham and Chancellor of Edward III*, ed. Ernest C. Thomas (New York, 1889), pp. 112–113.

144   Smalley, *English Friars and Antiquity*, p. 69. Richard of Bury bought from St Albans a volume containing the *Metalogicon* and the *Policraticus* (London, British Library, Royal 13 D. IV, fol. 1).

145   "Licuit enim Virgilio aurum sapientiae in luto Ennii poetae quaerere...": *Polychronicon Ranulphi Higden*, ed. Churchill Babington, 9 vols. (London, 1865–86), vol. 1, p. 16 (mentioned in Smalley, *English Friars and Antiquity*, p. 20). The influence of the *Policraticus* on Chaucer is still the subject of debate.

146   Smalley, *English Friars and Antiquity*, pp. 85 and 102.

147   Ibid., pp. 151 and 155. The Dominican Thomas Ringstead, bishop of Bangor (†1366), starts his book on Proverbs with a lengthy quotation of a passage from the *Policraticus* where John of Salisbury praises the knowledge of letters (ibid., p. 215).

Super sapientiam Salomonis: this work was heavily influenced by the *Communiloquium* of John of Wales and was just as successful.[148] The Franciscan theologian William Herbert (†1333/7?) also made use of the *Policraticus* in his sermons.[149]

The *Policraticus* is mentioned on numerous occasions by Roger Waltham, a secular cleric and administrator († 1332 X 1341), in his treatise on the moral virtues of the prince entitled *Compendium morale*.[150] For instance, at the start of the second part of the *Compendium*, Waltham borrows the definition of the *res publica* from *Policraticus* 5.2, as well as the metaphor of the body politic.[151] Nevertheless, it is with a long quotation from the *Liber de philosophia prima* of Avicenna – which is also found in Roger Bacon's work – that he sustains the idea of the necessary coordination of the different participants to the city. In the second part, he uses *Policraticus* 4.6 in order to demonstrate the importance of wisdom and learning for rulers, but quotes "Helinand" as his source for the image of the illiterate king as a crowned ass.[152] In the third part of his work, he quotes *Policraticus* 1, 4 on the entertainments of the powerful; he also reuses the beginning of *Policraticus* 5, with the letter of Plutarch to Trajan, and the four main principles that princes should be taught.[153] The passage dedicated to

---

148 Robert Holcot, *Super sapientiam Salomonis*, lectio 54 (ed. Cologne, before 1476), fol. 111; see Beryl Smalley, "Robert Holcot O.P.," *Archivum fratrum praedicatorum* 26 (1956), 5–97, esp. p. 47–48.

149 On this, see *The Works of William Herebert, OFM*, ed. Stephen R. Reimer (Toronto, 1987), sermons 3 and 6, pp. 63–64 and 96–104 (after *Policraticus* 7.13, 14 and 19). In sermon 3 (probably preached in 1314), quotations from *Policraticus* 7.19 are used in order to criticize simony: on this, see Lauren Moreau, "Saintly Virtue, Clerical Vice: John of Salisbury and St. Edmund Rich in Sermon 3 of William Herebert," in Catherine Royer-Hemet, ed., *Canterbury: A Medieval City* (Newcastle-upon-Tyne, 2010), pp. 161–176.

150 The text is extant in at least 15 manuscripts.

151 London, British Library, Cotton Vespasian B. XXI, fol. 6v: "Res publica secundum Plutarchum imperatores (sic) Traiani institutorem corpus quoddam, quod diuini beneficio numeris animatur, et nutu summe equitatis agitur, et quoddam racionis moderamine regitur. Et que ad religionem pertinent, anime uicem in ea optinent. Princeps est capud huius corporis uni Deo subiectus et his qui Dei uices agunt in terris; locum cordis tenent senatus siue consiliarii principis, officia oculorum et lingue et aurum sic uendicant rei publice prouisores et iudices ac presides prouinciarum et [priores] ciuitatum. Officiales ac milites manibus coaptantur. Et qui semper assistunt principi lateribus assimilantur. Rerum privatarum custodes uentris ymaginem ferunt. Pedes autem agricole sunt. Ex hiis inferuntur illa quatuor que idem Plutarchus principibus inculcare conatur ut dicitur inferius sub tria rubrica sequenti."

152 Ibid., fol.13r.

153 Ibid., fol.20v and fol.28r.

combatants in the fourth part also refers explicitly to the *Policraticus*.[154] When using the image of the laws that are similar to a cobweb, however, he quotes Valerius Maximus instead of the *Policraticus*.[155] Waltham probably had access to at least part of the *Policraticus*, but he sometimes mentions this work under the title *De nugis philosophorum* or he quotes the *Policraticus* through the mediation of Helinand of Froidmont.

Walter Burley (c. 1275–1344) was long credited with the authorship of the *Liber de vita et moribus philosophorum*, a collection of *exempla* about ancient philosophers; but recent studies suggest this text was probably composed in Italy.[156] The Pseudo-Burley refers explicitly to the *Policraticus*, Helinand of Froidmont and "Caecilius Balbus," but does not mention the name of John of Salisbury. The huge success of the work – more than 150 manuscripts – probably helped to disseminate some passages of the *Policraticus*. The notice on Chilon of Sparta refers to John of Salisbury's text and reproduces literally a passage from Book 1 of the *Policraticus*.[157] The *exemplum* on Homer, however, while claiming to follow *Policraticus* 1, in fact quotes the *Speculum historiale* 2.87 of Vincent of Beauvais.[158] The *exempla* on Socrates and Demosthenes are distant echoes of *Policraticus* 8.[159] The other two philosophers for whom the author seems to make use of the *Policraticus* are Plato and Plutarch. In the notice on Plato, the image of the body that must keep its balance matches *Policraticus* 5.7.[160] The *exemplum* on Plutarch seems to indicate some familiarity with the text of John of Salisbury, at least with the *Institutio Traiani*, which the author calls a *libellum pulcherrimum*: it reproduces the whole of the letter of Plutarch to Trajan, with a few modifications, and the beginning of *Policraticus* 5.3.[161]

---

154   Ibid., fol.39v.

155   Ibid., fol.43v.

156   Hermann Knust, *Gualteri Burlaei Liber de vita et moribus philosophorum et poetarum mit einer altspanischen Übersetzung des Eskurialbibliothek* (Tubingen, 1886). The work was probably written in Paduan circles before 1326. See Mario Grignaschi, "Lo pseudo Walter Burley e il *Liber de vita et moribus philosophorum*," *Medioevo* 16 (1990), 131–189 and "Corrigenda et addenda sulla questione dello Ps. Burleo," ibid., 325–354.

157   *Liber de vita et moribus* 3, p. 22; cf. *Policraticus* 1.5, Webb, vol. 1, p. 37.

158   Vincent of Beauvais, *Speculum historiale* 2.87 (p. 75 of the Douai edition).

159   On Socrates: *Liber de vita et moribus* 30, p. 126; cf. *Policraticus* 8.12, ed. Webb, vol. 2, p. 309. On Demosthenes: ibid., 37, p. 164; cf. *Policraticus* 8.14, ed. Webb, vol. 2, p. 330.

160   Ibid., 52, pp. 226–228; cf. *Policraticus* 5.7, ed. Webb, vol. 1, pp. 308–309.

161   Ibid., 119, pp. 364–366. What follows is the famous anecdote about Plutarch and anger, adapted from *Policraticus* 4.8, ed. Webb, vol. 1, pp. 265–266.

From the early 14th century, the *Policraticus* seems to have circulated widely in Italy.[162] The remarks of Benvenuto da Imola, in his commentary on Dante, demonstrate knowledge of the work, as well as the desire of the author to distance himself from some assertions of John of Salisbury.[163] He quotes *"Policraticus anglicus"* about the glorious fate of Rome,[164] as well as John of Salisbury's judgement on the respective merits of Seneca and Quintilian.[165] But he criticizes the origin of the foundation of Sienna given in *Policraticus* 6.17.[166] He mentions the fact that the *Policraticus* makes Brennus a native of Britain.[167] He also quotes John of Salisbury's praise of Caesar.[168]

Circles of Italian jurists seem to have been particularly receptive to the *Policraticus*. John of Salisbury's text was used by Guilielmo da Pastrengo,[169] Lucas de Penna, and Paride dal Pozzo. It was also a Bolognese jurist, the canonist and friend of Petrarch, Giovanni Calderini (†c. 1365), who decided to compile an alphabetical table of the *Policraticus* that was then systematically reproduced in the manuscripts of the work. Ullmann's studies on Lucas de Penna have traced the influence of the *Policraticus* on this Napolitan jurist (†c. 1390), especially in his *Lectura* on the *Tres libri* of the Code.[170] The concern of Lucas de Penna to use a non-legal source to shed light on law may account for this.[171] For instance, he adapts to his milieu and his time the criticisms levelled

---

162 Smalley, *English Friars and Antiquity*, p. 270, about Michele da Massa Marittima (d.1337), an ermit from the order of Saint Augustine, author of some commentaries which refer to John of Salisbury; she also mentions some lectures on Ecclesiastes given by an anonymous Franciscan active at Vicenza or Parma, who quotes Valerius Maximus and John of Salisbury.

163 Benvenuto de Rambaldis da Imola, *Comentum super Dantis Aldigherij Comœdiam*, ed. Jacobo Filippo Lacaita, 5 vols. (Florence, 1887).

164 Ibid., vol.1, pp. 83–84, on *Inferno*, Cant. 2, ll. 25–30. Cf. *Policraticus* 5.7, ed. Webb, vol. 1, p. 315.

165 Ibid., vol.1, p. 179, on *Inferno*, Canto 4, ll. 139–41. Cf. *Policraticus* 8.13.

166 Ibid., vol. 2, p. 410, on *Inferno*, Canto 29, ll. 121–39.

167 Ibid., vol. 4, p. 429, on *Paradiso*, Canto 6, ll. 28–48. Cf. *Policraticus* 6.17.

168 Ibid., vol. 4, p. 446, on *Paradiso*, Canto 6, ll. 70–111; also ibid., vol. 5, p. 245, on *Paradiso*, Canto 19, ll. 100–2.

169 Guglielmo da Pastrengo refers to *"Policratus"* and to *"Policraticus"* ("Policrato teste…ut Policraticus refert") as well as to Plutarch ("Traiani imperatoris instructor"), in his *De viris illustribus* and in his *De originibus* (*De viris illustribus et De originibus*, ed. Guglielmo Bottari (Padua, 1991), pp. 89, 182, 185, 209, 266).

170 Ullmann, *The Medieval Idea of Law*, esp. pp. 31–32; there is a convenient introduction to the author and his work by Emmanuele Conte, "Luca da penne (Lucas de Penna)," in *Dizionario biografico degli Italiani*, vol. 66 (2006), pp. 251–254.

171 Ullmann, "The Influence of John of Salisbury on Medieval Italian Jurists," p. 386.

by John of Salisbury to some forms of learning.[172] He also follows in the steps of John of Salisbury when he shows his interest in the organic structure of society, in law and justice, as forms of government.[173] He is equally close to the *Policraticus* when he discusses the issue of tyrannicide, though he omits the reservations expressed by John of Salisbury on the legitimacy of this act.[174] Nevertheless, if Lucas deems that the purpose of science is to demonstrate that man is subject to the law of God, he does not follow John of Salisbury in his estimate of the relationship between the two powers.[175]

All this may give the impression that the *Policraticus* deeply influenced Lucas de Penna when he was writing his *Lectura* and that the work was widely read in southern Italy. In fact Lucas may have discovered the *Policraticus* not in Naples, but in Avignon where he stayed in the 1370s, which means that the geographical diffusion of the *Policraticus* may have been more limited than what Ullmann assumed[176]: it was in Avignon that Lucas deepened his knowledge of classical authors, in particular Valerius Maximus, on whose work he wrote a *Summaria*.[177] Ullmann may also have given too much significance to the influence of the *Policraticus* on Lucas. The *proemium* of the *Lectura* mentions John of Salisbury's work,[178] and Lucas quotes it frequently in the rest of the work. Yet the *Policraticus* is only one source among the many he uses, and in reality, numerous statements that may seem at first sight to originate in John of Salisbury's text had long been part of the common stock of moral and political thought in the West.[179] Moreover, Lucas is often happy either to quote the *Policraticus* or to refer the

---

172   Ibid., p. 385.

173   Ullmann, *The Medieval Idea of Law*, pp. 165–166.

174   Ibid., pp. 188–189 and idem, "The Influence of John of Salisbury on Medieval Italian Jurists," pp. 387–388. Ullmann refers most notably to the passage at the very end of Lucas de Penna's work, the commentary on Book 12 of the Code, tit. 63 (fols. 333v and 340r of the Lyon edition, 1557).

175   Ibid., p. 391.

176   Walter Ullmann stresses the significance of the work for Napolitan jurists, in particular for subjects such as government and public administration. But they do not seem to have known the name of the author of the *Policraticus*: "The Influence of John of Salisbury on Medieval Italian Jurists," pp. 384–385 and 391.

177   On this, see Laure Hermand-Schebat, "Pétrarque et Jean de Salisbury: miroir du prince et conceptions politiques," in Maurice Brock, Francesca Furlan and Frank La Brasca, eds., *La Bibliothèque de Pétrarque. Livres et auteurs autour d'un humaniste* (Turnhout, 2011), pp. 177–195.

178   Ed. Lyon, 1557, fol. 1.

179   Among the medieval authors quoted by Lucas de Penna: John of Salisbury, but also Peter of Blois, Hugh of Saint-Victor, Richard of Saint-Victor, Alan of Lille, Giles of Rome and Thomas Aquinas, as well as Petrarch.

reader who would like to read more to the original text, without really commenting on it. This is for instance the case with the passages that deal with tyrannicide.[180] The same may be said of the sections which concern the body politic,[181] in which Lucas sometimes reuses the metaphor from *Policraticus* 5,[182] and at other times prefers to follow Aristotle or some other source.[183]

A similar point may be made for other Italian jurists. In the work of Paride dal Pozzo (c. 1411–93), who studied in Naples and Bologna, the *Policraticus* also seems on the face of it to be an essential source for the political reflections of the author. In his *De sindicatu*, a work that probably reflects both the needs of the practitioners and those of the schools, he mentions John of Salisbury's work several times.[184] He does this, for instance, when dealing with the issue of tyrannicide, which he considers lawful in some cases.[185] However, like Lucas de Penna, his approach consists in tapping both legal sources and a vast range of literary, historical and philosophical works. Consequently it may be argued that jurists like these were less interested in John of Salisbury's commentaries on specific passages in Roman law than in using his work as a means to broaden their discussions with reflections on the philosophy and history of Antiquity.

The place of the *Policraticus* in the early Humanists' work seems to confirm this view. There are similarities between the ideas of John of Salisbury and those of Petrarch,[186] who mentions the *Policraticus* in his letters.[187] In a letter

---

180 For instance fols. 54 and 153r of the Lyon edition, 1557.

181 Ibid., fol. 222r: "Hec et alia satis moralia et utilia quere si delectat in Poll. lib. vj. c. penul."

182 Ibid., fol. 318r.

183 For instance ibid., fol. 296v: "Et sicut anima regit corpus et conseruat ita rex statuitur ad regni gubernationem et regimen et sicut anima est salus et vita corporis sic et rex et huiusmodi principes si recte principantur sunt salus et vita regnorum ut patet per Aristotelem iiij politice."

184 The edition used here is *Tractatus illustrium...jurisconsultorum*, (Venice, 1583) vol. 7, fol.217 sq. The first edition dates from c. 1473; the definitive edition was printed in 1485.

185 Ibid., fol. 11 sq. The war against the tyrant is allowed "si a preside exerceatur."

186 On this point, see Hermand-Schebat, "Pétrarque et Jean de Salisbury"; also eadem, *Pétrarque épistolier et Cicéron. Étude d'une filiation* (Paris, 2011). According to Laure Hermand-Schebat, John of Salisbury was an essential intermediary in the reading of Cicero by Petrarch, although Petrarch does not admit to having used medieval authorities (ibid., p. 245). According to her, John of Salisbury and Petrarch are particularly close on a number of subjects, such as academic probabilism or the articulation between sceptical doubt and Christian faith.

187 Umberto Bosco, "Il Petrarca e l'umanesimo filologico. Postille al Nolhac e al Sabbadini," *Giornale storico della letteratura italiana* 120 (1942), 65–119. Bosco shows that about 1343–5 Petrarch still only had an indirect knowledge of the *Policraticus*. This was not the case any more in 1351 at the latest, as his correspondance shows (ibid., esp. pp. 100–101).

to Barbaro da Sulmona on the death of Robert the Wise, he borrows from *Policraticus* 7.6 the image of the sun that fell from heavens on the day of Plato's death.[188] However, his other references to the *Policraticus* are confined to the letter of Plutarch to Trajan.[189] The treatise on tyranny by the chancellor of Florence Coluccio Salutati (1400) demonstrates deeper knowledge of John of Salisbury's work, although in his letters he admires the style of the author he thinks is the "translator of Plutarch."[190] Wondering whether it is lawful to kill the tyrant, Coluccio Salutati contrasts the general assertion of John of Salisbury – according to whom one ought to kill the tyrant – and the multitude of examples John gives, that demonstrate that it is preferable to subject oneself to the power of the tyrant.[191] He then analyses, in *Policraticus* 3 and 8, several statements on the issue that seem contradictory,[192] and concludes that John of Salisbury did not approve of tyrannicide.[193] He also mentions *Policraticus* 8.19 about Caesar,[194] but there he mainly discusses the point of view of Cicero. The overall impression is that Salutati wishes to distance himself from the work of John of Salisbury, whose contradictions he does not hesitate to point out.

Reading the *Policraticus* in Later Medieval France

In the later Middle Ages, the *Policraticus* continued to be read in England, and was well known by some Italian authors: nevertheless, it is without any doubt on French writers that its impact was the strongest. Three authors – Christine of Pisan, Jean Gerson and Jean Juvénal des Ursins – relied heavily on it, in a context of civil conflict where the call to unity, as well as the strengthening of

---

188   *Fam.* 5.1: *Lettres familières*, t. 2, *Livres IV–VII, Rerum familiarium, Libri IV–VII,* (Fr.) trans. André Longpré, notices and notes Ugo Dotti (Paris, 2002), p. 132: "Itaque, si quo die Plato rebus humanis excessit, sol celo cecidisse visus est..." Also *Fam.* 15.7.10.

189   *Fam.* 11.5, 18.16 and 24.7.

190   Di Stefano, *La Découverte de Plutarque en Occident*, pp. 132–133. Rather ironically, his reflections on the style of Plutarch derive from his reading of John of Salisbury's work. See ibid., p. 50 on the confusion made by Salutati.

191   *Tractatus de Tyranno von Coluccio Salutati*, pp. xxx–xxxi: "Aliud enim est occisum aliquem esse, aliud iure cesum; ut michi visus sit vir eruditissimus Johannes de Saberiis, qui libro, quem, nescio quam ob rem, dicimus Policratum, determinat tyrannum occidere iustum esse, dum hoc exemplorum multitudine probare nititur, nichil agere. Non enim probant exempla tyrannos occidere iustum, sed potius usitatum."

192   Ibid., pp. xxxi–xxxii.

193   Ibid., pp. xxxii–xxxiv.

194   Ibid., pp. xxxiv.

military discipline, had become strong imperatives. In more than one way, this represented a break with the use that was made of the *Policraticus* in earlier periods: John of Salisbury's work reached a new type of readership in search of political and moral advice.

The early 14th-century *Liber de informatione principum* mentions the *Policraticus*. This text may have been compiled by a Dominican friar, and one version of it was dedicated to King Louis X.[195] In 1379, Jean Golein translated the work for Charles V. The author of the *Liber* borrows the organic metaphor from the *Policraticus* – but without ever quoting it literally – in order to describe "royal majesty."[196] The analogy he traces between the merchants and the legs does not appear in the *Institutio Traiani*; moreover, the organic metaphor is mainly used to stress the pre-eminence of the head, and the duty of obedience of the members.[197] Other passages of the *Liber* refer to the *Policraticus*, for instance 2.16, about corruption, where the author borrows the figure of Orpheus from *Policraticus* 5.10 in order to illustrate the extreme corruption of the people of the court, who are more ferocious than the wild animals Orpheus succeeded in taming with his music.[198] A distant echo of *Policraticus* 5.11 is found in Chapter 32 of the second part of the *Liber*, about the "office des prevoz et baillifs et autres justiciers du royaume."[199] There is also a reminiscence of the

195 Wilhelm Berges. *Die Furstenspiegel des hohen und späten Mittelalters* (Leipzig, 1938), pp. 336–340; Krynen, *L'Empire du roi*, p. 188.

196 Paris, BnF fr. 1950, fol. 4r (translation by Jean Golein): "...l'en doit savoir que la royal magesté est en la chose publique aussi comme un corps composé de divers membres ou quel le roy ou le prince tient lieu du chief. Et les seneschaulz, les prevoz, les juges ont l'office des oreilles, des iex et les sages conseilliers l'office du cuer. Et les chevaliers deffendeurs le lieu des mains. Et les marcheans courants par le monde sont a maniere des jambes. Les laboureurs cultiveurs des champs et les autres popules povres sont adjoins a manière des piez. Et ainsi il appiert que les princes sont au corps de la chose publique comme le chief."

197 For instance ibid., fol. 4v: "Et a bonne cause le roy est designé par le chief ou quiconques bon prince. Car aussi comme le chief est superposé a touz les membres et si est leur gouvernement a touz en haut eslevé et es doué de touz les membres et par singularité de dignité est ymaginé noblement, ainsi le roy ou le prince est a touz sousmis et a touz ses sojects a gouverner et mettre en ordenance et comme esleue par-dessus touz il doit les iex du cuer et la face de l'ame lever au ciel et doit par dessus touz en parfaite cognoissance preceller et en noblesse de meurs resplendir et apparoir. Et pour ce a bonne cause touz obeissent au roy ou au prince aussi comme les membres a leur chief servent et obeissent."

198 Ibid., fol. 72: "L'en raconte que Orphe sis [adebonnant] et aprivoisa les lyons et les tigres par le son de la harpe. Mais les curiaulz ne pueent estre aprivoisiez ne apaisiez se non que leurs cuers qui sont pesans comme [plomc] soient amoliez par les malz dor et d'argent."

199 Ibid., fol. 101. The Cistercian Pierre Ceffons, in his letter to Lucifer – a satire on the Curia – also mentions John of Salisbury as an authority (Smalley, *English Friars and Antiquity*, p. 260).

body politic as described in the *Policraticus* in the *Avis au roy* which was perhaps written to the order of John the Good about 1347–50; most importantly,
this section is illustrated by a unique iconographic representation of the body
politic.[200]

The inventory of the royal library drawn up by Gilles Malet in 1373 mentions a copy of the *Policraticus* in Latin,[201] and writers who revolved around
the royal court under Charles V and the young Charles VI knew of John of
Salisbury's text. In the *Songe du vieil pelerin*, for instance, Philippe de
Mézières advises the prince to undertake a number of readings, including
the *Policraticus*.[202] In his *De moneta* (written before he rallied to the
Dauphin), Nicole Oresme quotes *Policraticus* 5.2 about the nature of the *res
publica*, in the chapter on tyrants who cannot last long. However, in this
work, the sections on tyranny and the body politic are mainly influenced by
Aristotle's *Politics*.[203] In a sermon given in Avignon in 1363, Oresme resorts

---

200 New York, Pierpont Morgan Library 456, fol. 5r-5v: "La seconde raison est quar selon la
sainte escripture, li roys est li chies par dessus le pueple subget, qui sont li membre, et
pour ce fut il dit a Saul le premier roy: Cum esses paruulus in oculis tuis nonne caput in
tribubus Israel factus es. C'est a dire quant tu estoies petiz et humbles ne fu tu mie faiz
chief es lignees dou pueple d'Israel. Dont le roy si est le chief, seneschaut, baillif et prevost
et autre iuge ont l'office des eyls et des oreilles, li sage et li conseiller on l'office dou cuer,
li cheualier qui ont a deffendre le bien commun ont l'office des mains, li marchent qui
courent par le monde ont l'office des gembes, li laboreur des terres ont l'office des pies,
quar il sont tous iours a la terre et soustiennent le corps. Et ainsi li princes est le chief de
tout le corps de la communité. Et a l'exemple dou chief qui contient et comprent en li
touz les v sens humains et gouverne et addresce touz les autres membres li bons princes
doit comprendre en li en son pouoir toute protection pour touz les subgez gouvernier a
poinct et addrecier. Et pour ce est il mis au dessus a la meniere dou chief, si se doit moult
garder d'un mot que dit saint Bernart, qui dit ainsi: Symia in tecto Rex fatuus sederis in
solio. C'est a dire li roys fols qui se siet en trone est semblables au singe monté sur le toit,
quar ainsi comme le singe en tant que il est monté plus haut de tant apert plus la laideur
et son defaut. Ainsi est il de roy fol et non uertueus hautement assis quar lui defaut en
sont plus cogneu et plus manifeste." The picture shows the body of the king with labels
explaining the meaning of the different parts: "Seneschals baillis et tous iuges,"
"Conseilliers et sages," "Cheualiers," "Marcheans," "Laboureurs de terres." See also Julien
Lepot, "Un miroir au prince enluminé du milieu du xive siècle: l'*Avis aus roys*," unpublished doctoral dissertation, Université d'Orléans, 2014.

201 Léopold Delisle, *Recherches sur la librairie de Charles V*, 2 vols. (Paris, 1907), vol. 2, p. 85,
no. 500.

202 Philippe de Mézières, Chancellor of Cyprus, *Le Songe du vieil pelerin*, ed. G.W. Coopland,
2 vols. (Cambridge, 1969), vol. 2, no. 229.

203 *The De moneta of Nicholas Oresme and English Mint Documents*, ed. and trans. Charles
Johnson (London, 1956), pp. 43–44.

to the analogy between the *res publica* and the human body, while stressing the harmony between the members in the body: but this is to advocate a balanced *res publica ecclesiastica*.[204] Oresme also refers to the *Policraticus* when he translates and comments the passage of the *Politics* on the parts of the city.[205] For instance, he expands on the idea according to which each member of the human body fulfils its own office, as the parts of the political community do, and quotes the letter of Plutarch to Trajan for the definition of the *res publica*. Further on in the text, he again refers to Plutarch – but also to Augustine – in order to sustain his reflections on oversized kingdoms.[206] Developing ideas found in John of Salisbury's work, he sets out the problems found in an unbalanced body: imbalance in the body, which leads to bodily illness, finds its parallel in the excessive wealth of some members of the *res publica*, which Oresme considers as the consequence of "exactions," "mauvais contrats" and "lois mal mises ou mal tenues." Yet altogether these references to the *Policraticus* are not very many; nor do they reflect a significant influence of John of Salisbury's work on Oresme.

In the 14th century, the influence of the *Policraticus* in France seems to have been relatively limited; on the other hand, the decision to translate it certainly reflects the interest of curial circles in John of Salisbury's text.[207] In 1372, the Franciscan Denis Foulechat completed this work, and this vernacular version may have contributed to the diffusion of the *Policraticus* among a new public.[208] The style of Foulechat's translation offers a number of specific features. Repetitions, the systematic use of a concrete adjective for an abstract noun are typical of Foulechat's manner as a translator, and express both a desire for

---

204 Mathieu Caesar, "Prêcher *coram papa Urbano V*. Édition et commentaire d'un sermon de Nicole Oresme," *Revue Mabillon*, n.s. 19 (2008), 191–229, esp. p. 224.

205 Maistre Nicole Oresme, *Le Livre de Politiques d'Aristote*, ed. Albert Douglas Menut (Philadelphia, 1970), p. 209.

206 Ibid., p. 291. Oresme also refers to Augustine, *De civitate Dei* 3.10.

207 Delisle, *Recherches sur la librairie de Charles V*, vol. 2, p. 85, no. 501 (inventory of Gilles Malet, 1373).

208 There are three manuscripts of Foulechat's translation: Paris, BnF fr. 24,287, Paris, Arsenal 2692 (Books 1–6 only) and Paris, Bibliothèque Sainte-Geneviève 1144–1145. Ed. Charles Brucker: Denis Foulechat, *Le Policratique de Jean de Salisbury (1372), Livres I–III; Livre V* (Geneva, 2006); *Le Policraticus de Jean de Salisbury traduit par Denis Foulechat (1372) (manuscrit no 24,287 de la B.N., livre IV* (Nancy, 1985); Denis Foulechat, *Tyrans, princes et prêtres (Jean de Salisbury, Policratique IV et VIII)* (Montreal, 1987); Denis Foulechat, *Éthique chrétienne et philosophies antiques. Le Policratique de Jean de Salisbury, Livres VI et VII* (Geneva, 2013).

clarity and for concrete expression.[209] Foulechat is fully aware of the difficulty of his task and explains at length the techniques he has developed as a translator.[210] In the first prologue to the translation, he stresses the "hautesce du livre," the "tressoutil et ancien latin," as well as the "matiere restrange qui tout mon povoir seurmonte." In the dedicace, he also recalls the magnitude of his task, "la grant oeuvre, qui me seurmontait trop grandement."[211] This would account for the time it took for him to complete his translation,[212] as well as for his desire to revise it.[213] As Charles Brucker has shown, the first ten folios of the manuscript of the Bibliothèque nationale de France include a number of marginal glosses, that clarify the letter of the text, and these may represent Foulechat's attempt to start revising his translation.

The manuscripts of the French translation of the *Policraticus* contain a number of pictures. Iconography was not totally unknown in previous manuscripts. For instance, British Library Royal 12 F VIII, compiled in Rochester before 1202, includes three marginal drawings, which were probably added later on. The drawing on fol. 62 shows Demosthenes; on fol. 73v, there is a figure of a small scribe. On fol. 95, the margins contain the figures of a hanged man and of a woman mourning a dead: this illustrates the famous anecdote of the matron of Ephesus, borrowed by John of Salisbury from Petronius (*Policraticus* 8.11).[214] With the French translation of the *Policraticus*, however, the iconographic programme becomes both more elaborate and coherent. BnF fr. 24 287[215] includes ten miniatures of average size (on 15 lines of text) as well as a small miniature on fol. 5v, which may depict the translator.[216] Only the miniature on fol. 2r, which represents Charles V reading a book, is of a larger dimension; the book held by the king shows the words *Beatus uir qui in sapientia morabitur...*, an echo of a passage from the first prologue of the translator.[217]

---

209   See Charles Brucker in his introduction to his edition of Books 1 to 3 and 5: Foulechat, *Le Policratique de Jean de Salisbury* (1372), *Livres I–III*, pp. 67–69. Also *Livre V*, p. 220.

210   Ibid., pp. 86–87.

211   Ibid., pp. 86 and 250.

212   Ibid., p. 251.

213   Ibid., p. 87; also ibid., p. 250.

214   Ilya Dines has also brought to light two pictures that illustrate passages from the *Policraticus* in MS 22 of Westminster Abbey: a picture illustrating the anecdote of "Andronicus" and the lion in one of the "third-family" bestiaries, and the Wheel of Fortune, next to a passage from the *Policraticus*: "The earliest use of John of Salisbury's *Policraticus*," pp. 113, 117–118.

215   According to Charles Brucker, this may not be the manuscript offered to Charles V, but it is probably quite close to it: Foulechat, *Le Policratique de Jean de Salisbury* (1372), *Livres I–III*, p. 24.

216   For an examination of the miniatures, see ibid., pp. 25–26.

217   Ibid., pp. 25 et 86.

The most complex miniature in this iconographic program is that on fol. 12r, which opens Book 1. It is broken up into four sections: in the left compartment of the top register, a king sits under a canopy, a scepter in his hand, and looks to his left, to the next compartment, where several figures are depicted in front of a basket into which they seem to be depositing books. There are four figures with a halo behind their head, and the head of a fifth one in the background, without a halo, as well as the figure of a bearded king, perhaps a reference to Plato. The caption gives seven names: Jerome, Ambrosius, Augustine, Plato, Aristotle, Gregory the Great, and a mysterious "Salvidie de Tules," perhaps a signature.[218] The two scenes represented in the compartments of the lower register depict the entertainments of the *curiales*, mainly hunting. The whole miniature may refer to the tensions of curial life or simply to the denunciation of curial *mores* by philosophers. It is more difficult to justify the choice of the miniature which opens Book 2, and which seems to represent the storming of a city (fol. 31v). The manuscript of the Bibliothèque Sainte-Geneviève also includes three miniatures; the large painting on fol.1 was added later.

Christine of Pisan may be representative of the new lay readership created by the translation of Foulechat.[219] In the *Livre des fais et bonnes meurs du sage roy Charles V* (1404), she mentions the *Policraticus* among the books translated on the order of Charles V, and she certainly consulted Foulechat's translation.[220] Although her mastery of Latin is still a contested issue, she may nevertheless

---

218 I wish to thank Christophe Grellard for his suggestions concerning the interpretation of the various figures.

219 On the borrowings made from the *Policraticus* by Christine of Pisan, see Elsmann, *Untersuchungen zur Rezeption der Institutio Traiani*, p. 69 sq.; Jeannine Quillet, *Charles V, le roi lettré. Essai sur la pensée politique d'un règne* (Paris, 2002²), p. 225 sq.; Kate Langdon Forhan, *The Political Theory of Christine de Pizan, Women and Gender in the Early Modern World* (Aldershot, 2002), p. 47 sq.; eadem, "Polycracy, Obligation, and Revolt: the Body Politic in John of Salisbury and Christine de Pizan," in Margaret Brabant, ed., *Politics, Gender, and Genre. The Political Thought of Christine de Pizan* (Boulder, 1992), pp. 33–52; Karen Green and Constant J. Mews, eds., *Healing the Body Politic. The Political Thought of Christine de Pizan*, (Turnhout, 2005); Frédérique Lachaud, "'Plutarchus si dit et recorde...' L'influence du *Policraticus* de Jean de Salisbury sur Christine de Pizan et Jean Gerson," in Patrick Gilli and Jacques Paviot, eds., *Hommes, cultures et sociétés à la fin du Moyen Âge. Liber discipulorum en l'honneur de Philippe Contamine* (Paris, 2012), pp. 47–67. On the relationship between Christine of Pisan and Jean Gerson, see Earl Jeffrey Richards, "Christine de Pizan and Jean Gerson: an Intellectual Friendship," in John Campbell and Nadia Margolis, eds., *Christine de Pizan 2000. Studies on Christine de Pizan in Honour of Angus J. Kennedy* (Amsterdam, 2000), pp. 197–208.

220 Christine de Pisan, *Le Livre des fais et bonnes meurs du sage roy Charles V*, ed. Suzanne Solente, 2 vols. (Paris, 1936–40), vol. 2, p. 44.

also have had access to some of the Latin text of the *Policraticus*.[221] In the *Chemin de longue étude* (1402), the *Livre des fais et bonnes meurs* and the *Livre de la paix* (1412–3), she demonstrates knowledge of the *Policraticus*, though in these works, the influence of John of Salisbury's work remains secondary.[222] The *Livre du corps de policie* (1404–7), written for the Dauphin Louis of Guyenne, betrays the influence of the *Dicta et facta mirabilia* of Valerius Maximus, known

221   For instance, in the *Le Chemin de longue étude*, she is closer to the Latin text of the *Policraticus* than to Foulechat's translation: "Plutarchus si dit et recorde/Que ycelle publique concorde/Est un droit corps vivifié,/Du don de Dieu saintifié/Et gouverné par l'atrempance/De raison, par bonne ordenance." (*Le Chemin de longue étude. Édition critique du ms. Harley 4431*, ed. and trans. Andrea Tarnowski (Paris, 2000), ll. 5493–8, p. 412) See *Policraticus* 5.2, ed. Webb, vol. 1, p. 282 and the translation by Foulechat, *Livre V*, p. 271.
222   In the *Chemin de longue étude*, Christine of Pisan makes a superficial use of the analogy between a body and the *res publica*, and the passages she dedicates to combatants refer to Vegetius as well as to *Policraticus* 6: *Le Chemin de longue étude*, ll. 4268 sq., 4453 sq., 5493–514. The *Policraticus* is also used to give more substance to the sections on the wisdom of the prince and the action of the prince in government. Liberality as a princely virtue is illustrated with the anecdote borrowed from *Policraticus* about Titus, who deemed wasted a day spent without any liberality (ibid., ll. 5913–54, pp. 438–440). In the *Livre des fais et bonnes meurs du sage roy Charles V* (1404), the influence of the *Policraticus* is less patent. For instance, Christine mentions the distribution of tasks within society (as a founding act of the law-giving prince), but she does not use the organic metaphor (*Le Livre des fais et bonnes meurs du sage roy Charles V*, vol. 1, pp. 113–114). The influence of the *Policraticus* is also prominent in the *Livre de la Paix*: The "Livre de la Paix" of Christine de Pisan, ed. Charity Cannon Willard (La Haye, 1958). See Elsmann, *Untersuchungen zur Rezeption der Institutio Traiani*, pp. 77–82). In Chapter 15 of the first section, where she deals with the issue of flattery, Christine refers to *Policraticus* 3.4 (ibid., 1.15, p. 86). The picture of Charles V giving justice on the spot, while he is about to go hunting, is an echo of Trajan agreeing to give justice unexpectedly, while he is about to set out on a military expedition (ibid., 2.9, p. 100). The anecdote is mentioned in *Policraticus* 5.8, but it became a commonplace of parenetic literature in the later Middle Ages. See Priscille Aladjidi, "L'empereur Trajan: un modèle imaginaire de la charité royale dans les miroirs des princes de la fin du Moyen Âge," in Anne-Hélène Allirot, Gilles Lecuppre and Lydwine Scordia, eds., *Royautés imaginaires (XIIᵉ–XVIᵉ siècles). Actes du colloque organisé par le Centre de recherche d'histoire sociale et culturelle* (CHSCO) *de l'université de Paris X-Nanterre sous la direction de Colette Beaune et Henri Bresc (26 et 27 septembre 2003)* (Turnhout, 2005), pp. 53–73. Once again, in the *Livre de la Paix*, the metaphor of the "corps de policie" stresses the necessity of a harmonious society under the aegis of the prince. The prince heals equally all members of the *res publica*, in the way a physician heals the whole body (ibid., 3.2, p. 117). Only a united body may fight tyranny successfully (ibid., 3.6, p. 124). Christine also warns her reader against a confusion of functions within the kingdom. In particular, she is hostile to the nomination of common people to governmental offices in towns (ibid., 3.11, pp. 130–131).

to Christine in the glossed translation of Simon of Hesdin and Nicolas of Gonnesse;[223] but here one also finds distinct echoes from the *Policraticus*, as the title itself indicates.[224] Faced with civil dissension, Christine of Pisan's agenda consists in stressing the need for harmony between the different parts of the people of France: in this context, the image of the body politic is particularly apposite, for it binds together disparate elements.[225] As is the case in John of Salisbury's work, reciprocity and mutual obligations between the members enable the body to stay alive.[226] The body's harmony also relies on the virtuous accomplishment of the obligations of each estate: here Christine of Pisan agrees with John of Salisbury, but even more with Thomas Aquinas or Giles of Rome, in her vision of the economic distribution of tasks.[227] The prince ought to make sure that all his subjects fulfil their proper office, without interfering with the others' functions: this idea is at the heart of the *Institutio Traiani*, and Christine expresses it on several occasions.[228] Nevertheless, the use she makes of this is very specific, for her main imperative is to prevent civil discord.[229] Besides, the organic metaphor has lost its original meaning, since she uses it to describe different social categories, instead of offices of government.[230]

---

223 Several sections refer specifically to the text of John of Salisbury. This is the case with the passage on flattery, which Christine discusses by referring directly to the *Policraticus* (*Le Livre du corps de policie* 1.2, ed. Angus J. Kennedy (Paris, 1998), p. 16). Cf. *Policraticus* 3.4. When she deals with the theme of the liberality of the prince, she illustrates her subject (as in the *Chemin de longue étude*) with the example of Titus, like *Policraticus* 3.14 (ibid., 1.4, ed. Kennedy, p. 24).

224 See Elsmann, *Untersuchungen zur Rezeption der Institutio Traiani*, pp. 72–75; Jeannine Quillet, "Le Livre du corps de policie de Christine de Pizan," in *De Charles V à Christine de Pizan* (Paris, 2004), pp. 39–41.

225 See *Le Livre du corps de policie*, p. xxxvi.

226 Ibid., 3.1, p. 91.

227 Ibid., 1.23, p. 40; cf. Thomas Aquinas, *De regno* 4.23; Giles of Rome, *De regimine principium* 4.1.8 and 3.1.5.

228 Ibid., 1.10, pp. 16–17.

229 Ibid., 3.1, p. 92.

230 In addition, when she mentions the "communite du peuple," she essentially refers to the people in towns, "par especial en la cité de Paris et aussi en autres citez," and divides it into clergy, burgesses and merchants, on the one hand, and the common on the other (trade people and "laboureurs") (ibid., 3.4, p. 96). In 3.9, she returns to the description of the feet by reproducing more or less literally John of Salisbury's text (ibid., 3.9, p. 106). Christine illustrates the section on civil strife with a version of the fable of the Belly and the Members. This tale (also found in Philippe de Mézières's work) appears in the *Policraticus*, but this cannot be the source of Christine's version, since the end, as well as the morality of the tale, are different. The glossed translation of Valerius Maximus by

At about the same time Jean Gerson also refered to the *Policraticus* in his sermons and speeches.[231] *Vivat rex* – a sermon on the reform of the kingdom which the chancellor of the University of Paris delivered in the presence of Charles VI on 7 November 1405 – demonstrates the influence of John of Salisbury.[232] It quotes the letter from Plutarch to Trajan.[233] As in Christine's work, the image of the body, with its different members "selon divers estas et officez qui sont ou royaulme," coexists with that of the three estates: yet their definition is different from that given by Christine, since Gerson lists "l'estat de clergie, l'estat de chevalerie et l'estat de bourgoisie."[234] Moreover, this pattern fits into the triple life of the king: bodily, civil and political, spiritual and eternal. In particular, the civil and "mystical" life of the king relies on the unified entity he makes with his subjects, like the head with the members.[235] Gerson uses the organic metaphor in order to enhance the duty of mutual help and reciprocity between the different parts of the organism, against the idea that the king would have no obligation toward his subjects.[236] However, the members ought to keep to their place in the body; in particular, lords should not displace the subjects, nor the subjects usurp the place of lords.[237] Here, the usurpation of another's office, which is a central concern in the thought of John of Salisbury,

---

Simon of Hesdin and Nicolas of Gonnesse is not the source for Christine of Pisan's version either, since in their version the members repent in time: 2.1, Paris, BnF fr. 15,471, fol. 86va (p. 170 of the edition of Paris, 1500). In the *Livre du corps de policie* (3.1, p. 92) the tale ends with the death of the body, in the medieval Aesopian tradition (on this, see Laurence Harf-Lancner, "Les Membres et l'Estomac: la fable et son interprétation politique au Moyen Âge," in Dominique Boutet and Jacques Verger, eds., *Penser le pouvoir au Moyen Âge (VIIIe–XVe siècle). Études d'histoire et de littérature offerts à Françoise Autrand* (Paris, 2000), pp. 111–126, at p. 114). As for the morality of the tale in Christine of Pisan's version, it is a warning to the prince against excessive exactions at the expense of the people, and to the people against disobedience.

231 For the influence of *Policraticus* on Gerson, see Elsmann, *Untersuchungen zur Rezeption der Institutio Traiani*, pp. 232–234.

232 *Vivat rex*, ed. Palémon Glorieux, in Jean Gerson, *Œuvres complètes*, t. 7*, *L'Œuvre française. Sermons et discours (340–398)* (Paris, 1968), no. 398, pp. 1137–185.

233 Ibid., p. 1146.

234 Ibid., p. 1151.

235 The king is indeed "une puissance publique ordonnee pour le salut de tout le commun, ainsi comme de chief descent et despand la vie par tout le corps." The function of kings and princes is not arbitrary; it comes from an initial agreement, a contract, "par commun accort de tous." (ibid., p. 1155).

236 Ibid., p. 1155.

237 Ibid., p. 1156.

appears to be the source of civil strife: what follows can only be the death of the body politic.[238]

In *Vivat rex*, Gerson dedicates a long passage to the tyrant.[239] The tyrant wants his subjects to remain powerless and ignorant and is hostile to the idea of mutual love between them. He oppresses the people by recruiting mercenaries, by levying excessive taxes, "par murtriseurs secrez," he closes schools, forbids assemblies, and encourages civil strife.[240] Having to face a head or a member who is ready to introduce such venom into the body, the other members must do everything in their power to prevent it. Nevertheless, this should not go as far as amputating the sick member: it is best to heal it with sweet medicines and salutary words.[241] In the last resort, the "bons amys et loyaulz subiectez du roy" may act to preserve the health of the king, even if he does not agree to it,[242] but they have to avoid sedition at all costs, since this may be worse than tyranny. Clearly it was not in Gerson's intention to defend tyrannicide: in *Vivat rex*, it is Sedition who justifies the extermination of the "faulz traitrez," of those who are responsible for theft and tyranny.[243] Nevertheless this passage placed Gerson in an awkward position at

---

238   Ibid., p. 1156. The king and the subjects cannot survive long without each other: the four cardinal virtues will achieve this agreement and union, "en samblance des quatre qualitez premieres au corps naturel, moyennant l'operacion divine du saint Esperit qui fait ceste conciliacion ou corps mistique, comme l'influence dez cieulz ou corps naturel." (ibid., p. 1160). There are other reminiscences of the *Policraticus* in the text, for instance in the reflections on flatterers (ibid., pp. 1161–1162). The quotations from Juvenal (satire 3, ll. 104–6 and satire 4, ll. 70–1) are also found, albeit in a slightly different form, in *Policraticus* 3.4. The image of the body recurs in the section on prudence (ibid., pp. 1166–1167). The passage on fortitude includes some considerations that correspond to some sections of the *Institutio Trajani*, for instance on the discipline of combatants, or on the choice of officers of justice (ibid., p. 1175). Like Christine of Pisan, Gerson uses the fable of the Belly and the Members, but this is in order to prescribe a measured taxation of populations (ibid., pp. 1178–1179).

239   Ibid., p. 1158.

240   This is a reference to Aristotle, *Politics* 5.11.

241   Ibid., p. 1159. Kings and princes must listen to those who know how to prevent the venom of tyranny from entering the body, even if this means limiting their own power (ibid., p. 1159).

242   Ibid., p. 1147.

243   *Vivat rex*, pp. 1153–1154. Nowhere does Gerson allude, in *Vivat Rex*, to the passage from *Policraticus* 3.15 where John of Salisbury comments Cicero on tyrants, whom it is allowed to flatter since it is allowed to kill them.

the Council of Constance,[244] where Martin Porrée accused him of being in favour of killing the tyrant.[245]

Indeed, in the course of the debates following the murder of Louis of Orléans (23 November 1407), the sections of the *Policraticus* dedicated to tyrannicide had attracted much attention.[246] In his first *Justification du duc de Bourgogne* delivered in the king's presence on 8 March 1408, the Parisian master Jean Petit defined the crime of royal lese-majesty before defending the assassination of the "tyrant."[247] He then invoked a number of authorities, including John of Salisbury, in order to prove his case,[248] though here he did not go further in his use of the *Policraticus*. Besides, he defined tyrannicide narrowly, as the execution of the "tyrant" who wants to usurp power, and is therefore guilty of

---

244   On this point, see Mario Turchetti, *Tyrannie et tyrannicide de l'Antiquité à nos jours* (Paris, 2001), p. 325.

245   Jean Gerson, *Œuvres complètes*, ed. Palémon Glorieux, t. 10, *L'Œuvre polémique (492–530)* (Paris, 1973), no. 520a, p. 220: "Prima assertio. Non est fere ita modicus si vellet exponere vitam suam pro tollendo vitam tyranni, qui non possit invenire modum et viam ipsum interficiendi et ab eo liberare. [In tractatu qui incipit: Vivat rex]. Videtur erronea, sapere haeresim, quia est propositio multum propinqua vel eadem huic propositioni: Quilibet tyrannus, etc. Vergit etiam in subversionem totius reipublicae et uniuscujusque regis aut principis. Dat viam et licentiam ad plura alia." The reply of Gerson is in the *Summaria responsio*: "Haec propositio vera est in forma, sicut et aliae septem per episcopum Attrebatensem male tractae pro suo proposito, in quibus honorifica contumelia auctorem afficit, juxta verbum Hieronymi de Rufino. Unde propositio haec clare loquitur de posse facti, non juris; sicut sanctus Thomas scribit similiter libro I° de regimine principum, cap. xi, qui non favet huic errori: Quilibet tyrannus, etc." (ibid., no. 521, p. 226).

246   The debate is analysed in Alfred Coville, *Jean Petit. La question du tyrannicide au commencement du XVᵉ siècle* (Paris, 1932); see also Bernard Guenée, *Un Meurtre, une société. L'assassinat du duc d'Orléans, 23 novembre 1407* (Paris, 1992), pp. 232–264 and Turchetti, *Tyrannie et tyrannicide*, pp. 319–332. Part of the dossier is edited in Gerson, *Œuvres complètes*, t. 10, but some of the texts relating to the dispute remain unpublished.

247   The first *Justification* of Jean Petit is reproduced in Enguerran de Monstrelet, *La Chronique...en deux livres...1400–1444*, ed. Louis Douët-d'Arcq (Paris, 1857), vol. 1, pp. 177–244, here p. 206. It is a version different from the one that circulated in independent manuscripts (Coville, *Jean Petit*, p. 133 sq).

248   "La seconde auctorité si est *Salberiensis sacre theologie eximii doctoris, in libro suo Policrat, libro II, c. xv, sic dicentis: Amico adulari non licet, sed aurem tiranni mulcere licitum est*, etc. C'est à dire il n'est licite à nullui de flater son ami, mais il est licite de adenter et endormir par belles paroles les oreilles du tirant. Car puisqu'il est licite d'occire ledit tirant, il est licite de le flater et blander par belles paroles et signes." (Jean Petit, *Justification*, pp. 206–207). The passage to which Jean Petit alludes is in fact *Policraticus* 3.15, ed. Webb, vol. 1, p. 232.

lese-majesty. On 14 September 1408, Thomas du Bourg, abbot of Cerisy, pronounced a discourse where he set out to refute Jean Petit's arguments. Petit
replied in the following years with some new *Justifications*; shortly before his
death, he went back to this matter in his *Traité contre les édifieurs de sépulcres*. It
was against Jean Petit that Jean Gerson took up again the issue of tyrannicide in
Rex in sempiternum uiue.[249] In this speech, delivered on 4 September 1413, he vio-
lently attacks the theses of Jean Petit, in the shape of assertions which he refutes
one by one. He then demonstrates the significance of oaths and alliances: the execution of the tyrant is illicit if one has contracted with him an agreement attested
by oaths. Gerson does not mention the fact that John of Salisbury also considered
the oath as a major obstacle to tyrannicide, but he very probably knew the passage
of the *Policraticus* where this major *caueat* appears.[250] As Jacques Verger has noted,
the *Policraticus* was not listed among the books of the Dauphin's ideal library in the
Tractatus de considerationibus quas debet habere princeps that Gerson wrote for
the preceptor of Louis of Guyenne or of Dauphin Charles.[251] It may be speculated
that it was precisely the issue of tyrannicide that led Gerson to leave out John of
Salisbury's treatise from the list of books of political philosophy he recommended
for the heir to the throne.

Paradoxically, the influence of the *Policraticus* is much more perceptible in
the other parts of *Rex in sempiternum uiue*. In the first section, where Gerson
states that the king ought to be concerned with the common good, he quotes
Prov. 20:8, the king who sits on the throne of judgment puts all evil to flight by his
look (*rex qui sedet in solio iudicii dissipat omne malum intuitu suo*), also in
Policraticus 4.11. Nabuchodonosor's dream echoes *Policraticus* 6.27, but the treatment of this theme is different enough to suggest that Gerson resorted to other
sources[252]; however, it does introduce the image of the body politic drawn from
the *Policraticus*. What follows is a curious mixture of several metaphors – the

---

249 *Rex in sempiternum vive*, in Gerson, *Œuvres complètes*, ed. Palémon Glorieux, t. 7*, *L'Œuvre
française*, no. 389, pp. 1005–1030. On 9 June 1414, Jean Gerson reiterated his attacks in a
council gathered in Paris, with a *Réprobation* of the nine assertions drawn from Jean
Petit's *Justification*.

250 *Policraticus* 8.20, ed. Webb, vol.2, pp. 377–378.

251 Jacques Verger, "*Ad prefulgidum sapience culmen prolem regis inclitam provehere*.
L'initiation des dauphins de France à la sagesse politique selon Jean Gerson," in *Penser le
pouvoir au Moyen Âge* (*VIIIe–XVe siècle*), pp. 427–440, esp. p. 436. This absence is all the
more notable since Augustine's *City of God*, the political works of Aristotle and the treatise of Giles of Rome are listed by Gerson.

252 *Rex in sempiternum vive*, p. 1012. Gerson then unravels the different meanings of the
vision, referring to Richard of Saint-Victor for the tropological sense. cf. *Policraticus* 6.27,
ed. Webb, vol. 2, p. 81.

human body, the statue and the three estates. This leads Gerson to distinguish
between four parts in the kingdom: the king, knights, clergy and burgesses.[253]
The image of the body politic strengthens the idea that the head of the *res publica*
ought not to favour one member at the expense of the others,[254] and that the
upper members should help the popular estate. The king has to make sure that
all his subjects fulfil their office under him, without allowing for a confusion of
functions which would be detrimental to the good health of the *res publica*.[255]
This emerges again when Gerson resorts to the image of the mystical body of the
res publica.[256] Finally, several passages of *Rex in sempiternum uiue* deal with the
functions and duties of combatants, drawing on *Policraticus* 6.[257]

Echoes of the *Policraticus* may also be seen in the work of Alain Chartier.
In his *Quadrilogue invectif* (1422), Chartier uses the image of the "corps de policie" when he makes the people speak: but this is the body of a madman, who
tears apart his own members.[258] Chartier also reuses, albeit unevenly, the

---

253   Ibid., p. 1013.

254   Ibid., pp. 1016–1017. The considerations on the imperative of impartiality and justice are
      quite similar to what John of Salisbury writes on this matter, but it is not possible to estab-
      lish a direct link between the two texts. For Gerson, the transfer of the kingdom may hap-
      pen if the king does not judge justly, for instance by showing his favour to some persons
      instead of punishing them, "comme le dit le Sage: regnum de gente in gentem transfertur
      propter injustitiam" (ibid., p. 1017). *Policraticus* 4.11 comments on the same passage
      (ed. Webb, vol. 1, p. 270).

255   Here Jean Gerson quotes 1 Cor. 12:23, but this passage also recalls *Policraticus* 5.2 and the
      end of *Policraticus* 6.20, where John of Salisbury underlines the necessary reciprocity
      between the upper members and the feet (ibid., p. 1029).

256   Ibid., p. 1030.

257   The estate of knighthood ought to receive "loyer et gages publics" in order to defend the
      king and kingdom, but they have to be content with that. Gerson is here quite close to
      Policraticus 6.10 (ed. Webb, vol. 2, p. 25). And the knights ought to obey the king above
      their direct lord, which Gerson illustrates with a quotation from Terence. This also
      appears in *Policraticus* 8.3: but where Gerson uses the quotation in order to stress the
      importance of experience, John of Salisbury mocks the braggart soldier who prepares
      himself for the combat in the most splendid way, only to flee at the crucial moment.

258   Alain Chartier, *Le Quadrilogue invectif*, ed. Eugénie Droz (Paris, 1950²), pp. 23–24. This is
      probably a reference to the fable of the Belly and the Members, quoted by Menenius
      Agripa when he was trying to convince the people of Rome not to rise against the Senate.
      According to legend this episode would then have led to the institution of the Tribunes of
      the people. See Harf-Lancner, "Les Membres et l'Estomac." At several points in his text,
      Alain Chartier seems close to the *Policraticus*, as when he deals with princely virtues or
      when he recalls the importance of the discipline for combatants: but this ressemblance is
      relatively general.

passages John of Salisbury dedicates to the necessary wisdom of the prince. For instance in Prose 9 of the *Livre de l'Espérance* (c. 1429–30),[259] he deals with the topic of princely knowledge. The ignorant prince is similar to a crowned ass, "roy sans lettres est ung asne couronné." The ruler, who dominates other men, must also be their superior by his knowledge. Yet Chartier sustains this assertion not so much with passages from the *Policraticus* as with the authority of Plato and the figures of Solomon, Avicenna (the "prince d'Aboaly," for Abou-Ali), Averroes (transformed into one of the dukes of Greece), Caesar, Ptolemy king of Egypt, as well as several legislators and founders of principalities.[260]

In fact, the third writer to make extensive use of the *Policraticus* in 15th-century France was Jean Juvénal des Ursins.[261] The influence of John of Salisbury's treatise on his work is very noticeable, and in *Verba mea* he gives him the title of "venerable doctor." It also undergoes a transformation, as in Christine of Pisan's, and Jean Gerson's works.[262] In *Audite celi* (1435), Jean Juvénal quotes *Policraticus* 6.17 about Julius Caesar, who forbade his men to attack temples, so that he was always victorious in his military expeditions, and whose downfall was precipitated by the destruction of the temple of Delphi. In the original, however, the anecdote is not about Caesar, but about Brennus: this discrepancy suggests that Jean Juvénal may not have had direct access to the text of John of Salisbury when he was writing this passage.[263] In *Loquar in tribulacione* (1440), he occasionally follows the *Policraticus*, for instance when dealing with "Sapience."[264] He also draws his inspiration from John of Salisbury for the passage on Caesar and Alexander, although he attributes

---

259   Alain Chartier, *Le Livre de l'Espérance*, ed. François Rouy (Paris, 1989).

260   Ibid., pp. 72–74.

261   On the career and political writings of the archbishop of Reims, see Peter Lewis, "Jean Juvenal des Ursins and the Common Literary Attitude towards Tyranny in Fifteenth-Century France," *Medium aevum* 34 (1965), 103–121 and Albert Rigaudière, "Jean Juvénal des Ursins, précurseur de l'absolutisme," in *Absolutismus, ein unersetzliches ForschungsKonzept? Eine deutsch-französische Bilanz* (2007), 53–104, esp. p. 57 and note 10 for a summary of Jean Juvénal's writings.

262   Jean Juvénal des Ursins, *Écrits politiques*, ed. Peter Lewis, 2 vols. (Paris, 1978–85), vol. 2, p. 397. Jean Juvénal does not seem to know the name of John of Salisbury. He calls him several times "Pollicraticon" (for instance *Verba mea*, ibid., pp. 400.401), which suggests he did not have access to the translation by Foulechat, who entertained no doubt about the identity of John of Salisbury.

263   Ibid., vol. 1, pp. 245–246.

264   Ibid., vol. 1, pp. 331–332, which repeats aproximately the quotation from Aulus Gellius, *Noctes Atticae* 13.8.3, which is also in *Policraticus* 4.6.

this to Caecilius Balbus.[265] The section on military discipline claims to be
inspired by Vegetius, but in reality it is close to *Policraticus* 6.[266] But Vegetius as
well as John of Salisbury could be the source for the section on the combatants'
oath.[267] The passages on the king who is the soul (instead of the head) of the
body of the *res publica*, and on the illnesses that affect that body, distantly
recall the *Institutio Traiani*, albeit with some modifications and without the
Policraticus being quoted.[268] In his *Exortation faite au roy* (1458) written to ask
for royal grace for the duke of Alençon, Jean Juvénal purports to reproduce an
anecdote "que j'ay veue en Pollicraticon" about Philip of Macedonia. Here, he
deforms the meaning of his source considerably. Where John of Salisbury compared Philip's vices and virtues with Alexander's, stating that Alexander was
greater than his father – both in his virtues and in his vices – Jean Juvénal
writes that Philip had more "corpulence...prudence, sens et courage" than his
son, and that whatever Alexander did "fut par le conseil des vieulx chevaliers et
chefz de guerre qui avoient esté en la compaignie du père."[269]

It is in the epistle *Verba mea auribus percipe, domine* (1452 or before) that
Jean Juvénal is the closest to the *Policraticus*, which he reproduces at length.
This complex treatise, built around a theme drawn from Ps. 5: 2–3, examines all
aspects of the kingdom's government. In the first part (*Verba mea auribus percipe*), Jean Juvénal stresses the importance of thanking God for one's victories,
in the tradition of parenetic literature. In the second part (*Intellige clamorem
meum*), he offers a number of general observations on royal power. These are
divided into three sections: royal majesty, the king and war, and finally the relationship between the king and the law. A short exhortation concludes the work.
The influence of the *Policraticus* first surfaces in the section where the author
defines majesty: the place of the prince is determined in relation to the body
politic in a paraphrase of *Policraticus* 5.2.[270] Jean Juvénal then literally reproduces

---

265 Ibid., after *Policraticus* 3.14 (ed. Webb, vol. 1, p. 231). "Celcilius Balbus" occurs again in *A, A,
     A, nescio loqui* (written after 3 August 1445), but in fact Jean Juvénal seems to refer to
     Policraticus 3.14 (*Écrits politiques*, vol. 1, p. 476).
266 Ibid., vol. 1, pp. 408–409, after *Policraticus* 6.14 (ed. Webb, vol. 2, p. 37). There is no match-
     ing passage in Vegetius.
267 Ibid., vol. 1, pp. 409–410 (cf. *Policraticus* 6.7 and Vegetius, *De re militari* 2.5).
268 Ibid., vol. 1, p. 376. This passage is commented by Rigaudière, "Jean Juvénal des Ursins,
     précurseur de l'absolutisme," pp. 428–430.
269 Ibid., vol. 2, p. 411, after *Policraticus* 5.12 (ed. Webb, vol. 1, p. 336).
270 However, unlike the metaphor of the body as it is developed in the *Policraticus*, here the
     king or prince is the soul of the *res publica* (ibid., vol. 2, p. 203). Further on, Jean Juvénal
     explains to the king that he is the soul of the *res publica*, but also the head of the body
     politic (p. 272).

some passages from the *Policraticus* in order to flesh out his discussion of the necessary education of the prince.[271] Again, he invokes the authority of John of Salisbury in the section on military officers, and when discussing the exemplary role of the king in matters of courage.[272] The passages on chivalry are inspired by Vegetius and above all by *Policraticus* 6.[273]

Jean Juvénal also enters into a discussion of tyranny and of the relationship between the prince and the law. He reminds the king that he is the soul of the *res publica*, and that the soul has never been wont to destroy the body, a statement supported by a warning against the bad use of taxes. Nevertheless, the king is also the head of the body: Jean Juvénal sets his own text in the steps of John of Salisbury when he considers as tyrannical the actions of a head that would destroy the heart, the hands and the feet. The head would then have to perish. But nowadays, Jean Juvénal writes, the hands, the feet and the rest of the body are so sick that it would be difficult to believe that the king, who is the head, does not feel any pain.[274] Jean Juvénal also picks up passages from the beginning of *Policraticus* 4 where John of Salisbury gives his definition of the prince as public power and image of divine majesty: these Jean Juvénal translates, and then appeals to the king to consider the fate of his subjects.[275]

He also reproduces John of Salisbury's observations on the relationship between the prince and the law, and on the cooperation of the head and the members from *Policraticus* 5. He relies in particular on *Policraticus* 5.12 and 8.17:[276] he quotes the text but does not translate it, and is happy to comment on it in a summary way, with observations on good government through the laws. In the passages on counsel and on the exercise of justice, he repeats the *Policraticus*, but here again he is content to alternate Latin quotations from John of Salisbury's text and his personal reflections.[277] However, the way he translates the ambiguous statement from *Policraticus* 4.1, *hic legi obtemperat et*

---

271 Ibid., vol. 2, p. 205; cf. *Policraticus* 4.6, ed. Webb, vol. 1, p. 256.

272 Ibid., vol. 2, p. 226–227; cf. *Policraticus* 4.4, ed. Webb, vol. 1, p. 244.

273 Ibid., vol. 2, p. 240 sq.

274 Ibid., vol. 2, p. 272. For an examination of the position of Jean Juvénal des Ursins on kingship, see Rigaudière, "Jean Juvénal des Ursins, précurseur de l'absolutisme," p. 69.

275 Ibid., vol. 2, p. 273.

276 Ibid., vol. 2, pp. 298–299.

277 Ibid., vol. 2, pp. 330–333 (after *Policraticus* 5.9) and 337–340 (after *Policraticus* 5.11). Some quotations are erroneous: for instance when he writes "et treuve recité en Pollicraticon *quod sine legibus policia regulam nescit, et Romanis suis legibus suam policiam sublimarunt,* sans loys la chose publique ne scet tenir rigle et les Rommains par faisant loys et les garder ont sublimé et exaussé la chose publique" (ibid., vol. 2, p. 284). This sentence is not in *Policraticus*.

eius arbitrio populum regit cuius se credit ministrum, by "est ung vray prince celluy qui obtempere a la loy dont il est ministre et y gouverne son peuple," suggests he paid some particular attention to this passage. His translation tallies with that of Denis Foulechat, although it does not seem that Jean Juvénal had read this work.[278]

One striking feature of Jean Juvénal's use of the *Policraticus* is the awareness he demonstrates of its historical setting. He does not hesitate to situate the *Policraticus* and the *exempla* it contains in a bygone age. For instance, when he discusses oath-taking, Jean Juvénal explains that nowadays there is no proper military oath, but some kind of equivalent.[279] The correlation of this historical awareness is the tendency of Jean Juvénal to bring the *Policraticus* up to date by illustrating it with contemporary examples. *Policraticus* 4.1 on the relationship between the head and the members in the body politic leads him to reflect on contemporary politics, for instance the convocation of estates, taxes and sumptuary laws.[280] As with Christine of Pisan and Jean Gerson, the image of the body politic overlaps awkwardly that of the estates.[281] When he considers tyranny, Jean Juvénal stresses that Charles VII is not a tyrant, and that what he writes is merely a warning against bad advice.[282] He adds that the *Policraticus* always refrained from associating kings and tyrants.[283] He then attacks those who allow the prince to do what he wants, and distinguishes the will of the prince from that of the tyrant. Here the *Policraticus* leads him to warn the prince who is unreasonable in the exercise of his will against the consequences of his actions: the repercussions of the punishment of Adam and Eve are still being felt, he writes, since the prince who does not obey the laws when he can, cannot obey them when he wants.[284]

---

278   Ibid., vol. 2, p. 275. On this point, see esp. Yves Sassier, "Le prince, ministre de la loi? (Jean de Salisbury, Policraticus IV, 1–2)," in Hervé Oudart, Jean-Michel Picquard et Joëlle Quaghebeur, eds., *Le Prince, son peuple et le bien commun, de l'Antiquité tardive à la fin du Moyen Âge* (Rennes, 2013), pp. 125–144. This is Foulechat's version, Paris, BnF fr. 24,287, fol. 99rb: "Donques en ce est la seule ou la Greigneur difference entre le prince et le tyrant que le prince obeist a la loy et gouverne le pueple par la franchise de la loy dont il cuide et croist qu'il soit ministre. . ."

279   Jean Juvénal des Ursins, *Écrits politiques*, vol. 2, p. 244. In this section Jean Juvénal summons other authorities: Letter 94 of Peter of Blois and the *De laude novae militiae* of Bernard of Clairvaux. Rather curiously, he confuses this text with that of the *Policraticus* when he attacks the ostentation of knights. Ibid., vol. 2, pp. 248–9 (cf. *De laude novae militiae* 2.3).

280   Ibid., vol. 2, p. 276.

281   Once again the image of the body is borrowed from the *Policraticus* in order to promote the virtue of clemency (ibid., vol. 2, p. 307, after *Policraticus* 4.8).

282   Ibid., vol. 2, p. 299.

283   Ibid., vol. 2, p. 299.

284   Ibid., vol. 2, p. 300–1 (after *Policraticus* 8.17).

The last section of *Verba mea*, which deals with the relationship between temporal power and the Church, also relies heavily on the *Policraticus*, to the point that Jean Juvénal's own text is often mere paraphrase. Here and there, however, he seems to wonder about the position of John of Salisbury. For instance, he reproduces the beginning of the conversation between Adrian IV and John of Salisbury about the evils of the Church (*Policraticus* 6.24): he does not translate this passage, where John voices some sharp criticism of the Roman Church, and adds in veiled terms that things can only have degenerated since the time of John of Salisbury.[285] Nevertheless, he seems to adopt a more nuanced point of view when he explains that the criticisms addressed to tyrannical prelates were probably justified at the time of the *Policraticus*: but in our time, he writes, there are many prelates (including him presumably), who fulfil their office with dignity.[286] Besides, he follows the *Policraticus* when asserting that "l'excercice de la jurisdiction temporelle voire criminelle despend de l'esglise."[287]

In the cases of Christine of Pisan, Jean Gerson, and Jean Juvénal des Ursins, it was the contemporary political and then military crisis that led them to look for political and ethical lessons in the *Policraticus*. In particular, the teachings of John of Salisbury on the necessary coordination of the different members of the body politic gave a moral imperative to their political lesson. The image of the body politic was by then part of the common political terminology, but going back to the text of the *Policraticus* enabled them to flesh out their argument and to articulate it with the teachings of Roman history. What is quite remarkable in their approach to John of Salisbury's work is that they nevertheless realised that it was a text written in the context of a bygone age, and that not all of its aspects had to be taken literally.

---

285   Ibid., vol. 2, p. 389.

286   Ibid., vol. 2, p. 396. Further on, when dealing with the habits of prelates who haunt princely courts, Jean Juvénal states that his model (*Policraticus* 8.17) belongs to remote times: "Je ne veulx pas maintenir que, supposé que du temps de Pollicraticon les manieres de faire dessusdictes eussent lieu, que de present ilz se facent." (ibid., vol.2, pp. 400–1). Writing on *Policraticus* 8.17, where John pretends that he does not wish to criticize the legates of the pope and the Roman Church, Jean Juvénal notes that John of Salisbury seems to mean the opposite of what he writes: "toutevoye Policraticon dit au lieu dessus recité, par ung langage comme par manière qui voulsist dire le contraire, Ecclesiam Romanam..." (ibid., vol. 2, p. 398 about *Policraticus* 8.17).

287   Ibid., vol. 2, p. 358; cf. *Policraticus* 4.3, ed. Webb, vol. 1, p. 239. Also ibid., vol. 2, p. 359. By contrast, in Christine of Pisan's work, the order between temporal and spiritual power is the opposite of John of Salisbury's. For instance, the king may correct clerics (*Le Livre du corps de policie* 1.7, p. 11).

Conclusion

In the course of the three and a half centuries that followed the publication of the *Policraticus*, the way it was read, and borrowed from, underwent a number of transformations. While in the 13th century, the trend was to abbreviate and tone down the text, the borrowings made from the *Policraticus* in the later Middle Ages were closer to the original text; at the same time, interrogations about its meaning became more vocal.

Throughout the period most readers of the *Policraticus* express their admiration for the style of John of Salisbury, his wide learning, the elevation of his views.[288] This does not mean however that the *Policraticus* set a trend. There does not seem to have been any real effort to imitate its style. Besides, some central topics of the work were disregarded early on, sometimes to be taken up again later. This was for the instance the case with the criticism leveled by John of Salisbury against the *curiales*: these became secondary in the 13th century. It was only in the early modern period that this topic underwent a renewal, as suggested by the title of the translation of the *Policraticus* by François Eudes de Mézeray in 1639.[289] However, the *Policraticus* was used as a guide, without any real discontinuity, on the issue of the role of combatants in society. It is rare that a writer who knows the *Policraticus* does not quote it at some length, when he deals with combatants, in conjunction with Valerius Maximus, Vegetius and Frontinus.

At an early date, some of the themes and formulations of the *Policraticus* seem to have been present in the common stock of political vocabulary and thought. Was this the reflection of an early diffusion of this text? In fact, John of Salisbury may simply have voiced the concerns of his contemporaries and reproduced their debates, as well as expressing some personal views. Moreover, some topics of the *Policraticus* have parallels in other traditions, whether oral or written, so that it is sometimes difficult to delineate precisely its influence: this is for instance the case with topics such as the wisdom of the prince, or the relationship between the prince and the law. Most authors agree on the fact that the prince is the incarnation of the law, and that he ought to subject his

---

288 This is notably the case with Denis Foulechat, *Le Policratique de Jean de Salisbury* (1372), *Livres I–III*, pp. 86–87.

289 Moreover, his *Vanitez de la cour* includes only the first six books of the *Policraticus*. In the 1560s, Gabriel de Collanges translated the *Policraticus* into French, but this work seems to be lost. On these translations, see Nicolas de Araujo, "Une traduction oubliée du *Policraticus* de Jean de Salisbury par François Eudes de Mézeray (1639)," *Bibliothèque de l'École des Chartes* 164 (2006), 581–594 and Cullière, "Les Vanitez de la cour, de Mézeray (1639)."

own will to the laws. If one quotes the *Policraticus* on this issue, it is often as one authority only in a myriad of texts.

The contribution of the *Policraticus* is more distinctive in its discussion of tyranny, although the reading of Cicero for instance is at the origin of other filiations. Besides, many writers are aware of the ambiguous nature of the assertions of John of Salisbury on this point. It is the case, as has been seen above, with Coluccio Salutati. Some French authors of the 15th-century know the section of the *Policraticus* on tyrannicide, but they never apply it to the king. For Jean de Terrevermeille, as for Jean Gerson, any resistance to the king, who is the head of the mystical body of the kingdom, is proscribed, even sacrilegious.[290]

The influence of the metaphor of the body politic, which is one of the main elements of the *Institutio Traiani*, is also a matter for discussion. The first readers of John of Salisbury did not seem to have paid much attention to this. But from Helinand of Froidmont onwards the organic metaphor dominated borrowings made from the *Policraticus*. This raises a number of issues. The first is the adaptation of this metaphor in ways that are sometimes very distant from the text of John of Salisbury. The various organs often become interchangeable: in particular, the prince sometimes takes the place of the soul or the heart, instead of the head.[291] Nevertheless, whatever the modifications to the scheme, the ideas of solidarity and harmony within the body always remained. While for John of Salisbury, however, this concerned mainly (to the exception of the feet) administrative and governmental offices, and the exercise of power in a wide sense, including military service, it often became, with his readers, a grid for analysing society as a whole, overlapping the notion of order. Besides, much more so than John of Salisbury, they usually tended to place the whole of the body under the aegis of the prince: clearly, the metaphor contributed to strengthen monarchical authority.

The place of clerics in the body politic is another issue. The *Policraticus* contains several chapters on the soul of the body and on the reverence due to clerics, but some writers felt necessary to expand on this: an extreme case is John of Wales, who dedicated to the ecclesiastical body a whole part of his

---

290   Lewis, "Jean Juvenal des Ursins and the Common Literary Attitude," pp. 106, 109, 114, 121.

291   In the *Livre des trois âges* of Pierre Choisnet, for instance, the prince holds the place of the heart, not that of the head: "...et qu'est corps politique,/Et comme on peult icellui contempler/Par corps d'omme qui bien y veult penser,/Et que le roy est le cuer du dit corps/Politique, duquel par bons accors/Vie et vertu aux autres membres vient,/Parce que Dieu son cuer en sa main tient." (Pierre Choinet, *Le Livre des trois âges. Fac-similé du manuscrit Smith-Lesouëf 70 (Paris, Bibliothèque nationale de France)*, critical ed. Lydwine Scordia (Mont-Saint-Aignan, 2009), p. 164, ll. 79–85). Also ibid., p. 178 sq., l. 428.

Communiloquium, thereby leaving the civil body soulless. By contrast, in *Rex pacificus*, the pope holds the place of the head, the prince that of the heart; the two jurisdictions are separated, but the author of this tract seems to have defended the superiority of the heart over the head.[292]

A third issue arises from the very nature of the organic metaphor. In the *Policraticus* this was mainly a rhetorical device that John of Salisbury used in order to convince his readers to place common good before private good.[293] But in some of the works inspired by this metaphor the body politic became an autonomous entity. The image of the mystical body, borrowed from ecclesiological thought, strengthened this interpretation of the organic metaphor, as in the *Tractatus* (1419) of Jean of Terrevermeille.[294] Another series of difficulties concerns the existence of the organic metaphor within a complex intellectual tradition, which was ancient, transmitted in various ways, and reactivated according to context: the presence of the organic metaphor in a text does not necessarily mean that it is a direct quotation from the *Policraticus*. Even when John of Salisbury's text is quoted, it may be only in order to support a general assertion. The influence of Aristotelian texts – especially *Politics* 5.3.6 – also led to a significant transformation of the metaphor of the body politic. The natural analogy, which underlies many political texts, encouraged resorting to the organic metaphor. This demonstrates for instance the fundamental and inevitable nature of the kingdom's unity, which is anchored in stability, and in obedience to the king.[295]

In the later Middle Ages, and beyond,[296] the organic metaphor was a commonplace of political discourse: this does not necessarily imply that the *Policraticus*'s influence was systematically at work. The speech pronounced in October 1326 by Adam Orleton, bishop of Hereford, in favour of Queen Isabella, refers for instance to the fatal exercise of power by Edward II by discussing the

---

292   *Quaestio de potestate papae (Rex pacificus)/An Enquiry into the Power of the Pope. A Critical Edition and Translation*, ed. R.W. Dyson (New York, 1999), pp. 21–25.

293   This position is defended in Frédérique Lachaud, "Corps du prince, corps de la *res publica*: écriture métaphorique et construction politique dans le *Policraticus* de Jean de Salisbury," in *Le Corps du prince*, Micrologus. *Nature, Sciences and Medieval Societies* 22 (2014), 171–199.

294   Jean de Terrevermeille, *Contra rebelles suorum regum* (ed. Lyon, 1526), esp. the second treatise (fol. 48 sq); see Jacques Krynen, "Naturel, essai sur l'argument de la nature dans la pensée politique à la fin du Moyen Âge," *Journal des Savants* (1982), 169–190, esp. p. 180.

295   Krynen, "Naturel, essai sur l'argument de la nature," pp. 172, 174–175.

296   In particular in Jean Bodin, *Les six Livres de la République, un abrégé du texte de l'édition de Paris de 1583*, ed. Gérard Mairet (Paris, 1993), pp. 371–372.

theme of the "head that is hurting me."[297] Bishop Grandisson used the metaphor in a petition dating from early 1337.[298] The image is also recurrent in English parliamentary texts, in particular in the opening sermons of parliaments. For instance, the opening speech of the chancellor in January 1377 refers to the head/prince and to the members/subjects.[299] The metaphor occurs again in the opening speech of the parliament of January 1404, in order to support the call for a fiscal aid.[300] In 1407, in a sermon of the archbishop of Canterbury entitled "*Regem honorificate*," the argument of necessity was invoked, in order to ask for a fiscal aid, and this was reinforced by the image of the political body.[301] In 1431, as a justification for summoning parliament, the opening sermon of master William Lynwood underlined the foundations of government, from the theme "the throne of his kingdom will be established" (1 Chron. 22:10), drawing on the metaphor of the body politic, before deploring the factors that undermined the unity of the kingdom.[302]

Studies undertaken since the articles of Walter Ullmann and Amnon Linder have enlarged our knowledge of the diffusion of the *Policraticus*. Nevertheless, many questions remain unanswered, notably because some aspects of medieval political literature are relatively little known. This is in particular the case with the production of political texts in England: if the judgement delivered by historians on the reception of the *Policraticus* in England from the early 13th century is rather negative, it may also reflect the fact that some sources need exploring more in depth.[303] However, one may safely conclude that the multifarious nature of the reception of the *Policraticus* is indeed a striking feature of

---

297 *Chronicon Galfridi le Baker de Swynebroke*, ed. Edward Maunde Thompson (Oxford, 1889), p. 23 (after 2 Kings 4:19).

298 *The Register of John de Grandisson, Bishop of Exeter*, ed. F.C. Hingeston-Randolph, 3 vols. (London, 1894–9), vol. 2, p. 840.

299 *The Parliament Rolls of Medieval England, 1275–1504*, ed. Chris Given-Wilson, 16 vols. (Woodbridge, 2005), vol. 5, *Edward III, 1351–1377*, p. 396, no. 8 (parliament of January 1377).

300 Ibid., vol. 8, *Henry IV, 1399–1413*, p. 227 (parliament of January 1404).

301 Ibid., vol. 8, *Henry IV, 1399–1413*, p. 420, no. 6 (parliament of October 1407).

302 Ibid., vol. 10, *Henry VI 1422–1431*, p. 444, no. 2. The kingdom needs to be sustained by three virtues: union and unity, peace and tranquillity, justice and equity. For the virtue of union and unity, there is a threefold union. The first is collective, the second is similar to the connection between the members in a human body, the third is created by consent: this is found in the mystical body.

303 On this point see the remarks of Ilya Dines, "The earliest use of John of Salisbury's *Policraticus*," p. 115, who suggests that a close analysis of the manuscripts originating from Lincoln Cathedral in the late 12th and early 13th century may yield more information about the circulation of the *Policraticus* in England.

its posterity, as well as a reflection of its polysemous nature. Yet if John of Salisbury's discussions remained relevant during the whole period under examination, it may be because the conceptual framework of political thinking on power did not alter radically: the same vision of the relationship between power and law, as well as the exercise of virtues by the prince, dominated political reflection until the end of Middle Ages.

Sources and Bibliography

Primary Sources

Editions of the Works of John of Salisbury

NB: the whole work of John of Salisbury is printed in the *Patrologia Latina*, vol. 190.

John of Salisbury's Entheticus de dogmate philosophorum, Critical Text with English Introduction and Notes, ed. D.J. Sheerin, PhD Diss. (University of North Carolina, 1969).

"The *Entheticus* of John of Salisbury, a Critical Text," ed. R.E. Pepin, *Traditio* 31 (1975): 127–193.

Entheticus maior et minor, ed. and tr. J. van Laarhoven, 3 vols. (Leiden, 1987).

Historia pontificalis, ed. and tr. M. Chibnall (Oxford, 1986).

The Letters of John of Salisbury, ed. and tr. W.J. Millor and H.E. Butler, 2 vols. (Oxford, 1979 and 1986).

Metalogicon, eds. J.B. Hall and K.S.B. Keats-Rohan (Turnhout, 1991).

Policraticus I–IV, ed. K.S.B. Keats-Rohan (Turnhout, 1993).

Metalogicon libri III, ed. C.C.J. Webb (Oxford, 1929).

Policraticus sive de nugis curialium et vestigiis philosophorum, ed. C.C.J. Webb, 2 vols. (Oxford, 1909).

Vita Sancti Anselmi and *Vita Sancti Thomae*, ed. and Italian trans. I. Biffi, *Anselmo e Becket, due vite* (Milano, 1990).

Translations
English Translations

Anselm & Becket: Two Canterbury Saints Lives by John of Salisbury, trans. Ronald E. Pepin (Toronto, 2009).

The Metalogicon of John of Salisbury, trans. D. McGarry (Berkeley, 1962).

Metalogicon, trans. J.B. Hall, Corpus Christianorum in Translation (Turnhout, 2013).

The Statesman's Book of John of Salisbury [*Policraticus* Books IV, V, VI, and excerpts from Books VII and VIII], trans. J. Dikinson (New York, 1963).

Frivolities of Courtiers and Footprints of Philosophers [*Policraticus* Books I, II, III and excerpts from Books VII and VIII], trans. J.B. Pike (Minneapolis, 1972).

Policraticus [Selections], trans. M. Markland (New York, 1979).

Policraticus [Selections], trans. C. Nederman (Cambridge, 1990).

French Translations

Denis Foulechat (trans.), *Le Policraticus de Jean de Salisbury, livre IV, traduit par Denis Foulechat (1372), Ms 24287 de la BN*, ed. C. Brucker (Nancy, 1985).

————, *Tyrans, princes et prêtres: Jean de Salisbury "Policratique" IV et VIII*, ed. C. Brucker (Montreal, 1987).

————, *Le Policratique de Jean de Salisbury, 1372: livres I–III*, ed. C. Brucker (Paris-Geneva, 1994).

————, *Le Policratique de Jean de Salisbury. Livre V*, ed. C. Brucker (Paris-Geneva, 2006).

————, *Éthique chrétienne et philosophies antiques. Le Policratique de Jean de Salisbury, Livres VI et VII* (Geneva, 2013).

Les Vanitez de la cour, trans. F. de Mazeray (Paris, 1640).

Metalogicon, trans. F. Lejeune (Paris, 2009).

German Translations

Policraticus: eine Textauswahl. Lateinisch-deutsch, trans. S. Seit (Freiburg im Breisgau, 2008).

Italian Translations

Giovanni di Salisbury 'Policraticus.' L'uomo di governo nel pensiero medievale, trans. L. Bianchi and P. Feltri (Milano, 1985).

Giovanni di Salisbury, Il Policratico ossia delle vanità di curia e degli insegnamenti dei filosofi, 4 vols., ed. and trans. U. Dotti (Turin, 2011).

Anselmo e Becket, due vite, trans. I. Biffi (Milano, 1990).

Spanish Translations

Policraticus, trans. M.A. Ladero, M. Garcia Gomez, T. Zamarriego (Madrid, 1984).

Select Bibliography

Aladjidi, P., "L'empereur Trajan: un modèle imaginaire de la charité royale dans les miroirs des princes de la fin du Moyen Âge," in A.-H. Allirot, G. Lecuppre and L. Scordia, eds., *Royautés imaginaires (XIIᵉ–XVIᵉ siècles). Actes du colloque organisé par le Centre de recherche d'histoire sociale et culturelle (CHSCO) de l'Université de Paris X-Nanterre (26 et 27 septembre 2003)* (Turnhout, 2005): 53–73.

Anton, H.H., "Fürstenspiegel," *Lexicon des Mittelalters*, t. 4 (München-Zurich, 1989), cols. 1040–1149.

Arduini, M.L., "*Sola ratione* in Giovanni di Salisbury," *Rivista di filosofia neo-scolastica* 89 (1997): 229–268.

————, "Contributo alla riconstruzione biografica du Giovanni di Salisbury," *Rivista di filosofia neo-scolastica* 90 (1998): 198–214.

Aurell, M., "Aux origines de la légende noire d'Aliénor d'Aquitaine," in A.-H. Allirot, G. Lecuppre and L. Scordia, eds., *Royautés imaginaires (XIIᵉ–XVIᵉ siècles). Actes du*

colloque organisé par le Centre de recherche d'histoire sociale et culturelle (CHSCO) de
l'Université de Paris X-Nanterre (26 et 27 septembre 2003) (Turnhout, 2005): 89–102.

Barker, L.K., "Ms Bodl. Canon. Pat. Lat. 131 and a Lost Lactantius of John of Salisbury:
Evidence in Search of a French Critic of Thomas Becket," *Albion* 22 (1990): 21–37.

Barlow, F., "John of Salisbury and His Brothers," *Journal of Ecclesiastical History* 46
(1995): 95–109.

Barrau, J., "Jean de Salisbury, intermédiaire entre Thomas Becket et la cour capétienne?," in M. Aurell and N.-Y. Tonnerre, eds., *Plantagenêts et Capétiens:*
Confrontations et héritages (Turnhout, 2006): 505–516.

———, "Ceci n'est pas un miroir, ou le *Policraticus* de Jean de Salisbury," in F. Lachaud
and L. Scordia, eds., *Le Prince au miroir de la littérature politique de l'Antiquité aux*
Lumières (Mont-Saint-Aignan, 2007): 87–111.

———, "La *conversio* de Jean de Salisbury: la Bible au service de Thomas Becket?"
Cahiers de civilisation médiévale 50 (2007): 229–243.

———, *Bible, lettres et politique. L'Écriture au service des hommes à l'époque de Thomas*
Becket (Paris, 2013).

Barzillay, P., "The *Entheticus de dogmate philosophorum* of John of Salisbury,"
Mediaevalia et Humanistica 16 (1964): 11–29.

Bell, D.M., *L'Idéal éthique de la royauté en France au Moyen Âge, d'après quelques morali-*
stes de ce temps (Geneva, 1962).

Bellenguez, P., *Un Philosophe académicien du XIIe siècle, Jean de Salisbury: sa vie, son*
œuvre, sa pensée (Aire-sur-Lys, 1926).

Belmar-Lopez, P., "La destruccion de la razon metodica en el siglo xii: Cornificius,"
Estudios Filosoficos 37 (1988): 275–296.

Berges, W., *Die Fürstenspiegel des hohen und späten Mittelalters* (Leipzig, 1938[1]; Stuttgart,
1952[2]).

Bertrand, O., *Du Vocabulaire religieux à la théorie politique en France au XIVe siècle. Les*
néologismes chez les traducteurs de Charles V (Paris, 2005).

Biffi, I., "Anselmo nell'interpretazione di Giovanni di Salisbury," in *Anselmo d'Aosta e*
dintorni. Lanfranco, Guitmondo, Urbano II (Milan, 2007): 317–328.

Boczar, M., "Filozofia prawa w ujeciu Jana z Salisbury" (The philosophy of Law in John
of Salisbury), *Studia Filozoficzne* 10 (1979): 53–69.

———, "Jana z Salisbury znajomosc literatury antycznej" (John of Salisbury's
Acquaintance with the Classical Literature), *Meander* 36 (1981): 261–271.

———, "*Ratio naturae et officii* w filozofii spolecznej Jana z Salisbury" (*Ratio naturae et offi-*
cii in the Social Philosophy of John of Salisbury), *Studia Mediewistyszne* 24 (1986): 3–28.

———, "Koncepcja retoryki w pismach Jana z Salisbury" (The Concept of Rhetoric in
John of Salisbury), *Kwartalnik Historii Nauki i Techniki* 32 (1987): 139–155.

———, *Czlowiek i wspólnota: filozofia moralna, spoleczna i polityczna Jana z Salisbury*,
PhD Diss. (Warsaw, 1987) (with abstract in English).

Bollermann, K., and Nederman, C.J., "John of Salisbury's Second Letter Collection in Later Medieval England: Unexamined Fragments from Huntington Library HM 128," *Viator: Medieval and Renaissance Studies* 40 (2009): 71–91.

Bordier, S., "*Aenigma Somniorum*," *Bulletin de l'association Guillaume Budé* 50 (1991): 306–314.

Brasa Diez, M., "Lo que la historia ha pensado de Juan de Salisbury," *Escritos del Vedat* 5 (1975): 263–292.

———, "Quintiliano y Juan de Salisbury," *Estudios filosoficos* 24 (1975): 87–99.

———, "Las artas del lenguaje en Juan de Salisbury," *La Ciudad de Dios* 193 (1980): 19–45.

———, "Tres clases de logica en Juan de Salisbury," in W. Kluxen et al., eds., *Sprache und Erkenntnis im Mittelalter. Akten des VI. Internationalen Kongresses für mittelalterliche Philosophie der Société internationale pour l'Étude de la Philosophie Médiévale. 29 August–3. September in Bonn* (Berlin-New York, 1981): 357–367.

———, "Micro y Macrocosmos de Juan de Salisbury," in *L'Homme et son univers au Moyen Âge. Actes du 7e congrès international de philosophie médiévale* (Louvain-la-Neuve, 1986): 347–355.

Breck, J., "A Reliquary of Saint Thomas Becket Made for John of Salisbury," *The Metropolitan Museum of Art Bulletin* 13 (1918): 220–224.

Bride, M., "John of Salisbury's Theory of Rhetoric," *Studies in Medieval Culture* 2 (1966): 56–62.

Brooke, C.L., "Aspects of John of Salisbury's *Historia pontificalis*," in L. Smith and B. Ward, eds., *Intellectual Life in the Middle Ages: Essays Presented to Margaret Gibson* (London, 1992): 185–195.

———, "Adrian IV and John of Salisbury," in B. Bolton and A.J. Duggan, eds., *Adrian IV. The English Pope (1154–1159). Studies and Text* (Aldershot, 2003): 1–13.

Brown, A., "John of Salisbury," *Franciscan Studies* 19 (1959): 241–297.

Brown, C., *Contrary Things: Exegesis, Dialectic and the Poetics of Didacticism* (Stanford, 1988).

Brucker, C., "Le *Policratique*: un fragment de manuscrit dans le Ms BN fr. 24287," *Bibliothèque Humanisme et Renaissance* 34 (1972): 269–273.

———, "À propos de quelques hellénismes de Jean de Salisbury et de leur traduction au xive siècle," *Bulletin du Cange* 39 (1973–4): 85–94.

———, "La pensée morale et politique de Plutarque dans un Miroir des princes latin du xiie siècle et sa réception en moyen français (1372)," in M.C. Timelli and C. Galderisi, eds., "*Pour acquerir honneur et pris*". *Mélanges de moyen français offerts à Giuseppe Di Stefano* (Montreal, 2004): 87–99.

Brückmann, J. and Nederman, C., "Aristotelianism in John of Salisbury's *Policraticus*," *Journal of the History of Philosophy* 21 (1983): 203–229.

Brüschweiler, R., *Das sechste Buch des "Policraticus" von Ioannes Saresberiensis: ein Beitrag zur Militärgeschichte Englands in 12. Jahrhundert* (Zurich, 1975).

Burnett, C., "John of Salisbury and Aristotle," *Didascalia* 2 (1996): 19–32.

Campbell, C. and Nederman, C., "Priests, Kings and Tyrants: Spiritual and Temporal Power in John of Salisbury's *Policraticus*," *Speculum* 66 (1991): 572–590.

Camps, M., "A presença do *Policraticus* de João de Salisbúria na *Crónica de D. João I* de Fernão Lopes," *Mediævalia – Textos e Estudos* 22 (2003): 121–156.

Carbo, L., "La ley natural en el *Policraticus* de Juan de Salisbury," in A. Fraboschi, ed., *Conociendo a Hildegarda: La Abadesa de Bingen y su tiempo. 1a Jornada Interdisciplinaria, Buenos Aires, 22 de agosto de 2003* (Buenos Aires, 2003): 39–51.

Caverly, W., "The Political Theory of John of Salisbury," *Reality* (1962): 93–113.

Cazzola Palazzo, L., "Il valore filosofico della probabilità nel pensiero di Giovanni di Salisbury," *Atti della Academia delle Scienze di Torino* (1957–9): 96–142.

Colish, M.L., "The Virtuous Pagan: Dante and the Christian Tradition," in W. Caferro and D.G. Fisher, eds., *The Unbounded Community* (New York, 1996): 43–91.

Constable, G., "The Alleged Disgrace of John of Salisbury in 1159," *English Historical Review* 69 (1954): 67–76.

Cotts, J.D., "Monks and Clerks in Search of the *Beata schola*: Peter of Celle's Warning to John of Salisbury Reconsidered," in S.N. Vaughn and J. Rubenstein, eds., *Teaching and Learning in Northern Europe, 1000–1200* (Turnhout, 2006): 255–277.

Cullière, A., "*Les Vanitez de la cour*, de Mézeray (1639)," in V. Bubenicek and R. Marchal, eds., *Gouvernement des hommes, gouvernement des âmes. Mélanges de langue et littérature françaises offerts au Professeur Charles Brucker* (Nancy, 2007): 453–467.

Dal Pra, M., *Giovanni di Salisbury* (Milan, 1951).

Daniels, H., *Die Wissenschaftslehre des Johannes von Salisbury* (Freiburg-im-Breisgau, 1932).

De Araujo, N., "Le prince comme ministre de Dieu sur terre. La définition du prince chez Jean de Salisbury (*Policraticus*, IV, 1)," *Le Moyen Âge* 1 (2006): 63–74.

———, "Une traduction oubliée du *Policraticus* de Jean de Salisbury par François Eudes de Mézeray (1639)," *Bibliothèque de l'École des Chartes* 164 (2006): 581–594.

Delhaye, P., "Une adaptation du *De Officiis* au XIIe siècle," *Recherches de théologie ancienne et médiévale* 16 (1949): 227–258; 17 (1950): 5–28.

———, "Le bien suprême d'après le *Policraticus* de Jean de Salisbury," *Recherches de théologie ancienne et médiévale* 25 (1953): 203–221.

———, "L'enseignement de la philosophie morale au XIIe siècle," *Medieval Studies* 11 (1949): 81–94, repr. in idem, *Enseignement et morale au XIIe siècle* (Paris-Fribourg, 1988): 58–81.

De Rentiis, D., "Für eine Geschichte der Nachahmungskategorie. Imitatio und lectio auctorum im Policraticus VII, 10," in U. Schaefer, ed., *Artes im Mittelalter* (Berlin, 1999): 161–173.

Demimuid, M., *Jean de Salisbury* (Paris, 1873).

Denis, L., "La question des universaux d'après Jean de Salisbury," *Revue des sciences philosophiques et théologiques* 16 (1927): 425–434.

————, "Un humaniste au Moyen Âge: Jean de Salisbury, 1120–1180," *Nova et vetera. Revue d'enseignement et de pédagogie* 22 (1940): 5–22; 22 (1941): 125–152.

Desideri, S., *La institutio Trajani* (Genoa, 1958).

Dickinson, J., "The Medieval Conception of Kingship and Some of Its Limitations, as Developed in the *Policraticus* of John of Salisbury," *Speculum* 1 (1926): 308–337.

Dines, Ilya, "The Earliest Use of John of Salisbury's *Policraticus*: Third Family Bestiaries," *Viator* 44 (2013): 107–118.

Dotto, G., "'Artes liberales' come 'Sapientia' in Giovanni di Salisbury," *Annali della facoltà di lettere e filosofia. Università degli Studi di Perugia* 17 (1979–80): 229–240.

————, "Logica ed etica in Giovanni di Salisbury," *Annali della Facoltà di Lettere e Filosofia. Università degli Studi di Perugia* 18 (1980–1): 7–33.

————, *Giovanni di Salisbury. La filosofia come Sapienza* (Assisi, 1986).

Dowdell, V.L., *Aristotle's Influence on John of Salisbury*, PhD Diss. (Cornell University, 1930).

Dox, D., *The Idea of the Theater in Latin Christian Thought: Augustine to the Fourteenth Century* (Ann Arbor, 2004): 87–92.

Duggan, A.J., "Classical Quotations and Allusions in the Correspondence of Thomas Becket," *Viator: Medieval and Renaissance Studies* 32 (2001): 1–22.

————, "Totius Christianitatis Caput. The Pope and the Princes," in B. Bolton and A.J. Duggan, eds., *Adrian IV. The English Pope (1154–1159). Studies and Text* (Aldershot, 2003): 105–155.

Elsmann, T., *Untersuchungen zur Rezeption der Institutio Traiani* (Stuttgart – Leipzig, 1994).

Escobar, A., "*Duce natura...*Reflexiones en torno a la recepcion medieval de Ciceron a la luz de Juan de Salisbury," *Convenit selecta* 7 (http://www.hottopos.com/convenit7/escobar.htm).

Feldwick, A., and Nederman, C.J., "To the Court and Back Again: The Origins and Dating of the *Entheticus de Dogmate Philosophorum* of John of Salisbury," *Journal of Medieval and Renaissance Studies* 21 (1991): 129–145.

Ferruolo, S., *The Origins of the University: The School of Paris and Their Critics, 1100–1215* (Stanford, 1985).

Flori, J., "La chevalerie selon Jean de Salisbury (nature, fonction, idéologie)," *Revue d'histoire ecclésiastique* 77 (1982): 35–77.

Foreville, R., "Une lettre inédite de Jean de Salisbury, évêque de Chartres," *Revue d'histoire de l'Église de France* 22 (1936): 179–185, repr. in *Thomas Becket dans la tradition historique et hagiographique* (London, 1981).

Garfagnini, G.C., "Giovanni di Salisbury, Ottone di Frisinga e Giacomo da Venezia," *Rivista ciritica di storia della filosofia* 27 (1972): 19–34.

————, "Legittima potestas e tirannide nel Policraticus di Giovanni di Salisbury. Riflessioni sulla sensibilità di un clericus per i problemi politici," *Critica storica* 4 (1977): 575–610.

————, "Da Seneca a Giovanni di Salisbury: auctoritates morali e vitae philosophorum in un ms trecentesco," *Rinascimento* 2 (1980): 201–247.

————, "L'attività storico-filosofica nel secolo xii: Giovanni di Salisbury," *Medioevo* 16 (1990): 23–42.

Gerl, H.-B., "Zum mittelalterlichen Spannungsfeld von Logik, Dialektik und Rhetorik. Die Programmatik des Metalogicon von Johannes von Salisbury," *Tijdschrift voor Philosophie* 43 (1981): 306–327 (repr. in *Studia mediewistyczne* 22 (1983): 37–51).

Godman, P., "*Opus consummatum, omnium artium...imago.* From Bernard of Chartres to John of Hauvilla," *Zeitschrift für Deutsches Altertum und Deutsche Literatur* 124 (1995): 26–71.

————, *The Silent Masters: Latin Literature and Its Censor in the High Middle Ages* (Princeton, 2000).

Goeglein, T., "The Problem of Monsters and Universals in 'the Owl and the Nightingale' and John of Salisbury's *Metalogicon*," *Journal of English and Germanic Philology* 94 (1995): 190–206.

Gonzalez-Fernandez, M., "Corona in capite: Juan de Salisbury y Dante," *Revista española de filosofia medieval* 10 (2003): 207–218.

————, "Juan de Salisbury y los goliardos," *Revista española de filosofia medieval* 11 (2004): 213–225.

————, "Los limites del conocimiento: Juan de Salisbury y Francesco Petrarca," in M.C. Pacheco and J.F. Meirinhos, eds., *Intellect et imagination dans la Philosophie médiévale/Intellect and Imagination in Medieval Philosophy/Intelecto e imaginação na Filosfia Medieval. Actes du XIᵉ Congrès International de Philosophie Médiévale de la SIEPM, Porto, 26–31 août 2002* (Turnhout, 2006): vol. 2, 1039–1052.

Grellard, C., "Jean de Salisbury. Un cas médiéval de scepticisme," *Freiburger Zeitschrift für Philosophie und Theologie* 54 (2007): 16–40.

————, "Le sacré et le profane. Le statut des laïcs dans la *Respublica* de Jean de Salisbury," in P. Demouy, ed., *Les Laïcs dans les villes de la France du Nord au XIIᵉ siècle* (Turnhout, 2008): 167–187.

————, "Le socratisme de Jean de Salisbury," in S. Mayer, ed., *Réception philosophique de la figure de Socrate, Diagonale φ* 2 (2008): 35–59.

————, "La religion comme technique de gouvernement chez Jean de Salisbury," *Cahiers de civilisation médiévale* 53 (2010): 237–254.

————, "'Le roi est sujet de la loi de justice.' Loi des dieux, loi des hommes chez Jean de Salisbury," in B. Ribémont et S. Menegaldo, eds., *Le Roi fontaine de justice. Pouvoir justicier et pouvoir royal au Moyen Âge et à la Renaissance* (Paris, 2012): 85–103.

————, "Doxographie et anecdotes. L'écriture sceptique de Jean de Salisbury," in F. Lecercle et G. Navaud, eds., *Anecdotes philosophiques et théologiques de l'Antiquité aux Lumières* (Paris, 2012): 87–104.

————, "La seconde acculturation chrétienne de Cicéron: la réception des *Académiques* du IXe au XIIe siècle," *Astérion* 11 (2013): http://asterion.revues.org/2350

————, *Jean de Salisbury et la renaissance médiévale du scepticisme* (Paris, 2013).

Guglielmetti, R., "Varianti d'autore nel *Metalogicon* e nel *Policraticus* di Giovanni di Salisbury," *Filologia Mediolatina* 11 (2004): 281–307.

————, *La tradizione manoscritto del Policraticus di Giovanni di Salisbury, primo secolo di diffusione* (Florence, 2005).

Guth, K., *Johannes von Salisbury: Studien zur Kirchen-, Kultur-, und Sozialgeschichte Westeuropas in 12. Jahrhundert* (St. Ottilien, 1978).

————, "Standethos als Ausdruck hochmittelalterlicher Lebensform. Zur Gestalt des ethischen Humanismus in der Briefwelt des Johannes von Salisbury," *Freiburger Zeitschrift für Philosophie und Theologie* 28 (1981): 111–132.

Hall, J.B., "Notes on the *Entheticus* of John of Salisbury," *Traditio* 39 (1983): 444–447.

————, "Towards a Text of John of Salisbury's *Metalogicon*," *Studi Medievali* 24 (1983): 791–816.

————, "L'emendatio: il caso del Metalogicon di Giovanni di Salisbury," C. Leonardi, ed., *La critica del testo mediolatino. Atti del convegno (Firenze, 6–8 dicembre 1990)*, (Spoleto, 1994): 117–126.

Harf-Lancner, L., "L'Enfer de la cour: la cour d'Henri II Plantagenêt et la Mesnie Hellequin dans l'œuvre de Jean de Salisbury, de Gautier Map, de Pierre de Blois et de Giraud de Barri," in P. Contamine, ed., *L'État et les aristocraties (France, Angleterre, Écosse) XIIe–XVIIe siècles* (Paris, 1989): 27–50.

Haseldine, Julian, "Understanding the Language of *Amicitia*: The Friendship Circle of Peter of Celle (c. 1115–1183)," *Journal of Medieval History* 20 (1994): 237–260.

Hauréau, B., "Notice sur un pénitentiel attribué à Jean de Salisbury (n° 3218 et 3529 [A] de la Bibliothèque nationale)," *Notices et extraits des manuscrits de la Bibliothèque nationale et autres bibliothèques*, 24 (1876): 269–287.

Hebling-Gloor, B., *Natur und Aberglaube im Policraticus des Johannes von Salisbury* (Zurich, 1956).

Hendley, B.P. *Wisdom and Eloquence: A New Interpretation of the Metalogicon of John of Salisbury*, PhD Diss. (Yale University, 1967).

————, "John of Salisbury's Defense of the Trivium," in *Arts libéraux et philosophie au Moyen Âge. IVe Congrès international de philosophie médiévale. Montréal 1967* (Paris, 1969): 753–762.

————, "John of Salisbury and the Problem of Universals," *Journal of the History of Philosophy* 8–3 (1970): 289–302.

————, "A New Look at John of Salisbury's Educational Theory," in J.E. Murdoch et al., eds., *Knowledge and the Sciences in Medieval Philosophy. Proceedings of the Eight International Congress of Medieval Philosophy* (Helsinki, 1990): vol. 2, 502–511.

Hicks, E., "A Mirror for Misogynists: John of Salisbury's *Policraticus* (8.11) in the Translation of Denis Foulechat (1372)," in E.J. Richards, ed., *Reinterpreting Christine de Pizan* (Athens, Georgia, 1992): 77–107.

Hirata, Y., *John of Salisbury and His Correspondents: A Study of the Epistolary Relationships between John of Salisbury and his Correspondents*, PhD Diss. (University of Sheffield, 1991).

———, "John of Salisbury and Thomas Becket: The Making of a Martyr," *Medieval History* 2 (1992): 18–25.

———, *Collected Papers on John of Salisbury and His Correspondents* (Tokyo, 1996).

———, "St. Anselm and Two Clerks of Thomas Becket," in D.E. Luscombe and G.R. Evans, eds., *Anselm: Aosta, Bec, and Canterbury* (Sheffield, 1996): 323–333.

———, "John of Salisbury, Gerard Pucelle and amicitia," in J. Haseldine, ed., *Friendship in Medieval Europe* (Stroud, 1999): 153–165.

Hohenleutner, H., "Johannes von Salisbury in der Literatur der letzten zehn Jahren," *Historisches Jahrbuch* 77 (1958): 493–500.

Hosler, J.D., *John of Salisbury. Military Authority of the Twelfth-Century Renaissance* (Leiden, 2013).

Jaeger, C.S., "Irony and Role-playing in John of Salisbury and Thomas Becket Circle," in M. Aurell, ed., *Culture politique des Plantagenêt (1154–1224). Actes du Colloque tenu à Poitiers du 2 au 5 mai 2002* (Poitiers, 2003): 319–331.

———, "John of Salisbury, a Philosopher of the Long Eleventh Century," in Thomas F.X. Noble and J. Van Engen, eds., *European Transformations: The Long Twelfth Century* (Notre Dame, 2012): 499–520.

Jambeck, K., "The *Fables* of Marie de France: A Mirror of Princes," in C.A. Maréchal, ed., *In Quest of Marie de France: A Twelfth-Century Poet* (Lewiston, N.Y., 1992): 59–106.

Jeauneau, É., "Jean de Salisbury et Aristote," *Aristote, l'école de Chartres et la cathédrale* (Chartres, 1997): 33–39.

Keats-Rohan, K.S.B., "John of Salisbury and Twelfth-century Education in Paris from the Account of his *Metalogicon*," *History of Universities* 6 (1986): 1–45.

———, "The Textual Tradition of John of Salisbury's *Metalogicon*," *Revue d'histoire des textes* 16 (1986): 229–282.

———, "The Chronology of John of Salisbury's Studies in France: A Reading of 'Metalogicon,' II.10," *Studi Medievali* 28 (1987): 193–203.

———, "Marklandus in Policraticum Ioannis Saresberiensis," *Studi Medievali* 29 (1988): 375–421.

Kerner, M., "Zur Entstehungsgeschichte der *Institutio Traiani*," *Deustsches Archiv* 32 (1976): 558–571.

———, *Johannes von Salisbury und die logische Struktur seines Policraticus* (Wiesbaden, 1977).

————, "Natur und Gesellschaft bei Johannes von Salisbury," in A. Zimmermann, ed., *Soziale Ordnungen in Selbstverständnis des Mittelalters* (Berlin-New York, 1979–80): vol. 1, 179–202.

————, "Die Institutio Trajani – spätantike Lehrschrift oder hochmittelalterliche Fiktion?" *Fälschungen im Mittelalter. Internationaler Kongreß der Monumenta Germaniae Historica München, 16–19. September 1986* (Hannover, 1988): vol. 1, 715–738.

————, "Johannes von Salisbury im späteren Mittelalter," in J. Miethke, ed., *Das publikum der politischen Theorie im 14. Jahrhundert* (Munich, 1992): 25–48.

————, "Johannes von Salisbury und das gelehrte Recht," in P. Landau and J. Müller, eds., *Proceedings of the Ninth International Congress of Medieval Law* (Vatican City, 1997): 503–521.

Kleineke, W., *Englische Fürstenspiegel vom Policraticus Johanns von Salisbury bis Basilikon Doron König Jakobs I* (Halle, 1937).

Krynen, J., "*Princeps pugnat pro legibus...*, un aspect du *Policraticus*," *Droit romain, jus civile et droit français. Études d'histoire du droit et des idées politiques* 3 (1999): 89–99.

————, "Sur la leçon de législation ecclésiastique du *Policraticus*," in G. Constable and M. Rouche, eds., *Auctoritas. Mélanges offerts au professeur Olivier Guillot* (Paris, 2006): 497–502.

Kuhn, U., "Nodus in scirpo – Enodatio quaestionis: Eine Denkfigur bei Johannes von Salisbury und Alanus von Lille," *Antike und Abendland* 44 (1998): 163–176.

Laarhoven, J. van, "Die tirannie verdrijven...John of Salisbury als revolutionair?" in W.F. Dankbaar, ed., *Geloof en Revolutie, Kerkhistorische kanttekeningen bij een actueel vraagstuk* (Amsterdam, 1977): 21–50.

————, "Iustitia bij John of Salisbury: Proeve van een terminologische statistiek," *Nederland Archiv voor Kerkgeschiedenis* 58 (1977): 16–37.

————, "*Non iam decretam, sed Evangelium*! Jean de Salisbury au Latran III," in M. Fois, ed., *Dalla Chiesa antica alla Chiesa moderna. Miscellanea per il cinquantesimo della Facoltà di Storia Ecclesiastica della Pontifica Università Gregoriana* (Rome, 1983): 107–119.

————, "Titles and subtitles of the Policraticus: A Proposal," *Vivarium* 32 (1994): 131–160.

————, "Een humanist als exegeet? John of Salisbury en de bijbel," in D. Akerboom, ed., *Broeder Jehosjoea: Opstellent voor Ben Hemelsoet* (Kampen, 1994): 107–119.

Lachaud, F., "L'idée de noblesse dans le *Policraticus* de Jean de Salisbury (1159)," *Cahiers de recherches médiévales* 13 (2006): 3–19.

————, "*De tyranno et principe* (Cambridge, Corpus Christi College, ms. 469): un pamphlet 'britannique' contre la tyrannie d'Henri III?," in J.-P. Genet, ed., *Les îles Britanniques: espaces et identités, Cahiers de Recherches Médiévales et Humanistes. A Journal of Medieval and Humanistic Studies* 19 (2010): 87–104.

————, *L'Éthique du pouvoir au Moyen Âge. L'office dans la culture politique (Angleterre, vers 1150-vers 1330)* (Paris, 2010).

————, "La figure du clerc curial dans l'œuvre de Jean de Salisbury," in M. Gaude-Ferragu, B. Laurioux and J. Paviot, eds., *La Cour du prince. Cour de France, cours d'Europe (XIIIᵉ–XVᵉ siècles)*. *Actes du colloque international organisé du 18 au 20 septembre 2008 dans les Universités de Versailles-Saint-Quentin, Paris-12 et Paris-13* (Paris, 2011): 301–320.

————, "De la satire politique au 'miroir': Jean de Galles et la lecture du *Policraticus* de Jean de Salisbury au XIIIᵉ siècle," in C. Giraud and M. Morard, eds., *Universitas scolarium. Mélanges offerts à Jacques Verger par ses anciens étudiants* (Paris, 2011): 385–407.

————, "'Plutarchus si dit et recorde...' L'influence du *Policraticus* de Jean de Salisbury sur Christine de Pizan et Jean Gerson," in P. Gilli and J. Paviot, eds., *Hommes, cultures et sociétés à la fin du Moyen Âge. Liber discipulorum en l'honneur de Philippe Contamine* (Paris, 2012): 47–67.

————, "Corps du prince, corps de la *res publica*: écriture métaphorique et construction politique dans le *Policraticus* de Jean de Salisbury," in *Le Corps du prince, Micrologus. Nature, Sciences and Medieval Societies*, 22 (2014): 171–199.

————, "La simonie et les clercs simoniaques dans le *Policraticus* de Jean de Salisbury: un aspect de la réforme morale et religieuse en Angleterre au milieu du XIIe siècle" (forthcoming).

Ladero Quaesada, M.A., "El emperador Trajano como modelo de principes en la edad media (El principe en Policraticus)," *Annuario de Estudios Medievales* 29 (1999): 501–525.

Langdon Forhan, K., "A Twelfth-Century Bureaucrat and the Life of Mind: The Political Thought of John of Salisbury," *Proceedings of the PMR Conference (Patristic, Medieval and Renaissance)* 10 (1985): 65–74.

————, *The Twelfth Century 'Bureaucrat' and the Life of the Mind: John of Salisbury's Policraticus*, PhD Diss. (John Hopkins University, 1987).

————, "Salisburean Stakes: The Uses of 'Tyrany' in John of Salisbury's Policraticus," *History of Political Thought* 11 (1990): 397–407.

————, "Polycracy, Obligation and Revolt: The Body Politic in John of Salisbury and Christine de Pizan," in M. Brabant, ed., *Politics, Gender and Genre. The Political Thought of Christine de Pizan* (Boulder-San Francisco-Oxford, 1992): 33–52.

————, "The Not-So-Divided Self: Reading Augustine in the Twelfth Century," *Augustiniana* 42 (1992): 95–110.

Lapid, B., "Jana z Salisbury rozumienie zadan historiografii (The notion of history in the works of John of Salisbury)," *Studia Zrodloznawcze: Commentationes* 15 (1971): 85–107.

Lastra Paz, S., "Juan de Salisbury: su visión del miles christianus," *Stylos* 4 (1995), 75–89.

Lawson, N.E. and Nederman, C.J., "The Frivolities of Courtiers Follow the Footprints of Women: Historical Women and the Crisis of Virility in John of Salisbury," in C. Levin and J. Watson, eds., *Ambiguous Realities: Women in the Middle Ages and Renaissance* (Detroit, 1987): 82–96.

Leach, E., "'The Little Pipe Sings Sweetly While The Fowler Deceives The Bird': Sirens in The Later Middle Ages," *Music and Letters* 87 (2006): 187–211.

Lejeune, F., "Pierre Abélard et Jean de Salisbury. *Metalogicon*, 2, 10," in J. Jolivet, ed., *Pierre Abélard à l'aube des Universités. Actes de la Conférence internationale de Nantes* (Rennes, 2001): 247–260.

Lerer, S., "John of Salisbury's Virgil," *Vivarium* 20 (1982): 24–39.

Lesieur, T., "The *Policraticus*: a Christian Model of *Sapientia*?" in M. Aurell, ed., *Culture politique des Plantagenêt (1154–1224). Actes du Colloque tenu à Poitiers du 2 au 5 mai 2002* (Poitiers, 2003): 363–371.

Liebeschütz, H., "John of Salisbury and Pseudo-Plutarch," *Journal of Warburg and Courtlaud Institutes* 6 (1943): 33–39.

———, *Medieval Humanism in the Life and Writings of John of Salisbury* (London, 1950).

———, "Englische und europäische Elemente in der Erfahrungswelt des Johannes von Salisbury," *Die Welt als Geschichte* 11 (1951): 38–45.

———, "Chartres und Bologna: Naturbegriff und Staatsidee bei Johannes von Salisbury," *Archiv für Kultur Geschichte* 50 (1968): 3–32.

Liebeschütz, H. and Momigliano, A., "Notes on Petrarch, John of Salisbury, and the *Institutio Traiani*," *Journal of the Warburg and Courtauld Institutes* 12 (1949): 189–190.

Linder, A., "The Knowledge of John of Salisbury in the Late Middle Ages," *Studi Medievali* 18 (1977): 315–366.

———, "John of Salisbury's *Policraticus* in Thirteenth-Century England: The Evidence of MS Cambridge Corpus Christi College 469," *Journal of the Warburg and Courtlaud Institute* 40 (1977): 276–282.

Loundsbury, R.C., "The Case of the Erudite Eyewitness: Cicero, Lucan and John of Salisbury," *Allegorica* 12 (1990): 15–35.

Martel, J.P., "Rhétorique et philosophie dans le *Metalogicon* de Jean de Salisbury," *Actas del Congreso Internacional de Filosofià Medieval* (Madrid, 1979): 961–968.

Martin, J., *John of Salisbury and the Classics*, PhD Diss. (University of Harvard, 1968).

———, "John of Salisbury's Manuscripts of Frontinus and of Gellius," *Journal of Warburg and Courtauld Institutes* 40 (1977): 1–26.

———, "Uses of Tradition: Gellius, Petronius and John of Salisbury," *Viator: Medieval and Renaissance Studies* 10 (1979): 57–76.

Massey, H.J., "John of Salisbury: Some Aspects of His Political Philosophy," *Classica et Mediaevalia* 28 (1967): 357–372.

Mazzantini, C., *Il pensiero filosofico di Giovanni di Salisbury* (Turin, 1957).

McGarry, D., "Educational Theory in the *Metalogicon* of John of Salisbury," *Speculum* 23 (1948): 659–675.

McGuire, B.P., *Friendship and Community: The Monastic Experience 350–1250* (Kalamazoo, 1988).

McLoughlin, J., "The Language of Persecution: John of Salisbury and the Early Phase of the Becket Dispute (1163–66)," in W.J. Sheils, ed., *Persecution and Toleration: Papers Read at the Twenty-Second Summer Meeting and the Twenty-Third Winter Meeting of the Ecclesiastical History Society* (Oxford, 1984): 73–87.

———, *John of Salisbury (ca. 1120–1180): The Career and Attitudes of a Schoolman in Church Politics*, PhD Diss. (University College Dublin, 1988).

———, "Amicitia in Practice: John of Salisbury (c. 1120–1180) and His Circle," in D. Williams, ed., *England in the Twelfth Century* (Woodbridge, 1990): 165–180.

———, "Nations and Loyalties: The Outlook of a Twelfth-Century Schoolman (John of Salisbury, c. 1120–1180)," in D. Loades and K. Walsh, eds., *Faith and Identity: Christian Political Experience* (Oxford, 1990): 39–46.

Métais, C., "Découverte du tombeau de Jean de Salisbury, évêque de Chartres," *Bulletin monumental* 69 (1905): 501–504.

Michel, A., "Autour de Jean de Salisbury: la dignité humaine et l'honneur de Dieu," in C. Leonardi, ed., *Gli umanesimi medievali. Atti de 2 congresso dell internationes mittellateinerkomitee, Firenze, 1993* (Florence, 1998): 375–382.

Miczka, G., *Das Bild der Kirche bei Johannes von Salisbury* (Bonn, 1970).

Misch, G., *Studien zur Geschichte der Autobiographie, 5. Johann von Salisbury und das Problem des mittelalterlichen Humanismus, Nachrichten der Akademie der Wissenschaften in Göttingen* 6 (1960): 231–257, repr. in *Geschichte der Autobiographie, 3. Das Mittelalter, 2, Das Hochmittelalter im Angang*, pt. 2 (Frankfurt-am-Main, 1962): 1157–1295.

Molnár, P., "De la morale à la science politique. La transformation du miroir des princes au milieu du XIIIe siècle," in P. Odorico, ed., *L'Éducation au gouvernement et à la vie.' La tradition des " règles de vie " au Moyen Âge. Actes du colloque international, Pise, 18 et 19 mars 2005* (Paris, 2009): 181–204.

Monagle, C., "Contested Knowledge: John of Salisbury's *Metalogicon* and *Historia pontificalis*," *Parergon* 21 (2004): 1–17.

———, "The Trial of Ideas: Two Tellings of the Trial of Gilbert of Poitiers," *Viator: Medieval and Renaissance Studies* 35 (2004): 112–129.

Moos, P. von, "Lucans Tragedia im Hochmittelalter, Pessimismus, contemptus mundi und Gegenwartserfahrung," *Mittellateinisches Jahrbuch* 14 (1979): 127–186.

———, "'Fictio auctoris'. Eine theoriegeschichtliche Miniatur am Rande der 'Institutio Traiani'," in *Fälschungen im Mittelalter. Internationaler Kongreß der Monumenta Germaniae Historica München, 16–19. September 1986* (Hannover 1988), vol. 1, 739–780.

———, "Jean de Salisbury," in J.-C. Polet, ed., *Le Patrimoine littéraire européen*, IV/b (*Le Moyen Âge*) (Brussels, 1993): 220–236.

————, *Geschichte als Topik. Das rhetorische Exemplum von der Antike zur Neuzeit und die historiae im Policraticus Johanns von Salisbury* (Hildesheim-Zurich-New York, 1996).

————, "Die angesehene Meinung IV: Johannes von Salisbury," *Mittellateinisches Jahrbuch* 34 (1999): 1–55.

————, "L'anecdote philosophique chez Jean de Salisbury," T. Ricklin, ed., *Exempla docent. Les exempla philosophiques de l'Antiquité à la Renaissance* (Paris, 2006): 135–148.

Mora, F., "Virgile, le magicien et l'*Enéide* des Chartrains," *Médiévales* 26 (1994): 39–57.

————, *L'Enéide médiévale et la naissance du roman* (Paris, 2004).

Morizot, P., "Jean de Salisbury et la Champagne," *Mémoires de la société d'agriculture, sciences et arts du département de l'Aube* 99 (1939–42): 257–291.

Moulinier-Brogi, L., "Jean de Salisbury: un réseau d'amitiés continentales," in M. Aurell, ed., *Culture politique des Plantagenêt (1154–1224). Actes du Colloque tenu à Poitiers du 2 au 5 mai 2002* (Poitiers, 2003): 341–361.

Munk-Olsen, B., "L'humanisme de Jean de Salisbury, un cicéronien au 12e siècle," M. de Gandillac and É. Jeauneau, eds., *Entretiens sur la Renaissance du 12e siècle* (Paris-La Haye, 1968): 53–83.

Musseters, S., "Chretien and John of Salisbury," *Bibliographical Bulletin of the International Arthurian Society* 33 (1981): 304–305.

Nederman, C., "The Aristotelian Doctrine of the Mean and John of Salisbury's Concept of Liberty," *Vivarium* 24 (1986): 128–142.

————, "Aristotelian Ethics and John of Salisbury's Letters," *Viator: Medieval and Renaissance Studies* 18 (1987): 161–173.

————, "The Physiological Significance of the Organic Metaphor in John of Salisbury's *Policraticus*," *History of Political Thought* 8 (1987): 211–223.

————, "Nature, Sin and the Origins of Society: The Ciceronian Tradition in Medieval Political Thought," *Journal of the History of Ideas* 49 (1988): 3–26.

————, "A Duty to Kill: John of Salisbury's Theory of Tyrannicide," *Review of Politics* 50 (1988): 365–389.

————, "The Changing Face of Tyranny: The Reign of King Stephen in John of Salisbury," *Nottingham Medieval Studies* 33 (1989): 1–20.

————, "Knowledge, Virtue and the Path to Wisdom: The Unexamined Aristotelianism of John of Salisbury's *Metalogicon*," *Mediaeval Studies* 51 (1989): 268–286.

————, "Aristotelian Ethics Before the *Nicomachean Ethics*: Sources of Aristotle's Concept of Virtue in the Twelfth Century," *Parergon*, n. s. 7 (1989): 55–75.

————, "Nature, Ethics and the Doctrine of *Habitus*: Aristotelian Moral Psychology in the Twelfth Century," *Traditio* 45 (1989/90): 87–110.

————, "Aristotelianism and the Origins of 'Political Science' in the Twelfth Century," *Journal of the History of Ideas* 52 (1991): 179–194.

————, "Freedom, Community and Function: Communitarian Lessons of Medieval Political Theory," *The American Political Science Review* 86 (1992): 977–986.

————, "The Union of Wisdom and Eloquence before the Renaissance: the Ciceronian Orator in Medieval Thought," *The Journal of Medieval History* 18 (1992): 75–95.

————, "The Third Sex: The Idea of the Hermaphrodite in the Twelfth Century," *Journal of the History of Sexuality* 6 (1996): 497–517.

————, "Toleration, Skepticism and the 'Clash of Ideas': Principles of Liberty in the Writings of John of Salisbury," in J.C. Laursen and C.J. Nederman, eds., *Beyond the Persecuting Society: Religious Toleration before the Enlightenment* (Philadelphia, 1998): 53–70.

————, "Social Bodies and the Non-Christian 'Other' in the Twelfth Century: John of Salisbury and Peter of Celle," in A. Classen, ed., *Meeting the Foreign in the Middle Ages* (New York-London, 2002): 192–201.

————, "The Virtues of Necessity: Labor, Money and Corruption in John of Salisbury," *Viator: Medieval and Renaissance Studies* 33 (2002): 54–68.

————, "The Origins of 'Policy': Fiscal Administration and Economic Principles in Later Twelfth-Century England," in C.J. Mews, C.J. Nederman and R. Thomson, eds., *Rhetoric and Renewal in the Latin West 1100–1500: Essays Presented to John O. Ward* (Turnhout, 2003): 149–168.

————, "Body Politics: The Diversification of Organic Metaphors in the Later Middle Ages," *Pensiero Politico Medievale* 2 (2004): 59–87.

————, "Beyond Aristotelianism and Stoicism: John of Salisbury's Skepticism and Moral Reasoning in the Twelfth Century," in I. Bejczy and R. Newhauser, eds., *Virtue and Ethics in the Twelfth Century* (Leiden, 2005): 175–195.

————, *John of Salisbury* (Tempe, Arizona, 2005).

————, "Friendship in Public Life during the Twelfth Century: Theory and Practice in the Writings of John of Salisbury," *Viator: Medieval and Renaissance Studies* 38 (2007): 385–397.

Newmann, J., "Satire Between School and Court: The Ethical Interpretation of The *Artes* in John of Salisbury's *Entheticus in dogmata philosophorum*," *Journal of Medieval Latin* 17 (2008): 125–142.

Noonan, J.T., "Bribery of John of Salisbury," *Proceedings of the Seventh International Congress of Medieval Canon Law, Cambridge, 23–27 July 1984* (Vatican City, 1988): 197–203.

Olsen, G.W., "John of Salisbury's Humanism," in C. Leonardi, ed., *Gli umanesimi medievali. Atti de 2 congresso dell' "internationes Mittellateinerkomitee," Firenze, 1993* (Florence, 1998): 447–468.

Palacz, R., "Les manuscrits du *Policraticon* en Pologne," *Mediaevalia philosophica polonorum* 10 (1961): 55–58.

————, "Bezposrednia recepcja arystotelizmu w *Metalogiconie* Jana z Salisbury" (The Immediate Reception of Aristotelianism in the *Metalogicon* of John of Salisbury), *Studia Mediewistyczne* 5 (1964): 191–251.

Partner, N.F., "The New Cornificius: Medieval History and the Artifice of Words," in E. Breisach, ed., *Classical Rhetoric and Medieval Historiography* (Kalamazoo, 1985): 5–59.

Pepin, R.E., *The Entheticus of John of Salisbury: A Critical Edition and Commentary*, PhD Diss. (Fordham University, 1973).

———, "The *Entheticus* of John of Salisbury: A Critical Text," *Traditio* 31 (1975): 127–193.

———, "John of Salisbury: An American Tribute," *The Hatcher Review* 9 (1980): 17–19.

———, "John of Salisbury's *Entheticus* and the Classical Tradition of Satire," *Florilegium* 3 (1981): 215–227.

———, "*Amicitia jocosa*: Peter of Celle and John of Salisbury," *Florilegium* 3 (1983): 140–156.

———, "Master John's Hilarity," *The Hatcher Review* 2 (1985): 399–403.

———, "Fulgentius – The Enigmatic Furvus in John of Salisbury's *Entheticus*," *Mittellateinisches Jahrbuch* 23 (1988): 119–125.

———, *Literature of Satire in the Twelfth Century: A Neglected Mediaeval Genre* (Lewiston, N.Y., 1988).

———, "'On the Conspiracy of the Members' Attributed to John of Salisbury," *Allegorica* 12 (1991): 29–41.

Pézard, A., "Du *Policraticus* à la *Divine Comédie*," *Romania* 79 (1948–9): 1–36 and 163–191.

Pioletti V., "Giovanni di Salisbury e la *Cena Trimalchionis*," *Giornale italiano di filologia* 17 (1964): 350–358.

Poirel, D., "La patience, l'un et la Trinité. Un traité sur la Trinité de l'école de Jean de Salisbury," *Archivum Latinitatis Medii Aevii* (Bulletin du Cange) 61 (2003): 65–109.

Poirel, D. and Stirnemann, P., "Nicolas de Montiéramey, Jean de Salisbury et deux florilèges d'auteurs antiques," *Revue d'histoire des textes*, n. s. 1 (2006): 173–188.

Poole, R.L., "The Masters of the Schools at Paris and Chartres in John of Salisbury's Time," *The English Historical Review* 35 (1920): 321–342.

———, "John of Salisbury at the Papal Court," *The English Historical Review* 38 (1923): 321–330.

Raña Dafonte, C., "La ética en el Policraticus de Juan de Salisbury," in *Actas del II Congressos Nacional de Filosofia Medieval* (Saragossa, 1996): 431–438.

———, *Juan de Salisbury (1110/1120-1180)* (Madrid, 1999).

———, "El tema de los universales en Juan de Salisbury," *Revista española de filosofia medieval* 6 (1999): 233–239.

———, "La dimension practica de la filosofia segun Juan de Salisbury," *Revista española de filosofia medieval* 10 (2003): 219–226.

———, "Juan de Salisbury: Poema sobre La conspiracion de los miembros corporales," *Revista Espanola-de Filosofia Medieval* 11 (2004): 301–305.

———, "La responsabilidad del escritor en la Edad Media: Petro Abelardo, Juan de Salisbury," in M.A. Villaverde, ed., *Hermeneutica y responsabilidad: Homanaje a Paul*

Ricoeur. *Actas de los VII Encuentros Internacionales de Filosofía en el Camino de Santiago, Santiago de Compostela, Pontevedra, A Coruña, 20–22 de noviembre de 2003* (Santiago de Compostela, 2005): 109–120.

———, "Conocimento y verdad en Juan de Salisbury," in M.C. Pacheco and J.F. Meirinhos, eds., *Intellect et imagination dans la Philosophie médiévale/Intellect and Imagination in Medieval Philosophy/Intelecto e imaginação na Filosfia Medieval. Actes du XIe Congrès International de Philosophie Médiévale de la SIEPM, Porto, 26–31 août 2002* (Turnhout, 2006): vol. 2, 1053–1062.

Ray, R., "Rhetorical Skepticism and Verisimilar Narrative in John of Salisbury's *Historia pontificalis*," in E. Breisach, ed., *Classical Rhetoric and Medieval Historiography* (Kalamazoo, 1985): 61–102.

Richard, H. and Rouse, M.A. "John of Salisbury and the Doctrine of Tyrannicide," *Speculum*, 42 (1967): 693–709.

Richardson, H.G., 'The Early Correspondence of John of Salisbury," *English Historical Review* 54 (1939): 417–473.

Robertson, L., "Exile in the Life and Correspondence of John of Salisbury," in L. Napran and E. Van Houts, eds., *Exile in the Middle Ages. Selected Proceedings from the International Medieval Congress. University of Leeds, 8–11 July 2002* (Turnhout, 2004): 181–197.

Rota, A., "L'influsso civilisto nella concezione dello stato di Giovanni Salisberiense," *Rivista di storia del diritto italiano* 26–27 (1953–4): 209–226.

Sassier, Y., *Royauté et idéologie au Moyen Âge: Bas-Empire, monde franc, France (IVe–XIIe siècles)* (Paris, 2002).

Schaarschmidt, C., *Johannes Saresberiensis nach Leben und Studien, Schriften und Philosophie* (Leipzig, 1862).

Schebat, L., "Jean de Salisbury et Pétrarque: aspects et enjeux de leur jugement sur Cicéron," *Les Cahiers de l'humanisme* 3–4 (2003–4): 93–113.

Seit, S., "Die Orientierung des Denkens in der Unvermeidlichkeit der Sprache. Johannes' von Salisbury *ratio indifferentiae*," in J. Brachtendorff, ed., *Prudentia und Contemplatio: Ethik und Metaphysik in Mittelalter* (Paderborn, 2002): 120–141.

———, "Die Kunst, die Wahrheit in den Sternen zu lesen. Astrologie, Divination und die *ars coniectoris* bei Johannes von Salisbury," in C. Dietl and D. Helschinger, eds., *Ars und Scientia im Mittelalter und in der Frühen Neuzeit: Ergebnisse interdisziplinärer Forschung. Georg Wieland zum 65. Geburtstag* (Tubingen, 2002): 77–96.

Sénellart, M., *Les Arts de gouverner. Du* regimen *médiéval au concept de gouvernement* (Paris, 1995).

Sheerin, D.J., *John of Salisbury's 'Entheticus de dogmate philosophorum': Critical Text and Introduction*, PhD Diss. (University of North Carolina at Chapel Hill, 1969).

Sivers, P. von, "John of Salisbury: Königtum und Kirche in England," in P. von Sivers, ed., *Respublica Christiana: Politisches Denken des orthodoxen Christentums im Mittelalter* (Munich, 1969), 47–72.

Smalley, B., *The Becket Conflict and the Schools: A Study of Intellectuals in Politics* (Oxford, 1973).

Spörl, J., "Humanismus und Naturalismus: Johannes von Salisbury," in *Grundformen hochmittelalterlicher Geschichtsanschauung: Studien zum Weltbild der Geschichtschreiber des 12. Jahrhunderts* (Munich, 1968): 73–113.

Struve, T., "Bedeutung und Funktion des Organismusvergleichs in den mittelalterlichen Theorien von Staat und Gesellschaft," in A. Zimmermann, ed., *Soziale Ordnungen in Selbstverständnis des Mittelalters* (Berlin-New York, 1979): 144–161.

———, "Vita civilis naturam imitetur...Der Gedanke, der Nachahmung der Natur als Grundlage der organologischen Staatskonzeption Johannes von Salisbury," *Historisches Jahrbuch* 101 (1981): 341–361.

Stürner, W., "Die Gesellschaftsstruktur und ihre Begrüdung bei Johannes von Salisbury, Thomas von Aquin und Marsilius von Padua," in A. Zimmermann, ed., *Soziale Ordnungen in Selbstverständnis des Mittelalters* (Berlin-New York, 1979): 162–178.

Suchomski, J., *Delectatio und utilitas. Ein Beiträg zum Verständnis mittelalterlicher komischer Literatur* (Bern-Munich, 1975).

Swinford, D., "Dream Interpretation and the Organic Metaphor of the State in John of Salisbury's *Policraticus*," *The Journal of Medieval Religious Cultures* 38 (2012), 32–59.

Szlachta, B., "Prawo i aequitas w filozofi Jana z Salisbury" (Law and Equity in the Philosophy of John of Salisbury), in W. Sajdek, ed., *Czasy katedr–czasy uniwesytetow. Zrodla jednosci narodow Europy* (Lublin, 2005): 209–232.

Tachella, E., "Giovanni di Salisbury e i Cornificiani," *Sandalion* 3 (1980): 273–313.

Thomson, R.M., "William of Malmesbury, John of Salisbury and the *Noctes Atticarum*," in G. Cambier, ed., *Hommages à André Boutemy* (Brussels, 1976): 367–389.

Tilliette, J.-Y., "Jean de Salisbury et Cicéron," *Helmantica* 50 (1999): 697–710.

Tobin, R.B., "The Cornifician Motif in John of Salisbury's *Metalogicon*," *History of Education* 13 (1984): 1–6.

Trovato, M., "The Semantic Value of *Ingegno* and Dante's *Ulysses* in the Light of the *Metalogicon*," *Modern Philology* 84 (1987): 258–266.

Tschacher, W., "Die Entstehungszeit der *Historia pontificalis* des Johannes von Salisbury," *Deutsches Archiv für Erforschung des Mittelalters* 50 (1994): 509–530.

Türk, E., Nugae Curialium. *Le règne d'Henri II Plantegenêt (1145–1189) et l'éthique politique* (Geneva, 1977).

Ullmann, W., "The Influence of John of Salisbury on Medieval Italian Jurists," *English Historical Review* 59 (1944): 383–392, repr. in *The Church and the Law in the Earlier Middle Ages. Selected Essays* (London, 1975).

———, "The Knowledge of John of Salisbury in the Later Middle Ages," in K. Hauck and H. Mordek, eds., *Geschichtsschreibung und geistiges Leben im Mittelalter: Festschrift für Heinz Löwe zum 65. Geburstag* (Cologne-Vienna, 1978): 519–545, repr. in *Jurisprudence in the Middle Ages. Collected Studies* (London, 1980).

Verbaal, W., "*Teste Quintiliano*. Jean de Salisbury et Quintilien: un exemple de la crise des autorités au XIIᵉ siècle," in P. Galand-Hallyn, F. Goyet, F. Hallyn and C. Lévy, eds., *Quintilien ancien et moderne* (Turnhout, 2008), 155–170.

Veyrard-Cosme, C., "Jean de Salisbury et le récit de Pétrone, du remploi à l'exemplum," *Cahiers d'Études Anciennes* 39 (2003): 69–88.

Walberg, E., "Jean de Salisbury biographe de Thomas Becket, modèle ou copie?" *Mélanges de philologie et d'histoire offerts à M. Antoine Thomas* (Paris, 1927): 479–489.

Ward, J.O., "Some Principles of Rhetorical Historiography in the Twelfth Century," in E. Breisach, ed., *Classical Rhetoric and Medieval Historiography* (Kalamazoo, 1985): 103–165.

Webb, C., *John of Salisbury* (London, 1932, repr. New York, 1971).

———, "Notes on the Books Bequeathed by John of Salisbury to the Cathedral Library of Chartres," *Medieval and Renaissance Studies* 1 (1941–3): 128–129.

———, "Ioannis Sarresberiensis Metalogicon: Addenda et corrigenda," *Medieval and Renaissance Studies* 1 (1941–3): 232–236.

Wieruszowski, H., "Roger II of Sicily, *Rex-Tyrannus*, in Twelfth-Century Political Thought," *Speculum* 38 (1963): 46–78.

The World of John of Salisbury, ed. M. Wilks (Oxford, 1984[1], 1994[2]).

Zanoletti, G., *Il bello come vero alla scuola di Chartres. Giovanni di Salisbury* (Rome, 1979).

Index Rerum

Index Nominum